CW01337971

CHEYENNE WAR

CHEYENNE WAR
Indian Raids on the
Roads to Denver
1864–1869

JEFF BROOME

ABERDEEN BOOKS
Sheridan, Colorado

LOGAN COUNTY HISTORICAL SOCIETY
Sterling, Colorado

2013

isbn 978-09713852-4-5 (hardcover)
isbn 978-09713852-5-2 (paperback)
copyright © 2013 James Jefferson Broome
First printing, 2013

Library of Congress Control Number: 2013952990

Aberdeen Books
3890 South Federal Boulevard · Sheridan, Colorado 80110
303-795-1890 · aberdeentp@earthlink.net · www.aberdeenbookstore.com

Logan County Historical Society
P.O. Box 564 · Sterling, Colorado 80751

Design by Ariane C. Smith · Capital A Publications, llc · Spokane, Washington

Progress, far from consisting in change, depends on retentiveness. When change is absolute there remains no being to improve and no direction is set for possible improvement; and when experience is not retained, as among savages, infancy is perpetual. Those who cannot remember the past are condemned to repeat it.

GEORGE SANTAYANA
THE LIFE OF REASON OR THE PHASES OF HUMAN PROGRESS
(NEW YORK, NY: CHARLES SCRIBNER'S SONS, 1911), 284

Table of Contents

Illustrations *9*

Maps *11*

Preface and Introduction *13*

Acknowledgements *27*

CHAPTER ONE
The Beginning of the Denver Trail *29*

CHAPTER TWO
The Indian War Begins *37*

CHAPTER THREE
The War Is On *67*

CHAPTER FOUR
The War Continues *89*

CHAPTER FIVE
More War *113*

CHAPTER SIX
The 1865 Indian War *133*

CHAPTER SEVEN
The 1865 Indian War Continues *155*

CHAPTER EIGHT
The War Stays Hot *175*

CHAPTER NINE
Treaty Failures *219*

CHAPTER TEN
Out of Control 249

CHAPTER ELEVEN
Waging Actual War 305

CHAPTER TWELVE
Waging Heavy Peace 331

CHAPTER THIRTEEN
Colorado Indian War 359

CHAPTER FOURTEEN
Fights and More Raids 389

CHAPTER FIFTEEN
Tall Bull's Revenge 411

CHAPTER SIXTEEN
Bury My Heart at Spillman Creek 433

APPENDIX
Locating Stage Stations on the Denver Road 469

Bibliography 481

Index 499

Dedication 527

Illustrations

George Tritch   *80*

Rescued captives from the August 7–8 raids   *94*

Skeletons of 10 freighters killed July 18, 1864   *112*

Private Hugh Melrose   *129*

Fort Sedgwick   *218*

An attack on the Overland Stage Company   *221*

Brevet Major General George Armstrong Custer   *252*

The discovery of Lyman Kidder   *259*

Edward "Ned" Wynkoop   *273*

Fight near Fort Wallace   *286*

Sergeant Frederick Wyllyams   *291*

Veronica Ulbrich   *307*

Preserved scalp of William Thompson   *314*

Lon Schermerhorn and family   *345*

Apollinaris Dietemann   *371*

Henrietta and John Dietemann grave marker   *376*

Corporal Leander Herron, Company A, 3rd Infantry   *397*

Death of Malcolm Granstadt   *421*

Spillman Creek Raid   *436*

Tom Alderdice   436

Mary Zigler Alverson   437

The capture of Maria Weichell   441

Willis Daily   443

Summit Springs   451

Maria Weichell's rescue at Summit Springs   462

Maria Weichell   465

Minnie Grace Weichell   466

Riverside Station   474

Military artifacts recovered at Riverside Station   475

Mound Station artifacts   476

Mound Station Memorial Marker   477

Military artifacts recovered at Riverside Ranche   478

Artifacts recovered from Wisconsin Ranch   479

Willis Daily, Mary Twibell Daily, and their three children   480

Memorial Marker at Summit Springs   480

Maps

Denver road   *134–135*

Custer's 1867 summer campaign   *250*

August 1868 raids and the route of Tom Alderdice, May 30, 1869   *330*

Homesteads raided in Elbert County, Colorado, August 25, 1868   *358*

Military engagements with the Cheyenne   *412*

Custer's camp on July 4–5, 1867   *472*

The Native Americans say that a story stalks a writer and, if it finds you worthy, comes to live in your heart. The writer's responsibility is to give that story a voice.

WWW.DEBBIMICHIKOFLORENCE.COM/
AUTHOR_INTERVIEWS/2004/SALLYKEEHN.HTML
(ACCESSED JULY 11, 2013)

Preface and Introduction

THIS BOOK FOCUSES ON INDIAN RAIDS ALONG THE ROADS to Denver from 1864 to 1869. The road following the South Platte River was also called the Denver road and the South Platte road. The other two roads are the well known Smoky Hill trail and the Santa Fe trail. I refer to all three trails as roads. In addition, I have tried to account for all the skirmishes, battles and raids along settlements that were located in some sort of connection with the roads, as well as incidents well off the roads, but connected with the Indian war that I have chosen to call *Cheyenne War*. In writing this history of Indian raids along these roads, I have tried to produce new information not found in other works that cover parts of this war. The most unique source for this new information is the many individual Indian depredation claim files, housed in the National Archives, in Washington, DC.

Having been trained in philosophy, I have always had an appreciation for discovering and understanding truth. While there is an unavoidable subjective element involved in interpreting truth, one should always remember what the philosopher David Hume wrote more two hundred years ago, viz., truth is the basis of history.[1] I have tried to bring a clearer focus on truth by presenting the historically factual incidents that occurred along these roads during this era of a general Indian war, involving citizens living in Kansas and the territories of Colorado, Nebraska, and what would later become Wyoming, but was in 1864 Dakota Territory. The interpretation of truth is ultimately a philosophical question, and the perspective one brings when understanding facts will always leave open the possibility of disagreement. The perspective I am bringing in this work is primarily what I would call the civilian perspective. Obviously, the Indian perspective is understandably different, as is the military perspective. Those are the three understandings from

---

1   David Fate Norton and Richard H. Popkin, edited, *David Hume: Philosophical Historian* (New York, NY: The Bobbs-Merrill Company, Inc., 1965), 36.

which the facts of this particular past are embedded, civilian, Indian, and military. The facts, however, are still the facts. Facts, like historical artifacts, do not change. Often they become hidden through the advancement of time, but facts are still facts, and it should be the primary task of the historian to gather as many of the facts as can be known before presenting a history of something. Having said that, it is wise to recall what one author said on this subject: "As we all know, even the making of a 'true' story out of 'true' facts involves certain emphases and distortions of those facts; there's always some element of 'slant' or 'spin'."[2] My "spin" is to recover the lost civilian perspective, for I believe those who advance the other perspectives, while advancing our understanding of the Indian wars post Civil War, need to address the civilian perspective. They have been ignored for far too long. Bringing these out will hopefully swing the interpretive pendulum back to the center.

One might ask the question: Why is the story of all these raids important to read? What is being advanced in *Cheyenne War*? The answer mirrors what the late historian David Dixon said, in his review of my earlier work, *Dog Soldier Justice: The Ordeal of Susanna Alderdice in the Kansas Indian War*.[3] He wrote, "The purpose . . . is not to sensationalize the anguish of the victims, but to demonstrate that recent scholarship has diminished or discounted the degree of suffering endured by the settlers in favor of emphasizing the horror and despair experienced by the Indians."[4] That purpose continues with *Cheyenne War*.

Some historians do not feel there ever was an Indian war along the roads bringing people to and from Denver. Michael Tate, in his recent important study, *Indians and Immigrants: Encounters on the Overland Trails*, says the record rejects the "treasured image of the corralled wagon train under relentless assault by feather-bedecked warriors . . . immigrants had far more to fear from accidents, epidemics, and lack of sustenance than they ever had to fear from American Indians."[5] Tate is both right and wrong. If one wishes to make such a judgment about the trails *before* 1864, then it is true that Indian raids were generally not the concern for travelers. Tate is right.

2   Lincoln B. Faller, "Making Medicine Against 'White Man's Side of Story': George Bent's Letters to George Hyde," (*American Indian Quarterly*, Vol. 24, No. 1, Winter, 2000), 73.

3   Jeff Broome, *Dog Soldier Justice: The Ordeal of Susanna Alderdice in the Kansas Indian War* (Lincoln, KS: The Lincoln County Historical Society, 2003); Reprinted as a Bison Book (Lincoln, NE and London: University of Nebraska Press, 2009).

4   *The Western Historical Quarterly*, Volume XXXVI, Number 1, Spring 2005, 95.

5   Michael Tate, *Indians and Immigrants: Encounters on the Overland Trails* (Norman, OK: University of Oklahoma Press, 2006), x.

Even so, Tate goes on to claim that, after 1856, and "even in the bleakest of years, incidents of cooperation far outnumbered cases of conflict."[6] But when one looks at the period of time *Cheyenne War* covers, Tate's statement reeks of falsehood, as will be demonstrated in the ensuing pages. During these important years, 1864–1869, Tate is wrong.

While I have, when appropriate, used secondary source works and information found in contemporary newspaper accounts of the time, as well as contemporary authors, my main research focus has been the long neglected citizen affidavits found in the National Archives, unavailable on microfilm, and hidden in well over 13,000 individual files, known as Indian Depredation Claims. Record Group 123 contains the majority of these claims, and its storage space occupies nearly three football fields of shelf space.[7] I have located about seven feet of that storage space, from the files of hundreds of people who suffered losses from Cheyenne raids, from which this book draws its stories. In most claims, the Cheyenne were not acting alone. Arapaho, Kiowa and several Lakota tribes were also involved. Often the raids were conducted by conglomerates of both Northern and Southern Cheyenne.

Through these records I have tried to give a more permanent account of what the settler and freighter endured in the settlement of the west during that brief period of time when Indians were sharing the land. In the roughly five-year period covered by *Cheyenne War*, conflict inevitably occurred.

Finding this pioneer voice in the depredation claims has been laborious. Numerous trips were made to the National Archives Building in Washington, DC, over a 10-year period. With each trip I have been able to locate several hundred individual depredation claims that relate to this study.[8] The majority of these files contain first-hand affidavits detailing the specifics of a particular Indian raid.

---

6   Tate, *Indians and Immigrants*, xi.

7   *Preliminary Inventory of the Records of the United States Court of Claims (Record Group 123)*, compiled by Gaiselle Kerner (Washington, DC: The National Archives, 1953), 22.

8   The 158-page index of names for RG 123 (each page containing 80 names) does have in an appendix a file number for each claim committed by the various Indian tribes, sorted by tribe, and pulling all of those files involving the Cheyenne was also helpful. But I discovered that many of the files in the appendix were missing in the chronological file numbers. I also discovered many other files involving the Cheyenne were not in the appendix tribal list. Further, there is an additional alphabetical index list of 80 pages, containing names not included in the 158 page index, and that index does not have a tribal appendix. And of course, these two indexes only list the claims in 800 feet of records stored in RG 123. Hundreds of other claims are scattered throughout other record groups, especially RG 75, which contains at least 22 storage feet of files, but has no name index. To find those claims I had to individually pull each file box and examine each depredation claim. Even now, Cheyenne claims remain hidden in other boxes in RG 75.

As early as 1796 Congress enacted legislation, to provide monetary compensation for American citizens who suffered attacks by Indians that were in treaty with the United States. The generic idea behind the legislation was to teach the Indian that unwarranted attacks upon settlers must stop. This was done by reducing the monetary value of annuities provided by a particular treaty, proportionate to the amount of personal property stolen or destroyed in a given raid.[9] The early legislations were titled "Civilization and Education Acts." The educational component was to teach American citizens not to retaliate against Indians for their raids. The civilization component was meant to convince depredating Indians to abandon their long-held cultural practice of stealing and raiding against people outside the confines of friendly tribes.[10]

The various laws relating to these claims were tweaked over the ensuing decades, but regulations finally ended up with several requirements to complete a claim. First, each claim had to be filed within three years of the specific attack, and the Indian tribe had to be identified. Next, a sworn affidavit had to be obtained from the victim or surviving family, detailing the facts of the attack, along with at least two other sworn affidavits, from witnesses not benefiting from the claim. Eventually, the claim was sent to the Department of the Interior, and an investigation began through that agency to verify the claim's authenticity. The claim was then forwarded to the appropriate Indian agency, and the accused tribes were consulted about each depredation. Often, leaders of particular tribes denied any knowledge of the depredation; but surprisingly, many times they freely admitted their involvement.

The claim was then turned over to a special government agent, who then went to the affected community and investigated the particulars of the claim, determining whether the alleged victim was deemed truthful. This was usually accomplished by interviewing citizens not connected with the original affidavits, and in this way verifying or falsifying sworn statements. At one time, in the 1880s, there were six agents working full-time, investigating individual claims. Often at this stage in the investigation, the

9   By 1870, Congress had changed the law requiring compensation to come from annuities and instead declared it to come from special appropriations. See Larry C. Skogen, *Indian Depredation Claims 1796–1920* (Norman, OK: University of Oklahoma Press, 1996), 98.

10 "Depredations Report," Department of the Interior, Office of Indian Affairs, 18–24. Entry 96, Letters Sent, 1890, Record Group 75, National Archives Building, Washington, DC.

agent would modify the claim, reducing the monetary value to fit what was believed to be a more accurate figure of the actual property loss. A horse valued at $200 in the original claim might be re-valued at $125; furniture, clothes, etc., would also have their values lowered. When one studies the claims today, it seems that investigating agents had some kind of governmental duty to lessen the amount filed. Never was the amount increased, and rarely was the original amount accepted. To relate this today, insurance agents always deal with exaggerations of insured property lost. That kind of fraud is often detected in examining individual depredation claims. But seldom was it determined that an attack had not been made. The facts of the attacks were not challenged. The facts of the losses often were.

At this stage in the investigation, pending approval of the claim by the investigating agent, the claim then went back to Congress for approval, and the settler was then supposed to be awarded compensation, the money originally coming from approved treaty annuities already granted to the guilty tribe. That changed, including payment from annuities, when Congress turned investigation of the claims over to the Court of Claims in 1891, "hoping that the justices could sort out the whole mess."[11] It appears that the majority of the 10,841 citizens filing individual claims, now stored in Record Group 123, the files associated with the Court of Claims, did not receive compensation. Settlers who did receive compensation, noted by name and claim number in many of the uncompensated claims, are not found in Record Group 123. That claims were paid is certain, but how many is a mystery.[12]

There has been one important study focusing on Indian depredation claims, by Larry Skogen, *Indian Depredation Claims, 1796–1920*.[13] In the book, Skogen notes that by 1890, only about three percent of all claims filed were compensated. After that year, when the files were transferred to

---

11   Larry Skogen, "The Bittersweet Reality of Indian Depredation Cases," (*Prologue, the Journal of the National Archives*, Volume 24, Fall, 1992), 291.

12   In several trips to the National Archives, between 2002 and 2009, I investigated probably at least 3,000 of the claims in RG 123, copying several hundred for my own research files, and in each instance the claim was not compensated. Part of the problem is because the claims ended up in a court battle and were finally adjudicated to the U.S. Court of Claims, where after several years, and well into the 20th Century, most of the pending and other uncompensated claims were tossed out as unconstitutional. It appears to me that RG 123 includes all such claims.

13   Skogen, *Indian Depredation Claims*. Until my use of claims in *Dog Soldier Justice*, only John D. McDermott had consulted claims for publication. See John D. McDermott, *Forlorn Hope: The Battle of White Bird Canyon and the Beginning of the Nez Perce War* (Boise, ID: Idaho State Historical Society, 1978).

the Court of Claims, and from then until 1920, about 3,600 more claims were compensated. This amountd to as many as 33% of the nearly 11,000 claims in RG 123 that were eventually compensated, though it usually took almost three decades before compensation was finalized.[14] By that time, of course, the claimant in many cases was deceased, and the reduced amount was finally awarded to an heir. The attorneys who stuck with the process also received their percentage of the compensation. Those paid claims were eventually reduced by an average of 37% from what was originally claimed as losses.[15]

Beginning in the early 1870s, and through the 1880s, many congressmen and senators received repeated calls from their constituents to allow people to re-file claims that had earlier been turned down, or never filed in the first place because of the three-year requirement that claims had to be filed by. As a result, there were various laws passed between 1873 and 1891, allowing citizens to re-file claims, even if no claim had originally been filed. Notices like this were printed in nearly all of the local papers at the time:

INDIAN DEPREDATION CLAIMS

The Indian depredation bill will undoubtedly become law within a week and it is therefore of the highest importance for those who have been affected by its provisions to understand the limitations of the act. There seems to be a misunderstanding as to the date prior to which the claims can be prosecuted. Any claim on file or which shall be filed before the bill becomes a law, no matter when the depredation occurred, comes under the provision of the law, but no claim for depredations which occurred prior to 1865, unless they are on file when the bill becomes a law, can be adjudicated by the courts within jurisdiction for Indian depredation claims. All of the thousands of claims now on file and which have been presented either to congress or the interior department can be considered by the courts, and any claim filed with the interior department before the act takes effect can also be taken into consideration; but when the act goes into effect, as before stated, no claim based upon a depredation committed prior to the year 1865 will come under the provisions of the law. Claimants, therefore, who have not already filed their claims and whose claims were based upon injuries inflicted by Indians prior to 1865 should at once make out their affidavits, attach such evidence to them as they can secure and forward them at once to the secretary of the interior. Requests have come to several senators asking for petitions or declarations and blank forms for

---

14   Skogen, *Indian Depredation Claims*, 195, 208.
15   Skogen, *Indian Depredation Claims*, 119–120. These paid claims can be found in Record Group 217. See Skogen, *Indian Depredation Claims*, note 17, 249, and note 32, 256.

making out such claims. There are no such forms. All that is needed is a statement of the claim, property sworn to, and with corroborative evidence which should be forwarded to the secretary of the interior.[16]

Such notices brought out many people, who filed claims in an attempt to recover compensation for their losses. One quirk in the law was that there was no compensation for injury or death, nor was there any compensation for costs incurred in attempting to recover stolen stock or personal property, or in medical expenses as a result of injuries caused by the raiding Indians. Freighters who hauled goods for a month before losing everything in an Indian raid could not receive compensation for their labor up to the time of loss. The merchant they were freighting for could claim the loss of the property, and the freighter could apply for compensation for the loss of his wagons and other property associated with freighting. Still, with such favorable reports of Congress finally taking seriously the issue of victim compensation, the Department of the Interior was flooded with numerous depredation claims.

In 1885, nearly 4,500 claims remained unpaid, totaling almost $15,000,000 in compensation. In today's inflation calculation, that amounts to a staggering $377,450,946 in lost property.[17] A report from the Department of Interior noted these difficulties:

> Owing to the absence of papers in many cases, the imperfect preparation of others, and the general and confused condition of the records, it has been impossible with the most patient and careful investigation to obtain post-office addresses of all the respective claimants, as well as accurate abstracts of other requisite and important facts.[18]

By 1887, only 305 of these claims had been adjudicated, of which only 157 were approved for compensation, and in each case but one—a claim for

16   *The Omaha Daily Bee*, February 25, 1891. As a result of this Congressional effort to pay for depredation claims, many people filed for the first time. There was a general distrust that they would ever get compensation, which prevented several people from filing earlier. The claim of George Tritch is an example. When asked why he did not file a claim at the time of the depredation, he replied "I never thought the Government would pay any of these claims until they sent out an agent to look after Indian claims. I went to see him and stated my claim. That brought me notice that the Government was going to pay private claims. . . ." George Tritch Indian Depredation Claim #1174 and 3102. Record Group 123. Indian Depredations Claims Division. National Archives Building, Washington, DC.

17   http://www.westegg.com/inflation/infl.cgi (accessed July 10, 2013).

18   J. D. C. Atkins, Commissioner, "Letter from the Secretary of the Interior," *49th Congress, 1st Session, House of Representatives, Ex. Doc. No. 125* (Washington, DC: Government Printing Office, 1886), 2–3.

$50 was approved for $50—the amount approved was less than the amount sought. For example, a claim for $13,490 was reduced down to $4,000. A claim for as little as $70 was reduced to $50. A claim for $5,775 was approved for $4,620; a claim for $7,600 was reduced to $375. A claim for $19,100 was approved for $8,625. A huge claim of $51,600, from Foster & Company, along the Denver road in the attacks in January 1865—for loss of general merchandise, wagons, cattle, etc.—was approved for the reduced amount of $16,713. Another claim for $214.45 was only approved for $64.45.[19]

But it is these individual Indian depredation claims that provide important first-person accounts of incidents along the trails to Denver that otherwise would remain lost to history. While it is no doubt true that many of the claims included fraudulent statements as to the value of the property lost, the contents lost, the number of mules, oxen and horses lost, etc., it was seldom that the claimant was dishonest in putting forth an account of an Indian attack, who was there, what happened, how it happened, etc. There might not have been as many Indians involved, the fight might have been shorter than reported, but the time of the attack, the method of the attack, the persons killed and injured are all generally reliable statements regarding the facts of the raids, and therefore should be trusted as reliable and true, unless there exists positive grounds from other sources to dismiss the sworn affidavit. In modern philosophy, this is known as the principle of critical trust: it is reasonable and rational to accept an assertion as true, unless there are positive reasons to distrust it. Applying this to history, when a supporting eye-witness statement contradicts another statement, this should cause one to question the authenticity of the claim. When that happens, one must turn to other supporting documents which support one statement over another.[20]

It should be understood that individual depredation claims by themselves are not sufficient support for understanding this history from 1864 to 1869. Skogen advised researchers to be "very critical of any of the information contained in them."[21] He is certainly correct in his caution. But when one

---

19 J. D. C. Atkins, Commissioner, "Letter from the Acting Secretary of the Interior," *49th Congress, 2nd Session, House of Representatives, Ex. Doc. No. 77* (Washington, DC: Government Printing Office, 1887), 1–24.

20 John Hick, *Between Faith and Doubt: Dialogues on Faith and Reason* (New York, NY: Palgrave Macmillan, 2010), 57–58.

21 Email correspondence with the author, July 9, 2009. Skogen's analysis of the reliability of individual depredation claims can be found in "The Bittersweet Reality of Indian Depredation Cases," 295–296.

places these testimonials alongside all other available documents covering this history, a clearer story does emerge. Outside of these citizen affidavits, other sources come through military reports, newspaper accounts, pioneer reminiscences, Indian reminiscences, and letters and diaries written at the time. Historians know that all of these methods of recording facts are fallible; but generally, when there is no evidence to the contrary, the reliability of all fallible methods of documenting facts goes something like this: the closer the recorded event is to the time of the event the more likely the reported facts are true.

Of course, all of these documents must be found and studied; otherwise there would be no way to assess the events in question. And in fact, this has been done by many historians writing about these important times. But consider this: if any of the other noted methods of documentation was put through the critical scrutiny that the individual Indian depredation claims were put through, e.g., sworn affidavits, testimony of witnesses, and then an independent investigation for the truthfulness of the claim conducted by a hired agent of the United States government, well, we would no longer be arguing our facts. Instead we would be advancing our interpretations on those facts. This is where the individual Indian depredation claims, when containing sworn affidavits of an attack, are an outstanding lens into history.

An example of a fraudulent claim, easily detected by the stringent methods of verifying the facts in an individual depredation claim, is here summarized to show how the system worked. A claim was filed by George Knox under the name "Robert Williams & Co," for losses in three separate attacks on his ranch near O'Fallon's Bluffs during the summer of 1864, when the Indian war first broke out. The claim was very detailed in describing property lost, amounting to $18,410. The claim placed Williams at his ranch at the time of each raid, and reported that all of his buildings were burned to the ground. In addition, the claim had sworn affidavits of three other witnesses, one being Williams' partner, George Knox, and the other two men, Henry Clifford and Alfred Gay.

Indian agent V. T. McGillycuddy interviewed the principal chiefs at Pine Ridge, who were identified in the claim as the Indians responsible, and the chiefs admitted that they burned and destroyed all the property and ranches along the Overland Road during that time, implying their guilt in this instance. It appears that the claim was legitimate. But then the file was turned over to the investigating agent, L. H. Poole, who traveled to the area, and began a series of interviews with other witnesses and survivors of the violent raids in August 1864. Poole learned that the witnesses for Williams were at the time "Squaw men," who lived in lodges with the Indians, as did Williams, and were all witnesses "whose reputation for truth and veracity is not good among those who know them best." One local witness described them as "men of no reputation and that he regards their testimony . . . as unworthy of belief." Knox also was a "Squaw man," with an Indian wife and was never known to have been in business with Williams.

Agent Poole found an additional 10 witnesses, who all testified to the claim being fraudulent. He also noted that Williams' claim for losses was "ten times as great as the most liberal estimate placed upon the value of all the property in and about the claimant's ranche, and that their nearest neighbors have no knowledge of the alleged depredation and that at the date the ranche is claimed to have been burned, the Indians had committed no depredations in the vicinity of O'Fallon's Bluffs. . . ." Williams himself had been killed by Indians in 1865, and it was Knox who was filing in his behalf, trying to fraudulently claim substantial monetary remuneration for what was described by all the credible witnesses as the smallest ranch on the Overland road. The merchandise Williams offered along the road only amounted to "a little bad whiskey, cheap tobacco, Cove oysters, canned fruit, clay pipes &e." Yet Williams' claim stated the ranch house was valued at $4,000, the stolen 80 pounds of chewing tobacco was of fine cut and valued at $1,400, and so on, making the entire claim one big fraudulent enterprise.[22]

What is clear in studying this one depredation claim is that the credible witnesses who disputed the Williams' claim all suffered significant losses in 1864, and when Agent Poole went to investigate Williams' claim, he was told in no uncertain terms that the claim was fraudulent. Those who did suffer losses were not about to allow others to advance a claim that was not legitimate.

There are other motives for fraud than just overvaluing the property lost or destroyed. After Congress became proactive in soliciting claims, a business grew in successfully prosecuting depredation claims. Attorneys soon

---

22   Robert Williams Indian Depredation Claim #8356. Record Group 123.

specialized in claims and went into the affected settlements and solicited victims. Their reward was five dollars for each claim they processed, as well as a percentage of "what might be collected." Fraudulent claims were processed in this effort to secure customers.[23]

Many depredation claims often do show that property lost was valued higher than it was really worth. This human tendency is well known to insurance adjustors today. Larry Skogen warns the researcher of Indian depredation claims:

> First, a researcher must be prepared to find out a subject lied and tried to fraudulently obtain money through one of the Indian policies. Second, he or she cannot accept these documents at face value. A researcher must remember that these people were motivated to exaggerate their material possessions and to make Native Americans a larger-than-life threat to their well-being. He or she should use corroborating evidence apart from the claims to try to substantiate anything of interest in them.[24]

When Skogen advised the researcher that depredation claims cannot be taken at face value, one must understand that this basically applied to the amount of property lost and the value therewith. This is not an indictment against the depredation claims being reliable statements of what occurred, where it occurred, and how it occurred during an Indian raid. There was no need to exaggerate the raid itself, as there was no compensation for injury or death. In fact, often claims completely ignored describing an attack when people were killed or injured—not mentioning those facts—focusing instead merely on the property lost. Those facts regarding people injured or killed often surfaced in other claims, or in the statements of supporting witnesses, military reports, newspaper accounts, etc.

Nevertheless, many times, in an effort to state the facts of a claim, witnesses gave very detailed information about the raid itself, how the Indians surprised unsuspecting citizens, what happened during the raid, how someone was injured, etc. There is no reason to distrust such detailed statements, and therefore I have freely used these accounts in bringing out this history

---

23   An example of this comes from the claim of William Wild, in Lincoln County, Kansas in 1866, when a claim was processed for the loss of 5 cattle and one horse, attributed to Pawnee. Upon investigation it was learned that the stock starved to death because the Wild family had fled the area, fearing an Indian raid, when in fact no such raid occurred. See William Wild Indian Depredation Claim #3482. Record Group 123.

24   Skogen, "The Bittersweet Reality of Indian Depredation Cases," 295–296.

of Indian raids along the roads to Denver. When possible I have used corroborating statements from other sources to produce a clearer picture.

This I can confidently claim: without the testimony found in the many depredation claims consulted for this book, *Cheyenne War* would not have been possible. The military reports alone, often the only primary source document consulted in some books covering the Indian wars, are entirely insufficient to give one a complete picture of what really happened during these turbulent times.[25]

When the war began in the spring of 1864, fully erupting in Nebraska in early August, there were only a few attacks occurring along the South Platte road and elsewhere. That would change in January 1865, when the main acts of the war were along the South Platte. But to understand those events, it was necessary to extend this study beyond the South Platte road to include the other roads in Kansas, Nebraska, Wyoming and other parts of Colorado, especially in the spring and summer of 1864. Even so, this work only briefly covers important war events in Wyoming, such as the Battle at Platte Bridge near present-day Casper, on July 26, 1865; the Connor Fight along the Tongue River, near present-day Ranchester, on August 29, 1865; or the Fetterman Fight, on December 21, 1866 near present-day Sheridan.[26] Nor does this work give in-depth details of other fights in Colorado, such as the November 29, 1864, battle and subsequent massacre of unarmed women and

---

25   As an example of this, see Douglas C. McChristian, *Fort Laramie: Military Bastion of the High Plains* (Norman, OK: Arthur H. Clark Company, 2008). His entire well-written narrative of the attack on Julesburg and the subsequent war of 1865 came entirely from military sources, along with the four decades later, factually flawed memories of George Bent. The depredation claims relevant to this time, all studied together, corrects many errors in the military reports and both corroborates and corrects Bent's narrative of this war.

26   For accounts of these three fights see J. W. Vaughn, *The Battle of Platte Bridge* (Norman, OK: University of Oklahoma Press, 1963); John D. McDermott, *Frontier Crossroads: The History of Fort Caspar and the Upper Platte Crossing* (Casper: Fort Caspar Museum, 1997); David E. Wagner, *Powder River Odyssey: Nelson Cole's Western campaign of 1865 The Journals of Lyman G. Bennett and Other Eyewitness Accounts* (Norman, OK: The Arthur H. Clark Company, 2009); John H. Monnett, *Where a Hundred Soldiers Were Killed: The Struggle for the Powder River Country and the Making of the Fetterman Myth* (Albuquerque, NM: University of New Mexico Press, 2008). See also John D. McDermott, *Red Cloud's War: The Bozeman Trail 1866–1868* (Norman, OK: The Arthur H. Clark Company, 2010). McDermott has written extensively on the Indian Wars on the Northern Plains in the mid 1860s, in addition to the two books mentioned above. These include *Dangerous Duty: A History of Frontier Forts in Fremont County, Wyoming* (Lander, Wyoming: Fremont County Historical Commission, 1993); "'We had a terribly hard time letting them go': The Battles of Mud Springs & Rush Creek, February, 1865," *Nebraska History* 77 (Summer, 1996); *Circle of Fire: The Indian War of 1865* (Mechanicsburg, Pennsylvania: Stackpole Books, 2003); and "The Pacific Telegraph in Wyoming," *Annals of Wyoming* (Spring, 2011).

children at Sand Creek, near present-day Eads; and the September 17–25, 1868, battle and siege at Beecher's Island, near present-day Wray. Outside of the closing chapter, which includes the 1869 fight at Summit Springs, due to its proximity and connection with the Denver road, the emphasis in this study is to produce unknown details relating to Indian raids associated with the roads to Denver that followed the Platte and South Platte Rivers, the Arkansas River, and the Smoky Hill River.

This preface began with a reference to philosophy. It might be worthwhile to end it likewise. In his classic work, *Utilitarianism*, John Stuart Mill wrote that the two main things that produce unhappiness are selfishness and the lack of mental cultivation. Mill noted that opening up one's mind to the rich fields of knowledge is a lifelong quest, and then he said this about a cultivated mind: it "finds sources of inexhaustible interest in all that surrounds it: in the objects of nature, the achievements of art, the imaginations of poetry, *the incidents of history*, the ways of mankind, past and present, and their prospects in the future." Searching out "the incidents of history"[27] has filled my life with a great deal of pleasure and joy, and it is an unending quest. But it is important that we stay faithful to what can be known regarding the truth of these incidents.

Bringing alive the voice so often found in individual depredation claims will give the reader today a view into yesterday's incidents of history, and will result in a more complete understanding of life along the Denver roads, as people either journeyed to or from Denver, or settled somewhere along the way. Had we been alive around 1900, we would have heard this voice, when listening to our elders telling us about their experiences on the wild frontier. But, as is the case with most voices, that voice became forever lost when the old pioneer died, and unless one committed experiences to pen and paper, it then became filtered through those still alive who heard it; and usually, over a generation or two, it was finally lost. As time ventures forth, even that filtered voice is silent today. So we must turn to the printed word to find these stories.

The most prominent voice found in *Cheyenne War* is that which has been hidden for more than a century, in the dusty storage vaults of the National Archives. It is these long hidden "incidents of history" that will give us

---

27 John Stuart Mill, *Utilitarianism* (Indianapolis and New York: The Bobbs-Merrill Company, Inc., 1957), 19.

insight into understanding those dangerous and thrilling days of old. When reading them here, one can easily imagine sitting by a fire on a cold winter night, or, if it is summer, relaxing on a porch in the cool of evening, and listening to a first-hand account of the perils of journeying into the Wild West, by an old-timer who could never forget what it was like to be an unwilling participant in an Indian raid. So often, as I read an individual first-hand account, my mind "heard" the voice speaking, bringing alive once again what was in most cases repeated numerous times in the days of old.

Today, people realize the "voice" of the World War II veteran is rapidly disappearing. Efforts abound to preserve this fading voice of what we now call America's Greatest Generation. I am confident that in 1920, as the settler's voice was then rapidly disappearing, those people living then, like us now with our aging veterans, looked to those who experienced the American West as their "greatest generation." Today that voice is generally despaired as an unwitting arm of Manifest Destiny. It is my hope that *Cheyenne War* will help to move the pendulum of understanding to a more balanced perspective.

One final explanation is in order to the reader. In some of the testimonials found in depredation claims, the accounts were presented in the third person, which I changed to the first person for a better flow in reading. For example, a claim might have said "Affiant was in the house when the Indians entered." I changed that to "I was in the house when the Indians entered." I occasionally changed misspellings to avoid having to note that each time it appeared. Also, the Lakota were always identified as Sioux. When possible I changed that to the specific Lakota tribes, which were mostly Oglala and Brule. If the tribal affiliation was unknown but identified as Sioux I changed that to Lakota. I did not, however, change the wording in individual first-hand testimonials.

Cheyenne War can be read while ignoring the footnotes, but to the reader who consults them, a more complete understanding emerges with them.

Acknowledgements

My RESEARCH THAT RESULTED IN THIS BOOK HAS BEEN carried on for more than a dozen years. There are numerous persons and institutions that have helped me along the way, too many to mention them all. But among those I wish to particularly thank the following people:

Ed and Nancy Bathke, Deb Bisel, Chuck Bolam, Jr., Chuck and Sheri Bowen, Bill Chapman, Bill and Sandra Condon, Marilyn Carr, Thomas Carr, Mike Day, John L. Dietemann, Steve Friesen, Duane Gile, Hank Graepler, Jerry Greene, Ron Hagan, Dennis Hagen, Tracee Hamilton, Roger Hansen, John Harmon, David and Jana Harrington, David Hungate, Will Johnson, Chuck Jones, Kent Kooi, Dan Larson, Robert Larson, Bill and Gloria Leeper, Jeff Lubbert, John Ludwickson, Scott Lundin, Lisa Manuello, Billy Markland, Michelle Martin, Jack McDermott, Cynthia Meski, Greg Michno, Gene Miller, Doris Monahan, John Monnett, Ric Morgan, Jim and Sharon Nelson, Judy Penhiter, Vonnie and Ron Perkins, Tom Petteys, Nell Brown Probst, Gary Ramey, Tedd Remm, Kay Rich, Joseph Rosa, Peter Russell, Doug Scott, Larry Shirkey, Dan Siebersma, Larry Skogen, Mildred, Russ and Bob Talbot, Chuck Thomann, Lana Tramp, Willie Walker, Donald Westfall, Bob Welheim, Tracy White, Gary Wiggins, Stan Winder, Lee Whiteley.

Thanks to these following institutions/organizations: Buffalo Bill Museum and Grave, Golden, Colorado; Colorado State Historical Society, Denver, Colorado; Crook Historical Museum, Crook, Colorado; Denver Public Library, Western History Department, Denver, Colorado; friends in the Denver Westerners who have supported me; Ellis County Historical Society, Hays, Kansas; Fort Hays State Historic Site, Hays, Kansas; Fort Hays State University, Special Collections Archives, Hays, Kansas; Fort Sedgwick Historical Society, Julesburg, Colorado; Friends of Historic Fort

Logan, Sheridan, Colorado; Hays Public Library, Hays, Kansas; Kansas State Historical Society, Topeka, Kansas; Lincoln County Historical Society, Lincoln, Kansas; Logan County Historical Society, Sterling, Colorado; McCracken Research Library, Buffalo Bill Historical Center, Cody, Wyoming; Nebraska State Historical Society, Lincoln, Nebraska; Salina Public Library, Kansas Room, Salina, Kansas; Sidney, Nebraska Public Library, Sidney, Nebraska; White Swan Research Library, Little Bighorn Battlefield National Monument, Crow Agency, Montana; Overland Trail Museum, Sterling, Colorado.

This book—as it is in its final version—would not have been possible without the generous support of the Logan County Historical Society, Tom Petteys of Aberdeen Books, and the man whom this book is dedicated to, Mr. Bill Condon, Sterling, Colorado. My sincere thanks and appreciation to each.

CHAPTER ONE

The Beginning of the Denver Trail

IN 1858 THERE WAS NO COLORADO TERRITORY. WHAT IS TODAY Colorado was at that time mostly in Kansas Territory, and a bit in Nebraska Territory. Change began when traces of gold were discovered near the confluence of Cherry Creek and the South Platte River in what soon would be named Auraria. Shortly after that a rival settlement, located on the other side of the confluence, was called Denver City. A season later Denver City would be the remaining settlement. By 1859, gold discoveries extended into the mountains just west of Denver City and South Park. The gold rush began. By 1860, 36,000 citizens would occupy Colorado, the majority young men.[1] In January 1861, Kansas was admitted into the Union, and one month later the western half of what had been Kansas Territory was designated Colorado Territory.

Prior to the discovery of gold, the long traversed Santa Fe trail took travelers through the southern part of the old Kansas Territory and now the new Colorado Territory, but that was about the extent of any interest in what would become the Centennial State in 1876. Gold changed all of that. To be sure, the white man had an interest in what was in Colorado, but before the discovery of gold that interest was in animal pelts acquired in trade with the Plains Indians. Bent's Fort along the Arkansas River and Fort St. Vrain along St. Vrain Creek, southwest of present-day Greeley, were the two enduring trading forts. These early settlements are not to be confused with military posts which came later, such as Fort Sedgwick and Fort Morgan. These earlier "forts" were fur trading posts with no connection to the United States military.

---

1   Emma Burke Conklin, *A Brief History of Logan County, Colorado With Reminiscences by Pioneers* (Denver, CO: Welch-Haffner Printing Company, 1928), 39.

These trading posts, along with others such as Fort LeDuc near present-day Wetmore, Fort Vasquez, southwest of today's Greeley, Fort Lupton (present-day town), Fort Cass near present-day Pueblo, and Fort Uncompahgre near present-day Delta indicated a strong trading presence among the Indians of the region, going back into the early 1800s. But white settlements during this trading era did not exist beyond the posts; that is, until the discovery of gold. Once gold was found, the need arose for pathways into the western edges of modern-day Colorado. Along with the Santa Fe trail that followed the Arkansas River in the southern part of the state, the Smoky Hill trail, with various branches into Colorado, soon developed. However, the main road to the gold fields and Denver City, the trail used the most until the railroad reached Cheyenne in 1867, was the Denver City trail—the Denver road—along the south side of the South Platte River, coming to Denver from northeastern Colorado and east of that into Nebraska.

By early spring, 1859, William H. Russell and John S. Jones, belonging to the larger firm of Russell, Majors and Waddell, were responsible for acquiring the first mail contract to Denver City and the surrounding mountain communities. Named the Leavenworth and Pike's Peak Express Company, their route to Denver first followed what became the middle—starvation—branch of the Smoky Hill trail, but soon after that followed the South Platte River, and within a short time various stage stations were built to accommodate the mail and stage service.[2] Originally the stage went from Fort Leavenworth through what is today Benkelman, Nebraska, up the Republican River to the Big Sandy near present-day Limon, and then on what became a branch of the Smoky Hill trail to Denver. Once the mail contract to Denver had been procured in late spring, the preferred route to Denver followed the south side of the South Platte River. This was because of the purchase of the mail contract of John Hockaday, who had the contract to deliver mail to Salt Lake City. As a result of that obligation it was necessary, after only three weeks of operation, to change the route to Denver from the first route to one following the South Platte River. Mail could then be

---

2   Glenn R. Scott, "Historic Trail Maps of the Sterling Quadrangle, Northeastern Colorado," *Historic Trail Maps of Eastern Colorado and Northeastern New Mexico* (Denver, CO: U.S. Department of the Interior, U.S. Geological Survey, 2004), 2. George A. Root and Russell K. Hickman, "Pike's Peak Express Companies: Part I—Solomon and Republican Route," *Kansas Historical Quarterly*, Volume XIII, Number 3, August 1944, 167.

conveniently carried on through to Salt Lake City, since that contract also carried the mail to Fort Kearny, Nebraska Territory.[3]

Shortly after this was established, William Russell and John Jones in 1860 created the Pony Express, which originated in St. Joseph, Missouri. It followed the South Platte River from Nebraska, west to Julesburg, and then north to the North Platte River, and from there on to its destination at Sacramento, California. However, it was short lived and by the end of 1861, it was abandoned. Also by this time, Ben Holladay had taken over the stage and mail service to Denver.[4] The company name was changed to the Central Overland California ("C.O.C.") and Pike's Peak Express Company.[5] To be sure, this Platte River route was known long before the beginning of mail service to Denver. Traders used it as early as the late 1700s, Indians used it long before that, and the buffalo and wild animals had always traversed it as a source for food and water. It was a convenient water access people could use coming to and from Denver, and it presented no major difficulties in travel. With the building of stage stations to accommodate the needs of the stages and travelers there now began the permanent intrusion of white settlement in land that had long been an important part of Indian life on the plains.

The earliest buildings erected along the Denver trail were built to accommodate the stage/mail service. The two earliest stations between what would later become Fort Sedgwick and Fort Morgan, which preceded the mail contract to Denver, were Lillian Springs (east of present-day Proctor) and Beaver Creek (east of present-day Fort Morgan).[6] Other early stations included Spring Hill Station, Washington Ranche (owned by brothers Charlie and Jim Moore), Valley Station, Wisconsin Ranche, Godfrey's Ranche and nearby American Ranche. The difference between a ranch and a ranche was that the former was a private, individually owned property

---

3 George A. Root and Russell K. Hickman, "Pike's Peak Express Companies: Part II—Solomon and Republican Route—Concluded," *Kansas Historical Quarterly*, Volume XIII, Number 4, November 1944, 221. See also "Part III—The Platte Route," *Kansas Historical Quarterly*, Volume XIII, Number 87, November 1945, 485.

4 Nell Brown Probst, *Forgotten people: A History of the South Platte Trail* (Boulder, CO: Pruett Publishing Company, 1979), 45. Joseph J. Di Certo, *The Saga of the Pony Express* (Missoula, MT: Mountain Press Publishing Company, 2002), 39–40.

5 Root and Hickman, "Part III—The Platte Route," 506.

6 Doris Monahan, *Destination: Denver City The South Platte Trail* (Athens, OH, Chicago, London: Swallow Press/Ohio University Press, 1985), 49.

not seeking economic contact with travelers, whereas a ranche was a place that offered services to those traversing the road.[7] By the mid-1860s, moving west from Fort Sedgwick, the more important ranches/stations and their distances apart were as follows: eight miles west of Fort Sedgwick, Gillette's Ranche; 4.25 miles further west, Antelope Station; 5.45 miles west to Harlow's Ranche; two miles west to Spring Hill Station; 6.25 miles west to Riverside Ranche; 2.3 miles west to Mound Station; 1.7 miles west to Lillian Springs Station; 5.25 miles west to Chicago Ranche; 2.2 miles west to Riverside Station; 4.2 miles west to Dennison Station; 2.5 miles west to Washington Ranche (also called Moore's Ranche); 3.5 miles west to Valley Station; 8 miles west to Wisconsin Ranche; 10.6 miles west to American Ranche; 1.7 miles west to Godfrey's Ranche (Fort Wicked); 12.25 miles west to Beaver Creek Station; 15.9 miles west to Fort Morgan.[8] They would all encounter Cheyenne war by 1865.

Ben Holladay was the single most influential business connoisseur affecting the Denver trail. In late 1861, he acquired the Central Overland California Stage Company, which included a subsidiary to Denver, the Pike's Peak Express Company. Through Holladay's investments, stage stops along the Denver trail were sponsored. Stages ran once a day from the Missouri River town of Atchison, Kansas, to Denver, a route of 653 miles. Drivers and horses were changed at "home" stations, while horses alone were changed at "swing" stations. Passengers were fed at home stations, at a cost of anywhere from 50 cents to two dollars.[9]

The stage service to Denver was influential in developing the freighting route following the same path. Stage service went to and from Denver daily, with as many as three stages leaving each day.[10] During the winter months freighting continued, but not at the tempo it kept during spring, summer and fall. The South Platte road to Denver was the first "interstate highway" linking travelers to the growing city. In just the month of May 1860, it was

---

7   Probst, *Forgotten People*, 39. Though this distinction is easily understood today, people at the time did not always make this distinction and thus often referred to their ranche as a ranch. I will use the word "ranch" to describe both dwellings.

8   Scott, "Historic Trail Maps," 18. Unless appearing in quotations, hereafter I will be referring to all ranches as ranch.

9   Root and Connelley, *Overland Stage*, 42, 70.

10 Root and Hickman, "Part II—Solomon and Republican Route—Concluded," endnote 120, 216.

estimated that no less than 10,000 vehicles passed along the Denver trail through the Platte valley. With such traffic as that it was obvious that the valley in this section of northeastern Colorado Territory offered great opportunity for establishing profitable ranches along the way. Most new stations were built in 1863–1864. The stations owned and operated by Ben Holladay in this section were Julesburg, Antelope, Spring Hill, Dennison's, Valley Station, Kelley's (later renamed American Ranche) and Beaver Creek.[11]

The stage service alone is a fascinating story. Passengers were carried in sturdy Concord coaches manufactured in Concord, New Hampshire, by the Abbot-Downing Company. Each coach cost $1,000 to build and deliver. In today's money, that is more than $14,450 per coach.[12] Holladay had about 100 coaches in operation during his heyday. The coach was made to carry nine passengers inside with another passenger or two alongside the driver. The coaches stopped only to change horses and drivers, or to allow for meals to be purchased by passengers at home stations. Holladay operated 49 stations between Atchison, Kansas, and Denver, 25 of them serving as stations that offered meals to passengers. The journey from Atchison to Denver and from Denver to Atchison lasted on average six days and six nights and about every 12 hours a west-bound coach would pass an east-bound coach. Every Monday coaches at Atchison and Denver were designated to carry only express mail and no passengers, unless there was room to fit a passenger or two on top of the mail. Express packages cost one dollar per pound, and the express coach could be expected to contain hundreds of pounds of express mail. When one purchased a ticket in Atchison or Denver, it guaranteed a seat, in the order that one became available. Often passengers had to wait days to get a seat. A one-way fare to Denver in 1859 cost $75, but by the end of the Civil War the fare had jumped to $175, an equivalent of $2,588 in today's dollars.[13] Stations averaged 12½ miles apart, all the way from Atchison to Denver. About a dozen animals were kept at every station. One hundred miles west of Atchison was the Kansas town of Marysville, just below the Nebraska border. Marysville was considered in 1860 to be the end of civilization. From there on into Denver, it was "wilderness," or

11   Root and Connelley, *Overland Stage*, 162–163; 222; 384.
12   http://www.westegg.com/inflation/infl.cgi (accessed May 20, 2013).
13   http://www.westegg.com/inflation/infl.cgi (accessed May 22, 2013).

uncivilized territory.[14] When the Cheyenne war began in 1864, these stage stops were extremely vulnerable to Indian attacks.

For many of these ranches/stations, little is known other than brief comments from a rare first-hand account of travel along the route. Englishman Maurice Morris, writing in 1863 of his travel that summer over the trail, said this:

> we came, without further adventure than killing a watersnake mottled beautifully like a panther, to Spring Hill Station, which bore evidence of the saw-mills near Denver. We then camped at Lillian Springs, where the heaven was illuminated with lightening more fantastic than any fireworks; but there was no rain. At this ranche I felt convinced, by a fence that I saw, that an Englishman or Irishman had been at work, so I went in, and found it tenanted by a North of Ireland man; he had left a good farm in Illinois on account of the war, which he disapproved of, and, as he considered talking a thirsty process, he insisted on my joining him in some whiskey, modified by a cordial much approved of, I believe, called the "good Samaritan." I had my fears as to the results, but they proved groundless.[15]

An even earlier account comes from C. M. Clark, who ventured along the trail in 1859:

> Thirty miles further travel over the high prairie, and along the river bottom, alternately from one to another, brings us to Lillian Springs, where there is an adobe building, occupied as a trading post; and there is also one of the best springs of water that is to be met with on the whole line of travel.[16]

Incidental comments like that those just noted, giving specific details of particular stage stations are rarely found in published literature. However, records housed in stored government files in the National Archives contain a wealth of information regarding these individual ranches along all three roads to Denver. Those files are the long neglected individual Indian depredation claims. These records provide important details as to what was supplied at various ranches, specifics as to numbers of buildings and building structures as well as who owned or operated particular stations.

The depredation claim of Charles Moore contains much information about the Denver road and Washington Ranch. From his claim and others

---

14 Root and Connelley, *Overland Stage*, 11, 22–23, 49, 64, 66–67, 69, 74, 84, 93, 96, 102, 190, 486.

15 Maurice O'Connor Morris, *Rambles in the Rocky Mountains: With a Visit to the Gold Fields of Colorado* (London: Smith, Elder and Co., 1864), 68–69

16 C. M. Clark, M.D., *A Trip to Pike's Peak & Notes by the Way, etc.* (Chicago, IL: S. P. Round's Steam Book and Job Printing House, 1861. Reprinted The Talisman Press, 1961), 57.

one can gain a better understanding of the Denver trail. Early Logan County historian Emma Burke Conklin claimed that Valley Station was owned by "'Jim' and Charley Moore," and that they had built a toll road "east of the bottom and, after making a hard, dirt road, charged for immigrant wagons one dollar each" to pass through their self-imposed toll.[17] This is confirmed in Charles Moore's testimony in his claim that sometime after 1864 he acquired a contract with the stage company, and Valley Station was then abandoned. He with some other men then took the better buildings from Valley Station and brought them three miles east to Washington Ranch. But these details will come out later, as the accounts of the various Indian raids will make clear.

17   Conklin, *History of Logan County*, 74.

CHAPTER TWO

The Indian War Begins

. . . we all took matches, and we were to wait until the Indians came on to us and then each man with the powder wagons had orders to set fire to the powder wagons, and we knowing what would happen was to scatter and lie on the ground, and give the Indians a surprise. This of course was only to be resorted to as a last measure.

AARON HOEL INDIAN DEPREDATION CLAIM #7528

THE DENVER ROADS DID NOT EXPERIENCE OPEN HOSTILI-ties with Plains Indians prior to the year 1864. With each passing year after 1859, more and more travelers used the trail, both coming and going. When Indians were present along the trail, it was common for them to seek food from parties operating the various wagon trains. Freighters often fed and traded with the Indians. It was not uncommon for small bands of Indians to remain camped for several days at or very near the various stage stops. But by the spring of 1864 that would change, when a combination of hostilities—the causes were varied and many—commenced involving Southern Arapaho, Cheyenne, Kiowa, Comanche and Apaches from the southern part of the territory, and Northern Cheyenne, Lakota and Arapaho from the north. Both Southern and Northern Cheyenne, along with various Lakota and Arapaho bands brought their anger along the Denver trail. From then until the war effectively ended in the summer of 1869, both Northern and Southern Cheyenne Indians were involved with nearly every raid. Even when Lakota were primarily responsible for a particular raid, Cheyenne were among the warriors present. It was a Cheyenne war.

Among Indian accounts of this war, the memories of George Bent remain the most comprehensive. Bent was the son of William Bent, the well-known trader who ventured into present-day Colorado, with three other brothers, and established Bent's Fort in 1835, along the Arkansas River near where Fort Lyon was established in 1860. George was born July 7, 1843, the son of Owl Woman, a Southern Cheyenne. Bent's half-brother Charles, who was born in 1847, was four years younger. He was the son of Owl Woman's younger sister, Yellow Woman, whom William Bent married after Owl Woman died. The Bent brothers spent time in their youth receiving formal education in St. Louis. When the Civil War broke out, both brothers briefly served in the Confederate service. And both brothers survived the 1864 attack on Black Kettle's sleeping village at Sand Creek. Together, after Sand Creek, both Bent boys participated in many of the well-known incidents comprising the Cheyenne war. Charles Bent died of wounds received in fighting the Pawnee in 1868. George lived a long life, dying in Colony, Oklahoma, in 1918. But it was the letters George Bent wrote, most of them to George Hyde, beginning in 1904, that constitute the material that Hyde shaped into the book, *Life of George Bent*. The book, however, was not published until well after both George's were dead, in 1968.[1]

According to George Bent, the Cheyenne had six warrior societies: Wohsihitaneo—Kit-fox Men; Himoiyoqis—Crooked Lance or Bone Scraper Society, which included Bent and Roman Nose; Mahohivas—Red Shields, or Bull Soldiers. This band of warriors carried red shields and favored the Republican River valley; Himatanohis—Bowstring Men or Wolf Warriors; Hotamimasaw—Foolish or Crazy Dogs, a Northern Cheyenne warrior society; Hotamitaneo—Dog Men. Dog Men, the principal warrior society as the Cheyenne war played out, were called Dog Soldiers by the whites. Famous warriors from other divisions joined the Dog Men. Bent recalled: "For a long time the Dog Soldiers were looked upon almost as outlaws by the rest of the tribe; but when the big wars came with the whites, and the Dog Soldiers took such a leading part in the fighting, the rest of the tribe came to show them the greatest respect."[2]

The Dog Soldiers were interested in raiding and plunder, which was the impetus for the Cheyenne war. They were not led by council chiefs, such as Black Kettle, but rather were guided by their own individual leaders. It was

---

1   Dan L. Thrapp, *Encyclopedia of Frontier Biography*, Volume I (Glendale, CA: The Arthur H. Clark Company, 1988), 96–100.

2   George E. Hyde, *Life of George Bent Written From His Letters*, edited by Savoie Lottinville (Norman, OK: University of Oklahoma Press, 1868), 337–338.

these warriors, especially the young ones—"wild and reckless"—who got the rest of the Cheyenne tribe in trouble with the Army. The Dog Soldiers freely mixed with the Brule and Oglala Lakota, so in any given excursion there was always a mix of Cheyenne and Lakota. "Throughout the 1860s, the soldier bands conducted hundreds of raids in Kansas, Nebraska, and Colorado, as recorded in the official War Department records."[3] This was the Cheyenne war.

Governor John Evans, appointed by President Abraham Lincoln to replace William Gilpin, the first territorial governor of Colorado, reported a grave concern in late fall, 1863, which was a prelude of things to come. Sources warned him that all of the above mentioned bands of Indians had confederated together for the purpose of forcing all the white settlers out of the country and that they would forcefully take back their land from the whites. The main source for this information was Robert North, a white man married to an Arapaho Indian. North had lived among the Indians since he was a boy, and after recovering an Arapaho female captive from the Ute Indians, he "obtained the confidence of the Indians completely." He warned Evans about what he has witnessed, that the Indians had for some time only been trading for arms and ammunition, and as soon as they felt they had sufficient quantities, they would then commence a general war to drive out all white people and close all trails of commerce. North prepared a statement for Evans noting he observed "the principle chiefs pledge to each other that they would be friendly and shake hands with the whites until they procured ammunition and guns, so as to be ready when they strike. Plundering to get means has already commenced, and the plan is to commence the war at several points in the sparse settlements early in the spring [1864]."[4]

---

3   John H. Moore, *The Cheyenne Nation: A Social and Demographic History* (Lincoln and London: University of Nebraska Press, 1987), 197–198.

4   Robert North statement dated November 10, 1863 and included in report to the Secretary of Interior 1864, 368. Anderson Sharp Indian Depredation Claim #1520, 1526, 6–7. Record Group 123, National Archives Building, Washington, DC. See also *The War of the Rebellion: A Compilation of the Official Records of the Union and Confederate Armies* (Washington: Government Printing Office, 1891), Series I, Volume XXXIV, Part IV, 100. See also *Report of the Commissioner of Indian Affairs for the Year 1864* (Washington, DC: Government Printing Office, 1865), 224–225. Eldridge Gerry confirmed this when he reported later in August, when the war was in full swing, that "nearly all the old [Indian] men were opposed to war, but the young men could not be controlled; that they were determined to sweep the Platte and the country as far as they could." Gerry stated he received this information from two old Cheyenne chiefs, Long Chin and Man-shot-by-a-bee. See *Report of the Commissioner of Indian Affairs for the Year 1864*, 232.

North's statement was soon confirmed in early April 1864, when a Denver newspaper said that "People coming in from the river report that Indians are offering large prices in buffalo robes for rifles and ammunition and seem to be in need of little else."[5]

It is a difficult task today to lay out all the causes for the war that eventually broke out in 1864, and continued for five years. Governor Evans cited misunderstandings among the Indians regarding the stipulations of the Fort Wise Treaty of 1861, which reduced their land, as one cause. He was certainly right about that. But he also believed the Sioux coming from the north, having escaped "unconquered" from their violent 1862 Minnesota uprising that resulted in hundreds of dead settlers, were urging the Plains Indians to continue the war they had started up north. He would have that verified by Cheyenne Chief Bull Bear five months later when questioned at Camp Weld about which Indians were expected to continue raiding. Bull Bear replied that about one half of all the Missouri River Sioux "and Yanktons who were driven from Minnesota are those who have crossed the Platte."[6] They wanted their Cheyenne and Arapaho allies to begin committing raids along the Denver roads and join their Lakota comrades in a general outbreak. In August, Mr. Elbridge Gerry reported that two Indians told him that "nearly all the old men are opposed to war, but the young men could not be controlled; they were determined to sweep the Platte and the country as far as they could; they know that if the white men follow up the war for two or three years they would get rubbed out, but meanwhile they would kill plenty of whites."[7] The attention to the Civil War also encouraged the warriors anxious for war, leaving, as Evans feared, "the plains to an easy and successful conquest by the alliance."[8] In addition, Confederate emissaries had encouraged this

5   *The Commonwealth*, April 9, 1864. This story and all other events relating to the Indian war of 1864 can be found in Scott C. Williams' compilation, *Colorado History through the News (a context of the times). The Indian Wars of 1864 through the Sand Creek Massacre* (Aurora, CO: Pick of the Ware Publishing, 1977).

6   John M. Carroll, Introduction, *The Sand Creek Massacre: A Documentary History* (New York, NY: Sol Lewis, 1973), "Report of the Secretary of War," 39th Congress, 2d Session, Ex. Doc. No. 26, 217. For a recent account of this violent episode in Indian war history, see Greg Michno, *Dakota Dawn: The Decisive First Week of the Sioux Uprising, August 17–24, 1862* (New York, NY: Savas Beatie, 2011). Bull Bear confused his Lakota tribes. It was the Dakotas that initiated the deadly 1862 Indian outbreak in Minnesota, not the Yanktons (Nakotas).

7   *Report of the Commissioner of Indian Affairs for the Year 1864* (Washington, DC: Government Printing Office, 1865), 232.

8   John Evans report dated October 15, 1864. Anderson Sharp Indian Depredation Claim #526, 12–13. Record Group 123.

affiliation of tribal warriors. Indeed, intermittent violent encounters with various Lakota, Cheyenne, and Arapaho Indians can be traced back to the mid-1850s, and the prospect for improvement by 1864 was not good.

Diminishing land and food sources, however, seemed to be the common thread in the various Indian grievances. The once vast buffalo herds were beginning to thin by 1864, and it was obvious that the nomadic Indian way of life, following the buffalo herds, could not survive for many more years. Open land was vanishing with the coming of the white man. The erecting of buildings and the continuous stream of traffic, both to and from the west along the major water thoroughfares connecting Kansas with Colorado Territory, including the important Denver road, was especially troubling. Among other things, it caused the buffalo migration to change the pathways of its annual northern trek, which interfered with the Indians hunting buffalo.[9] Timber was disappearing due to its use both as building material and as a means of fuel.[10] Indian populations were declining due in part to the many diseases brought to them by white expansion. Depending on which Indian was heard, various complaints of discontent grew. Governor Evans was well aware of his and everyone else's isolation in Denver should a general war erupt.

Newspapers later reported that the building of the railroad was also causing Indian anger: "The Indian has learned that the Railroad is his enemy, and he makes that his objective point. The Railroad like the cabin of the settler, indicates the advance of civilization, and the Indians are making an aggressive fight against it."[11] In 1864, the Indian had not yet developed hostility toward the building of the railroad. That was soon to come, however, when he realized the consequences this big iron machine brought to the long revered hunting grounds. One Indian expressed his frustration by asking a freighter how he would like it if the Indians came into his country

---

9   Kiowa chief Satanta outlined his complaints in 1867 this way: "that the white man must build no more houses out here, must burn no more of their wood, must drink no more of their water, must not drive their buffalo off, that the railroad must not come any further, and that the [trail] must be stopped." Captain Henry Asbury, "Report, Headquarters, Fort Larned, Kansas, February 27, 1867." Letters received, Department of the Missouri, Record Group 393, Part 1, Entry 2593, National Archives Building, Washington, DC.

10 Arapaho chief Little Raven was especially upset by the cutting of timber, especially for use at military posts. See Major Henry Douglass, "Report, March 14, 1867." Letters received, Department of the Missouri, Record Group 393, Part 1, Entry 2593.

11 *Leavenworth Times & Conservative*, May 30, 1869.

and killed his cows and dogs. Well, that was what the white man was doing by coming into Indian country and killing their buffalo and wolves.[12]

The brooding contempt against the continuing intrusion of the white man into Indian country continued and by early April 1864, it appeared that North's warning of an impending Indian war was coming to fruition. The signs of war sprang forth. Rancher W. D. Ripley rode from Bijou Creek to Camp Sanborn (on the north side of the South Platte River north of present-day Roggen, Colorado) and reported to Captain George L. Sanborn, commanding the 1st Colorado Cavalry, that on April 11 a band of Indians had stolen stock from several people living on and near Bijou Creek, Ripley himself barely escaping with his life. Captain Sanborn sent 2nd Lieutenant Clark Dunn and 40 men from companies H and C in pursuit. Lieutenant Dunn split his command prior to encountering about 15 or 20 Indians near Fremont's Orchard (present-day Orchard). Dunn later reported his effort to parley with the Indians, numbering about 25, hoping they would surrender the stock. The Chief replied with "a scornful laugh" and immediately fired at the troopers. Dunn: "I ordered my men to return the fire, and after a short time they fled, and I pursued them. . . ." Four soldiers were wounded, two severely. After a running fight of about an hour the Indians escaped north, the army horses having played out. Private J. G. Brandly, wounded in the back with an arrow, and Private A. J. Baird, wounded with an arrow in the right shoulder, later died and were buried at Camp Sanborn. Dunn reported 20 Indians were either killed or wounded. He noted the Indians were well armed with "rifles, navy and dragoon pistols, and the carbine pistol, carrying an ounce ball, besides their bows and arrows."[13] For all intents and purposes, the Cheyenne war had commenced.

At about this time, another interesting incident occurred along the Denver road involving a freighting excursion that coincided with Dunn's escapade. Aaron Hoel owned most of the wagons in the train, and apparently bad weather was a contributing cause in the loss of his oxen. It began in late fall 1863, but culminated at the time of Dunn's fight. Hoel had bought the

---

12 Augustine Holland Indian Depredation Claim #3290. Record Group 123.

13 *War of the Rebellion*, Volume XXXIV, Part I, 883–885. See also Jacob Downing's report, found in the report of the special joint committee on the condition of the Indian tribes, 1867, a copy of which is in the file of George Shrouf Indian Depredation Claim #2170. Record Group 123. See also Gregory F. Michno, *Encyclopedia of Indian Wars: Western Battles and Skirmishes, 1850–1890* (Missoula, MT: Mountain Press Publishing Company, 2003), 134–135.

trading post at the old California Crossing near Julesburg from a French-man who was married to a mixed-blood Indian woman. She "was the daugh-ter of old Bouvier [Beauvais], a French man who had married a full blood Indian squaw, and who kept the trading post, on the old California crossing of the South Platte."[14]

After Hoel bought the trading post, Truman B. Hays was freighting one wagon from Omaha to Denver in the fall of 1863. He got caught in a snow-storm about Thanksgiving, which closed the trail until the next spring. The storm came when he was at Hoel's recently bought trading post. He stayed the winter at the post. The next spring, in late March or early April, he finally was able to resume his journey to Denver. Hoel also had freight he was bringing to Denver and the mining camps, hauled in 13 wagons, along with another man named Millard who had two wagons. Hays also had a wagon, which made the train leaving Hoel's ranch 16 wagons long. They were hauling mostly blasting powder for the mines, along with some general merchandise. Each wagon had at least six oxen pulling it, but most were pulled by four yoke (two oxen per yoke), making more than 80 oxen hauling the heavy freight. Hays' story gives one a clear understanding of the beginning of the war:

> On the night of the second day, we camped at the Wisconsin Ranch, to remain there over night, and turned our cattle [oxen] out as was customary; during the night a storm came up, and the boys staid at the wagons; in the morning when we went to look for our cattle we found most of them gone; the boys of the train went out on foot to hunt up the cattle, and that night they returned with about half the cattle, so we were unable to proceed any farther; the next day following the return of the boys with those cattle, Mr. Hoel, and I went out on horse back hunting the lost cattle; we went South to a place called the White Man's fork, a creek; it was some where between a hundred miles and eighty miles from the Wisconsin Ranch, and there we hunted all around, back and forth, East and West; we spent seven days on this trip, and then we started back, and when we got about twenty miles or so from the Wisconsin Ranch, a blizzard came up so that it was impossible for us to travel so we lay in a buffalo wallow, until the worst of the Blizzard was over; the next day the wind was so strong that we could not face it; Mr. Hoel, who had been in that neighborhood said that there was a ranch on Beaver Creek, west of where we were, but we missed Beaver Creek, learning after that we had passed it where it ran under ground; this we did not know at the time, we rode west all day and just before sun

---

14   Aaron Hoel Indian Depredation Claim #7528. Record Group 123.

down we saw an Indian buck, who tried to get away from us, but he at the time was on a pony and we headed him off and tried to get some information from him; he acted so suspicious and so dumb that we got no information from him at all, he would not tell us any thing at all. From where we met this Indian we rode due north all night following the North Star, until about two o'clock in the morning; we were then up on a Bluff, and it was bright moonlight, and from there we saw a valley and some water, which proved to be the Platte River; we also saw some wagons right under the bluff with a camp fire still burning and close by was a ranch. At the time we did not know where we was, we went around the bluff, and as soon as we got down to the valley we recognized the place; Hoel then went to the Ranch and woke the man, he being acquainted with him; he was a Frenchman, who was married to a Squaw; Hoel after waking up the man told me that he could not eat any thing that Squaw cooked, as he had eaten there some time before this at a big dinner, and that after eating the dinner he made the discovery, that it had been dog meat that he had eaten, and that it made him so sick that he was not able to eat any thing that she might cook. We got some crackers and whiskey from this man and waited there until nearly day light then went six miles east, to a ranch owned by a white man, who had a white wife, and there we got our breakfast; these Ranches were about sixty or sixty five miles west of the Wisconsin Ranch, where we had left our wagons.

After breakfast we went east towards our camp; at dinner time we came to Beaver Creek, ate our dinner at a ranch house there, and parties there told us they had heard of a bunch of cattle being seen on Beaver Creek quite aways from there, so we got the woman at this ranch to bake us some biscuits and boil a shank of a ham, and we started the next morning. After resting our selves and horses all afternoon and night, for the place we were told that those cattle had been heard of up on the Beaver, we hunted all up and down there along Beaver and the sur-rounding country, and got back to about the same place as we were before about twenty miles from the Wisconsin Ranch, near some bluffs, and there we ran into another blizzard, much worse than the one before; we picketed one of the horses and hobbled the other, and hunted up a place to stay. We discovered a small cave, and we got into it and we stayed in the cave all of eighteen or twenty hours, before this blizzard subsided; when we got out of the cave we got our horses and started for our camp, they were very weak, after going a few miles one of them played out entirely. We took the saddle and bridle of that one and put them on the stronger one, leaving the worn out horse on the road (this horse was afterwards recovered) and then with one of us at the head of this horse and the other behind driving we went on towards camp; that night we stopped at a ranch just a short distance from the Wisconsin Ranch, where our outfit was, all but the lost cattle. We got to the camp the next day, after being gone on this hunt, Hoel and I, about fourteen days in all.

After getting back to camp at the Wisconsin Ranch, some Indians came to the ranch, and that evening an Indian buck came to our camp and we made inquiries of him, about the lost cattle, and he told us that he had seen some with a brand; on describing by signs what they were like and where the brands were, the sign he made was an "H" and gave the location of the brand on the cattle. This was Hoel's brand exactly; he said he knew where the cattle was and pointed the directions, and that he had seen them. Immediately Hoel made arrangements with the Indian to go with him after the cattle; they were to go the next morning, so Mr. Hoel bought a good horse there at the ranch to go on this hunt. The next morning the Indian did not want to go, and wanted to back out, but Hoel placed him on his honor, and then the Indian said if Hoel would give him so much he would go with him and show him the place; this Hoel did, and they started from the camp, Hoel and this Indian; after they started the Indian wanted Hoel to get him some thing at the camp, this Hoel did coming back after it. What followed after I only know from what Hoel told me after he got back from that trip. Hoel and the Indian got back at night, next day.

Hoel had a fine horse that he had bought to go on this trip, with this Indian; after they got started from camp the Indian wanted Hoel to stay back when they would come to a raise [rise], and let him go ahead and reconnoiter and see what was to be seen. This Indian appeared to be very nervous, and excited, [and] at last the Indian went up on a hill, stopped a while and then went over the hill and disappeared. This aroused Hoel's suspicions, and he left his horse, crawled up on top of the hill, and looked over and there in the distance Hoel saw a large band of Indians; he watched them for a while and then he saw an Indian leave the band and come towards him. He crawled back to the draw where he had left his horse, and soon the Indian who had gone out with him came back to where he had left Hoel; Hoel noticed that he did not have the package that he had given him and was much more excited and nervous apparently, and told Hoel that the cattle was gone, that they had been taken to Big Belly's Ranch, and when Hoel wanted to go on he insisted on returning to the Wisconsin Ranch, and Hoel, having seen this big bunch of Indians, and knowing they were so close to him, was willing to return to the camp without the cattle. I know that he returned without any of the cattle, and it was at that time told me to what occurred and what he had seen on that trip with this Indian.

After starting from Wisconsin Ranch, we traveled two days and about nine miles east of Fremont's Orchards, and had passed the stage station about three miles, and the men from the stage station came after us and tried to get us to return to the station, telling us that the Indians had assembled together, and that the Soldiers that was stationed at Fremont's Orchards, had gone out to disperse them, but that the Indians were so numerous that they had driven the soldiers back to Fremont's Orchards [Dunn's fight], and they were afraid the Indians would gather and attack the Stage Station; those men wanted us all to gather at the Stage Station for self protection, for them as well as for us. We had seen the signal fires that night, and it appeared in some places as balls of fire in the skies, and we could see them all around where we were, at that time.

We held a consultation, Mr. Hoel, I and the others who were with us, and we decided to go right on to Denver, taking the River Road, and we also decided what we would do if we were attacked; so we got some dry grass and put it in the powder wagons, and we all took matches, and we were to wait until the Indians came on to us and then each man with the powder wagons had orders to set fire to the powder wagons, and we knowing what would happen was to scatter and lie on the ground, and give the Indians a surprise. This of course was only to be resorted to as a last measure; we then continued on our way and reached Denver unmolested.[15]

On April 15—three days after Dunn's fight—another violent encounter occurred with the command under Lieutenant George S. Eayre. Again, stolen cattle were the cause. On April 5, government contractors Irwin, Jackman and Company lost 175 head of cattle from the headwaters of the Big Sandy. The cattle were lost along what would the following year become the Smoky Hill stage route, not far from present-day Cheyenne Wells, Colorado. When this was reported to Colonel John M. Chivington, commanding the district which included Colorado Territory, he ordered Eayre in pursuit. Eayre's column consisted of 26 men, Company D, First Colorado Cavalry, and 54 men and two 12-pound mountain howitzers of the Independent Battery, Colorado Volunteer Artillery.[16] By April 11, he was at Beaver Creek, 80 miles east of Denver. There he was joined by a guide named Routh. Routh had been herding the cattle when they were stolen.

On April 13, Eayre picked up the trail of the Indians who had stolen the cattle, and followed them northwest to the headwaters of the South Fork of the Republican River near present-day Flagler, Colorado. He was soon informed by one of his scouts of a small encampment of Cheyenne about one mile away. Halting his command, he sent a lieutenant and two men to the village, which had only five lodges, to demand return of the cattle. Within minutes one of the men galloped back to report that the Indian men were advancing toward his command, while the women were fleeing in the other direction. As Eayre approached the village with his men, a concealed Indian fired upon the soldiers, wounding one critically. Dividing his men into groups of 10, Eayre ordered them to advance against the Indians, who did not stay to greet them, but instead fled, abandoning their small village. Eayre then burned the village and destroyed the vast stores of Indian food and supplies.

---

15   Aaron Hoel Indian Depredation Claim #7528.
16   *War of the Rebellion*, Volume XXXIV, Part III, 113.

Following the fleeing Indians further north, two days later he found another village near present-day Wray, Colorado, again abandoned, which he promptly destroyed. His scouts surmised that the Indians were following the Republican River east. Believing his horses were not able to continue pursuit, he abandoned the chase and returned to Denver. Near this second village his men recaptured 19 of the contractor's stolen cattle.[17]

On April 19, Indian Agent Samuel G. Colley wrote to Governor Evans from Fort Lyon south on the Arkansas River, and reported that Cheyenne down there had taken several horses that had strayed from the post. He was concerned because Captain Hardy had been sent to recover the stock and if the Cheyenne resisted Hardy would fight them. He feared this might start an Indian war. John Powers, a young man married to a Cheyenne, confirmed to Colley that the Lakota had come down from the north and smoked the war pipe with the Cheyenne. Robert North's earlier warning to Governor Evans was proving true. Things indeed were looking ominous. Meanwhile, the next day another report came in from Kansas, stating that Kiowa were attacking wagon trains, stealing and killing stock. Lieutenant W. D. Crocker noted that in two years on the plains he had never seen the Indians so insolent. He wanted reinforcements to ensure peace.[18]

Once Lieutenant Eayre returned to Denver from his battle, he was almost immediately sent back out to find and chastise the Cheyenne and recover the remaining stolen stock of Irwin and Jackman. Leaving on April 24 with 84 men, 15 wagons and two mountain howitzers, he headed in the direction of the Smoky Hill River. On May 1, near present-day Cheyenne Wells, he wrote to Col. Chivington that he had found a large trail containing 100 lodges, which had come from the direction of the Republican River. He intended to follow the trail and overtake the Indians.[19] The trail continued east along the Smoky Hill River. On May 13, Cheyenne Indians stole four mules and one horse from post sutler Jesse Crane at Fort Larned, a post along the older Santa Fe trail. He had been post sutler since 1862.[20] Warriors returned June 5, and took three more mules and another horse.[21] Fort

---

17   *War of the Rebellion*, Volume XXXIV, Part III, 218–219. Volume XXXIV, Part I, 881–882. See also Michno, *Encyclopedia*, 135.
18   *War of the Rebellion*, XXXIV, Part III, 234, 241.
19   *War of the Rebellion*, XXXIV, Part IV, 101, 403.
20   Jesse Crane Indian Depredation Claim #1164. Record Group 123.
21   Jesse Crane Indian Depredation Claim #1165.

interpreter Henry Bradley went out to try and recover the stock stolen on May 13, but came back and reported that the Cheyenne had the mules and horse. When asked to return them the Indians refused and all they would talk about was "going to war with the whites." Licensed Indian trader F. R. Curtis further confirmed the warlike attitude of the Cheyenne, saying the other tribes had been for the past month warning him that the Cheyenne were hanging around the post "to get information and murder, and to steal and run off horses and mules."[22] Captain J. W. Parmetar confirmed these rumors, in a report sent May 17: "the Cheyenne Indians will commence hostilities against the whites in a very few days. They have all left the vicinity and gone to the Platte country for the purpose of preparing for war."[23]

At the same time these men were gathering this information, on May 16, near today's Schoenchen, Kansas, and south of present-day Hays, Eayre found his Indians in what was then called Big Bushes. They were in all likelihood the same warriors that had stolen Crane's stock so close to Fort Larned three days earlier.

Accounts of what then happened next vary depending on who made the claim. According to the Indian version, Cheyenne hunters alerted the village of the coming soldiers and peace chiefs Black Kettle and Lean Bear, wearing a large peace medal he had received when visiting Washington the year before, approached Eayre's column. However, before any communications had been made, Eayre ordered his men to open fire on the chiefs. Lean Bear and two other Indians immediately went down. The Indians then returned fire, killing four soldiers and wounding three. Shortly after the fight began the two howitzers were deployed and opened fire into the village, which consisted of at least 500 warriors. This action angered the Indians, who were ready to counterattack and wipe out Eayre's column, which they could have easily done, given their large numbers. Black Kettle, however, intervened and kept the Indians from retaliating. The soldiers were thus able to retreat to the safety of Fort Larned about 40 miles to the south.[24]

The military version, however, is quite different. The first report to come out—May 25—simply reported that the Indians were driven from the field after several hours of fighting, losing 28 killed.[25] Two days later Major

---

22   Crane Indian Depredation Claim #1165.
23   *War of the Rebellion*, XXXIV, Part III, 643.
24   Hyde, *Life of George Bent*, 130–132.
25   *War of the Rebellion*, XXXIV, Part IV, 39.

Edward "Ned" Wynkoop, commanding Fort Larned, wrote that from 25 to 30 Indians had been killed. Among those dead, he erroneously included Black Kettle. Eayre lost several horses "killed, wounded, and stampeded in the fight." The terrain was not suited for howitzer fire or the entire village would have been destroyed. The soldiers made a gallant display of courage in the fight. Eayre appended a brief report with Wynkoop's account and added that the fight began when he was attacked by 400 Cheyenne. It took seven-and-a-half hours to drive the Indians from the field. Eayre said three chiefs and 25 warriors were killed.[26]

Major Thomas I. McKenny, Inspector General of the Department of Kansas, was at Fort Larned when Eayre came into the post, and he added different details than what Wynkoop or Eayre gave. Saying Eayre had wandered out of his district, the Indians found his command scattered, his wagons well behind without any rear guard, the artillery almost two miles to their front and the cavalry an additional mile further. With Eayre's command thus situated the Indians saw their opportunity and attacked, "killing 3 instantly and wounding 3 others, 1 dying two days afterward, the Colorado troops retreating to this place."[27]

Regardless of which version one chooses to accept—McKenny's version may be the most truthful—from this point on, there was no question about the intentions of the Indians: the Cheyenne war had begun. Bent: "The Cheyennes were so stirred up over the killing of Lean Bear that the chiefs could not control the young warriors. They made up a war party and raided the stage road all the way from Fort Larned to near Fort Riley, killing several white men and plundering all the stations."[28]

Bent was accurate in his assessment. Indeed, on the day after Eayre's fight, John Dodd was leaving Fort Larned when he met Eayre with his command a few miles away from the post. Eayre informed Dodd of his fight on the 16th and told him to go back to the fort, as it wasn't safe to travel north to the station he worked at near present-day Great Bend. Dodd soon learned that the station on Walnut Creek had been raided at 9 A.M., on April 17. He lost

---

26 *War of the Rebellion*, XXXIV, Part I, 934–935.

27 *War of the Rebellion*, XXXIV, Part IV, 403.

28 Hyde, *Life of George Bent*, 133. Of course, the statements in Crane's Indian depredation claim testify to the fact that the Cheyenne were already preparing for war and had already begun when Eayre killed Lean Bear. If the statements in Crane's claims are true, then Bent is wrong to blame Eayre for starting a war that the Cheyenne had already begun.

two horses.[29] Charles Rath lost more, six mules and two horses.[30] Nearby at the Great Bend of the Arkansas River Harvey Rickford suffered the theft of three mules and a horse, along with a bunch of household goods, including, interestingly, one Indian lodge.[31] His horses were taken from a trading post run by T. R. Curtis and a man named F. Cole.[32] Curtis and Cole were licensed Indian traders and had operated a trading post east of the Great Bend, at a stream called Big Turkey, near where Fort Zarah would be built. Curtis was married to a Lakota woman, Winty Curtis, the sister of Red Cloud. They were married about 1847.[33] The Cheyenne Indians came to the post between 10 and 11 o'clock in the morning and pilfered the store of whatever they wanted, destroyed the rest of the goods and set the building afire. Everything was lost. Their trading goods were valued at over $2,100, the ranch valued at $1,500. In addition nine horses, four mules and a donkey were stolen, together valued at $1,430. An investigation into the losses later determined that the attack was made by a band of Kiowa, Arapaho and Cheyenne and stated "that it was a fact notorious among the whites located in the neighborhood of the scene of these outrages, that the tribes designated committed the depredations, but on account of their hostility it was impossible and impracticable, literally, to submit claims to them for reclamation."[34]

Eight miles up Walnut Creek from where the Indians made the raid against Dodd, William ("Dutch Bill") Ennis kept a station for the Kansas Stage Company. He reported the attack at his ranch was carried out by a band of Kiowa, Apache and Cheyenne warriors. His ranch was burned to the ground, destroying all of the contents of the stage station. In addition he lost 40 cattle, 17 mules and 25 horses.[35]

---

29 John Dodd Indian Depredation Claim #1168. Record Group 123.

30 Charles Rath Indian Depredation Claim #1167. Record Group 75. See also report of Captain James W. Parmetar, commanding the post at Ft. Larned, which confirms this attack. *War of the Rebellion*, Volume XXXIV, Part III, 661.

31 Harvey Rickford and Orson Stanley Indian Depredation Claim #2351. Record Group 123.

32 T. R. Curtis Indian Depredation Claim #10728–10730. Record Group 123.

33 T. R. Curtis Indian Depredation Claim #198. Record Group 75, entry 701. T. R. Curtis died in 1874, and Winty took over his depredation claim, testifying to her marriage and stating that she was the sister of Red Cloud.

34 T. R. Curtis Indian Depredation Claim #10728.

35 William Ennis Indian Depredation Claim (no claim number noted in file). Record Group 75, entry 700. John Dodd, in his depredation claim (RG 123, #1168), says at the time of his loss his neighbor eight miles up Walnut Creek was also attacked. He identified him as "Dutch Bill." Ennis says in his claim that his station was 30 miles east of Ft. Larned on Walnut Creek. Northeast is more accurate, which would place his ranch near present-day Heizer, Kansas, and would be about eight miles up the creek from Dodd's ranch. "Dutch Bill" was the nickname for William Griffenstein. See J. A. Cary Indian Depredation Claim #3439. Record Group 75. See also p. 298.

The Indian raids at this time were rather widespread. On May 16–17 settlers living near Salina, about 60 miles east from where the raids were happening on Walnut Creek, abandoned their farms and sought protection inside the town. W. W. Morrison was living two miles south of Salina, where Indians took a cow and pony.[36] Benjamin Gardner lost his crops outside Salina because he could not attend to them. In addition, his house was ransacked, it later being determined that soldiers sent to the settlements for protection themselves broke into several houses, including Gardner's house. There was a scare at this time that the Cheyenne were being aided by white Confederate sympathizers, and that the raids were being made to divert attention away from General Sterling Price's anticipated raid into Kansas later that fall.[37] The same thing happened to James Sharp, he too fleeing to Salina for protection, just two days after his youngest child was born. Rumors abounded that several men had been killed 10 miles west of Salina.[38] Lenox Baxter also fled his farm near Salina and reported a loss of eight hogs, a crop of corn and much timber that was cut to build a blockhouse in Salina for all the settlers' protection.[39] Peter Giersch fled his farm, losing a horse and all his crops.[40] Thomas Boyle reported that a man by the name of Walker was killed at the Prather Ranch in Ellsworth County, about 35 miles west of Salina. Boyle was living with his young family eight miles northwest of Salina when all of this was happening. His family fled to Abilene, and while gone Indians burned six miles of the Saline valley, which included his 18 acres of land, most of it growing corn and wheat. He believed, however, that the Indians responsible for this were Kaw and not Cheyenne.[41]

Two families from the Salina settlement decided to move west into Lincoln County, but were soon chased back to town by the May raids. Albert L. Brown, brothers William and Charles Case, and brothers John and Thomas Moffitt all lived in Brown's cabin while the other men were working to build their own. But when the raids began in the spring, they all fled back to Salina. By early August, the two Moffitt brothers decided it was safe enough to return and work the land again. They took with them two other men, John Houston and James Taylor. Taylor was married, and his wife also

---

36   W. W. Morrison Indian Depredation Claim #3623. Record Group 75.

37   Benjamin Gardner Indian Depredation Claim #7513. Record Group 123.

38   James Sharp Indian Depredation Claim #7523. Record Group 123.

39   Lenox Baxter Indian Depredation Claim #3117. Record Group 75.

40   Peter Giersch Indian Depredation Claim #7520. Record Group 75.

41   Thomas Boyle Indian Depredation Claim #3536. Record Group 123.

came along. They weren't there long before they became the first victims of the Indian war in Lincoln County. On August 6, the four men had left the cabin to hunt buffalo but had gone barely a mile when the Indians attacked them. While the men fought desperately they were soon overwhelmed and killed. The Indians apparently never discovered the cabin along Beaver Creek and Mrs. Taylor was able to escape back to Salina.[42]

While Lieutenant Eayre was pursuing Indians east into Kansas and settlers were fleeing to Salina, more trouble was brewing in Colorado along the Platte River road. On April 18, Major Jacob Downing of the 1st Colorado Cavalry, stationed at Camp Sanborn, received a report that Cheyenne attacked Morrison Ranch [American Ranch] along the road to Denver, which was owned and operated at that time by partners James Moore and William Kelley.[43] With 60 men he marched out and reached the ranch the next day. The Indians were believed to have traveled north, whereupon he sought to find them but failed. By April 20, he had returned to Camp Sanborn, having traveled a distance of 140 miles in three days. Downing then divided his command into two columns, sending one down the river just east of present-day Fort Morgan—which did not exist as a fort at that time—at what was known as Beaver Creek Station, and the other back down another 27 miles east to American Ranch.[44] On April 27, Downing reported to Colonel Chivington that he had reunited his command at American Ranch and there learned that the Cheyenne had returned, stealing $800 worth of horses from Moore

---

42   A. L. Brown Indian Depredation Claim #1841. Record Group 123. See also Elizabeth N. Barr, *Souvenir History of Kansas* (self-published, 1908), 18–20; C. Bernhardt, *Indian Raids in Lincoln County, Kansas 1864 & 1869* (Lincoln, KS: The Lincoln Sentinel Print, 1910), 6–13.

43   *War of the Rebellion*, XXXIV, Part III, 250. Morrison Ranch is what others refer to as Morris Ranch. It was 1.7 miles east of Godfrey's Ranch. Godfrey's Ranch was later known as Fort Wicked. Morrison Ranch was owned by James Moore and William Kelley from 1861 until they terminated their partnership in August 1864. While they owned it, it was known as the American Ranch, the name most frequently used in reference to the same place as Morrison Ranch, Moore & Kelley Ranch, Kelley Ranch, and American Ranch. For the definitive source, see Charles Moore Indian Depredation Claims #1240–1244, and 1248, Record Group 123. In addition, the Indian Depredation Claim of Holan Godfrey, #2559 (Record Group 123) states that in January 1865 William Morrison owned the ranch and that it was still called American Ranch. William was killed and his wife Sarah Morrison (not Sarah Morris) was taken captive. The Morrison last name for Sarah and William is further corroborated in *War of the Rebellion*, XLVIII, Part I, 42 (Lieutenant J. J. Kennedy report) and 43 (Lieutenant Albert Walker report). However, the Census Record of 1870, in addition to the marriage certificate for Sarah and William on March 3, 1860 in Delaware County, Indiana, confirm Sarah's married name was Morris and not Morrison. See Census Record, Niles Township, Delaware County, Indiana, 1870. Her maiden name was Iams (see 1850 Census Record, same township, for her family under her father's name, Rezin Iams).

44   *War of the Rebellion*, XXXIV, Part III, 251.

and Kelley. Downing pursued the Indians south to the Republican River. In about 25 miles he found their village of 11 lodges abandoned, which he promptly destroyed. He continued his pursuit down to the Republican, and then turned back north in the direction of Cedar Bluffs (today called Cedar Canyon, about 50 miles north of present-day Fort Morgan).[45]

By May 1, Major Downing had returned to American Ranch, and soon after captured an Indian, whom he was going to shoot until he learned he was half-Lakota. He then agreed to spare his life if the Indian would lead him to the Cheyenne camp, which the warrior consented to do. Leaving American Ranch on the afternoon of May 2, the command went northwest about 15 miles and then rested until 10 P.M., and then marched another 15 to 20 miles until 6 o'clock on the morning of May 3, when the Cheyenne were discovered in a canyon near Cedar Bluffs. In the ensuing fight about 25 Indians were killed and as many as 40 wounded. One soldier was killed and another wounded.[46] The Indian version of this fight denied any warriors died and said the village consisted of only five lodges. Downing, unable to draw the Indians away from the bluffs, withdrew but took their ponies, which the soldiers later divided among themselves.[47]

Within the next three weeks, Indians carried on a series of raids lasting several days in the vicinity east and southeast of Denver for about 30 miles. Early in June, Cheyenne warriors raided a wagon party on Bijou Creek, taking two horses and two mules belonging to Ezekiel Reynolds.[48] Back on the Denver road, James Moore had brought 45 horses from American Ranch to his brother Charles' Washington Ranch, three miles east of Valley Station. They were soon taken, along with an unspecified number of additional mules and horses from Charles Moore.[49] On June 9, 13 miles east of Denver, brothers John and Junius Brown lost 28 mules after they had been turned out to graze and rest. The mules were used hauling freight in six wagons on what was to have been their last stop before reaching Denver. Shortly after the mules were unhitched and allowed to graze, two Indians—from a larger band of Kiowa, Arapaho and Cheyenne—suddenly came "dashing by the mules, flirting buffalo robes. It frightened the mules and drove them away."[50]

45   *War of the Rebellion*, XXXIV, Part III, 314.
46   *War of the Rebellion*, XXXIV, Part I, 907–908.
47   Hyde, *Life of George Bent*, 129–130.
48   Ezekiel Reynolds Indian Depredation Claim #1043. Record Group 123.
49   Charles Moore Indian Depredation Claim #1244. Record Group 123.
50   John Sydney Brown Indian Depredation Claim #2196. Record Group 123.

Surprisingly, of the seven men with the wagons, only three were armed, but only with pistols. A few of the men pursued the Indians, but after several miles, more Indians had joined the ones being followed. Realizing they were outnumbered, the freighters ended their quest. As the raiding warriors were joined with other Indians, each had loose stock taken from other raids. The Indians had divided up and were raiding throughout the whole area. At the same time Thomas Darrah lost stock, as did Philip Gomer. Indeed, the Indians had stolen 113 mules in the vicinity between June 9 and June 11.[51] Included in that number were seven horses belonging to Philip Gomer.[52] The fact that the freighters in the Brown wagon train only had three pistols among them shows very well that until the violent outbreak in the spring of 1864, the freighters and other people traveling along the Denver road were not that concerned about Indians attacking them along the trail. A handful of pistols or rifles among the travelers were believed sufficient for protection.

But it was an ugly incident that would occur outside Denver on the last day of this raid that would bring both fear and anger to all Colorado residents. It was the first innocent white blood drawn in the 1864 Cheyenne war. And it was probably done by Arapaho warriors, perhaps a few Cheyenne with them. Sometime in the early morning hours of June 11, probably near sunrise, Indians surrounded a cabin on Running Creek/Box Elder Creek, 30 miles southeast of Denver, that was occupied by the young family of Nathan Ward Hungate. The family consisted of wife Ellen Eliza Decker Hungate, 25 years old, and daughters Laura, not yet three, and Florence, just shy of five months. Nathan was 29. The young family had only been at their home for two months when tragedy struck, having moved to Colorado Territory from Nebraska Territory.

The likely scenario for the murderous attack was to avenge a killed or wounded raider. Nathan the day before probably shot one of the warriors trying to steal his stock. Numerous bands of warriors were stealing stock from a wide area for at least a day before this incident. The warriors returned for their revenge, carefully taking their time to burn the family out of their home, where Nathan was desperately making a defense to protect his family and drive them away. Fate dictated otherwise. Contrary to a newspaper

---

51   Brown Depredation Claim, Statement of Loss, 12. See also Philip P. Gomer Indian Depredation Claim #693. Record Group 123.

52   Philip Gomer Indian Depredation Claim #2495. Record Group 123.

article in 1892 that said Nathan was not at his house when his family was attacked and killed, but had died coming to his family while another man (Mr. Miller) reported the murders in Denver—Hungate's body was found more than a mile north on the other side of the creek, while his murdered family was discovered not far from the house. The very first report in a Denver newspaper said Nathan was present at the house when the Indians attacked.[53] Further, modern archaeological excavations at the homestead have produced numerous weapons that were burned and no doubt used in the family's defense, including the breach of a new Warner carbine, which had exploded due to its continuous fire in the family defense.[54] The terrified family had no choice, once the house was engulfed in flames, but to run from the home. They had made a desperate defense during the time it took to burn them out. But once they fled from the house, it was all over. Mrs. Hungate and her daughters were found about 100 yards from the cabin, southwest in the direction of Running Creek. The little daughters had their throats slashed from ear to ear, and other parts of their bodies were mutilated and mangled. Ellen was likewise mutilated and scalped, and from signs found on her body, had been brutally raped before death. Nathan was able to escape north—down the river—as far as he did before he was killed because he had fled the burning house with a loaded Henry rifle, which held several rounds of ammunition, and was thus able to keep the Indians from overtaking him—that is—until he fired his last shot.[55]

---

53 *The Denver Commonwealth*, June 15, 1864. The *Rocky Mountain News* was not in business at this time because of an earlier devastating flood that hit Denver and washed away its printing press.

54 This author has developed the thesis that the Hungates were killed after they were burned out of their home in the following publications: "Indian Massacres in Elbert County, Colorado: New Information on the 1864 Hungate and 1868 Dietemann Murders," *The Denver Westerners Roundup*, January–February 2004, 3–30; and "The 1864 Hungate Family Massacre," *Wild West*, June, 2006, 48–53. Part of the evidence for this thesis included the weapons and personal family items found at the burned cabin site, which the Indians would have taken had the traditional story of Nathan being away when his family was killed been true. The wrong story holds that Nathan was away from the home when the Indians made their raid, burning the home after they plundered it and killed his family. Supposedly, Nathan was killed when he saw the smoke from his burning cabin and raced back to the cabin in a failed attempt to rescue his family. This false account permeates nearly all published accounts of the family murders.

55 At the burned home site were found numerous Henry shell casings, which support the thesis that Nathan left the house with his Henry rifle, which holds several rounds, thus giving him a bit of security from immediate capture. But after a mile or so, with warriors probably circling him at a wide distance and individuals running their ponies towards him from various angles, forcing Nathan to fire his Henry to keep them at bay, he eventually used up his ammunition, and then they descended upon him in Nathan's final moment of life.

The dead family was discovered later that day, temporarily taken to Philip Gomer's mill, the closest settlement to the Hungate home site, and transported the next day to Denver, where they were for a short time openly displayed, showing their ghastly death wounds, inciting fear and anger among Denver residents.

At the time the Hungate bodies were being displayed in Denver, 16 Indians caught William Kelley on the Denver road, a little distance from his American Ranch. He had been hunting when they surprised him. Fortunately for him, he was able to race his horse back to his ranch before the Indians could overtake him and kill him.[56]

Two weeks later, in Platte County, Nebraska Territory, about 15 to 25 Cheyenne and Arapaho Indians—professing to be Sioux—descended upon a party of five men and one woman out cutting hay on a government contract for the 7th Iowa Cavalry. The hay party was working on Looking Glass Creek, about four miles east of the Pawnee Reservation. Professing peace and asking for food, the Indians were then fed by Bridgette Murray, wife of the contractor Patrick Murray. She was cooking for the work crew while her husband, Patrick, was away in Omaha procuring supplies. At a given signal during their meal, the Indians threw their food down, drew their weapons and started firing on the unsuspecting party. One man named Jack was killed instantly. Adam Smith, Patrick Murray's brother-in-law, was wounded and died the next morning. Another man died three weeks later from his wounds. Two other men were wounded, but recovered. Bridgette was hit with three arrows and bedridden for three months before she recovered. For this the Indians were able to escape with five mules.[57]

At about the same time as this raid was going on, down south on the Santa Fe trail, at Cow Creek, freighter George Green was returning back to Council Grove after delivering goods at Fort Lyon, when a band of Cheyenne suddenly attacked his train, running off two mules, eight cattle, and one horse.[58]

---

56 Report of Governor John Evans dated June 16, 1864. Anderson Sharp Indian Depredation Claim #1520, p. 22. Record Group 75.

57 Patrick Murray Indian Depredation Claim #1217. Record Group 123. Later reports in the file indicate the Cheyenne denied being involved in the raid and that at that time, in that part of the country, it was the Lakota who were making raids. On the other hand, the man named Jack, had earlier told the other workers that he had lived among the Arapaho for nine years and married an Arapaho woman, but when he left he stole a bunch of horses and knew if the Arapaho ever saw him again they would immediately kill him. Jack was the first person shot.

58 George Green Indian Depredation Claim #3352. Record Group 75.

George Green later settled in Lincoln County, Kansas, endured the violent August raids of 1868, and then joined George A. Forsyth's 50 scouts, fought in and survived the September 17–25 siege known as Beecher's Island.[59]

On July 12, back north and not far from present-day Douglas, Wyoming, a small wagon train was attacked. Some Cheyenne may have been involved, but the warring party was composed of mostly Lakota, primarily Oglala. The small wagon party earlier had left Kansas. They were traveling to Virginia City, Montana, where they hoped to set up a business supplying goods to miners.

One version of what happened says that they were preparing supper when about 100 Indians came to their camp, professing to be friendly and asking to be fed. While the party was preparing food, the Indians suddenly attacked, killing two men and a boy, and wounding two others. Josiah Kelly was gathering firewood nearby, when the Indians made their attack and was able to escape detection, hiding in the brush. His wife Fanny, and adopted seven-year-old daughter, Mary, were not so lucky. They were captured. The war party put Fanny and Mary on a horse and all rode through the night. Fanny slipped little Mary off her horse sometime during the night, with instructions to remain silent until the Indians were gone, and then make her way back to the trail, where it was hoped another wagon party would soon find her and rescue her. But it was not to be, as the Indians soon discovered her missing, and a few warriors went back to find her. When they found her, they "cruelly murdered and mutilated her." Fanny remained in captivity until December 9, when a Blackfoot Lakota, who had purchased her for three horses, delivered her to the commanding officer at Fort Sully in present-day South Dakota. Fanny reported during her captivity that she was made to be "the squaw of an Ogallalla Chief, who treated her in a horrible manner, and during her captivity she was forced from chief to chief and treated in the same way."[60]

---

59 For the story on Beecher's Island, see John H. Monnett, *The Battle at Beecher Island and the Indian War of 1867–1869* (Niwot, CO: University Press of Colorado, 1992); Orvel A. Criqui, *Fifty Fearless Men* (Marceline, MO: Walsworth Publishing Company, 1993); Broome, *Dog Soldier Justice*.

60 Fanny Kelly Indian Depredation Claim (no number noted). Record Group 75, Entry 700, Box 7. Fanny Kelly would later write a book about her experiences, and in this way gain fame for being an Indian captive. Her *Narrative of My Captivity Among the Sioux Indians* was originally published in 1871 and went through many editions in her lifetime. See the edition edited by Clark and Mary Lee Spence (Chicago, IL: The Lakeside Press, R.R. Donnelley & Sons, Company, 1990). Fanny Kelly's story is fascinating to read, but the reader should be aware of the fact that in her book *(continued)*

Another version exists of what happened, providing additional details. With Fanny Kelly and her husband was the young family of William J. Larimer, which included his wife Sarah L., and their seven-year-old son Frank.[61] They had two wagons loaded with jewelry and art goods, as Sarah was a photographer and an artist. The young family intended to set up a portrait business in Virginia City, Montana Territory. Freighters drove two other wagons carrying additional goods. Both freighters were killed in the attack. They also had with them seven horses. In 1862, William was a lieutenant in the Eighth Kansas Volunteers but had become ill, left the service and was still recovering when the young family ventured on the Overland trail.

Sarah recalled what happened on the day of the attack:

> My husband and child and myself were about 80 miles beyond Fort Laramie. We were attacked by a large band of Sioux Indians; my husband was wounded; our property was taken and destroyed; my child and I were carried into captivity by the Indians; on the second night of my captivity I escaped from the Indian camp with my child on my arms, and returned unaided and alone to Deer Creek Station, about 15 miles beyond where we were captured. . . . We were moving along the road in the afternoon when a large band of Indians came upon the bluff and surrounded us, and came up to us, and had us go along a little, and finally our men stopped the teams, and pretty soon the Indians commenced firing, and three men were killed and myself and child carried off by the Indians. Those who pursued the Indians said that the Indians had carried myself and child about 70 miles off in the hills in the direction of the Missouri River."[62]

---

she denies any sexual abuse during her captivity, which is contrary to what she puts forth in her depredation claim. It appeared to me that someone else wrote her story after gathering the facts from her. It strikes me as an embellished effort to restore her dignity, which was commonly lost for women who survived brutal Indian captivity during this era.

61   Mrs. Sarah L. Larimer, *The Capture and Escape; or, Life Among the Sioux* (Philadelphia, PA: Claxton, Remsen & Haffelfinger, 1870), 41, 67.

62   William J. Larimer and Sarah L. Larimer Indian Depredation Claim #1275. Record Group 123. The depredation claims of both Fanny Kelly and Sarah Larimer present their claims without any acknowledgement of the other woman being carried into captivity at the same time. Both women wrote books of their experience, Sarah's book coming out one year earlier that Fanny's book. Both women earlier agreed to write a book together and sought a publisher. But what they produced was not good enough for publication and when a ghost writer was contracted by Fanny, apparently Sarah took the earlier manuscript and, using that published her book without the knowledge of Fanny. This eventually led to a lawsuit in Kansas, which Fanny won. See Alan W. Farley, "An Indian Captivity and Its Legal Aftermath," *The Kansas Historical Quarterly*, Vol. XXI, 1954–1955, 247–256. The records of this lawsuit are available on microfilm from the Kansas State Historical Society. While there is material in both books that is identical, there are important differences too. Fanny is credited in her book for warning

Captain Jacob S. Schuler was at Deer Creek Station when Sarah arrived. He wrote:

On the 13th day of July, [I] was captain of and in command of Co. [H] of the 11th Ohio Cavalry, and with my command was stationed at Fort Laramie, Wyoming Territory, and that on or about that date having information that the Sioux had made a raid on the emigrant road, captured and destroyed a train of emigrants and had carried into captivity . . . Mrs. Sarah L. Larimer and her little child, I immediately moved against the Indians up Platte River in a north-westerly direction a distance of about 115 miles to a place called Deer Creek Station. I there learned that the capture of Mrs. Larimer and her child and the destruction of her property and the murdering of several persons who were with the train had taken place on Box Elder Creek, and as I was about to move against the Indians with the force I had, which consisted of my own company and a force under Captain Marshall, the said Sarah L. Larimer came into camp carrying her little child in her arms, she having escaped from the Indians, after having been carried by them about 75 miles, and returned on foot to the emigrant road where she met my command. When she came into our camp her condition was most deplorable, her clothes had been nearly all torn off her body, her arms and limbs were lacerated from making her way through the thorns, bushes, and cactus on her way after her escape, and she and her little child were nearly famished. As soon as she could be resuscitated by nourishment, which was only a very short time, she gave me a detailed account of the position of the Indians and their plans and movements, and designs against my command, and also their numbers and the position they occupied and the ambuscades they had prepared. So that by taking proper precaution my command was enabled in a short time to move forward and thwart their designs, not only against the pursuing troops but against other exposed points, and trains that were on the emigrant road.[63]

Coincidentally, when Sarah arrived at Deer Creek Station, her husband was there too, having been found wounded at the attack two days after it occurred. The man who found him, Alfred M. Atkinson, brought him back to the station where he was given medical aid.[64]

---

the military of a planned attack upon a fort, when she was able to slip some letters to an officer warning him of the attack. But Sarah herself has a similar story in her depredation claim, which is verified by the affidavit of the officer that spoke with her. Each captivity book focuses on the story of the captivity author, and both are worthy of study separately and together. Sarah's book is extremely rare in the 1st edition due to the fact of the lawsuit, which resulted in the destruction of all copies of Sarah's book. I am a lucky recipient of owning one copy of the original edition.

63   William J. Larimer and Sarah L. Larimer Indian Depredation Claim #1275. Record Group 123.

64   William J. Larimer and Sarah L. Larimer Indian Depredation Claim #1275. Record Group 123. Sarah's book gives a differing account of her rescue, which, when compared to what is in her Indian depredation claim, may well be embellishment. See her *The Capture and Escape*, 85–122.

While Sarah Larimer and Fanny Kelly were enduring their hardships, other warriors were continuing to spread their havoc upon the trails to Denver. Back in Kansas on July 17, Jesse Crane, sutler at Fort Larned, was again attacked by Indians, this time losing 12 mules and 21 horses. But in addition to his loss, the Colorado Battery stationed at Fort Larned lost at least 100 horses, and the stage line and other people lost an additional 33 mules and horses. This time Kiowa Indians were at fault, the Cheyenne now pretty much carrying on their depredations nearer the Platte. Kiowa chief Sa-tan-ke (Sitting Bear/Satanta) led the raid. It was a bold raid. The Indians had come to the fort to beg for food and ask for a parley. Several Indians were admitted into the post and given beef, bacon and hard-tack. This, however, did not satisfy the Indians and Captain Parmetar, commanding the post, was warned that the Indians meant mischief. He ignored their warnings, got drunk and fell asleep. Crane's herd of stock was about 80 rods from the post, and when his herder began to move the stock closer to the fort the Indians began to follow. The sentinel ordered the Indians to move back, but when he raised his gun the chief shot the sentinel in the arm with an arrow: "The sentry then fired his gun at the chief but missed him. Immediately the war whoop was given, and instantly the command of the chief was all mounted on their ponies and dashed into the herd . . . stampeding the horses and mules and carrying them away."[65] At the same time the Indians ran off all of the horses of the Colorado Battery, amounting to over 100, along with the stock belonging to the stage line. Captain Parmetar was finally aroused from his drunken stupor but by the time he was able to order pursuit—there were now no horses at the post—the Indians were over a mile away.

Because of this and other complaints, efforts were finally made to remove Parmetar from the post. Major Thomas McKenny wrote on June 15 that Captain Parmetar "is reported by every officer and man that I have heard speak of him as a confirmed drunkard." On June 27 Major General Samuel R. Curtis demanded that Parmetar be removed from command.[66] One month later, orders were issued at Fort Larned to prevent further brazen attacks upon the post. Among the changes were instructions to construct stockades for securing all stock at night along all the military posts west of the Kansas and Nebraska settlements. Further, any Indians visiting any

---

65   Jesse Crane Indian Depredation Claim #1164.
66   *War of the Rebellion*, XXXIV, Part IV, 403, 575.

post must be blindfolded before entering and "kept totally ignorant of the character and number of our forces."[67]

The Kiowa, no doubt emboldened from their easy success at Fort Larned, then went north and caught a freight train just east of where soldiers were camped at what would by September become Fort Zarah, about three miles east of present-day Great Bend, Kansas. Jerome Crow had contracted with Fort Union to deliver 22 wagons of flour and other goods, mostly wagon-bows. Having started from Fort Leavenworth, on July 17 he had joined up with nine additional wagons of Richard Barret under the charge of John Hiles, also hauling freight to Fort Union. Early in the morning of July 18, the two trains were only about a third of a mile east of the military camp where Fort Zarah would be built, when about 125 Indians approached the long wagon train from the west. The 31 wagons were stretched out for about half a mile. The Indians acted friendly and had spread out on both sides of the train, shaking hands with several of the freighters. James Riggs, one of the assistant wagon masters under Crow, said "I gave tobacco to several of them, and talked with one of them for about five minutes. When they got about half way down the train—the two trains were then about a half mile long—they commenced firing upon our teamsters with bows and arrows and some fire-arms." From Riggs' description, soldiers at the military camp concluded one of the Indians involved was Southern Cheyenne White Antelope.[68] Ten men were killed and an additional five wounded. Eight of the dead men belonged to the smaller train of Barret, while two belonged to Crow's train. One of Barret's teamsters was wounded, while four from Crow's train were wounded. Ten men were scalped. Two of the dead from Barret's train were Negroes and were not scalped. One of the wounded was shot with several arrows and scalped but he recovered. One of Crow's wounded men was also scalped.[69] They then plundered the wagons, destroying 132 sacks of flour. Nine wagons were completely destroyed and several mules killed. At least 30 oxen were either killed or stolen.[70] One of

67 "Massacre of the Cheyenne Indians," *Report of the Joint Committee on the Conduct of the War, Volume 3* (Washington, DC: Government Printing Office, 1865), 76.

68 Jerome Crow Indian Depredation Claim. Record Group 75, Entry 701. "Letter from the Secretary of the Interior," *House of Representatives, 42d Congress, 3d Session, Ex. Doc. No. 62.*

69 "Letter from the Secretary of the Interior." Jerome Crow Indian Depredation Claim. Record Group 75.

70 Jerome Crow Indian Depredation Claim #998. Record Groups 75 and 123.

the leaders of the Kiowa was recognized as Little Heart. Captain Dunlop was commanding the men of Company H, 15th Regiment of Kansas Cavalry. He wrote that the attack was about three miles away from his camp. When he learned of it, he immediately preceded to the scene but when he got there the Indians were gone. He saw a dead horse in the field and knew that it had belonged to Kiowa chief Kicking Bird. Albert Gentry, one of the teamsters, shot both the horse and the rider.[71]

That same day, July 18, another large freighting train of 50 wagons was on the road nearby and they too were attacked. The various owners of the trains were all of Mexican descent and from New Mexico. They had a contract to deliver 25,000 pounds of government goods from Fort Leavenworth to Fort Union in New Mexico. The drivers had just gone into camp and put the mules out for grazing when the Indians rode past the camp. One Indian stopped and took water from the men while the others rode on. When they came to where the mules were grazing they charged into them, scared the dumb animals into stampeding, and then chased them away from where they were grazing. Twenty-five mules and one mare were taken. A party of men pursued the Indians for about 25 miles, but was not able to catch up with them.[72]

Because it was customary for freighters to bring along additional stock to cover for losses during the long freighting trip caused by sickness or injury to the working stock, Vicente Otero, one of the freighters, had enough replacements and was able to continue on south to Fort Larned, where he was denied a military escort to continue to Fort Union. Otero did, however, unload a few of his wagons at the fort, and then continued west along the Santa Fe trail. When they came to the Cimarron cutoff—a little west of present-day Dodge City—they turned south, and by August 5 had stopped at the first springs south of the Cimarron River, which was called Palomas Springs (the arroya de Las Palomas). They put their stock out to graze about a half-mile away from the springs, as that was the closet place to find grass for the mules to eat. A heavy guard was placed around the stock, and even a few sentries on the surrounding hills, but that didn't stop the Indians from charging into the stock. This time they got all of the wagons' horses and mules, leaving Otero without any mules to haul his freight.

---

71 Richard Barret Indian Depredation Claim #1679. Record Group 123.
72 Vicente Otero Indian Depredation Claim #88. Record Group 123.

Eight men were able to follow the raiding warriors for a few miles and then engaged them in a battle lasting for over an hour. One of the freighters was wounded and one Indian and two horses were killed. Now stranded at Palomas Springs, Otero and his men waited a few days until some Americans passed them, returning from Fort Union, carrying empty wagons. Otero contracted with the Americans to use their oxen, attach them to his newer wagons, and deliver the freight to Fort Union. For that each American was paid $250 and Otero gave them his new wagons.[73]

One Indian was recognized as one of the party that was involved in the first raid near Fort Zarah. It was believed that Comanche were also in confederation with the Kiowa in both raids. The Indian recognized at both raids must have been Comanche, because Satanta and his Kiowa, after their raids near Fort Zarah, appeared two days later, on July 20, nearly 100 miles east of Fort Zarah, in Marion County. There they stole 11 horses from licensed Indian traders Harvey Bickford and Orsen Stanley. Earlier in February, the Kiowa also stole two mules from the traders, and when Bickford found them in Satanta's village two weeks later Satanta refused to give them up, though he was willing to trade them back for whiskey.[74]

While Satanta was making his raid in Marion County, the Kiowa raided a nearby ranch on the same day and stole a horse belonging to C. R. Roberts. Roberts, who was operating a ranch on Big Turkey Creek, knew the Kiowa well and recognized the leader as chief Kicking Bird. If this was the case then Kicking Bird was not killed in the July 18 raid two days earlier. The Kiowa would return a year later and steal four more horses and kill several cows. W. A. Douglas, a soldier in Company D, 2nd Colorado Cavalry was killed at the same raid. This raid was carried out by Kiowa chief Little Heart.[75]

Also on July 20, and near the Roberts raid, Kiowa and Comanche attacked the wagon train of Samuel Martin, who was at Charr's Creek Ranch. He lost the contents of his wagons in addition to three horses, 34 oxen and eight cows.[76] On July 22, the Kiowa attacked P. H. Green's wagon train while at Cow Creek Ranch, along the Santa Fe trail. He lost his wagon and its entire contents, which included blacksmith tools, several hundred pounds of lead,

---

73   Vicente Otero Indian Depredation Claim #88.

74   Harvey Bickford and Orsen Stanley Indian Depredation Claim #1249. Record Group 123.

75   C. R. Roberts Indian Depredation Claim #181. Record Group 123.

76   Samuel Martin Indian Depredation Claim #2940. Record Group 123.

half a keg of black powder, boxes of sardines, oysters, peaches, strawber-
ries, apples, bananas, farming equipment, a feather bed, nine buffalo robes,
trunks, housewares and books. In addition to what was in his wagon he also
lost two mules, seven horses, and 46 cows, calves and work cattle. John H.
"Jack" Cosbyn noted that the Kiowa in 1867 bragged about their raids in
August 1864, that they cleared the road for a distance of 75 miles, took and
destroyed all property they could, and that it was an easy job. He noted
that Kicking Bird was the leader of the raiders.[77]

Meanwhile, the Cheyenne were doing their best to keep the raids going.
On July 18, back in Colorado Territory, about 65 miles east of Denver, Cheyenne raided the freight outfit of Stephen Battey and H. H. Wentworth's
while they were camped at Bijou Creek Ranch, and stole three horses from
Wentworth and six horses from Battey. Soldiers were able to recover one
of Wentworth's horses. Having lost their horses to haul their freight, the
freighters were compelled to pay $200 to deliver their goods to Denver.[78]
The horses had been turned out to graze after the owner of the ranch chided
Battey for being concerned about Indians stealing the lose stock. He was
promised by the ranch operator there had been no Indians within 100 miles
of the station. It wasn't long after the horses were put out to graze when
seven Indians appeared and chased them off. The freighters pursued the
Indians, hoping to recover their stock; but in their pursuit a second band of
warriors appeared, followed by still more Indians, numbering at least 25. It
was useless to try and recover the stock and they returned empty-handed
back to their camp.[79]

On July 21, from Salina, Kansas, Major General T. R. Curtis sent a telegram to General H. W. Halleck stating that the stage from Fort Laramie
just arrived. "The damage done by Indians amounts to ten teamsters killed,
five wounded, two of them scalped, and the stealing of about three hundred
cattle."[80] Two days later Curtis sent another message stating that stages
were not getting through and that the Indians "have run off our stock from
Larned and Walnut creek, murdering some men."[81]

---

77 P. H. Green Indian Depredation Claim #125. Record Group 123.
78 H. H. Wentworth Indian Depredation Claim #1838. Record Group 123.
79 Stephen Battey Indian Depredation Claim #4951. Record Group 123.
80 William McLennan Indian Depredation Claim #1576. Record Group 123.
81 Major General S. R. Curtis to Major General H. W. Halleck, July 23, 1864. "Massacre of the Cheyenne
    Indians," 62.

On July 25, Indians struck the Denver road, raiding stock all the way from Beaver Creek Station to Washington Ranch. Twenty-nine horses and 18 mules were stolen, property of Charles A. Moore and Joseph H. Nesbitt, along with another 45 horses belonging to Moore's brother, James. Moore and Nesbitt had founded Washington Ranch in the spring of 1862, and by the summer of 1864, it was described as the largest trading store between Fort Kearny and Denver. Situated about three and a half miles east of Valley Station—a station owned by Ben Holladay that included a telegraph office which was protected by soldiers—Washington Ranch was established so that travelers could purchase whatever they needed along the road.

Charles Moore ran the ranch and kept a hotel, while Nesbitt operated a joint freighting venture, making several trips along the trail each season. Anywhere from two to eight ranch hands were hired to help run the ranch, including Joseph's brother, John. The ranch consisted of a large adobe house, one-and-a-half stories high, which included a pilgrim's house attached to it, providing lodging and meals for travelers; in addition there was a general store housing a large amount of merchandise and supplies. Two large corrals held both cattle and horses, in addition to a large sod stable capable of holding over 100 horses. A blacksmith shop and large well rounded out the facilities. Charles had worked for two years as a stage driver for the Pike's Peak Express and Stage Company, earning $60 a month before he went into business as a freighter. After doing that for about a year, he entered into partnership with Nesbitt, opening Washington Ranch. He remained in partnership with Nesbitt until his brother James Moore bought out the freighting part of the business in early August. For the remainder of the life of the ranch—now also called Moore's ranch, until the spring of 1864, James and Charles Moore were the proprietors. Prior to Jim Moore buying out Nesbitt, he had been in business with William Kelley since 1861, operating American Ranch several miles up the trail near present-day Merino. At the time, Jim bought out Nesbitt, and a man named William Morris bought American Ranch from Kelley and Jim Moore.

For the two years prior to the Indians attacking on July 25, Indians frequently visited and traded with Charles Moore and Joseph Nesbitt, often staying at Washington Ranch for several days at a time. They were never given liquor as this was forbidden by law and rigidly enforced by military authorities, who would confiscate and destroy all liquor supplies if a proprietor was caught selling to the Indians.

Shortly before the raid at Washington Ranch, Moore and Nesbitt purchased all of the stock (50 head) belonging to the owner of Dennison Ranch about nine miles east because "the Dennisons wanted to get away." These cattle were part of the loss. The raid occurred about 7 o'clock in the morning, when a herder came running into the ranch, where everyone was sitting at breakfast, and announced that Indians had run the stock off. Only one horse was left behind, and that was because it was tethered just outside the ranch building. When Charles Moore ran outside he could see about a dozen Indians running the stock southeast over a small rise about a half-mile away. It was useless to immediately pursue them, because there was only one horse available, so instead Moore raced up to Valley Station, hoping to get a military escort to try and recover the stolen stock. There he learned from the telegraph operator that raids were occurring all the way to present-day Fort Morgan. The soldiers were not sent in pursuit, probably because of the concern for the other raids and what this might mean throughout the valley, so Charles himself trailed the Indians for about 12 miles before he gave up and returned to the ranch.[82]

---

[82] Charles Moore Indian Depredation Claim #1241–1244. Record Group 123. All of the information on Washington Ranch and the Moore brothers was taken from the lengthy file in Charles Moore's claim.

CHAPTER THREE

The War Is On

We stayed at the Pawnee Ranch guarding ourselves until I think it was the 11th, of August. And we gathered up all of the settlers that were there with what teams we could get, and made a break for Fort Kearney. We put sticks in the hands of the women and children so as to make it appear to the Indians that we were better armed than we really were.

WILLIAM MUDGE INDIAN DEPREDATION CLAIM #4123

THE MURDEROUS INCIDENTS IN NEBRASKA TERRITORY ON the Denver road just north of central Kansas without question alerted everyone to a full-scale war with the Cheyenne and any other Indians banding with them. It was the beginning of what was to come. Many of the surviving victims fled to Atchison, Kansas, and once there they filled new travelers' thoughts with "first hand stories of Indian savagery, told with an intensity of bitterness born of personal suffering."[1] When these stories arrived in Denver, Governor Evans knew action had to be taken, to protect the territorial residents. There were two sets of Indian raids that were both very deadly. Near present-day Oak, Nebraska, from August 7–9, the Little Blue River attacks occurred, led by a mixed party of Northern Cheyenne, Sioux—Oglala and Brule—and Northern Arapaho warriors. Included with these bands was another mixed band of Lakota under a chief named Two-Face. When it was over at least 38 settlers and freighters had been murdered, nine wounded and five captured.[2] About 100 miles northwest from these deadly attacks, near present-day Lexington,

---

1   Frank C. Young, *Across the Plains in '65* (Denver, CO: Privately printed, 1905), 33.

2   Michno, *Encyclopedia of Indian Wars*, 147. A fuller account of this deadly raid is in Ronald Becher, *Massacre along the Medicine Road: A Social History of the Indian War of 1864 in Nebraska Territory* (Caldwell, ID: Caxton Press, 1999).

Forts & Stage Stations on the Little Blue

Platte River

NEBRASKA

80

Big Blue River

Little Blue River

Thompson Ranch

Kiowa Station
Hackney Ranch
Oak Grove Ranch
Eubanks Ranch
Little Blue Station
Buffalo Ranch
Liberty Farm
The Narrows
Pawnee Ranch
Lone Tree Station
Spring Ranch
Elm Creek Ranch
Thirty-Two Mile Station
Summit Station
Junction Ranch
Ft. Kearny

Waterville

DENVER TRAIL

Republican River

KANSAS

0   25   50 miles

Courtesy Joan Pennington, Fairfax Station, Virginia.

Nebraska, the Plum Creek massacre happened on August 8. Cheyenne Dog Soldiers were behind this raid. A train of 12 wagons was attacked by a party of 100 Cheyenne. In the aftermath 11 freighters were strewn on the ground, dead, and a woman and child were captured.[3]

The killing of these citizens, and capturing of women and children, was gruesomely violent, and no doubt the voices of eye-witnesses spread quickly along the Denver road. The story of what happened to the extended Eubanks family must have excited the fearful imaginations of all who heard the details. Anyone along the trail potentially could be the next victim. Joseph Eubanks came from Missouri to homestead along the Little Blue River in the summer of 1864, near present-day Oak. His younger sons, Joseph, Jr., and Fred had earlier moved out there to ranch. Joseph, Sr.'s, family included his wife Ruth, and daughters Hannah, Dora (Madora), Bell, and sons Joseph, Jr., Fred, George, William, James, Henry, Andrew, and grandson, Ambrose Asher. William Eubanks was married to Lucinda and had two children, three-year-old Isabelle and six-month-old Willie.[4] Joseph Eubanks, Jr., was also married. He and his wife, Hattie, who was about two months pregnant with her daughter at the time of the raid—and her brother, John Palmer, were living with Henry Eubanks when Joseph, Sr., and the rest of his family moved from Missouri to be near them. It was a large family, but in a few short weeks most of them were dead, victims of the ugly Indian war that without question showed that a man was a fool to venture unarmed along the roads through Kansas and into Nebraska, Colorado and Wyoming. By the end of the day on August 7, at least eight and perhaps nine members of the Eubanks family were dead. Joseph, Sr.,

3   Michno, *Encyclopedia of Indian Wars*, 147–148. The two captives were a boy, Daniel Marble (his father killed) and Mrs. Nancy Morton (her husband and other relatives killed). Both captives would eventually be rescued from their captivity. For a fuller account of this event, see Gregory and Susan Michno, *A Fate Worse Than Death: Indian Captivities in the West, 1830–1885* (Caldwell, ID: Caxton Press, 2007), 136–142, and Russ Czaplewski, *Captive of the Cheyenne: The Story of Nancy Jane Morton and the Plum Creek Massacre* (Kearney, NE: Dawson County Historical Society/Baby Biplane Books, 1993).

4   In 1926, William Eubanks wrote to John Ellenbecker and said he was 9 months old at the time of his capture. He spelled his name Eubank and not Eubanks, which is also the spelling of his grave stone in Eaton, Colorado, where he died in 1935. However, in his letter he asks Ellenbecker if he could help to reconnect him to his Eubanks relatives. He apparently never met any of them after his rescue, as nearly all of the extended family had been killed, and there was nothing for his mother to return to. His mother, Lucinda, died in Crawford County, Kansas on April 4, 1913, where she was living with William and his family in her old age. Apparently William dropped the "s" at the end of his name and went by Eubank. See John C. Ellenbecker, *Tragedy at the Little Blue: The Oak Grove Massacre and the Captivity of Lucinda Eubank and Laura Roper*, Revised Second Editon (Kearney, NE: Morris Press, 1993), 16.

was killed, along with all of his seven sons, Joseph, Jr., (found scalped with three arrows in his back and an arrow in his arm), William (Bill), James (Jimmie), Henry, George, Fred, Andrew, and daughter Dora, and little Bell. William's young wife, Lucinda, was taken captive, along with her children, Isabelle and Willie. Those few family members that survived, like the pregnant Hattie, were all quite fortuitously just beyond the scene of the deadly attack, or they too would have been victims.[5]

The deadly raid began on Sunday, about four o'clock in the afternoon. Harriett (Hattie) Eubanks was not feeling well and was at her home at the stage stop known as Kiowa Station. She and her husband, Joseph, Jr., had lived there about eight months, along with her brother, John Palmer. Hattie had asked her brother to go near the river and secure some sulphor for her, which she hoped would make her feel better (she was probably experiencing the normal ill feelings of early pregnancy). When he came back the attack had began. He saw one of the Eubanks men dead on the ground, not far from the cabin. Fortunately for John and Hattie, there was an ox-train heading east, consisting of 25 or 30 wagons, less than 100 yards from the station. They quickly darted to the train for protection. The train had about 25–30 teamsters, and up to this point only 10 Indians had been seen coming towards the train and station. The freighters fired their muzzle-loading rifles at the warriors and kept them from advancing. Because the Indians were outnumbered they didn't attack the train, though Hattie saw them kill a boy off in the distance. That night the Indians set the buildings at Kiowa Station afire and burned them to the ground. Lost too were over 30 horses and 120 head of cattle. What stock and property the Indians did

---

5   Michno, *A Fate Worse Than Death*, 295–305. See also Becher, *Massacre along the Medicine Road*, Chapter 2 and 12. Both Michno and Becher fail to list all of the Eubanks family, according to the testimony of the widow of Joseph Jr., Harriett, found in the Indian depredation claim she later filed as the heir to Joseph Eubanks, Jr. I used her testimony to determine the family members, which include a second daughter, Bell. Further, I spell their name as Eubanks, not Eubank, as that is the spelling in the various Indian depredation claims. However, in another affidavit in her depredation claim, she testifies to a different number of the family being killed: the two Josephs, Dora and three brothers, William, Fred, and James. This would mean six victims, not 9. See Harriett Adams (Joseph Eubanks) Indian Depredation Claim #1117, Record Group 123. The Colorado U.S. Census for 1870 indicates that Josephine A. Eubanks, the daughter of Joseph Eubanks, Jr., was born in Marysville, Kansas, March 15, 1865, thus making Harriett Palmer Eubanks pregnant by almost two months at the time of the raid. In the Joseph Eubanks, Sr., depredation claim (#2733, Record Group 123) it is reported that Joseph, Sr., along with eight members of his family was murdered. However, in the same claim is the testimony of Lucinda Eubanks, who was captured, and she claims that there were eight victims, leaving out the name of Bell.

not steal they destroyed. The wagon train did not move that day. The next day it went east, and after going only four miles about 25 Indians attacked it, wounding two freighters. The train was able to reach Big Sandy Stage Station, where they remained until the Indians left.[6]

John Palmer recalled what happened:

In the month of May 1864 the Eubanks family composed of Joseph Eubanks [Sr.]—and—Eubanks, his wife, their two married sons Joseph [Jr., 22 years of age] and William with their wives [Harriet and Lucinda]; also three younger sons and two younger daughters . . . my sister Harriet and myself settled . . . in the state of Nebraska. Our settlement was about 50 miles west of the present city of Beatrice. . . . This land had been surveyed by the U. S. government and was open for settlement. The Eubanks and myself had taken claims. . . .

The massacre of the Eubanks took place late in the afternoon between 4 and 5 o'clock . . . this was a Sunday evening. The Eubanks were all at their house excepting one of the younger sons who was with me—we were pulling up some hay. Young Eubanks was raking hay while I was going to a spring about a half mile distant for water. I was absent about half an hour—upon my return I found young Eubanks dead and scalped. He had been shot with arrows.

Joseph Eubanks, Jr., & his wife who was my sister—the young Eubanks just mentioned & myself lived together. About an hour before the massacre I saw Joseph Eubanks, Jr., and his wife at our house. After the younger Eubanks and myself had gone into the field . . . Joseph Jr. left the house to go look for [document fades]. . . . He was found dead and scalped 3 days after about 1 ½ miles from his house.

Where I found the younger Eubanks dead in the hay field upon my return with the water from the spring I at once ran to the house to see if my sister . . . was safe. When I got to the house I saw the Indians ride to the top of a hill about 300 yards north . . . from the house; a train of freighters was corralled about 600 yards east from the house. I found my sister unharmed and we ran with all possible haste to the freighters . . . the Indians then left and I did not see any more of them

My sister and I remained with the freighters that night and the next day I went to where the Eubanks lived about 4 miles northwest of where I lived. When I reached their house I found five dead bodies, i.e., those and two younger sons aged about 14 and 16 years and a daughter aged 17 of Joseph Eubanks, Sr., William; two children of William and a boy about 7 years old, a grandchild of Joseph, Sr., were captured. All had been shot with arrows except William—he was shot in the head with a bullet. All except Joseph E., Sr., were scalped and entirely stripped of their clothes. I with some of the freighters before mentioned buried all of them. The wife of Wm. Eubanks was taken captive and was with the Indians over a year [sic]. At the same

6   Harriett Adams (Joseph Eubanks) Indian Depredation Claim #1117. Record Group 123.

time Miss Roper who lived about a mile from the house of the Eubanks was taken captive & kept by the Indians about 6 weeks. . . .

I would further say that the houses were all burned, the furniture destroyed and carried off—all of their horses were taken away by the Indians and the oxen and cattle shot with arrows and killed.

When the Indians began their initial assault on the Eubanks, Lucinda (Lucy) was out walking with her two children and a neighbor girl, Laura Roper. They witnessed the killing of some of the family, hid in some nearby bushes, hoping to escape detection. But Isabella screamed, alerting the Indians to their hiding place. They were captured, as was seven-year-old Ambrose Asher nearby. He had been riding in a wagon with his grandfather Joseph, Sr., and his 13-year-old uncle, James Eubanks. The Indians surprised them, killed young James and Joseph, Sr., and took Ambrose captive. Lucinda's Indian captivity was brutal, as was the treatment of 16-year-old Laura Roper, captured with her and little Isabella and William.

Laura Roper was rescued 37 days after the August 7 raids. Major Edward N. Wynkoop secured her release from Black Kettle, along with nine-year-old Daniel Marble, whose father was killed August 8 at the Plum Creek attack. In addition, Lucinda's daughter, Isabelle, and seven-year-old Ambrose Asher were also given to Wynkoop. Black Kettle took responsibility for their release, and denied any Cheyenne under him were involved in their capture. Lucinda reported, however, upon her rescue the following spring (along with her infant Willie and Mrs. Nancy Morton, who was captured with Daniel Marble August 8), that she was captured by Cheyenne and Arapaho Indians, and later traded to the Sioux.[7]

Lucinda was able to keep her nursing son, William, with her throughout her ordeal, which extended through the winter, until her rescue near Fort Laramie in early May 1865. On June 22, she made a statement to Lieutenant Jeremiah H. Triggs of the 7th Iowa Cavalry. When taken to the Cheyenne village she was brought to the lodge of an old chief whose name she had forgotten:

He forced me, by the most terrible threats and menaces, to yield my person to him. He treated me as his wife. He then traded me to Two Face, a Sioux, who did

---

7   Harriett Adams (Joseph Eubanks) Indian Depredation Claim #1117. Greg Michno, *A Fate Worse Than Death*, 295–305. Lucinda by 1870 had remarried, to James Bartholomew and was living in Illinois. In 1893 she married Dr. D. F. Atkinson in Vernon County, Missouri. She died in McCune, Kansas, in 1913.

not treat me as his wife, but forced me to do all menial labor done by squaws, and
he beat me terribly. Two Face traded me to Black Foot, (Sioux,) who treated me
as his wife, and because I resisted him his squaws abused and ill-used me. Black
Foot also beat me unmercifully, and the Indians generally treated me as though
I was a dog, on account of my showing so much detestation towards Black Foot.
Two Face traded for me again. I then received a little better treatment. I was better
treated among the Sioux than the Cheyennes—that is, the Sioux gave me more
to eat. When with the Cheyennes I was often hungry. . . . During the winter the
Cheyennes came to buy me and the child, for the purpose of burning us, but Two
Face would not let them have me. During the winter we were on the North Platte
the Indians were killing the whites all the time and running off their stock. They
would bring in the scalps of the whites and show them to me and laugh about it.
They ordered me frequently to wean my baby, but I always refused; for I felt convinced if he was weaned they would take him from me, and I would never see him
again. They took my daughter from me just after we were captured, and I never
saw her after. I have seen the man today who had her; his name is Davenport. He
lives in Denver. He received her from a Dr. Smith. She was given up by the Cheyennes to Major Wynkoop, but from injuries received while with the Indians, she
died last February. . . . While encamped on the North Platte, Elston came to the
village, and I went with him and Two Face to Fort Laramie. I have heard it stated
that Two Face's son had saved my life. I never made any such statement . . . and I
think if my life had been in danger he would not have troubled himself about it.[8]

George Bent said Two Face and Blackfoot were Oglala Sioux, and contradicted Mrs. Eubanks' testimony that she was captured by Cheyenne
and then traded to the Oglala later.[9] It appears Bent was more interested
in denying Cheyenne participation in the raids on the Little Blue than he
was in reporting the truth. In this case of conflicting testimony one must
accept Eubanks' testimony over Bent's. But it also illustrates a problem that
will in all likelihood remain forever unresolved in learning the truth, viz.,
just which tribes of Cheyenne Indians were involved in the outbreak of the
1864 Cheyenne war. What will be clearly seen in the events that unfolded
the next day on Plum Creek is that the Cheyenne were the perpetrators
there, including both Northern and Southern Cheyenne.

Young Ambrose Asher described his grandfather, Joseph Eubanks, Sr., as
having long, gray whiskers. He had moved out with his grandfather from
Missouri only a short time before the murders. His mother had remained
back in Missouri with Joseph's wife, Ambrose's grandmother.

8   Carroll, *The Sand Creek Massacre*, Appendix, 90–91.
9   Hyde, *Life of George Bent*, 208.

Ambrose recalled the violent day:

I was on the wagon with my [grand] father and two uncles going after hay. One Indian rode up out of the tall grass which is higher than a man on horse back. The Indian asked my grandfather for a chew of tobacco. My grandfather took a twist from his pocket cut it in two and handed one piece to the Indian. The Indian took a chew and put the remainder of the piece in a sack he had with him. The Indian then got his bow and arrow and made a motion as though he would shoot one of the oxen. My grandfather told him by sign and words not to do that, and the Indian then presented the bow successfully at my grandfather's son, then at me, and finally at my grandfather himself. The Indian ended his performance by shooting my grandfather with a number of arrows. My grandfather's two sons started to run back to the ranch when a large number of Indians, maybe fifty or seventy-five, arose from the tall grass with a yell, and killed my two uncles. At this time I was hanging to the wagon, as a boy would, and one of the Indians rode up, dismounted, and threw me on the horse behind him. The Indians taking me with them then went on to the ranch where they killed another one of my uncles, and my aunt, Dora. They took prisoners also my aunt Lucy and her two children, and at a point some distance from the ranch they killed also my uncle Fred who was in the hay field. The Indians then tied my feet under a horse, and tied my hands under the horse's neck and in this way I rode to where the Indians stopped a few moments—I suppose for water—they then proceeded until some time the next day when we reached their camp. They untied me then from the horse, and when I got off began to kick and cuff me around until a squaw came and took me away from them. I was with the Indians some months, but was finally taken away by some soldiers, and after some delay sent back to Missouri or Illinois to my mother.[10]

When the Eubanks family members were killed on August 7, their bodies were gruesomely hacked, disfigured, and scalped. Daniel Freeman was a member of the party that found the bodies and assisted in their burial.

---

10   Joseph Eubanks, Sr. Indian Depredation Claim #2733. Record Group 123. The claim includes a statement from Valentine T. McGillycuddy, Indian agent at Pine Ridge Reservation, and he confirms the following Indians responsible for the Little Blue and Plum Creek raids: Cutoffs of Pine Ridge, Upper Brules of Rosebud, Northern Arapahos of Shoshone Agency, Northern Cheyennes of Pine Ridge, and also a dispersed band of Sioux Indians under a chief named Two Face. The claim also has interesting testimony regarding the amount and worth of property taken or destroyed. Along with a claim of $10,000 for the abuse and damage to the character of Mrs. Eubanks, rescued 10 months after her capture, the family filed an additional $5,603 in lost property. However, testimony of neighbors described the family as quite poor, and they did not see the value of their property as totaling more than $600. It did not matter however, for the claim was denied on the technicality that it was filed after the three year grace period to produce a claim. This was a typical action with hundreds, if not thousands of claims filed by citizens seeking compensation for their losses, which did not include injury or death (Lucinda's claim for $10,000 was denied because such compensation was not a part of the law). No wonder so many citizens overvalued their property losses.

He described what he saw: "the men were scalped, their limbs unjointed, privates cut off; the women were scalped their bodies mutilated and the private parts scalped, ..."[11] Another witness said that "one of the females, beside having suffered the latter inhumane barbarity, was pinned to the earth by a stake thrust through her person in a most revolting manner."[12] These victims were left on the stage road and the passing stages, as well as freighters who saw the remains soon after, reported what they observed when they arrived in Denver. Almost immediately Governor Evans issued his call for volunteers to form the 3rd Colorado Cavalry. If the atrocities that later occurred at Sand Creek had a motivation, it was the many victims in Nebraska and not the young Hungate family that had been killed almost two months earlier.

The raids in Nebraska actually began earlier than the deadly outbreak of August 7–8. Daniel Freeman owned a ranch about 60 miles east of Fort Kearny, and 16 miles southeast of Liberty Farm, just a little east of the Eubanks' ranch. His ranch was on the road connecting Fort Leavenworth to the Overland trail. On August 1, Indians stole a horse. They continued to steal stock here and there along the trail until they began their murderous raids one week later. Freeman's house was burned to the ground and additional stock stolen, on August 7.[13]

On August 6, a large wagon train of 65 wagons, as well as a mail coach, was attacked about 11 miles east of Little Blue Station. Twenty-five or 30 Indians fired on them and then retreated. The wagon party then proceeded to Little Blue Station and camped for the night. Coincidentally, on this same day, back on the Denver road in Colorado Territory, nine Indians rushed at horses grazing near Washington Ranch and ran off 36 horses belonging to Charles and Jim Moore. One was recovered at Sand Creek later in November.[14]

When the Indians began their deadly raid against the Eubanks family, all the surrounding ranches along the road were attacked. Just a couple miles

11 Charles Emery Indian Depredation Claim #1620, Record Group 75. That Freeman mentions the Eubanks women as plural is further evidence that Harriet Adams was correct in listing two dead Eubanks children.

12 Thomas Harmon Indian Depredation Claim #4942. Record Group 123. It was this kind of testimony from the Nebraska raids that enflamed Denver residents against the Indians, more so than the earlier June 11 murders of Nathan Hungate and his family.

13 Daniel Freeman Indian Depredation Claim #4943. Record Group 123.

14 James and Charles Moore Indian Depredation Claim #1248. Record Group 123.

east of the Eubanks' house, Mrs. Johanna Uhlig had lived since 1860. Already a widow when she came to the Little Blue, she and her three sons, aged 26, 23 and 15, set up a ranch and stage station along the trail. They had prospered until the raids. Her youngest son, Theodore, was coming home after visiting Kiowa Station, two miles further east. Indians surprised him and shot him off his horse, just as he was about home. From the front of her house Mrs. Uhlig witnessed an Indian scalp her son while he was still alive and conscious. Screaming for the help of her oldest son and a hired man, they ran to young Theodore's assistance. The Indians scampered away from the armed men and went into the house, which they then plundered. Just as more Indians appeared, "the timely arrival of a party of armed neighbors and freighters from Kiowa Station" came to the Uhlig's rescue. Theodore quickly died but they were able to save his mutilated corpse from further desecration. The Indians burned the family house down, and destroyed all of its contents.[15]

Kiowa Station was not immune from attack; on August 9, after everyone had fled the station, the Indians plundered it and burned the buildings down. James Douglass, who operated the station, lost four horses, 12 cows and a bull, in addition to the entire contents of his two-story home.[16]

Two days after the deadly August 7 attacks, Isaac Varney, George Constable and Melvin Brown had all joined their westbound freighting wagons together into one big train, comprising about 65 men, nearly all experienced freighters. However, of all the men, there was only one rifle among them. Nearly all were armed with a pistol, but no one expected any violence with Indians. The freighters and ranchmen simply were not prepared for what happened. There hadn't been any violence in the years before and there was no reason to expect it would happen. On the other hand, nearly all of the Indians "had rifles and very good ones."[17] When the wagon train got to Little Blue Station, just to the west of where the Eubanks had been murdered two days earlier, the Indians attacked them. Melvin Brown remembered that the train had come to Douglas Ranch on the Blue on Saturday, and

---

15 Johanna Uhlig Indian Depredation Claim #4024. Record Group 123. The claim states the raid happened on August 6, but this is a mistake, confirmed by Edmund Uhlig's depredation claim, which correctly dates the raid as August 7. In his claim Edmund says the Indians came back on August 9, and that was when the house was burned down. Conflicting testimony from other witnesses say the house was and was not burned. See claim #2496. Record Group 123.

16 James Douglass Indian Depredation Claim #2337. Record Group 123.

17 William Young Indian Depredation Claim #2328. Record Group 123.

stayed over on Sunday when the outbreak began. Three men were killed a half mile from the ranch on that day. The freighters stayed until August 9, when they ventured back on the trail. Soon they met a coach full of passengers going west. Wisely, the stage driver and passengers stayed with the large wagon train. It was driven by Bob Emery, the brother of Charles Emery, who operated Liberty Ranch.[18] The train rolled out with the stagecoach leading the way. Brown tells what happened next:

> The coach got about a mile ahead and the Indians attacked it. They were laying in a ravine. The coach turned around and run back. The Indians shot through the coach; shot through a lady's hat; shot through a man's hat, but done no damage to the coach or to the passengers further than shooting into it. Then we marched on to where the Indians were in the valley and there we found two dead men that they had killed. We passed on up the road and found seven more laying in the road. We pulled them out of the way so we could get by and when the Little Blue was reached it was decided to camp there and we sent out several men. We saw no more Indians that day until they attacked us. We went into camp and put the cattle across the river with a guard [of nine men] around them and put the horses up a ravine, mules and all, to graze, and the Indians made a raid on the horses and mules. We headed them off on that and run the horse stock and mules inside [the corral], and then the Indians struck for the cattle and they took four hundred and fifty six head. . . . They set a trap for us right there. There was only six Indians that made the dash for these horses and mules and when they did not get them they took the cattle and as they went with them they beckoned us to come on. Perhaps there was twenty five horses and mules saddled in no time to go and try and [re] capture the cattle, but the guard saw the trap. There was a big band of them on the Little Blue in the timber, waiting for us.[19]

Brown's wagons had been loaded with mostly corn, bound for Fort Collins in Colorado Territory.[20] When the cattle were taken the men didn't have enough horses left to haul their wagons, so they made the decision to load just one wagon with necessities and in the dark of night they made their escape. They hadn't traveled far when they observed smoke from where their wagons had been abandoned. The Indians had set them afire. The escaping party went east, back to St. Joseph.[21]

---

18   William Young Indian Depredation Claim #2328.

19   William Young Indian Depredation Claim #2328.

20   Thomas R. Smith Indian Depredation Claim #8666. Record Group 123. Smith, representing the claim of William Young, lost four freight wagons and 102 mules in the attack. Young was in partnership with Melvin Brown.

John Bicktold had his house burned too, losing everything in it, along with two oxen, three cows and six horses.[22] So did Albert Halladay, who operated Hackney Ranch about a mile east of Bicktold's place. He lost several oxen and had all of his household contents plundered and destroyed, which he said included several kegs of whiskey. His ranch, however, was not burned.[23] On the day of the Eubanks murders, August 7, just east at the Oak Grove Ranch, 36 Indians had been well-fed as guests at the ranch. After two hours of resting, suddenly, at a given signal, "they fired on the men at the Ranch, killing Melan C. Kelly, and a man named—Butler, from Topeka, Kansas, and wounding two others." The surviving men were able to run to another room where guns and ammunition were stored. Now armed, they defended themselves and wounded two Indians, causing the warriors to retreat. Nelson Ostrander, out herding Comstock's cattle, was also killed at this time. George Hunt was wounded. The surviving men, along with their wounded, were able to flee the next day. The entire ranch was then burned to the ground and everything destroyed. The Indians took 16 horses, one mule and five cows.[24] George Comstock's father Erastus was running the ranch at Oak Grove, which was owned by James Douglass.[25] George was running Thirty-Two Mile Station several miles further west along the stage road. Brother James was operating Little Blue Station about a mile west of where the Eubanks had been killed. All three stations were burned to the ground and all property was either stolen or destroyed.[26] No person in the area escaped being attacked.

A few miles west of the Oak Grove Ranch was Spring Ranch, owned and operated by James Bainter. For several days before the raid Bainter had noticed that the Indians "acted as though they contemplated mischief, they seemed shy and would sneak around, and they did not seem as friendly as

---

21 Isaac Varney Indian Depredation Claim #1161. William Young Indian Depredation Claim #2328. Record Group 123.

22 John Bicktold Indian Depredation Claim #1191. Record Group 123.

23 Albert Halladay Indian Depredation Claim #1022. Record Group 123. In Hallady's claim William Blakely testifies that Hackney Ranch was owned by Fred Roper. Ron Becher, in *Massacre Along the Medicine Road* (190–191), says that Roper owned the ranch until shortly before the raids. Becher also says the ranch was burned down and the timbers thrown into the well to render it useless. However, Charles Emery testified in the Halladay claim that the ranch was not burned, and Halladay himself made no claim for the loss of his ranch, but only the contents inside it. It is thus likely that the ranch was not burned.

24 George Comstock Indian Depredation Claim #2493. Record Group 123.

25 James Douglass Indian Depredation Claim #2337. Record Group 123.

26 George Comstock Indian Depredation Claim #5156.

they had been." For a few days they disappeared, and when they reappeared they began their murderous campaign. Cheyenne Dog Soldier Tall Bull and the Lakota White Horse were active leaders of the raid.[27] On the morning of the 7th, Bainter was on the road near his ranch when he saw an Indian try to hide in a ravine. Avoiding the ravine he soon saw the warrior join with another and continue down the road:

> About this time I noticed a man coming along the road from the east. He was in a wagon, driving a team,—the wagon appeared to be loaded with sacks of corn. I saw one of the Indians after they had met and passed this man who was driving the wagon, turn and shoot the man; he fell from the wagon and I saw the Indians dismount and scalp him. In a short time my son and hired man came up and we drove the Indians off. In a short time after this Mr. Emery . . . and his hired man, myself, my son and hired man placed the man who was shot [and scalped], and who was a Mr. [Patrick] Burke of Beatrice, Nebraska, in a wagon and took him to Pawnee Ranch, which was a mile east of Spring Ranch.[28]

Burke died soon after reaching the station. Pawnee Ranch, a stage stop operated by Louis M. Hill,[29] was in the open prairie and easier to defend,

---

27 Charles Emery Indian Depredation Claim #1620. Record Group 75.

28 Charles Emery Indian Depredation Claim #1620. Charles Emery identifies Burke's first name as Patrick and notes that in addition to being shot he was also scalped. See his testimony in the Albert Halladay Indian depredation claim #1022.

29 Harriett Adams (Joseph Eubanks) Indian Depredation Claim #1117. Becher, in *Massacre along the Medicine Road* (p. 144), says Pawnee Ranch was operated by Newton Metcalf. However, Louis Hill testifies under oath in the Harriett Adams claim that Pawnee Ranch at the time of the raid was owned by Ben Holladay and that he (Hill) was the keeper of the ranch. The Ben Holladay depredation claim confirms that Pawnee Ranch was owned by Holladay. See "Testimony as to the Claim of Ben Holladay," 46th Congress, 2d Session, Mis. Doc. No. 19 (Washington, DC: Government Printing Office, 1880), 17. Newton Metcalf's real name was Merritt Metcalf, and he filed a fraudulent claim for losses at Pawnee Ranch. He argued that the ranch was burned after it was abandoned and he lost all of his supplies and household goods totaling $13,653.50. Upon investigation of the claim, however, the survivors of the raid all confirmed that the ranch was not burned, and that in fact it was used by soldiers for several months following the raid. Metcalf's character was disparaged by everyone that knew him. William Mudge reported that Metcalf was later hanged in Montana "by Lynch Law for crooked transactions." Charles Emery reported "he was hanged by a Vigilance Committee in Montana for stealing government mules." Thomas Stevenson, who had served as a captain in the Nebraska Militia, stated that most of the ranches at that time provided mainly tobacco and whiskey (Metcalf reported losing 64 gallons of bourbon whiskey) and that the ranchmen providing such goods were as a class "tough characters, in some instances escaped convicts with a few honorable exceptions, but as a class not worthy of belief under oath in the claims against the government." While Thompson's statement may be true regarding the particulars of the value and amount of individual losses of personal property, Metcalf serving as a good example, the individual depredation claims nevertheless provide accurate and useful testimony regarding the details of the attacks, as do the supporting witnesses in the Metcalf claim regarding the fight at Pawnee Ranch. See Merritt Metcalf Indian Depredation Claim #9850. Record Group 123.

GEORGE TRITCH, SUCCESSFUL
DENVER MERCHANT, WHOSE
WAGON OF GOODS WAS LOST IN
THE INDIAN RAID ON THE
LITTLE BLUE, ON AUGUST 7, 1864.
Had Tritch been with the wagon train,
he would have likely died as did all the
freighters that day. He lived until 1899.
Courtesy Ed Bathke, Roxborough, Colorado.

so Bainter and all the other settlers in the area flocked to that ranch for protection. The next day, viewing through binoculars, Bainter observed the Indians torch his house. What was not stolen was destroyed by the warriors prior to burning the house. His oxen and cows were killed and his horses stolen.[30]

Between Bainter's Spring Ranch and Andrew Hammond's Elm Creek Ranch further west, a train of six four-horse wagons was hauling hardware freight to Denver. Horace G. Smith was the wagon master and was in partnership with T. H. Simonton and/or John Nye to deliver freight from St. Joseph, Missouri, to Denver. The Indians attacked the six-man party when they were near a large ravine and quickly killed all of the men, except one who was mortally wounded and died the next day. The wagons were burned and destroyed, the freight likewise, and the horses stolen. The wounded freighter was found in a thicket near where the other dead men lay. An arrow was stuck in his head but he was alert and able to talk about the attack. When the arrow was removed from his brain—after he

---

30   James Bainter Depredation Claim #1019. Record Group 123.

was brought back to the ranch—he immediately died.[31] Indians directly responsible for this attack were Arapaho Dock Billy, Roaring Wind and Big Thunder. All of them were under Two Face, whose mother was Cheyenne and father was Arapaho.[32]

One of the Denver merchants who had contracted with Simonton and Smith to deliver merchandise to Denver was George Tritch. Among the freight was "pocket cutlery, table cutlery, plated ware, silver-plated spoons, knives and forks, scissors, and quite a large line of desk and drawer locks, both brass, iron and nickel; quite a stock of carpenter tools, planes, saws, squares, and . . . monkey wrenches."[33] Tritch had been a successful hardware and general merchandise dealer in Denver at 15th and Wazee. But before that he was almost a victim of smallpox.

Frank A. Root, an early supervisor for the Overland Stage Company, gave an interesting story of meeting Tritch in 1863. Root was traveling to Denver on an express stage, one carrying only mail and no passengers. When the stage stopped at Fort Kearny, Root learned of a sick man who had for three weeks been isolated in a lone cabin away from all human contact. Travelers feared the spread of his disease—smallpox—which he supposedly was just getting over. No one visited him in the isolated cabin. He wanted desperately to go to Denver where his young family was and where he kept his business. He had earlier paid for his stage seat from Atchison but had been removed because of his illness. Root himself had earlier survived smallpox and was thus immune to its spread, and he agreed to meet with Tritch who was begging each stage and wagon train passing through for assistance. Root:

---

31   T. H. Simonton and Horace G. Smith Indian Depredation Claim #2498 & 3102. Record Group 123. Ronald Becher, in *Massacre along the Medicine Road*, 148, says there were six wagons. The Simonton claim indicates only five wagons. However, this same incident is noted in John Nye's Indian Depredation claim, and Nye says there that there were six trains and six men. He also said that he (Nye) was in partnership with D. Tom Smith (Horace Smith's brother) and another man by the name of John Kinna. He also testified that he was the person who provided the money to purchase the goods being freighted to Denver and that Smith and Kinna shared in the profits by providing the labor in bringing the goods to Colorado and distributing them to miners and other people in need of the hardware goods. Obviously, one of the claims is fraudulent, for both Simonton and Nye cannot be the principal partner, the claims not mentioning each other. It appears from reading both claims that Simonton's claim might be the fraudulent one. See John Nye Indian Depredation Claim #4635.

32   George Tritch Indian Depredation Claim #1174, p. 14. Record Group 123.

33   George Tritch Indian Depredation Claim #1174, p. 8.

His face, as he looked at me, presented a horrible sight. It resembled a pounded beefsteak more than it did that of a human being, and I hardly knew, under the circumstances, what to do. There was no seat for him or anyone else in the stage. He was a stranger to me and had his passage paid to Denver; but the agent at the stage line at Fort Kearny refused to allow him a seat in the coach, owing to the vigorous protests that had been made by the passengers. For five minutes or more we talked the matter over. I told him there was no room on the coach for a passenger; besides, I thought it dangerous, not only for himself but for others going overland, to take him along. . . . He assured me that he was perfectly willing . . . to take all the risks. . . .There was something in the man's eye and the tone of his conversation that pleased me. . . . He assured me that he could put up with anything.

I rearranged the boxes and packages as best I could, and spread his robe and blankets on top of them so he could lie down quite comfortably, but it was out of the question to fix one of the coach seats for him. The fact that he was allowed to go with me appeared to be one of the happiest events of his life. At once his heretofore despondent feelings changed, and he appeared like a different person. I inquired of the stranger his name, and learned it was George Tritch. He kept a small stove and tin-shop in a little rough, one-story frame building on the west side of F street (Fifteenth), a few doors north of Blake street.

For nearly 400 miles we had the coach all to ourselves. At night . . . slept together all the way up the Platte for four nights. Several way-passengers along the route wanted a seat in the stage, but the sight of the "gentleman from Denver" scared them away in a hurry, particularly after learning he had just got out of bed from a terrible siege of smallpox. . . . Every hour we seemed to get better acquainted. We had both traveled the "rough and rugged road" years before, and soon became the warmest friends. During those four days and nights we had a jolly good time, for the sick man had somehow forgotten that he had ever been sick. I found him a pleasant, warm-hearted, genial traveling companion, a pleasant conversationalist, and we became quite devotedly attached during the long, monotonous stage ride. . . . I am pleased to learn that, for a quarter of a century, he was one of the foremost business men of Denver, independently wealthy, an honored, highly esteemed citizen, of whom the entire city and the great state of Colorado could justly feel proud.[34]

East of Bainter's Spring Ranch, Charles Emery operated Liberty Farm, a stage stop and hotel, which included, in addition to the hotel and stables, a blacksmith shop. When Burke had been mortally wounded Emery took his wife and children and, like other ranch owners, sought protection at Pawnee Ranch. Pawnee Ranch was soon fortified with wagons and logs,

---

34   Root and Connelley, *Overland Stage*, 507–509.

and the men awaited the anticipated attack from the warriors. But it didn't happen right away. Instead, the Indians first plundered and burned all the abandoned ranches.

Coincidentally, the night before the August 7 raid, several wagons met at Pawnee Ranch. Some were empty and going east, others were loaded and going west to Denver. It was their fortune to camp that night at Pawnee Ranch, for when the raids began the next morning they were left unmolested. Had the wagons been anywhere else along the trail near this point, they would have in all likelihood suffered the violent fate that befell others. James Whiten was in charge of the empty wagons going east, and E. S. Graves was freighting the loaded wagons, bound for Central City to the west. Settlers from nearby homes as well as additional wagon trains coming on the road all converged at Pawnee Ranch for protection. On August 9, the anticipated attack finally began, and lasted four hours.[35] Just prior to this attack Charles Emery's Liberty Farm had been torched.[36] Emery described what happened:

On Sunday, August the 7th, 1864, a man by the name of Burke, stopped at my place and watered his team. He had a wagon load of corn with him. I asked him to stop and take dinner at my ranch, and he said, No, he would go to Pawnee Ranch and take dinner there, as he wanted to make Elm Creek that night. Pawnee Ranch was a ranch about 6 miles west of my ranch [Liberty Farm]. He didn't stop but went on toward Pawnee Ranch. Right after dinner this same day, myself and one of my hired men started on horseback for Pawnee Ranch. When within a mile and a half of Pawnee Ranch we found this man [Patrick] Burke shot and lying in the road scalped, but not yet dead. I jumped down off my horse and went to him and he told me that the Indians had shot and scalped him. I could do nothing for him, so I mounted my horse and we went to Pawnee Ranch and notified the ranchmen. They at once got out a team and wagon; we went back to where Burke was; I helped put him in the wagon and then we rode home as fast as we could. We had not been at home a great while before nine Indians came down from the Bluffs on the north, and I then saw them go into my herd of cattle on my ranch, shoot one

---

35   James Whiten Indian Depredation Claim #7168. Whiten's depredation claim has a statement by
      Lorenzo M. Freas, the merchant in Central City whose goods were lost at Pawnee Ranch when the
      freighters later fled the ranch for military protection at Fort Kearny. He claimed that a Captain Murphy
      [Captain John Murphy] stationed at Fort Kearny went with Graves back to Pawnee Ranch on August
      13. The wagons were unmolested, but instead of providing an escort to bring the wagons back to Fort
      Kearny, Murphy ordered his soldiers to raid the wagon of seven boxes of boots that were meant for
      the miners at Central City, each box containing a dozen pairs of boots.

36   Charles Emery Indian Depredation Claim #1620. Record Group 75.

of my two-year-old heifers and cut a piece out of her hind quarter, stampeded the balance of my herd, and then crossed the Little Blue River and went South toward the Republican Valley. After the Indians had left, myself and man went to gather up my herd of cattle and drive them up to my corral, which we finally succeeded in doing, with the exception of the one they killed. I then concluded that these Indians, who were members of the Sioux and Cheyenne tribes, had started out on a raid along the Overland Stage route. The stage was due at my place at 10 P.M. daily, but didn't come this time until the next morning at 9 o'clock. As this was before any railroads had been constructed across the plains, this stage carried the Government mails and was the only public conveyance across the plains. The driver and passengers told me that a large party of Sioux and Cheyenne Indians were on a raid and were coming toward my ranch, and were killing and taking prisoners everybody they came across, and burning and destroying all property in their way. I knew it wouldn't do for me to stay at my ranch with my family, especially as all of my men but one had left on the Saturday before and gone east to Oak Grove on a hunting and fishing expedition, taking with them all the arms and ammunition which we had. I took my family, which consisted of my wife and two children, the children being the one 3 and the other 5 years old. Neither I, nor any of my men or family had up to that time ever had had any trouble with any Indian, and we consequently [were] not apprehending any danger from them and were therefore not prepared to resist their attack. As I was saying I took my wife and family and put them in the coach with the coach passengers, and I told the driver to go to Pawnee Ranch and stop until I came. I knew that there was a big ox train camped there, which consisted of twenty-six wagons, six yoke of oxen to the wagon, and about forty men. I then took the stage horses which were kept at my station, and I told my man to take my mules and stallions and lead them, and I would drive the stage horses loose, and we would go to Pawnee Ranch for protection. My man, however, was greatly excited and badly scared and consequently some how mismanaged the stallions so that they broke loose and ran in among my mules and stampeded them, so that one of the mules and stallions and four of the stage horses made their escape and had to be left by us at the ranch where they were subsequently captured and driven away by Indians, and they were never recovered by me. We found that we could not save all of the horses and we managed to get to Pawnee Ranch with the eight stage horses and the two horses which I and my man were riding. We had also to leave at the ranch all of my herd of cattle, consisting of work oxen, beef cattle, and milch [milk] cows; we also had to leave behind us all of my hogs, and my other personal property. We went as rapidly as we could from my ranch to Pawnee Ranch because from what the passengers had seen and the driver told of the outrages the Indians had been committing just east of us the night before, we had the very best reasons to expect an attack from the Indians any moment, and as soon as we got to Pawnee Ranch everybody at once commenced to prepare for an attack from the Indians. We reached Pawnee Ranch between 10 and 11 o'clock on the morning of the 8th of August, 1864. Just after we got there the Overland stage coach from the west arrived, and we learned from its driver and passengers that the Indians had been destroying property, burning ranches, and killing many freighters between there and Kearney, and that all the ranchmen and station-keepers west of us had fled to Kearney for their lives. The passengers on this coach were six men, old Californians, and were all well armed, and I insisted that they all stop at Pawnee Ranch and assist in its defense; the driver however, wanted at once to drive on east; I finally prevailed on them to stop. We then went to fortifying the ranch. In the first place I went and got this ox train to move up to the ranch—Pawnee Ranch—we formed a half circle with the wagons around the front and exposed side of the ranch; we then tore down a large log building, took the logs and laid them up on the inside of the corral made with the wagons, as high as the wagon beds, which being all loaded made a strong breast-works. The Indians, however, did not put in an appearance that day. About noon on Tuesday, the 9th of August, 1864, myself and another man went out to reconnoiter in the direction of my ranch, Liberty Farm, and got within about 2 miles of my place. We then saw that my buildings were burning, having been set on fire by the Indians. Just at this time thirteen Indians came riding down toward us directly from my ranch and burning buildings. They were well mounted on ponies and armed with rifles and bows and arrows and opened fire on us as soon as within gun shot. The man with me was shot through the arm. We then started back to Pawnee Ranch. Just then nine more Indians came up and joined the thirteen and all together chased us clear up to Pawnee Ranch, shooting and yelling, and we had a very narrow escape with our lives. The man with me, and who was shot through the arm, was named Joseph Markham. . . .[37]

William Mudge was a part of the defense at Pawnee Ranch. His ranch had also been abandoned when he learned of the deadly raids being conducted against his neighbors. He had a young family, and fortunately, they were able to escape undetected to Pawnee Ranch.

His story adds details to what happened at Pawnee Ranch:

I was living and also Joseph Milligan my partner living on the Little Blue River in what was then the territory of Nebraska in what is now the northern part of Nuckolls County and on a ranch known at that time as Buffalo Ranch. On the 7th day of August 1864, a marauding tribe of Indians composed of the Sioux and Cheyennes made a raid upon a settlement in our neighborhood and on that day they attacked nearly every ranch in that part of the country. On that day there happened to be a train of wagons at our ranch so that we were reasonably well protected on that

37   Charles Emery Indian Depredation Claim #1620.

day, and were not attacked on that day. I had a wife and three small children and hearing of the killing of a number of the settlers on that day among them a Mr. Burke and a family of nine [Eubanks] not far away from us. The next morning on the 8th of August, being in danger of our lives and without sufficient protection we and the most of the other settlers in that country congregated at the Pawnee Ranch, about ten miles from our ranch, and combined together for self-protection. My teams were out on the range and we were unable to get them on account of the danger of being killed in going after them. We were obliged to walk from our ranch a-foot carrying our little children. I took a gun and what ammunition I had; my wife carried one child and led the others and was obliged to leave our home and everything behind us to the Indians. Joseph Milligan my partner at that time was at Nebraska City after a load of groceries for our ranch and was not there at the time of the raid.

After we got to Pawnee Ranch the settlers who had got there made the best fortification we could and we were there attacked by the Indians who surrounded the ranch, yelling and shooting at us and they kept that up for three or four hours during the evening of the 8th, or 9th, of August 1864. My best recollection is it was on the 9th. We were so well fortified and made such a stout resistance that we were successful in keeping the Indians at bay, only one or two of our party were wounded. One man was shot through the arm as well as I can recollect from observation I should judge that we saw about eight hundred around the Pawnee Ranch the day we were attacked. They were all mounted on ponies and well mounted at that. They were armed with guns, bows and arrows, spears and shields and were painted up and dressed in their regular war uniforms and style.

We stayed at the Pawnee Ranch guarding ourselves until I think it was the 11th, of August. And we gathered up all of the settlers that were there with what teams we could get, and made a break for Fort Kearney. We put sticks in the hands of the women and children so as to make it appear to the Indians that we were better armed than we really were. We went towards Fort Kearney as far as Valley City and near there met a company of United States soldiers who were on their way to relieve a detail of soldiers on the Little Blue who were there cutting wood. We remained at Valley City over night and there concluded to make up a party and come to Beatrice. We got to Beatrice safely along about the 20th of the month.

After the company was raised under the command of Captain A. G. White, we went out under orders to report to Fort Kearney. On our way to Fort Kearney we passed over the scenes of depredation of the Indians between here and there, seeing many dead white people settlers whom the Indians had killed. I saw a young boy, one of the Eubanks family. He was lying about seventy-five yards from the Eubanks residence. They lived on the Little Blue about ten miles south-east of our ranch. I also saw William Kennedy lying dead, killed by the Indians. It was about thirteen miles south-east of our ranch. His body had at that time been almost devoured by wolves. I also saw what was left of two men by the name of Kelley and Buckley who had been killed by the Indians at Oak Grove ranch about twelve miles from our ranch. The Indians after they killed them burnt their bodies so that they were almost unrecognizable. We could only tell them by portions of their cloths that were not burned.

The ranches generally were plundered and burned. The property was all either destroyed or stolen by the Indians, and the country left in a state of desolation. Some of the women and girls were taken prisoners and carried off by the Indians. I now recall two—Mrs. Hugh Banks [Lucinda Eubanks] whose husband was killed and Miss Laura Roper. They did not get back again for something like a year after their capture.

On this march I went by our ranch [and] every particle of personal property was either destroyed or stolen by these Indians. The buildings were not burned but the windows were knocked out, broken up and destroyed. The house was a double log house with three rooms in it. We were detained in the militia for about five months and as soon as the militia was dismissed and I could gather up something we went back again unto the ranch. My recollection is that it was the last of March 1865.[38]

This fight at Pawnee Ranch was kept up until the Indians tired of their inability to storm the fortified defense. Three Indians were known to be killed in the fight.[39]

Daniel Freeman also gave details about the devastation the Indians wreaked upon the settlers and their property:

I owned a ranch about 14 miles from there [Buffalo Ranch] and I delivered from my ranch to this Buffalo ranch quite a lot of shelled corn just a few days prior to this time and was going back and forth, and was pretty well acquainted with their ranch and property. I know that they kept quite a stock of groceries and provisions for sale to the travelling public that travelled over this overland stage route. This was the main overland route from the states to California [and Denver] at that time. About the 7th, of August, a hostile band of Sioux and Cheyenne Indians came to my place and destroyed my property and ranch and all the other ranches in that community, burning the ranches, stealing what property they wanted and destroying the rest and murdering all of the inoffensive settlers that were not able to get away from them. I left my ranch on the 6th [11th?], of August 1864; and came to Beatrice and stayed at Beatrice a few days and got up a company of settlers to go out there and drive the Indians off. We reached Mudge & Milligan's ranch on the 14th of August on my way back with the company. I found the furniture all broken, everything in the house was destroyed, dishes of every description broken,

---

38   William Mudge Indian Depredation Claim #4123. Record Group 123.

39   William Mudge testimony in Merritt Metcalf Indian Depredation Claim #9850.

copper boilers was shot full of arrow holes, tin pans and dishes of every description shot full of arrow holes, groceries, corn and oats mixed together on the floor of the store room; there was shelled corn scattered all over the prairie. It seemed as though the Indians took sacks of corn on their ponies and ran races with it to see how far they could string it by letting it run through a small hole cut in the sack. There was always two strings of corn close together. There were quite a number of cattle laying dead around with arrows shot through them, among others were his nice cows that I had seen a few days before lying dead there. There was nothing left of any value on the place, nothing but bare walls of the building were standing there. I could see the broken stoves and other articles of household furniture had all been broken into little pieces and the chairs and tables were all hacked to pieces with hatchets, they had killed the chickens and I saw them lying dead around [Elizabeth Mudge, William's wife, testified that the dead chickens were thrown into their well], feathers were scattered around about the place, I supposed at the time that the feathers came from the feather beds. . . .

They killed at this outbreak a good many, quite a number that I knew. They killed a young man by the name of Ulich, another by the name of Kennedy, a man by the name of Butler, another by the name of Kelly. They shot fifteen arrows into a man by the name of Ostrander and he afterwards died. They wounded George Hunt in the thigh, they killed five persons of the Eubanks ranch and took two women prisoners. Further up the road they killed John Burke and seven other teamsters were killed in a bunch, I don't know their names. These persons and others I helped to bury. Butler and Kelley were burnt in the Cumst [Comstock] Ranch, but we gathered up what bones we could find and buried them.[40]

---

40   William Mudge Indian Depredation Claim.

CHAPTER FOUR

The War Continues

*Daniel is a mighty smart boy I took a liking to the boy when I first saw him
on the Smoke Hill. there was an old squaw maid him a kind of a coat and
I tried to get him to take it with him but he said he dident want any thing
to do with any thing they had. . . .*

W. F. SMITH, 1ST COLORADO CAVALRY
ANN MARBLE INDIAN DEPREDATION CLAIM
INDIAN DEPREDATIONS CLAIMS DIVISION, RECORD GROUP 75

WHILE INDIANS WERE LINGERING ABOUT THE TRAIL ON
the Little Blue River prior to their renewed attacks on August 9,
a day earlier and about 100 miles northwest along Plum Creek,
paralleling the south side of the Platte River and near the present-day town
of Lexington, the Plum Creek massacre occurred. Cheyenne Indians were
the perpetrators of this raid. Cheyenne White Antelope, killed at Sand
Creek, confessed the next month to Governor Evans, saying his Cheyenne
took two prisoners and destroyed the freight trains.[1]

The August 8 raid began early in the morning, about two miles west
of Plum Creek Station, when the Cheyenne attacked a wagon train just
breaking camp to begin their day's journey west. The Indians failed in this
attack and left two of their own dead along the road. Three teamsters were
wounded.[2] The ranch of Bernard Blondeau, situated less than a mile east of
Plum Creek Station, was also raided at this same time and everything inside
was either destroyed or taken. Blondeau also lost 14 head of cattle. There
were several men at Blondeau's ranch when the wagon train was attacked to
the west, about two and a half miles away. Seeing the train under attack in

---

1   Carroll, *The Sand Creek Massacre*, 406.
2   Michno, *Encyclopedia of Indian Wars*, 148.

the distance, the ranchmen wisely fled to Plum Creek Station, where there were soldiers stationed.[3] Blondeau was a Frenchman who had married his wife, Rose Marie, in 1854. He had earlier been married and had a son living with them, who escaped the ranch on horseback, along with Blondeau's Canadian partner, a man named Mr. Dupries and his wife Eteinne. They took with them Rose Marie's daughter, who was 10 at the time of the raid. Rose Marie and Bernard did not have horses and fled a few hundred yards to the river, where they jumped in and hid among the limbs and brush overhanging the river.[4]

At about the same time that this attack was going on, and about 10 miles further east, Indians raided the ranch of Frederick Smith, known as Twenty-Five Mile Point Ranch. Fortunately for Smith, he and his wife had earlier that morning driven a wagon east to Fort Kearny and missed all the subsequent raids. Smith had left his ranch hand, Austin Rainey, in charge of the ranch. The Indians killed him, then burned and plundered the ranch.[5]

Just two miles east of Plum Creek Station, or eight miles west of where Rainey was killed, another wagon party had just started their day's journey west when they were quickly surprised on the road. They were unable

---

3 Bernard Blondeau Indian Depredation Claim #5520. Record Group 75.

4 Bernard Blondeau Indian Depredation Claim #10761.

5 Frederick Smith Indian Depredation Claim #4568. Record Group 123. Becher, in *Massacre Along the Medicine Road* (p. 262), says Smith and his wife went to Dobytown the morning of the raid, while Smith, in his depredation claim, says he went to Fort Kearny. Dobytown was just west of Fort Kearny, so he would have passed through Dobytown on his way to Fort Kearny. The Smith depredation claim, while providing details of the raid, is an excellent claim to study for its fraudulent intent. The process for filing a successful claim required affidavits of witnesses, which served as a safeguard to prevent fraud, as was the case in Smith's claim. While Smith's ranch was burned and destroyed and his ranch hand killed, Smith nevertheless filed a claim for a total of $13,198.75 in losses. He overinflated his house by hundreds of dollars. Neighbors and soldiers who served along the trail were interviewed as a part of the investigation of Smith's claim, and they all testified that his ranch was quite small and that the goods he had were scant, not totaling more than $500 in groceries at any time, while Smith claimed that he had just prior to the raid returned from Nebraska City with two wagon loads of goods to sell at his ranch worth $2,200 (the file produces no receipts for proof). Benjamin Gallagher, at the time the post trader at Cottonwood Springs (later Fort McPherson), testified that Smith's goods consisted in "a barrel of whiskey or two bags of coffee and probably some course goods, cheap beads and Indian goods to trade with the Indians for robes." Another witness testified that Smith did not have any cattle, though he claimed a loss of 30 head worth more than $100 each. Another neighbor testified that Smith did have cattle, but not very many and that their worth did not exceed $25 each. Yet another witness testified that Smith did not think he would be paid but made the claim large enough that if he got half or two-thirds of what he was filing for, then he would be compensated the amount he really lost. Before the raid, prices along the trail were reasonable, but after the raid they became quite expensive, no doubt due to the increased risk of running a ranch while a war was going on.

to defend themselves against more than 100 screaming warriors, as the Cheyenne war party—Bull Bear's Dog Soldiers—descended upon the train.[6] In a matter of just a few terrifying moments, 11 men were killed and a boy and woman were taken captive, Daniel Marble and Mrs. Nancy Jane Morton. There are many incidents connected with the Plum Creek massacre that are worth noting. Young Daniel Marble, whose father was one of the dead, was eventually given over to the authorities by Black Kettle later that fall, along with three captives from the August 7 raid along the Little Blue River—Laura Roper, and children Isabella Eubanks and Ambrose Asher. Isabella suffered permanently from her captivity ordeal and never recovered. She died in early 1865.[7]

Though Black Kettle professed peace by returning the captives, he was dishonest in saying three more captives were in the possession of the Sioux, implying they were elsewhere from where he was camped, when in fact they were hidden in the same cluster of Indian lodges where he was. This was later learned when two of them were rescued—the third was hanged in an Arapaho tepee shortly after Black Kettle released four captives. He also misstated the truth when he said the captives he released were victims that he had traded for, implying that his band of Indians were not involved with the violent outbreak in early August. Technically he was correct. It was not his band. But many in the guilty party were Cheyenne that often camped with or near his band.

William Marble began his portion of the train from Council Bluffs on July 23. He was being paid to freight goods, mostly corn owned by George Marshal, to Julesburg and Denver. With his three wagons—which he owned—along with the horses and mules used to freight the goods, were his two young sons, Daniel and Joel. Daniel was nine and Joel was 12. Working with him were James Smith, W. [Charles] Iliff and a man by the name of St. Clair. Shortly after leaving Council Bluffs, Joel became sick and arrangements were made to return him home to his mother, Ann Marble. He thus

---

6   Father Peter John Powell acknowledges the Cheyenne were responsible for this raid, along with some Brule Lakota. See *People of the Sacred Mountain: A History of the Northern Cheyenne Chiefs and Warrior Societies 1830–1879*, Volume I (San Francisco, CA: Harper & Row, Publishers, 1981), 279. White Antelope told Governor Evans at the Camp Weld conference in Denver "We (the Cheyennes) took two prisoners west of Fort Kearney, and destroyed the trains." Carroll, *The Sand Creek Massacre*, 406.

7   Michno, *A Fate Worse Than Death*, 139, 141–142, 302. Michno lists her death as occurring on March 18. Lucinda Eubanks, in her affidavit dated June 22, 1865, said her daughter died "last February." See Carroll, *The Sand Creek Massacre*, Appendix, 91.

left the freight train and avoided capture or death. However, his future was not promising. He continued in poor health after returning to his mother in Council Bluffs and died in January 1870.

When Daniel was rescued in September—he had been a captive for 31 days—he was under the care of one of the soldiers who was there at his rescue, and later at Fort Lyon, prior to the released captives being brought into Denver. W. F. Smith took a strong liking to little Daniel and wrote to Mrs. Marble about him. He first wrote on October 12, to inform her that Daniel had been taken from Fort Lyon, where Smith was caring for him, to Denver, preparatory to his return to his mother. Company D of the 1st Colorado Voluntary Cavalry donated $72.50 to help Daniel get back home. Smith even sewed new clothes for him. He wrote—in poor grammar—that Daniel "was well pleased with me and wanted to stay with me I would been glad to of kept him but I am in hopes he will get home this winter. I think he will. Please write and tell me if he gets home safe and if he is not at home let me no if you halve heard from him." Smith wrote again on October 24, noting that he anticipated that Daniel was probably by then home with his mother. He noted:

> Daniel hated to leave me might bad I felt sorrow for the poor little fellow. He told them he wasent going unless I went with him But I couldent go with him. Daniel is a mighty smart boy I took a liking to the boy when I first saw him on the Smoke Hill. there was an old squaw maid him a kind of a coat and I tried to get him to take it with him but he said he dident want any thing to do with any thing they had....[8]

But Daniel's homecoming was not to be. Some time after he arrived in Denver—about September 23—he took sick with typhoid fever. A doctor, W. F. McClelland, wrote to Mrs. Marble on October 13, stating that Danny had become ill three weeks earlier. He was hopeful for his recovery, however, and reported that Danny would soon be able to travel. On November 12, McClelland wrote again and reported the sad news that Daniel had died three days earlier: "I have to disclose to you a sorrowful report your little boy was taken to the military hospital three days from the time he was taken sick and was attended by the surgeon of the hospital for some time . . . and died last Wednesday the 9th of November." McClelland wrote in the spirit of a spiritual advisor: "He is gone & you must be reconciled to your fate which is a bitter one . . . God does all things well and we have to submit & hope that God will support you in your sad affliction."

---

8   Ann Marble Indian Depredation Claim. Record Group 75.

Rescued captive Laura Roper also shared her condolences to Mrs. Marble, telling her that if she was not able to get another photograph of little Daniel, she would cut his image out of the picture that was given to her, showing all four captives together. When she last saw Daniel, he had told her that he thought he was out of danger, "that he would soon be well and then he would go home and see his mother."[9]

The other captive taken when Daniel Marble was captured, Nancy Morton, whose husband Thomas was killed in the attack—as well as her brother William Fletcher and cousin John Fletcher—was later sold to the Lakota. She remained in captivity until bought by traders six months later in Wyoming Territory.

The man responsible for her rescue, Joseph Bissonette, Sr., added more information about Nancy and her rescue. He had lived on the frontier for many years, and in 1864 was living in what would become Wyoming, operating Deer Creek Station, about 20 miles east of Platte Bridge, which was in present-day Casper. In December, some friendly Indians came to him and reported that the Cheyenne—not Lakota—had Mrs. Morton as prisoner but would be willing to give her up in trade. Bissonette telegraphed Fort Laramie and received permission from Major John Woods, commanding the post, to obtain her "by any means in his power." Mrs. Morton was being held by a Cheyenne chief named Medicine Arrow. John Richmond,[10] under the direction of Colonel Collins, had earlier failed to gain her release.

---

9   Ann Marble Indian Depredation Claim. All of the information relating to the Marble family comes from this file. The original letters written to Mrs. Marble were all in her Indian depredation claim and never returned to her. That she would give these letters to the government as a part of her claim must have been painful, as they were the original reports of the last days of her young son's short life. The famous photograph taken of the four rescued captives often errs in identifying Daniel Marble as the boy on the left, when in fact he was the smaller boy—though two years older than Ambrose—on the right. The mystery is solved in the photograph—showing three and not the four captives—used in Margaret Coel's *Chief Left Hand Southern Arapaho* (Norman, OK: University of Oklahoma Press, 1981, p. 227). In Coel's research she was given the original photograph that Laura Roper kept, which had Daniel's picture cut out, on the right, confirming Laura's promise to send Daniel's mother the image of him from her own photograph if she was unable to procure another copy. Margaret Coel later told me that the University of Oklahoma, who published her book, never returned to her the original photographs she sent to the publisher when she sent all her documents for publication, despite repeated requests over many years for their return. Fortunately, today's digital technology prevents like travesties from occurring.

10   A report filed with the Bureau of Indian Affairs says Richmond's name was John Richard. See Russ Czaplewski, *Captive of the Cheyenne: The Story of Nancy Jane Morton and the Plum Creek Massacre* (Kearney, NE: The Dawson County Historical Society, 1993), 45.

RESCUED CAPTIVES FROM THE AUGUST 7–8 RAIDS ON THE LITTLE BLUE RIVER AND PLUM CREEK, NEBRASKA TERRITORY. Cheyenne Chief Black Kettle surrendered these captives to Major Edward Wynkoop, who then delivered them to Denver in late September 1864. From left to right: seven-year-old Ambrose Asher (captured on Little Blue); 17-year-old Laura Roper (Little Blue); three-year-old Isabella Eubanks (Little Blue); nine-year-old Daniel Marble (captured on Plum Creek). At Camp Weld, White Antelope admitted that his Southern Cheyenne Indians were responsible for the Plum Creek raid. Isabella never recovered from her captivity ordeal, and died in Denver six months later, March 18, 1865. Daniel Marble died of typhoid fever at Camp Weld, November 9, 1864, less than a month after his rescue. Because Daniel was two years older than Ambrose, people often identify the taller boy as Daniel. This is a mistake, as revealed in the Indian depredation claim of Mrs. Marble. *Courtesy Nebraska State Historical Society, Lincoln, Nebraska.* RG1507-2.

The first attempt by Bissonette also failed. He had sent his half-breed son, Joseph Bissonette, Jr., along with Jules Coffey with a wagon load of supplies, including horses, but the attempt was unsuccessful and nearly cost both men their lives. Apparently the Cheyenne were riled up, as they had recently become aware of "some transactions on the South Platte [probably Sand Creek], and demanding further remuneration." Young Joseph "had very hard work in getting away with his life, he was pursued for near fifty miles from the village, but succeeded in making his escape."

After this failed rescue, the ransom was enlarged to include four horses, two revolvers, four pairs of blankets, 20 yards of bed ticking, 150 pounds of sugar, 45 pounds of coffee, three sacks of flour, 60 pounds of rice, three pounds of gunpowder and four pounds of bullets, two shirts, three yards of calico, one bridle, 33 pounds of tobacco, two gross gilt buttons, 24 bunches of beads, one pound of brass tacks, six dressing combs, two dozen ebony handled knives, 32 pounds of bacon, half a bushel of corn, one hat, one rifle, one shot-gun, and one saddle. In January 1865, a second expedition was begun, with the above provisions, and three men were hired. The rescuers all knew the expedition to rescue Mrs. Morton might cost them their lives. This time, the ransom was accepted and Mrs. Morton was set free, finally arriving at Fort Laramie on January 30, 1865. What is interesting in Mr. Bissonette's account is his repeated insistence that, along with her husband and the other people killed at the Plum Creek massacre, Nancy's sister was also with the wagon party during the attack and was killed. Nancy Morton later never affirmed that claim, though it is possible that her sister or sister-in-law—possibly her cousin John Fletcher's wife—was one of the victims of that deadly August raid.[11]

When Mrs. Morton was rescued in 1865, Lieutenant Jeremiah Triggs, commanding Company D, 7th Iowa Cavalry, interviewed her about her ordeal. The Utah *Union Vedette* on August 19, 1865, published what Triggs learned. Nancy said the war party consisted of only 65 warriors, of which 10 were Sioux, 10 Arapaho, one Kiowa and the rest Cheyenne. The Indians all got drunk the evening of her capture.[12] Mrs. Sarah L. Larimer, herself

11   Jules Coffey, Joseph Bissonette, Senior, and Joseph Bissonette, Senior Indian Depredation Claim #2208. Record Group 75. Donald Berthong identifies Medicine Arrow as Medicine Arrows. See *The Southern Cheyennes* (Norman, OK: University of Oklahoma Press, 1963), 258.

12   Czaplewski, *Captive of the Cheyenne*, 30.

a captive in 1864, but who was able to escape her Lakota captors after two days, was apparently at Fort Laramie when Mrs. Morton was brought in, late in January. In 1870, she wrote a now rare account of her captivity and mentioned Mrs. Morton's story, saying there were several cases of liquors found in some of the wagons when the massacre occurred. All but two Indians—guards for the revelry—got drunk that night consuming the plundered booze. Mrs. Larimer shared other details that Mrs. Morton told her she witnessed. One involved the capture and sad death of a seven-year-old girl taken from somewhere along the warriors' path of destruction, either from a home or a wagon train. Mrs. Morton met her when she was brought into the first camp, the little girl having been captured shortly before:

> She was an intelligent little creature, but, alas! Could not understand that her only safety lay in obedience. The child cried continuously for her mother, frequently declaring she knew that the Indians intended to kill her. The savages admired the little girl, and evidently intended to take her to their village; but at length, weary of her continual fretting, a council was held to decide her fate. It was decided that she was unprofitable, and, at the close of the council, the child was placed a little apart from the others.
>
> "I believe you are going to kill me," she cried, as she held her little, trembling hands imploringly toward her companion in bondage. "I always feared they would kill me, and I would never see my dear mamma!" At this instant a deadly arrow pierced her heart, and she lay dead.
>
> The savages evidently were sorry for what they had done, though conceiving it their duty, and laid her to rest with all the honors due to a beloved one of their own tribe.[13]

The poor, little unknown girl proved true American philosopher William James's dictum that there are times "where a fact cannot come at all unless a preliminary faith exists in its coming."[14] Her unfortunate and uncontrollable fear created her reality.

Years later Mrs. Morton put her story to pen:

> At Plum Creek station we were rejoined by nine wagons. This made our train consist of twelve wagons which made it better for all of us. As our trains were loaded with freight which we were taking to Denver and one of the men was obliged to stand guard for fear robbers might make an unexpected assault.

13 Mrs. Sarah L. Larimer, *The Capture and Escape*, 130–131.
14 William James, *The Will to Believe and Other Essays in Popular Philosophy* (New York, NY: Dover Publications, Inc., 1956. Originally published in 1897), 25.

When we camped at Plum Creek that night my brother and Mr. Marble stood guard the former part of the night and my husband the latter.

About six o'clock in the morning we again started on our western course. My husband being quite fatigued requested that I should drive which I gladly consented. While I was driving and my husband fast asleep all of my time was spent in viewing the beautiful landscape. Which I supposed we would soon reach. But alas! That was only a momentary thot [thought] for far in the distance I could see objects which seemed to be approaching but on account of the great distance they were indistinguishable. What could it be? I called to my husband and he at once came to my side when I told him to look in the distance and tell me what that large group of objects could be. He thought it was only a herd of buffalo so soon reclined on the couch and was soon fast asleep. But it wasn't long, only a few moments until I observed they were Indians and I again called my husband and he said he knew they were Indians. Soon the landscape before us was covered with the savages. Soon we observed they were warriors and were painted and equipped for battle. Soon they uttered a wild cry and fired a volley from their guns, which made us realize our helpless condition.

This terrible and unsuspected apparition came upon as with such startling swiftness that we had no time to make preparation for defence [defense]. Soon the whole band of warriors encircled us and gave the war whoop. Which I shall never forget. None but those who had had personal experience in Indian warfare can form a just conception of the terror which this war whoop is calculated to inspire. With wild screams and yells they circled around and around which frightened our teams so they became uncontrollable. Thinking there might be some faint hope of escape I sprang from the wagon. When my husband called "Ah my dear! Where are you going?" Those were the last words I heard him say. But our team was running and I jumped. I fell to the ground and before I could recover myself one of the back teams came dashing by and the wheels passed over my body. I thot I could never make another attempt to rescue myself. But soon I was so nerved by fear or by the dread of death by such demon hands I again made a desparate effort for life with all the strength I could procure I started for the river. When I met my brother and my cousin and they said we have no hope of escape. As the Indians had encircled us, and the air was full of arrows. At that moment an arrow struck my cousin which proved fatal and he fell dead at my feet. In another instant three arrows penetrated my brother's body, he too fell at my feet and his words were "Tell Susan I am killed. Good by my dear sister."

With naturally a sensitive nature, tenderly and affectionately reared, shuddering at the very thot of cruelty, you can my dear reader, imagine but only imagine the agony I endured. But neither the gloom of the forest nor the blackness of night, nor both combined could begin to symbolize the darkness of my terror stricken heart.

My first impulse was to kneel by my brother when upon kneeling I discovered two arrows lodged in my side. Just as I went to remove them a horrible old warrior came up to me and demanded me to go with him. When I immediately told him no! I was going to stay by my brother. Before I could utter another word he drew a large whip from his belt and began whipping me severely. But I soon made an effort to escape him and started to run, when two warriors came after me and ordered me to stop or they would kill me. I told them I would rather die than to be led into captivity and I told them I was going to search for my husband. But those two Indians soon overtook me and demanded me to mount an old pony or they would shoot me. I was almost paralyzed with fear for I had seen these Indians on our previous trip to Denver but they had been at peace and did not molest us. They were the Sioux and Cheyennes the most savage Indians at that time. This band was commonly called the Ogallalla band and to be taken captive by them almost made me pray to die instantly. But I still bitterly resisted to mount the old pony, but before I could make another resistance they tossed me on the old pony and took me to the wagons.

Such a sight as human eyes could behold was before me. The wagons had all been plundered, and the mangled forms of the dear were about me, and our teams were running at large over the prairie with the Indians after them and war whoops resounding from every direction. Only one of the horses escaped and found his way home and with good care he soon recovered as the Indians wounded him many times with the arrows.

After the Indians succeeded in capturing several of the horses and killing the rest they were ready to return to their camp. They had massacred all of my comrades except little Dannie Marble. Two old chiefs and two old Squaws came up to Dannie and I and told us we were obliged to go with them so one of the warriors tossed me back of the saddle of one of the old Chiefs ponies and Dannie back of the other old chief. As we were leaving, I took a look at those dear to me lying dead upon the ground, perhaps to be devoured by wild beasts and the war whoops resounding till I was almost deaf. . . .

As Dannie and I traveled along the Indians talked very mean to us, threatening our lives all the while. . . .

After we had traveled until almost noon, we reached a lake. Here the whole band stopped to eat, rest and divide the provisions they had taken. . . .

As soon as Dannie and I dismounted we sat down on the bank to rest for we were both so fatigued we were unable to stand. The arrows in my side I knew would prove fatal if allowed to remain much longer. Fortunately a Frenchman that made his home with the Indians came to me and asked me if those arrows in my side weren't almost unendurable. I told him I knew that they would soon prove fatal for the agony I endured was almost indescribable. He then offered me his pen knife and I removed the arrows. I suffered dreadful from those wounds and soon discovered I had two ribs broken which rendered my condition much more horrible. While I was sitting here suffering and trying to comfort little Dan who was crying like his heart would break. Several warriors came near us then they would toss scalps into the air, and laugh with all the vengeance they could procure. Then Old Chief Big Crow came up and threw a scalp into my face which I soon recognized was taken from my own dear brother's head and their clothes were still wet from the lifeblood of my dear ones lying upon the battlefield.

After they had tortured me with scalps all they deemed satisfactory, they departed but one returned with a piece of raw buffalo meat which he compelled me to eat. . . .[15]

Nancy Morton's claim against the Indians, filed after she was rescued, asked for an additional $5,000 for damages she incurred in her captivity. It "was one of hardship and having undergone great wrongs and sufferings at the hands of her barbarous captors." She noted that she "suffered from all the abuse and indignity that could be practiced toward her not only by one Indian, but many." In her claim, she identified the Indians as Cheyenne Dog Soldiers. She noted in a June 11, 1865 deposition that when she got to the lake mentioned in her written account, she met a white man, "who told her the Indians were Cheyennes, under Chief 'Bull Bear'."[16]

The massacred wagon party was composed of three or four wagons owned by Thomas Morton and Matthew Pratt, who was not present, one wagon driven by Morton and the others by teamsters, two of them Nancy's brother and cousin. As Nancy recalled, just before the massacre their wagons joined seven or eight more, totaling either 11 or 12 wagons.[17]

---

15 Czaplewski, *Captive of the Cheyenne*, 14–17.

16 Mrs. Morton Indian Depredation Claim #1642. Record Group 75. It is significant that Mrs. Morton identifies Bull Bear as responsible for her capture. Bull Bear was one of the chiefs who went with Black Kettle to Denver in September 1864, in an attempt to profess peace. This affidavit clearly and without question shows that the Indians associated with Black Kettle were indeed, at the very least, partially responsible for the violent outbreak along the Denver road in early August. Brigadier General Robert Mitchell wrote in a report, dated March 6, 1865, that Mrs. Morton said the Indians were all gathered high up the North Fork of the Powder River, which included "the Cheyennes, Arapahoes, Kiowas, Brule and Ogalalla Sioux, and Minneconjous are banded together, and determined to make war to the knife." *War of the Rebellion*, Series I, Vol. XLVIII, Part I, 1105. It should be noted, too, that in Mrs. Morton's later reminiscences about her captivity she said that she had never been traded away from the Indians who captured her. Further, she was in the village with Mrs. Eubanks when the four captives that Major Edward Wynkoop had released to his custody were given up. At that moment of rescue of Danny Marble, Laura Roper, Isabelle Eubank and Ambrose Asher, the Indians "ordered Mrs. Eubanks and I to the ground with buffalo robes thrown over us so we would not be noticed. And warriors stood near us with bows and arrows drawn ready to murder us if we should make one faint murmer [*sic*]." Czaplewski, *Captive of the Cheyenne*, 22.

17 Pratt, in his affidavit in Mrs. Morton's depredation claim, said the Morton party consisted of four wagons. Nancy, in her memoirs, said it was three wagons pulled by her husband, brother and cousin. See Mrs. Morton Depredation Claim #1642, and Czaplewski, *Captive of the Cheyenne*, p. 13.

It is generally reported that the remaining teamsters were unknown men. Ronald Becher, in *Massacre Along the Medicine Road*, claims that the train consisted of six wagons belonging to Michael Kelly, three to Thomas Morton, and three belonging to William Marble. Becher cites no reference for Michael Kelly.[18] The name Kelly is identified in a report made by Lieutenant Charles F. Porter to the *Omaha Nebraskan* for August 17, 1864: "The names of those certainly killed are Charles Iliff, Marble and boy, Smith and Smith's partner all of Council Bluffs; Wm. Fletcher, Colorado; and five others not known. Six wagons loaded with corn and machinery from St. Joe, belonging to Michael Kelly, and outfit belonging [to] . . . Morton from Sidney, was destroyed. . . ."[19] Michael Kelly was probably confused for freighter Michael Tulley.

Becher writes that the 11 wagons were stretched out several hundred yards apart, with James Smith riding a mule in the front with Mr. St. Clair, and Smith's wife riding in one of Marble's wagons. William Marble and Charles Iliff were further back, and behind them were the Morton wagons, and then further back were the remaining wagons.[20] St. Clair, Iliff and Morton were the first killed. Mrs. Smith miraculously escaped by jumping off her wagon and hiding among cattails in a marshy area near the road.[21]

Indian depredation claims help to identify all but two of the other freighters. Patrick Harmon was apparently one, though his claim was filed many years later by his sister Margaret Joy, administrator of the estate, who confused the date, believing the massacre happened August 4. But she did confirm a woman escaped. She said the unnamed woman and her husband left the train just before the attack to visit at Plum Creek Station, which was only about a half-mile away. The station operator—Laurence Hays—and the unidentified man and wife witnessed the attack. Harmon was delivering a wagon of iron piping to Denver.[22]

---

18 Becher, *Massacre along the Medicine Road*, 252.
19 This story is also produced in Czaplewski, *Captive of the Cheyenne*, 14.
20 Becher, *Massacre along the Medicine Road*, 255.
21 This is the account that Becher gives, *Massacre along the Medicine Road*, 258.
22 Patrick Harmon Depredation Claim #4942. It is slightly possible that this depredation claim identifies an earlier attack in the same vicinity as the well-known Plum Creek massacre. First, the distances from Plum Creek Station and the August 8 attack, as noted in all other accounts, are between one and two miles, depending on sources, but generally closer to two miles. The distance from Plum Creek Station in the August 4 attack is less than half a mile. Military reports are scant in reporting the August 8 massacre (one short telegram, dated August 10, stating 10 men were just killed). Military reports about the Indian attacks in the area did not surface until several weeks later, and thus it is possible a

Calvin C. Woolworth and David H. Barton operated a company involved in freighting and their wagons and goods were also destroyed in the massacre. Freighters Peter Dolan and Michael Tulley—two of the 11 victims—were contracted to deliver $3,433.64 of goods in seven cases, weighing 1,993 pounds and consisting of books and stationery goods. They were to go to Woolworth and Moffat, who operated a book and stationery store in Denver. In addition to this, the wagon included three cases of cigars weighing 950 pounds. That was to go to Casler and Company in Denver.

Woolworth and Barton loaded the freight at St. Joseph on July 22, and gave to Peter Dolan "bills of lading of said goods." Barton noted that he had seen on file in the governor's office in Colorado "a bill of lading . . . taken from the body of a Cheyenne chief, called 'Big Wolf,' after said chief was slain in a battle near Valley Station, which occurred in October last [October 10, 1864. See Chapter 5, p. 123]. I recognized said bill as one . . . shipped by Woolworth and Barton, to Woolworth and Moffat, and given to said Peter Dolan."[23]

David Moffat was the owner of the stationery store in Denver, which went out of business around 1872. His lost goods represent a side of early Denver history mostly unknown today. Moffat's depredation claim reproduces the entire contents of the goods meant for sale in his store. It gives one a nice glimpse into the literary and social culture of early Denver:

---

first massacre was overlooked. The bodies of the August 8 massacre were buried within a day after they were killed, but in the Margaret Joy account, the bodies of the August 4 massacre were not buried for several days. The Indians stayed at the massacre site of the August 4 murders for three or four days; the Indians stayed at the August 8 massacre only long enough to burn, pilfer and destroy the wagons. Also, accounts of all the murderous raids along the Little Blue and Plum Creek, as well as the Platte River further west, reveal at least 51 Americans killed in the August raids, yet the identities of who were killed can only be established at about 36, thus leaving unknown the names of nearly 20 victims, most likely freighters, as the settlers knew each other and witnesses identified all of the dead settlers. Thus, it is possible that there were two wagon trains near Plum Creek Station four days apart, each attacked and resulting in equal casualties of 11. Though this appears unlikely, still, it cannot be ruled out. Who, if there was not an August 4 massacre, were the man and woman from the August 8 massacre that fortuitously escaped their deaths by leaving the train and going forth to the station just before the massacre was reported in the August 4 depredation claim? Becher says only a woman escaped, who was the wife of James Smith. Further, the *Omaha Republican*, on August 19, reporting the massacre of August 8, noted in addition that "news arrived last night that several more men have been killed in the vicinity of Dan Smith's and Gillman's [sic] Ranche." Gilman's Ranch was about 12 miles east of Camp Cottonwood, later named Fort McPherson. If this report is true then indeed several men were killed a few miles west of Plum Creek Station, and could indeed be the men noted in the August 4 massacre, as revealed in the Harmon depredation claim. Still, this seems unlikely.

23   Woolworth and Moffit Indian Depredation Claim #4958. Record Group 123.

2 bound books, Cape Cod, at $1.75	$3.50
2 bound books, Thurstons, at $1.50	$3.00
2 bound books, Eldorado, at $1.50	$3.00
4 bound books, Irving Sketches, at $1	$4.00
4 grosses, Blk. gilt tablet pencils at $6.50	$26.00
5 grosses, Blk. gilt tablet pencils tipped, at $9.50	$47.50
3 grosses, Blk. gilt tablet pencils at $8.50	$25.50
1 and five twelfths grosses Blk. gilt tablet pencils at $7, — (9.91)	$9.09
2 grosses red and blue polished pencils, at $4.50	$9.00
One fourth gross Artists polished pencils, at .25	$6.25
One fourth gross Artists polished pencils, at .40	$10.00
One fourth gross Artists polished pencils, at .45	$11.25
One half gross Artists propelling pencils, at .42	$21.00
One half gross Artists propelling pencils tipped, at .24	$12.00
6 Photograph Albums, No. 100 at 90 cts.	$5.40
3 Photograph Albums, No. 115 at $2.75	$8.25
4 Photograph Albums, No. 117 at $3.50	$14.00
5 Photograph Albums, No. 121 at $6.00	$30.00
2 Photograph Albums, No. 128 at $5.75	$11.00
2 Photograph Albums, No. 134 at $4.75	$9.50
2 Photograph Albums, No. 136 at $6.00	$12.00
2 Photograph Albums, No. 137 at $7.00	$14.00
4 Photograph Albums, No. 140 at $4.50	$18.00
6 Photograph Albums, No. 141 at $4.75	$28.50
2 Photograph Albums, No. 150 at $7.00	$14.00
2 Photograph Albums, No. 151 at $7.50	$15.00
3 Photograph Albums, No. 153 at $9.00	$27.00
2 Photograph Albums, No. 154 at $11.00	$22.00
2 Photograph Albums, No. 156 at $7.50	$15.00
2 Photograph Albums, No. 160 at $2.00	$4.00
1 Photograph Albums, No. 160 at $16.00	$16.00
1 Photograph Albums, No. 170 at $25.00	$25.00
5 Photograph Albums, No. 123 at $4.50	$22.50
6 Ambrotypes, at $2.25	$13.50
15 Ambrotypes, two thirds, at 88 cts.	$13.20
8 Prayer books, at $2	$16.00
3 Prayer books, at $2.25	$6.75
2 Bound books, Cave Life at $1	$2.00
2 Bound books, Vicar of W, at $1.25	$2.50
2 Bound books, Queen Mab, t $1.50	$3.00
1 Bound book, Love	$1.50

2 Bound books, Lights and S. at $1.25	$2.50
2 Bound books, Madge, at $1.25	$2.50
2 Bound books, Round Table, at $1.50	$3.00
7 Bound books, Guliver, at $1.00	$7.00
2 Ambrotypes, at 20 cts.	$.40
6 Ambrotypes, Face, at 88 cts.	$5.28
1 Engraving, Evangeline, at 88 cts.	$.88
3 Engravings, N. and S. at $2.64	$7.92
1 Engraving, Ball Slippers, 88 cts.	$.88
2 Engravings, Midsummer Dream, at 88 cts.	$1.76
1 Engraving, Empress Eugenie, — $2.25	$2.25
2 Engravings, Joy and Sorrow, at $2.25	$4.50
1 set cloth bound L. S. Tales, $6.25	$6.25
1 set cloth bound Sea Side Tales, $12.50	$12.50
2 Bound books, Rubina, $1.50	$3.00
2 Bound books, Dennis, $1.50	$3.00
2 Bound books, Life before Him, $1.25	$2.50
12 Bound books, St. Nicholas, 50 cts.	$6.00
12 Bound books, Banner, 25 cts.	$3.00
1 Bound book for Mechanics, $2.50	$2.50
7 Lithograph pictures, Pres. Lincoln, $1.33	$9.31
4 Lithograph pictures, Washington, $1.67	$6.68
3 Lithograph pictures, Central Park, $2	$6.00
10 Lithograph pictures, Voyage of Life, $1.50	$15.00
9 Lithograph pictures, Stag at Bay, 33 and a third	$3.00
13 Lithograph pictures, Evangeline, .80	$10.40
4 Lithograph pictures, Jefferson, $1	$4.00
4 Lithograph pictures, Clay and Webster, $1.50	$6.00
11 Lithograph pictures, Gen. Grant, 75 cts.	$8.25
100 Cooper's papers bound, .36	$36.00
2 Bound books, Linnets Trial, $1.50	$3.00
2 Bound books, Tanner Boy, $1.25	$2.50
1 Bound book, Woman's Philosophy, $1.50	$1.50
4 Bound books, Marchia, $1.50	$6.00
4 Bound books, Cudjo's Cave, $1.75	$7.00
4 Bound books, Pique, $1.75	$7.00
2 Bound books, Gen. B. Butler, $2	$4.00
4 Bound books, Robinson Crusoe, $1.50	$6.00
7 Doz. Morocco wallets, $12.00	$84.00
5 and a half doz. Morocco wallets, $10	$55.00
3 Doz. Morocco wallets, at $5	$15.00

10 doz. Morocco wallets, at $5.50	$55.00
1 Doz. Morocco wallets, at $7.50	$7.50
1 Doz. Morocco wallets, at $8.50	$8.50
1 Doz. Morocco wallets, at $16.50	$16.50
1 doz. Morocco wallets, at $13.50	$13.50
6000 American Tales, Novels, at .08	$480.00
220 Harpers Monthly, 22 cts.	$48.40
55000 heavy buff envelopes, $3.60	$198.00
33000 heavy buff envelopes, $7.50	$247.50
20000 heavy buff envelopes, $6.75	$135.00
179 Quires Blnk. Books, 90 cts.	$161.10
195 Quires Full Bnd., 42 cts.	$81.90
420 Quires half Bnd., 28 cts.	$117.60
60 Quires Long days, 20 cts.	$12.00
4 Reams Medium Ledger, $16.50	$66.00
1 gross of Pass Books, $4.50	$4.50
18 Quires Long days Blk. 18 cts.	$3.25
20 Quires Record, 26 cts.	$5.20
163 Quires Journal, 29 cts.	$47.27
8 Quires Long Days, 20 cts.	$1.60
70 Quires Ledger, 29 cts.	$20.30
2 Doz. R. R. files, $1.25	$2.50
63 Quires Journal full bound, .42	$26.46
96 Quires Ledger, full bound, .42	$40.32
28 Quires Record, full bound, .42 (1176)	$11.70
35 Quires Journal, .90	$31.50
30 Quires, half bound, .28	$8.40
10 and a half reams Legal Cap, $3.25	$55.13
8 Reams Parson's wave flat, $3.90	$31.20
6 Reams E & S. $11	$66.00
87 Quires full bound blk. books, .42	$36.54
40 Reams letter ruled, $3.99	$159.60
15 Reams letter ruled, $3.50	$52.50
13 and a half Reams letter ruled, $3.85	$51.97
1 Chandelier and Globe,	$30.00
1 lamp, $3, 1 doz. R. Chimneys	$14.38
1 half doz. chimneys and wicks	$1.80
2 doz. wicks	$.90
4 Reams E & S. Medium Cap	$52.00
6 Reams Roulston note paper	$11.25
Cases, drayage, and freight to St. Joseph Mo.	$84.05
	$3433.64

Michael Tulley was another Plum Creek victim. He rode one wagon, pulled by just two mules. He left a wife, Elizabeth, who filed a claim to recover her husband's losses, which included the two mules. She noted that her husband was to be paid eight cents per pound for the 2,405 pounds of freight that he was carrying on his wagon, for a total of $192.40. Elizabeth identified Cheyenne chief Bull Bear as the principal leader of the raid. G. C. Barton, of Woolworth and Barton, oversaw the loading of Tulley's wagon in St. Joseph, and verified that it contained goods to be delivered to Denver. Tulley's body was recognized "among the parties who were killed, by a Pike's Peak gold ring which he wore." He had made several trips to Denver prior to being murdered. In 1884, U.S. Indian agent V. T. McGillycuddy interviewed the Indians at his Pine Ridge agency and they named the principal chiefs involved in the massacre as a "Sioux chief called 'Two Face' and a Cheyenne chief called 'Bull Bear'."

Yet another Denver merchant filed a claim for his losses at Plum Creek, and for losses the day before on the Little Blue, where he had separate wagon trains carrying merchandise. John A. Nye had contracted to haul to Denver a long list of goods consisting of mostly tools valued at $3,727.39. His depredation claim has a long account given by Lieutenant Charles Porter, the soldier who earlier gave information published in the *Omaha Nebraskan*. Stationed at Fort Kearny, he was First Lieutenant of Company A, First Nebraska Cavalry. He reported the wagon train at Plum Creek consisted of 12 wagons and that the Indians doing the attack numbered 150. Interestingly, he identified the three principal Indians who did the deadly August 7–8 Nebraska raids as Spotted Tail of the Sioux, White Antelope "and a half-breed named Bent."[24] His first-hand account is worth noting:

---

24 John A. Nye Indian Depredation Claim #4635. Record Group 123. White Antelope was killed at Sand Creek, November 29. As I was researching and writing this chapter, I received a phone call from Melvin Melrose, a descendant of Hugh Melrose, an early Colorado pioneer, who in 1866, married the sister of my great-great grandfather, William A. Watson, who homesteaded the section of land that became Wetmore, Colorado (see *Portrait and Biographical Record of the State of Colorado*, Chapman Publishing Company, Chicago, 1899, 770–772). What is highly coincidental about this is that Hugh Melrose served in the 3rd Volunteer Colorado Cavalry, and was credited with killing White Antelope at Sand Creek. See Greg Michno, *Battle at Sand Creek: The Military Perspective*; Upton and Sons, Publishers, 2004, 215. See also "A. J. Templeton Manuscript," Archives Location 4C. A41.189, Colorado Springs Pioneers Museum, Colorado Springs, Colorado. Lieutenant Andrew Templeton was Melrose's commanding officer, and this is what he said: "White Antelope led the fight [at Sand Creek] until he was killed. White Antelope was one of three principal chiefs. He was killed by Hugh Melrose, one of our company [Co. G, 3rd Cavalry]." Thus my great-great-uncle— unknown to me as I (*continued*)

In the months of July and August A.D. 1864, I was in the Military Service of the United States, and was First Lieutenant of Co. "A" 1st Battalion Nebraska [Cavalry and] stationed at Fort Kearney, Nebraska Territory. I was well acquainted with all that section of country from the "Little Blue River" in Kansas, along the routes of travel, from west via Republican and Platte Rivers—to Denver Colorado and Fort Laramie Nebraska [*sic*], having been on scouting duty a great deal during a previous term of service in said section, during the latter part of July and early part of August 1864. I was in a command of a detachment of Cavly., sent from Fort Kearney to make search for some mules stolen by Indians from the train of Jas. K. Wall of Omaha, Neb., while in camp ten miles east of Plum Creek Neb. We followed the trail of the mules through the Plum Creek Country, found the dead body of McGarret (a teamster who had gone out in search of the mules) very badly mutilated by the Indians—and thence the trail led us into the "Brule" Sioux Indian Camp on the Platte River ten miles east of Cottonwood. The Indians with [their] stolen mules had passed through a few hours previously, crossed the Platte River and gone north; with my small force it was useless to follow them any further. The Indians in camp were about three hundred warriors and exhibited many signs of hostility. "Little Thunder" the chief was very insulting and demonstrative in his talk and actions the few hours we [remained] to rest our horses. I got back to Fort Kearney on the second or third of August. on the morning of August 8th, 1864, about seven o'clock I was in the telegraph office at Fort Kearney, while the dispatches came from Plum Creek thirty miles west giving an account of an attack that was then taking place in sight of the station by about (150) one hundred and fifty Indians, upon a train of twelve wagons; they murdered the men, took the women away with them, took all the mules and horses, what goods they wanted, and destroyed the wagons and contents as far as they could. This Indian raid on the (8th) eight of August 1864 was a general attack on trains—mail coaches—and "Ranches" that were not heavily guarded—all along the line of overland travel from the Kansas line to one hundred miles east of Denver, Colorado. The Arapahoes, Cheyennes, Brule, & Ogallah Sioux with smaller bands from the Kiowas and other tribes in large numbers combined—then divided into parties one hundred to two hundred strong—and made the attack a number of places about the same hour on the same day and were

was researching and writing on these incidents, likely killed one of the principal perpetrators involved in planning and carrying out the deadly August Nebraska raids, who was also one of Black Kettle's principal chiefs. This implication of White Antelope's participation in the Nebraska murderous raids is further evidence that Black Kettle was not the 1864 peace chief people today believe him to be. Still, this claim is highly controversial and illustrates again the difficulty in naming guilty leaders. As early as January 10, 1865, the conclusion of the governmental investigation into the atrocities committed at Sand Creek claimed Northern Cheyenne Dog Soldiers were responsible for the Nebraska raids, "but all the testimony goes to prove that they had no connection with Black Kettle's band, but acted in despite of his authority and influence." See "Massacre of the Cheyenne Indians," II [follows page 120].

successful in capturing and destroying trains and "Ranches" at nearly every point where they attempted it. A few hours after the news from Plum Creek came Col. S. W. Summers—of the 7th Iowa Cavly Vols.—with a detachment of troops [left] for Plum Creek about noon August [8]. A courier arrived from the valley [?] about ten miles east from Fort Kearney—stating that Indians had attacked the stage coach, below them and that they had <u>captured</u> and <u>destroyed</u> a <u>train</u> of fourteen wagons near Thirty Two Mile Creek or "Dead Man's Hollow" and that night we had the information that the Indians were on the war path, all the way east to the Kansas line. On the morning of the 9th of August a detachment of troops under command of Capt. Murphy, 7th Iowa Cavly, and Lieut. M. B. Cutler of Neb. Vet. Cavly—started down the road eastward, to render all the assistance possible to the settlers and mail stations. On the [11th] Eleventh of August I followed with my command and saw the destruction as far east as Kiowa Station near "Dead Man's Hollow" or Thirty Two Mile Creek Station. There had evidently been a desperate struggle—the prairie on each side of the road for several hundred yards was covered [with] all kinds of merchandise and broken wagons—they had run some of the wagons together and burnt them and their contents. Others had been fired separately and were only partially burnt. Among the merchandise destroyed and scattered at this point was hardware and some mowers or harvesters mark[ed] Jno. A. Nye, Denver Colorado—these machines were broken up so as to be entirely useless. Some of this stock had been burnt or carried away. I saw several tags and parts of boxes mark[ed] Jno. A. Nye, Denver, Colorado—shipped by Woolworth and Barton, St. Joseph Mo. at the ravine where some wagons had been run over the bank and burnt—most of the articles so scattered about were rendered totally unfit for use. I don't think any of the property at this point of any value was ever recovered . . . the Indians that committed these depredations east of Fort Kearney were of the Arapahoe & Cheyenne tribes and with them bands of Sioux from the Ogallahs and that "White Antelope," Spotted Tail and a half breed named Bent were the principals in command.[25]

The number of persons killed in the Plum Creek massacre is believed to be 13.[26] The known victims are William Marble, Mr. St. Clair, Charles Iliff, James Smith, Thomas Morton, William Fletcher, John Fletcher, Thomas Harmon, Michael Tulley and Peter Dolan. Three remain unidentified.

There were other victims in the area. About 75 miles west of Fort Kearny, John Gilman operated a ranch with his brother, J. G. Gilman. The ranch was about 15 miles east of Camp Cottonwood (soon to become Fort McPherson).

---

25   John A. Nye Indian Depredation Claim #4635. Record Group 123. Words underlined in testimony.
26   Michno, *Encyclopedia of Indian Wars*, 149.

On the day of the Plum Creek massacre, raiders also struck near the Gilman ranch. The Gilmans had taken in two families and another man who had entered partnership with them to operate a new ranch five miles east of the Gilman ranch. The new ranch would provide hay for feed to the freight stock along the road. One family consisted of a young man named John Andrews and his wife. They were living out of a wagon while the new ranch was being constructed. The other family consisted of Chauncey Gillett, his wife Dorothy and daughters Mary (24), Louise (23), Clara (21), Ida May (8) and one son, 17-year-old Jefferson. They had recently come from Boulder to enter this new venture. Herman Angell was also in partnership with the other men. The way the partnership broke down was like this: Andrews supplied a team and wagon, harnesses and cooking utensils, Angell provided a haying machine and labor.[27] Andrews and Jefferson Gillett were just finishing up the final touches on the newly constructed log house and had begun to move furnishings from the Gilman home to their new home when tragedy struck. On August 8, they left to work at the new ranch but did not return. Chauncey was worried for his son and early the next morning he borrowed a horse from John Gilman, and armed with a revolver he ventured out to look for his missing boy.

He soon found his son and Andrews, both dead amid the ruins of the new home. He crossed the arms of his dead and scalped boy and was returning to the Gilman ranch to report what he found, when numerous warriors overtook him about a mile from the ranch, well within sight of the ranch. Those inside the ranch saw him fall from his horse, while several Indians surrounded him. When his body was recovered, he had five arrows in his back, and had also been shot with his own pistol.[28] Jeremiah Gilman remembered seeing the elder Gillett fall: "I saw him coming back toward me on horseback, running, with 18 Indians chasing him, all mounted; they fired at him repeatedly and shot him and scalped him within 150 yards of me."[29] After Chauncey was killed the Gilman brothers, along with Angell, prepared to defend themselves at the Gilman ranch, but the Indians ran past them and instead took the stock, which had just been put out to graze. The Indians were not interested in attacking the people inside the ranch

27   Herman Angell Indian Depredation Claim #8351. Record Group 123.
28   Chauncey Gillett Indian Depredation Claim #2350. Record Group 123.
29   Herman Angell Indian Depredation Claim #8351.

after they stampeded nearly 100 cattle and several horses and mules. The Gilman brothers and Angell later ventured out to the newly built Gillett ranch and secured the bodies of young Jefferson and Andrews, and also brought back Chauncey's body. They then rode a wagon with the families and three dead bodies to Camp Cottonwood for protection.[30]

There is an interesting story connected with the release of captives Lucinda Eubanks, taken on the Little Blue August 7, and Nancy Morton, taken near Plum Creek August 8. Although captured on separate days more than 100 miles apart, they were soon in the same village. They apparently remained together as long as six weeks[31] and were then separated, both later rescued far north of their capture. Both were released in present-day Wyoming, Morton near present-day Casper and Eubanks near Fort Laramie. Mrs. Morton was freed in late January 1865, and Lucinda Eubanks about three months later.[32] They both spent time at the post—not together—and both were the reason for the subsequent hanging of three chiefs at Fort Laramie.

Not long after Morton's rescue and during her journey to Fort Laramie, she saw one of the Indians responsible for her August 8 capture. He was visiting Deer Creek Station, on the road between Fort Casper and Fort Laramie, when she passed through. Recognizing who he was, she reported this to Lieutenant Triggs, who had the warrior arrested. He was a Cheyenne named Big Crow, who was brought to the brig at Fort Laramie on February 9.[33] Later that month, some soldiers returned to the fort from an expedition. Learning of Big Crow's arrest and ill treatment of Mrs. Morton, they took matters into their own hands and escorted the chief outside the post where

---

30   Chauncey Gillett Indian Depredation Claim #2350.

31   Larimer, *The Capture and Escape*, 134;

32   Larimer said Mrs. Eubanks was rescued in April. Other accounts have her rescued close to May 18. See Larimer, *Capture and Escape*, 133. John McDermott suggests May 15. See *Circle of Fire: The Indian War of 1865* (Mechanicsburg, PA: Stackpole Books, 2003), 60. Ron Becher indicates May 18. See Becher, *Massacre along the Medicine Road*, 371.

33   Larimer, *Capture and Escape*, 133. She identifies the Indian as Black Crow; McDermott, *Circle of Fire*, 57, probably correctly names the Indian as Big Crow. Doug McChristian, citing Bent's letters, said the Big Crow hanged was a Northern Cheyenne, and not the Southern Cheyenne Big Crow, who was one of the principal leaders in the attack on Julesburg in January 1865. See Douglas McChristian, *Fort Laramie*, 196; Hyde, *Life of George Bent*, 171. This, however, is probably not true for the simple fact that the principal warriors responsible for the Plum Creek massacre, where Nancy Morton was captured, were Southern Cheyenne, as admitted by White Antelope at the Camp Weld Conference. See "Report of the Secretary of War," in Carroll, *The Sand Creek Massacre*, 406.

they prepared him to be hanged. They would have succeeded, except that Colonel William O. Collins intervened. He told the soldiers the Indian would be hanged after a trial. Big Crow remained in arrest until April 24, when he was hanged according to orders.[34]

If Nancy Morton felt any sense of relief in the hanging of Big Crow, then perhaps Lucinda Eubanks had a similar sense of justice when she arrived at Fort Laramie shortly after her rescue. After she and her little boy were rescued, she said it was Cheyenne who abducted her and that she had been sexually abused. After a time, she was traded to the Oglala Two Face, who "terribly" beat her. He then traded her to Oglala Black Foot, who also sexually abused and beat her. She was then traded back to Two Face, and finally Two Face brought her into Fort Laramie.[35] But once the commanding officer heard of the abuse Lucinda had endured with Two Face and Black Foot, he ordered both men arrested. They were brought to trial and found guilty of their mistreatment of Lucinda. They were ordered hanged on gallows next to where the rotting body of Nancy Morton's tormentor—Big Crow—remained suspended from his hanging a month earlier. The double hanging was done on May 26.[36] Ohio cavalryman Hervey Johnson was there for the hanging. In a letter written on June 4, he said this about the two warriors:

> They wanted half a bushel of silver and were equally as extravagant in their demands for provisions. The ire of the "powers that be" at the fort were aroused, (Col. Collins aint in command now) and "Mr. ingen" was swung up, and it didn't cost a cent to get the woman and child. It is "bad medicine" for an Indian to be hung. They think he never goes to the "happy hunting ground."[37]

George Bent later condemned the hangings and said the Oglala chiefs had actually been responsible for Lucinda's rescue, and claimed "these two Sioux were not the captors but the ransomers of the woman and her child."

34   Czaplewski, *Captive of the Cheyenne*, 41–42, says the hanging was April 23, or perhaps April 27; McDermott, *Circle of Fire*, 57, indicates the chief was hanged two days after General Patrick Connor sent a telegram on April 22, ordering the warrior to be hanged and his body left suspended on the gallows. A soldier writing to his sister, on April 27, said the hanging occured April 23. See William E. Unrau, edited, *Tending The Talking Wire: A Buck Soldier's View of Indian Country 1863–1866* (Salt Lake City, UT: University of Utah Press,1979), 243.

35   Appendix, "The Chivington Massacre," Carroll, *The Sand Creek Massacre*, Appendix, 90–91.

36   McChristian, *Fort Laramie*, 203–206.

37   Unrau, *Tending The Talking Wire*, 251–252.

He said the officers responsible for their hanging were drunk at the time of the trial and soon removed from command "on general incompetence and drunkenness."[38] Obviously Bent did not have Lucinda's sworn testimony which contradicted his claims. She clearly identified the two Lakota chiefs participating in the raids when she was captured, and claimed they were the principal abusers of her during her captivity.

---

38   Hyde, *Life of George Bent*, 208.

Skeletons of 10 freighters killed July 18, 1864,
east of where Fort Zarah was later erected.
(See p. 61.) The eight white freighters were buried together, and the two
Negro freighters buried nearby. Two freighters were scalped but survived.
Several other freighters were also wounded. The remains were discovered
after a 1973 April flood on Walnut Creek. See http://www.kshs.org/
kanapedia/massacre-at-walnut-creek/12139 (accessed October 23, 2013).
Courtesy Archives Division, Kansas State Historical Society, Topeka, Kansas.

CHAPTER FIVE

More War

*My brother and I unhitched the cattle from the wagon, and both got on the
old mare, and started for home, which was about a mile distant. Before
we could get there, the Indians attacked us, shooting us several times, and
finally pinned us together with an arrow, when we fell off the horse. In
the fall, the arrow pulled through my body, and remained sticking in my
brother's back.*

GEORGE MARTIN INDIAN DEPREDATION CLAIM #4393

T HE NEWS OF ALL OF THESE AUGUST MURDERS IN NEBRASKA
quickly reached Denver, and by August 11, with the Indians still
conducting their Nebraska raids, Governor Evans issued a proclamation authorizing all Colorado citizens to engage in war against all factious Indians. That same day, he received permission from Washington, DC,
to recruit a regiment of Colorado volunteers to fight them.[1] This regiment
would soon make their mark in Colorado history with their November 29
dawn attack upon Cheyenne Black Kettle's sleeping village, along the banks
of Sand Creek—the Big Sandy—in southeastern Colorado Territory, not
far from present-day Eads.

On August 12, Charles Autobees, a farmer since 1853 living at the mouth
of the Huerfano and Arkansas River about fifteen miles east of Pueblo,
Colorado, had an unwelcome visit by a large party of Arapaho and Cheyenne Indians, led by the son of Arapaho Little Raven.[2] They stole 19 horses,
one of which was later found in the village of Black Kettle after the fight at

---

1   Gregory F. Michno, *Battle at Sand Creek: The Military Perspective* (El Segundo, CA: Upton and Sons,
     Publishers, 2004), 134–135.
2   Carroll, *The Sand Creek Massacre*, Appendix, 216.

Sand Creek, yet more direct evidence of Indians under Black Kettle were involved in the ongoing war.[3] The next day, about 45 miles farther east along the Arkansas River from the Autobees' theft, a war party came upon the Upper Arkansas Agency under construction by engineer H. M. Fosdick. Housed at the agency were about 50–75 persons, including some women and 20 soldiers from nearby Fort Lyon serving for protection. Nearly 30 horses were stolen, and the cavalry did not have a single horse to pursue the Indians. The raid was violent; the Indians killed two men employed by Fosdick, along with other men, the total number dead unknown.[4]

Two days after the Arapaho theft of Autobees' stock, the same warriors murdered three men on the Santa Fe road on the north side of the Arkansas River, about eight miles east of Booneville and very close to Autobees' ranch. In addition, the Indians took captive the wife of John Snyder, a soldier who was a blacksmith at Fort Lyon. Snyder arranged for his wife, Anna, to come to Denver, where he had procured a small ambulance from the quartermaster at Fort Lyon, as well as four mules, a driver, himself and another blacksmith named William Smith, to escort Mrs. Snyder down to Fort Lyon. Their trip to and from Denver to Pueblo was without incident, but when they stopped at Booneville, five miles west of Charles Autobees' ranch, a lady there remarked to Mrs. Snyder that her long hair would be a treat for the Indians to get. Mrs. Snyder replied "Oh, don't say that, for I have heard such terrible stories of how they abuse their prisoners." Having just come from Denver, no doubt by way of stage past the Little Blue—that was the only way into Denver at that time, unless one went via Fort Lyon from the south—it is possible she may have ridden one of the first stages west to Denver that witnessed the deadly raids on the Little Blue earlier in August. If so, then the stories of the murders on the Little Blue and Plum Creek would have been fresh in her frightened mind. When the wagon and party of four departed Booneville east for the day-long ride to Fort Lyon, they were never seen alive again. Arapaho Little Raven's son—some say brother—again led the war party, which included some Cheyenne. A stage coming from the east came upon the carnage, left after the Indians did their damage. So did a man named Captain Bullock. Mrs. Snyder was nowhere to be found, but several items of clothing belonging to her were scattered

---

3   Charles Autobees Indian Depredation Claim #825. Record Group 123.
4   H. M. Fosdick Indian Depredation Claim #1290. Record Group 123.

about the scene, leaving the sad witnesses to infer a woman had been taken captive. John Snyder was horribly mutilated, scalped, his testicles cut off and put inside his mouth, one leg completely cut off and the rest of his mangled body attached to a wagon wheel, leaving his grisly remains hanging off the plundered wagon. The other two men were so horribly mutilated they could not be identified.[5]

What happened to Mrs. Snyder was later reported by other captives who were eventually rescued. She was brought to the village where Black Kettle was, the Arapaho erecting their lodges next to the Cheyenne. At some point she was able to escape, only to be tracked down and brought back into the Arapaho village. That night she is said to have hanged herself, high on a lodge pole inside a tepee. The *Rocky Mountain News* reported on September 29—while covering the Camp Weld Conference Governor Evans held with Black Kettle and other chiefs—that Mrs. Snyder committed suicide. Whether her hanging was a suicide or a murder remains speculative, though the likelihood is she was hanged by an Indian. Julia Lambert reported in 1916 that Laura Roper said Mrs. Snyder hanged herself. Laura was troubled in understanding Snyder's hanging, noting

> How she accomplished this no one knew as the poles are high in the center. The lodges are round like a Sibley tent, the poles crossing in the center in a manner that braces them one against another. There they found the poor creature's body hanging lifeless. They took me in to see her. I never knew what disposition was made of the corpse.[6]

Laura Roper's account, however, contradicts that which Mrs. Morton told Lieutenant Jeremiah Triggs, when she was rescued in Wyoming Territory. She was in the camp where Laura and the other captives were, and said the Arapaho village consisted of 60 lodges. While with the other captives, Mrs. Morton said the Arapaho "had two white women, both of whom they hung."[7] Perhaps Mrs. Snyder was hanged as punishment for escaping. If she

---

5 The following sources were used to reconstruct this story: Julia S. Lambert, "Plain Tales of the Plains," *The Trail* (Volume VIII, No. 12, May 1916), 8; Carroll, *The Sand Creek Massacre*, Appendix, 57, 216; *Rocky Mountain News*, August 24, 1864. My great-great-grandfather, William A. Watson, in 1864 was living near Booneville, and upon learning of the murders, moved west of Pueblo, near present-day Florence, believing it was safer to be where the Ute Indians were still hunting. See *Portrait and Biographical Record*, 770–772.

6 Lambert, "Plain Tales of the Plains," 7.

7 Czaplewski, *Captive of the Cheyenne*, 30.

was killed by her captors there would be no problem in explaining how she could hang herself so high up lodge poles. She didn't. The Arapaho hung her.[8]

On the same day Mrs. Snyder was captured, other Indians further east continued their violent forays. Near present-day Lakin, Kansas, about 75 miles west of Fort Dodge and close to the Colorado border, the freighting train of Charles Wiley was attacked. Wiley had left from Fort Union after delivering goods there and was returning to Fort Leavenworth. The empty train consisted of 20 wagons comprising 190 oxen and three horses. The day before the attack about 60–90 Indians came to their camp, mingled with the men and received provisions. They made no signs of being threatening. But in fact they were scouting the men to see if they were armed and how many men there were. The wagon party consisted of 27 men. The next day the wagon train again went into camp, and about dusk three men went off to gather buffalo chips for the dinner fire, while three more men took the stock away from the camp to graze where there was abundant grass. It was nearly a half mile away.

Wiley had made two freighting trips to Fort Union in 1862, two more in 1863, and was returning on his first trip in 1864. Every year during the excursions, Indians would visit with the freighters all along the way. There had been no violence, and as Wiley noted, nearly all Indians on the plains at that time could speak Spanish. English speaking wagon bosses always had Mexicans accompanying the train as freighters in order to communicate with the Indians and other Spanish speaking people who were met along the way. About half of Wiley's freighters were Mexican. When the Indians visited the camp the day before, they had three Mexican captives with them, a woman and two children. The captives told the Mexican freighters that the Indians were Kiowa and Cheyenne, and identified Satank and Satanta as the leaders. An Indian by the name of Old Torchee was their head chief.[9]

Wiley gave a good description of how a wagon train would camp, and what happened in the attack on August 14:

8 A later account, covered in the *Weekly Rocky Mountain News*, November 15, 1865—more than a year after the incident—said Mrs. Anna Snyder was killed alongside her husband. It was a sworn, notarized statement by N. D. Snyder, perhaps the brother of John. Regarding John Snyder, the account said he was stripped of his clothing and scalped. The Indians mutilated him, "cutting off his testicles and putting them in his mouth, cutting off one of his legs, then tying him to the upper part of the ambulance by his other leg, leaving his head hanging down. The Indians then stripped Mrs. Snyder, tied her upon her back to stakes driven in the ground, and a number of them ravished her, and then killed her; then cut her throat, cut out her heart, and mutilated her body in an awful manner. Wm Smith was scalped, stript of all his clothing, his body cut to pieces and arrows shot through them."

9 Charles Wiley Indian Depredation Claim #1105. Record Group 123.

In trains we have what we call a right and left wing to a train. The lead team of one wing will lead the train one day, and the other wing of the train will lead the other day; it is easier on the cattle. In corralling or getting into a camp your lead team, or half of your train, would go in a circle and haul up a little, the right on the right hand. The next wagon following the cattle go right outside the preceding wagon, and run the forward wheel of their wagon against the hind wheel of the preceding wagon, forming a half circle. You continue that until that half of your train has formed a line, circular. When half of your train is pulled in, the other half, which you call the left wing, comes and runs parallel with the first wagon, leaving a gap in your train, say 20 or 25 feet wide, then the next wagon runs right in the same way until you are formed into a half circle corral.[10]

After the wagons had formed their corral the oxen were taken to graze. The mess wagon was about 250 yards from the corralled wagons. Three night herders, two mounted and all three armed, were with the stock. One was Mexican and two were white. Three Mexicans took gunny sacks and went to look for buffalo dung fuel for their evening fires. While this was going on 15 or 20 Indians charged the mess wagon. The men there were all able to flee safely into the corralled wagons. While these Indians were plundering the mess wagon another 275–300 Indians charged past them and attacked the night herders and fuel gatherers:

> As they neared the camp, within 200 yards, probably or possibly a little more, they were shooting and screaming, and came up and circled off to the left, cutting off our herd from our assistance, and charged right on the herd, stampeding the cattle and every hoof of stock. They massacred the 6 men, scalping them; they took the one pony, both saddles, their guns and pistols, and left the men there dead. This whole thing occurred probably within ten minutes' time, and within ten minutes from the time of the attack the cattle and Indians were stampeding over the bluff. We saw them no more.... We watched the entire night with our guns in our hands, expecting any moment to be re-attacked, but we saw no more of the Indians, and at the break of day, as soon as it was light enough to see, we could see at the camp a few head of cattle, and we could see that our men were lying there; we all went from the camp; we found the men dead; we found one horse there with a broken leg and six or seven cattle wounded and dead, one pony gone, both of the saddles, the night herders' guns and pistols. The regular night herders were armed with a carbine and a Colts revolver, and the three Mexicans who went with them to pick up buffalo chips all had pistols.[11]

10   Charles Wiley Indian Depredation Claim #1105.
11   Charles Wiley Indian Depredation Claim #1105.

Having safely journeyed across several times from 1862 to 1864, having fed and mingled with the Indians numerous times, and indeed again just the night before, this violent attack upon Wiley's wagon train was both unexpected and most terrifying. And that is how the Indian war showed itself on the plains this violent summer of 1864. Nearly every attack was unexpected. It was not going to end.

On August 16, six soldiers of Company H, 7th Iowa Cavalry, left Salina for Fort Ellsworth which would soon become Fort Harker. Late in the afternoon a war party of at least 100 and possibly 300 Indians attacked them, killing four. Two soldiers got away and reported the fight.[12] On August 18, north in Nebraska Territory several soldiers caught 500 Indians on Elk Creek north of the Republican River (a few miles north of present-day Arapahoe, Nebraska) and had a stiff fight. Ten Indians were killed, as well as two soldiers. The Indians were chased 10 miles but when the troops withdrew, the Indians reversed their direction and then pursued the soldiers 30 miles.[13] That same day, Indians entered the premises of Lewis Baker's house, where he lived with his family along the Platte River, about three miles from O'Fallon's Bluffs. His family "suffered every indignity they [the Indians] could heap upon them." Fortunately he and his family were not killed.[14]

After the murderous raids along the Little Blue and Plum Creek in early August, most of the ranch owners fled their buildings. Many later returned to find everything burned and destroyed. Lewis Baker's experience was typical. After suffering his attack he went with other neighbors to the nearby ranch of Jack Morrow, and from there left for Nebraska City. When he returned the next spring everything was burned up, his barn, his dwelling house, his store house, his pilgrim house, his blacksmith shop and his corrals. When he had left in the middle of August he did not have any wagons to remove his household goods, as his wagons were used by a neighbor at that time to procure merchandise from Nebraska City. Thus he had simply nailed his house shut to keep people out, but when the Indians burned everything down he also lost all of his household goods. He had to rebuild from scratch.[15]

---

12   *War of the Rebellion*, Series 1, Vol. XLI, Part 1, 264.

13   "Massacre of the Cheyenne Indians," *The Sand Creek Massacre: A Documentary History*, 64.

14   Lewis Baker Indian Depredation Claim #2492. Record Group 123.

15   Lewis Baker Indian Depredation Claim #615.

Not everyone abandoned their ranches after the August 7–8 deadly raids. Some would later pay for staying. George Martin's family endured the violence of the Indian war, and yet remarkably, all would survive. George had taken up a homestead about 30 miles east of Fort Kearny along the Overland trail. Somehow he and his family were apparently oblivious to all the violence perpetrated in early August, and were unaware that their lives were in danger. On August 19, a small party of six to eight warriors attacked George as he was hauling hay in a wagon to his ranch. He was hit three times with arrows, one of the horses carrying his hay was shot and killed, but he was close enough to his house that his wife and two young daughters came to his rescue, running to him and firing two guns at the Indians. This caused the Indians to pause and retreat from the house, allowing the wounded husband and father to make it safely inside. George recognized one of the Indians as a Cheyenne known as Indian Charley [half-blood Charles Bent]. George's seven-year-old son William recalled this moment:

> The day he was attacked by the Indians . . . I was herding cattle. As I was driving the cattle up in the evening, my mother ran out and cried to me that the Indians were after my father, and told me to run to the house. I left the cattle and ran to the house, and tied my pony to the door. My father was harvesting hay when he was attacked, and he ran to the house, the Indians following him tolerably close to the house, where they got my pony, saddle and bridle. When the Indians started to go to where my brothers were, about a half mile from the house, we all left the house and started for a place of safety, taking with us 2 stallions and leaving 2 colts, and 4 stage horses, in the stable. When we had gone about 400 yards, one of the stallions that had been shot, staggered, laid down, and died. We went on, and came back to the house the next day and found that the Indians had stolen the 2 colts, but not the stage horses; they probably did not see them; they had also taken the mare which my brothers were riding. The most of the things were taken, and that which they did not take, they destroyed.[16]

When the Indians retreated from the daughters' gunfire, the warriors spotted George's other young sons, 14-year-old Henry and 12-year-old Robert, riding together on a horse in a frantic attempt to get home before the Indians could overtake them. It was a futile race. The Indians caught them, shooting at them several times with arrows until one arrow pinned both brothers together, which caused them to violently fall from the horse.

16   George Martin Indian Depredation Claim #4393. Record Group 123.

While the Indians were attacking the boys, as young William recalled above, the family fled in the opposite direction with their injured father and made their escape. They were sure the two older boys had been killed. However, that is not what happened. The severely wounded boys fooled the Indians into thinking they were dead. Henry gave an account of life at their ranch and included moving testimony about what happened:

My father was a native of England, and came to this country about 1850. . . . In 1862, my father located on the same piece of land which he subsequently took up as his homestead; situated in the Platte valley, on the emigrant road, from Nebraska City to Fort Kearney, about 30 miles from the latter place, in what is now Hall County, Neb. At this time he had about 32 head of cattle, 2 mares, 2 stallions, and 1 gelding. He built a sod house, dirt roof and dirt floor, two rooms in the house. He also built a sod barn with dirt floors and roof. About a year later his place was made a Stage station, and remained such until the Union Pacific Railroad was built. It was an eating station, and a stock tender was stationed there to take care of the stock. In the latter part of August, 1864, as near as I can recollect, my father, my younger brother, and I, were engaged in making hay. On that day, the stock tender (whose first name was Charley, and whose last name I have forgotten), had gone down the road to Bateman's ranch, 4 or 5 miles, taking a horse that had come into the ranch that morning, and which had the Government brand on it. We afterwards learned that it belonged to a party of soldiers, who had had a fight with the Indians a day or two before about 17 miles south, on the West Blue.

There was no one at the ranch that day, except my father's family. There had been no Indian depredations in that part of the country, up to that time, of which we had heard, and we did not know of the fight on the Blues until afterwards. We were cutting hay wherever we could find it, along the Platte, but could only get it in small patches, and had to haul it in to the house as soon as we had got enough for a stack, to keep the freighters from using it. It was early in the hay season, and we had got enough for one stack hauled, and about half of it hauled, having a big stack started, and about 10 tons in it, and were hauling in more. My father was driving the team, with the 2 stallions, and was about half a mile ahead of me and my brother. About a week before this, one of the mares had been bitten by a snake and died, leaving us with only the 3 horses, my father having sold the gelding before, so that we had to hitch up a pair of raw steers, and hitch the other mare in front as a leader, and that was the team my brother Robert and I had. As we were going home with our loads of hay, I saw a party of 8 or 10 Indians attack my father, and shoot at him with bows and arrows, and finally he ran his team into the house. My brother and I unhitched the cattle from the wagon, and both got on the old mare, and started for home, which was about a mile distant. Before we could get there, the Indians attacked us, shooting us several times, and finally pinned us together with an arrow, when we fell off the horse. In the fall, the arrow pulled through my body, and remained sticking in my brother's back. When the Indians came up to us, we pretended to be dead; they took the lines tied to the mare, and which had been tangled up with us, and untwisted them from us, cut the harness off the mare except the bridle, struck my brother on the head several times, to be sure he was dead, and then left us. I saw them go to the house, load their ponies, and ride off south. Brother and I went on to the house, and got there a little before dark, to find it all torn up and deserted.

The corn, fed, flour, meal, and everything, was strewed together; there was about 300 bushels of corn, 20 bushels of oats, and about 700 lbs. of flour; they took off about 500 lbs. of the flour, and mixed the remainder up with the grain. The bedding was all gone, the feather beds torn open and the feathers scattered over the house, the trunks and boxes all broken open and their contents gone, except my box,—cracker box,—and the under part of mother's trunk; they did not know enough to raise the till of the trunk; the stove was mashed; that is all I can say about the house.

They had gone to the stable and taken the 2 sucking colts; there were 4 stage horses in the stable, and the doors were standing open, but they had not been taken; it was supposed they did not look in. They took off the mare that my brother and I were riding.

We stayed that night in the house, as I was too weak to go away. The next day my father and his family got back to the ranch with a train going east; they had started to go to Bateman's, when they saw us fall off the mare, and thought we had been killed. They had not gone far when they met the stock tender, Charley, coming back; but before that, one of the stallions lay down and refused to go any further; he had been shot right behind the fore leg; the Indians cut the stallion's throat, so my father told me afterwards. After meeting Charley, they went on westward, by Bateman's ranch, and overtook a train going west; they went with that train till they met the one going east, and then returned to see what had become of us. They found us in the stable, and we all started for Nebraska City; we went on down the road, but I was not able to travel far, so we took possession of a deserted house on the road, and remained there several weeks, during which time my father returned the horse with the Government brand, to the Commanding officer, at Fort Kearney.[17]

The Indians appear to have remained in the vicinity. On August 27, a wagon train headed by William Slusher and William Watson was taking freight (their second trip) from Omaha to Salt Lake City. They had camped for the night along Plum Creek about 30 miles west of Fort Kearny. A man named Beson was selected as night guard, and as the men were about to fall asleep several Indians attacked the train, killing Beson and desperately wounding three other men. They made off with several mules and horses.[18]

17 George Martin Indian Depredation Claim #4393.
18 William Watson Indian Depredation Claim #40. William Slusher Indian Depredation Claim #65. Record Group 123.

After the raid upon the Martin family and the killing of Beson, subsequent attacks upon the Nebraska settlements lessened. But that did not mean the war was halting. In Colorado, a band of Indians thought to be Cheyenne but possibly Arapaho—or both—made another raid southeast of Denver, several miles south of where the Hungate family had been killed on June 11. By August of that year, several settlers had banded together in one house called California Ranch, south of present-day Franktown near today's Castlewood Canyon. Accounts later emerged describing what happened. In one account three men had left the ranch to gather stock, and while returning were attacked by a party of about 12 Indians. Lorenz Welte and George Engel were able to escape. Thirty-year-old Conrad Moschel, father of two young children, was shot and fell from his horse at the beginning of the attack, which occurred in Castlewood Canyon. When he was later found by a search party he had an arrow in his side and had been hit with a shotgun. He was also scalped. Another account said the men were part of a military command and were caught away from where they were camped at California Ranch. Moschel had been shot with an arrow in his back and a bullet in his forehead.[19]

Back in Kansas, warriors were active on the Santa Fe road. On August 23, near Fort Dodge, Arapaho and Comanche Indians attacked a wagon train freighting supplies from Fort Leavenworth to Fort Union, New Mexico Territory. They succeeded in running off 134 oxen, one horse and a mule.[20] Prairie fires, believed to have been set by Cheyenne and Lakota, destroyed several houses in Washington County, just south of the Little Blue River in north-central Kansas.[21]

On September 25, General James G. Blunt, with about 500 men, caught about 1,500 warriors—Arapaho and other tribesmen—about 100 miles west

---

19 Josephine Lowell Marr, *Douglas County: A Historical Journey* (Gunnison, CO: B & B Printers, Gunnison, Inc., 1983), 37–38. Marr said there were four men attacked, the fourth man named Caspar Courts. She does not date the incident but said 30 Indians were involved. She also said Welte, spelled "Welty," was at the time of the attack a member of Company M, 3rd Colorado Cavalry. However, the Muster Rolls do not list him in either spelling. See Michno, *Battle at Sand Creek*, 302. Susan Consola Appleby says the killing happened August 4, which contradicts the marker erected where Moschel was killed, dating it August 21. See *Fading Past: The Story of Douglas County, Colorado* (Palmer Lake, CO: Filter Press, LLC, 2001), 57. The more reliable account is found in Bea W. Barton, *The Mormon Battalion Mississippi Saints and Pioneers Douglas County, Colorado: Honorable Remembrance to the Latest Generation* (Aardvark Global Publishing, 2008), 919–922.

20 Alexander Repine Indian Depredation Claim #87. Record Group 123.

21 J. Bowmaker, Sr. Indian Depredation Claim #6894. Record Group 123. See also Thomas Kinsley Indian Depredation Claim #6662.

of Fort Larned. A hot fight ensued, and when it was over 91 Indians were killed. Only two soldiers died, but seven were wounded.[22] On September 29, a wagon train returning to the east after freighting to Denver camped two miles west of Plum Creek Station in Nebraska Territory, when Indians attacked them, killing one man and wounding two others.[23]

At about this time, but further west on the trail, 28 wagons of Brigham Hamilton Young, delivering freight to Salt Lake City, came under attack. The freighters had been repeatedly harassed by Cheyenne Indians. Young was able to buy them off with coffee and sugar several times, until one wagon fell behind the train. Young sent five teamsters back to repair the wagon and bring it forward to the rest of the train. It wasn't to be. "There the Indians came up on them, massacred them, took all the dry goods, what few nicknacs there was they stuck their hatchets into, and cut the spokes out of the wagon, and left the men to bleach." Lost in the wagon were goods destined for Boughtenburg and Kahn, merchants in Salt Lake City. The plundered property included "broad cloths, silks, fine dress goods, and a variety [of] general merchandise."[24]

Back in Colorado, the 3rd Colorado Volunteer Cavalry Regiment was formed and sent out to give added protection along the trails leading to Denver. Their first "response" to what the Indians had done on the Little Blue and Plum Creek occurred near Valley Station in October. Captain David H. Nichols, commanding a company of the newly formed cavalry, was patrolling along the Denver road, when he learned of the appearance of Cheyenne warrior Old Wolf, dressed in his war paint, on the bluffs just south of Wisconsin Ranch. Old Wolf was shaking his fist at the people at the ranch and seemed to be taunting them. When Nichols was informed that Summit Springs was about 12 miles further south from that point—and was a preferred camping spot for Indians—he decided on an early morning surprise raid, anticipating that the springs would be where the Cheyenne warrior would be found. The command left Wisconsin Ranch on October 10 at about 2 A.M., with as many as 30 soldiers joined by an additional 10 soldiers at the ranch, as well as one of the Coad brothers, owners of the ranch, and two other guides, Grant Ashcraft and a man nicknamed Dunk.

---

22   Carroll, *The Sand Creek Massacre*, Appendix, 69.

23   *War of the Rebellion*, Vol. XLI, Part I, 829.

24   Brigham Hamilton Young Indian Depredation Claim #5344. Record Group 123.

The men arrived at the springs near daybreak. There they surprised two lodges containing six warriors, three or four women, one 15-year-old boy and two children.[25] In the ensuing fight, no quarter was given and all of the Indians were killed, including the children. Found inside one of the lodges was the scalp of a white woman along with her bloody shoes, and other evidences of attacks upon freighters.[26]

One of the soldiers there was Morse Coffin. He later penned his memories, admitting guilt over what happened to the women and children.

> Two of these squaws were rather young, and two middle aged ones had the babes in their arms. One of these was killed with her feet in a pool of water, and bent over her child as if to shield it, and as we came up it opened wide its eyes and looked up at us. I said "boys don't kill it, it is too bad," etc., but one of the guides (glad it was not a soldier) came up and coolly shot it, at the same time making a remark not indicative of pity. I strongly denounced this part of the work, using cusswords.[27]

In his report of the affair, Captain Nichols noted that in addition to the scalp and bloody shoes of a white lady, also recovered were "freight bills, from parties in St. Joseph to Denver merchants, and signed by one Peter Dolan, who no doubt went under."[28] Captain Nichols, of course, had no way of knowing that Peter Dolan was killed at the Plum Creek massacre of August 8. Nevertheless, the connection of Dolan's freight bill, recovered at Summit Springs in the possession of the dead Cheyenne Big Wolf, is further evidence that links the Cheyenne to the murders on the Platte River, and confirms their hostility throughout the region.

Meanwhile, back on the Platte, near Plum Creek Station in Nebraska Territory, Indians had returned. On October 12, 25 Indians attacked a westbound stage eight miles west of the station. The stage was able to drive to a nearby abandoned ranch where the passengers and stage hands fought for two hours before driving the Indians off. When it was over two Indians were dead, one stage guard was severely wounded with a shot to the head, and a passenger was wounded in the leg.[29] Two days later, 40 Cheyenne warriors led by White Antelope attacked a small detachment of soldiers, killing two,

25   David Berthong, in *The Southern Cheyennes*, fails to mention two children and says there were only three women. See p. 213.
26   *War of the Rebellion*, Vol. XLI, Part III, 798–799.
27   Morse Coffin, *The Battle of Sand Creek* (Waco, TX: W. M. Morison, Publisher, 1965), 7–8.
28   *War of the Rebellion*, Vol. XLI, Part III, 799.
29   *War of the Rebellion*, Vol. XLI, Part I, 830.

wounding two, and killing and wounding several cavalry mounts.[30] Three Indians were killed in this skirmish, including one who spoke broken English and was thought to be a chief.[31] A week earlier, in the same area Indians killed Lieutenant F. J. Bremer and wounded a trooper.[32] On October 20, west of Alkali Station at present-day Ogallala, Nebraska, Indians caught and killed one citizen and stole 50 oxen.[33]

Things had become so bad along the Platte River road it had become evident the Indians must be punished and punished severely. One radical move commenced on October 22, when the winds were conducive to enhance a huge firing of the prairie. Colonel Robert R. Livingston, commanding the First Nebraska Cavalry, ordered the burning of all land north and south of the Platte River Valley from a point 20 miles west of Fort Sedgwick, at Spring Hill Station, to 10 miles east of Fort Kearny, Nebraska Territory. In a report dated November 1, Livingston outlined the extent of this burning:

> On the 22d of October last, the wind being from the north and favorable, I caused the prairie south of the Platte River Valley to be simultaneously fired from a point twenty miles west of Julesburg continuously to a point ten miles east of this post, burning the grass in a continuous line of 200 miles as far south as the Republican River. In some places the fire went out owing to the grass being too thin to burn readily. But since then detachments have been sent out and the work has progressed favorably; every canyon and all the valleys of streams along this line have been thoroughly burned, thus depriving hostile Indians of forage for their animals in their hiding-places and driving all the game beyond the Republican River. From a point ten miles east of this post [Fort Kearny] to Little Blue Station I have burned only the creek valleys and canyons, compelling the Indians to graze their stock on the high prairie if they remain in that part of the country, and leaving the game in that section undisturbed for the use of the [friendly] Pawnee....
>
> The firing of the prairie has been commenced on the north side of the Platte Valley from Mullahla's Station to a point twenty-five miles west of Julesburg, Colorado Ter. [where the highway runs to present-day Crook, Colorado], extending north in some distances 150 miles. Universal consternation has spread among the Indians, to whom this mode of warfare is apparently new, and their presence along the road through this sub-district need not be apprehended during the winter. Officers from Fort Laramie tell me already the effect of this grand burning of the prairie is manifest among the Indians, and that they are anxious to make peace, but whether

---

30   *War of the Rebellion*, Vol. XLI, Part I, 841–841.
31   *War of the Rebellion*, Vol. XLI, Part I, 830.
32   *War of the Rebellion*, Vol. XLI, Part I, 843.
33   *War of the Rebellion*, Vol. XLI, Part I, 830.

their propositions are induced by fear of starvation, the game being driven off by the fires, or only to check the process of burning until they can renew hostilities in the spring, I am not prepared to say. . . . One thing is certain, the burning of the prairie has produced a marked effect on the Indian tribes along the road, and they begin to dread the white man's power.[34]

Livingston went on in his report to note that this burning did not include the vegetation within the traveled parts of the valley itself, thus maintaining the meager amounts of natural forage to be found along the trail on both sides of the Platte River, which was preserved for the many freight trains traveling along the road.

Livingston ended his report with the conclusion that

unless a terrible example is made of them—for instance, the total annihilation of some of their winter encampments, by which they will be brought to feel the power of the Government to avenge the terrible butcheries committed by them this past summer—they will from their past successes be encouraged to a more vigorous and audacious warfare as soon as the grass is green next spring.[35]

Colonel Livingston's burn order did not clear all the Indians out of the Platte River Valley. Around November 10, about two miles west of Eagle's Nest Stage Station, near present-day Orchid, Colorado, 10 Indians—probably Oglala—came to Coleman Laurance's ranch and burned 120 tons of hay and stole four or five horses and a mule. Some of the hay belonged to John H. Harris, who ran Eagle's Nest for the Overland Stage Company. The Indians fled north with the stock. Because of several reports that warriors were raiding all along the Platte River, Laurance and several other families had banded together for protection at Camp Osborn, a few miles east of Eagle's Nest. Thus, no one was at the ranch when the raid was made, but

---

34 *War of the Rebellion*, Vol. XLI, Part I, 830–831. Eugene Ware, in *The Indian War of 1864*, 488–491, said this burning occurred January 27, 1865, and was ordered by General Robert B. Mitchell. Ware goes on in some detail to describe how this burning occurred, in some cases by tying small bales of hay in metal chains, lighting the hay and then dragging it via horseback across the prairie to assure large portions of prairie catching fire. While Ware may be correct in explaining how the prairie was fired, surely he must be wrong in who ordered the burning and when it occurred. Many historians use Ware to claim the prairie was burned two times, three months apart; but, if critically thought through, if the burning in October was the success that Livingston reported it to be, then there was no prairie to burn three months later. It would take another season of growth for the prairie to have burnable grass in the dry winter season. Further, the *War of the Rebellion Documents* bear no report from Mitchell acknowledging a second burn. Ware, then, clearly got his dates wrong.

35 *War of the Rebellion*, Vol. XLI, Part I, 832.

a party of men followed the trail north and observed moccasin tracks and other Indian signs which convinced them that the Indians did the deed.[36]

Back in Kansas, two days later, on November 12, near Fort Larned, five freight wagons were destroyed and two freighters killed by a party of about 30 Indians.[37] That same day a train was freighting corn from Fort Leavenworth to Fort Larned. They had arrived at Ash Creek, 10 miles east of Larned, when they went into camp. William Kersten, John Herd, August Siegenfuhr and Conrad Henning were among the freighters. At around nine that night as many as 100 Cheyenne came charging into camp, firing guns and arrows at the men, overpowering them and driving off the stock. One man was killed and several severely wounded. Forty-three mules and 16 horses were stolen, along with seven wagons, either taken or destroyed.[38]

The Indians were still in Nebraska Territory. On November 15, along the Platte trail, nine miles west of Plum Creek, William McLennan was leading 14 wagons loaded with corn under a government contract to deliver the freight to Camp Cottonwood. The wagons were individually owned by several men. They were about 20 miles from the fort when at about four o'clock that afternoon, 100–200 Cheyenne warriors attacked the train. The Indians were able to separate and capture three teams of oxen (28 total), which they promptly killed, shooting and lancing them on the road. They also destroyed the wagons the oxen were attached to. That part of the train had fallen behind the other wagons and was thus exposed to the attack. The men driving those wagons were able to run several hundred yards into the safety of the remaining train. George W. Shrouf suffered most of the loss, including two of his three wagons and 18 of the oxen, along with his own personal possessions.[39] His son Daniel, a mere 15 years old, was driving one of the wagons. Jesse Graham lost one wagon, 10 oxen and his possessions in the wagon.[40] Four and a half tons of corn was also lost. Realizing the freight was just corn, the Indians did not try to overpower the remaining five wagons and thus no men were lost.[41]

---

36   Coleman Laurance Indian Depredation Claim #10103. Record Group 123.

37   Carroll, *The Sand Creek Massacre,* Appendix, 71.

38   John Herd Indian Depredation Claim #1221. Record Group 75; William Kerston Indian Depredation Claim #3305; August Siegenfuhr Indian Depredation Claim #7793; Conrad Henning Indian Depredation Claim #8955. Record Group 123.

39   George W. Shrouf Indian Depredation Claim #2170. Record Group 123.

40   Jesse Graham Indian Depredation Claim #2947. Record Group 123.

41   Benjamin Rue testimony, William McLennan Indian Depredation Claim #2172. Record Group 123.

The Indians remained active in Kansas, on the Santa Fe road. Milton Clarke was in charge of moving 1,200 head of cattle and 20 horses from Council Grove to Fort Union, New Mexico. He had with him 15 additional men to protect the herd.[42] One of the men with him was James L. McDowell. Early in the night of November 23, the men were in camp about 15 miles east of Fort Zarah, and guards had been assigned to oversee the herd. As McDowell recalled, it was very dark when about 8:30, one of the sentries fired a pistol shot to warn everyone of the presence of Indians.

> Immediately about 175 Indians began to pour a steady fire from rifles & arrows, into our camp, & as quickly as possible our men turned out and began firing upon the Indians who we found had completely surrounded the camp, and they continued the attack until about eleven o'clock, when the moon rose & the Indians left us, but during the fight B. H. Dunlap & two of the other men were wounded & we had to leave them at [Fort] Zara. At this time the Indians drove off 25 head of cattle, 2 black horses, 1 sorrel horse & 1 bay horse, all number one stock.

Dunlap had been in charge of the herd until he was wounded. Four or five men were placed as night guards, all armed with breech loading rifles and colt revolvers. The herd was a quarter of a mile away from the camp. Additional guards were placed at the camp. Dunlap vividly recalled that night:

> I and McDowell were sleeping in the same wagon, and just before the guard had given the alarm, I had blown out the light and heard the horses trampling. I awoke McDowell and told him it was either the cattle stampeding or Indians. We both got out of the wagon and immediately a heavy fire was poured into the camp, which riddled the wagons. Our men returned the fire, and it was kept up some five or ten minutes. During the fight I was shot in the leg and six others were wounded [two seriously]. I shot one of the Indians, that we knew of, but from the appearances the next morning there were probably more of them shot. It was said by the soldiers at Fort Zara, that there were some 250 Indians in that party, and they were said to be Kiowas, and a few Arapahoes and Cheyennes.

The shot that wounded him was a large ball. It broke his leg. Dunlap "killed a Cheyenne that was cutting the ropes of the horses, and he fell with a large knife in his hand, at the place where one of the horses was picketed."[43]

---

42 Mary Hacker Indian Depredation Claim #4887. Record Group 123.
43 Milton Clark Indian Depredation Claim #526. Record Group 123.

PRIVATE HUGH MELROSE,
3RD COLORADO CAVALRY.
Melrose was reported to have killed Southern
Cheyenne Chief White Antelope at Sand
Creek, November 29, 1864. He enlisted at
Colorado City. After his 100-day service,
Melrose married the author's great-great
aunt, Sarah Watson, on July 20, 1866. *Author's
collection, courtesy Kathy Lambert Maez,
Saguache, CO.*

The Indians were not through molesting the cattle train. The freighters
continued on their journey to Fort Union, and three days later the warriors
made another attack. McDowell: "On the night of 26 November, at Pawnee
Rock [15 miles northeast of Fort Larned] the Indians attacked us again &
stampeded the cattle, & quite a bunch of them were cut off by the Indians,
& drove off, & they were seen going through [Fort] Zara about daylight on
a run." At least 175 cattle were lost in this second raid.[44]

While all of this was going on in central Kansas, Colonel John M.
Chivington was carefully maneuvering from near Denver 450 men of the
3rd Colorado Cavalry, and an additional 100 men of the 1st Colorado Cavalry, down to the Santa Fe trail. He arrived at Fort Lyon on November 28,
where an additional 125 soldiers of the 1st Colorado Cavalry joined the regiment. From there, under cover of darkness, the command marched 35 miles
northeast to the Big Sandy where more than 120 lodges belonging to Black
Kettle and White Antelope, and a few Arapaho lodges under Left Hand
were camped. At dawn on November 29, with the surprise commencement
of cannon fire, the fight at Sand Creek began. This was a desperate engagement, lasting more than eight hours and covering that many miles. When
the fight was over, more than 130 Indians lay dead. Among the dead were a
good number of women and children. Chivington lost 24 men killed, and

---

44   Milton Clark Indian Depredation Claim #526

an additional 52 wounded, for a total casualty count of 76. To put these soldier losses into perspective, from 1850 to 1890 west of the Mississippi, there
were over 1,450 fights between whites and Indians that produced white
casualties. Of all of those, only six fights in that 40-year period produced
more white casualties than happened at Sand Creek.[45] Because a portion of
Chivington's men participated in the senseless murder of unarmed women
and children, apparently with the knowledge and approval of Chivington
himself, this fight has forever been mired in justifiable controversy. But
what should not be lost in this controversy is the fact that the very warriors in the village who fought so desperately and caused so many army
casualties at Sand Creek were among the same warriors who had banded
for war against the white man, and participated in the many deadly raids
along the immigration trails starting in earnest, earlier in August. If they
were peaceful, their peace was only begun some time after the deadly raids
along the Little Blue and Plum Creek three months earlier. [46]

After Sand Creek, primarily because of the unwarranted atrocities committed upon several unarmed Indians, many of whom were women and
children, an investigation was begun. The results were eventually published
as an off-print of the 38th Congress, Second Session.[47] From testimony
recorded in the investigation of Sand Creek, the government concluded
that "Black Kettle and White Antelope . . . were and had been friendly to
the whites, and had not been guilty of any acts of hostility or depredation."
Instead a northern band of Cheyenne, known as Dog Soldiers, had been

---

45   Michno, *Battle at Sand Creek*, 279, 304.
46   Many books have been written on Sand Creek, the majority of which advance the agenda of blaming the
     Colorado military forces for criminal genocide, which was true with a limited number of men, and thus
     prevent the reader from being able to separate the military murderer from the military soldier doing
     his duty. Thus it is difficult to learn the facts about Sand Creek from the printed sources, especially
     the fact that Black Kettle's principal chief, White Antelope, and many of his warriors were intimately
     involved in the outbreak of the 1864 Indian war. To start to understand Sand Creek, however, would
     be to read the entire documents created in the government investigation of Sand Creek [see Carroll,
     The Sand Creek Massacre]; see also Michno, *Battle at Sand Creek*, to read evidence which understands
     the fight as a battle in which terrible atrocities occurred. The Indian depredation claims used for
     this book have many incidental comments relating to Sand Creek, some of them quite interesting.
     For example, one freighter, a man named Samuel Monk, testified under oath that the subordinate
     officers under Chivington, who opposed his attack upon Black Kettle, "were supposed, and I think
     justly too, to be friendly to these Indians, selling them government supplies, and of course they did
     not wish the Indians disturbed. They were profiting from these Indians. That was the general report
     and belief at the time." See Sallenna Grant Indian Depredation Claim #9942. Record Group 123.
47   Carroll, *The Sand Creek Massacre*, 1–108.

guilty.[48] But, as has been seen throughout the settler reports of the Indian attacks in 1864, especially along the Little Blue and Plum Creek in August, indeed, White Antelope especially, and thus by implication Black Kettle, were both involved in this violent Indian war of 1864, contrary to the testimony presented to the government in its investigation of the atrocities at Sand Creek. White Antelope admitted his Cheyenne participated in these raids, aligned with the northern band of Dog Soldiers, while Black Kettle remained silent and thus was likely in at least tacit partnership with this violent war. Had not a small number of soldiers committed unspeakable atrocities to several of the innocent women and children caught at Sand Creek, there probably would not have been a subsequent investigation, and today critics of Sand Creek would be as silent as critics of Summit Springs in 1869. But of course, to speculate this is merely that, speculation; for the facts are, there were atrocities committed and a subsequent investigation, and today the fight at Sand Creek remains highly controversial. It can be added to this that the resulting war along the trails to Denver, which continued through 1869, was emotionally fueled by the soldier atrocities committed at Sand Creek.[49]

---

48   Carroll, *The Sand Creek Massacre*, ii.

49   The controversy continues to grow even today. For an account of modern issues associated with Sand Creek, including finding the actual battle site, see Ari Kelman, *A Misplaced Massacre: Struggling Over the Memory of Sand Creek* (Cambridge, MA: Harvard University Press, 2013). See also Jerome A. Greene and Douglas D. Scott, *Finding Sand Creek: History, Archeology, and the 1864 Massacre Site* (Norman, OK: University of Oklahoma Press, 2004).

CHAPTER SIX

The 1865 Indian War

The first we saw of the Indians was when my brother-in-law, Mark Coad, and one of the men were getting up the horses and had them saddled to look for stock. I got on a horse and went up the road for about a mile and I was attacked there by about ten or fifteen Indians who ran me to the ranch. I went to the dwelling house, which was about sixty or seventy-five feet from the store, to get my wife and children and take them to a safer building.

JANUARY 15, 1865, BENJAMIN DANIELSON AFFIDAVIT
JOHN F. & MARK M. COAD INDIAN DEPREDATION CLAIM #7665

THE SURVIVING INDIANS FROM BLACK KETTLE'S VILLAGE on the Big Sandy, on November 29 fled northeast, first finding shelter with other Cheyenne Indians camped on the Smoky Hill River just at the Colorado/Kansas border, and eventually arriving at a large camp of assembled Indians on Cherry Creek, near present-day St. Francis, in northwest Kansas. It was here that plans were set for retaliation. The focus for attack was the Platte River road to Denver. In this village were numerous Cheyenne lodges, 80 Northern Arapahoe lodges, and an untold number of Lakota lodges. There were enough Indians to assemble as many as 1,000 warriors to begin their avenging raids. Some of the Indians assembled here included Dog Soldiers under Tall Bull, warriors from Spotted Tail's Brule village, as well as Oglala under Pawnee Killer.[1] Their intended targets? Julesburg and as many stations as they could hit west and east of that important stop on the Denver road.

Camp Rankin was established in mid-September 1864, at several fords crossing the South Platte River near Julesburg. Its name would be changed to Fort Sedgwick on September 27, 1865, in honor of Major General John

---

1   Hyde, *Life of George Bent*, 168.

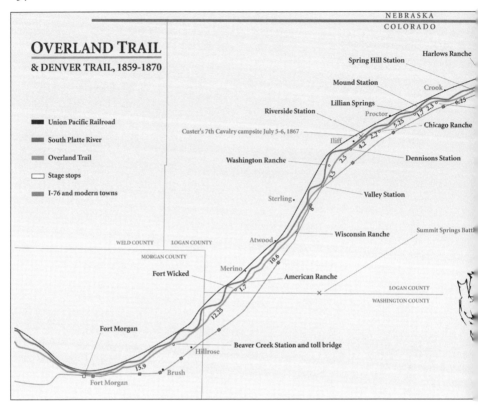

OVERLAND TRAIL
& DENVER TRAIL, 1859-1870

NEBRASKA
COLORADO

Union Pacific Railroad

South Platte River

Overland Trail

Stage stops

I-76 and modern towns

WELD COUNTY | LOGAN COUNTY

MORGAN COUNTY

Harlows Ranche

Spring Hill Station

Mound Station

Crook

Lillian Springs

Riverside Station

Proctor

Chicago Ranche

Custer's 7th Cavalry campsite July 5-6, 1867

Iliff

Washington Ranche

Dennisons Station

Valley Station

Sterling

Wisconsin Ranche

Summit Springs Battle

Atwood

Merino

Fort Wicked

American Ranche

LOGAN COUNTY

WASHINGTON COUNTY

Fort Morgan

Beaver Creek Station and toll bridge

Hillrose

Brush

Fort Morgan

Sedgwick, who had been killed in the Civil War battle at Spotsylvania in May the year before. The fort had originally been a ranch built by Samuel Bancroft, with whom the government negotiated a purchase. The Indians attacked Camp Rankin on January 7, 1865.[2]

Hundreds of warriors had approached the area the night before, and at daybreak remained hidden about three or four miles away in the sand bluffs to the southeast. Their plan was to lure the few soldiers at Camp Rankin away from the river and into the sand bluffs where they would be easy to ambush. It almost worked. A few Indians approached the fort and taunted the men, and soon a party of 38 soldiers and civilians under the command of Captain

2   Ware, *The Indian War of 1864*, 326. Robert W. Frazier says the camp was established May 17, 1864. See *Forts of the West* (Norman, OK: University of Oklahoma Press, 1963), 41.

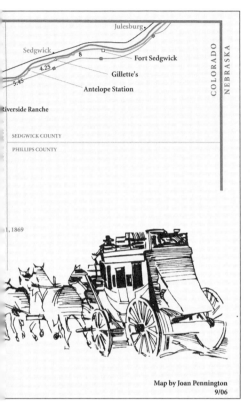

DENVER ROAD, SHOWING STAGE
STATIONS FROM FORT SEDGWICK
TO FORT MORGAN.
Indians made several violent forays at
each ranch and stage station, beginning in
January 1865, and continuing through 1868.
The road was actively used from 1859 until
late fall, 1867, when the railroad completed
tracks to Cheyenne, Wyoming. At that
time, freighters brought goods 100 miles
south from Cheyenne, into Denver and
the mining communities. The South Platte
road ranches were individually abandoned
after that time, and by 1868 all ranches and
stations were vacant. The Indians burned
Fort Morgan in 1868. Nearly every ranch/
station had a small military presence after
Sand Creek, until the railroad opened
to Cheyenne. *Courtesy Joan Pennington,
Fairfax Station, Virginia.*

Map by Joan Pennington
9/06

Nicholas J. O'Brien went off in pursuit. But, as was often the case with Indian
surprise tactics, a few impatient young warriors emerged from their hiding
places before the command could be fully trapped. A running fight ensued
and the soldiers were able to make it back to the fort. Still, casualties were
high with 14 soldiers and 4 civilians killed, and two soldiers wounded.[3] While
scampering back to Camp Rankin, the men passed Bulen Ranch (also called
Benton's, Beuler's, Buler's and Bullin's Ranch[4]), which was located about one

---

3   Hyde, *Life of George Bent*, 170–174; Michno, *Encyclopedia of Indian Wars*, 161. One should be aware
     that this account comes from Bent decades after the fight, and thus might not be accurate. It is quite
     possible there were no impatient warriors ruining a trap. It might simply be that so many warriors
     emerged from the hills that the soldiers perceived the necessity to withdraw.
4   Actually, the correct name of the ranch was Connally and Bulen Ranch. See Connally and Bulen
     Indian Depredation Claim #2619. Indian Depredation Claims Division, Record Group 123.

and a half miles east of Julesburg. The soldiers warned the ranchmen that the Indians were in great numbers and to retreat to the fort. Earlier the ranchmen could see the soldiers engaged with the Indians about three quarters of a mile southeast of the station. The men fled to the fort, but the contents of their ranch were destroyed, including a stage coach loaded with valuable express mail. One of the civilians at the ranch that day was a doctor named Alexander Hamilton. He had practiced medicine since 1864 at Julesburg. He lost $772 in medical equipment and supplies.[5] The stage had earlier that morning been attacked, about four miles to the east of the station. The driver raced the horses pulling the coach west to the ranch, shortly before Captain O'Brien and his troopers arrived. O'Brien continued his pursuit of the taunting Indians who were trying to draw the soldiers into a trap.[6]

Another man, a contract surgeon with the Army, was present at a nearby ranch that morning. Apparently, this ranch was also the post hospital. It was the Julesburg Stage station, midway between Bulen Ranch and Camp Rankin.[7] Joel Wisely had several soldiers at the ranch under his medical care. The hospital was a small one-story log house consisting of two rooms. Wisely had recently contracted with the Army as a surgeon and was attending to the medical needs of the soldiers stationed at the new Camp Rankin. Described as a very competent surgeon wholly dedicated to his profession, he had an unusual face, with "the most grotesque and disproportionate nose" as could grace a face. "It was more than a nose—it was a combination of beak and snout." The soldiers came to call him Dr. Nosely.[8]

Captain Nicholas O'Brien reported that he passed the hospital about seven that morning, when he and his men were in pursuit of the Indians. At about noon, he sent a courier from where he was hotly engaged with the warriors, stating that he was retreating and that Surgeon Wisely should immediately remove the men under his care to the safety of the fort. By one o'clock, O'Brien retreated past the station and observed that the hospital

---

5   Alexander Hamilton Indian Depredation Claim #931. Record Group 123.

6   "Testimony as to the Claim of Ben Holladay," *The Miscellaneous Documents of the Senate of the United States for the Second Session of the Forty-Sixth Congress, 1879–1880*, Mis. Doc. No. 19 (Washington, DC: Government Printing Office, 1880), 25–27.

7   Colonel R. R. Livingston identified each camp as follows: Buler's Ranch two miles east of Camp Rankin and the Julesburg Stage Station one mile east of the camp. Thus these camps were one mile apart from each other. See *War of the Rebellion*, Series I, Vol. XLVIII, Part I, 41.

8   Ware, *Indian War of 1864*, 331.

men were then being transported in a wagon. All of the men made it safely to the fort.[9] O'Brien's fight with the Indians lasted about four hours.

Captain Edward B. Murphy of Company A, 7th Iowa Cavalry, gave more details of the events of January 7. He said the stage coach that ran to safety at Bulen's Ranch had been attacked before daylight that morning, and chased about two miles west to the ranch, which was about a mile east of Julesburg. At sunrise a report was sent of the attack to Captain O'Brien at Camp Rankin, and then a company under command of O'Brien left Rankin to investigate this attack.[10] It was learned that two men had been killed on the stage during its frantic jaunt to the ranch. Hearing at Bulen's Ranch that the Indians retreated south to some sand hills, O'Brien's small command then marched in that direction in an attempt to catch the Indians, thinking they comprised the small number of warriors involved in the stage attack. Instead, the Indians surprised them with overwhelming numbers, causing the men to retreat back to the ranch, and then west to the fort. Fifteen men were killed in this fight, all from a platoon that had been surrounded while trying to withdraw. Once the men at the fort saw the retreating soldiers racing back, they fired their howitzer into the Indians, which prevented the warriors from further advancing and ransacking the small town of Julesburg. It didn't prevent them from plundering Bulen's Ranch, however, and everything there was destroyed, including a loss of over $15,000 from the contents of the stage, which was loaded with express mail satchels.[11] One of the satchels contained specially ordered shirts, pants, silk cloth, gloves, hose, ribbons, collars and lace by Nelson Sargeant in Denver. His loss was valued at $353.70.[12]

---

9   Joel Wisely Indian Depredation Claim #2348. Record Group 123. This claim is interesting because of the bogus amount of loss that Wisely sought compensation for, including $75 for a fur overcoat, which was a buffalo coat valued at $6, and purchased in trade with the Indians at that time for about $1.50. Wisely's losses were valued by him at $499.50, but determined upon investigation to be worth no more than $100. This happened with some regularity with particular depredation claims, i.e., American citizens asking for significantly larger amounts of property loss than they were legitimately entitled to. That this type of fraud occurred with some regularity with many individual depredation claims cannot be denied. However, this does not distract trusting in the sworn affidavits in the individual depredation claims which detail the particular actions happening in the various raids. Wisely's recollections of the events can be trusted for accuracy as an important and new primary source account of this fight in 1865. Captain O'Brien's account of the January 7 raid, in Wisely's depredation claim, is an authentic first-hand source for learning important details of this raid.

10 This account is different from the account give by George Bent in Hyde, *Life of George Bent*, 171.

11 Affidavit of Edward B. Murphy, "Claim of Ben Holladay," 23–25.

12 Nelson Sargeant Indian Depredation Claim #709. Record Group 123. Gemenien Beauvais also filed a claim for property losses somewhere in the same vicinity for January 9. He claimed the (*continued*)

The soldiers killed in this fight were Sergeant Alanson Hanchett, Corporals William Gray, Anthony Koons, Walter Talbott and privates George Barnett, Hiram Brundage, Henry Hall, David Ishman, James Jordan, Davis Lippincott, Edson Moore, Amos McArthur, Thomas Scott and Joel Stebbins. Another soldier died with these men, John Pierce, but he had not been formally inducted into the service before he was killed, having just enlisted before Christmas. There were no enlistment papers at Camp Rankin and the company was awaiting papers from Omaha to officially enlist him.[13]

One of the wounded soldiers who made it back to Camp Rankin suffered a unique arrow wound. The arrow was improvised from the handle of a common frying pan and struck him in the back part of his hip. Lieutenant Eugene F. Ware, assigned to the company, but who was away at O'Fallon's Bluffs during the fight, later described the wound:

> The frying-pans of that day used on the plains were little, light steel utensils, with slender, heavy hoop-steel handles with a ring in the end. The Indian had a large arrow, and about nine inches of this frying-pan handle sharpened on both sides, and pointed, was fixed into it. The arrow went in several inches, and through the pelvic bone. Although the soldier got out of the fight alive, he could not pull the arrow out. He succeeded in getting back to the post. Then one of the soldiers got the company blacksmith's pinchers, and, laying the wounded man down on his face, he stood on top of him, got hold of the arrow-head with his pinchers, and finally succeeded in working and wrenching it out. The poor fellow was in great pain, but subsequently recovered all right.[14]

Charles T. Johnson was the operator at the station, owned by Connelly and Bulen.[15] He reported that when the Indians attacked on January 7, they drove off several dozen work cattle and killed two herders. Including the 15 soldiers killed, another seven civilians were killed (which includes the two herders), bringing a total of 22 men killed in this fight.[16] Julesburg Station

---

loss of 34 oxen, three wagons and a wagon train of sellable goods bound for Denver. His loss totaled more than $15,000, but his file does not contain any details. Gemenien Beauvais Indian Depredation Claim #7104. Record Group 123.

13   Ware, *Indian War of 1864*, 419, 448–449.

14   Ware, *Indian War of 1864*, 442, 453.

15   This would mean the station called Beuler's, Buler's, Bullin's Ranch, and Conley and Bullins is the same station called Conley [Connally] and Bulen. That the correct spelling is Bulen is verified in the depredation claim of Guilford D. Connally and E. D. Bulen. See Indian Depredation Claim # 2619, Record Group 123.

16   Charles T. Johnson affidavit in Abram T. Litchfield Indian Depredation Claim #4843. Record Group 123.

was the home station of the Overland Stage Company. Bulen's Ranch was a trading ranch, well stocked with various goods and liquors for traveling immigrants. It, along with the Julesburg Station, was eventually burned in another raid, on February 2.[17]

While the attack on the soldiers near Julesburg was happening, further attacks were being made many miles west on the trail. A few miles west of Valley Station, Indians surprised a stage traveling east. A running fight ensued. One passenger was killed, the driver wounded and finally, after a frantic chase, the coach toppled, crashing hard onto the trail. The remaining six passengers, all of them already wounded, made a dash for the cover of the river and were able to escape to Valley Station. Two Indians were killed. A few miles east of Valley Station, near Dennison's Ranch, Indians attacked a large wagon train and killed four to 12 men.[18]

Within a week more attacks were made, this time on various ranches all along the Denver trail. Colonel Livingston, reporting from Camp Rankin on February 5, said that several attacks occurred on January 14–16. Beaver Creek Station, 82 miles to the west, was burned down, as was American Ranch 68 miles west. Godfrey's Ranch, one and a half miles further west from American Ranch, wasn't burned but that was because Holan Godfrey and others successfully fought off the Indians for two days. Wisconsin Ranch was attacked and burned on January 15. Valley Station was attacked on January 26, as well as Washington/Moore Ranch. Lillian Springs Ranch, 33 miles west of Camp Rankin, was attacked and burned on the 27th. Antelope Stage Station, 15 miles west, was burned, as were Buffalo Springs Ranch, Harlow's Ranch, and Spring Hill Stage Station, all on January 28. Also burned were Bulen's Ranch and Julesburg Stage Station.[19] The Indian war was being waged all along the Denver road.

George Bent got his dates wrong years later when he wrote about the

---

17 Charles T. Johnson Indian Depredation Claim #2578. The four civilians killed, then, were the two on the stage and the two herders at Bulen's ranch.

18 Michno, *Encyclopedia*, 161–162. Probst, *Forgotten People*, 73. See also *War of the Rebellion*, Series I, Vol. XLVIII, Part I, 23. Monahan, *Destination: Denver City*, 208–209, citing a newspaper account, says this was not a stage coach but rather a four-mule wagon carrying six passengers. The owner of Dennison's Station was St. Ledger Beck, and in his depredation claim he says there were four men killed and seven wounded. When he finally fled the ranch with his family on January 20, prior to its being burned on January 25, he took four of the wounded men with him and named them as Mr. Bills of Chicago, and Jones, Palmer and Cross, all of Leavenworth.

19 *War of the Rebellion*, Series I, Vol. XLVIII, Part I, 41.

raids, but he admitted to being present, and said the Indians who participated in this second attack on the ranches along the Denver road included
about 700 Cheyenne, Sioux and Arapaho.[20] Holan Godfrey's ranch was
attacked the morning of January 15, when more than 100 Indians swooped
down upon the building. The 47-year-old Godfrey, who lived at the ranch
with several other men as well as his wife Matilda and daughters Martha
(20), Celia (12) and Carrie (four months), lost 88 head of cattle in the attack,
mostly oxen.[21] Eli Perkins and his wife Margaret were living at the ranch
and working for Godfrey, as was a man by the name of Dunlap. When the
Indians attacked the men were outside but were able to escape to the buildings, running four horses inside the main building. The women helped to
load weapons while the men fired at the Indians from inside the ranch.
Godfrey's adobe buildings were strong and solid and the Indians were
unable to burn them.[22]

But that wasn't the case less than two miles down the river. The American
Ranch attack on January 15 was one of the most deadly of all the attacks along
the Denver South Platte road.[23] The ranch earlier was called Kelley's Station,
but it had been sold to William Morris and his brother shortly before the
raid.[24] It was established in 1861 by James Moore and William Kelley. When
sold to William Morris in early August 1864, James Moore then joined his

20   Hyde, *Life of George Bent*, 178.

21   Probst, *Forgotten People*, 46–47.

22   Holan Godfrey Indian Depredation Claim #2559. Record Group 123. Probst, *Forgotten People*, relying
     on later reminiscences, says the fight at Godfrey's ranch lasted two days (78–79), but the depredation
     claim lists the incident as happening in one day.

23   Historians have given different dates for this attack. Doris Monahan gives the date of the attack as
     January 15 (*Destination: Denver City*, 211). Luella Shaw, reporting the account of Watson Coburn, says
     the ranch was attacked January 14 (*True History of some of the Pioneers of Colorado*, 23). Nell Brown
     Probst also says it occurred January 14 (*Forgotten people*, 75). In Colonel R. R. Livingston's report of
     February 5, he states American Ranch was attacked about the 14th, with the date of the 15th in brackets
     next to the 14th (*War of the Rebellion*, Series I, Vol. XLVIII, Part I, 41). Lieutenant Judson Kennedy's
     report of January 16 implies the fight happened on that day (*War of the Rebellion*, 41–42). Accounts
     from Sarah Morris at her rescue, in June 1865, states the attack occurred on January 10 (*Frontier Scout*,
     June 22, 1865). Holan Godfrey's Indian depredation claim notes he was attacked on January 16, and
     while his attack was going on he could see one and a half miles down the river American Ranch was
     being attacked and burned at the same time (Holan Godfrey Indian Depredation Claim #2559). The
     Indian depredation claim of Mark and John Coad at Wisconsin Ranch provides the most details of
     the attacks, and insists through the testimony of multiple witnesses that the attack was made on Janu-
     ary 15 and not January 16, as Godfrey claims. The Coad brothers saw the smoke from the burning of
     American Ranch shortly before they were attacked on the same day. This testimony lends credence
     that the attack happened on January 15. Coad Indian Depredation Claim #7665. Record Group 123.

24   Testimony of Charles Moore in John F. & Mark M. Coad Indian Depredation Claim #7665.

brother Charles at Washington Ranch, buying out partner Joseph Nesbitt. Nesbitt and Charles Moore had been in partnership operating Washington Ranch since the spring of 1862.[25] Prior to the Indian raids beginning in the spring of 1864, American Ranch had been a very profitable traveler's station along the Denver trail. Indeed, when Kelley and James sold it they received $3,800 for the transaction, a very high price in those times. In today's dollars, it would be equivalent to more than $55,000.[26] The war changed all of that.

William Morris brought to the ranch his wife Sarah J. Iams, along with an adopted son, four-year-old Joseph and a biological son, 18-month-old Charley. Sarah was a twin daughter of Rezin Iams and Eleanor Riley, and was born August 20, 1837, in Pennsylvania. William and Sarah married March 3, 1860, in Delaware County, Indiana. Their dreams for a happy life on the frontier came to a violent end on the Sunday morning of January 15.

Later pioneer reminiscences say that William was playing his fiddle in the back room of the home when 27-year-old Mrs. Morris heard a noise in the front room. Upon checking what his wife heard, William found several

---

25   James Moore and Charles Moore Indian Depredation Claims #1240–1245. Record Group 123. Doris Monahan, in *Destination: Denver City*, 165, cites a newspaper article in the *Rocky Mountain News*, which speaks of American Ranch burning down in August. It seems unlikely that the entire ranch would be rebuilt in late summer/early fall in order for it to be burned to the ground again in January 1865. Further, the Moore depredation claim makes no mention of American Ranch being destroyed by fire. Instead it states that James Moore in his partnership with William Kelley owned the stock, and Kelley owned the buildings, and that when the partnership dissolved in August 1865, James Moore moved his stock to Washington Ranch and bought out Joseph Nesbitt's half of the partnership with Charles Moore. It is difficult to conceive of William Morris taking over a burned out ranch in August and immediately rebuilding it. Perhaps there was a smaller fire at American Ranch that the *Rocky Mountain News* was reporting.

26   See http://www.westegg.com/inflation/infl.cgi (accessed October 5, 2012).
      James Moore Indian Depredation Claims #524. Record Group 75, Entry 700. In this depredation file is a letter written by Charles Moore, in which he stated: "My brother and Kelley was [sic] the oners [sic] of the American Ranch up to the early spring of 64. Then they dissolved Kelley took ranch and goods Jim took all the live stock about five hundred cattle and about seventy eight head of horses. Then I and bro went into copartnership. I at that time had a partner and running a ranch twenty two miles east of the American Ranch and my partner got frightened [sic] on account of the Indian trubles [sic] and I bought him out stock—ranch and everything pertaining to ranch . . . will inform you of the fate of the American Ranch and ocupants [sic]. Kelley sold out to Morison Bro the Indians captured the ranch and kiled [sic] all in ranch including one of the Morisons but the wife and child carried all the goods of they could and set fire and burned ranch. Kelley sold ranch for 3800 dollars." Charles Moore is one of several contemporaries at the time that identified Sarah's last name as Morrison, not Morris (e.g., see Holan Godfrey depredation claim). However, census records confirm the correct spelling was Morris. It is also interesting to note that the partnership at American Ranch was with two brothers, one of whom was not present when the Indians made their deadly assault. Charles Moore's letter is dated July 16, 1888.

Indians had entered the premises. When the Indians saw him they tried to kill him, but William quickly shot three Indians, and the rest fled out the front door. The warriors then started a siege, and by the end of the day they succeeded in burning down the ranch, forcing the five men in the house to flee out the back in a desperate attempt to reach the Platte River and hopefully conceal themselves in the thick willows and banks. William yelled to Sarah to take the children and go out the front door and surrender, thinking the Indians would not kill her and the children. The men, however, didn't get far before they were overtaken, killed and scalped. William probably made it as far as the river, for his body was not found until early April, with 17 arrows in it.[27] Sarah and the children were taken captive.[28] According to Holan Godfrey, whose own ranch was under attack at the same time, he could see the attack at American Ranch. He stated two of Morris' men survived, Gus Hall and a boy named Tom. Both were severely wounded but were able to hide along the banks of the South Platte.[29]

Later reminiscences changed the name of the boy to Big Steve, and added further details. The two men were not at American Ranch when the attack started but had coincidentally, just as it began, returned from an earlier jaunt to retrieve wood several miles north in the canyons. They were unaware the ranch was under attack. Eleven Indians saw them cross the frozen river from the north and charged at them, just as they got across the river. Big Steve was killed but Gus Hall, severely wounded in the right leg, was left alone along the bank. After a period of time, the wounded Hall saw the Indians preparing to leave the burned out ranch. He peered up from the bank and instantly an arrow hit him in the chest, going through his body and landing several feet behind him. When the Indian who fired the arrow came to scalp him, Hall killed him with a pistol shot. Apparently no other Indians witnessed this, for he was left alone with the dead

27 Frank C. Young wrote in his journal for Saturday, April 15, that "...it is only a week or two ago that the soldiers found his body in the Platte, close by, with seventeen arrows in it (he was missing for some weeks after the fight); while there are four graves across the road, about two hundred yards from the house, where his three defenders sleep beside him." *Across the Plains in '65* (Denver, CO: privately printed, 1905), 197.

28 Shaw, *True History*, 26–27. This account also claims that before fleeing the fire-engulfed home, William took time to lace two decanters of whiskey with strychnine, to poison the Indians. But this idea really doesn't make sense because the house was engulfed in flames, so the whiskey would have been destroyed before the Indians could drink it.

29 Holan Godfrey Indian Depredation Claim #2559.

warrior on top of him. After the Indians left, Hall crawled for 17 hours, on his hands and knees, down the mostly frozen river, 10 and a half miles to the Wisconsin Ranch. It too had been attacked and burned earlier that day. Finding warmth in spilled grain next to a sod wall in one of the burned buildings, Hall curled up there, where he was soon found by men in a large wagon train, still alive but unconscious. He was rescued and then taken to Omaha, where he later recovered.[30]

But a January 17 telegraph from Valley Station reported a different story, saying instead that apparently Hall and another man were rescued by the telegraph operator from Junction Station (Beaver Creek). This other man was probably the boy named Tom that Holan Godfrey said was severely wounded when Hall was wounded:

> The telegraph operator from Junction Station arrived here this morning. He had an escort part of the way. He came the last twenty-two miles alone, and in the night. He found two wounded men at a ranch [Wisconsin ranch] five miles west of this place. An escort was sent from here, which brought the wounded men in. He found the American ranch, 17 miles west of here, again on fire, and seven bodies burned to the cinders, among them two children and one woman. A large number of Indians were along the road. Signal fires are burning at night in every direction. It is expected the Indians will butcher every person on the road unless speedy assistance is sent us.[31]

The telegraph operator from Junction Station likely was Michael Murray, owner and operator of a ranch called Douglas Ranch (also sometimes called Murray Ranch), which was situated about five miles up from Beaver Creek Station, near present-day Fort Morgan. His reminiscences stated that he was looking for Gus Hall and another laborer of American Ranch, who had gone north across the river to pick up firewood when the Indians attacked them. "I found the other man dead and took care of his body and thought Hall was dead too but . . . found him alive at Valley Station. He had been shot through the heel and later had his leg amputated in Denver." Hall told Murray that it was about half a dozen Indians who chased him and his partner, who was gunned down. Hall got under the bank of the Platte River and escaped. Murray does not mention an arrow wound.[32]

30 Shaw, *True History*, 27–30.
31 *Syracuse* [New York] *Daily Courier and Union*, January 19, 1865.
32 Michael Murray Affidavit, Coad Indian Depredation Claim #4665.

Later pioneer reminiscences conflict with the report that Sarah Morris gave when she was rescued June 21, 1865, at Fort Rice, Dakota Territory. She said the Indians numbered about 100 and made their attack about 10 o'clock that morning. They set the house and stables on fire, forcing everyone into "the pilgrim room." When that finally caught fire, everyone had to flee the flames.

> We ran out towards the river, through the corral, hoping to make our escape. My husband said perhaps we could escape that way. When we got to the corral we found we could not. He told me to stop, that they would probably take me prisoner, and he possibly might get away. They surrounded, and killed him and another man as they were running to the river. The Indians stood so thickly about me, I could not see him when he was killed. He had no arms of any kind with him.[33]

Sarah also reported that in addition to her husband, three other men were killed in the attack, making a total of four men killed, not five. She received "five wounds from arrows and six wounds from knives. They also struck me across the head with their whips." Her captivity was one of suffering and hardship. When the Indians left the ranch with their three captives—Sarah and her two small boys—they went south to their Cherry Creek camp where they stayed for several days, while the warriors celebrated their success with several scalp dances. The Indians then moved north, where they remained until Sarah was finally released in June. Her adopted son, Joseph, was separated from her during her captivity and was never heard from again. Little Charley stayed with her, but about seven weeks before her rescue the Minniconjou Sioux chief White White got tired of his crying—"My baby was afraid of him and would cry"—took little Charley by the neck, "threw him down, and stamped on him." Charley suffered and died in about three weeks. While Sarah spoke of the chief's cruelty in killing her son (she said he was still alive—barely—when they tried to bury him in a coffee sack), she also said White White was responsible for saving her life. According to Sarah's understanding, he had joined the Cheyenne in their planned raid along the Denver road because his daughter was married to a white man who lived in one of the ranches and he was afraid she might be harmed in the raids. When the Cheyenne were stabbing Sarah and shooting arrows into her, White White jumped to her rescue and shielded her from certain death. He then bought her from the Cheyenne with an American horse, and

---

33 "History of Mrs. Sarah Morris," *The Frontier Scout*, June 22, 1865.

she remained with him until her rescue. She also reported that he treated her fairly well, "making me do scarcely anything except pack on my back a few kegs of water, and saddle my pony."[34]

Sarah's claim of being fairly well-treated, however, goes against what an officer recorded, who was present at her rescue. Colonel Charles Augustus Dimon was stationed at Fort Rice in Dakota Territory. In his unpublished memoirs he painted a very different picture of Sarah at her rescue:

I shall never forget the heart-rending story of a white lady who was captured by them, and passed a living death with them, given to me when she had just been rescued from a fate indescribable and worse than death. On the 21st of June, 1865, "White White," leader of a band of Minnecongues, had sent me word that his band wanted to make peace with the whites. Learning that they had a white woman prisoner in their camp, I stipulated that they should give up this woman; they agreed, and the next day the band appeared near the post with a flag indicating peace; we went out to meet them. It seems the woman, not understanding their language, had no knowledge of their intentions. When about two hundred yards from them, a commotion among the Indians was noticed, and soon a form darted from their midst and flew toward us, with nothing but a buffalo robe girt about her loins, with hair flowing and unkempt, with hands extended—this poor woman, flying from the gates of a living hell, with hope long ago left far behind, but now returning so suddenly as to nearly take from her her reason, this saved soul threw herself at the feet of my horse, and clinging to the stirrups of the saddle, with streaming eyes could only say, "MERCIFUL GOD! Have you at last heard me? Am I dreaming? God bless you! God bless you!" For many weeks, she lay in our Fort hospital between life and death; her cries during the delirium of her fever were fearful as she seemed to be again going through her terrible sufferings. When reason was restored, she gave me an account of atrocities, that if it were permissible to repeat, you might think possible and probable in some far away wild land of India or Africa, but could NEVER imagine took place in one of our border states or territories. It was learned that this woman's name was Mrs. Wm. Morris, a daughter of Reason Imes, Esq., of Granville, Delaware County, Indiana, a refined educated lady, who had been brought up as an only daughter, amid luxuries and comforts. She had started with her husband, Mr. William Morris, his brother, a son aged six years, and an infant about one year old, to go to Colorado, there to settle in a new home, with prospects in life before her, and these bright. They were captured by a band of hostile Indians on the 10th of January, 1865, about one hundred and thirty miles north-east of Denver, Colorado; She was wounded in several places. Her husband was wounded

---

34   "History of Mrs. Sarah Morris," *The Frontier Scout.* George Bent, getting the dates wrong, said that the Sioux capturing Sarah was Cut Belly. Hyde, *Life of George Bent*, 179.

and after tortured, scalped, and murdered before her eyes; the brother-in-law was killed at the first attack; her son was sold to another band the second day, and she never saw him again. The fourth day, the Indian possessing her, becoming enraged at the constant crying of her sickly babe, in a passionate moment, took it by its limbs and dashed its brains out on the frozen ground. She had been sold to three different chiefs. When opportunity offered, she was sent down to her father in Indiana, who welcomed her as one from the dead.[35]

When one compares Sarah's account with Dimon's memoirs, there are some errors of fact. For instance, both state she was captured January 10, but this in all likelihood cannot be, for all eyewitness testimony of the attack place the raid on January 15–16. Sarah was not an only child. Both accounts also conflict with each other. Dimon said Sarah was sold to three chiefs, White White being the last, while Sarah said she was in White White's company the entire time. Dimon said her son Charley was killed in the first week while Sarah said it was in the last month of her five-month ordeal. But their biggest discrepancy comes in Sarah's treatment during her captivity. According to Dimon it was brutal, not permissible to repeat, ". . . a fate indescribable and worse than death." According to Sarah she was treated not badly and only had to carry water and care for her captor's pony. So where might the truth lie? It is probably found in Dimon's remembrances, for there is scarcely a single account of Lakota, Cheyenne, Kiowa, Comanche or Arapaho white female captivity that does not bear out a vicious and sexually tortured ordeal, unless one turns to the journalistic press, where efforts were made to restore a sense of dignity in young women surviving Indian captivity.[36]

---

35 Charles Augustus Ropes Dimon Papers, Yale Collection of Western Americana, Beinecke Rare Book and Manuscript Library.

36 This fact is borne out in the excellent documentary study by Greg and Sue Michno, *A Fate Worse Than Death*. See especially pp 457–480. See also Broome, *Dog Soldier Justice*, 127–146. A somewhat different perspective of white Indian captivity comes from John Monnett. See "Reimagining Transitional Kansas Landscapes: Environment and Violence," *Kansas History: A Journal of the Central Plains* (Volume 34, Number 4, Winter 2011–2012), 259–279. Monnett claims "there are many cases of decent treatment of captive women, both white and Indian, *after* their captor's initial rage had subsided, . . ." (274–275). He does not cite a single source, and the suspicion is any source cited also has a source denying it, as is the case with Sarah Morris' captivity ordeal. Monnett does go on to make the strong claim that psychological factors prominent among all humans in all cultures throughout history, where the violent rape of captives occurs, is more likely brought about by "discrete emotional states caused by a sudden, specific, localized scene or event" and not by other causes, such as political beliefs or cultural moods, etc. (275). In other words, sexual abuse of captives is more the product of attempting to shame a victim more so than a cultural practice of an existing entity, in this case, Indian society.

Some time during the attack and burning of the American Ranch, other Indians also attacked Wisconsin Ranch. Historian Donald Berthong erroneously reported that one woman and two children were killed at the Wisconsin.[37] In fact, only Indians were killed in the attack.[38] The ranch was owned and operated by two brothers, Mark M. and John F. Coad. They had owned the ranch since 1862, and kept it until 1867, at which time it was sold to a stage company. The ranch consisted of a store house, a dwelling house with an attached kitchen and dining room, and several stables and corrals. Twenty-two-year-old John was freighting on the trail, and was in Nebraska City at the time of the raid. Thirty-three-year-old Mark was at the ranch, along with ranchmen Francis "Frank" Jacques, James Hinds and 34-year-old brother-in-law and ranch manager and bookkeeper, Benjamin Danielson, his wife (Coad's sister) and their two small children. Danielson and his family had arrived at Wisconsin Ranch in June 1864 and remained there until June 1866.

The attack happened on the morning of January 15. Mark Coad vividly recalled:

> Between ten and eleven o'clock in the morning the Indians made an attack on the ranch. I was standing at the door of the store and had a saddle horse with me which I was going to mount to go out after some milk cows, which were running with the cattle [a total of 44]. About twenty-five or thirty Indians made a dash on the ranch. They were mounted and had guns, bows and arrows, tomahawks and spears with them. Mr. Danielson saw the Indians and ran into the dwelling house from the store to get his wife and two children. I was standing at the door and trying to get the horse into the store but the Indians commenced hallowing at me. I could not get the horse in so I let him go and went to the counter to get a gun. We had four loaded guns on the counter. The horse ran down to the stable and one or two of the Indians ran after him. They kept shooting at us all the time and we returned their fire until they fell back. By this time Danielson got into the store with his wife and children. The Indians were all the time firing at him but shot over his head.

37   Berthong, *The Southern Cheyennes*, 227. Berthong carelessly cited reports of Lieutenant Judson Kennedy in the *War of the Rebellion* (Vol. XLVIII, part I, 41–42), where Kennedy mentioned rescuing the women and children at Wisconsin Ranch but then also reported a woman and two children killed, which was from American Ranch, not Wisconsin. And of course that report was wrong, for they were not killed (at that time) but rather captured. Other historians quote Berthong, which confuses the truth by advancing falsehoods. See, for example, John McDermott, *Circle of Fire*, 27.

38   The following account of the fight at Wisconsin Ranch comes from the lengthy depredation claim of the Coad brothers in John F. & Mark M. Coad Indian Depredation Claim #7665. Record Group 123.

We then got our guns and went on the outside. By this time they fell back and left their horses and commenced coming on foot. There were seven Indians coming from the west and seven from the east, all on foot. They were still firing on us and we at them until they came too thick. We kept them away from the corrals and stables all this time. We thought that they might cut us off from the store house and when we found that we could not defend both the corrals and the store house we fell back to the store house. We were skirmishing back and forth for about an hour and a half, when we fell back to the store house and they jumped into the hay corrals and set fire to them. They then came up to the store house and knocked on the doors and windows. They, as I have stated, had set fire to the hay corrals [150 tons of hay was estimated destroyed] and the smoke blew across to the store house and all the time they kept shooting at us but on the account of the smoke they could not distinguish where we were. When one squad got tired they would retreat and another would take their place. There were six or seven in a squad. The Indians were six or seven yards from the store and the main body of them kept out of site. Along in the middle of the afternoon Lieutenant Kennedy came up with a squad of men but did not come up close to us. He said he would have come up nearer but he would probably lose men in doing so. Everything was on fire at that time except the store house we were in and the dwelling house. The stables and corrals and lumber [twenty cords] and hay that was in the yard were all burning. Lieutenant Kennedy retreated back down the valley [to Valley Station eight miles east] and the Indians pursued him to the station five [sic] miles east of the Wisconsin ranch, where he was in camp. The Indians kept reinforcing all the time. Another crowd had captured the American ranch about this time and destroyed it. Toward evening, I think about four or five o'clock, they got armfulls of wood and hay and came around to the back door of the store to set it on fire. We did not have time to cut port holes in the wall. We had a string of wagons around the yard forty or fifty steps from the store in a half circle. The Indians who had the wood and hay came around to the back door without giving us a chance to fire at them. The door was cased on the inside and outside with pine lumber and pine boards. As the casing was perfectly dry it would take but little fire to set it afire and then the fire would go to the roof. We had the doors and windows piled up with flour and corn to keep the bullets from getting through. The Indians would shoot at the doors and windows but with the sacks of grain and flour and other stuff which were piled up in front of them the bullets could not come through to us. When they got ready to fire the wood I had Danielson pull the flour away from the door and I went out. There were three Indians at the back door. In the meantime I ordered Frank Jacques, one of the men with us, to shoot out of the side window and draw the attention of the Indians away from me. There was an old stove by the side of the store and an Indian there was trying to light a match on the stove to light a fire with some hay which he had in his hand. I saw the Indian and shot him with my gun [rifle]. I then threw the gun back into the house and took two pistols and rushed among the Indians. The Indian who I first shot, who was lighting the match on the stove, fell. The Indians were all naked except their breech clouts. One Indian had a tomahawk with him. I shot him through the breast and I wounded the other one. They shot at me but shot over my head. I jumped in through the back door but kept on my hands and knees. When I went through the door they fired a volley of bullets into the door. Danielson stood inside the door with an ax ready to assist me if I needed him. That was our plan. That was pretty near the winding up of the fight.[39]

Coad then saw the Indians take their cattle and shoot them, killing most of them. Between eight and nine that night, Lieutenant Kennedy sent a squad of men back to Wisconsin Ranch, to bring any survivors back to Valley Station. The besieged men had only three bullets left by the time the Indians withdrew. Coad tried to get some of the soldiers to remain and assist in bringing with them the undamaged goods inside the store house and dwelling house but the soldier in charge refused, saying there weren't enough men. With the promise that they would return early the next morning, everyone went to Valley Station. However, the next morning, when soldiers were sent to retrieve the goods, when they got within two miles of the ranch they saw so many Indians they retreated back to Valley Station for reinforcements.

By the time they returned, everything at the ranch was either taken or destroyed. When all had fled the dwellings the night before, Coad left a lamp burning on the table, and next to it a bottle of liquor. When he returned the next day, the lamp and liquor bottle, untouched, had been removed from the building and set out on the road, as the Indians "evidently thought it contained poison." The Indians had not yet burned the buildings and wagons, but everyone remained at Valley Station until it was thought safe to return. Six days later the Indians returned and burned down the vacant buildings and wagons.

Benjamin Danielson remembered more details relating to the January 15 attack. When it began between 10 and 11 o'clock, it initially involved from 20 to 25 Indians.

> The first we saw of the Indians was when my brother-in-law, Mark Coad, and one of the men were getting up the horses and had them saddled to look for stock. I got on a horse and went up the road for about a mile and I was attacked there by about

39   John F. & Mark M. Coad Indian Depredation Claim #7665.

ten or fifteen Indians who ran me to the ranch. I went to the dwelling house, which was about sixty or seventy-five feet from the store, to get my wife and children and take them to a safer building. In the meantime Mr. Coad tried to get his pony into the store. The Indians kept prodding him with their spears [taking coup] all the time. Finally we got in the back door of the store. While we were there they took two horses and one mule. They then left us and followed on after Lieutenant Kennedy and his soldiers who were going to Valley Station to take charge of the government corn there which was left on the prairie at that time. The soldiers came from Denver. They fought the Indians all the way down to the Valley, five miles. After the soldiers got into quarters the Indians came back to our ranch and fired our hay, stable and wood.[40]

When the Indians returned from chasing Kennedy's troopers, they put brush all around the store house and dwelling building, keeping the men and family trapped inside until about 4:30 that afternoon. When Mark Coad realized the Indians were going to burn them out he told Danielson "We have got to charge those Indians."

He [Mark Coad] could understand the Sioux language and said they meant to fire the place. We had the back door barricaded with sacks of flour. I told him it was foolish for two men to charge that band of Indians but he said it must be done as they were going to set the store on fire. I said "all right." We removed the flour from against the door and fired and we got rid of those Indians. I could not tell how many Indians we killed but, I think some of them. The others picked them up and carried them off. After we opened up and charged on the Indians they quit us and went up a mile or a mile and a half up the Platte River and camped.[41]

After the warriors had withdrawn to the west, Danielson wrote a letter for Lieutenant Kennedy at Valley Station, asking for six wagons to bring the stored goods at Wisconsin to Valley Station. He gave the letter to the young boy, "Frank" Jacques, but Jacques only proceeded a quarter of a mile before two Indians chased him back to the ranch. Danielson:

I gave him a six shooter and started him out again [on foot] and told him to keep along the river bank and he could stand off the Indians and could also keep out of sight if he did not see any and also the soldiers could see him from the Station as they were on the lookout for him. I had a field glass and I could see for a distance of five miles and I kept watch of him and I saw when he got a little over half way. Twenty-seven head of horses came out saddled on the east side of the station and

40   Benjamin Danielson Affidavit, John F. & Mark M. Coad Indian Depredation Claim #7665.
41   Benjamin Danielson Affidavit, John F. & Mark M. Coad Indian Depredation Claim #7665.

I could see one horse that had no rider. I was satisfied then that the soldiers had discovered that this man was on his way with some news. They did not know whether we were killed or not but they met this boy and took him back to Valley Station. He gave the letter to Lieutenant Kennedy but instead of him sending the wagons up he sent an escort of fifteen soldiers and an ambulance. It was about seven o'clock when we left the ranch that evening and the ambulance was too small for us to take anything in it.[42]

Everyone from Wisconsin Ranch remained at Valley Station for about two weeks. Joining them there was another company of soldiers and, according to Danielson, a seemingly unbelievably large train of 2,600 wagons heading east from Denver, where the earlier attacks along the trail caused all wagons heading in either direction to halt until now.[43] John Reynolds accompanied this train, and gave a more reasonable estimate of about 144 wagons, which included 340 men "and a great many women and children. The train was under a regular military organization [Lieutenant Albert Walter] and John Wanless, captain of the train."[44] On January 9, the train left Denver, Lieutenant Walter having been ordered to protect it at least through to Julesburg. Indians periodically harassed them through their Platte River valley jaunt, but no one was injured. They arrived in Julesburg on January 22.[45]

Another freighter named Frank Dimick accompanied this train. He provided further details:

> In the winter (January) 1865 the Indians had sent word to the settlers, or at least we understood that they sent us word that we could not get a sufficient force to go back and bring in provisions [to Denver], that they were going to starve us out. We organized a company of about five hundred of citizens with one hundred and twenty-two wagons, including a company of soldiers, headed by Major Wanless, who escorted us through. We were under strict orders to corral every night. We started for Missouri River. Our pickets were driven in one night by Indians, not far from Fort Lupton. As we got down to Godfrey's ranch we found he had been attacked. At American ranch, the Wisconsin ranch and Baker's ranch we found signs of fights with Indians, dead Indians and dead white people and the ranches

42   Benjamin Danielson Affidavit, John F. & Mark M. Coad Indian Depredation Claim #7665.

43   Doris Monahan, relying on a newspaper account, said this train consisted of 105 wagons and 300 freighters, under the command of Lieutenant Albert Walter of the 1st Colorado Cavalry. See *Destination: Denver City*, 211.

44   Frederick Z. and Hyman Z. Salomon Indian Depredation Claim #1889. Record Group 123.

45   Report of Lieutenant Albert Walter, 2nd Colorado Cavalry, February 1, 1865. *War of the Rebellion*, Vol. XLVIII, 43. Reynolds states the train left Denver on January 14, but his memory no doubt failed him when he made his affidavit nearly two decades later.

deserted, and more or less signs of Indian troubles, and all ranches deserted until we struck a body of soldiers encamped about six miles above Moore's ranch.[46]

In 1923, Mark Coad published his memoirs of the fight at his ranch. He added further details about this violent encounter on January 15. But so too, his memory of certain events back in 1865 was different than earlier recorded and some details were probably exaggerated. He noted that Lieutenant Kennedy had 25 soldiers and a few emigrants coming from Denver, and had passed American Ranch earlier in the morning, shortly before the Indians attacked that ranch, killing the men and capturing Sarah Morris and her two children. By the time that fight ended, Kennedy and his men had reached Wisconsin Ranch. When the soldiers had gone about a half-mile east of this ranch, Indians descended upon both the soldiers and the ranch. There were about 60 Indians, dividing in half for the two assaults. "The old man [James Hinds] and the young boy [Frank Jacques] were only capable of loading the guns, so the fighting was left to two men [Coad and Danielson]." After about two hours of fighting the Indians were reinforced by those warriors who had just attacked American Ranch. Soon after, the Indians began to attack the ranch simultaneously from the east and west. But they were also now under the influence of alcohol, captured at American Ranch, which made them reckless and bold, and which also explains why they continually shot over the heads of both Danielson and Coad. The Indians "made several attempts to force the door and windows of the store house open but as often as they came up we poured volleys of shot and bullets into them, killing and wounding quite a number."[47]

Early in the afternoon Lieutenant Judson Kennedy returned from Valley Station with 18 men, but could only get within a few hundred yards of the ranch before being repulsed. Coad:

After driving the soldiers back the Indians returned with a determination to capture us. They charged the doors and windows with clubs and axes and tried to force them in but we kept up a steady fire on them from the inside which soon slackened their courage. Towards sundown they concluded it was useless to try to force the ranch, so tried another plan. They left fifteen Indians behind a string of wagons that ran in a half moon circle around the store and which we used as a

46   Watson S. Coburn Indian Depredation Claim #8988. Record Group 123.
47   Mark M. Coad, "Indian Fighting in 1864," *Nebraska History*, Vol. VI, No. 4, October–December 1923, 103.

breastworks in the fore part of the fight. They sent another party with dry wood and hay which they threw against the door, the casing of the door being made of dry lumber and running to the roof. Three Indians were in the act of igniting the hay when I had Ben Danielson remove the merchandise which was piled against the door and stand at one side with an ax in case the Indians would try to rush in as soon as the door was opened. I took a Hawkins rifle, loaded and cocked, two pistols at my waist, jumped out the door, shot the first Indian with a rifle, threw the gun back into the store, jerked the pistols from my belt and went after them, shooting as fast as possible. We four were all mixed up together. I shot two down and wounded the other one. Then, squatting down close to the ground, [I] jumped back into the store. As I went to the door the fifteen Indians fired at me, but the shot passed over my head. Thus the Indians were defeated and foiled in their strategy.[48]

What a fight it had been at the Wisconsin Ranch. Near sundown Coad narrated a story different than earlier noted. Instead of the young Jacques walking to Valley Station with a letter from Danielson asking for relief, Coad says it was he who walked to Valley Station, the soldiers at first thinking he must be dead. He was so exhausted he collapsed and fainted. When he awoke the next morning, everyone had been rescued from the ranch and brought to Valley Station. Coad went on to say that he had seven muzzle loading guns that were used in the defense, firing them over 150 times. No one except some of the soldiers had breech loading rifles. Coad said he later learned from Mrs. Morris, after her rescue, that the Indians said they lost 22 dead and about 30 wounded in the fight. "When the fight ended we had only three bullets and a handful of shot left."[49]

---

48   Coad, "Indian Fighting in 1864," 103–104.
49   Coad, "Indian Fighting in 1864," 104–105.

CHAPTER SEVEN

The 1865 Indian War Continues

At the river my brother and I took charge of the horses and the other members of the party dismounted, formed a line of defense on our right and rear where the Indians were numerous and continuously exchanging shots with our men. We continued our retreat in this manner to within four or five hundred yards of our ranche, when one of the Indian shots from the rear wounded my brother and he fell, releasing the horses which he was leading. I also let loose my horses, but all the horses, being frightened, ran to and into our corral, and we lost no horses that day. I found my brother was still able to walk with the assistance we could and did give him and in this way we continued to slowly retreat to the ranche, exchanging shots with the Indians the entire distance.

CHARLES MOORE INDIAN DEPREDATION CLAIM #1240

A FTER THE FIGHT AT THE WISCONSIN RANCH, MOST OF the Cheyenne retreated back to their camp in western Kansas on Cherry Creek near present-day St. Francis, celebrating their exploits but also no doubt mourning their losses.[1] Other Indians remained along the Denver road, stealing stock wherever possible. The Cheyenne, joined with their northern brethren, along with Northern Brule and Arapaho, soon returned. St. Ledger Beck, who operated Dennison Station near present-day Iliff, Colorado, feared an attack upon his ranch similar to what happened at Wisconsin Ranch. He wisely abandoned his station on January 20, and took his family and the four wounded freighters from the earlier January 7 attack on a wagon train near his premises, six miles west to Valley

---

1   Hyde, *Life of George Bent*, 175. George Bent many times states that Indians losses were non-existent or minimal (only three Sioux killed in all the attacks along the trail that winter), 178, when they clearly were not.

Station, where there were soldiers stationed. On January 25, the Indians returned and burned his station to the ground, destroying all household contents he had left behind. He could see the flames from Valley Station, and knew his ranch was destroyed. In addition to his dwelling house, he also lost his barn and corrals, two wagons, 45 tons of hay and 16 work oxen and five cows, which he had left behind when he fled with his family the week before. On the 26th, when he tried to check on the safety of his stock, he found a party of 75 Indians still lingering about his destroyed station.[2]

On January 22, Lieutenant Walter arrived at Julesburg with the earlier noted big train that was being escorted east from Denver. He had stopped the night before at Gillette's Ranch, where another train was temporarily camped. Gillette's ranch was nine miles west of Julesburg. The day after arriving at Julesburg, Walter received a telegram instructing him to escort a freight train that was coming west to Denver. It was the train that he encountered the night before at Gillette's.

Gillette's Ranch was also known at the time as Ackley Ranch. The ranch by 1865 was owned by 25-year-old Lewis B. Gillette. In 1862, Gillette was half-owner with George B. Ackley, "selling groceries, provisions, grain, and whiskey, dealing in cattle, trading, and buying and selling them." In 1864, Gillette bought Ackley out and hence the change in the name of the ranch. Later that spring, he sold a partial interest of the ranch to William J. Cady for $1,600. The ranch consisted of a dwelling house, 22 by 44 feet, matched wooden flooring with windows and paneled doors. In addition there was a milk house, a store house measuring 24 by 36 feet with a counter and shelves across one end, a 150 foot long corral joining the store, plus two stables, each 100 feet long, and a large fenced haystack yard containing 45 tons of hay in 1865. Part of the furnishings of the dwelling house came from Samuel Bancroft, probably after he sold his ranch to the military when it then became Camp Rankin. Both Gillette and Cady were married, and Cady was Gillette's brother-in-law.[3]

On January 24, Lieutenant Walter left Julesburg, to catch up with the train at Gillette's Ranch and from there escort it to Living Springs, a ranch

---

2   St. Ledger Beck Indian Depredation Claim #2491. Record Group 123.

3   Lewis Gillette Indian Depredation Claim #2346. Record Group 123. Hugh McKan said Walter arrived at Gillette's Ranch on the evening of the 22th. Walter said he arrived the day before. See Hugh McKan Indian Depredation Claim #1889. Record Group 123. *War of the Rebellion*, Series I, Vol. XLVIII, Part I, 43.

about 45 miles from Denver. Horatio M. Foster was in charge of 19 wagons Walter was to escort. The train included 140 oxen. Using six oxen per wagon (three yoke), this left a surplus of 24 oxen to replace any stock that came up lame, etc. The freighters with Foster were Nahum C. Roswel, Robert P. Wilson, Frank Pennock, James Sutherland, brothers James and David Bogart, and Hugh McKan. Foster was in partnership with Philip Gomer, and was supervising the train when it stopped at Gillette's Ranch. Two of the wagons were owned by James Sutherland, who was freighting to Central City for merchants William Roworth and L. M. Trees, along with another merchant, Lorenzo Freas. Roworth was to receive more than 5,000 pounds of codfish, sugar, paper and glassware. L. M. Trees had ordered more than three tons of freight of various goods and groceries. Freas had ordered a ton of codfish and mackerel, more than a ton of molasses, 353 pounds of liquor, 248 pounds of sugar, 337 pounds of soap, and 562 pounds of boots.[4] The freight had been loaded at Nebraska City, and left there on November 2, which was late in the season to freight across the road to Denver. Included in the freight were 600 sacks of flour, each weighing 98 pounds, to be delivered to Frederick and Hyman Salomon in Denver. In addition, the wagons carried more than 15 tons of various foods and liquors for other merchants. They had stopped at Gillette's on January 21.

The next day, they were unable to move, since much of the stock of 140 head of oxen had scampered away the night before. Both Lieutenant Walter in his report, and Foster in his affidavit, said that Indians ran them off. But freighters James Sutherland and Hugh McKan claimed that a storm had come up and scared the stock away.[5] Both Sutherland and McKan were there and had no good reason to dispute either Walter—who may well have been told by Foster that it was Indians that caused the loss of stock—or

4   James Sutherland Indian Depredation Claim #3367. Record Group 123. See also Horatio M. Foster Indian Depredation Claim #123, Lewis Gillette Indian Depredation Claim #2346, Lorenzo Freas Indian Depredation Claim #7168, and Hugh McKan Indian Depredation Claim #1889. Record Group 123. In Horatio Foster and Philip Gomer Indian Depredation Claim #692, Frank Pennock identified the Bogarts as Daniel and Bridger. Foster died in Leadville, February 7, 1880, and left his wife Mary at the Parker Stage house with 5 children. Wilson died in the fall of 1865 in Denver.

5   Hugh McKan Indian Depredation Claim #1889, Lorenzo Freas Indian Depredation Claim #7168, and H. M. Foster and Philip Gomer Indian Depredation Claim #692. Record Group 123. *War of the Rebellion*, Series I, Vol. XLVIII, Part I, 43. James Sutherland gave his testimony that it was a storm that scattered the stock contemporaneous with Lt. Walter's report. His affidavit was dated February 20, 1865. Central City merchant Lorenzo Freas was having bad luck with freighters, for his freight was lost in the raid on the Little Blue in August 1864, and now another freight of goods was lost at Gillette's Ranch.

Foster, who might have been motivated to be untruthful because he wanted Walter to remain with the train while several of the freighters were off in an effort to find the lost stock. McKan was probably the truthful one.

Because the storm scattered the stock, there was now a delay to find them, before the train could proceed to its destination in Denver. Nevertheless, Lieutenant Walter only remained one day and then took his command and proceeded west up the road, leaving the trains he had been ordered to escort with no protection. In his report, Walter said he had ordered eight men and a guide to locate the stock and to return by nightfall. Only five soldiers returned and brought back 22 oxen. Three of his men were missing. Their names were Peter Brine, Frank Thompson and Ed Kelso. Walter remained another day, sending out more soldiers with two guides to try and find the missing soldiers. They were never found and were either victims of the Indians or perhaps deserters, though that would seem unwise in the dead of winter far out from civilization. On the 26th, Walter left Gillette's Ranch, the train unable to join him because of the failure by that time to recover the scattered stock. The freighters were upset and pleaded with Walter to remain longer until the animals could be brought in, which lends credence to McKan's claim that a storm and not Indians had scattered the stock. If Indians had taken the oxen, it was unlikely that a few men could recover them, plus the longer they were missing the farther away they would be. It took two more days—not until January 28—before all the oxen were located and brought back to the ranch. The missing soldiers had now been gone that long.[6]

The day the stock was finally recovered, 36-year-old William H. Harlow, owner of Harlow's Ranch 10 miles up the river, had stopped for the night at

---

6   McKan and Gillette Depredation Claims #1889 & 2346. Record Group 123. In 1886, Oliver Perry Wiggins stated that he was a scout stationed at Ft. Kearny in 1865 and that during this time all wagons on the road were detained at the fort until there were 100 armed men to accompany the trains, and that the Foster train had been held up until there were 100 men, and that when they preceded west they left the bigger train to go on their own. The same thing then happened at Camp Rankin, and that was why they were attacked, and that was also why Lt. Walter was ordered to find and accompany the train. Had 100 men been with the train the Indians would not have attacked them. See Horatio Foster and Philip Gomer Indian Depredation Claim #692. But, one should be careful trusting Wiggins's testimony. See entry on him in Thrapp, *Encyclopedia of Frontier Biography*, Volume III, 1563. Thrapp says "very little of what he said at various times can be substantiated. . . ." Still, it seems there is no reason to distrust Wiggins here, for his untrustworthiness came in his talking about his own exploits. It indeed might have been the case that Foster was impatient to deliver their supplies in Denver and get paid.

Gillette's. With him was his neighbor, John H. Hiteman.[7] Hiteman owned the Buffalo Springs Ranch in partnership with Hiram Davis. Davis had several months earlier bought the site from 38-year-old Mexican War veteran Guilford D. Connally for $500. He then erected the ranch, and in April 1864, entered co-partnership with "Buffalo John" Hiteman. Buffalo Springs was on the trail four miles east of Harlow's Ranch. After Connally sold the site to Davis, he then erected a ranch one mile east of Julesburg Station, and joined a partnership in running it with E. D. Bulen, together operating the Connally and Bulen Ranch. Bulen did not have the capital in the ranch that Connally had, but he was given a share for working the ranch, while Connally stayed with his family at his home ranch and headquarters in Nebraska City. In addition to the store, their ranch was located at one of the crossings of the Platte River, and they made a good amount of money assisting travelers in crossing the river. Both men also were heavily involved in freighting, having at various times as many as 30 wagons delivering goods anywhere from Nebraska City to Fort Kearny and on to Denver, in addition to supplying groceries and general merchandise for sale at their ranch east of Julesburg. Both men were present during the earlier January 7 attack at their ranch, but shortly after that Connally left for his home station in Nebraska and Bulen and four ranchmen were left to continue to run the Connally and Bulen Ranch.[8]

William Harlow and his wife soon learned of the fights at Godfrey's, the American and Wisconsin ranches west of their living quarters. Mrs. Harlow's father owned one of the ranches in the fights, and had come east to warn them. They then went east to Buffalo Springs Ranch, to warn John Hiteman and Hiram Davis of what they had learned. Davis then went to Julesburg, to find out what he could of the Indian troubles. Arriving at Julesburg, he was told the Indians had another fight there the day before and that one citizen had been killed. Davis returned to his ranch and then went with Harlow back to his ranch, where they stayed the night. The next

7   The Harlow Depredation claim has Hiteman's affidavit, which is typed, and his name is wrongly spelled John H. Hutchinson, not Hiteman. However, in all other depredation claims he is named John H. Hiteman, co-partner with William Harlow of Buffalo Spring Ranch. Captain Nicholas O'Brien said he was known at the time as Buffalo John. See Hiram Davis Indian Depredation Claim #2332. See also Connally and Bulen Indian Depredation Claim #2619. Record Group 123.

8   Connally and Bulen Indian Depredation Claim #2619. See also Guilford D. Connally and James G. Romine Indian Depredation Claim #7173. Record Group 123.

morning, Davis tried to take Mrs. Harlow to her father's ranch up the river, but after about five miles they returned to Harlow's Ranch, fearing it was not safe to be on the trail. When they returned only a sick boy was inside the ranch, as Harlow and his two ranch hands were on the other side of the river, trying to retrieve two of Harlow's wagons, which they were unable to do because of the ice on the river. They left the wagons and stayed one more night at Harlow's place. Only having two horses among them, it was agreed that Davis would ride one to Julesburg and get a military escort to bring the Harlow party in. But before he left, his partner John Hiteman brought two wagons to the ranch and escorted everybody to Julesburg. They arrived unmolested. In fact, the entire road from Harlow's Ranch to Julesburg was quiet and peaceful.[9]

Having seen no Indians on their trek to Julesburg Station—and with the protection of the soldiers at nearby Camp Rankin—Harlow decided to venture back to his ranch. He wanted to fill the wagons left on the other side of the river with the many valuables he had left inside his ranch and then return to Julesburg. With his two men he returned, retrieved the earlier abandoned wagons back across the river, loaded them up with corn and other goods, and then proceeded east to Julesburg. They arrived at Gillette's Ranch, nine miles from their destination, just after sunset, on January 28. Afraid to continue on in the dark through the sand hills, they decided to stay the night at the ranch before proceeding on to Julesburg the next morning.[10]

When dawn came Harlow was preparing to resume his journey back east to Julesburg while Foster's 19 wagons were now ready to depart west, but without the military escort under Lieutenant Walter. It was Foster's unfortunate fate that just before sunup—January 29—as they were eating breakfast three Indians were observed placing a black flag on a pole (a sign of death) and sticking it in the ground in front of the ranch. They then ran off the stock. Harlow and two other men quickly saddled horses and went after the Indians. However, they soon encountered countless warriors coming at them from all directions. They hurriedly retreated back to the house and then the fight was on. There were four men at the ranch—one of whom was a Negro—and 14 freighters—18 men in all—defending each other from the attack. They fought until five o'clock that night. The wagons were close

---

9   William H. Harlow Indian Depredation Claim #2990.
10 William H. Harlow Indian Depredation Claim #2990.

to the ranch, which allowed the men to be able to keep the Indians from molesting them, though there were several charges made throughout the day try to get at the wagons. The Indians did set fire to the two stables, the hay stack and the wood yard, which created quite a fire. They also tried to set fire to the house but were unable to get close enough to succeed.[11]

When the Indians retreated at sundown, Harlow and others went outside and found four dead Indians near the house. Cheyenne Chief Graybeard later stated that the Cheyenne were not part of this raid but that the Sioux were, and that four Sioux were killed in the fight.[12] Captain Nicholas O'Brien, on the other hand, insisted that Cheyenne were involved in the fight and said the two leaders were Black Kettle and White Antelope. However, he clearly could not be right about this, as White Antelope had been killed at Sand Creek. George Bent said Black Kettle had taken the main portion of his tribe, consisting of 80 lodges, and moved south of the Arkansas River just before other Cheyenne went back up to the Platte River valley to join the Sioux and continue their raids. O'Brien also named Bad Wound, Blue Nose, Man Afraid of His Horse, and Little Thunder as Lakota leaders of the raid.[13] Friday, an Arapaho chief, admitted that there was a large party of both Cheyenne and Arapaho who participated in this attack. But these probably would have been northern bands. He remembered how easy it was to run off the stock.[14] Indian Agent Valentine T. McGillycuddy later identified the bands as the "Cut-Offs, the Upper Brules, the Northern Arapahoes and Northern Cheyennes. There was also a mixed band of predatory Sioux under a chief called Two Face."[15] If McGillycuddy was right about the Indians involved, they were the same ones that did the deadly Nebraska raids in August 1864, on the Little Blue and Plum Creek. They were merely continuing the war they had begun before Sand Creek.

---

11   William H. Harlow Indian Depredation Claim #2990. Hugh McKan stated that 12 Indians were killed—probably an exaggeration—though this is also the total dead that James Sutherland said were killed in the fight. Harlow gave a different account of how the fight occurred, saying the wagon train had just departed Gillette's ranch when 500 Indians descended down upon them from nearby bluffs, and that the fight happened away from the ranch. All of the other witness affidavits place the fight at the ranch store house. See McKan testimony in H. M. Foster Indian Depredation Claim #692. See Sutherland testimony in Lorenzo Freas Indian Depredation Claim #7168.

12   Saloman Indian Depredation Claim #1889. Record Group 123.

13   Hiram Davis Indian Depredation Claim #2332. Record Group 123. Hyde, *Life of George Bent*, 77.

14   Red Cloud Agency Indian Agent J. J. Savaille interview with Friday, Salomon Depredation Claim #1889.

15   William Harlow Indian Depredation Claim #2990.

It was good the fight ended when it did, because the defenders had used up nearly all of their ammunition.[16] Around eight o'clock that evening the barricaded men, having seen the Indians grow in strength during the day-long fight, realized there was no way they could withstand a night attack or another attack the next day. Prudently they sought to escape east under cover of darkness. In order to avoid detection in their retreat, they made a bright light in the store house, and then crawled on their hands and knees out the back of the building until they reached the river, where they then walked on the frozen ice down to Julesburg Station and the protection of the soldiers at nearby Camp Rankin.[17]

A young woman was with a military escort coming east from Denver a few days later and she recalled what she was told had happened. During the day long fight the Indians were able to plunder one of the wagons which contained whiskey.

> At night the fire-water circulated around the [Indian] camp fire, and by two o'clock the [warrior] guards stationed near the house fell asleep too. There was a tiny window at the back of the station which the Indians either didn't see or thought too small for a man's head to pass, so no guard was placed at the back of the house. A man can creep through a very small hole when his life is depending on it, and the eighteen men got through, dropped to the ground, and crawled to the river, which was frozen, and thus escaped to Julesburg. . . .[18]

Further east at Beauvais Station, Indians made a raid and stole 12 oxen and two cows. Gemenien P. Beauvais actually operated two ranches, one called Beauvais Ranch, which was situated along the Platte River about five miles east of Fort Laramie, and the other called Beauvais Station, which was on the south side of the South Platte River about 20 miles east of Julesburg. It was an important stop along the Denver road. Beauvais experienced many Indian raids at both places. Later in the fall, on November 2, Indians again raided his station on the South Platte, stealing 41 work oxen and two more milk cows.[19]

By this time there were as many as 140 people congregating around

16   William H. Harlow Indian Depredation Claim #2990. William M. Roworth Indian Depredation Claim #5864. Record Group 123.

17   Gillette Depredation Claim #2346. Sutherland Depredation Claim #3367.

18   Mrs. Halie Riley Hodder, "Crossing the Plains in War Times," *The Colorado Magazine*, Vol. X, Number 4, July 1933, 133.

19   G. P. Beauvais Indian Depredation Claim #6498. Record Group 123.

Julesburg, 40–45 of them soldiers at Camp Rankin. Things turned even uglier on February 2. Captain Nicholas O'Brien, along with Lieutenant Eugene Ware, a sergeant and five enlisted men were returning to Camp Rankin from Camp Cottonwood near present-day Maxwell, Nebraska.[20] Fortunately they had carried with them a mountain howitzer. When they reached Alkali Station on January 31, they were joined by a stage carrying two passengers and two riders.[21] On February 2, they were about 17 miles east of Julesburg when they stopped at Big Springs Station, a ranch serving travelers, operated by Richard Cleave. From there they could see smoke coming from the direction of Julesburg. Richard and his wife, fearing for their safety, joined the entourage in its trek to Camp Rankin. Shortly after leaving they saw a party of Indians on the opposite side of the Platte take Cleave's cattle and spirit them away to the north. He lost over 200 head of cattle.[22]

Colonel Robert R. Livingston, commanding the First Nebraska Cavalry, had about 300 men with him at Alkali Station 25 miles east of Big Springs, having arrived there in the early afternoon on February 2. Several days earlier, about 70 Indians had robbed the stock of Mahlon H. Brown who was camped near the station. He lost 275 of his 300 cattle.[23] From there people could see the smoke of the fires at Julesburg during the day. In his report filed two weeks later, Livingston elucidated details of the events as they unfolded during the attack. Although Captain O'Brien was in command of the 7th Iowa Cavalry stationed at Camp Rankin, it was Lieutenant John S. Brewer who was commanding the troops left at the camp. Captain O'Brien and Lieutenant Ware were away at the time. Fearing that O'Brien would come under attack as he was returning west on the trail to Camp Rankin, Brewer sent 30 men from the post east to find and safely escort O'Brien and his small party back to camp. The two groups of men apparently did not meet. But in sending out the men to find O'Brien, Brewer was left with only 15 men to defend Rankin and nearby Julesburg.

According to Livingston, the Indians were aware of the few soldiers left

20   Report of Nicholas O'Brien, Richard Cleave Indian Depredation Claim #2151. Record Group 123.

21   Ware, The Indian War of 1864, 495–496.

22   Richard Cleave Indian Depredation Claim #2151. Ware, in The Indian War of 1864, notes Cleave's name as Cleve (497). The depredation claim corrects the name as Cleave. Cleave had been a Pony Express rider in 1860–1861 and worked for the Overland Stage company from that time up until 1864, when he built his own ranch. Testimony in the claim places the ranch anywhere from three miles to 12 miles east of Julesburg.

23   Maylon H. Brown Indian Depredation Claim #10580 & 10819. Record Group 123.

behind, and it was Camp Rankin that the Indians were hoping to destroy on February 2. They used the burning of Julesburg as an attempt to get the soldiers to leave the confines of the camp and then overwhelm and kill them. A telegram was quickly sent—the wire not yet destroyed—from Julesburg east to Alkali Station when the attack began, and where Colonel Livingston had just arrived with his large body of troops. After receiving the telegram, Livingston ordered his command west. Marching all afternoon and through the night, they finally arrived at Camp Rankin at four o'clock on the morning of February 3.

Meanwhile, the Indians had divided into three bodies to descend upon Julesburg, each comprising more than 600 warriors. Lieutenant Brewer, realizing the futility of trying to come to the defense of the men at Julesburg Station, kept his small command inside the post and tried to help by occasionally firing a howitzer in the direction of the Indians. Julesburg, however, was just beyond range. Each building at the small town was separately burned, "the Indians firing one and then waiting to see the effect; then another, and so on till all were consumed." In addition to the burning of Julesburg, the Indians had destroyed the telegraph line for 12 miles on the Denver road, and 33 miles along the road to Fort Laramie. Brewer fought for several hours to protect the post from a direct assault.[24]

George Bent later confirmed the details of Livingston's report to such an extent that one must conclude that he had Livingston's report on hand when he wrote his reminiscences.[25] Bent:

> I went with the war party [February 2], and again the Indians tried the old trick of luring the soldiers out of their stockade by hiding the warriors among the hills and sending out a small party to tempt the soldiers out; but the troops this time were on their guard and would not stir outside their defenses, so after waiting among the sand hills for some time, our whole body charged out and raced across the flats to the stockade.... The Indians circled around the stockade, yelling and shooting and taunting the soldiers, to get them to come out and fight; but it was

24 Colonel Robert R. Livingston, "Report," February 18, 1865. *War of the Rebellion*, Series I, Vol. XLVIII, Part I, 89. George Bent says the telegraph was destroyed to the west all the way to Valley Station, and about 20 miles of wire on the route to Ft. Laramie. See Hyde, *Life of George Bent*, 186.

25 Lincoln Faller has extensively studied Bent's letters, noting that they require "reading between the lines to be understood." Faller also wrote that Bent worked with a man named B. W. Butler, who lived in Washington, DC, and contributed "a significant amount of work . . . through his access to government archives." See Faller, "Making Medicine," 72, 75.

no use . . . so after a while we withdrew east to the stage station. Here the warriors, about six hundred strong, broke into the store and stage company warehouse, and completely plundered both. The stage company had a big supply of shelled corn in bags in their warehouse, and the Indians took this corn on the pack ponies, and carried it north of the river, later sanding the ice of the Platte so the ponies would cross without slipping. In the hope of drawing the soldiers out, as soon as they plundered the buildings, the Indians set fire to them, one by one, burning the stage station, telegraph office, store, warehouse, stables, etc., each separately.[26]

While the Indians had nearly finished the burning and sacking of Julesburg, Captain O'Brien and his small party of soldiers and civilians were cautiously approaching from the east. They knew something was amiss with all the smoke they could see coming from Julesburg. When about four miles from the post, they reached a place O'Brien called Devil's Dive. O'Brien slowly peered over the hill, the ground from where they were approaching providing the small group some protection in being observed. He then saw the various buildings at the stage station all afire, with Indians pillaging and running about killing stock and taking goods.[27] The smoke from the burning dwellings acted as concealment for the small detail and allowed them to get within a couple miles from Camp Rankin. But from there they would be exposed if they continued on to the post. However, according to the reminiscences of Lieutenant Ware, they had their howitzer loaded with canister and ready to fire and they had the element of surprise, knowing the Indians would not realize that their charge into the post was not a regiment of soldiers coming to the rescue. They stopped for about two hours, made repairs on the howitzer, and plotted their bold move.[28]

Lieutenant Ware described the ruse:

> As we came over the hill we deployed at intervals of about twenty yards, with our artillery and coach up in the center of the line. Some of the Indians began to see us; then we went a-howling and yelling towards the post. It did not take us long to pass the burning stage station. The Indians were rallying on both sides of us, shooting at us from a distance; they did not know but what a regiment was coming from behind us.

---

26 Hyde, *Life of George Bent*, 182–183.

27 O'Brien testimony in Hiram Davis Indian Depredation Claim #2332. This land is today owned by Jay Goddard.

28 Ware, *Indian War of 1864*, 500–501. Richard Cleave Indian Depredation Claim #2151, testimony of Cleave.

Continuing on past the Julesburg Stage Station the howitzer canister was ordered fired. The post was still a mile away. The soldiers at the post saw the men coming and ordered their howitzer fired toward the Indians. This confused the warriors and kept them from realizing it was all a bluff:

> They did not know what was behind us, or what the smoke might conceal. They did not dare to charge us, but got out of our way and hovered on our flanks. We, all the time, were going as fast as our horses would carry us toward the post. We went through with the Indians firing and cavorting all over the prairie. Not a man in our party was injured. The Indians, like a hive of bees, showed great alarm, and were dashing around in groups.[29]

Captain O'Brien later described the approach to the fort this way: "We had a lively little run getting in and were attacked several times and once or twice the Indians came pretty near and I heard them hollering in their language."[30]

There is conflicting first-hand testimony regarding this escape into the safety of Camp Rankin. Andrew Hughes, the stage driver accompanied by O'Brien's small detail, gave a different account, which calls to doubt Ware's riveting story. According to Hughes, the fires from Julesburg were noticed about two o'clock that afternoon.

> We halted some distance east of the place [Julesburg] for a time, *until the Indians evacuated the premises*, and crossed the Platte River to the north side. After this halt for, say, an hour, *and the departure of the savages*, we went to the station, and found everything in the shape of a house, or a building of any sort, on fire, and too far advanced to be extinguished. . . . *After we had been there a short time, some troops came to the station from the post near there, then called Fort Rankin, and we passed on with them to that post the same evening.*[31]

Given that Hughes made his statement four days after the incident and Ware wrote his reminiscences 46 years later, one must accept the account

---

29 Ware, *Indian War of 1864*, 503–504.
30 O'Brien affidavit in Richard Cleave Indian Depredation Claim #2151. In 1889, testifying in the claim of Abram T. Litchfield's depredation claim, O'Brien said that he observed the fight from about four miles east of Julesburg and that when he came in he and his men helped to put out some of the fires at Julesburg, implying his party had waited until the Indians left and then came into Camp Rankin. See Abram T. Litchfield Indian Depredation Claim #4843. Record Group 123. See also Litchfield claim #1127, Record Group 123.
31 Andrew S. Hughes affidavit, December 6, 1865. Italics added. Testimony in the Claim of Ben Holladay, 28. Emphasis added.

of Hughes and dismiss Ware's enthralling but inaccurate remembrance of the O'Brien party's jaunt into Camp Rankin.

It is hard to find accurate information as to the number of people killed in this February 2 attack upon Julesburg. George Bent, who was present at both the January and February attacks, and who implicated Southern Cheyenne as accomplices in the Platte valley fights, does not mention any white casualties, nor does George Bird Grinnell in *The Fighting Cheyennes*. But there were casualties. At least four civilians were killed near Julesburg. One of the freight trains there at that time was a large train of 25 wagons owned by Abram Litchfield. Having arrived at the station about a month earlier, the perishable goods were stored in the warehouse at Julesburg, while the train was waiting better weather to venture on the road to its Denver destination. A few of the wagons along with the stock and five herders were in camp a few miles out from Julesburg, at the American Fork of the Platte. On the morning of the fight, Thomas Sergent and four other herders were attacked by several warriors. All were killed and scalped except Sergent, who was able to escape to Julesburg. Four wagons and their contents were burned. Several of the cattle were killed, the rest taken.[32]

With this attack and burning of Julesburg, other attacks were made in the ensuing days, and nearly all of the ranches and stage stations for several miles in both directions from Julesburg were either attacked and then burned or simply burned, the owners having earlier left the premises for protection at Camp Rankin to the east or Valley Station to the west. The Indians had been camped on the north side of the Platte River for at least a week prior to the burning of Julesburg, committing violent sorties up and down the valley. Ben Holladay, at that time the owner and operator of the Overland Stage Company, suffered losses at Julesburg Station, which included the telegraph office, station house, barn, warehouse, blacksmith's shop, corrals, 30 tons of hay, 3,500 sacks of corn weighing 196 tons, along with one horse.[33]

Because the ranches and stage stations had been abandoned before the final assault on Julesburg, it is difficult to ascertain exactly when they were burned. Colonel Robert Livingston, in his report dated February 5, gave the following breakdown: At Lillian Springs three Indians were killed in an all

---

32   Abram T. Litchfield Indian Depredation Claim #4843.
33   "Claim of Ben Holladay."

day fight on January 27, after which the ranch was burned. Antelope Station, Buffalo Springs Ranch, Harlow's Ranch and Spring Hill Station were all burned on January 28. Gillette's Ranch was burned after their fight, which Livingston says occurred on January 25. He also said that Julesburg, as well as the Connally and Bulen ranch were burned on January 28.[34] Given that he is wrong in his dates with the burnings at Gillette's, Julesburg and Bulen's, we cannot know for sure when each of the other ranches was burned. That the burnings occurred sometime between January 25 and February 3 is likely. The destruction of these ranches, however, was extensive, severely hindering accessibility to the Denver road, both to and from Denver.

Philip Gomer, who was in the fight at Gillette's Ranch on January 29, lost 140 oxen, 19 wagons and goods, the value of which he over-inflated the value at nearly $30,000 ($20,000 more for the oxen and wagons).[35] Lewis Gillette claimed a loss of $21,511.10 for the burning of his ranch and theft of merchandise. Gillette gave impressive details of his ranch, which included a stable 100 feet long, another double stable, underground milk house, and the dwelling his family lived in. Gillette:

> The size of the dwelling in 1865 was 22 by 24, wooden floors, good dressed and matched flooring; the casings, mopboards and windows were of good material and the doors were paneled. The house was plastered, and the roof was made of pine poles brought from the mountains, with plank laid on top of them, then a sod cut two inches in thickness was laid on top of the plank, then the pole or piece of joist was pinned or spiked on the edges of the rail, then about four inches of loose dirt put on the top of the sod. The milk house was about 10 by 12 feet, dug in the ground about five feet and then a sod wall was laid up a couple of feet more, and then a roof the same as that of the dwelling house: that was also plastered inside. The store building was 24 by 36 feet, floored with fencing, and had a counter across one end, and shelves on that end; the windows were half sash, and the doors home-made, and the roof was the same as the dwelling house. The corral joined the store and was 150 feet long: it was built of sod seven or eight feet high with a gate 7 or 8 feet high made of pine lumber. There were two stables 100 feet long, double stables. I don't know how wide: I think they must have been 24 feet wide. The stables were covered with poles and hay; there was a fence built around the hay stack yard.[36]

---

34   Colonel Robert R. Livingston, Report, February 5, 1865. *War of the Rebellion*, Series I, Vol. XLVIII, Part I, 40–41.

35   Philip Gomer Indian Depredation Claim #2347.

36   Lewis Gillette Indian Depredation Claim #2346.

Hiram Davis and John Hiteman operated Buffalo Spring Ranch/Antelope Station, which was situated a little over four miles west from Gillette's Ranch. Like Gillette's, Buffalo Springs was also burned. The loss at this ranch was valued at $9,625, and included a two-room dwelling house built of shingled pine lumber, including the floors, each room 16 by 18 feet, a 20-by-100-foot sod barn, and a 300-foot-square corral. In addition to having 75 tons of hay burned at their ranch they also lost ten oxen at the Gillette's Ranch fight.[37]

William Harlow was also in the Gillette fight. He owned Harlow's Ranch, 10 miles west from Gillette's Ranch. He valued his loss at $16,670, which included his two wagons and stock lost at Gillette's. He believed his ranch was burned on January 29, because during the fight at Gillette's they could see the fires from the direction of his ranch and two others; they assumed all the ranches were torched. Harlow described his ranch as follows:

> A dwelling house with four rooms, 12 by 14 feet, the others were smaller. They were principally made of adobe, or dried sod, covered with boards and dirt. The storehouse was 16 by 24. Some of the rooms had floors in them and some not. I had one general storage room, a stable for the accommodation of 100 head of stock, and barns. I had 3 or 4 corrals about 75 feet square. The walls were about five feet high and two feet thick.... The store room had counters through one side, with shelves running up to the ceiling, and well fixed for selling goods. I did not remove any of my property before its destruction. My recollection is that my wife took some of her clothing away when she left, but very little of it.[38]

Albert Thorne operated Spring Hill Stage Station, the next station two miles west of Harlow's Ranch. He did not own the ranch there, but rather operated the station for Ben Holladay since 1863. As a stage station it did not accommodate freighters or other travelers. It was strictly there for stage passengers. Consequently, there was not a large stock of goods on hand. It did however provide meals for the stage passengers. Thorne had apparently abandoned the station when the earlier attacks happened in January. While he claimed a loss of 120 tons of hay at a cost of $9,000 ($75 per ton), Hiram Davis said it was no more than 30 tons. Further, however, Ben Holladay claimed a Spring Hill Station loss of 20 tons of Hay at $50 per ton for a total

---

37 Hiram Davis Indian Depredation Claim #2332.
38 William Harlow Indian Depredation Claim #2990.

loss of $1,000.[39] The stage building was smaller than the common ranch buildings in the valley. Holladay claimed a loss of $6,000 for "a framed barn, and dwelling house with four rooms, with furniture complete, destroying stores, &c."[40]

G. D. Connally and E. D. Bulen had a loss they valued at $29,292.50. They claimed that for the 18 months prior to the burning of their ranch, on either January 29 or February 2, they had a net monthly profit of $700, which is equivalent to today at over $10,000 profit each month, which seems incredible. Their ranch included two buildings accommodating public travel, a barn, corral and various outbuildings, all of which they valued at $3,000. Their biggest loss included 150 fat work oxen valued at $100 each. In addition they lost four freight wagons and all the contents of the houses and other buildings when burned.

Connally described his burned property:

> My buildings consisted of what they call dobe [sic], covered with logs split and dirt over. The dimensions of them . . . was about 18 feet wide by 36 long—one story, partition through the center and also another building, the dimensions of which were about 18 or 20 feet wide and pretty much the same length. My stable was of a capacity to hold at least 125 or 130 head of horses—stalls on each side with regular mangers for hay purposes and covered the same, as I mentioned my house—logs and dirt. My corral was large enough, I suppose, to hold three or four hundred head of cattle. . . .[41]

Freighter James G. Romine was at Connally and Bulen's Ranch when the Indian attacked it. He had arrived there about Christmas and remained assisting four other men at the ranch when the Indians made their final raid.

---

39   Albert Thorne Indian Depredation Claim #2333. Record Group 123. "Claim of Ben Holladay," 22. This is a good example of potential fraud in the Indian depredation claims system. Not only does Thorne misrepresent himself as the owner of the Spring Hill Ranch, when in fact it was Spring Hill Station, he also extremely overinflated both the amount and value of hay. Fortunately, however, such claims, in the process of investigation, were generally rooted out as fraudulent, as is exactly what happened with Thorne's claim. Nevertheless, Thorne's claim has a signed affidavit from John Coad saying Thorne operated Spring Hill Station in 1862 and 1863, but after that time he quit his employ there and opened a private ranch "in the vicinity of the station and named it Spring Hill Ranch." If what Coad says is true, the Holladay's claim for Spring Hill Station is different than Thorne's claim for Spring Hill Ranch. Though Thorne's depredation claim has this affidavit, the final adjudication rejected upon insufficient evidence the entire claim.

40   "Claim of Ben Holladay," 34.

41   Connally and Bulen Indian Depredation Claim #2619. Record Group 123.

All apparently were able to escape into nearby Camp Rankin. Romine lost three wagons and 22 oxen.[42]

Freight business partners William Dillon and John Maxwell had their wagon train under wagon master G. D. Todd, who left four empty wagons and three lame oxen at Connally and Bulen's Ranch earlier in December. Seven more oxen were left at Moore's Ranch. Their wagons were burned and the oxen stolen. Indeed, all the cattle up and down the valley at the various ranches and stage stops were either stolen or killed. The total loss of cattle killed and stolen was about 1,500.[43]

Among the victims of theft and attack were the Moore brothers, operating Washington Ranch (also called at the time Moore Ranch), three miles east of Valley Station. They lost between 400 and 600 oxen, mules and cattle. Brothers Charles A. and James A. were born in Poland, Portage County, Ohio. When James Moore bought out Charles's partner Joseph Nesbitt in the early spring of 1864, Charles took 48 mules and drove them to Platts-mouth on the Missouri River and procured four six-yoke teams, attached them to freight wagons loaded with general merchandise along with a span of horses attached to another freight wagon loaded with goods. He then proceeded to Washington Ranch, arriving safely about December 15, just before the general attacks along the Platte valley. Early in the morning of January 28, about 100 Indians succeeded in driving off about 600 cattle which had been grazing, as they always did, on the north side of the Platte.[44] This was necessary because all freight animals traveling on the south side had used up all the grazing feed available there.

When the Moore brothers saw the Indians taking their cattle on the north side of the river, James hurriedly traveled west all the way to present-day Fort Morgan, soliciting help from soldiers and other ranchers to pursue the Indians and recover the stock.[45] A party of soldiers numbering 18 men

---

42   Guilford D. Connally and James G. Romine Indian Depredation Claim #7173. Record Group 123. See also Romine's testimony in William Dillon and John Maxom Indian Depredation Claim #2503.

43   Livingston, Report, February 5, 1865. *War of the Rebellion*, 41.

44   This is the date set by Lieutenant J. J. Kennedy in his report dated January 29. See *War of the Rebellion*, 42. Colonel Livingston said this happened on January 26. See *War of the Rebellion*, 41. The Moore depredation claim said it was late in the month.

45   James was in error in his recollections, saying he went west to Fort Morgan, as Fort Morgan had not been erected in early 1865. He must have meant Valley Station where he secured the help of soldiers. He probably ventured as far west as Beaver Creek Station, near where Fort Morgan would be erected, and solicited ranchers and other men to assist in the recovery of his stolen stock.

under the command of Lieutenants Judson Kennedy and Albert Walter, along with about 20 ranchers, which included Mark Coad and a man named Perkins, accompanied Moore and together the party pursued the Indians for about 15 miles north of the Platte to a canyon called Lewis's Canyon, where a fight then ensued the next morning. Kennedy reported killing 10 Indians along with seven ponies, and recovered about 300 of the cattle. Walter reported killing nine Indians and having three of his men slightly wounded. He said they recovered about 200 head of cattle. The cattle were brought back to Washington Ranch, but only about 100 were corralled. That was a mistake, because the Indians soon returned and took all the cattle not corralled. This led to yet another pursuit with Kennedy's men and another 20 soldiers under the command of Lieutenant Walter. According to Lieutenant Kennedy the Indians were again caught and another fight happened. Kennedy reported killing 20 Indians and recapturing 400 cattle.[46]

When the soldiers left on this second foray, Washington Ranch was left with 11 soldiers for protection. Charles Moore tells what happened next:

The following morning after the party returned to the ranch [with the recovered cattle] my brother with Sergeant Smith and ten Colorado volunteer soldiers rode out on the prairie in quest of those cattle which were not corralled the night before at the time of their return. They left at the ranch only myself and a few employees of ours. Shortly after their departure we at the ranch observed some indistinguishable dark objects on either side of the stage road about a half mile east of our ranch on a hill. I rode rapidly to the top of this hill and these objects were not there any longer, but in the next valley, three or four hundred yards distant, were a large number of Indians, not less than seventy-five or one hundred, mounted on horses; on seeing me they pursued me to within range of the guns of my men stationed at our ranch. I encouraged our men at the ranch to defend themselves and the ranch as best they could and I continued to run my horse in a southerly direction to the top of a hill about a half mile distant from our ranch, hoping to locate my brother and his party and warn them of the presence of the Indians. I was unable to see my brother's party from the hill but on looking toward the ranch I observed several mounted Indians on the open prairie completely cutting off my retreat to the ranche. My only refuge then was Valley Station, three miles west of our ranche. I immediately ran my horse in that direction the Indians following closely. One of them having a better horse than mine was about overtaking me, having shot several arrows at me, when on arriving at a small elevation of the road I came suddenly in front of

46 Charles Moore Indian Depredation Claim #1240. Kennedy Report, *War of the Rebellion*, 42. *War of the Rebellion*, 41–42.

my brother and his party. This caused the race to change its course, the Indians now taking the lead.[47] This situation continued but a short time, as the Indians were reinforced with a larger part of their party, and we were compelled to take a detour to the left of the road, to seek protection of the river bank. At the river my brother and I took charge of the horses and the other members of the party dismounted, formed a line of defense on our right and rear where the Indians were numerous and continuously exchanging shots with our men. We continued our retreat in this manner to within four or five hundred yards of our ranche, when one of the Indian shots from the rear wounded my brother and he fell, releasing the horses which he was leading. I also let loose my horses, but all the horses, being frightened, ran to and into our corral, and we lost no horses that day. I found my brother was still able to walk with the assistance we could and did give him and in this way we continued to slowly retreat to the ranche, exchanging shots with the Indians the entire distance.

The Indians continued to occupy the high ground surrounding the ranch during the day, shooting several shots into the cattle in the corral from the hill top south of the ranch and wounding several of the cattle, but they did not make any further assault upon us during that day but collected all the cattle they could find in the vicinity of said ranch and drove them away. The numbers of these was not less than one hundred head. We were confined to our ranch without any help or assistance for five days after the fight last stated, when Lieutenant Murphy came up the road with five companies of cavalry and a large caravan of freight and immigrant wagons. He was repairing the telegraph line, the poles of which had been burned for a distance of twenty-five miles in our section of the road. After the departure of the Indians our men reported the counting of over two hundred beef heads found on our range and the hill north of us, showing that the Indians had killed that many cattle for immediate use while camped near us at the time of the raid I have mentioned.[48]

The injury to Jim Moore was serious, and it was uncertain whether he would live or die. Mrs. Halie Riley Hodder was with the military escort that Charles Moore recalled coming to the ranch five days after his brother was severely wounded. Mrs. Riley recalled that when the escort stopped at Valley Station, one group of men with 10 wagons—unfortunately she was in one of those wagons—decided to venture five miles further to the Moore ranch. Before the wagons left Denver, they had been warned to carry their own provisions as all the ranches on the road east had been destroyed by

---

47 It appears this change in course meant that the men turned about and went toward Washington Ranch. This makes sense when Moore next said the men veered to the left to get to the river.

48 Charles Moore Indian Depredation Claim #1240.

the Indians, so no goods could be purchased. But at Valley Station, they were told the next ranch east was still operating and thus the decision to go unescorted an additional few miles to the ranch. The ride from Valley Station to Washington Ranch was fast and perilous. She remembered being thrown about in the wagon like baseballs. When they arrived at the ranch there were only three men inside, and one— Jim Moore—was severely wounded. Her memory remained vivid with what she saw: "... there the poor man lay—the most terrible sight I have ever seen, with his head swelled almost to the width of his shoulders. Why he didn't die I cannot say."[49]

By early March, Jim Moore was recovering well enough to get back on his feet. Frank Root, who later left his memoirs in *The Overland Trail to California*, visited overnight at Washington Ranch on his way from Denver to Atchison. Leaving Denver on a stage on March 1, the coach arrived at Moore's place on March 4, one month after Riley was at the ranch. Root found both Moore brothers narrating their recent fight and Jim's wounding. He described Jim Moore as "the same genial, good natured fellow he had always been, and jokingly remarked that he was ready for another brush with the murderous scalp-lifters."[50] Moore's sense of humor was further shown at this time in the placing of an old churn mounted on wooden wheels, to give it the appearance of a howitzer, which was placed in front of the ranch to keep the Indians away. Root felt it worked; but the truth was, there was little left for the Indians to come back and raid. Supplies were desperately needed in Denver, and the attacks only temporarily stopped the large caravans of freight wagons along the trail. At Beauvais Ranch Root passed a wagon train consisting of 180 wagons loaded with supplies traveling west to Denver.[51]

---

49 Mrs. Hodder, "Crossing the Plains in War Times," 132. Hodder's reminiscences came years later and she did not remember Jim Moore's name, or the name of the ranch. But it is clear in reading her story, coupled with when the train left Denver, that this was the person she saw severely wounded.

50 Root and Connelly, *Overland Stage*, 386.

51 Root and Connelly, *Overland Stage*, 387.

CHAPTER EIGHT

The War Stays Hot

*During my conversation with them, the Cheyennes stated that their home
was on the Arkansas River, that many of them had served in the late Rebel
Army under General Price; ... that they had been but a short time in this
part of the country, and on their way up, attacked and killed Lieut. Collins
and twenty-seven men at or near Platte Bridge, also that they had captured
a citizen wagon train somewhere on their route. They seemed very anxious
to enter into a treaty with the whites, provided that they be permitted to go
to their homes on the Arkansas River but under no other condition would
they make peace.*

REPORT OF GEORGE W. WILLIFORD
OCTOBER 9, 1865, RECORD GROUP 393
DEPARTMENT OF THE MISSOURI, PART 1, ENTRY 2639

AFTER THE WARRIORS LEFT THE SOUTH PLATTE RIVER
valley, the violence shifted north, as well as east along the Platte
River road. The devastation along the Denver road was significant
and little was left to attack and plunder for the Indians. They moved north,
settling their large village on Lodgepole Creek, south of Mud Springs Station near present-day Dalton, Nebraska. On February 4, 1865, Indians stole
a herd of horses at the station. A telegram reporting the loss was sent from
the station to Fort Laramie, and soon a party of 120 soldiers, comprising
volunteers from the 11th Ohio Cavalry and the 7th Iowa Cavalry, was sent
down to Mud Springs. In addition, Lieutenant William Ellsworth brought
36 men, also of the 11th Ohio Cavalry, from Fort Mitchell. Ellsworth's small
party arrived first, on the morning of February 5. The Indians, 1,000 strong,
soon attacked the station, keeping the soldiers pinned down.[1]

---

1   Michno, *Encyclopedia*, 165–166.

On the morning of February 6, the day after the fight with Ellsworth's men, Col. William O. Collins and his soldiers arrived at the station, some in a forced march arriving in the dark about two o'clock, the rest arriving by eight o'clock that morning. The cold was so bitter several of the men suffered from frostbite. Another skirmish ensued that day, lasting four hours. At one point, about 200 warriors were able to get close enough to the station, protected by the surrounding hills and gullies, to lob numerous arrows into the compound, wounding several animals and soldiers. Two parties of soldiers were sent out to attack the Indians, which forced them to withdraw. The fight ended about mid-afternoon. Seven soldiers were wounded, three seriously. The Indians were thought to have lost about 40;[2] however, George Bent, who was there, denied any Indians were killed.[3]

February 8–9, near Broadwater, Nebraska, warriors attacked soldiers on Rush Creek, killing two privates and wounding nine others. Indian casualties might have been as high as 100 wounded, but probably only two or three Indians killed.[4] After this attack the natives withdrew further north, and attacks stopped until May. During this time things were silent along the Denver road. Several of the burned ranches were rebuilt and commerce again flowed to and from Denver. But while things were peaceful along the South Platte valley, this wasn't the case with events in Wyoming. The Indians had shifted their focus for raids and plunder up north.

On May 12, about 30 Lakota attacked a ranch owned by Dan Smith, a few miles southwest of present-day Gothenburg, Nebraska. The ranch was being guarded by a small detachment of four soldiers. One soldier was killed and two others wounded. Thirty horses were stolen.[5] Six days later, south of present-day Hastings, Nebraska, near Elm Creek Station, an army detachment of 15 unarmed convalescent soldiers was accompanying a single wagon driven by a civilian teamster. Twenty Indians, whose tribal affiliation was unknown, attacked the men, no doubt first observing they were unarmed. Two soldiers were killed and six others wounded. The wagon was

---

2   Agnes Wright Spring, *Caspar Collins: The Life and Exploits of an Indian Fighter of the Sixties* (New York, NY: Columbia University Press, 1927), 61–63. See also Robert Jones, *Guarding the Overland Trails: The Eleventh Ohio Cavalry in the Civil War* (Spokane, WA: The Arthur H. Clark Company, 2005), 196–203.

3   Hyde, *Life of George Bent*, 190. Given that Bent has proven his testimony false in enumerating Indian casualties in other fights, we may assume he is wrong here too, though the military often exaggerated Indian losses. Perhaps less than 20 Indians were killed.

4   Michno, *Encyclopedia*, 166–167.

5   Michno, *Encyclopedia*, 169–170.

plundered.[6] On May 25, near present-day Fort Collins, Colorado, Indians stole five horses and 17 cattle from Joseph Mason.[7]

Things stayed calm for a couple weeks, and then more violence erupted in early June, near present-day Casper, Wyoming. At about three in the afternoon of June 3, 10 Indians dashed down the opposite side of the river at Platte Bridge Station and fired upon soldiers stationed there. They then fell back, but Colonel Preston B. Plumb soon learned about it, from a messenger sent to his campsite about seven miles away. He immediately mounted 10 men and went to the station, leaving word at his camp for 20 more men to follow as soon as possible. From Platte Bridge Station, Col. Plumb started in pursuit of the Indians. After five miles, his men caught up with the warriors, and a skirmish ensued and two Indians were wounded. But suddenly, as many as 60 warriors came charging at Plumb's men, from the bottom of Dry Creek about a half-mile away. It was clear that a trap had been set by the warriors Plumb had been pursuing. Fortunately, however, at just this time the 20 other soldiers coming to join up with Plumb's small command arrived, and together they pursued the Indians in a chase that lasted about two miles. Eight soldiers left the main body of cavalry to pursue a number of Indians who had split off from the fleeing warriors, but this left them vulnerable to a counter-charge, which the Indians soon did. Unable to keep their position until reinforced, the warriors were able to kill two soldiers. At least one Indian was killed during this stand and several more wounded.[8]

On June 8, about 100 Lakota and Cheyenne attacked a small detachment of five soldiers stationed on the Overland trail at Sage Creek Station near present-day Saratoga, Wyoming. After an hour-long fight the men, running low on ammunition, decided to try and escape to the next station several miles away. In their run, which went eight miles, three soldiers were killed, as well as two civilians. The two soldiers who made it to Pine Ridge Station were wounded.[9] Three days later, back in Kansas, near Alden, a mail coach was attacked by about 100 Indians. Two of the six soldiers of the 7th Iowa Cavalry who accompanied the stage were wounded, and at least one Indian was killed. Soldiers nearby at Cow Creek Station witnessed the

6   Michno, *Encyclopedia*, 170.

7   Joseph Mason Indian Depredation Claim #525. Entry 700, Record Group 75.

8   *War of the Rebellion*, Series I, Volume 48, Part I, 305–306.

9   *War of the Rebellion*, Volume 48, Part I, 295; Jones, *Guarding the Overland*, 244; Michno, *Encyclopedia*, 172.

attack and the officer in charge of the troopers sent nearly 30—mostly of the 2nd Colorado Cavalry—off in pursuit of the Indians. After a chase of several miles, the Indians crossed the Arkansas River. About 15 Indians were killed or wounded. The soldiers thought the Indians were Kiowa.[10]

During this time, the Denver road from Julesburg to present-day Fort Morgan had remained calm from Indian attacks. It was a lucky time to travel to and from Denver. Wagon trains were not permitted to travel unless they were in parties of at least 25 wagons. During this month, Mallie Stafford was with a wagon party returning east from Denver. She recalled the fear of traveling over the road, everyone knowing of the deadly events happening less than six months earlier. Unlike before hostilities broke out in 1864, now all travelers on the road were armed, including the women. When Stafford's train camped near the ruins of American Ranch, where William Morris and his helpers had been killed earlier in the January raids and his wife and children taken captive, several men in the party, along with two women, were curious to visit the burned out site. They had been told the bodies of two dead Indians were still lying on the ground near the ruins. When they returned to the camp after visiting the site and viewing the dead warriors, they said the Indians had not decomposed in the dry Colorado air. Rather, "they merely dried up, their skin adhering to the bone and their hands and feet resembling claws." Mallie could not understand the fascination to view such a spectacle: ". . . as for myself, thoroughly wearied with life in the wilderness, I would gladly have traveled as far again to avoid their vicinity."[11] Mrs. Halie Riley Hodder remembered seeing one dead Indian at the ranch when she traveled through in February, just a month after the attack. "He was burned to a cinder."[12]

With all of the Indian raids throughout the winter and continuing in late spring, the government had decided a campaign against the warring warriors was necessary. They were now all congregated north of the South Platte River. As part of that campaign, the military authorities ordered the friendly Indians camped in and around Fort Laramie in Wyoming

10   *War of the Rebellion*, Volume 48, Part I, 313–314; Michno, *Encyclopedia*, 172–173.
11   Mrs. Mallie Stafford, *The March of Empire Through Three Decades* (San Francisco, CA: Geo. Spalding & Co., 1884), 125–126.
12   Mrs. Hodder, "Crossing the Plains in War Times," 132.

Territory, to move all the way to Fort Kearny in Nebraska Territory, making it easier for the military to find the elusive warriors. In preparation for the upcoming military campaign, 1,500 Indians were sent south under guard of 135 soldiers. Because they professed being friendly they were allowed to keep their weapons. Three days into the journey, however, the Indians began fighting among themselves over whether they were going to continue their escort to Fort Kearny, or instead return back to the north across the North Platte River. The Indians stalled and did not follow the soldiers on the morning of June 14, and after the column traveled a couple miles, an officer and several troopers went back to order the hesitating Indians to join the march. The warriors turned on the men, killed Captain William D. Fouts and three other soldiers, and wounded another four. Ironically, with this military escort were Lucinda Eubanks and her son Willie, who had earlier been freed from their August 7, 1864 captivity. The Indians escaped across the deep and wide North Platte River. Captain John Wilcox, in his report of this affair, noted why he was unable to pursue the fleeing Indians, a fact which was repeated throughout the Indian wars: "Indian ponies are trained and accustomed to cross in every stage. All Indians, great or small, can swim; one third of white men cannot."[13]

From Mrs. Eubanks, Sarah Larimer heard a different story about what really happened. After traveling with the soldiers for one day, the Indians became convinced there was some sort of treachery going on with their removal and that they were going to be killed. The reason was because some of the soldiers that first day took some of the Indian toddlers and "amused themselves by throwing the papooses into the [North Platte] river, and watching their dexterity in swimming out." This angered the men and changed their hearts against the soldiers. While the Indians had been allowed to keep their weapons, they did not have ammunition. But the warriors pleaded with Captain Fouts to give them "powder" to hunt. The ruse worked and they kept the ammunition and used it when they attacked the small party under Fouts the next day.[14]

George Bent also said why the Indians grew distrustful. The Indians were Brule under Spotted Tail, a few Oglala under Red Cloud, and several

---

13   *War of the Rebellion*, Volume 48, Part I, 322–324; Michno, *Encyclopedia*, 174–175.

14   Sarah Larimer, *The Capture and Escape*, 136.

Northern Arapaho. All of these "friendly" Indians were opposed to the war that Bent's Southern Cheyenne had been involved in since the summer of 1864, and were always assisting the military in locating the warring factions, many even offering to fight the factious warriors. But when they learned they were going to be taken to Fort Kearny down in Nebraska Territory, they feared it was a trap and that their hated enemy—the Pawnee—would kill them all, once they were down there. Still, they agreed to go south. Bent said the Indians were armed, and after being mistreated by the soldiers—Sarah Larimer's account explained that mistreatment—the final straw occurred when some of the soldiers selected young Indian women, "and took them to their own tents for the night."[15]

Once these Indians escaped across the North Platte, almost immediately an escort of over 200 soldiers was dispatched out of Fort Laramie, under the command of Colonel Thomas Moonlight, to overtake them. Over 120 miles were marched in just two days. Moonlight's command was near present-day Crawford, Nebraska, when the Indians discovered they were being trailed. The soldiers had marched 20 miles early on the morning of June 17, when they went into camp for breakfast. Not waiting for the soldiers to attack them, the Indians, about 200 strong, instead attacked the soldiers' camp and succeeded in capturing 74 horses. About 30 men pursued the Indians but soon encountered more than 400, "who, in the English language, dared them to fight." Obviously the Indians who escaped after killing Captain Fouts three days earlier were too many for such a small number of soldiers, and they wisely retreated. In this skirmish two men were wounded, and perhaps four Indians killed, as they were observed falling "over their horses, but being tied on around the knees by a thong, [their] horses galloped off with them hanging."[16]

One Indian, however, was not able to escape when the warriors fled after killing Fouts. He had earlier been arrested for some unknown act prior to the departure from Fort Laramie. He had been chained to a wagon as a prisoner when Fouts was killed. Sarah Larimer said what happened next:

> This Indian fell a victim to the wrath of the soldiers, who took him from the wagon and shot him. On perceiving intimations that they would destroy him, he turned a look of defiance and a scornful smile upon his white captors. When he lay dead,

15   Hyde, *Life of George Bent*, 209.
16   *War of the Rebellion*, Volume 48, Part I, 325–328; Michno, *Encyclopedia*, 175–177.

a mountaineer, who had witnessed the whole proceedings, and who was a friend to the Indians, sprang upon the lifeless form, and with one stroke of a knife severed the scalp, offering it to a soldier. Next he cut off an arm, and so continued to mutilate the body till the pieces were all distributed among the lookers-on, all the while giving way to vituperation against the soldiers. A reason given by some for this unexpected outbreak was a feeling of ill-will for this officer. Captain Fouts had been a Methodist clergyman for twenty-five years before entering the army. He left a wife and several children, who witnessed his untimely fate.[17]

It seems the Indians did not fare well with Methodist ministers. Colonel John Chivington, responsible for what earlier happened at Sand Creek, was also a Methodist minister.

Following these events June, things were quiet for a little over a month. This did not mean that the militant Indians had no plans to continue their war. Indeed, now over 2,500 strong, the Indians showed their resolve to continue war when they attacked soldiers stationed at Platte Bridge Station in present-day Casper, Wyoming. Platte Bridge at that time housed about 120 soldiers from various commands. It was a strategic station along the Overland trail, and it had an important wooden bridge which immigrants used to take their wagons across the North Platte River to continue their journey west. In addition, Platte Bridge was located at a junction of three branches of the Overland/Oregon trail, and it contained an important telegraph link to Fort Laramie.[18] The Indians knew its importance and wanted it destroyed.

On the morning of July 26, Lieutenant Caspar Collins, observing numerous warriors across the river, feared for the safety of an expected small military freight train from the west. He put together a small command of 25 men and proceeded across the bridge in an effort to find the anticipated wagons that were guarded by 25 soldiers under Sergeant Amos Custard, returning from Sweetwater Station. Collins had not proceeded far before as many as 1,000 warriors surprised him and his men. The soldiers immediately swung their horses around and made a desperate attempt to race back across the bridge.

As this was going on, Lieutenant Bretney with 40 soldiers had crossed the bridge in an effort to reinforce Collins. Two hundred Indians surprised them once they crossed the river, preventing them from joining

---

17   Larimer, *The Capture and Escape*, 137.

18   Vaughn, *Platte Bridge*, 8.

with Collins. Meanwhile, Collins' command was able to make it back across the bridge, but not without a loss of five men dead, including Caspar Collins, and another eight men wounded. Two more soldiers were killed later in the day when yet another detail ventured out to repair the damaged telegraph wire.[19]

The concern for Custard's wagon train was well founded. When he was half-way to Platte Bridge from Sweetwater Station, he camped on the night of July 25. He there met with 30 soldiers who warned him of the Indians near and around Platte Bridge. He was advised to return to Sweetwater. Feeling compelled by his duty to follow his original orders, Custard declined the advice, and continued on towards Platte Bridge on the morning of July 26. As he got closer he heard gunshots, probably those of Lt. Collins' command, and sent five of his men to scout the cause of the gunfire. The five men went to investigate and were themselves soon under attack near Platte Bridge.

They made a desperate run to cross the bridge, as the warriors fired to keep them from their destination. Two soldiers were killed, but three made it across the river and into the safety of the station. But that was all of Custard's command that lived. Indians surrounded the remaining 20 men and two wagons a few miles north/northwest from the station. A hot fight ensued, lasting four hours, and when it was over Custard and 19 soldiers were dead. Indian casualties were at least 12 dead and 18 wounded.[20]

For the rest of the summer, most of the warring Cheyenne remained north in the Powder River country with their Lakota brethren, "to hold the usual summer medicine ceremonies."[21] While up there on July 31, a band of Cheyenne and Arapaho Indians—led by Cheyenne Sand Hill's Aorta band, made an attack upon the family of Jasper Fletcher in southwest Wyoming Territory, about 35 miles east of Fort Halleck and just east of Rock Creek Station. The Fletchers were with a larger train of 75 wagons—perhaps as many as 200–300 people, delayed at Fort Laramie until the wagon party was large enough to proceed. A part of the wagons included a military escort,

19   Vaughn, *Platte Bridge*, Chapter 6 (55–70); Spring, *Caspar Collins*, Chapter 12 (79–104). The most comprehensive and complete account of the fight can be found in John D. McDermott, *Frontier Crossroads: The History of Fort Caspar and the Upper Platte Crossing* (Casper, WY: City of Casper, Publisher, 1997), Chapter Five (61–76). Casper, Wyoming, is named after Caspar Collins, and Fort Collins, Colorado, is named after Caspar's father, Colonel William Oliver Collins. For Bent's Indian version of this fights, see Hyde, *Life of George Bent*, 215–220.

20   Vaughn, *Platte Bridge*, 22–34; Spring, *Caspar Collins*, 90–92; Michno, *Encyclopedia*, 179–181.

21   Hyde, *Life of George Bent*, 225.

taking supplies for Camp Douglas, outside of Salt Lake City. The family had left Illinois May 10. They went to Omaha, and from there followed the Platte River west, and then took the South Platte from Julesburg to Denver. There they stayed a couple weeks and then went north to Fort Laramie. When they arrived at the fort, the family was ordered to attach with a wagon party numbering 75, which left the fort the evening the family arrived at the post. It seems odd that they traveled to Denver and then up north to Fort Laramie, as they went about 80 miles out of their way on their journey to California. But all knew at this time that the Indians were hostile on the roads, so perhaps they went to Fort Laramie on the wise advice of people they met while in Denver. They were lucky to make it on the Denver road without being molested.

As the wagon train neared Rock Creek Station, the family's two wagons—one carrying their possessions and the other a "convenience" wagon to allow the women to travel in leisure—were slightly beyond the other wagons, when they stopped near the station to prepare their noon meal. The young family had come to America from England in 1861. The family included Jasper and his wife Mary Ann; 13-year-old Amanda; 11-year-old William Henry; six-year-old Jasper, Junior; four-and-a-half-year-old Oscar D.; and two-year-old Elizabeth—Lizzie. After resting and eating, the wagon train was going to cross the creek at the stage station. While preparing camp, Mary Ann and her two daughters walked beyond their wagons about 400 yards towards the station when the Indians—300 in number—suddenly sprang on them. They quickly killed Mary Ann, and captured Amanda and Lizzie. They charged at the two wagons and wounded Jasper, shooting him in the wrist. It was his first time he had seen an Indian. He and his three small sons were able to run back to the wagon train, leaving their wagons and the captured females to the warriors. Before departing, the Indians plundered the wagons, taking what they wanted and then destroyed the rest of the contents and set the two wagons on fire. They stole the three horses used to carry the wagons.[22] Neither the military escort with the government wagons, nor any of the armed freighters tried to come to the rescue of the Fletcher family. After setting the wagons on fire, the Indians retreated at a leisurely pace. Mary Ann Fletcher's body was buried at the stage station the next day.[23]

---

22   Jasper Fletcher Indian Depredation Claim #5072. Record Group 123.
23   Jasper Fletcher Indian Depredation Claim #5072.

The Indian who captured Amanda was a Southern Cheyenne, Minimic—also spelled Minimick, Min-im-mie, Mah-min-ic (Eagle Head). He was one of the Indians with Cheyenne One Eye, when both took great risks to communicate with Major Ned Wynkoop at Fort Lyon in September 1864, to beg for peace.[24] The letter was written as part of Black Kettle's effort to create peace after the violent August attacks on the Little Blue River and Plum Creek in Nebraska Territory, the bloody events that precipitated Sand Creek later that fall. Minimic was there and survived. However, he lost his wife and two daughters, victims at Sand Creek.[25] After Sand Creek, Minimic joined his warrior brethren in making war against the whites. The Fletcher family was victims of this tit-for-tat war.

Amanda recalled her ordeal:

> We were just camped for dinner, and a party of the Indians just came right down on us,—about three hundred of them as I afterward learned,—Cheyennes and Arapahoes. There were three Sioux [Brule] with them, but as to whether they were adopted into the tribe or not, I do not know. They came on the train as we were in camp, and just went into fighting. Of course they came on their ponies in regular fighting order. I had my mother by her hand and my sister under the other arm. My mother was killed by my side and my sister taken. Then I was taken, picked up and put on horseback and taken back to the wagons. Where I was picked up I could not tell just exactly, but it must have been 300 or 400 yards from the wagons.[26]

With the 300 warriors were two squaws. Three days after Amanda was captured, the Indians attacked another single family travelling alone on the road. Amanda said the entire family was killed, "with the exception of the white woman. She was captured, and killed shortly afterwards." Just how many unidentified families, like the one Amanda reported, were caught and killed on the various roads during the Cheyenne war will never be known.

The day after the Fletcher daughters were captured, Lizzie was separated from Amanda. Lizzie was observed by various white people almost two years later, owned by Cut Nose, but she was never seen after that and disappeared.

Amanda was in captivity for seven months before she was rescued. Shortly after Amanda's rescue, Custer learned of Lizzie's captivity and Amanda's ordeal. He recalled the Fletcher family in his book:

24   Louis Kraft, *Ned Wynkoop and The Lonely Road From Sand Creek* (Norman, OK: University of Oklahoma Press, 2011), 106. Jasper Fletcher Indian Depredation Claim #5072.

25   Ida Ellen Rath, *The Rath Trail* (Wichita, KS: McCormick-Armstrong CO., Inc., 1961), 27.

26   Jasper Fletcher Indian Depredation Claim #5072.

The child [Lizzie] now held by the Indians was kept captive. An elder daughter [Amanda] made her escape and now resides in Iowa. The father resides in Salt Lake City. I have received several letters from the father and eldest daughter and from friends of both, requesting me to obtain the release of the little girl, if possible ... all trace of the little white girl was lost, and to this day nothing is known of her fate.... "Cut Nose" with his band was located along the Smoky Hill route in the vicinity of Monument Station. He frequently visited the stage stations for purposes of trade, and was invariably accompanied by his little captive. I never saw her, but those who did represented her as strikingly beautiful; her complexion being fair, her eyes blue, and her hair of a bright golden hue, she presented a marked contrast to the Indian children who accompanied her. "Cut Nose," from the delicate light color of her hair, gave her an Indian name signifying "Little Silver Hair." He appeared to treat her with great affection, and always kept her clothed in the handsomest of Indian garments. All offers from individuals to ransom her proved unavailing. Although she has been with the Indians but a year, she spoke the Cheyenne language fluently, and seemed to have no knowledge of her mother tongue.[27]

Once Amanda was rescued both she and her father tried to get Custer's help in rescuing Lizzie. Custer wrote to Amanda on January 27, 1867, and said Lizzie was in the village of a Cheyenne chief called "Cutnose." Lieutenant Owen Hale and William Comstock had seen her in the village a little south of Fort Wallace, near Big Creek.[28] Surprisingly, though Amanda thought her sister had died early in captivity, genealogy research shows Lizzie apparently lived a long life among the Indians and married an Arapaho by the name of Broken Horn. The 1900 U.S. Census shows her name as Kellsto Time (Sometime Kills To Time or Killing Horn), living with her husband at the Shoshone Indian Reservation in Fremont, Wyoming.[29] The records also indicate Lizzie was born in Rock Island, Illinois on August 6, 1863, which is confirmed in Jasper Fletcher's Indian Depredation Claim. She died May 31, 1928, at the Wind River Indian Reservation in western Wyoming.[30]

After her capture, Amanda was soon brought by her captors back to Kansas, where she remained a captive in Minimic's village, until an Indian trader, Charles Hanger, found her in late February 1866. He was able to

27   Gen. G. A. Custer, *My Life on the Plains, or, Personal Experiences With Indians* (New York, NY: Sheldon and Company, 1874), 45–46.

28   Jasper Fletcher Indian Depredation Claim #5072.

29   http://search.ancestry.com/cgi-bin/sse.dll?rank=1&new=1&MSAV=1&msT=1&gss=angs-g&gsfn= kells*&gsln=time&msrpn——ftp=wyoming&cpxt=0&catBucket=rstp&uidh=uh1&cp=0&pcat= ROOT—CATEGORY&h=74467689&db=1900usfedcen (accessed August 2, 2013).

30   http://trees.ancestry.com/tree/24796863/person/1305288696 (accessed August 2, 2013).

purchase her for $1,665 in trade goods. She was in a village 45 miles southeast of Fort Dodge. Once ransomed, she was brought into Fort Dodge. From there she was escorted to Fort Larned, and then turned over to Cheyenne agent Wynkoop. Charles Hanger was partners with a man named Morris and together they had a license to trade with the Indians under Agent Wynkoop's care. Hanger found her in a camp of Dog Soldiers in February 1866. He stated he "bought her from the Indian who captured her . . . that it was a party of Cheyennes who attacked the train, and that no other Indians were with them at the time."[31] When he was trading with the Indians, he stayed in the Cheyenne Dog Soldier camp. There were about 1,000 Cheyenne camped together. About 1,200–1,500 Arapahos were camped, one or two days' ride from the Cheyenne village. Also camped nearby were between 600 and 800 Apaches. When Hanger purchased her, he sent her down to the Arapaho village. His interpreter—Poysell—was there with his wife, and they took Amanda into their home, where she remained until a company of soldiers went for her and brought her back to Fort Dodge.[32]

One of the items the Indians stole from the Fletcher wagons was a box—12 by 18 inches—containing all of the money Jasper owned, which was substantial, all in British notes or gold coin. The paper notes amounted to "17,000 pounds in Bank of England notes and 3,000 in gold sovereigns." This seems like a large amount of money, and probably the sovereigns are exaggerated in number. The sovereigns were each a pound (English money roughly equivalent at that time to an American dollar). If the family had as many as 3,000 sovereigns, they would have weighed a little more than nine pounds, which could fit into a box with the dimensions of 12 by 18 inches. The Fletcher family came from an upper class family in Derbyshire, England, and Jasper had sold his claim in a coal mining business before coming to America. They were hoping to bring that money to California and begin a new life.

Minimic kept much of the money in Fletcher's box, and throughout

---

31 Hanger testimony comes from Jasper Fletcher Indian Depredation Claim #5062. Record Group 123. He noted in his testimony that he remained friends with Amanda for the next several years, and that after she married William E. Cook 10 years after her rescue she received a substantial inheritance from family in England. See also Michno, *A Fate Worse Than Death*, 144–150; Kraft, *Ned Wynkoop*, 164–165.

32 Jasper Fletcher Indian Depredation Claim #5062. Kraft, *Ned Wynkoop*, 164–165. Captain G. A. Gordon, 2nd Cavalry, "Headquarters, Fort Dodge, Kansas, March 5, 1866." *Annual Report of the Commissioner of Indian Affairs for the Year 1866* (Washington, DC: Government Printing Office, 1866), 277–278.

Amanda's captivity he had her count it and note the value of paper money, which he then spent with traders, including a substantial amount he gave to Charles Hanger—$14,000 worth—who then used a small portion of that to purchase Amanda back from Minimic. But Minimic wasn't the only warrior who got some of the money. Several other Indians had substantial amounts. Before Amanda was rescued, Minimic brought her to William Bent, George Bent's father. Bent had brought several wagons down to the Indian village to trade with them. He knew the value of the money, and traded with Minimic for much of it. As Amanda recalled Indians and money:

> They didn't know the value of the bills, but they knew it was money. They knew they could buy something with it. Repeatedly several Indians came into the tent where I was, and would have the money in handkerchiefs, and in the handkerchiefs there would be bills laid in different shapes. They wanted me to count them. I would count the number. There was one that had 1700 bills. One Indian in particular had 2400 pounds of English money. . . . There was one that had 700 bills. I knew this money. It was a different kind from the American. I knew it was the same. The gold was divided among them. The squaws had the coins, after making holes in them, strung in their ears. Something grand and something that was very nice in their idea.[33]

There is no historical record found which shows William Bent reported his knowledge that young Amanda was a captive in a Cheyenne village. If this is because he made no report, one can only assume his desire for trade trumped his desire for seeking her freedom from captivity. Trader Hanger stated that Bent got money belonging to the Fletcher family, and told Hanger he got it.[34] But this Fletcher money apparently led to a white man's death. Captain G. A. Gordon was with Wynkoop when he was down in the Cheyenne village, just about when Hanger had traded for Amanda. Wynkoop was trying to get the Dog Soldier Cheyenne to sign the Treaty of the Little Arkansas that Black Kettle had signed the prior fall. Gordon concluded his report of his excursion, by noting that on February 21, a son of Mr. Boggs was killed and scalped by four Cheyenne, six miles east of Fort Dodge. The reason? He had gone to trade with them and traded with 1 Indian ten, one-dollar bills for 10 ten-dollar bills. The Indians knew money had value but did not know the specifics, and once the Cheyenne learned

---

33   Jasper Fletcher Indian Depredation Claim #5062.
34   Charles Hanger testimony, Jasper Fletcher Indian Depredation Claim #5062.

they had been cheated, they returned and killed the young Boggs. Gordon: "I think this case needs no further comment."[35]

After Amanda was rescued, it was several years before she was reunited with her father. But both she and her father did what they could to try and gain little Lizzie's release. Amanda:

> I was for some years after my captivity separated from my father. I met him again in Colorado and Utah [1871]. He had saved the boys and with them resided in Utah and I went there to him and found him. I found him mentally not the man he was before the attack on our train in 1865. The worry over us girls' captivity, and the murder of my mother had had their affect. He was not the business man that he had been before these depredations. I found that the depredations had impoverished him and that his earnings, much of same he had expended in looking for us captive girls, that his constant thoughts were on his sore affliction and losses.[36]

Jasper Fletcher died suddenly in Salt Lake City, October 15, 1875. In her efforts to find her sister and gain compensation for her family's loss, Amanda even corresponded with George Bent, who recalled she—he called her Mary—was captured by Sand Hill's band of Cheyenne. Bent wrote that he received a letter from her and she said she was well treated while a captive, that Sand Hill's wife was very kind to her during her captivity. He erroneously stated that John Smith, working for Morris and Hanger, traded for her. Bent acknowledged that Amanda was turned over to Wynkoop, while he was trying to negotiate with the Dog Soldiers to sign the Treaty on the Little Arkansas that Black Kettle had earlier signed. But, according to Bent, Big Head and Rock Forehead refused to put their signatures on the treaty.[37] In Captain G. A. Gordon's report, dated March 5, 1866, he noted that Big Head rejected the treaty, and "said that he and his tribe objected strongly to the Smoky Hill route, and to living south of the Arkansas: that the road lay through their best hunting grounds, and the country south of the Arkansas was not his, but belonged to the Apaches and Arrapahoes, and he and his tribe preferred to live in the country north of the Arkansas, where they were born and bred." Gordon went on to say Wynkoop told the Dog Soldiers to stay friendly to the whites, and all warriors then professed peace. At Wynkoop's request, Gordon sent a company of troopers under Lt.

---

35 Captain G. A. Gordon, "Headquarters, Fort Dodge, Kansas, March 5, 1866," 277–278.
36 Jasper Fletcher Indian Depredation Claim #5062.
37 Hyde, *Life of George Bent*, 251.

Bates, to Little Raven's Arapaho camp and retrieved Amanda, and brought her back to Fort Larned.[38] When Wynkoop returned from his council with the Dog Soldiers, he stated—contrary to what Bent wrote—that all the chiefs signed the treaty, and naively concluded "I have now got all the hostile bands in, and can safely declare the Indians to be at peace, and consequently the different routes of travel across the plains perfectly safe."[39]

At the end of July, the Powder River campaign was initiated to fight the Indians up north. It consisted of three different columns of soldiers. Colonel Nelson Cole commanded 1,400 men, leaving Omaha with the destination of Bear Butte in present-day South Dakota. Lt. Colonel Samuel Walker led 600 men from Fort Laramie and went north to the Black Hills in the same general vicinity of Cole's destination. Brigadier General Patrick E. Connor led the third column of over 400 soldiers and 90 Pawnee scouts from Fort Laramie, in an effort to locate the guilty parties in the Powder River country in present-day Wyoming and Montana.[40] On August 17, in northeastern Wyoming, about 50 of Connor's Pawnee Scouts, under the leadership of Captain Frank North, found a band of Cheyenne. In a sharp, mostly one-sided engagement, the Pawnee killed 27 Cheyenne.[41] Meanwhile, General Connor continued north with his men. On August 28, his scouts informed him of their discovery of a large Indian village just 40 miles distant. On August 29, a spirited fight ensued.

The village, located on the Tongue River at present-day Ranchester, Wyoming, turned out to be an Arapaho one under the leadership of Black Bear. The Arapaho had earlier split from their Cheyenne allies, who remained at the mouth of Crazy Woman's Fork of the Powder River.[42] Black Bear's village was large, with about 300 teepees and 700 Indians. The fight lasted

38   Captain G. A. Gordon, "Headquarters, Fort Dodge, Kansas, March 5, 1866," 277.

39   Major E. W. Wynkoop, "Fort Larned, Kansas, April 8, 1866." *Annual Report of the Commissioner of Indian Affairs for the Year 1866*, 278.

40   Jerry Keenan, *Encyclopedia of American Indian Wars 1492–1890* (Santa Barbara, CA: ABC-CLIO, Inc., 1997), 51–52. This long neglected campaign has recently been given due study in two works by the late David Wagner. See *Powder River Odyssey: Nelson Cole's Western Campaign of 1865* (Norman, OK: The Arthur H. Clark Company, 2009), and *Patrick Connor's War: The 1865 Powder River Indian Expedition* (Norman, OK: The Arthur H. Clark Company, 2010).

41   George Bird Grinnell, *Two Great Scouts and Their Pawnee Battalion: The Experiences of Frank J. North and Luther H. North* (Lincoln, NE: University of Nebraska Press, 1973), 89–92; Wagner, *Patrick Connor's War*, 108–113; Hyde, *Life of George Bent*, 227. Bent says only five Indians were killed, one of them his step-mother.

42   Hyde, *Life of George Bent*, 226.

most of the morning. When it was over, two soldiers and three scouts were dead, and several soldiers wounded. Indian casualties were anywhere from 35 to 63 dead. Seven women and 11 children were captured.[43] George Bent, who was not there at this fight, reported what one of the warriors told him years later. While not listing Indian casualties, Bent did say that the exiled warriors continually harassed Connor's men throughout the remainder of the day, in a valiant but unsuccessful effort to rescue the captured women. Nevertheless, a few days later the Arapaho met with Connor and made peace. Connor then released the captives. Bent also reported that all of the captured women and children were taken by Pawnees and not the soldiers.[44]

Connor's successful fight against Black Bear was the only significant encounter of the Powder River Expedition. A series of skirmishes did ensue between Cheyenne and the men under the columns of Cole and Walker, who had joined together northwest of the Black Hills. As many as 14 men were killed in these skirmishes, along with perhaps 20 Indians, but early winter weather took a harsher toll against the government horses and mules. About 700 died, which forced the men to destroy the accoutrements associated with the campaign. It was an expensive venture to get at the Indians.[45] It did, however, keep the Indians away from the Denver road and allowed time for the burnt ranches to be rebuilt and commerce to safely flow once again. Things along the trail stayed quiet through the spring and summer of 1866, though orders were issued throughout the forts along the trail that emigrant and freight wagons could not travel beyond the forts until they had at least 20 wagons and 30 armed men among each wagon party.[46]

One other encounter at this time in the Powder River country is worth mentioning. In addition to the three military columns making up the Powder River Expedition, there was also a civilian party of 53 men, a road building expedition into the Powder River, under the leadership of James Sawyers. Leaving northwestern Nebraska on June 13, it had a military escort of 143 men under the command of Captain George Williford. By August

43 Michno, *Encyclopedia*, 184–185; Wagner, *Patrick Connor's War*, 153–166.

44 Hyde, *Life of George Bent*, 230–231.

45 Michno, *Encyclopedia*, 187. See also Wagner, *Powder River Odyssey*. For a first-hand account of events under Cole's command, see Charles H. Springer, *Soldiering in Sioux Country: 1865*, edited by John W. Hampton (San Diego, CA: Frontier Heritage press, 1971).

46 Report, August 27, 1866, Fort McPherson. Record Group 393, Department of the Platte, part 1, Letters Received, Box 1, 1867.

9, they were near present-day Gillette, Wyoming, when the Cheyenne attacked them. A civilian was killed and eight horses stolen.[47] Six days later, on August 15, the Indians reappeared, this time in huge force. Williford estimated them at 2,000–3,000 strong, and comprised of Cheyenne, Arapaho, and the Lakota bands of Oglala and Brule. The fight lasted 8 hours. Two soldiers were killed and several more wounded, though most just slightly. Williford had artillery and used it effectively, probably resulting in about 40 Indian casualties, of which at least 11 were mortal.[48]

About one o'clock that afternoon, the Indians ended their siege and requested a parley. Williford met with about 20 of their chiefs outside of the protective wagon corral. Williford:

> During my conversation with them, the Cheyennes stated that their home was on the Arkansas River, that many of them had served in the late Rebel Army under General Price; they were anxious to know if the war was over between the North and South; they also stated that they had been but a short time in this part of the country, and on their way up, attacked and killed Lieut. Collins and twenty-seven men at or near Platte Bridge, also that they had captured a citizen wagon train somewhere on their route. They seemed very anxious to enter into a treaty with the whites, provided that they be permitted to go to their homes on the Arkansas River but under no other condition would they make peace. Many of them were dressed in the U.S. uniform, that of an officer.[49]

After the parley, Williford agreed to give the Indians a wagonload of provisions, which ended the fighting. Indeed, fighting waned for the next few months in the Powder River country. But it wasn't all peaceful along the trails to Colorado. In July, Evan Davis was bringing a small freight train from Golden to Nebraska City, to get supplies to bring back to Colorado. When he got to Camp Cottonwood (Fort McPherson), the commander stopped the train and informed Davis he could not pass "without a certain number of men and wagons, and as I did not have enough, they made me stop there to wait until I could get some more." While Davis was awaiting more freighters at his camp, two miles distant from the military post, Indians made a surprise night attack and made off with several horses, which they took north across the Platte.[50] On July 15, near Denver, Cheyenne

47   Michno, *Encyclopedia*, 182–183.
48   Wagner, *Patrick Connor's War*, 125–140.
49   Report of George W. Williford, October 9, 1865. Record Group 393, Department of the Missouri, Part 1, Entry 2639.

Indians stole five mules belonging to Fleming Logston.[51] Again, on September 10, Indians stole four mules and a horse from Patrick Guthrey, on the Denver road just east of Julesburg at the Nebraska line.[52]

By September 1865, the Smoky Hill trail had opened and was well in operation, running both freight and stages along the road from Leavenworth to Denver. This was in direct competition to the Denver road following the South Platte River valley. It was also a shorter route, thus tempting freighters to use it over the South Platte trail. Though shorter, it was also more dangerous. By July, Fort Morgan had been established to complement the protection in the building of Fort Sedgwick the summer before. Likewise, in September, Fort Wallace was established in western Kansas. providing protection for the newly established Smoky Hill trail.

As these forts were being built and commerce continued to build into Colorado Territory, Indians were still making forays across the trails to Denver. Edmund Verney was on a stage coming all the way from San Francisco to Atchison, a journey that began in early June, and included stops at Salt Lake City and Denver. He left Denver on August 1, and, following the South Platte River, arrived at Julesburg August 3. Just four days earlier, a two freight-wagon party had been attacked nearby; the freighters were "shockingly mutilated, the waggons [sic] burned, and their contents carried off, with the team of horses."[53] A newspaper article on August 3 confirmed this attack, noting that it was a party of 40 Indians and the attack happened 40 miles west of Julesburg, which would be near Riverside Station. Two men were killed. At the same time soldiers were attacked near Valley Station. At least three soldiers were slightly wounded and their stock driven off. In addition, the telegraph lines were again cut. Indian sorties were showing up all along the Denver road.[54]

On the day Verney left Denver, another freighting excursion of 15 to 20

---

50   Evan Davis Indian Depredation Claim #5928. Record Group 123.

51   Fleming Logston Indian Depredation Claim #10371. Record Group 123. The depredation file contains no details of this raid and does not exactly place where it happened, other than saying "in the vicinity of Denver, Colorado."

52   Patrick Guthrey Indian Depredation Claim #6936. Record Group 123. Like the Logston claim, Guthrey's depredation file contains no details, and places the raid "at or near the Nebraska and Colorado line, on the Platte River." He claims Sioux Indians were responsible.

53   Edmund Hope Verney, "An Overland Journey From San Francisco to New York, by way of the Salt Lake City," *Royal Good Works and Sunday Magazine* (Vol. 7, June 1, 1866), 392.

54   *Janesville Weekly Gazette*, Janesville, WI, August 3, 1865, page 3.

wagons was attacked several miles northeast of Julesburg near Ash Hollow. Chester Spencer owned his own freighting firm, and was in charge of three of the wagons which had joined in a larger train. Each of Spencer's wagons was pulled by six yoke of oxen. He was taking his freight of groceries and liquors from the Missouri River to Salt Lake City, but was traveling with another freight train owned by John M. Chivington, the commander of the military forces at Sand Creek the year before. Chivington, now out of the military and in the freighting business, had just crossed the South Platte to join Verney in his jaunt. Together they went into camp near O'Fallon's Bluffs, where they ended their day's journey. It was about sundown and the men were eating supper, when Lakota warriors suddenly appeared from all directions, commenced yelling and driving off the untethered herd. While about 10 Indians focused on running off the stock, the remaining warriors commenced to plunder the wagons. The freighters, unprepared for an attack, retreated, several of the men going back across the Platte River to the south. The Indians, after taking what they desired, destroyed the wagons by setting them on fire.

When the warriors made this initial assault, Spencer escaped with his horse across the river, and the next morning, along with several other men, organized a rescue party to try and recover the stolen stock. Only about half of the dozen men in the pursuit had horses, the rest losing theirs in the raid the night before. Those with the horses were out but a few hours when they found the Indians and a short skirmish ensued. The warriors had the upper hand, killing one of the freighters. Spencer was badly wounded in the arm from an arrow, and eventually convalesced at Fort Sedgwick, where the fear was that the arrow which pierced him was poisoned.[55] Poisoned arrows were a great fear in an Indian attack. The usual method to produce a poisoned arrow was to capture and pin a rattlesnake, poke him several times to get him angry and then put the liver of a deer on a stick and let the snake strike that several times. A sharp dogwood stick would then be put into the poisoned liver at the point of the snake's fang incisions. When the wood dried the metal arrow would then be attached to the poisoned tip of dogwood and then the arrow was ready for use. "To be wounded with such an arrow is almost certain death."[56]

---

55   Chester Spencer Indian Depredation Claim #4938. Record Group 123.
56   Theodore Davis, "A Stage Ride to Colorado," *Harper's New Monthly Magazine*, Vol. 35, No. 206, July 1867, 149.

At the end of August, another wagon train consisting of 26 wagons was journeying to Denver. For several days they had encountered as many as 60 Indians on the trail. A couple of times the natives, in small groups of two or three, came into the camp when the men had retired for the day and shared a meal with the freighters. The wagon master and owner of the wagons, Sallenna Grant, being an experienced freighter, had the policy of letting the Indians alone, "as long as they would let us alone." The Indians said they were Arapaho. When the train camped about 30 miles east of Julesburg, the friendliness suddenly ceased. Just before midnight, the men "were awakened by whoops and yells and cattle, horses and mules running, and war whoops of the Indians." All the men were able to escape the attack in the darkness, but when the Indians were finished over 300 of the oxen had been stolen, and all of the wagons plundered and burned. None of the freighters were injured, but all their property was lost. The Indians fled to the south in the direction of the Republican River.[57]

At about this same time, either on August 29 or early in September, at a point half-way between Julesburg and Fort Kearny, another train was making its way east, after delivering goods in Virginian City, Montana. Near Julesburg, the train passed as many as 150 Cheyenne Indians. The caravan consisted of three wagons, 40 mules and three horses. It had joined up with two other wagon parties, their numbers unknown. William Phipps, employing four other men, owned his outfit and made his living freighting all over the plains, including California. He had just gone to sleep when he was suddenly awakened by the night guard. About 40 to 60 Indians had sneaked into the camp along the Platte River, unshackled the stock and then made their war whoops and stampeded the herd away. No men were hurt, but there was not a single animal saved in Phipps' and the other parties' outfits. The men were forced to walk 14 miles east to the next station before they could get a ride to Fort Kearny, and there connect with other people and continue east. They did not have any means to acquire other stock, and thus were forced to abandon their wagons, along with what freight was inside, including a keg of whiskey and several kinds of groceries.[58]

Meanwhile, on August 15 and 18, 24 chiefs of the Cheyenne, Arapaho, Kiowa, Apache and Comanche met with a peace agent at the juncture of

57   Sallenna Grant Indian Depredation Claim #9942. Record Group 123.
58   William Phipps Indian Depredation Claim #7081. Record Group 123.

the Little Arkansas and Arkansas River, just west of present-day downtown Wichita, and there promised to commit no more raids. They gave their word to remain at peace through early October when all could sign the treaty agreement.[59] To the Cheyenne, at least, this promise apparently did not extend to the entire tribe, as shown by their murderous attack upon a train of nine wagons, about 12 miles west of Fort Dodge along the Santa Fe road one month later, on September 20. The wagon train had earlier traveled from Las Vegas, New Mexico, to Leavenworth, where they loaded their wagons with groceries and other supplies to take back to New Mexico. After passing Fort Dodge earlier in the day, and no doubt hearing of the new peace accord with the Cheyenne, the freighters went into camp near the Arkansas River. While preparing evening chores, Peodoro Armijo and Miguel Gonzales y Baca went south across the river in search of a single buffalo they had espied just before calling it a day, near present-day Sears, Kansas. The men rode a few miles before killing the buffalo, and as they were returning with fresh meat for supper, they got about 400 or 500 yards from the camp, when they observed about 150 Cheyenne Indians attacking their comrades across the river. They quickly hid under a bank in the Arkansas, to avoid detection, and then watched as their relatives and traveling partners were slaughtered. Killed were Ramone Baca y Ortiz, Servando Baca y Ortiz, Juan Torrez, Monico Baca and Jose Baca. Tino Torrez was gravely wounded and Daloreo Martinez, a young boy about 13, was captured.

Just when the freighters had been killed and the Indians were plundering the captured goods, coincidentally, a guarded mail stage was seen coming from the west. The Indians quickly dispersed. The soldiers found the wounded Torrez and the stage then hurriedly continued to Fort Dodge. Once the soldiers departed, the Indians reappeared and continued to plunder the wagons, destroying several and taking what they wanted in groceries. They killed what oxen they did not take, all of which was witnessed by the watchful eyes of the two freighters hiding along the Arkansas River. Armijo and Gonzales y Baca continued to hide along the river bank. Finally, the Indians left and the two men then emerged from their hiding, crossed the river and cautiously walked to the plundered site. Soon after that a military escort returned from Fort Dodge, buried the dead men, and took the two survivors back to the fort where they remained for about a month with

---

59   Leo Oliva, *Soldiers on the Santa Fe Trail* (Norman, OK: University of Oklahoma Press, 1967), 165.

the wounded Torrez. The young captive boy, Daloreo Martinez, incredibly, remained a captive of the Cheyenne for over 20 years, before he was able to return to his people in the late 1880s. He confirmed the raiding party was Cheyenne. Living with them for about 24 years certainly removes any question that the attack was done by the Cheyenne, almost immediately after they pledged their word on the Little Arkansas to cease hostilities along the Santa Fe road.[60]

Major Scott Anthony confirmed this attack in a report to *The Denver News,* on September 30. Though there is some variation from Anthony's report in the newspaper and the sworn statements of the surviving men, Anthony added the further detail that a party of 12 Indians, thought at the time to be Comanche, came to the men in their camp, laid down their arms, professed their friendship, "and saying they had come from the treaty where peace had been made with the whites." But soon a cloud was seen of the approaching soldiers from the west, and the Indians yelled "Utes!," grabbed their arms and immediately pounced on the men in the camp, all of whom were unarmed, the two men who earlier left to hunt having the only weapons. The Indians then fled and the advancing soldiers found the dead men and the other freighter severely wounded.[61]

On the same day that these murders happened along the Santa Fe road near Fort Dodge—September 20—Oglala warriors approached a train of three wagons in camp along the road from Fort Collins to Fort Laramie. Elias W. Whitcomb had been contracted to bring 5,000 pounds of potatoes and other groceries from Colorado. While his men were in camp at the crossing of Pole Creek, the Indians fired several rounds into the wagons and then spoke in Sioux, asking the men if they were not aware that the Sioux were at war with the whites. They then warned the men that if they did not flee in the night they would all be killed and scalped the next morning. The men took the warning seriously, and abandoned their freight and retreated back to Colorado. Whitcomb soon gathered a large posse and

---

60 Miguel Gonzales y Baca Indian Depredation Claim #6565. Record Group 123.

61 *Madison County Courier,* Edwardsville, Illinois, October 19, 1865. Anthony says the murderous party was only 12 Indians, not 150. He does not name any of the men killed or wounded and reports that two boys, not one, was captured. He says four men were killed instead of five, as the depredation claim notes by name. He also does not report on the Indians returning and burning the wagons, after the soldiers left with the wounded man. He does, however, say the date of the incident was September 20, while the depredation claim just says it was in September.

returned to his wagons, but found all the goods either gone or destroyed, though the wagons were not burned. Surprisingly, his cattle were recovered at the abandoned camp.[62]

Back on the Denver road, seven miles west of O'Fallon's Bluff, Indians made a raid on a small quartermaster train of two wagons. James H. Temple was in charge. With him were 10 men and a woman. At about 10 o'clock in the evening of September 30, Indians surprised the party in their camp. Temple was killed and two teamsters were critically wounded. The unknown warriors made off with 12 mules. One of the uninjured teamsters escaped and ran to O'Fallon's Bluff, where Captain John Wilcox of the 7th Iowa Cavalry commanded a small garrison of soldiers. Wilcox immediately ordered 15 troopers and two lieutenants (Parker and Akin) to the scene of the attack, with orders to investigate what happened. If the Indians could be overcome by the small command, they were instructed "to fight them & take no prisoners." Otherwise they were to report back to O'Fallon's Bluff. The soldiers returned on the afternoon of October 1. When they reached the train the Indians had already left. While still dark, the soldiers brought Temple's body and the two wounded men to Lewis Baker's ranch, situated two and a half miles west of O'Fallon's Bluff. It was a station operated by the stage company and had five soldiers stationed there for protection.[63] The next morning it was discovered that the Indians, "true to Indian sagacity . . . had made trails to the south to delude pursuit to the north (their true direction)." When the soldiers finally found the main trail later that morning, the war party was too large for 17 cavalrymen to pursue, and they then returned to their station.[64]

The Treaty of the Little Arkansas was signed on October 18, and it was then thought that hostilities along the trails would finally cease. They did, for about as long as the signed papers took to reach Washington and be filed in the War Department. At about the time of the signing of the treaty, the Southern Cheyenne who had been north in the Powder River country came back south. George Bent reported that the Indians "reached the Platte about October 20 and made some raids along the road, capturing trains loaded

62   Elias W. Whitcomb Indian Depredation Claim #6059. Record Group 123.

63   Lewis Baker Indian Depredation Claim #2005. Record Group 123.

64   Captain John Wilcox, "Report, October 1, 1865," "Diary of John Wilcox" (n.d.) assembled and typed by Barbara Wright Blair, 72 pages, from surviving John Wilcox papers. Courtesy of John Ludwickson, Lincoln, Nebraska. See also James E. Potter, *Standing Firmly by the Flag: Nebraska Territory and the Civil War, 1861–1867* (Lincoln & London: University of Nebraska Press, 2012), 204–205.

with goods for Denver."[65] He was certainly correct about his timing and the raids. During the night, on or about October 11, Indians tore the corral down and stole 39 cattle from Lewis Baker's ranch, where Temple's body and the two wounded freighters had been brought 11 days earlier. Indians returned again on October 31, and stole 48 more oxen and 20 milch [milk] cows. Baker and a helper followed the trail but could not recover the stock.[66]

During October, one company of the Nebraska Veteran Volunteer Cavalry was stationed at both Pole Creek and Mud Springs Stations on the Fort Laramie Road, northwest of Julesburg. Captain William W. Ivory commanded Company C. Late in the evening of October 18, 30 Indians made a bold attack on a two-wagon government train under the charge of Corporal Riley Cain and eight troopers, near Sand Hill Station. In a desperate fight lasting 30 minutes, the soldiers held off the warriors. Cain—he would soon be promoted to sergeant—kept his troopers from panicking, as the Indians came within 10 feet of the wagons. Private John Boyle was hit in the leg with an arrow but did not quit firing his carbine. He pulled the arrow through his body, shooting several more rounds before anyone realized he had been hit. The number of Indian casualties was unknown. Indians would again attack Company C, on November 6, at Pole Creek Station. Two soldiers were wounded, and the Indians made off with nine horses.[67]

On the night of October 22, Cheyenne and Lakota warriors raided the newly established Chicago Ranch along the Denver road, stealing three horses. Operated by Watson Coburn, the ranch was "an overland feed ranch and supply station, for emigrants and freighters." The ranch was 2.2 miles east of Riverside Station, south-east of present-day Iliff, Colorado. Earlier that day, a government train was attacked near Coburn's ranch. Eight Indians were killed in this skirmish, three of whom were left on the ground, the warriors unable to retrieve them.

The *Daily Rocky Mountain News*, November 7, confirmed the attack on the train near Coburn's ranch. Henry F. Lentz saw the battlefield shortly after the skirmish. He said that one man was wounded and another killed in the fight:

65   Hyde, *Life of George Bent*, 243.

66   Lewis Baker Indian Depredation Claim #2005. Record Group 123. The interesting thing about Baker's claim is that he thought it was Brule who did the raid. When the claim was brought to their council, they denied doing it. They were correct. George Bent implicated the Southern Cheyenne. Hyde, *Life of George Bent*, 243.

67   Captain Wm. W. Ivory to Maj. Geo Armstrong Comdg 1st N.V.V.C., dated Ft. Sedgwick, Julesburg Col. Terr., 31 Jany, 1866, pp. 10–11. Courtesy John Ludwickson, Lincoln, NE.

The battlefield was an open piece of ground, favorable for defense. We saw two dead Indians and several head of stock. I learned from one of the parties engaged the following particulars: The Indians came across the Platte, advanced on and into the train on ponies, retreated, dismounted, and charged en masse in military style. About fifteen men did the fighting, as the balance were unarmed, and succeeded in killing eight of the Indians, three of whom were left on the ground, the others being lariated and dragged off as soon as despatched. At the ranch below [Chicago] I saw the man that was wounded. He had three arrows shot into him, one of which it required the strength of two men to extract. One man only was killed in the fight.[68]

Watson Coburn stated that about four weeks after the fight near his ranch, "there was a white boy who had been raised by the Indians who ran away from them and came to my place. He gave me to understand that he was with the Indians during this fight [October 22], and he wanted to know how many Indians were killed and where they were. I took him down to where the Indians were lying; he took one by the arm and turned him over and says 'This is old Roman Nose, the Cheyenne Chief'."[69]

One might think such a story was more fiction than fact, but it was confirmed in a diary kept by John J. Pattison, a trooper in Company B, 7th Iowa Cavalry. Pattison was stationed at various posts along the Denver road during these attacks. He wrote:

A boy some 10 years old escaped from the Indians (Sioux) at Republican River, 24th of November, 1865, and came to Mount [Mound] Station on South Platte on the 28th of November, 1865. Clad in Indian costume and speaking the Indian Dialect, he knows not who were his parents—where he was taken prisoner, nor the length of his captivity—he supposes that his parents were killed and he taken captive by the Indians in his infancy. He is now [December 30] with Lieutenant Sallee, 13th Missouri Cavalry.[70]

There is yet another source about this escaped young captive, in a letter from Captain John Wilcox, to John A. Kasson, written from Fort Heath:

68 J. G. Lane Indian Depredation Claim #10273. Record Group 123. The diary of John Pattison said the attack was made at Lillian Springs, the next ranch east of Chicago Ranch, on October 21. Coburn said the fight was near his ranch. Perhaps it was between Chicago Ranch and Lillian Springs. Pattison said nine Indians were killed. See John J. Pattison, "With the U.S. Army Along the Oregon Trail, 1863–1866," *Nebraska History*, Volume 15, 1934, 87.

69 Watson S. Coburn Indian Depredation Claim #8988. Record Group 123. Roman Nose, the Cheyenne warrior and not a chief, was killed at Beecher's Island September 17, 1868. It is possible this is another Roman Nose, but it is not the famed warrior Roman Nose.

70 Pattison, "With the U.S. Army," 88. Mound Station was seven miles east of Chicago ranch. It might be that Coburn, after meeting with the boy, took him to Mound Station, where soldiers were stationed.

In the month of November 1865, a white boy some ten years of age, dressed in Indian costume and speaking the Indian dialect escaped from the Sioux on the Solomon River & came to Mound Station on South Platte C.T. November 27, 1865.

He is apparently transformed to an Indian—having all their peculiarities of motion and gesture. He states that his parents were killed by Indians in the Minnesota massacre—he does not recall where, how long since nor what were their names. He had for a long time sought an opportunity of escaping to his own race, and accomplished it finally by running a fast pony, till it fell exhausted beneath him, then made the last tedious miles on foot—by careful skulking marches by day & building fires around him at night to keep off the wolves. He reports two white women captives with the Indians that they persuaded him to escape etc. with hopes of being themselves rescued by their own race.[71]

Wilcox, however, was likely mistaken in stating the boy's age and that he was captured in the 1862 Minnesota Sioux uprising. The mystery of who this little boy was is solved in an account of another captive, who in 1864 escaped from the Indians after just two days. Sarah Larimer published her account in 1870. From her is learned what became of the little boy:

A little boy of fourteen years, whose name proved to be Charles Sylvester, from Quincy, Illinois, had been stolen, when but seven years old, from his parents, who were at that time in Humboldt Valley, Utah Territory. The knowledge that he was not an Indian, but a white child, never left him, though he had forgotten his people, language, and even his own name. He had been so domesticated in the habits of the Indians that no fears of losing him ever seemed to occur to them, and he was allowed full liberty. He had been with these Indians seven years, when he escaped and came to a military station [Mound Station], where he had some difficulty in convincing the officer that he was not an Indian boy. Eventually, however, he succeeded in making his story intelligible, and was sent to St. Louis, where he was advertised, and, it is said, his portrait was widely circulated. A gentleman from Quincy, Illinois, furnished satisfactory proof that the boy was his nephew, and he was allowed to take him home. Little Charles proved to be very bright, and in a few months had acquired quite a knowledge of the English language, learning also to read. His love for his own people, however, was not strong enough to draw his affections from the habits of his [Indian] life, and the restraints of his city home

---

71   "Diary of John Wilcox." The letter is dated August 24, 1865, but the account of the white Indian boy was added by Wilcox at a later, undated time, and included as a PS to his August 24 missive. The two white women would have been Mrs. Nancy Morton and Mrs. Lucinda Eubanks, both of whom were later rescued in present-day Wyoming, though Fanny Kelly claims it was just her that he knew. See next footnote. The little boy must have yet understood some English, in order to converse with the women captives.

were irksome to him. Having a hasty temper, he became offended at some remark made by his uncle, and immediately started to join the Indians, among whom he still remains, acting as a trader and interpreter, at North Platte City, Nebraska, on the Union Pacific Railroad.[72]

While the fight was occurring that Charles Sylvester witnessed near Coburn's ranch, a bigger fight was happening at the same time, about 70 miles further east, near Alkali Station. Alexander James Walker, Thomas McGee, Mike Whalen (also called Black Hawk) and James Stapleton, while stopped at Fort Kearny, had all bunched together with their individual freight trains to make a party of at least 15 wagons. They were freighting to Denver when they had camped for their midday break, a short distance

72 Larimer, *The Capture and Escape*, 139–140. Given Larimer's account, it is likely that Charles stayed at Mound Station for a few weeks before he was sent to St, Louis. It would also explain why he visited with Mr. Coburn at Chicago Ranch, seven miles west from Mound Station, so that he might be able to identify the dead Indians left on the ground after the skirmish on October 22. Alongside Larimer's account is a conflicting account from Fanny Kelly, who was captured with Sarah in 1864. Fanny remained in captivity five months before being rescued, while Sarah and her boy escaped after two days. In Kelly's book, she said in one of the villages she saw a 14-year-old white boy named Charles Sylvester, from Quincy, Illinois, who had been stolen seven years earlier. This all accords well with Larimer's account, but then Kelly changes the story, saying Charles was unable to remember his name or incidents of his capture, etc. It seems very strange the boy didn't know his name but Fanny Kelly did. Kelly goes on to state that Charles was still able to converse in English. Kelly's conflicting account:

> About a year after, when this boy was out hunting, he killed a comrade by accident, and he dared not return to the village; so he escaped on his pony to the white people. On his way to the states, he called at a house where they knew what tribe he belonged to, and they questioned him as to whether he had seen a white woman in the village. He replied in the affirmative and from a bundle of pictures given him he picked out mine saying "That is the white woman whom I saw."
>
> After a while, being discontented with his own people, he returned to his adopted friends on the North Platte and became an interpreter and trader. He still remains there doing business at various posts. (Kelly, *Narrative of My Captivity*, 160–161.)

What is strange about this story is that the beginning and end of her account reflects information Sarah had acquired in her narrative. The middle part, however, seems highly questionable and is probably imaginative writing. The possibility that the people whom Sylvester escaped to would have Kelly's picture to show him is extremely unlikely. Further, all the other accounts indicate the boy did not know his name when he appeared at Mound Station, leaving the reader to assume this part of Kelly's narrative uses information from Larimer and fashions it into a connection to herself. For further information about the two captivity narratives of Sarah Larimer and Fanny Kelly, see Farley, "An Indian Captivity and Its Legal Aftermath," 247–256. On May 28, 1869, a man named Charles Sylvester—quite likely the same man—was wounded in a raid Tall Bull's warriors made at Fossil Creek Stage Station at present-day Russell, Kansas. See Chapter 15; Adolph Roenigk, *Pioneer History of Kansas* (Self-published, 1933), 170–174. See also *New York Tribune*, June 3, 1869, Vol. XXIX, Issue 8784, p. 1.

west of Alkali Station. Part of the reason for going into camp was that a bigger train of about 40 wagons had stopped less than a mile to the east while one of the wagons was being repaired. Sometime between two and four o'clock that afternoon, anywhere from 200 to 500 Indians—mixed bands of Lakota, Cheyenne and Arapaho—attacked the 15-wagon camp, scattering the stock, which had been unhitched to graze a short distance from the corralled camp. The cattle had been grazing near the bluffs to the south of the trail when the Indians suddenly appeared and charged the men at their wagons, as well as the stock grazing several hundred yards to the south. They successfully stampeded the grazing herd to the top of the bluffs, while at the same time killing the herder that was with the stock. As soon as they had secured the freight stock, the Indians then resumed their attack upon the men, where their wagons had been unhitched. A short fight ensued, and two freighters were killed. Once the Indians withdrew, the men walked back east to Alkali Station.

Coincidentally, soon after this deadly skirmish, soldiers fortuitously appeared on the road from both the east and west. About 120–200 infantrymen and citizens came from the west, and about 150 cavalrymen came from the east. The stampeded stock was still in sight on the distant bluffs, and to that point the soldiers and citizens advanced. But it was soon discovered the Indians numbered about 1,000; and once the soldiers realized how outnumbered they were, the countercharge was abandoned.

Alexander Walker was making his second freighting excursion to Denver, both times delivering groceries and assorted goods. He witnessed the events and vividly recalled:

> We saw them [the Indians] about a mile west of us; they crossed—they were on the opposite side of the river, but crossed over to the south side—the side we were on—and when they came over there they dismounted, and stopped there about two minutes, I guess. We didn't know but what it was soldiers. . . . We heard a bugle, a bugle sounded, and they all dismounted. Of course, I did not understand anything about what the bugle meant [he had never served in the military]; one man said it did not mean to dismount. They all got off and we supposed they tightened their cinches on the horses; in about two minutes, I guess, they gave a yell, and then we got our guns, knowing there was going to be a fight . . . . They came right east for our wagons, right down the road; the road was near the Platte, I guess about 200 yards from it . . . we thought there was about 200 [warriors]; that is, that came there then, and when they made the charge on us, as quick as they got near enough, they

began firing on us, and we opened fire on them. . . . We were corralled, . . . stopped for dinner at noon; there was a wagon had broken down beyond us [about half a mile] and we thought we would wait in them [40 wagons]. . . . They [the Indians] did not accomplish anything right there at present; they fought us there for about ten minutes, I guess, probably 20, and we had our cattle out about 200 yards from the corral, and one man with them looking after them. They [then] went out there and killed him and took the stock, and drove them back in the bluff, 40 head of them [belonging to Walker], and as quick as they took the stock, they got away as quick as they could, and the boys that were hired [freighters], there was only three of us that owned the outfit, the boys that were hired thought there was no use to stop there, and they left . . . back to the other train, about half a mile back. . . . Well, [James] Stapleton and me stood there at the corral; we said we thought probably we could hold it ourselves. When we saw there was a big crowd, there was about a thousand of them. . . . It was probably half an hour; we was there at the corral alone. . . . Oh, they got to be a thousand of them, there was only about 200 of them at the start. . . . They came from everywhere—out of the bluff, we thought they were coming out of the ground; it was level prairie, they raised up 15, 20, 50 and 100 at a time; we supposed there was about a thousand altogether. . . . [When they came back] they just walked into the corral. . . . We walked off; we was within 30 feet of them; we did not run at all, we walked; we each had a gun and six shooter apiece; we didn't fire a shot and they didn't.[73]

It was very unusual that the Indians did not try to kill Walker and Stapleton, and Walker thought he knew why: "Stapleton was very red-headed, and had a big bunch of hair, and of course it was sticking up and very red; they was a little afraid of it. He had very fiery red hair. We stood there until they came within 30 feet of us."[74] Walker and Stapleton slowly walked from their corral, now inundated with Indians, to the other corral of 40 wagons about a half-mile distant to the east. At about the same time, soldiers approached from the west, but seeing so many Indians on the prairie in their front they quickly aborted their feeble attempt to retrieve the stock on the bluffs a few

---

73 Alexander J. Walker Indian Depredation Claim #7274. Record Group 123. See also the depredation claims of James Stapleton (#1264) and Thomas McGee (#948). One of the hired freighters was Michael Stapleton, the brother of James Stapleton. He must have been a shiftless brother, for years later he filed his own depredation claim, saying he owned the goods belonging to James Stapleton. As the claim was investigated it was proven to be a fraud. Years later, in 1889, James Stapleton testified that he was the owner of the goods destroyed by Indians, and his brother was making a fraudulent claim. The record went on to say that Michael's whereabouts had been unknown for years and it was believed that he was dead. They obviously drifted apart in the ensuing years. See Michael Stapleton Indian Depredation Claim #2329. Record Group 123.

74 Walker Depredation claim #7274.

hundred yards away. After this the civilians and most of the soldiers went back to Alkali Station two or three miles to the east. Four soldiers and an officer stayed at the corral until about five o'clock, and then started east to Alkali Station, when the Indians on the bluffs made a swoop upon them and, according to eyewitness Alexander Walker, killed them all. When the day was over, the wagons and contents, abandoned on the road at both corrals, were burned and destroyed and at least 130 mules were lost. One herder, two freighters, and five soldiers were dead.[75] The dead soldiers included 27-year-old Sergeant James Gruwell, 27-year-old Corporal Dewitt Chase, and 23-year-old Corporal Francis M. Stanley (or Standley), all of Company C, First Regiment of Nebraska Volunteer Cavalry. Twenty-two-year-old Private James Waugh survived with a shoulder wound. He was rewarded with a promotion to corporal 13 days later.[76]

The Indians probably felt they were in an ideal spot for taking advantage of unsuspecting freighters. If that was the case, then they remained in the area, for six days later, on October 28, they made another deadly attack at the same spot. In this raid, reports varied in stating anywhere from four to seven freighters were killed, but it was probably just four killed. The caravan attacked was much larger than the earlier train on October 22. Anywhere from 70 to 100 wagons were heading west, destination Denver and the mountain communities, bringing mostly groceries, flour, dried vegetables, etc. There were several different groups put into one long train. When they all joined together at Fort Kearny, Hamilton B. Garton was put in charge. His own freight wagons numbered 23. J. G. Lane had several more wagons, as did John Adle. When stretched out and rolling west, the wagons covered a distance, from front to back, of almost a mile.

The wagons had stopped at Alkali Station earlier in the day, and about noon or one o'clock they headed west, their destination the next station, Sand Hill. It was snowing lightly and a chilly day. They got about half-way, perhaps four or five miles from Alkali, when the Indians—60–75—were able to separate about a dozen wagons at the end of the long train. About 100 soldiers were near Alkali Station, commanded by Brevet Brigadier General

---

75   Walker, McGee and Stapleton Depredation claims. Pattison exaggerated the dead at 25. See Pattison, "With the U.S. Army," 87.

76   *Roster of Nebraska Volunteers From 1861–1869*, compiled by First Lieutenant Edgar S. Dudley (Hastings, NE: Wigton & Evans, State Printers, 1888), 31–43. Potter, *Standing Firmly by the Flag*, 205.

Herman H. Heath, but the train had gone beyond sight of the post, making it a perfect place for an ambush. J. G. Lane was hauling food wares to the mining towns, filling up several large wagons, pulled by five and six yoke of oxen. Lane described what happened:

> We were coming across with teams and the Indians were lying in hiding in the willows in the bed of the river; we were following along up the Platte River and it was pretty near dry, just a few little pools along here and there, and the bed of the stream had growed up to brush, mostly willows, and these bands of Indians were hiding there in the willows, and when the train came along they cut off I think it was 12 or 13 wagons off from the rear of the train, and ham-strung the oxen [cut the tendons], burned the wagons and killed four men.[77]

John Adle was also hauling groceries to the mining district. He had one wagon that got caught by the warriors. His wagon-load of dried onions was pillaged and his wagon burned. His oxen were yoked together, and all of them had their tendons cut while yoked to the wagon.[78]

It was the wagons belonging to Hamilton Garton that comprised the majority of those the Indians captured. Charley Bent and his group of Dog Soldiers were there, as well as Oglala under Standing Elk, and some Northern Cheyenne. Mr. Garton was shot with several arrows and bullets, dying where he fell. He was later found on the road, with his gun still at his side. Freighting with him were two sons, 16-year-old Elijah, and 20-year-old Ellis. Elijah had not been feeling well and had been riding in a wagon. When the attack came he made an effort to retreat west to the wagon train but he did not make it. Also killed were George Selby and Albert Gaskell.

Another wagon train was going east, and came upon the attack just as it was happening. One of the men was in advance of the wagons saw the fight. He raced back and reported what he saw. The freighters then drove their train into the corralled wagons that were ahead of Garton's captured wagons. The next day Henry F. Lentz, accompanying the train going east, observed the results of the fight:

> In the morning we started on and soon found the bodies of three of the party, as follows: Hamilton B. Garton, Elijah Garton, and George Selby, all of Wayne County, Iowa. The body of Albert Gaskell, of Decatur County, Iowa, was not found until the afternoon. On nearing the scene of slaughter we found the body of the

77   J. G. Lane Indian Depredation Claim #10273. Record Group 123.
78   John Adle Indian Depredation Claim #6373. Record Group 123.

first man lying on its face, with two arrows in the body and perfectly stripped, as were all but one. The second and third were but a short distance from it. The body of the boy had been partially burned and lay at the edge of the fire. Our men coming up saved the body of the fourth from being stripped. Since leaving Denver on the 19th day of October no less than twelve men have been murdered between the former point and Fort Kearney.[79]

The dead men were taken to Alkali Station and buried. Ellis Garton was put on a stage east. He was described as crazed over the incident, and the loss of his father and brother.[80]

Oliver Perry Wiggins was at Alkali Station, employed by the Overland Stage Company. He claimed his position was Chief of Scouts, in charge of 42 Omaha and Winnebago Indians. When Alkali was burned in the January attacks on the ranches and stage stations that included the attacks at Julesburg, the men running Alkali quit. Wiggins, then living in Denver, was hired to help at Alkali. He had been at the stage station since early April. Also at Alkali were about 20 soldiers used to escort stages east and west. They were Confederate prisoners—Galvanized Yankees—who had taken the Oath of Allegiance and were sent away from the Southern states and used for protection along the roads to Denver. Wiggins recalled they were commanded by Capt. Coffey, and had arrived from Johnson's Island in Detroit. Mostly Tennesseans, he said they were excellent soldiers and did fine duty at Alkali.[81]

When a report came back that the Garton train was under attack, Wiggins saw the smoke from Alkali and went to the scene. One of the first to arrive, he described what he saw:

> Well, the old man [Hamilton Garton] was shot and fell right by his wagon and his gun was alongside of him. They had taken the little boy, who was sick, from the wagon and put a large bread pan that was there on his breast and built a fire in it and tortured the little, sick fellow. There were five [sic] of the drivers lay dead there. The cattle were all driven [south about two miles] over the hills, horses, cattle and mules, by the Indians, except about five—from five wagons; they had ham-strung the oxen, five yoke to each wagon, they could not unhitch them, so they ham-strung them.[82]

---

79   The *Daily Rocky Mountain News*, November 7, 1865. J. G. Lane Indian Depredation Claim #10273. Record Group 123.

80   H. B. Garton Indian Depredation Claim #7075. Record Group 123.

81   John Adle Indian Depredation Claim #6373. Record Group 123.

82   H. B. Garton Indian Depredation Claim #7075.

Wiggins went on to report that the 7th Iowa Cavalry had come on the Denver road about May 1865, and soldiers were stationed at several stage stops. Alkali had a military post about a mile from the station, and, according to Wiggins' memory, at times included soldiers of the 16th Kansas Cavalry, under the command of Col. Sam Walker. In addition, more soldiers were ordered to Alkali on the day of the raid, after report of the attack via telegraph. They had come from O'Fallon's Bluff, about 25 miles east, ordered by General Heath. The cavalrymen raced westward, arriving at Alkali later that night. Wiggins said several horses died after arriving at the post, having been ridden so hard to get there. It also rendered the unit unfit for immediate pursuit of the raiders. Instead, after a stormy night, the next morning, October 28, Wiggins remembered two companies of the 7th Iowa Cavalry picked up the Indians' trail to the south. Wiggins went with them, as did several Indian scouts. The warriors appeared to try and divert the soldiers from following them, sending the stolen stock with a few Indians north, thinking any pursuit would follow the stock. Instead the soldiers and scouts, about 50 in number, followed the fainter trail to the south. The next day, October 30, the soldiers came upon the Indian camp on Frenchman's Creek, called White Man's Fork in 1865, probably not far from present-day Palisade, Nebraska. It was about 70 miles southeast of Alkali Station. Wiggins said the Indians were "eating supper under a bank, down in the creek bottom. . . . We crawled to the top of that bank and got a good shot at those Indians and we killed thirty-two of them; they were completely off their guard."[83]

Wiggins was rather accurate in his recollections, except it was one company of soldiers from the 1st Nebraska Cavalry, commanded by Captain Henry Krumme that surprised the Indians at Pointed Rock. The Battle of Pointed Rock was a decisive fight, and immediately punished the guilty Indians. A Report from the War Department summarizes the events:

On the evening of the 28th Genl. Heath reached Alkali with detachments of Cos. 'A' and 'B', 7 Iowa Vols. and Cos. 'E' and 'K'. 1 Neb. Vet. Cav. Vols., numbering in all seventy-five men. At eleven o'clock of the same night a report was made to Gen. Heath that the Indians had attacked and set fire to a wagon train about six miles distant [west]. Boots and saddles were at once sounded and as soon as possible Genl. Heath with the detachments spoken of were on the ground where

---

83   H. B. Garton Indian Depredation Claim #7075. Record Group 123.

the depredations had been committed. The enemy fled after killing four men, two of whom had been scalped, one terribly burned.[84] Six loaded wagons had been burned and sixteen mules stolen and a large number of cattle hamstrung and otherwise rendered useless. Owing to the darkness of the night immediate pursuit was impossible. At daybreak of the 29th Capt. [Henry] Krumme and Lt. [Martin B.] Cutler, 1st Neb. Cav. with 36 men were ordered out as an advance on the trail of the enemy followed by Genl. Heath on the 30th.[85] He was instructed to attack and hold the Indians, if possible, until Genl. Heath could come up with a larger force. Lt. Col. [Rufus] Fleming, 6th W. Va. Vet. Cav. Vols. with 45 men & Capt. [George] Norris, commandg Co. E, 7 Iowa Cav. Vols. with 40 men had in the meantime reported to Gen. Heath making the whole expeditionary command number 170 officers & men. The advance under Capt. Krumme met on the 30th, & engaged the enemy, 150 strong at Rocky Point. The fight lasted from 11 o'clock A.M. until 5 P.M., resulting in killing from 30 to 35 Indians. Capt. Krumme, fearing his ammunition would give out was compelled to fall back about 20 miles, at which place he met the main body at 11 o'clock the same night. Early on the following morning the whole command moved forward as rapidly as practicable but on reaching the camp of the Indians it was very obvious that they, the enemy, had made a hasty flight upon the approach of the troops, as quantities of flour, sugar, coffee & many articles captured from the train they had destroyed were left on the ground. The march was continued during the day & at dark the command went into camp without having found the enemy.[86]

The day after Krumme left Alkali, General Heath followed with a larger command. Each man had carried six days rations. Heath brought an ambulance to carry any soldiers that might get wounded, should the Indians be found. Heath left early on October 30, the same day Krumme had his fight 70 miles away. He also brought along a 12-pound mountain howitzer. Heath's command marched 50 miles the first day, and by the end of the day—Krumme's fight had now ended—several of Heath's men had suffered frost-bite. Krumme found Heath's camp about eleven o'clock that night, and reported his fight with the Indians earlier that day. Krumme's fight incurred just one soldier wounded. The Indians suffered 30–40 wounded, in addition to nearly three dozen killed. Heath's column reached Krumme's battle site

---

84   Pattison reported in his diary, "Train burned, oxen ham-stringed; four men killed and burned." Pattison, "With the U.S. Army," 87.

85   Pattison's diary said 48 men pursued. Perhaps the additional numbers represented Wiggins and some of his scouts. Pattison, "With the U.S. Army," 87.

86   War Department military report appearing upon a return of the East Sub-District of Nebraska for the month of October 1865, in H. B. Garton Indian Depredation Claim #7075. Record Group 123.

about three o'clock the next day, October 31. They then continued down White Man's Fork—today's Frenchman Creek—halting to camp at dark. Rain and snow fell on the soldiers that night. The next day, November 1, the command continued to follow the Indian trail. During the day the trail split, the larger one continuing south, in the direction of the Smoky Hill River. Heath followed that trail until late in the day. He wisely anticipated the Indians might attack his camp, so he placed more pickets out than usual. And indeed, about 11 that night, as many as 300 Indians attacked the camp from three sides, first firing on the six men stationed as pickets. The skirmish lasted about 30 minutes. The Indians tried unsuccessfully to stampede the horses. Forty troopers were ordered in pursuit, but the Indians crossed the river and got away. In this second fight, Heath estimated as many as 30 warriors were killed. No soldiers were wounded. The command began their return to Alkali the next morning, arriving there on the afternoon of November 3.[87]

Though the raiding warriors had been severely punished, it did not stop them from taking advantage of freighters using the Denver road. On October 31, Indians found an unsuspecting target in William Jones' small freight crew. "Billy" Jones was freighting mostly groceries from the east to Denver, in three wagons. The men had gone into camp at what was known as the Alkali Bottoms, two or three miles east of Beauvais Ranch (about 35 miles east of Julesburg). Sometime later in the night, Lakota and Cheyenne warriors succeeded in running off the stock, consisting of 24 steers and two horses. The freighters were unharmed and fled from their camp, and the Indians then got possession of the wagons. What the plundering warriors didn't take they destroyed, burning the wagons and the remaining contents. Jones' freight included 5,000 pounds of bacon valued at $1,400; 3,000 pounds of sugar worth $1,800; 2,000 pounds of coffee at $1,600; 3,000 pounds of flour at $750; 250 pounds of tea at $500; 76 gallons of whiskey at $950; 500 pounds of tobacco at $375; 300 blankets valued at $1500; and eight cases of boots worth $1,152.[88]

The next day, November 1, Jacob Penny was nearby, ready to cross the Platte and travel on the south side. He and his sons, Joseph, John, Thomas

---

87 Heath's report, in John Ludwickson, "Trouble at Alkali Station," unpublished manuscript, courtesy John Ludwickson, Curator of Anthropology, Nebraska State Historical Society. See also James E. Potter, *Standing Firmly by the Flag*, 205.

88 William Jones Indian Depredation Claim #7326. Record Group 123.

and Harvey, had recently delivered several wagons of freight up north to Fort Reno. They were returning with an unknown number of other independent freighters—all with their empty wagons—when they went into camp just a few miles west, on the north side of the Platte River from where Jones had been attacked on the south side the night before. The moon was full and sometime after 10 at night, anywhere from 25 to 75 warriors suddenly came screaming into the camp, coming to within 10 feet of the sleeping party. They succeeded in scattering the freight herd, which had been picketed several yards to the north of the camp. Penny lost 20 mules. About that number, along with a few horses, were taken from the other freighters. The next day, November 2, Jacob Penny reported that he met with a Captain Kelley, who was stationed with a small detachment of soldiers at a nearby ranch he called Rising Sun Ranch. With those soldiers an attempt was made to recapture the lost stock. When they got near Ash Hollow, some 15 miles away, they discovered several thousand Indians in camp nearby. Wisely, they gave up their quest to recover the stolen stock.[89]

The Indians continued their attacks upon the Denver roads through November. On November 5, Evan Davis—who had suffered a loss from an Indian raid back in July—had gone into camp at Sand Hill station, about nine miles east of Alkali Station.[90] Davis owned eight wagons loaded with freight destined for Denver. He had a total of 86 oxen to pull them, five yoke to a wagon with six to spare. He was a part of a larger wagon train, numbering 25 wagons and about 100 men. The train had gone into camp between seven and eight o'clock in the evening. The oxen were driven out about 250 yards from camp, where grass was available away from the well-traveled road. As Davis and some other men were walking back to camp, about 100 Indians suddenly appeared on horseback, shooting at the men and scattering the stock. Davis recalled the night: "The Indians shook their buffalo robes and yelled. I can hear them yet. They made these robes crack like a whip, and every steer was on the jump." Davis lost all 86 of his oxen, Joshua Hudson lost 80, and altogether 328 cattle and horses were stolen. The night

---

89 Jacob Penny Indian Depredation Claim #4634. Record Group 123.

90 This station is not to be confused with another station, also called Sand Hill, which was at the western terminus of the trail following the Little Blue River to the Platte River, much further east in Nebraska. The station Davis was referring to would be just south and near present-day Roscoe, Nebraska, east of Ogallala. The reader should be aware, however, that the depredation claim has conflicting testimony, saying both that Sand Hill was nine miles west and nine miles east of Alkali Station. In fact, the station was west of Alkali.

herder was shot and later found unconscious with a serious wound in the arm. His mule was killed. Stripped of his arms and spurs, the herder did not die. The 25 wagons were now stuck nearly 200 miles from Denver, with no stock to drive them. Oliver Wiggins, who operated Alkali Station and was also in charge of a contingent of Omaha scouts, identified the perpetrating Indians affiliated with Oglala Spotted Tail and Northern Cheyenne under Standing Elk. The warrior leading the raid was Standing Elk.[91]

The stranded freighters stayed with their wagons for nearly two months, finally selling everything to other freighters passing by, at a great loss. That was probably their best option, as evidenced by what happened five days later to the eight wagon freighting excursion of Frederick Ingham, S. A. Ingham and Augustus Christie. They had contracted with merchants to haul groceries and other goods from Nebraska City to Denver. When they got near Julesburg, the hired men put their stock out to graze for the night. Later that night about 20 Indians stampeded the stock, stranding the men with their wagons. The freighters felt they had no choice but to leave the wagons and go to Denver to get more animals to pull the wagons to their destination. They were only contracted to deliver the freight and thus were not authorized to sell it at a loss on the road. And of course, no freighter was anxious to remain with the wagons and protect the goods. Consequently, by the time they returned, the wagons were all destroyed and nearly all of the goods gone.[92]

While these raids were happening along the Denver road, the new Smoky Hill trail was also under attack, in all likelihood by the Southern Cheyenne contingent that George Bent was associated with, who were returning south to their winter quarters below the Arkansas River. On November 15, a stagecoach left Atchison, Kansas, for Denver, carrying eight people. When it got to Downer Station, Cheyenne Indians attacked the men, compelling them to flee for their lives. Lewis Perrin "and the four others who were able to escape from the pursuing Indians took refuge in a buffalo wallow, and there a running fire [fight] was kept up for several hours between them and the Indians; at nightfall, the Indians retiring from the field, they made good their escape."[93] Earlier in July, Perrin also lost a wagon, loaded with furs, in eastern Colorado, which he was transporting from Denver back east.

---

91 Evan E. Davis Indian Depredation Claim #6303. Record Group 123.
92 Frederick W. Ingham, S. A. Ingham, and Augustus Christie Indian Depredation Claim #6580. Record Group 123.
93 Lewis K. Perrin Indian Depredation Claim #4935. Record Group 123.

The 51-year-old Perrin lost his suitcase to the Indians. In it were new dresses for his wife and daughters, who were in Denver. When the men fled the wallow after nightfall, they made it to the next station 12 miles east, a stage stop known as Blufton Station.[94] It was found abandoned and the station burning. The Indians got there first. The men continued their foot journey east, when about midnight they met up with another stage driving west. Inside this coach was the famed Civil War sketch artist for *Harper's Weekly*, Theodore Davis. When it was learned of the murderous attack at Downer Station, the stage turned back to the next station east—bringing along the rescued men—Ruthden Station, which was also known as Louisa Springs. From there a messenger was sent back to Camp Fletcher—five miles south of present-day Walker, Kansas[95]—where Lt. Col. William Tamblyn had a small command of men. The stage waited almost 24 hours for the arrival of troops before venturing further west on the morning of November 21.

Lewis Perrin shared the details of the attack with Theodore Davis. The coach in which he was riding had arrived at Downer Station at two o'clock the day before. According to Davis, the eight men involved in the attack included the workers at the station: two stock herders, two carpenters and a blacksmith. There were only three men riding the stage, Perrin being the only passenger. Not long after the animals were unharnessed from the stagecoach and turned loose, Indians suddenly appeared from all directions. Everybody quickly ran into the station house and prepared for defense. One of the Bent brothers, thought to be Charles, was with the war party, and after identifying himself as a son of William Bent, began to parley with the white men.[96] He wanted to know if the new treaty [Treaty of the Little Arkansas] had been signed yet. Told it had been signed, the Indians then professed peace. They asked for the men to come out unarmed, and they would lay their weapons down too, and all could meet in the open and shake hands. The men agreed and came out from the building. The peace parley went on for just a short time, when the warriors suddenly pulled out hidden bows, arrows and pistols and began shooting at the men. One man, Fred Merwin, was killed instantly, and two other men, herders of the

---

94   Wayne C. Lee and Howard C. Raynesford, *Trails of the Smoky Hill: From Coronado to the Cow Towns* (Caldwell, ID: The Caxton Printers, Ltd., 1980), 55. See also 85, note 4.

95   Debra Goodrich Bisel and Michelle Martin, *Kansas Forts and Bases Sentinels on the Prairie* (Charleston and London: The History Press, 2013, 100. Camp Fletcher was later known as Old Fort Hays.

96   Thrapp, *Encyclopedia of Frontier Biography, Volume I*, 96.

stock, were captured and soon killed. The remaining men, unable to escape back into the adobe station house, fled to some nearby bluffs, where they took refuge in a buffalo wallow. In their hasty retreat they must have been able to retrieve their weapons, for they fought until dark, and then made their escape.

When the men were finally rescued by the stage Davis was riding in, they had used up all their ammunition, were hungry and very cold. Davis listened intently as Lewis Perrin gave his account of the fight in the buffalo wallow. Davis recorded Perrin's story, misspelling Perrin's name as Mr. Perine:

They formed a circle about us, riding dexterously and rapidly; occasionally one more bold then the rest would come within range of our revolvers, but he was careful to keep his body on the side of his pony away from us. Arrows came from all directions; a rifle or revolver bullet would whistle past us or strike the earth near. It was evidently their purpose to exhaust our ammunition, when they would be able to take us alive. Of this fact we were painfully aware and only fired at them when we were sure of a good shot. This kept them at a distance. The Negro blacksmith was armed with a Ballard rifle, with which he was a capital shot. He bravely exposed himself to obtain a shot, and came near losing his life by so doing. A bullet struck him in the head, when he fell, as we supposed, dead. I took his rifle, rolled the body up to the edge of the wallow to serve as a breastwork to shoot from, and commenced to fire. I had made several shots in this way, and had the rifle across his neck with a dead aim on an Indian when the darkey came to and remarked, "What you doing dar, white man?" thus discovering to us the fact that he was anything but a "gone coon dis time." He had been deprived of speech and power of motion by the shot, but was fully aware of what was going on about him. He was not disposed to regard the use of his body as a breastwork as altogether a pleasing performance.

While we were fighting from the wallow, we could plainly see the Indians that still remained about the adobe, at work torturing the stock-herders that they had succeeded in capturing alive.

One poor fellow they staked to the ground, cut out his tongue, substituting another part of his body [live castration] in its place. They then built a fire on his body. The agonized screams of the man were almost unendurable; about him were the Indians dancing and yelling like demons. The other stock-herder was shoved up to look at the barbarous scene, the victim of which he was soon to be, but they reserved him until nightfall, evidently hoping that we might be added to the number of their victims.

There could not have been less than a hundred and fifty Indians in the entire party—that is, those who were about us and those near the adobe. Bent told us that Fast Bear, a Cheyenne Chief, had command, but Bent is worse than any Indian, for he knows better. Had there been a possible chance to rescue the stock-herders, we should have attempted it. When darkness came the Indians withdrew, and as soon as we were convinced of the fact, we followed their example, going, it is unnecessary to remark, in the other direction [west]. Chalk Bluffs we found deserted and burning. Then we heard the coach coming and came to it. The Indians probably would have taken you in [Theodore Davis] if we had not.[97]

Once the soldiers joined with the stage at Ruthden Station, the party proceeded on their way to Denver, Perrin included. When they got to Downer Station, everything was burned and destroyed, including the abandoned stagecoach, but the three dead men were not to be found. A little further west they came upon a body, "or rather the remains of a man, evidently killed the night before. The wolves had stripped the bones of all flesh; face, hands and feet alone were unmarked. As we came near the wolves withdrew."[98] The stage traveled a day before coming to a station that wasn't deserted. There they found a corralled government wagon train. The Indians had earlier attacked it and killed one soldier. From these soldiers it was learned that they had come upon the dead men at Downer Station the day after the attack. They buried the men there and had beaten the graves down to prevent the wolves from digging them up.

Back on the Denver road, passage was still unsafe. On December 1, wagon master Andrew Brugh went into camp about nine miles west of Julesburg. He was returning three wagons to Nebraska City, after having delivered corn to Camp Collins earlier. There were other wagons with them, but the number is unknown. Around midnight, Lakota warriors stole about 60 oxen, nine of which belonged to Edwin Barnard, and another nine belonged to Spangler Brugh. The night herders had aroused the camp that Indians were stealing the stock. The men could hear the Indians taking the cattle across the Platte, but could not see them because it was too dark. The next day about 10 of the men tried to follow the warriors and retrieve the stock, but after several miles they gave up. Two days after the raid, soldiers from Fort Sedgwick came upon a party of Indians driving a large amount of stock about 35 miles north up Lodgepole Creek, and recovered about 40, four belonging to Barnard and five belonging to Brugh.[99]

Oliver Wiggins was at Alkali Station with his wife and children, running

97   Davis, "Stage Ride," 144–145.
98   Davis, "Stage Ride," 145.
99   Edwin Barnard Indian Depredation Claim #6239. Spangler Brugh Indian Depredation Claim #6236. Record Group 123.

the station there and tending stock. On the morning of December 5, Oglala and Cheyenne Indians appeared on the bluffs nearby, and immediately pounced on the grazing stock, which numbered 150–200 oxen. At the same time, a sharp fight ensued with a number of cavalrymen stationed at the nearby Alkali Post. The soldiers were forced to withdraw into the fort. Casualties are unknown.[100]

The next day, December 6, an unknown party of Indians appeared on the Denver road, all the way west at Wisconsin Ranch. The Coad brothers had diligently repaired their ranch from the attack earlier that year on January 15, when the Indians had burned all the buildings down. It had taken several men nearly a month of labor in rebuilding the ranch. The stables were rebuilt, 48 feet longer than the original stable. The stables, containing adobe walls nearly three feet thick, were large, 175 feet long and 28 feet wide. The original stable contained 44 double stalls, 10 feet deep and eight feet long, so the rebuilt ones were one fourth larger, being 228 feet long and 28 feet wide. The stalls were so large that when rebuilt, 500 pounds of nails had been used to reconstruct them. A squad of 10 soldiers from the 13th Missouri Cavalry was stationed at the ranch to provide protection for the mail route. The troopers rode with the mail stages back and forth as they passed, but that didn't stop at least two Oglala from sneaking up to the stables and setting them on fire. Fires were set in several places within the stables, which succeeded in burning them down. After this the brothers gave up rebuilding their important ranch.[101]

Mark Coad remembered the day very well:

John F. Coad, my brother, Benjamin Danielson [brother-in-law] and a squad of the Thirteenth Missouri Cavalry was at the ranch. I had started across the river

---

100 Oliver P. Wiggins Indian Depredation Claim #1323. Record Group 123. Oliver Wiggins lived a long life, finally settling in Denver. As the aging pioneers began to die off, Wiggins began to tell stories that seemed to grow in stature with each telling. He influenced early historians who freely quoted him in his claims to have traveled and fought with Kit Carson. In 1968, authors Lorene and Kenneth Englert called to task Wiggins's many claims. See Englert, *Oliver Perry Wiggins Fantastic, Bombastic Frontiersman* (Palmer Lake, CO: Filter Press, 1968). They cite a newspaper article confirming that Wiggins was a stage agent at Alkali in 1866 (p. 28). It is known from the depredation claim that he was already there in 1865. He thus lived there with his family for at least two years. Englert's study inspired Dan Thrapp to caution researchers that very little of what Wiggins said can be substantiated. (Thrapp, *Encyclopedia of Frontier Biography, Volume III*, 1563). While this is perhaps true regarding his claims associated with Kit Carson and earlier pre-territorial encounters, Wiggins' Indian Depredation Claim contains nothing of such experiences, and there appears nothing there to reject as not true.

101 Coad Brothers Indian Depredation Claim #7665. Record Group 123.

on the north side to go to Cedar Canyon after wood. . . . [After going about five miles] one of my men called to me and said there was a fire at the ranch. I looked around and saw one of the buildings was on fire [the stable]. I then went to the mess wagon and got out my field glass and looked at the ranch and saw the men rushing around as though they were fighting Indians. I saw two men going from the ranch on horseback, one ahead of the other and one standing and looking toward the buildings. I looked at one and saw he was an Indian as I could see the feathers tied to his pony and he had a war bonnet on. I could not see the other one near enough to know what he was but I am satisfied he was an Indian too. They were going from the ranch toward the hills [south]. I turned the train around and went back to the ranch to see what the trouble was. I saw the large stable which we had was burning and a quantity of corn that was piled against the side of the stable, a span of horses, a cow and some harnesses that we had in the stable. They were all burned.[102]

In addition to the burned stable and lost stock, 150 tons of hay had been stacked against the stable, and it was also burned. John Coad, who had just arrived at their ranch the day before with a load of supplies from Nebraska City, recalled what he and Danielson experienced.

It was somewhere about one o'clock, and we had been sitting at the table but a short time when Danielson [Danielson's wife and two children were in the house at the time] discovered smoke passing the window and he went to the door to see what it was and on looking out yelled "Indians." I went to look for the key to the store, as our arms were locked up in the store. That is why I did not get out in time to see the Indians. I rushed over to the store and unlocked it and got our arms and then went over to the stable, which I entered at the side door. When I arrived there the roof of the stable was all in flames.[103]

The soldiers' horses were in the back of the stable, but they were able to be rescued from a rear door. The Coads' stock was in the front of the stable where the fire was started, and they perished.

Danielson's memory gave his perspective:

I did not see the fire set but Mr. [John] Coad and myself were sitting inside of the dwelling house as we had closed the store on account of the soldiers being there. There was no one in sight when we saw the fire but we rushed out the front door and I saw two Indians riding not a quarter of a mile away and they were going up the hill [south]. We could not get into the stable but both the back and front doors

---

102   Coad Brothers Indian Depredation Claim #7665.
103   Coad Brothers Indian Depredation Claim #7665.

were open. The stable was afire the whole length of it and there were no one in sight until the soldiers came out of their quarters [small tents]. It appeared to have been set afire in a great many places at about the same time just as though the Indians had ridden through on horseback and fired it as they went along and there being hay on the roof it went like powder.[104]

The burning of the stable at the Wisconsin Ranch ended the raids in 1865 along the roads to Denver. Regarding the Denver road, Indians remained around the area until April 1866. There would be more activity along the Smoky Hill trail in the ensuing year.

---

104 Coad Brothers Indian Depredation Claim #7665.

ETCHING OF FORT SEDGWICK,
SHOWING THE 3RD REBUILT TOWN OF JULESBURG,
ACROSS THE RIVER.

Fort Sedgwick was originally Camp Rankin, but was commissioned Fort Sedgwick in September 1865, and remained active until closed in the spring of 1871. *Courtesy History Colorado (Scan #10038534), Denver.*

CHAPTER NINE

Treaty Failures

White men must build no more houses out here, must burn no more of their wood, must drink no more of their water, must not drive the buffalo off, that the railroad must not come any further, and that the Santé Fe line must be stopped.

SATANTA TO CAPTAIN HENRY ASBURY

"HEADQUARTERS, FORT LARNED, KAS., FEBRUARY 27, 1867"

RECORD GROUP 393, PART I, LETTERS RECEIVED 1867

DEPARTMENT OF THE MISSOURI, ENTRY 2593

T HE WINTER OF 1865–1866 WAS A MILD SEASON FOR SNOW and cold weather in Kansas and the territories of Nebraska and Colorado.[1] Unlike 1867, which was an extremely wet summer, the summer of 1866 had both wet and dry episodes, the spring being dry and midsummer wet.[2] The issues angering the Cheyenne continued to build into a gathering storm. A review of treaties they had made can magnify some of their motivation to continue on the warpath. Their first treaty with the United States was the confederated 1851 tribal treaty of Fort Laramie. For the Cheyenne and Arapaho, it gave them the land roughly from present-day Casper, Wyoming, all the way south along the foothills of the Rocky Mountains to the Arkansas River at present-day Pueblo, Colorado, and extending all the way east to roughly present-day Dodge City, Kansas, and up north to present-day North Platte, Nebraska. Within 10 years it was clear that this Indian region was too vast to allow for western expansion. Continued white encroachment, along with the discovery of gold in what would

---

1   Watson Coburn Indian Depredation Claim #8988. Record Group 123.
2   James C. Malin, "Dust Storms Part Two, 1861–1880," *Kansas Historical Quarterly*, Vol. IV (August 1946), 268.

become Colorado Territory, led the government to introduce a new treaty in 1861, the Treaty of Fort Wise. Soon after this treaty was hammered out the fort's name was changed to Fort Lyon. But in this treaty, the Cheyenne and Arapaho conceded nearly all of the land given to them in the 1851 treaty. What was left was a small section of eastern Colorado, roughly along the Arkansas River from present-day Rocky Ford to present-day Lamar, and extending north to about present-day Kit Carson. That changed with the signing of the Treaty of the Little Arkansas in 1865. The land given in the 1861 Fort Wise treaty was taken away, and the Cheyenne and Arapaho were removed from Colorado Territory and given land from present-day Great Bend, Kansas, down to present-day Enid, Oklahoma. After the violence of Indian raids in Kansas in 1868, the Indians were removed to their present reservation land in Oklahoma.[3]

As the Indians experienced their land losses via the various treaties, there was the further problem that large numbers of Cheyenne tribal leaders were not involved in the treaty-making process, and they therefore felt that the treaties did not apply to them. George Bent recalled the Fort Wise treaty this way:

> it had been signed by only a few men and without the consent of the tribe; these men had deeded away most of the tribe's lands and had consented to the cooping up of the people on a small reservation; they had not even understood what they were signing, and had been induced to put their cross-marks on the paper by bribery, by the liberal distribution of presents. The Cheyenne therefore said the treaty was worthless, ...[4]

Bent was not as critical of the Treaty of the Little Arkansas in 1865, though he said of it that only one-sixth of the Cheyenne tribe was there, and that "it was always easy to induce Indians to sign a treaty, even if they do not like its provisions."[5] Still, as a result of this treaty, the year 1866 along the

3   Charles J. Kappler, compiled and edited, *Indian Treaties 1778–1883* (Mattituck, NY: Amereon House, 1972), 594–595; 807–810; 887–891; 984–989; Jerome A. Greene, *Washita: The U.S. Army and the Southern Cheyennes, 1867–1869* (Norman, OK: University of Oklahoma Press, 2004), 11–13; Kraft, *Ned Wynkoop*, 159–165.

4   Hyde, *Life of George Bent*, 118.

5   Hyde, *Life of George Bent*, 248. Elsewhere Bent said that the six Cheyenne who signed the treaty, only four of whom were of the Council of 44—the Cheyenne leadership hierarchy—was a "slap in the face" to the other appointed chiefs. See Thom Hatch, *Black Kettle: The Cheyenne Chief Who Sought Peace but Found War* (Hoboken, NJ: John Wiley & Sons, Inc., 2004), 82; William Y. Chalfant, *Hancock's War: Conflict on the Southern Plains* (Norman, OK: The Arthur H. Clark Company, 2010), 35–36.

ARTIST RENDITION OF AN ATTACK ON THE
OVERLAND STAGE COMPANY ALONG THE SMOKY HILL ROAD.
Courtesy National Archives Building, Washington, DC.

trails to Denver was the least violent of the years from 1864 to 1869.[6] But, though the 1865 treaty was believed sufficient to stop the Cheyenne and other tribes from continuing the war, there was still the need to align their Lakota allies in a separate treaty. In January 1866, runners were sent from Fort Laramie to the various Lakota camps in the Powder River, urging them to come to Fort Laramie for a peace council. Spotted Tail, the new leader of the Brule, was one of the first to respond. By March 9, Colonel Henry Maynadier, commanding the post at Fort Laramie, reported that Spotted Tail was coming to the fort for council, but that he first wanted to bury his 17-year-old daughter, who had just died. She was his eldest and favorite daughter.[7]

Brings Water (Mini-Aku), also called Monica, became ill while in camp on the Powder River, most likely suffering from tuberculosis, and while en route to Fort Laramie, she died. Before she died, she made a request of her

6 George Bird Grinnell, *The Fighting Cheyennes* (Norman, OK: University of Oklahoma Press, 1956), 246.

7 George E. Hyde, *Spotted Tail's Folks: A History of the Brule Sioux* (Norman, OK: University of Oklahoma Press, 1961), 108; John D. McDermott, "No More Snowstorms, Tears or Dying," (*Wild West*, February 2006), 26. An excellent account of this is in McChristian, *Fort Laramie*, 255–260.

father to be buried at Fort Laramie. Colonel Maynadier had known Brings Water when she was twelve, when he was stationed out west in 1861.[8] When he learned of this request from Spotted Tail, he prepared a coffin and had her body put in the northwest section of the post cemetery. The post chaplain conducted a Christian burial service, which was translated to the grieving family. A scaffold was erected, and after the reading of the burial service her coffin was raised upon the scaffold.

This kindness by Maynadier, perhaps partially motivated to make a positive impression upon Spotted Tail for the ensuing peace talks, had its desired effect. Three days later the first peace talks were held with about 150 Lakota present. Significant among those present was Red Cloud, Oglala leader of the Bad Face band, one of the more prominent allegiances of Indians engaged in the attacks in the Powder River country through 1865. One principal complaint from the Indians was the increasing presence of travelers into the Powder River country, especially through the newly opened road known as the Bozeman trail. This is significant because the principal violence throughout 1866 and into 1867 centered upon this road. Nevertheless, these initial peace talks were productive, and all agreed to return in early June and sign a new peace treaty.[9]

By early June, throngs of Indians had congregated near Fort Laramie, ready for the peace council. It began June 6, and lasted two days. Hundreds of warriors were present, while 1,000 remained nearby at their river camps. Included among the Lakota were several Northern Cheyenne and Arapaho. Their principal complaint, again, was the traffic along the Bozeman trail, which they felt affected the buffalo migrations, keeping them away from the Powder River country. Unknown to the Indians, however, was the fact that the government was just about to formally announce the new road, and had plans to immediately construct forts along its path. That changed, however, when Colonel Henry B. Carrington arrived at Fort Laramie with the Second Battalion of the 18th Infantry. This large command had recently left Fort Kearny to establish the proposed forts along the Bozeman trail. Red Cloud perceived this as mistrust in the negotiations, refused further

---

8   Hyde says this meeting occurred near Deer Creek on the North Platte River in 1859 (*Spotted Tail's Folks*, 108). McChristian says it happened in 1861, which would be the more likely date if she was 17 when she died in 1866. *Fort Laramie*, 255.

9   McChristian, *Fort Laramie*, 260.

involvement and left with his band.[10] Spotted Tail, on the other hand, was not vested in the Powder River country, doing most of his hunting and camping down on the Platte. He and other inclined chiefs signed the treaty at Fort Laramie, and the consequences were that most of the violence of 1866 occurred in the Powder River country, while the trails to Denver were generally safer than they had been in 1865. Spotted Tail's influence down south was a big factor in the lessening violence on the Platte River trail.

This does not mean there weren't raids along the Denver roads, for there were. Sometime between April 10 and 15 Lakota and Cheyenne again visited Watson Coburn's Chicago Ranch on the South Platte, and stole 84 work cattle. The cattle were grazing on a nearby range and Coburn had gone to check on them in the early morning when he noticed them missing. He followed their trail for about half a mile when he came upon three men on horseback on a nearby hill. Approaching them he came within 100 yards when he discovered they were Indians. The warriors fled to the north and Watson retreated to his ranch. He then returned to where he had first discovered the Indians and followed their trail for a few miles "to convince myself that they had the cattle, and that it was useless for me to go any further alone. Not only useless but dangerous."[11]

More killings happened in May. Indian interpreter John S. Smith, who was in the village at Sand Creek in 1864 and survived, reported that in early June 1866, he was with Black Kettle's village south on the Arkansas River. While there he was invited to a council where he was told that Dog Soldiers, one of whom was from Black Kettle's village, had recently killed six settlers "somewhere on the headwaters of the Solomon." The reason the men were killed was because the Dog Soldiers, being hungry, approached their camp and were fired upon, one Indian being wounded.[12] Smith was no doubt referring to the party of six hunters mentioned in Roenigk's *Pioneer History of Kansas*. The party consisted of an old trapper named Lewis Cassil, a man named Walter Haynes, two other men named Roberts and Talbert, and two sons of William Collins. Out on a buffalo hunt they were camping on Buffalo Creek, in the southeastern part of Jewell County, southwest of present-day

10   McChristian, *Fort Laramie*, 269. See also John McDermott, *Red Cloud's War*, Volume 1, 59–61.
11   Coburn Indian Depredation Claim #8988.
12   Report of John S. Smith, August 15, 1867. *Difficulties With Indian Tribes*, 41st Congress, 2d Session, House of Representatives, Ex. Doc. 240, 144–145.

Jamestown, when the Indians attacked them. In a letter dated October 6, 1867, written from Clifton, Kansas, John Haynes named the victims as Louis Castle, Walter Haynes, Mr. Robberts, Mr. Talman and two Mr. Collins.[13]

According to Roenigk, the men had retreated to the southeast, fighting the Indians until they were finally overtaken and killed at Little Cheyenne Creek:

> The scene of the massacre showed that a desperate fight had taken place. In one of Cassil's hands when found was his empty revolver, in the other several cartridges, as though the last death-grip had clutched them and had not been relaxed, although he had been killed several days previous, showing that he had made a brave defense to the last. The fact that the Indians only took the horses, leaving the wagon and the revolver in the lifeless grasp of Cassil, was evidence that they had suffered a heavy loss in killed and wounded, whom they conveyed away.[14]

Another raid was made along the Denver road near Fort Morgan, at about the same time that the peace council was concluding up north at Fort Laramie. Edson (Ed) Boughton, along with his brother M. V. Boughton, was the post trader at the newly constructed Fort Morgan. They also ran the

13 John Haynes, "Letter to Governor Crawford, Oct. 6, 1867," Kansas State Historical Society, Document 970 495e, Archives Department, Topeka, Kansas. Haynes said that these people were killed in May 1866.

14 Roenigk, *Pioneer History*, 346. There is a dispute as to the names of the victims and, more importantly, the year of their deaths. Roenigk said it happened in 1866, acknowlededged there was a discrepancy in date, but said that his sources convinced him the massacre happened in 1866. M. Winsor and James Scarbrough, in 1878 published a pamphlet titled *History of Jewell County, Kansas, with a full account of its early Settlements and the Indian Atrocities Committed Within its Borders* (Jewell City, KS, 1878). The authors reported the massacre happening in the middle of May 1868, not 1866. The men's names were spelled Lewis Castle, Walter Haines, two brothers named Roberts, and two sons of a man named Collins (see p. 11). Roenigk's 1866 account is the correct year, supported by the Smith report of the killing of six men near the headwaters of the Solomon and the Haynes letter to Governor Crawford mentioned in the footnote above. If the headwaters of the Solomon is meant to be where the north and south forks join, then the place where Cassil (or Castle) was killed is about 20 miles from where Smith said the Indians reported killing six men in May 1866. Further, a newspaper report dated September 19, 1866, says that Kansas Governor Crawford reported via telegraph of the killing of seven settlers at the forks of the Solomon River. See *West Eau Claire Argus*, September 19, 1866, West Eau Claire, Wisconsin, p. 2. This also supports the Roenigk/Haynes/Smith timeframe. More verification comes from *The Janesville Gazette*, September 7, 1866, Janesville, Wisconsin. It reports from Kansas the following: "In May seven settlers were killed on Republican and Salmon [sic] rivers. The whole neighborhoods were driven from their homes on White Rock, abandoning improvements and crops. Several women were repeatedly ravished and otherwise savagely treated." Colonel Edward Wynkoop also verified the killing of six white men by Cheyenne, which he said was justified, no doubt hearing the same story that John Smith reported. See Major General W. F. Cloud, Kansas State Militia, "Letter to Maj. Gen. W. S. Hancock, December 22, 1966, Record Group 393, Part I, Letters Received, Department of the Missouri, Entry 2593, 1867. In General Cloud's letter he also reported two other settlers killed in the vicinity of Buffalo Creek west of Lake Sibley. These men were probably John Fott and Mr. Smith. See John Haynes, "Letter to Governor Crawford."

store at Junction Ranch next to Fort Morgan. Edson also had a freighting outfit separate from his sutler pursuits. It was his freighting outfit that was hit. On June 12, he had two or three wagons and was proceeding west from Junction Ranch, when he stopped at 11 o'clock that morning, about 400 yards east of Fremont Station. The men with him, James K. Maloney, James Thompson, and Thomas Donohue went into their noon camp and set the stock to graze. The stock consisted of 12 mules and four work horses. Boughton was riding in a two horse carriage. On the back of the carriage he had tethered an expensive race horse. He was proceeding to Fremont Station, when suddenly two dozen Indians came charging from a nearby sand hill. They quickly spooked the grazing stock and drove them away, while some of the Indians made a feint at Boughton in his wagon. The race horse got spooked and broke his tether, which caused the charging Indians to stop chasing Boughton and instead capture the prized horse.

Samuel Ashcraft was a witness to the theft. He coincidentally had just arrived at Fremont Station from the west when he observed the raid:

> I got to the station a few minutes before this happened and I had just picketed my horses out across the road, and I looked right down the river and I saw these Indians upon a sand hill. Then they made a dash for these mules and horses and they drove them off. Boughton was coming up one of the roads and his wagons was camped down on the other road, the Indians drove the mules and horses across the road behind Broughton and then is the time his race horse jerked loose and the Indians run after Broughton a ways but he outran them.[15]

Boughton's excursion along the Denver road in June was a part of an increasing number of freighters entering the new freighting season, despite the very real threat of Indian attack. From June 14 to June 20, records at Fort Morgan—named Camp Wardwell at the time—confirm the passing of 172 wagons, 88 of them going to Denver, the rest going to Leavenworth. Wagons were not permitted to travel in either direction unless they were banded in groups of twenty or more. No less than 247 men accompanied the wagons, carrying a total of 287 rifles and pistols.[16] If this was averaged out into the month, it would mean more than 350 wagons bringing freight into Denver, or 12 wagons a day, with about the same number traveling east.

---

15   Edson Broughton Indian Depredation Claim #587. Record Group 123.

16   "Tri-monthly report of trains passing Camp Wardwell (Fort Morgan) en route east and west, from the 14th of June to the 20th of June, 1866." Record Group 393, Part I. Department of the Platte, Letters Received, Box 1A.

Some of the raids happening in 1866 were actually committed by Indians other than Cheyenne or Lakota, which confirms that the two peace treaties did have an effect along the Denver trails, at least in 1866. On July 7, Robert Smith and four other men were on a buffalo hunt in Mitchell County, in north-central Kansas, when Pawnee Indians sneaked into their camp at about one o'clock in the morning, cut the ropes tethering their horses and mules and took them all. The theft was discovered at dawn. Smith lost a horse and a mule.[17] Four months later, the Cheyenne were blamed for the death of Andrew W. Smith. He had been out on a buffalo hunt with neighbors in Osborne County, but stayed back to trade with the Otoe after his partners left. While with the Otoe, an unknown number of Cheyenne had come into the vicinity and killed Smith as he was on his way back home.[18]

At the time of the theft of Robert Smith's stock, a more sinister raid took place on White Rock Creek in Jewell County, just to the north. John Marling had just claimed a site to homestead and had been there for only three weeks when a band of Indians, thought to be Cheyenne, came to the wagon he was living in with his wife and child. The Indians stole or destroyed everything in the wagon, scattering and tearing the feathers from the mattress and pillows. They then took Mrs. Marling into the nearby woods, where she was repeatedly raped. She could not say how many men raped her, but the trampled ground and the countless pony tracks indicated it was a large number.[19] An account written 12 years later gave more details. Saying the rape happened in August, not July, 40 Cheyenne were seen approaching Marling's home. Upon seeing them Marling jumped on his horse and went to the nearest settlement about 10 miles away to get help. The relief party returned the next morning and discovered Mrs. Marling in a dazed condition. The Indians had placed a rope around her neck, then "dragged her a short distance into the timber, where the whole party outraged her in the most brutal and fiendish manner, and left her in an insensible condition." When she was found the next morning she

was perfectly wild, and when she discovered her relief party, she could only see
in them her late fiendish and inhumane persecutors, and in order to escape being

---

17   Robert W. Smith Indian Depredation Claim #3300. Record Group 123. Other residents in the area also filed claims against the Pawnee, saying that their property was destroyed after they fled to Minneapolis for protection. They didn't return until the next year. See Alfred Shull Indian Depredation Claim #3702 and John Rees Indian Depredation Claim #3677. Record Group 75.

18   Uriah J. Smith Indian Depredation Claim #3741. Record Group 75.

19   John Marling Indian Depredation Claim #2944. Record Group 123.

retaken she continually darted from place to place as fast as her little child, who accompanied her, would permit. It was with considerable difficulty that her husband could get near enough to make her hear her name—"Elizabeth"—called. Hearing her name called, she knew they were friends, and stopped.[20]

While these infrequent but violent raids were occurring, General W. T. Sherman was making a long tour of the various Army posts and commands through the territories of Nebraska, Wyoming and Colorado. He observed an active commerce and what he felt was no real threat of Indian hostilities. Sherman wrote on August 21: "There seems to be no danger or apprehension of danger, for the telegraph line and the stage line have never been seriously molested [in 1866], and you are never out of sight of a train or a ranche." Still, he admitted that there lingers "a general apprehension of danger, though no one seems to have a definite idea of whence it is to come."[21]

After agreeing to the peace treaty at Fort Laramie, Spotted Tail moved his tribe down to the Platter River, about eight miles north of Beauvais Stage Station on the Fort Laramie road, near present-day Ogallala, Nebraska. On July 31, a mere month after Spotted Tail agreed to peace, a few of his young warriors left their camp and met a white man, about three miles away from Beauvais Station, at a station called Diamond Springs. There they procured whiskey and got roaring drunk. With the whiskey inside him, one Indian became very belligerent, and with his bow and arrow attacked several white men at Diamond Springs. The Indians then fled back to their camp. A stagecoach coming from the east learned of the attack while stopped at Beauvais Station, and when they got to Fort Sedgwick on August 1, the driver reported the incident to Colonel Carroll H. Potter, commanding the post. The driver reported one citizen had been killed and two were severely wounded. Col. Potter immediately took some of his men and went to the station to investigate. When he got there he learned the truth of what happened. Actually, no men were killed but two were severely wounded and another man was only slightly hurt.

What happened next is a testament to the resolve of Spotted Tail to keep

---

20   M. Winsor and James Scarbrough, *History of Jewell County*, 5. In the depredation claim Marling makes it clear that there was no cabin from which he fled, as they were living in their wagon. Probably, had not Marling fled, he would have been killed, as with the case with William Morris at the American Ranch in January 1865.

21   General W. T. Sherman, "Report from Fort McPherson, August 21," and "Fort Sedgwick August 24, 1866," 39th Congress, 2d Session, House of Representatives, Ex. Doc No. 23 (Washington, DC: Government Printing Office, 1867), 5–7.

the peace. It says a lot about his ability to control his young men who might cause trouble. After wounding the white men, the guilty Indians went back to their village and reported a different and false story than what really happened. The Indian who wounded the white men had apparently been beaten, for he went back and reported the abuse to the tribe and demanded revenge. Several of the young warriors were preparing to retaliate against the men at Diamond Springs, but before they could leave, Spotted Tail stopped them. A couple Indians from Standing Elk's Brule band—who also had signed the treaty a month earlier at Fort Laramie—were present when the drunken Indian made his violent attack and was beaten. They had come to Spotted Tail at the urging of an interpreter at Diamond Springs who witnessed the incident, and feared that the justly beaten Indian would go back to Spotted Tail's people and urge the other warriors to return and kill the white men. Indeed this was exactly what was happening when they arrived at Spotted Tail's village. The Standing Elk Indians reported to Spotted Tail the truth of what really happened, and when Spotted Tail heard this he took charge. He publicly whipped—severely—the drunken Indian, killed his pony, and then whipped the guilty Indian's father for taking the side of his son. And he let that be a lesson to his tribe that he would punish anyone who unjustly tried to engage in such violence against whites. He meant peace and he was going to do whatever was in his power as chief to preserve it.

When Colonel Potter learned what Spotted Tail had done to keep the peace, he sent word that he would like to visit with the chief. He was told Spotted Tail was ill and could not visit with him. Potter was then informed by his interpreter, who had seen Spotted Tail, "that he had been drinking which was the cause of his sickness, and that he was ashamed to see me, until he was perfectly sober." By six o'clock that evening, Spotted Tail had recovered enough and came down to visit with Potter. He apologized for the transgression of his unruly brave and offered to the injured white men, as further recompense several ponies, professing again his commitment to the new peace. Potter felt the guilty Indian had been punished enough and turned down the ponies. Spotted Tail told Potter who had sold the Indians the whiskey, which started all the trouble in the first place. The guilty white man was a trader at Diamond Springs, a man named D. D. Jennings, whom Potter immediately arrested and brought back to the jail at Sedgwick.[22]

---

22   Colonel Carroll H. Potter, "Report," Headquarters, Fort Sedgwick, August 2, 1866. Record Group 393, Part 1, Department of the Platte, Letters received, 1866. Box 1A. It is interesting how Spotted Tail

On September 6, Cheyenne Indians stole a mule and horse from A. D. Teasley and another horse from his neighbor, Anderson Bagwell, in Cloud County, Kansas.[23] At about the same time, 14 horses were taken from settlers down by the Huerfano River southeast of Pueblo. On November 10, a Cheyenne named Fox Tail killed a New Mexican herder near Fort Zarah.[24] George Bent identified him as a Dog Soldier and said the killing happened after Fox Tail got drunk and began a quarrel with the Mexican herder, who was employed by William Bent, George's father.[25]

It was hoped that the new treaty would end such attacks. But while it is understandable that the new treaty did lessen problems along the roads to Denver in 1866, this did not mean there was not a major conflict brewing. There was, but not on the Denver trails during the winter of 1866–1867. Instead it was along the Bozeman trail through present-day Wyoming and into Montana. Red Cloud's camping grounds were in the Powder River country, and the Bozeman trail directly affected his hunting areas. And so, the warring activities that were carried out in this area in 1865 continued into 1866 and included the contested Bozeman trail. The biggest event happened at the end of the year, on December 21, just outside of Fort Phil Kearny. Captain William J. Fetterman, with two other officers, two civilians, and a mix of both infantry and cavalry, a total of 81 men, left Fort Phil Kearny in pursuit of a band of Indians attacking a wood train party a few miles west of the fort. By the time the command went in relief, the attack had been called off, but the Indians—thought to be about 100—were seen retreating to the north of the fort. Captain Fetterman, in charge of the command, went off in pursuit, while Lieutenant Grummond, in charge of the cavalry, soon bolted off beyond Fetterman's marching infantry. When out of sight of the fort, but not out of hearing, the 100 Indians turned out to be over 1,000 waiting to ambush the soldiers. The surprise was complete and

acted to keep the peace. One wonders whether Black Kettle tried any similar means to control his unruly young warriors who did their fair share of stirring up trouble in 1864, prior to the affair at Sand Creek. If he had not, but would have, perhaps there would not have been the nasty affair of November 29, 1864. There is no evidence that he did take such measures as Spotted Tail took, so one may never know. For a recent study of alcohol and the Indian, see William E. Unrau, *Indians, Alcohol, and the Roads to Taos and Santa Fe* (Lawrence, KS: University Press of Kansas, 2013).

23   A. D. Teasley Indian Depredation Claim #3752. Record Group 75.

24   *Difficulties With Indian Tribes*, 116, 144. See reports in Ray Sparks File, Orvel Criqui Collections, Kansas State Historical Society, Topeka, Kansas. Reports from H. R. Wyatt, William Comstock and James Wadsworth. Also see Report of 1st Lieutenant Joseph Hale, 3rd Infantry, Fort Wallace, December 19, 1866, Record Group 393, Part I, Letters Received 1867, Department of the Missouri.

25   Hyde, *Life of George Bent*, 253.

in a short time Fetterman's command was annihilated to a man. This killing of Fetterman's command stood as the largest defeat during the 1860s–1870s Indian wars, until surpassed by Custer's more famous defeat at the Little Bighorn in 1876.[26]

By early 1867, incidents along the southern river routes began to increase. On January 8, 1867, Arapaho Indians burned 60 cords of wood on Pawnee Fork, between Fort Larned and Fort Dodge. The wood had been cut and stacked by eight men under the charge of Benjamin H. Clark, in preparation to freight it to Fort Dodge, where Theodore Weichselbaum and Calvin Dyche were post traders and had a contract to sell the wood to the government at $15.72 per cord. It cost $10 per cord in labor to cut and deliver the wood to Fort Dodge, so their profit was slightly over $5 per cord, the equivalent of about $81 in today's income.[27] But before it could be hauled away, Arapaho Indians under Little Raven set it on fire and destroyed it. Coincidentally, as the wood was burning, scout Charles Christy was delivering dispatches from Fort Dodge to Fort Zarah. The Indians saw him, chased him and then shot him in the right side with an arrow. Christy escaped but was severely wounded.[28] Yet another burning of wood would occur seven weeks later in the same vicinity.

Meanwhile, back on the Denver road, on January 15, a large party of Indians was seen near Fort Sedgwick. But they were not interested in attacking the post, for they quickly disappeared.[29] Their chances were better with a wood party about 80 miles northwest. Thirty-three-year-old Mark Coad, who with his younger brother John, had earlier operated Wisconsin Ranch, which was attacked and burned twice in 1865, were in 1867 living in

---

26 Three recent books have been published, that cover important incidents in Red Cloud's War, all of them dealing with the Fetterman defeat. See Monnett, *Where a Hundred Soldiers Were Killed*; Shannon D. Smith, *Give me Eighty Men: Women and the Myth of the Fetterman Fight* (Lincoln and London: University of Nebraska Press, 2008); McDermott, *Red Cloud's War*.

27 See http://www.westegg.com/inflation/infl.cgi (accessed April 27, 2013).

28 Theodore Weichselbaum and Calvin Dyche Indian Depredation Claim #1007. Record Group 123. Ben Clark was later a scout with Custer at the Washita fight and left accounts of his experiences with Custer, and Charles Christy was a scout with Colonel Carpenter in the relief of Forsyth's scouts at the Battle at Beecher's Island in 1868. In this depredation claim, Christy refused to turn over his diary to the court when he gave his deposition, which has confirmation of the burning of the firewood, saying "it is my private diary in which I have a great many incidents recorded and it is very precious to me in my old age."

29 Col. George A. Armes, *Ups and Downs of an Army Officer* (Washington, DC; Published by the author, 1900), 204.

Julesburg. Mark had secured a contract to cut wood to supply Fort Sedgwick for fuel during the harsh and cold winter. Twenty-four-year-old John was working with several men in the canyons at Lawrence Fork, about twenty miles southwest of the Platte River near present-day Bridgeport, Nebraska. About two dozen men were with the wood party. They spent several days cutting wood in the sub-freezing temperatures. There was a lot of snow on the ground, which drifted to several feet in many places. Two cabins gave the woodcutters shelter at their camp.

During the day on January 19, John Coad, with three other men, were loading wood onto one of the wagons when several Oglala suddenly appeared. The other men with him were Michael Quinn, Scotch Tom and a man nicknamed Kentucky. John's recollections are vivid:

We saw one band about a mile and a half to the southwest of us which was riding down the valley. They halted a few moments, then started to capture horses and cattle which were in front of the cabins. Another party came up the valley and met them at this point, so the Indians divided, one party took the stock along the valley and the other party started for us where we were loading the wood upon the wagons. This completely cut off our retreat from making any attempt to reach the cabins. We were unarmed and the only alternative left for us was to run to the bluffs and try to make our escape on foot. We started to the bluffs and got in a part where it was quite rough, being cut up by canyons, and as the snow was deep upon the ground and badly drifted we had the advantage in getting away from the mounted Indians. By starting from the wood pile each man grabbed a club with the intention of using the club should we come to close quarters. The Indians dismounted at this point and here occurred one of the most exciting foot races that has ever been run in the western country. There were three men with me in the party, and we devested [sic] ourselves of all surplus clothing, some of the men pulling off their boots, notwithstanding the thermometer was twenty-five degrees below zero, and the snow quite deep. The Indians ran after us for the space of half a mile or three quarters of a mile. We got to the head of one of the canyons, followed it down to where the country is quite broken and remained there until after dark, building a fire to keep from freezing. After dark we returned to the cabins and were informed by the men who held possession of the same during the day that the Indians attacked them and remained there until about three or four o'clock in the afternoon. In the evening some men who had been hunting in the vicinity came to our cabins and also two or three men who had been chopping poles for the use of the post at Fort Sedgwick. The latter had a very narrow escape from the Indians during the day. That evening I wrote a note to the commanding officer at Fort Sedgwick in Colorado, stating what had happened during the day and asked for assistance. We remained there several days. No assistance arrived. On the 23rd of January I started alone across the country to procure assistance in case the troops did not come. On that evening about nine or ten o'clock at night I met Lieut. Arms [*sic*] of Company M, Second Cavalry, who was coming to our assistance. Lieut. Arms informed me that he had routed a party of Indians about three miles below this point where we met and captured some of our cattle and one horse. I unsaddled the horse I was riding, left him at the creek and saddled the horse which had been recaptured. He gave me a sergeant and two or three men to drive the cattle back to our cabins on Lawrence's Fork.[30]

Lieutenant Armes received the message for assistance. Commanding a column of the 2nd Cavalry, he had left Sedgwick just before the urgent request had arrived. He had been ordered to find a load of stolen goods that was reported to be in a canyon about fifty miles away. It took until the next night, January 22, when he was awakened by guards and told that Indians were trying to break into their camp. It turned out to be a sergeant with 25 men, sent to him with the new orders to bring relief to the Coad wood party. Early the next morning, Armes left with his five wagons and 55 men to rescue to woodcutters who were about 40 miles further up the canyons. About half way there a band of Indians dashed out at the soldiers. Leaving 10 soldiers with the wagons, Armes and the remaining men went off in pursuit. Lieutenant Armes:

> Then I deployed my men, placing Lieutenant Jenness in command of the left, and charged the Indians, who wheeled and ran over the hills into the deep ravine full of snow, my little command after them, firing our carbines, yelling and making as much noise as we could. After a chase of three miles the Indians disappeared, and all we got was one Indian pony with a war-bag full of dried meat, saddle and bridle, bow and quivers, shield and a number of Indian trinkets, with six or seven head of cattle they had stolen and driven from the wood-chopper's camp, which is only ten miles further on.[31]

Armes reported that one soldier was lost in the chase and either killed or captured. He had special praise for Lieutenant John C. Jenness, not assigned to the 2nd Cavalry, but rather, temporarily at Sedgwick on his way north to report as an officer of the 27th Infantry, part of the replacement of officers killed in the Fetterman fight the month before. When Jenness learned that Armes was going out, he asked for permission to accompany him.[32] Having

---

30   Mark M. Coad Indian Depredation Claim #7667. Record Group 123.
31   Armes, *Ups and Downs*, 206–207.
32   Armes, *Ups and Downs*, 211.

Jenness with him proved fortuitous. "If it had not been for the assistance of Lieutenant Jenness I hardly believe one of us would have been left, but he helped to cheer the men forward and charge when, judging by the large band of Indians, it was hopeless."[33] Unfortunately for Jenness, his military career would be very short. He arrived for duty at Fort Phil Kearny within a few weeks, but lost his life less than seven months later, on August 2, in what is today known as the famous Wagon Box Fight, near present-day Story, Wyoming. Standing up behind the wagon boxes used for defense —wagons with their wheels removed—his last words were "Boys, look out! There are a good many Indians here, but—."[34] No doubt he was about to encourage the men. Instead a bullet struck him in the head and killed him instantly. As Armes first reported on Jenness, Captain James Powell, who wrote the report about the Wagon Box fight, repeated his praises. "In the death of Lieutenant Jenness the service has lost a gallant and promising young officer, one who had endeared himself to his comrades and who on the morning of his death fell while setting a noble example of coolness and daring to those who were serving with him."[35]

After Coad arrived back at the two cabins on Lawrence Fork, the wood cutters waited another day before Armes arrived with the rest of the men. Coad recalled what happened next:

> The next morning the troops started down to where the Indians had been camped and recaptured quite a number of work oxen. There were a great many of the work oxen that had been killed and small portions of the animals taken away. On that same evening Lieut. Arms and five of my men started again in pursuit of the Indians. Lieut. Arms left his wagons and disabled men with the out fit [sic] to start for Fort Sedgwick on the following day. We rode all that night and arrived on Pole Creek about four o'clock in the morning, at a point that is known as Little Pine Bluffs, or is called the narrows. This point is about five miles west of where Liet. Arms encountered the Indians and about sixteen miles west of Sidney, Neb. [In] the morning after daylight we commenced to scour around that section of the country and found four head of our oxen, also carcasses of two head and the signs and indications that there had been quite a band of Indians camped at that point. We then started in a southerly direction expecting to find a trail, and traveled about twenty-five miles south. About two o'clock of that day we gave up the chase

33   Armes, *Ups and Downs*, 207.
34   Jerry Keenan, *The Wagon Box Fight: An Episode of Red Cloud's War* (Conshohocken, PA: Savas Publishing Company, 2004), 84.
35   Keenan, *Wagon Box Fight*, 61.

and returned in a northeast direction, hoping and expecting to obtain shelter that night. The thermometer was thirty degrees below zero and our men were freezing. We arrived at Louis [*sic*] Ranch about eight o'clock that night. We had thirty-six men in the party, all were frozen with the exception of four men. The command haulted [*sic*] until ambulances could be obtained from Fort Sedgwick to haul the men in, they being so badly frozen they were unable to ride horses. Louis Ranch was situated about four miles east of what is now Sidney, Neb.[36]

Lieutenant Armes' memory of relieving the woodcutters appears embellished, according to what John Coad had recalled, for Armes said that the Indians had kept the men under siege at the cabins until his command arrived. He recalled their condition: "They had been without provisions for two days, and were boiling their shoes and boots to appease their hunger."[37] Armes did confirm the frozenness of the men. At Lewis Ranch he sent an escort to Fort Sedgwick to send ambulances to retrieve the frozen men. The men were in such agony that they couldn't even sit on their horses "without great suffering." Armes and his soldiers did not fare much better. Armes had to be bathed in cold water and rubbed with towels in order not to lose his fingers or toes. He reported that 27 of his men were frozen so bad they would no doubt be disabled through the rest of the winter. He also reported that the Indians were dressed in blue overcoats, rode American horses and were armed with Spencer rifles. This led him to conclude they were probably the same Indians involved with the Fetterman massacre.[38]

While Armes was involved north of the Denver road, a band of about 15 Cheyenne were committing depredations down along the Smoky Hill trail. Two stock tenders at Chalk Bluffs Station were killed. Arrows collected at the scene were identified as Cheyenne. On January 16, Cheyenne Indians stole 14 horses and two mules from Fort Wallace. H. R. Wyatt was at Pond Creek Station, two miles west of the post. He wrote a report to Captain Myles Keogh at Fort Wallace, and identified the Indians as Cheyenne. Fifteen of them, before the theft, had come into the station to escape the cold and take some coffee and bread.[39] The Indians doing this theft were probably the same Indians who

---

36   Mark M. Coad Indian Depredation Claim #7667. John Coad's descriptions of his experiences make for an interesting read. He went on to settle in Omaha where he became President of the Packers National Bank in South Omaha, and also Director of the Merchant's National Bank of Omaha.

37   Armes, *Ups and Downs*, 208.

38   Armes, *Ups and Downs*, 208–211.

39   H. P. Wyatt, "Letter to Captain Keogh from Pond Creek Station January 16, 1867." Record Group 393, Part I, Letters Received, Department of the Missouri, 1867.

a month earlier burned the station and killed two stock tenders at Chalk Bluffs Station 60 miles to the east of Fort Wallace. James Wadsworth was working at Monument Station, and he reported that the day before the murders at Chalk Bluffs, the same Indians appeared at Monument Station and attacked him. The leader of the Indians was identified as the Cheyenne Bull Bear.[40]

Captain Myles Keogh was asked to investigate the murders at Chalk Bluffs. He reported the following:

> The Indians connected with the Chalk Bluff outrage were Cheyenne, as horses and ponies lost by them on that occasion and picked up by the Overland Stage drivers, were afterwards claimed and turned over to a Cheyenne chief called Bull Bear and a party of his tribe, some of this party were recognized by an escaped ranch man from Chalk Bluffs as having been present at the massacre—also from arrows found that had been shot off around the station, it was seen that they were fashioned peculiar to the Cheyenne tribe.[41]

Shortly after Armes returned to Sedgwick following his rescue of the wood cutters, Colonel Richard I. Dodge was preparing to bring a detachment of recruits to Fort Sedgwick from Fort McPherson, 95 miles to the east. The extreme cold that Armes encountered lingered. A big snowstorm with high winds and bitter cold fell on February 7, and delayed Dodge's march until late in the morning on the 8th. Leaving from Jack Morrow's Ranch a few miles west of McPherson, the road was frozen hard which made the march easy. Only 11 miles were made before going into camp at Bishop's Ranch. The command had carried their fuel and hay. The next day the weather remained bitterly cold which kept the road frozen and the march not difficult for the men and animals. However, because of the bitter cold they only went 10 miles, and then camped at a ranch owned by Mr. Brown. Brown let the soldiers sleep inside the stables, which gave shelter against the wind. The officers were guests inside the ranch house. Brown fed the officers without charge. Dodge reported Brown's ranch was "the best place to stop on the route, Mr. Brown being supplied with everything."[42]

40   See Lieutenant Frederick Beecher's reports dated January 16 and January 19, 1867, Record Group 393, Part 1, Letters Received 1867, Department of the Missouri. Copies are also on file in the Ray Sparks Files, Kansas State Historical Society, Topeka, Kansas.

41   Captain Myles Keogh, "Report, headquarters Post of Fort Wallace, Kansas December 20, 1866." Record Group 393, Part I, Letters Received, Department of the Missouri, 1867.

42   Colonel Richard I. Dodge, "Journal of March of Detachment of Recruits for 30th U.S. Infantry from Morrow's Ranche to Camp near Fort Sedgwick," Record Group 393, Part I, Letters Received 1867, Department of the Platte, Entry 3731.

The weather improved the next day, and consequently the road became very slippery, making the march strenuous. After 13 miles they camped at a ranch owned by a man named Mobley. Dodge called him a "rascall," when it was reported that some of his soldiers were selling some of their clothing to Mobley. A search of the buildings did not find what he bought. On February 11, the men resumed their march. The weather was described as moderate and the road bad. They marched 15 miles, and camped at Murphy's Ranch, which Dodge said was also known as Alkali. The ranch was well supplied and the camp was comfortable. During the night, two carbines were reported stolen. But when Dodge investigated he learned that they were really sold to one of the men at Alkali. Dodge threatened to bring the man under arrest to Fort Sedgwick, where he would then be transferred to Omaha for trial. That was enough to gain a confession and the return of the carbines. The journey continued with the road still wet, causing many of the men to become footsore. Seventeen miles were marched until they came to a ranch Dodge called Pacific Ranche. He apparently did not like the ranch, because he placed guards out to prevent any soldiers from entering the main building. During the night another bad snow storm developed, bringing strong winds and more snow. It was again bitterly cold.

The next morning, Dodge was running short of rations so he marched the men past Beauvais Ranch 11 miles distant and kept on until reaching Cleave's Ranch 22 miles away. This was the hardest march of the journey, as the storm that came in the night before did not abate during the next day. Fortunately the strong winds were at the troopers' backs, or else it would have been impossible to move forward. At this ranch Dodge was able to purchase fuel and hay. The camp was comfortable and the men resumed their westward march the next morning. Fourteen miles later, the journey ended at Fort Sedgwick, on February 14. Colonel Dodge had some interesting observations about the ranches. He noted that nearly all of the ranchmen were easily tempted to trade a canteen of whiskey for a good gun. Indeed, at almost every ranch was found a number of Spencer carbines "many of which I doubt not have been purchased from soldiers."[43]

Colonel Dodge was not the only officer who understood this. Two weeks earlier, another column of troopers had come from Fort Riley with a destination of Fort Morgan, 75 miles further west from Fort Sedgwick. Henry

---

43   Dodge, "Journal of March."

Harrison Abell had just received his first assignment in the newly formed 7th Cavalry, commanding Company L.[44] He was responsible for several wagons and 46 new recruits on the journey. His trip, however, was a disaster from the beginning, and if the events weren't actual facts, it would seem nothing but a humorous fantasy best left for Hollywood to depict. Leaving Fort Riley on January 22, he proceeded north up the Big Blue River. Two days later, just a few miles south of present-day Blue Rapids, the first disaster struck. It had commenced snowing on the 23rd and didn't stop until the morning of the 24th. Six wagons fell off an embankment and plunged down the riverbank. Two wagons fell into the river. It took all of the next day to retrieve the wagons and continue the march. The weather was so bad that once the wagons were secured they could only march four miles in one day. But that was just the beginning. It took two more days to go 18 miles to Marysville.[45]

On the march to Marysville new problems arose. On the night of the 28th, seven men deserted, including the night guard. Lieutenant Abell was not able to pursue them for two reasons: the deserters took the best horses, and he had no men that he had any confidence in to follow his orders. Two nights later, six more soldiers deserted, including his first sergeant and two other non-commissioned officers. Again, part of the guard deserted with them. At Marysville Abell had to confiscate all of the soldiers' carbines because the men were selling them and their equipment, to citizens living in the vicinity, and then lying that the deserters had stolen them when they deserted. Abell stayed an extra day in Marysville, in order to purchase provisions for his men. While staying this extra day six more men deserted.

On February 3, the diminishing command reached "Cottonwood"—the early name for Fort McPherson, from which Col. Dodge would leave with his command five days later, and from there marched an average of 20 miles each day until they arrived at Little Blue Station. Here another snowstorm, accompanied with extremely cold temperatures, forced the command to wait a day before resuming their journey. They then made it to Rock Creek Station, where seven more men deserted. Their next stop was "Holaday's Ranch," where 12 men deserted. Once again the guard went too, as well as

---

44 James B. Klokner, *The Officer Corps of Custer's Seventh Cavalry 1866–1876* (Atglen, PA: Schiffer Military History, 2007), 40.

45 Lieutenant H. H. Abell, "Report from Fort Kearney February 14, 1867," Record Group 393, Part I, Letters Received 1867, Department of the Platte, Entry 2593.

all of the remaining non-commissioned officers. At Thirty-Two Mile Station two more men deserted. The deserters tried to take several horses and mules with them but were thwarted. Finally, on February 12, Abell arrived with his train at Fort Kearny. The six remaining soldiers were suffering from extreme frostbite, or perhaps they might have been tempted to desert too. One man was frozen so bad his toes had to be amputated.[46]

By the time the remnants of Abell's command reached Fort Kearny it was again snowing, and continued snowing for two days. Abell felt the citizens along the road provided the temptation for his men to desert. He said that they "tried to induce the men to desert by assisting them and offering them money for horses and equipments. . . ." He noted the terrible weather also was a major inducement for the massive desertions.[47]

Lieutenant Abell's company was not the only 7th Cavalry command sent to Fort Morgan that met with disaster. Earlier in December, Captain Michael Sheridan, younger brother of Lieutenant General Philip Sheridan, was sent from Fort Wallace to garrison his company L at Fort Morgan. The 14-day trip was an effort in endurance. Sheridan took 15 wagons, an ambulance and rations and forage for 25 days. On the night of their fourth day out, a terrific snowstorm stopped their march for a day. They finally moved on December 6, but were only able to make 10 miles. The temperature never got higher than 26 degrees, and it was necessary to make the soldiers walk to prevent their feet from freezing. Still, he lost two horses and two mules, and when he arrived at Fort Morgan on December 14, 22 of the soldiers had frostbitten feet.[48]

Sheridan's woes with his company were just beginning. Apparently the men did not like their new station at Fort Morgan. Within a month they were planning mass desertions, just at the time Lieutenant Abell was being ordered to join Company L at the post. They were apparently tempted by men from the east promising them $2,000 bounties for joining the Mexican Army as mercenaries, in Mexico's internal conflicts going on at that time.

46 Abell, "Report from Fort Kearney." Abell does not say in his report, but he must have had civilian freighters with the wagons because by the time he arrived at Fort Kearny there were only enough soldiers left to account for the wagons that earlier fell off the Little Blue River embankment. He spoke of the men being too frozen to ride their horses anymore.

47 Abell, "Report from Fort Kearney."

48 Captain Michael V. Sheridan, "Report from Fort Morgan," January 18, 1867. Record Group 393, Part I, Letters Received 1867, Department of the Platte.

On February 9, the men received their pay and the next night, Captain Sheridan averted a mass desertion by appearing at the stables at 11 o'clock, having earlier been warned of the upcoming desertions. He found most of the horses mounted, with arms and ammunition and ready to go. But the men fled on foot in the darkness, and Sheridan was not able to identify a single one, as the mounted horses were selected "without regard to ownership." He was left guessing who wanted to desert and did not know which enlisted men to trust with information. Four nights later, the soldiers successfully absconded, a whopping 29 from the company. Among the deserters was his first sergeant, three other sergeants that Sheridan described as his best, and all of the company corporals. All but two of the men on guard duty that night deserted with them.

This left Sheridan with only 38 men at the fort. He took 10 troopers he thought were reliable, and pursued the deserters, but after 25 miles gave up the chase, knowing he could not overtake them, especially as they took the best horses at the garrison. Of the remaining 38 men, Sheridan confined six in irons, convinced they would escape if given the chance. That left him with only 32 active men. Sheridan said he had only one non-commissioned officer who did not desert, and only one reliable soldier to replace the NCO ranks of the deserters. In his report, he noted that he would not make any promotions "till the recruits arrive which General Hancock telegraphs me are on the way up the Platte." Of course those recruits were under Abell's command, and it ended in disaster at Fort Kearny with only six recruits who had not deserted.[49]

While all of this was happening at Fort Morgan, warriors returned to the Denver road. On February 18, Indians made a raid 50 miles west of Fort Sedgwick, again at the Washington/Moore Ranch, which had been victimized several times in 1864–1865. Five Indians, thought to be Northern Cheyenne, chased off five mules and 23 horses. Jim Moore had recovered from his neck wound in 1865, when he and his brother Charles had a fight at their ranch. In 1867, Charles was away from the ranch while Jim

---

49   Michael V. Sheridan, "Report from Fort Morgan." In Sheridan's report in his Muster Roll, January/February 1867, he said 40 men deserted instead of the 29 he identified in his official report on the incident. See also Jeff Broome, *Custer into the West With the Journal and Maps of Lieutenant Henry Jackson* (El Segundo, CA: Upton and Sons, Publishers, 2009), 48–49; and Don Rickey, Junior, *Forty Miles a day on Beans and Hay: The Enlisted Soldier Fighting the Indian War* (Norman, OK: University of Oklahoma Press, 1963), 150.

was handling the ranch duties. Apparently, by this time Valley Station, three miles to the west, had been dismantled and the buildings moved to Washington/Moore Ranch, which was now called both Valley Station and Moore's Ranch. When Jim Moore learned from the herders that his stock had been stolen, he mounted a horse and rode to Fort Sedgwick to report the theft. A detail of at least 64 soldiers, under the command of Captain John Mix and Lieutenant George Armes, were sent in pursuit. Four wagons carried supplies. In addition a three inch ordnance gun (artillery) was carried. Moore named two of the Cheyenne as Little Horse and his son, Horse in the Road. The *Rocky Mountain News* named the Indians as Sioux under the leadership of Big Hoo.[50] The weather was still atrocious when the expedition began, and the soldiers suffered much in their 11-day pursuit, which was terminated after riding over 100 miles south to the Republican River. Another biting snowstorm engulfed the men during their journey, forcing Captain Mix to abandon two wagons and finally call off the pursuit due to the intense cold and heavy snow. Several of the men suffered frostbite.[51]

Lieutenant Armes gave details of this campaign. Spotted Tail had a prominent part in his narrative. When the soldiers first left there was a cold rainstorm, thoroughly chilling the men and freezing everything. Things were easier to manage during the march when they finally reached the sand hills. At night the men buried themselves in the sand to keep warm. They finally arrived at the Republican River, on February 28. Just as they were going into camp an Indian was spotted on a nearby hill. Captain Mix ordered Armes and 30 men to trail the Indian and try to locate their village. Not far from sight of the camp about 30 Indians appeared in the front of Armes' advancing column. Armes immediately charged the warriors, but in a few minutes discovered hundreds more encircling his small command. Armes ordered his men to a high bluff and prepared for a life-ending fight. He ordered his men to dismount, "giving orders to be very careful and let each shot make one Indian less." The drama continued:

---

50   James A. Moore Indian Depredation Claim #524. Record Group 75. Entry 700. Armes, *Ups and Downs*, 216, 219. *Rocky Mountain News*, February 23, 1867. George Bent said Little Horse was a Northern Cheyenne. See Hyde, *Life of George Bent*, 230.

51   Fort Sedgwick Post Returns, February/March 1867. See Dallas Williams, *Fort Sedgwick Colorado Territory: Hell Hole on the Platte* (Julesburg, CO: Fort Sedgwick Historical Society, 1996), 104–105.

Only a few moments elapsed before I was entirely surrounded by the red devils, who made up their minds I was going to fall an easy prey, judging by the slow manner they formed their circle around us. First, they made their ponies almost fly, then come to a run, a gallop, a trot and down to a slow walk, all the time getting nearer and nearer, until they were within easy reach of our carbines.

Having every man on his knees with his gun at a "ready" and in a circle around our horses, which were held by six men, we were in a pretty good position to defend ourselves for a while at least. Just as I was about to give the order "Fire!" an Indian and a half-breed rode out from the mass of Indians and called out "Don't shoot! Don't shoot!" Taking a sergeant, I met them half way between the lines, when I discovered my old friend Spotted Tail, chief of a large tribe of Northern Sioux. The half-breed was a Mr. [Billy] Lee, owner of a ranch on the Platte River, who had a number of wagons loaded with goods in the Indian village, where he was trading.

After shaking hands and saying "How, how," I explained that I was after horse-thieves and was not trying to get up a fight with them. Spotted Tail stood straight up, saying, "My men no steal horses from white men. Cheyennes steal horses. Cheyennes thieves gone south. My men good. Fight no white men unless white men shoot first."[52]

After this parley Armes invited Spotted Tail and several other Indians into the camp of Captain Mix, and there again Spotted Tail professed his peace. Mix generously shared with them what were quickly becoming meager supplies. Before leaving, Mr. Lee shared with Armes what almost happened, which again speaks powerfully for Spotted Tail's resolve to maintain peace. Armes:

Before leaving Mr. Lee told me that it was just as much as Spotted Tail could do to control his warriors, as they were so anxious to fight; that *he ordered one young chief shot on the spot and had several others punished*, and that some twenty or thirty of the young men left him and threatened to kill us anyway; that it took great determination on Spotted Tail's part to prevent an attack upon us, and that if we had fired first he could not have stopped them all. Under the circumstances, I feel that I am in luck.[53]

---

52 Armes, *Ups and Downs*, 216–217.
53 Armes, *Ups and Downs*, 218, emphasis added. Again, Spotted Tail emerges as a powerful chief for peace. It must have taken great leadership, intelligence and resolve to keep his people at peace. Unfortunately there are not similar documents showing Black Kettle demonstrating any ability to control the young warriors under him, which probably was why General Sheridan referred to him as a "worn out and worthless old cipher." See Sheridan's report to General Sherman, Forty-First Congress, 2d Session, Volume I, Executive Document, Pt. 2 (Washington, DC: Government Printing Office, 1869), 47. When Armes returned to Fort Sedgwick, he accepted a promotion to captain and then departed Fort Sedgwick to his new post in Kansas, commanding a company of newly formed buffalo soldiers.

Watson Coburn, owner of Chicago Ranch on the Denver road about seven miles east of the Moore brother's ranch, was with Jim Moore and the soldiers when this meeting with Spotted Tail occurred. His recollections provide more details and a slightly different perspective on Spotted Tail and the parley than Armes:

> In the spring of 1867 they [Indians] seemed to have been worse than any spring since I had been there [Coburn came in late August 1865 and hence missed the deadly raids in January that year]. There was a little party headed by Little Horse—a Cheyenne Indian—camped at Valley Station, owned by Jim and Charley Moore. This Little Horse seemed to have communication with the hostile Indians; they hung around there until they had a good opportunity to commit some depredations. Along the last of February, 1867, they gathered up 52 head of horses and mules and started south. I with Mr. Moore and several others went with Captain Mix, of the Second Cavalry, and 80 of his men, and followed the Indian's trail for nine days, when they run us into Spotted Tail's band of 800 warriors. I, with another scout, ran on to their scouts on the last day of February. We then prepared ourselves to fight, and in about three hours there were eight hundred warriors come on to us. Spotted Tail—being an old Indian—was inclined to be peaceable; and he threw up a flag of truce and wanted a council. After counciling [sic] some three hours we made what we called a treaty, that is, they gave us the [sic] until the next morning at sun-up to get out of there; and gave us to understand that if we didn't go that he would turn all his warriors loose and kill and scalp every one of us. And we accepted the terms. During the council, he (Spotted Tail) pointed to the Indian he called To Strike, who had five hundred followers of young bucks, and he gave us to understand that he could not control them with his three hundred old men, who were inclined to be peacable [sic]. Spotted Tail said that little bands of these young Indians would break away from him every few days, going different directions, and he would send a party of his old men after them and bring him back whever [sic] he could catch them; and our presence in that country fired the ambition of these young warriors until, if it was continued, that he could not control them.[54]

Captain Michael Sheridan, commanding Fort Morgan, filed a report on March 1, adding a bit more to this incident. Not having any scouts or interpreters at the deserter-depleted post, and upon learning of the theft of the stock at Moore's Ranch, he sent a sergeant alone on a mission to scout the area and find what he could in relation to the stolen stock. He left on February 24, and returned five days later. He reported that the stock was stolen by a band of Northern Cheyenne. The sergeant went east on the Denver road about 30

---

54   Watson S. Coburn Indian Depredation Claim #8988. Record Group 123.

miles, and then went south 40 miles to the Republican River valley. There he found fresh trails of many Indians, occasionally observing Indians on hills in the distance. He found some hunters down there who reported that the Indians were not molesting them but acted unfriendly, and they feared something was brewing. The Indians would hold no communications with the hunters and were obviously agitated, perhaps at the soldiers sent down there from Fort Sedgwick. The citizens living on the road between Forts Morgan and Sedgwick were greatly excited over the theft, "and all are of the opinion that frequent raids will occur in the Platte route in the spring."[55]

Back down on the Santa Fe road, on February 25, Arapaho Indians again burned wood which had been corded under a contract to deliver at Fort Dodge. This time, 260 cords were burned at a wood camp on Saw Log Crossing, a branch of the Pawnee Fork, located 12 to 15 miles north of Fort Dodge. Ben Clark, employed by the post sutlers at Fort Dodge, was still in charge of the woodcutters, who numbered 20. Twelve-hundred cords of cottonwood, elm and hackberry had already been successfully cut and delivered, but another 260 cords remained awaiting delivery. This represented a year's supply of fuel at the post. Arapaho Chief Little Raven, who was camped nearby with his village, had approached Clark during the cutting and demanded that the men stop, declaring that the wood belonged to the Cheyenne and Arapaho and the men had no right to cut it. Clark replied that the wood was cut on the military reservation and to take it up with the commander at Fort Dodge. Shortly after the Indians departed their camp and burned the remaining cords.[56]

---

55 Captain Michael V. Sheridan, "Headquarters, Fort Morgan, C.T., March 1, 1867." Record Group 393, Part I, Box 1A, Letters Received 1867, Department of the Platte.

56 John Tappan Indian Depredation Claim #722. Record Group 123. Curiously, Tappan's depredation claim is similar to the Theodore Weichselbaum and Calvin Dyche Indian Depredation Claim noted as occurring January 8. Both Dyche and Tappan claim they were post sutlers in partnership with Weichselbaum at Fort Dodge, and yet both claims do not acknowledge the additional burning or the other sutler in partnership with Weichselbaum. This is not evidence that one of the burnings did not occur, as both, when investigated, were admitted to by the Arapaho; but it does raise suspicion that both men were not in partnership with Weichselbaum and that one of them was trying to claim something that did not rightfully belong to him. My guess is, if this is the case, it might be Dyche because in his claim Ben Clark did not directly give sworn testimony, whereas in the Tappan claim Clark's sworn affidavit is there. In the Dyche claim there is a copy of a report of the burning submitted to Wynkoop and acknowledged. In the Tappan claim, Wynkoop acknowledged that burning too, and also, there is the confirmation of the burning noted by Indian depredation claims agent Michael Piggott, confirming the truth of the claim. Another possibility is it might be that Dyche was replaced in partnership with Weichselbaum by Tappan between the burnings and indeed there were two separate partnerships.

The burning of the wood represents just one of the issues simmering in early 1867, indicating an inevitable "new" war was brewing. On February 27, Third Infantry Captain Henry Asbury wrote an informative letter from his post at Fort Larned, of a recent conversation with Kiowa leader Satanta at Fort Zarah. It represented a classic clash with Manifest Destiny. Satanta stated that the hearts of the Indians had grown bad and that the "white men must build no more houses out here, must burn no more of their wood, must drink no more of their water, must not drive the buffalo off, that the railroad must not come any further, and that the Santé Fe line must be stopped."[57] Captain Asbury clearly saw the inevitable war soon emerging. In addition he reported that a band of Sioux, very possibly the ones involved in the Coad/Armes woodcutting attack north of Fort Sedgwick a few weeks earlier, passed south of the Arkansas to have a talk "with the tribes belonging to that region probably to determine the time for another outbreak." He then pleaded for the appointment of cavalry troopers at Fort Larned to compliment the small number of infantry stationed there. He was correct in every detail. In another letter, written on March 6, he reported that a man named Parker, living at a ranch six miles down the river from Fort Larned, came in and reported a small band of Cheyenne had come to his home and demanded to be fed. When he said he had no sugar they threatened to kill him.[58]

Captain Asbury wrote another report on March 15, and summarized things he had recently learned. Black Kettle feared an outbreak of war in the spring and, to protect his Indians, was moving his village south of the Arkansas, all the way to Texas. Several Lakota under Spotted Tail and Pawnee Killer had camped on Pawnee Fork, because officers north at Fort Laramie advised them to travel down to the Arkansas to avoid the war continuing up there, contesting the Bozeman trail. All the Kiowa were talking bad and ordering all whites to leave the region. And, Asbury said, the Cheyenne talk little but are the most dangerous because they are the superior soldiers.[59] Asbury added yet another report, dated March 26, and

57   Captain Henry Asbury, "Headquarters, Fort Larned, Kas., February 27, 1867," Record Group 393, Part I, Letters Received 1867, Department of the Missouri, Entry 2593.

58   Captain Henry Asbury, "Headquarters, Fort Larned, Kas., March 6, 1867," Record Group 393, Part I, Letters Received 1867, Department of the Missouri, Entry 2593.

59   Captain Henry Asbury, "Headquarters, Fort Larned, Kas., March 26, 1867," Record Group 393, Part I, Letters Received 1867, Department of the Missouri, Entry 2593.

said that the Cheyennes were "having a grand time" over learning of the Fetterman Massacre on December 21, 1866; "they all are rejoicing over the massacre, and say it was a great victory."[60]

A series of reports out of Fort Dodge in March continued the rumors of an impending war. On March 4, Satanta was down at Fort Dodge and left the next day to the villages south of the Arkansas River. Accompanying him was a man named John Adkins, an interpreter and guide, who reported three days later his impressions of Satanta. When they had proceeded about 15 miles Satanta ordered Adkins to leave him. Prior to that he spoke "highly insulting to whites generally, and especially toward officers and men of this garrison [Fort Dodge]." He felt strongly that Satanta was preparing for war.[61] Trappers south of the Arkansas reported, on March 11, that Little Raven's Arapahos were also heading south for a rendezvous with the Cheyenne and Kiowa.[62] Little Raven sent a message to Major Douglass on March 14, stating "that no more wood must be cut by this command on the Pawnee Forks, and that the troops must move out of the country by the time grass grows." Further communication came from Satanta, stating that the cavalry horses must be fattened because he is coming to take them, and that "all the Indians had agreed to stop the railroads and roads at Council Grove—that no roads or railroads would be allowed west of that point." To Major John H. Page, he declared that he "must gather together their soldiers, & leave, if they don't I will help them to leave. No wagons will be allowed on the road except those that bring presents; if any are found they will be taken."[63]

To the surprise of Major Douglass, Satanta came to Fort Dodge on March 18 and conferred with him. He brought about 35 men, women and children. He spoke of friendliness to the whites, and asked for provisions. And he warned the commander of the growing war interests of the Cheyenne, saying they were trying to entice him to join them in a series of raids along

60 Captain Henry Asbury, "Headquarters, Fort Larned, Kas., March 15, 1867," Record Group 393, Part I, Letters Received 1867, Department of the Missouri, Entry 2593.

61 John Adkins, "Letter to Lieutenant Wallace, Post Adjutant Fort Dodge," Record Group 393, Part I, Letters Received 1867, Department of the Missouri, Entry 2593.

62 Major Henry Douglass, 3rd Infantry, "Report from Headquarters Fort Dodge, Kansas March 11, 1867," Record Group 393, Part I, Letters Received 1867, Department of the Missouri, Entry 2593.

63 Major Henry Douglass, 3rd Infantry, "Report from Headquarters Fort Dodge, Kansas March 14, 1867," Record Group 393, Part I, Letters Received 1867, Department of the Missouri, Entry 2593.

the roads, but he refused to join them. The day before, a trapper named Mr. Baker came into the post and reported the theft of his stock by the Cheyenne. He said he had lived and traded with them for 23 years and was convinced by their manners, "that they would break out into open hostility this spring." Further, he was recently in a camp with them and witnessed many Cheyenne practicing with their arms. They were "splendidly armed with rifles and revolvers, with an almost inexhaustible supply of ammunition . . . they practiced continuously at target firing and were for the most part very good shots." The Indians had over 300 rounds each for practice and said there was much more in camp.[64]

Major Douglass then decided to send Mr. Jones, the post interpreter and guide, to villages north of Fort Dodge to ascertain why the Indians up there were moving toward the fort. Jones reported back that the main village of 200 lodges was under the leadership of Cheyenne Dog Soldier Chief Bull Bear. Bull Bear expressed nothing but peace and said that the Indians were making their villages along the Pawnee Fork in anticipation of a meeting later in the spring with General Hancock. Jones said Bull Bear's band was the friendliest band of Indians on the plains. The rumors of war were coming from other bands, bands Bull Bear and Jones were not in contact with. Bull Bear feared that the warriors causing trouble north of the Platte would soon come down south and cause trouble, but that all Indians presently encamped on Pawnee Fork were all Indians who wanted peace.[65]

While it seems obvious that the Indians were preparing for war, George Bent later wrote that this was not the case:

> The stories that during the winter of 1866–67 the Indians were planning to begin war in the spring were untrue. The winter camps of all the tribes had white traders in them that winter. If the Indians had been plotting an outbreak, these traders would have been the first to learn the facts and would soon have packed up their outfits and left the camps.[66]

Clearly, traders did report the rumors of war. But it gets better. Bent went on to say that during this time he was employed as a trader with David

---

64   Major Henry Douglass, 3rd Infantry, "Report from Headquarters Fort Dodge, Kansas March 19, 1867," Record Group 393, Part I, Letters Received 1867, Department of the Missouri, Entry 2593.

65   Major Henry Douglass, 3rd Infantry, "Report from Headquarters Fort Dodge, Kansas March 31, 1867," Record Group 393, Part I, Letters Received 1867, Department of the Missouri, Entry 2593.

66   Hyde, *Life of George Bent*, 267.

Butterfield, and that Butterfield had warned him just the opposite was the case, viz., it was the military that was bringing trouble, not the Indians.[67] And indeed he was working for Butterfield. But there was more to this connection than Bent shared. On March 3, David Tramp had a wagon and was trading in Black Kettle's village, 45 miles south of the Arkansas River. With him were W. E. Thurmond and Daniel Moran, driving two wagons for David A. Butterfield. All had been trading with Black Kettle and were moving to another camp when Kiowa, under Kicking Bird, came to them and demanded from them whatever goods the warriors wanted. After taking what they wished, a group of Cheyenne then came to the wagons and also freely pilfered what was remaining. Butterfield filed a claim against the Indians for a loss of $4,278, which included such things as canned goods, flour, coffee, clothing, military coats, officers' jackets, beads, tobacco, saddles, bridles, etc. When the theft was presented to Indian Agent John D. Miles, and through him brought to the Cheyenne, they admitted taking the goods. Bent himself admitted his knowledge of the theft but denied the value of what was stolen. He said that he and David Tramp were in the employ of Butterfield "as traders, at the time this raid is said to have been committed; that they had opportunity to know just how much property was taken and by whom, that the Indians were Cheyenne and Kiowa, but that the property taken did not amount to any great sum of money, and they pronounce the claim a fraud."[68] Tramp too remembered the events:

> In March 1867, [I] was on Bluff Creek about 45 miles south of Fort Larned, Kansas, with one wagon of [my] own loaded with . . . household goods, and there was at the same time and place two wagons belonging to D. A. Butterfield, . . . [his] wagons were on the way back to Fort Larned from "Black Kettle's" (Cheyenne) camp, south of the Arkansas River, where they had been trading with said Indians; that the goods on [Butterfield's] wagons were saddles, *guns, Remington revolvers, lead, powder, gun caps,* common tin ware, blankets and dry goods, which *they were trading to the Indians* for buffalo robes; . . . they were met by a band of Kiowa Indians led by Kicking Bird who desired the wagons to go to his camp. They turned back and went to within a mile of the previous night's camping ground, where they camped. Kicking Bird compelled W. E. Thurmond, who had charge of Butterfield's

---

67   Hyde, *Life of George Bent*, 268. Hyde notes that Butterfield was formerly the operator of the Overland Dispatch Stage Line.

68   D. A. Butterfield Indian Depredation Claim #531, Entry 700. Record Group 75.

wagons, to give his men guns and revolvers, after which the Kiowas left. About dark of the same day [March 3], a band of Cheyennes took forcible possession of the wagons and took therefrom such goods as they wished, and then left without destroying the wagons, harness or any of the animals belonging to [Butterfield]. Early the next morning, the ... wagons were loaded with buffalo robes and goods not taken by the Indians and the party went to Fort Larned, reaching there the 2nd day after the attack.[69]

Bent gave his testimony on this attack in 1889, and admitted he was employed by Butterfield then, but said he was 10 miles away from the wagon camp when the Indians attacked them. He remembered, though, being at the Medicine Lodge Treaty in the fall of 1867, that Butterfield was compensated for his loss there, that he (Bent) "acted as interpreter at the time of the settlement and [Butterfield] gave [Bent] a handsome present afterwards."[70] No doubt if Butterfield was compensated handsomely for his loss, as Bent says, he would not have included in his losses any weapons, for at this time all traders were prohibited from selling any arms to the Indians. Indeed, Butterfield's depredation claim was tossed out specifically because "the rules of the Office [Bureau of Indian Affairs] at the time prohibited the sale of Remington revolvers to the Indians and that the claimant [Butterfield] was violating the rules when the depredation occurred."[71] What is more important to note here, however, is the fact that the Indians were indeed trading, illegally, for arms and ammunition at the very time reports were filtering in to the various military posts that the Indians were arming themselves for an anticipated war come spring. And Bent knew it because he was there when the arms were being traded ... in Black Kettle's village.

It was in the midst of all this information gathering that General William T. Sherman sent General Winfield Hancock into Kansas, in an effort to stymie this war talk. If the Indians want war, Hancock was more than willing to oblige them; if they didn't, then the might of his army would deter them to stay on the road to peace.

---

69   D. A. Butterfield Indian Depredation Claim #531. Emphasis added.
70   D. A. Butterfield Indian Depredation Claim #531.
71   D. A. Butterfield Indian Depredation Claim #531.

CHAPTER TEN

Out of Control

The war was one of depredations. The Indians did not seek to fight the troops, but sought to evade them, and the troops could not find the Indians and could not overtake them in time to fight a battle with them.

TWO DEVELOPMENTS IN LATE 1866 WOULD HAVE A BEARING on the Indian war growing in the following year along the Denver trails. First, the 7th Cavalry was being organized in the fall, at Fort Riley. Brevet Major General George Armstrong Custer, now a Lieutenant Colonel in the post–Civil War army, took field command of the regiment. By early 1867, the recruits were assembled and ready to go about their duties protecting the roads through Kansas, Nebraska and into Colorado. Also at this time General Winfield S. Hancock took command of the Department of the Missouri, which included Kansas and Colorado. Just prior to his appointment, he was ordered to Kansas to seek council with all of the tribes that had been committing the attacks since 1864. His purpose was to call them to account for the attacks made since the signing of the Treaty of the Little Arkansas in 1865, and to engage them in war if that was what the Indians preferred. It was felt that by showing a large military presence the Indians would acquiesce for peace. Instead the opposite occurred, and before the spring was out the deadly raids on the roads to Denver recommenced.[1]

General Hancock has received the brunt of the blame for starting the 1867 war, but a look at the correspondence in the War Department reveals

---

[1]   For Custer's 7th Cavalry involvement, as well as all the relevant military reports relating to this campaign, as well as Custer's summer 1867 Indian campaign, see Broome, *Custer into the West*.

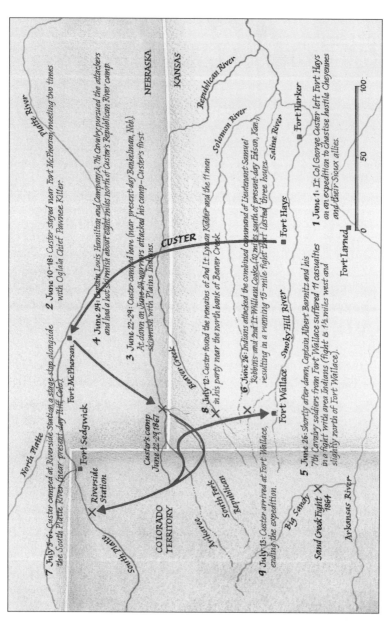

7 July 5-6: Custer camped at Riverside Station, a stage stop alongside the South Platte River (near present-day Iliff, Colo.)

2 June 10-18: Custer stayed near Fort McPherson, meeting two times with Oglala Chief Pawnee Killer.

4 June 24: Captain Louis Hamilton and Company A, 7th Cavalry, pursued the attackers and had a hot skirmish about eight miles north of Custer's Republican River camp.

3 June 22-24: Custer camped here (near present-day Benkelman, Neb.) At dawn on June 24 warriors attacked his camp—Custer's first skirmish with Plains Indians.

8 July 12: Custer found the remains of 2nd Lt. Lyman Kidder and the 11 men in his party near the north bank of Beaver Creek.

6 June 26: Indians attacked the combined command of Lieutenant Samuel Robbins and 2nd Lt. William Cooke (10 miles south of present-day Edson, Kan.) resulting in a running 15-mile fight that lasted three hours.

1 June 1: Lt. Col. George Custer left Fort Hays on an expedition to chastise hostile Cheyennes and their Sioux allies.

5 June 26: Shortly after dawn, Captain Albert Barnitz and his 7th Cavalry soldiers from Fort Wallace suffered 11 casualties in a fight with area Indians (fight is 1½ miles west and slightly north of Fort Wallace).

9 July 13: Custer arrived at Fort Wallace, ending the expedition.

NEBRASKA

KANSAS

COLORADO TERRITORY

CUSTER

Custer's camp June 22-24 1867

North Platte

Riverside Station

Fort Sedgwick

Fort McPherson

Platte River

Republican River

Solomon River

Saline River

Smoky Hill River

Fort Hays

Fort Harker

Fort Larned

Beaver Creek

South Platte

Arikaree

South Fork Republican

Big Sandy

Sand Creek Fight 1864

Arkansas River

Fort Wallace

0   50   100

CUSTER'S 1867 SUMMER CAMPAIGN.

Map details Custer's 704 mile march. Leaving Old Fort Hays June 1, the expedition effectively ended on July 13, when the command marched from the Kidder massacre site to Fort Wallace, camping one mile west on the Smoky Hill River. *Courtesy Joan Pennington, Fairfax Station, Virginia.*

that he was merely carrying out the orders of his superiors.[2] On February 19, General U.S. Grant, commanding all the Armies, notified General William T. Sherman that Hancock was to carry out his duties. General Sherman forwarded Grant's order to Hancock on the same day, adding this to his orders: "You may therefore take these Indians in hand in your own way and *let them feel our power and anger.*"[3] By March, however, the military learned a little about government agencies and the extent of military power within those agencies, which was limited.

When Hancock began his campaign he was demanding the tribes to release for punishment all Indians guilty of earlier depredations. General Sherman, learning the War Department's authority did not extend to the Department of the Interior, wrote to Hancock to clarify how far his authority extended. Noting that the Department of Interior had the authority to deal with all depredations committed by Indians under treaty, Hancock was informed that he did not have the power to demand any guilty Indians be turned over to him for punishment. That power rested with the Indian agents and commissioners, and not the military. Instead, the duty of the military was to protect American citizens who were lawfully on settled land or engaging in lawful commerce upon the roads, including all mail routes and especially the posts and military reservations established to protect the roads, as well as area settlements. Any Indians interfering with these "cannot be tolerated for a moment." Sherman then amended his orders to Hancock:

> I therefore authorize you to organize, out of your present command, a sufficient force to go among the Cheyenne, Arrapahoes, Kiowas, or similar bands of Indians, and *notify them that if they want war they can have it now;* but if they decline the offer, then impose upon them that they must stop their insolence and threats, and make their conduct conform more nearly to what we [decree] right. . . .[4]

Sending the Indian agents of the various tribes to call their leaders all together to council near Fort Larned, Hancock brought out about 1,400 soldiers for what turned out to be a failed council. The council finally began

---

2   This traditional criticism of Hancock is represented strongly in Chalfant, *Hancock's War.*

3   Telegraph from St Louis from General Sherman to General Hancock, February 19, 1867, emphasis added. Record Group 393, Part I, Letters Received, Department of the Missouri.

4   General W. T. Sherman, Letter to General W. F. Hancock, March 14, 1867, emphasis added. Record Group 393, Part I, Letters Received, Department of the Missouri.

ETCHING OF BREVET MAJOR
GENERAL GEORGE ARMSTRONG
CUSTER.
Author's collection.

on April 12, after snowy weather prevented it starting earlier. But immediately the Cheyenne were reluctant attendees, with only a few reporting,
with the explanation that their ponies were weak and also many of the
warriors were out on a buffalo hunt. When only a few chiefs reported at
Fort Larned, Hancock decided to move his men next to where the Indians
had their villages, which were on Pawnee Fork about 30 miles away. When
he arrived there he found two large villages, one Cheyenne and the other
Lakota, belonging to Pawnee Killer. Warned by Pawnee Killer and others
not to come near the villages, Hancock disregarded their warning and
moved even closer, promising not to molest them. It was not a wise move,
for in the villages were a number of women and children who had survived
the attack on Sand Creek 29 months earlier. Fear overcame them and that
night both villages were abandoned, the Indians fleeing under cover of
darkness. They left all their camp provisions in the tepees.

Custer was ordered with four of his companies in pursuit. In several days
chasing the Indians, another chilling snowstorm descended upon the area
and Custer was never able to overtake them. His command finally ended
up at Fort Hays—the original site 15 miles southeast of present-day Hays,
Kansas—his horses in need of rest and nourishment. But the supplies that

were supposed to be at the post were not there, and Custer found his command stuck with jaded horses and no supplies to feed them. The pursuit was terminated. He remained there until June 1, when he began a 43-day campaign that took his 350 troopers to the Platte River road in Nebraska, down south to an earlier branch of the Smoky Hill road, then back north to the Denver road along the South Platte River, and finally back down to Fort Wallace and the Smoky Hill road. Sixty men deserted at various camps during the campaign, 34 at Riverside Station along the Denver road near present-day Iliff, Colorado. Custer also had his first skirmish with Indians, his men fighting warriors in three separate engagements.[5]

In April, when Custer was first pursuing the Indians along the Smoky Hill road under Hancock's orders, he came upon the remnants of a vicious attack at Lookout Station, located about 22 miles west of Old Fort Hays. It was his first encounter of Indian atrocities committed upon the dead. There he found three men, employees running the station, all horribly mutilated and burned. The Indians had killed them shortly before Custer arrived. It appeared other people found them first and made a hasty burial for the men, whose extremities had been eaten by wolves. Custer reported: "The hair was singed from their heads; the skin and flesh burned from their breasts and arms, and their intestines torn out (not from wolves, however, as they could only reach their legs.)"[6] Three days before this report, Custer wrote another account, the first Hancock received, when he arrived at Downer Station west of Lookout. From the station workers he learned of the killings at Lookout. He was told that the Indians burned the station and all the hay and stole "eight horses and four mules. They scalped one of the men before burning the men, they also robbed the station west of Lookout."[7] When Custer reported this, Hancock, believing the Indians who killed the civilian workers at Lookout were those who earlier fled their villages, ordered the two Indian villages on Pawnee Fork burned, which he had kept under protection after the Indians abandoned their villages. Hancock felt the Indians had no intent for peace, and the fleeing from the villages was meant to escape responsibility of earlier attacks upon freighters, settlers and stage

5   All of the events related to Custer's movements are detailed in *Custer into the West.*

6   *Difficulties With Indian Tribes*, Report dated April 19, 1867, 72.

7   G. A. Custer, "Camp of the 7th Cavalry, Downer's Station, April 17, 1867," Record Group 393, Part I, Letters Received, Department of the Missouri, Entry 2593.

ranches. Regardless of the veracity of his perception, the 1867 Indian war was turning from lukewarm to hot.

Back on the Denver road, Indians again made a raid at Chicago Ranch. On April 20, at about nine o'clock in the morning, 30 warriors, believed to be Cheyenne, set fire to 100 tons of baled hay stored on the north side of the river about a mile from the ranch, which was a feed and supply station for the Overland Stage and Express. When Watson Coburn saw the fire—the flames roaring high—he summoned the other men to accompany him to the river. The Indians could be seen around the fire. "They danced around and had a regular jubilee there for an hour, until the hay was all burned up." When the Indians saw the men approaching they "commenced to dance and yell." They then mounted their ponies and went east down the river.[8]

On the same day Coburn had his hay burned at Chicago Ranch, a much more sinister act was occurring in Republic County, Kansas, on White Rock Creek, where the year before Elizabeth Marling had been brutally gang-raped. It took the miraculous survival of a young boy to get the details of the murder of four settlers. H. Lapier had spent the night of April 20 at the cabin of a neighbor, Daniel Davis, and the next morning started up White Rock Creek. After about five miles he found a wounded boy, an adopted son of Nicholas Ward. The boy told him that further up the creek Indians had attacked the day before and killed several people and wounded him. His adopted mother, Mrs. Ward, was taken captive. Lapier took the wounded boy to the house of Samuel Fisher. Fisher was gone obtaining provisions, but his wife and children were there. Lapier then took them, along with the wounded boy, back down to Davis' house, and they all started, with other settlers, for Lake Sibley further down the river. From there they went to Clyde. Fisher lost six horses and several household provisions, which were left when his wife and son fled. As Fisher was returning home with his supplies, neighbors stopped him and prevented him from entering the dangerous situation on White Rock Creek.[9] All the settlers on White Rock Creek had fled the area. From Clyde a party of men, including soldiers who had just arrived, returned to the scene of the raid and buried the victims. The dead were Nicholas ("Nick") Ward, a man named Bartlett, a widow named Mrs. Sutzer and her young son. Lapier stated that the wounded boy

8   Watson S. Coburn Indian Depredation Claim #8988. Record Group 123.
9   Samuel Fisher Indian Depredation Claim #1106. Record Group 123.

told him that "the Indians when they first came to the settlement professed to be friendly, asked and received dinner, claiming to be Sioux. . . ."[10]

General Hancock received a telegram from Kansas Governor Samuel Crawford, sent May 5, telling him about the killings. Hancock had earlier left orders that when the grass was up, some soldiers should be sent from Fort Harker northwest to the White Rock Creek area to provide protection for the settlers. When he received Crawford's telegram, he learned that his earlier order had been ignored. He immediately re-ordered a detail of men to the area.[11] The officer leading this company of soldiers was Captain Daingerfield Parker of the 3rd Infantry. He wrote two reports about the White Rock Creek murders. He noted that Samuel Fisher told him the murders had been committed on the 27th—not the 20th—"by Indians reported to be Pawnee." The murders occurred at two different homes. At one home the Indians killed Mrs. Sutzer,[12] her 10-year-old son and a man named Bartlett Rice—not Mr. Bartlett—who was living at the home. At the second house, Richard—not Nicholas—Ward was killed, his wife taken captive, and an unnamed boy was "desperately wounded." The soldiers and several locals followed the trail of the Indians for 40 miles in an attempt to rescue Mrs. Ward, but the trail (indicating eight or nine Indians) disappeared. They had gone to the mouth of the Little Solomon on the Solomon River, where the trail was lost "on account of their going over buffalo grass."[13] Parker reported that the settlers were convinced the Indians were Pawnee and he concurred. "I am decidedly of the opinion (as I was last summer) that the Indians professing to be friendly are the guilty ones. I am assured that no 'wild Indians' have been as far down as White Rock for the past three years."[14] Of course he was mistaken about this, for the year before Dog Soldiers admitted killing six settlers just a few miles east of where this atrocity occurred.

The wounded boy's story was also shared with settler Thomas Lovewell. Lovewell:

---

10   Daniel Davis Indian Depredation Claim #8763. Record Group 123.

11   Hancock's Report, *Difficulties With Indian Tribes*, 90. See also Broome, *Custer into the West*, 155–156.

12   John Marling Indian Depredation Claim #2944. Record Group 123.

13   John Marling Indian Depredation Claim #2944.

14   Captain Daingerfield Parker, "Headquarters Camp Hoffman Buffalo Creek Kansas, May 20, 1867," Record Group 393, Part I, Letters Received, Department of the Missouri, 1867. The depredation claims associated with this raid indicate the Indians were Dog Soldiers, mostly Cheyenne and Sioux. See, e.g., Samuel Fisher Depredation Claim #1106.

It was reported through the neighborhood by the boy that was wounded, and left for dead, that he was wounded by a band of 9 Indians; that these Indians had killed Ward, the man with whom he was living; that they took all the horses and mules on the place; and when the boy reported to us, we went and found that Ward had been killed as stated by the boy. We then went to Bartlett's and found Bartlett killed apparently with a knife, a dagger was yet sticking in his mouth. We also found the widow Setzer [sic] at Bartlett's house, dead, killed apparently by a blow from a large stone; and we followed the trail of parties from these [sic] place, by the tracks of horses and mules, to the Solomon River. . . .[15]

An even more detailed account came out in 1878:

The Indians came to Mrs. Sutzer's cabin, where Bartlett was boarding, and demanded dinner, which she proceeded to prepare, in the mean time sending her little son across the creek to Ward's to inform them of the presence of the Indians. Bartlett was down in the timber, splitting rails, and returning for dinner, was met by the Indians and tomahawked as he was passing around the corner of the house. He was found lying on his back, his iron wedge near his right hand and his own knife—a dirk—sticking in his throat. It is thought that when Bartlett was killed Mrs. Sutzer started to run. She was found dead about thirty yards from the house with her skull crushed with a rock. It appears that the cunning fiends had refrained from using firearms for fear of raising an alarm. After completing their bloody work at Mrs. Sutzer's the Indians crossed the creek to Ward's cabin, and again called for dinner, which Mrs. Ward prepared for them. They eat [sic] their dinner, smoked their pipes and chatted away in the most friendly manner. At the conclusion of their "smoke," one of them very coolly loaded his gun and asked Ward if he thought it would kill a buffalo. Ward replied that he thought it would. Whereupon the Indian instantly leveled his gun at Ward's breast and shot him through the heart, killing him immediately. The two boys—Ward's and Mrs. Sutzer's—then started to run. The Indians pursued them, following them to the bank of the creek, and shooting them down in the bed of the stream. The Sutzer boy was shot through the heart; instantly killed. The Ward boy was shot through the neck and left for dead. Some time during the succeeding night, however, he recovered his senses, and groping his way back to the cabin in the dark, found the door broken down and entered. Feeling around in the dark with his hands he stumbled and fell over the dead body of his adopted father. Procuring some blankets from one of the beds, he returned to the timber, where he remained the balance of the night, and was found the next morning by a party of claim hunters, to whom he told the above sad and harrowing tale.[16]

---

15   John Marling Indian Depredation Claim #2944.
16   Winsor and Scarbrough, *History of Jewell County, Kansas*, 5–6.

Mrs. Ward was never rescued from her captivity, and was probably killed shortly into her ordeal. But a story in the *Junction City Union* about two months after her capture led her neighbors to believe it was about her. The story told of buffalo soldiers finding a crazy woman wandering along the Saline River. When they approached her she ran off in a terrified manner, mistaking the buffalo soldiers for Indians. It was thought that this was Mrs. Ward and that she eventually starved to death, unable to recover from her hysteria of captivity to regain her senses and seek help.[17] The story also appeared later that summer in the *New York Times*:

> A wild romance is now attached to one of our lonely streams. While out scouting the other day, along Fossil Creek some of our [buffalo] soldiers came suddenly upon a white woman. She was dressed in black, with disordered hair and haggard eyes, and fled in a crazy manner when approached. An Indian camp had been supposed to exist near, and the soldiers were afraid to pursue beyond short distance. There are various opinions held regarding the matter. Most probably the woman's relatives were murdered in one of the attacks upon immigrant wagons, and she, escaping, became crazy from fright and grief. Or she may have strayed from the Indian camp, and been a poor captive, made insane by cruelty. Negro soldiers are not very fascinating in appearance, and, meeting in the lonely creek bottom the crazed wandered probably imagined them hostile Indians, and either fled for protection to those who held her captive, or wandered aimlessly on among the Smoky Hills. As more troops come into the country, she may again be found and the mystery solved.[18]

More troops did come into the country, but this woman disappeared, as did Mrs. Ward. Because of the timely appearance of this story to Mrs. Ward's captivity, settlers in Jewell County always believed this crazed woman story was indeed Mrs. Ward, and that her fate was probably that she died soon after being spotted by the soldiers.

On May 5, on the Denver road, a band of Cheyenne and Lakota Indians stole 50 head of stock at Julesburg belonging to George Lang.[19] The Indians remained in the vicinity, because on the 15th, five warriors sneaked right up to Fort Sedgwick and stole 17 ponies belonging to the friendly Sioux Red Bead, who was employed as a scout for the military at Sedgwick. Captain Mix was immediately sent after the thieves but returned, having lost their trail. Colonel Richard I. Dodge reported that Fort Sedgwick was "surrounded

---

17   Winsor and Scarbrough, *History of Jewell County, Kansas*, 6.
18   *New York Times*, July 22, 1867
19   George Lang Indian Depredation Claim #1943. Record Group 123.

with small thieving parties and can do nothing against them."[20] In little more than a month, Red Bead led Lieutenant Lyman S. Kidder and 10 men of the 2nd Cavalry from Fort Sedgwick down to the Republican River to find Lieutenant Colonel George A. Custer and give him important orders that had been telegraphed to Fort Sedgwick from Omaha. Kidder missed Custer's trail after his command left their camp near present-day Benkelman, Nebraska and Kidder and his men were all killed on July 2, on the banks of Beaver Creek, about 40 miles north of Fort Wallace.[21]

Colonel Dodge was correct about Indians making thieving sorties all around Fort Sedgwick. Late in the day on May 15, Indians stole 17 mules belonging to two men named T. W. Vollintine and William Hain. They had been in partnership for a little over a year running a ranch at Big Springs, 18 miles east of Fort Sedgwick. Before that Vollintine was a clerk employed for more than a year at Sedgwick. Three years before clerking at Fort Sedgwick, Vollintine had traded with Spotted Tail and other tribes along the Republican River, living with them each year for several months. The partners knew that their business at the ranch was soon to be a thing of the past because the quickly approaching railroad would drive them out of business. But they had just accepted an offer to run the sutler's store at Fort Phil Kearny in present-day Wyoming, but was in 1867 Dakota Territory. In April 1867, Colonel Henry Carrington met with them at their ranch and made them the post sutler offer. Carrington told them that the present sutler was bad and he wanted them to replace him. They accepted the offer and had the provisions to stock the sutler store in their camp near Big Springs. Young warriors belonging to Spotted Tail came into the herd and ran off the mules. Soldiers were sent out to try to recover the stock but returned a few days later without any success.

Three or four weeks after the theft, William Hain was stopped at Fort Laramie, on his way to Fort Phil Kearny. One of his freighters awoke him from a nap he was taking under one of his wagons. The man reported that some of Hain's stolen mules were at that moment in the possession of Indians who were visiting at Fort Laramie in anticipation of a council to negotiate a new treaty. The driver

---

20 Colonel Richard I. Dodge, "Report, headquarters Fort Sedgwick C.T., May 15, 1867. Record Group 393, Part I, Letters Received, Department of the Platte, Entry 3731, 1867.

21 Broome, *Custer into the West*, 78–90. See also Jeff Broome, "On Locating the Kidder Massacre site of 1867," *The Denver Westerners Roundup*, July—August, 2000, 3–18, as well as "Custer, Kidder and Tragedy at Beaver Creek," *Wild West*, June, 2002, 30–37.

THEODORE R. DAVIS' ETCHING,
SHOWING THE DISCOVERY OF 2ND LT. LYMAN KIDDER,
10 MEN OF THE 2ND CAVALRY, AND INDIAN SCOUT, RED BEAD.
The men were sent from Fort Sedgwick to deliver important dispatches to Custer, delivered via telegraph to Fort Sedgwick, from Omaha. Kidder missed Custer's trail and he and his small party were soon overwhelmed by at least 200 warriors. They were all killed on July 2, 1867, and discovered by Custer on July 12. At least one soldier was tortured alive, by fire. *Harper's Weekly* (August 17, 1867). *Author's collection.*

came up hurriedly, saying—"Bill, there is the old gray mule." She was kind of a gray mule. I rolled out from under the wagon and I knew the mule immediately and up to the fort I started, and by the way Captain Grimes was a particular friend of mine that I had known during the war. I told him about the mules and he said he would go with me to the general. The case was laid before the general and he stated that he had the Indians there trying to effect a treaty or compromise, so they will behave themselves and that it would be rather dangerous for him to try to get the mules. I then asked permission to retake them myself. And then he got red-headed and would not allow it at all; that is the kind of satisfaction I got.[22]

22   T. W. Vollintine and William Hain Indian Depredation Claim #7089. Record Group 123.

The misfortunes of Vollintine and Hain would follow them to Fort Phil Kearny, for the negotiation or "compromise"—as Hain described it— involved the closing of that fort the next year. When that happened, the Indians immediately burned it to the ground.

It wasn't just on the Denver road that Indians were causing problems. Back on the Smoky Hill road in Ellsworth County, Moses Strew had a ranch. On May 18, Cheyenne raiders attacked his ranch, destroyed his household goods, a wagon and mowing machine, and stole five horses and 27 cattle.[23]

On May 17, warriors made a deadly raid back on the Denver road, seven miles east of Julesburg on the north side of the river. A large freight train operated by Jacob Penny was returning east after delivering freight to Fort Laramie. Their destination was North Platte, the terminus at that time for the Union Pacific Railroad. They had just gone into their noon camp and had their large stock, numbering 260 oxen, unhitched and grazing. Three herders were watching the stock when, shortly after 11 o'clock, Indians charged into the grazing herd, chased down the three herders, killing each, and then drove off the entire stock. This was a bold attack, especially as it was so close to Fort Sedgwick. Captain Mix was immediately ordered to pursue the Indians and punish them. He was provided with four mules to carry provisions for six days.[24] Mix led a company of soldiers accompanied by 28 local citizens. After 60 miles the men went into camp on Smith Fork just before sundown. They had just picketed their horses when warriors charged at them. Jacob Penny was there and he recalled what happened next:

> We had orders to saddle our horses and prepare to go for them [the Indians]; we marched down the creek and charged upon the Indian camp which was about a half a mile away, and the Indians retreated over the hills in all directions; and we had orders to go for them, we followed them from five to eight miles. It was so dark that we couldn't get a shot, but we could hear them retreating. We went back to the soldier's camp, and the next morning the citizens went down and gathered up the cattle; and Captain Mix and a party of the citizens followed the Indians the next morning, and the rest of us turned back with the cattle.

Having recovered his cattle, Penney and his freighters drove the herd back to their camp near Julesburg. Not all of his stock was recovered. Still

---

23   Moses Strew Indian Depredation Claim #3770. Record Group 123.

24   Colonel J. H. Potter, "Orders to Captain John Mix," May 19, 1867. Record Group 393, Part I, Letters Received, Department of the Platte, Entry 3731, 1867.

lost were 21 oxen and three saddled horses.[25] The *Frontier Index*, a newspaper in North Platte, added more details about the events. The freight train included two trains run by Penny and a man named Galbreth. When the train camped near Julesburg, the three herders, thinking it was safe, left their weapons at the wagons. It was a fatal mistake and was the cause of their deaths. It was raining that day when the men

> were attacked by a party of Sioux and being unarmed spurred their horses towards the wagons, but were overtaken and in a twinkling were pierced with arrows, killing all three of them. One received four arrows, one two and the other one. This was done within sight of the wagons but too quick to get assistance. The cattle were all run off and also three ponies taken. The next day Penny and Galbreth started for Fort Sedgwick to report their loss and get assistance, and were pursued by a large band of Indians to within a mile and a half of the fort but their horses were to [*sic*] fleet for their pursuers, and they escaped uninjured.[26]

Captain Mix's account of this expedition gave more details. It rained every day. They didn't leave until five o'clock in the evening on the 19th and were unable to find where the freighters were camped until early the next morning. At daylight they marched 36 miles northeast to Henry's Fork of the North Platte. The mules assigned to carry supplies were entirely worthless and impeded the command. When they went into camp some scouts went on further and were chased back by about 12 Indians. They reported to Mix that the Indian village was about four miles away. Captain Mix immediately ordered his men to attack the village but they couldn't get there until it was dark. The Indians, instead of fighting, abandoned their camp and fled in the dark. Mix ordered everything destroyed. He reported recovering only 35 oxen. The next day he continued his pursuit of the warriors but gave it up and returned to Fort Sedgwick in the early afternoon of May 25th.[27]

While Mix was out on this six-day excursion, Indians attacked another train near Alkali Station, 30 miles east of Julesburg, and stole 70 cattle from a freighter named Ward. When Mix returned to Sedgwick he was immediately ordered back out by Colonel J. H. Potter to pursue these warriors who, like the last party, had retreated north. He was given three days' worth

25 Jacob Penny Indian Depredation Claim #4634. Record Group 123.

26 *Frontier Index*, Friday, June 14, 1867.

27 Captain John Mix, "Report," Fort Sedgwick, Col. Ter., May 25, 1867. Record Group 393, Part I, Letters Received, Department of the Platte, Entry 3731, 1867.

of rations and again used what Mix called worthless mules. With his same fatigued men and horses he left at daylight the next morning and followed the Indians' trail through the following day, May 27. Meanwhile Colonel Potter received a telegram sent from the stage operator at Pole Creek Station, reporting that Indians had made an attack on yet another freight train near that station and killed three men. Potter replied back that Captain Mix had already been sent out and was currently in the vicinity.[28] No doubt it was the same tribe involved in all the recent raids. Mix followed their trail to the North Platte, where the Indians crossed with their stolen stock. He ended the chase there, convinced that if he tried to send his men across the Platte many would drown as well as the horses, especially as his horses were nearly spent, having just returned from a 250 mile jaunt. In fact his horses were so exhausted and broken down that when he returned to Fort Sedgwick on the 29th, he had to camp on the north side of the South Platte, as the horses were unable to cross over the river where the fort stood.[29]

Meanwhile, back in Kansas, on the Smoky Hill road, things were heating up with several raids occurring. About May 19, Indians attacked a railroad crew and stole three wagons and the mules about 25 miles north of Monument Station. The wagons were owned by the Union Pacific Railroad and were under the charge of Mr. Greenwood.[30] A series of reports out of Fort Wallace made clear that Indians were on the warpath. 7th Cavalry Captain Myles Keogh stopped the eastbound stage at Fort Wallace and hastily wrote a report that Indians attacked soldiers stationed at Big Timbers (also called Blue Mound Station), 36 miles west of Fort Wallace the day before. A stage was also attacked. One of the troopers was slightly wounded, a corporal, M. Bernhardt, of the 37th Infantry.[31] Bernhardt reported that the attack was made about one o'clock in the morning as he was walking his post outside the station. He had just checked the stables and house and was making his way to the barn:

28 Colonel J. H. Potter, "Telegram to Col. Litchfield, Fort Sedgwick, C.T., May 24, 1867." Record Group 393, Part I, Letters Received, Department of the Platte, Entry 3731, 1867.

29 Colonel J. H. Potter, "Orders to Captain John Mix," May 26, 1867; Captain John Mix, "Report," May 29, 1867. Record Group 393, Part I, Letters Received, Department of the Platte, Entry 3731, 1867.

30 Captain M. S. Keogh, "Report, Fort Wallace" May 25, 1867. Record Group 393, Part I, Letters Received, Department of the Missouri, Entry 2593, 1867.

31 Captain M. S. Keogh, "Report, Fort Wallace" May 24, 1867. Record Group 393, Part I, Letters Received, Department of the Missouri, Entry 2593, 1867.

I saw the flash of a gun right in my face and felt a stinging in the back of my neck. I turned around to see where the fire came from and saw an Indian running about 30 paces from me. I immediately fired at him and I think I hit him for he gave a loud yell and stooped down and then walked off. And just as I was reloading my piece another shot was fired at me from the corner of the barn so I went into the fort then, and the Indians after trying several times to get into the barn went off carrying two or three men with them either dead or wounded. There have some been seen several times today. They also attacked the stage above here. One of the balls fired at me cut my coat blouse and shirt colors, but did not hurt me or anybody else.[32]

Bernhardt's neck injury was probably nothing more than a flesh wound. He reported the next night the Indians again attacked the stage station. They were easily driven off.[33] On May 25, Indians attacked the men at Russell Springs—also called Eaton Station—24 miles east of Fort Wallace. The stage going east was also attacked near the station, but Keogh had an escort of soldiers riding with it and they were able to drive the Indians away. Keogh noted that the stage road was becoming increasingly dangerous. Scurvy was also becoming rampant among the soldiers protecting the various stage stations.[34] Soldiers would ride on the stage from one station to the next and then ride the stage going in the opposite direction back and thus return to their posted station.

In another report, Keogh gave more details of the attack at Russell Springs. The station itself was not attacked but rather some soldiers were fired on near the station. The Indians were easily driven off. The stage attack ended as soon as one of the soldiers on the coach fired back. Keogh issued orders to his men to preserve any Indians killed so that their tribe might be identified. As yet he was not sure which Indians were making the raids. He also noted how miserable the weather was. It had been raining five days straight and "the prairie is a perfect morass."[35]

Keogh's report identified a serious problem in catching the guilty parties. The Treaty of the Little Arkansas permitted peaceful Indians to still hunt in

---

32   Corporal M. Bernhardt, "Report, Big Timbers Station," May 25, 1867. Record Group 393, Part I, Letters Received, Department of the Missouri, Entry 2593, 1867.

33   Captain M.S. Keogh, "Report, Fort Wallace" May 25, 1867. Record Group 393, Part I, Letters Received, Department of the Missouri, Entry 2593, 1867.

34   Captain M. S. Keogh, "Report, Fort Wallace" May 26, 1867. Record Group 393, Part I, Letters Received, Department of the Missouri, Entry 2593, 1867.

35   Captain M. S. Keogh, "Report, Fort Wallace" May 27, 1867. Record Group 393, Part I, Letters Received, Department of the Missouri, Entry 2593, 1867.

the areas where the roads were developed and the new settlements were being built. This was exactly where the militant raiders were showing their hostilities. By permitting treaty Indians to hunt all the way north of the Smoky Hill River and west of Plum Creek (in Nebraska), it made it nearly impossible for anyone who fell victim to an Indian raid to distinguish whether an Indian belonged to a peaceful hunting party or a warring band. Keogh strongly suspected, and correctly, that the two groups of Indians—the hunters and the raiders—were one and the same. He feared that the stages west of Fort Wallace were under siege, as no stage had come from that direction for two days. The last one from the west arrived at Wallace on May 27.[36]

On May 28, two miles west of Fort Wallace, 16 Indians approached Pond Creek Station and absconded with the herd of stock stationed there. When Keogh learned of it, he ordered mounted a command of soldiers and followed in pursuit. The warriors' tracks were easy to see in the soggy ground. He followed their trail nine miles west along the stage road and then five miles south of Goose Creek Station where he found their small campsite hastily abandoned. He recovered the stock there, except for five which had been killed before the Indians fled. He then followed the Indian trail northwest and soon encountered what was a frequent tactic warriors used when being followed. They all scattered in different directions, leaving no trail to follow, and Keogh was left to report "... I had to relinquish the attempt as an utter failure." Another problem he encountered was a lack of forage for his horses, which caused them to be unfit for quick pursuit. With all the rain they were not able to get much from grazing, and the post had been without grain for 20 days.[37]

The activity heating up around Fort Wallace was just a part of the attacks that were increasing at this time and shortly before. About 38 miles east of Fort Dodge, along the Arkansas River, a party of about two dozen Cheyenne Indians raided the bull train of Jesus Saracino and absconded with 48 oxen, a mare and a mule. Saracino was moving east on his way to Kansas City when he lost his stock.[38]

---

36   Captain M. S. Keogh, "Report, Fort Wallace" May 29, 1867. Record Group 393, Part I, Letters Received, Department of the Missouri, Entry 2593, 1867.

37   Captain M. S. Keogh, "Report, Fort Wallace" May 28, 1867. Record Group 393, Part I, Letters Received, Department of the Missouri, Entry 2593, 1867. National Archives Building, Washington, DC.

38   Jesus Maria Saracino Indian Depredation Claim #7143. Record Group 123.

The attacks upon the stage stations of the United States Express Company, later purchased by Wells Fargo and Company, were astounding. Their property losses for this period in 1867 in Kansas and Colorado Territory amounted to a whopping $242,512.32, just in property losses alone.[39] This would be the equivalent to $3,842,997.08 in today's ecomony.[40] The stage company began trying to collect for the damages incurred in their losses in late fall, 1867. In one letter, dated October 7, W. H. Cottrill noted that the guilty Indians were now asking for their annuities. He asked Commissioner of Indian Affairs E. B. Taylor that their annuities be withheld and that the stage company instead be paid. Cottrill:

> The Indians . . . have attacked our coaches, murdered our employees and passengers, burnt our stations, stole our stock, robbed and destroyed large quantities of hay, grain and provisions: they are now hostile, and we are for safety obliged to run two coaches in company with a military escort to protect them, and a large military force is kept upon the line at our stations to prevent attacks being made. Two hundred thousand dollars is a low estimate of the property of our company destroyed by these savages, besides the loss of nearly all the revenue from passenger traffic during the past summer.[41]

It was simply stunning to Cottrill that the government would even consider giving the Indians their annuities, while permitting them to make their attacks all summer long with what appeared to him to be clearly a case of immunity from any liability.

Depositions were taken from all Wells Fargo employees—Cheyenne and Arapaho warriors were usually identified as the perpetrators—and other witnesses to each attack, and then the entire report was forwarded to the government in an effort to receive compensation. The company noted astutely what the 1867 war was all about: "The war was one of depredations. The Indians did not seek to fight the troops, but sought to evade them, and the troops could not find the Indians and could not overtake them in time to fight a battle with them."[42]

---

39   Wells Fargo and Company Indian Depredation Claim #10573, in four files, File Four. Record Group 123. See also claim #10032.
40   http://www.westegg.com/inflation/infl.cgi (accessed April 27, 2013).
41   Letter from W. H. Cottrill to E. B. Taylor, October 7, 1867. Entry 700, Record Group 75. Indian Depredations Claims Division.
42   Wells Fargo and Company Indian Depredation Claim #10032.

A chronological rundown of all Wells Fargo raids follows, as well as additional raids that occurred at the same time.

April 14: Chalk Bluffs Station was attacked, 24 horses stolen, 45 tons of hay burned, as were the station house, barn, corral, and three freight wagons. Thomas D. Marshall and Frederick Heigele were "stock tenders" at Chalk Bluffs when the Indians attacked it. Samuel Dicus was a stage driver and was also at the station when it was attacked.

April 15: John Ferris drove a stage to Lookout Station and found the station "had just been burned by the Indians;" three men were found dead and scalped, and eight horses were stolen. William Sanders, stock tender at Deering Springs, also arrived at Lookout shortly after the attack and found the dead men. "Station had just been attacked by Indians." W. H. Cottrill, Division Superintendent, was also with the stage when it arrived at the station "while it was yet burning."

April 16: Joseph Brown, Train Master, was delivering two wagons of provisions for the United States Express Company and was attacked near Downer Station. The Wagons were burned and 10 mules stolen. P. L. Leonard was driving one of the wagons. The men were not killed.

April 17: Chalk Bluffs was again attacked. The station was burned and 24 horses stolen. Forty-five tons of hay was also burned. Witnesses who were there were not named.

April 18: W. H. Cottrill, Division Superintendent for the stage company, was at Walker's Creek Stage Station—probably the same station called Willow Creek—when Indians set fire to the prairie surrounding the hay stack and stage house. Both were burned to ground. H. Nichols, station keeper, was there, as was Jacob Stultzman, stock tender. Sixty-five tons of hay and the stable and station house were lost. The Indians also stole two horses.

April 18: Indians also attacked Goose Creek Station, the next station east of Willow Creek. Robert Boyd, stock tender, was there when Indians set fire to the hay stack and station buildings. One hundred fifty tons of hay was burned and eight mules were stolen.

April 20: J. W. Barron and Lent Maloney, stock tender, reported that Downer Station was attacked at night. The Indians burned the hay stack and station house and drove off eight horses.

April 21: Thomas D. Marshall was a stock tender at Chalk Bluffs when the station was attacked and eight horses stolen.

April 24: Richard Wright, driving a stage, was at Russell Springs when warriors set fire to the hay stack and corral. They also burned one freight wagon and captured eight horses and one mule. John Collins, stock tender, was also there at the time of the raid.

April 29: Goose Creek Station was attacked about 10 or 11 o'clock at night. L. C. Bursell, a carpenter, was there. The station house was again burned, as was the hay and stables. Eight mules were stolen. One hundred fifty tons of hay was burned.[43] Victor Clark, stock tender, was there. The presence of a carpenter at this time of attack indicates the stage station was being rebuilt when it was burned again.

May 9: Willow Creek Stage Station was attacked. L. J. Prentice, driving a stage, whose residence was at Lake Station, was there when the Indians attacked and stole eight horses and two mules. Timothy Gleason, a Blacksmith, was also there.

May 9: At one o'clock in the morning, Oliver Perry Wiggins, station keeper ("master") at Monument Station, was awakened when two Indians crept up and burned 75 tons of hay and the corral. Martha Wiggins, Oliver's wife, was there as were Frederick Heigele and John Collins, stock tenders. When Wiggins and his wife made their affidavits on November 16, Wiggins was then serving at Bijou Station as station keeper. He had earlier been stationed at Alkali Station when raids occurred there the year before.

May 10: Lake Station, located about three miles southeast of present-day Limon, Colorado, was attacked at night. John Ferris, Chief Division Agent of the Overland Mail Route, was there when the Indians made their assault, burning everything at about 11 o'clock. They fired the hay and all the buildings, "the fire spread so rapidly that it was impossible to turn loose the horses from the stable or save property from the storehouse." Twenty horses were burned to death, as was 70 tons of hay, one road buggy wagon, one express wagon, four freight wagons, one blacksmith's wagon, three mowing machines, 12 Ballard rifles, 10 Springfield muskets, as well as five ammunition boxes. The reason so much stuff was lost was because Lake Station served as a place storing supplies to keep the other stations functional, a "stable of depot for supplies." The total loss was valued at $32,058, or $508,010.48 in today's value.[44] Nathan

---

43   The April 18 attack also noted 150 tons of hay was burned. It therefore seems improbable that an additional tonnage of hay was there to burn 11 days later.

44   http://www.westegg.com/inflation/infl.cgi (accessed May 22, 2013).

Roberts, stock tender and stage driver, was there. The stable, storehouse and commissary building were all burned down. Daniel Maloney, driving a stage, came to Lake Station and said the "station had just been attacked by Indians who had set fire to the buildings and hay stack which was entirely destroyed." John L. Cisco was an Express Messenger and arrived at Lake Station on the stage with Maloney.

May 20: Monument Station was attacked and one horse was stolen. Back on the Denver road on the South Platte River, Riverside Station telegraphed Fort Sedgwick on May 29, reporting a flock of sheep at the Moore ranch was stolen, and that passengers on the stage going east saw about 50 warriors on the north bank of the river near Moore's place.[45]

Down on the Santa Fe road another raid happened, on May 23. Indians attacked the stage station at Pretty Encampment and ran off the stock. Eight days later Indians caught two soldiers of Company I, 37th Infantry out hunting near Fort Aubrey, a new post erected along the Santa Fe road about 60 miles east of Fort Lyon, not far into Kansas, killing them both.[46]

Meanwhile, at Old Fort Hays, Custer had six companies of the 7th Cavalry preparing for his summer campaign. His men had remained at the post since he arrived there last April, during his jaunt away from Hancock's campaign when he had been sent to locate the Indians who had fled their villages during Hancock's planned parley with the Indians. By early May, plans were drawn up for this campaign, and finally on June 1, Custer departed Old Fort Hays. His orders were to proceed north up to the Platte River, where Generals Sherman and Hancock believed the marauding Indians would be making their forays. Custer's command consisted of 350 men and 16 wagons. As it was later learned, his presence along the Platte River was not where the Indians were making their raids, and in early July he was ordered back down on the Smoky Hill trail.[47]

June 1: Attacks were not just on the Smoky Hill where Custer was operating. A stage was driving east from Denver on the Denver road. It carried only one passenger and another employee was leading four horses when

45   Colonel J. H. Potter, "Letter to General C. C. Augur, Fort Sedgwick, C. T., May 29, 1867," Record Group 393, Part I, Letters Received, Department of the Platte, Entry 3731, 1867.

46   Major Henry Douglass, 3rd Infantry, "Report from Headquarters Fort Dodge Kansas, June 12, 1867." Record Group 393, Part I, Letters Received, Department of the Missouri, Entry 2593, 1867. For information on Fort Aubrey see Bisel and Martin, *Kansas Forts*, 67–70.

47   For a full account of this campaign see Broome, *Custer into the West*.

they were attacked between Godfrey's Ranch—"Fort Wicked"—and the burned "Fairview" Ranch (American Ranch). When the stage was attacked the passenger jumped out and ran north towards the South Platte River. He escaped and made it to Godfrey's Station. He reported both the driver and man leading the horses were killed and the horses taken. At Godfrey's Ranch was a telegraph operator, who was out repairing the line at the time. He had his repair instruments with him and used them to telegraph the attack. "[Holan] Godfrey was attacked the same day and made a narrow escape fighting his way from cover to cover until he made it to his ranch."[48]

David Street, Superintendent of the stage company, in an undated report, noted that another stage carrying 10 passengers was also attacked nearby. At least one man was killed and a passenger badly wounded. The passengers were left at Moore's Ranch, about 30 miles east of where the other passenger escaped into the river. A report from Fort Sedgwick said the attack happened June 2. It also noted the telegraph was down at Riverside Ranch, two other stages going west were captured near Moore's Ranch and all wagon trains were stopped.[49] *The Chicago Tribune* shed more light on the lucky passenger who escaped in the earlier stage. He was a minister from Denver and was going east when the stage was attacked:

> it was a hot day and he had his shoes and coat off and was dozing, when "Bang! Bang!" went a lot of guns, and he looked out and saw a lot of Indians whooping and digging out for the stage-coach. He saw the driver keel over, shot through the head, and the horses swerve from the road off onto the prairie. His first impulse was to get the lines and fetch the horses back into the road, and he believed he could beat the Indians in a race. So he climbed out of the window and got upon the box, but the lines had dropped on the ground and the four horses were just more than streaking it. He climbed down on the pole to pick up the lines, the Indians popping away at him all the time, and just then the coach struck a wallow, a sort of gutter about two feet wide and perhaps nine inches deep, and down he went into the mud, and the stage went on without him. "Well," thinks he, "It's all up with

---

48   Wells Fargo and Company Indian Depredation Claim #10032. The depredation claim lists another stage burned and the driver killed on June 11, near Wisconsin Ranch, about 10 miles further west. These are likely the same event as the driver in both cases is identified as E. B. Kilburn. It must have been a typo from June 1 to June 11. If this is the case, then perhaps "Fairview" was an early name for Riverside Station, and not another name for American Ranch. This, at least, is what Doris Monahan writes in *Destination: Denver City*, 233.

49   Lt. Col. J. H. Potter, "Report, Fort Sedgwick, June 3, 1867." Record Group 393, Part I, Letters Received, Department of the Platte, Entry 3331, 1867.

me now. They'll torture me sure." But whether they thought he was dead or that they would come back after him, they rode around him, and made for the coach. Then the thought came to him that he might give them the slip. "I prayed to God Almighty for all I was worth," he said, "and then I slid along on my stomach in the mud till I got to where the ground sloped down toward the Platte River. But they saw me, and three of them came after me on their ponies. "Well sir," says he, "I had only my socks on, and the place was as full of cactus thorns as a flax hackle, but I got away from them in a hurry, I tell you. I was a pretty good swimmer, and if I could get into the water I was pretty near all right. Just then the three Indians stopped and looked west. I turned, too, and there were two men with guns coming down the river bank on my side, as if to cut me off. But I had prayed, and I wasn't going to give up then; so I made a bee line for the river, and got on the other side and was shaking myself when I heard somebody holler in English, 'Come over! We won't hurt you.' I told them I was just as safe where I was. Then they hollered back that they were two soldiers from Fort Sedgwick come out hunting, and, would you believe it? They hadn't heard that there were Indians in the neighborhood."[50]

The stage driver shot dead was a man named E. B. Kilburn. According to David Street, when Kilburn was killed his falling stopped the stage:

Instantly the savages made a rush and secured the horses, taking all the trimmings from the harness. They also cut the front and hind leather boots from the coach; then cut open and rifled the mail-sacks. There was only one passenger aboard—a minister of the Gospel, from Denver—and he, having his boots off, hurriedly jumped from the stage and ran back along the river bank to the station. Closely behind the coach was a boy with four stage horses, riding one and leading the other three. When he saw the Indians fire and Kilburn fall from the box, he instantly turned loose the three animals he was leading and ran them back to Godfrey's, thus saving the team and, what was of far more value to him, his own scalp. He escaped, but it was a very close call.[51]

The same Wells Fargo report noting the attack on the two stages had information concerning further undated attacks: Ferguson's Ranch was 15 miles west of Bishop's Ranch, which was five miles west of Fremont's Springs. At Ferguson's, the ranch was attacked late in the afternoon and two men were killed. A Frenchman, apparently the owner of the ranch, fought back and killed a chief. The men killed were the Frenchman's clerk and herder. According to David Street's report, "I sent a coach and ten (10) men up and

50   Root and Connelley, *Overland Stage*, 362–363.
51   Root and Connelley, *Overland Stage*, 362.

found the bodies of the murdered men lying where they were killed in the store, ..." George Smith found a train owned by a man named Gillespie near Ferguson Ranch. The train was also attacked, and the men reported "there was about 40 Indians in the band, they were very drunk, and they drove them back, killing one Indian. The Indians got 300 gallons of whiskey at Fergusons." The report is dated June 8, 1867, so the attack was shortly before that date.

At about this same time, a large train was driving to Denver on the Denver road, when two wagons owned by Aquila Hogbin had fallen back because one of the wagons had broken down. They were about half-way between Forts Sedgwick and Morgan, which would be somewhere near Washington/Moore's Ranch. After an hour or two spent repairing the wagon, Hogbin and his driver proceeded west to catch up with the other wagons at their evening camp, which was supposed to be about four miles distant. However, when they arrived the wagons were not there, so the men decided to rest and water their eight mules in the South Platte River about half a mile north of the road. As soon as the mules had waded into the shallow water, six Lakota and Arapaho warriors appeared in the river, mounted and armed. They had come out from a nearby hill, surprised the mules and drove them north across the river, where a larger number of Indians were waiting. Hogbin vividly recalled his scare:

> I [had] stopped and unharnessed my mules, and turned them out to let them graze a little bit, and rest; this was about an hour before sundown, and get something to eat for ourselves and after we had got our lunch, William Richards, my driver, gathered the stock up and started into the river to water them. While he was watering the stock, I went into the wagons to prepare the feed for the animals. After I had been in the wagons for some time I heard a hollowering [*sic*], I looked out and saw Richards a coming back without the mules, and hollowering that the Indians had got the mules, then I jumped out of the wagon, and I saw the Indians in the river and the mules also, about a half a mile away from me. I gathered my carbine and fired into the river with the intention of turning the mules, or scaring the Indians, I didn't care which, and about this time I saw a large lot of Indians on the opposite side of the river, and there was probably sixty or seventy of them, and a lot of ponies that were run out on the bank to attract the mules' attention, and of course the mules would run right to them, and they just took the whole bunch of stock and drove them right off into the hills. And that is the last I ever saw of the mules. I then left the wagons and started across to the rest of the train. They were camped three or four miles ahead. We had intended to go on and join the rest of

the train that evening after supper, but the reason that I stopped was that my mules were tired and fagged out.[52]

Down on the Santa Fe road below Fort Dodge, Indians made a raid on a wagon train owned by Don Jesus Luna. Colonel Edward Wynkoop investigated and reported the attack occurred on June 4. Two men were killed, three men wounded and a young boy taken prisoner. Sixty head of cattle were stolen. Wynkoop said the attack was done by Kiowa and not Cheyenne.[53]

Major Henry Douglass, commander at Fort Dodge, reported that a large wagon train from New Mexico was attacked south of the Arkansas River on Mulberry Creek near present-day Ford, Kansas. Ninety-six cattle were taken as well as several horses and mules. Four men were killed, and another four were missing and presumed dead. Douglass blamed the freighters for their losses, "owing to the gross carelessness of the men in charge," noting that the men guarding the stock were all unarmed, as were nearly all of the 20 men with the train. The theft and injury was committed by only seven Indians. Douglass also noted that the attack occurred on the south side of the river and not on the north side, the "prescribed" route which soldiers can protect. Further, he said "the Indians believe that the treaty confers no right on parties to send their trains south of the Arkansas between Forts Larned and Lyon—they therefore the more readily, and with greater impunity attack them."[54]

June 5: Henshaw Springs Station on the Smoky Hill trail 11 miles east of Fort Wallace was attacked and eight or nine horses were stolen. Henry Finley, stock tender, was there as was George Darrow, also a stock tender. One report stated eight horses stolen, and another report said nine were taken.

David Street sent a telegram on June 7, noting "Plum Creek Telegraph Station [Nebraska] was attacked yesterday & two men killed." The attack Street was referring to probably was associated with the killing of one man and the severe wounding of another, on a train of two four-horse wagons traveling east with groceries. The attack occurred on Plum Creek on June 6,

---

52   Aquila Hogbin Indian Depredation Claim #7002. Record Group 123.
53   E. Wynkoop "Letter to Maj. Gen. W. S. Hancock, Fort Larned, June 13, 1867." Record Group 393, Part I, Letters Received, Department of the Missouri, 1867.
54   Major Henry Douglass, 3rd Infantry, "Report from Headquarters Fort Dodge Kansas, June 8, 1867." Record Group 393, Part I, Letters Received, Department of the Missouri, Entry 2593, 1867.

EDWARD "NED" WYNKOOP, INDIAN AGENT FOR
THE CHEYENNE, ARAPAHO, KIOWA
AND KANSAS PLAINS APACHE DURING
MOST OF THE TIME *CHEYENNE WAR* COVERS.
Wynkoop (pronounced "Winecoop," according to several Indian depredation
claims) is shown with interpreter Dick Curtis, who accompanied General
Winfield Hancock during his spring, 1867 campaign. Hancock's campaign
contributed to the escalation of the Cheyenne war. Etching by Theodore R.
Davis, *Harper's Weekly* (May 11, 1867). *Author's collection.*

about 30 miles west of Fort Kearny. Joseph Fancher was driving two wagons
loaded with three tons of groceries, destination Colorado. A total of nine
horses and four mules were taken when the small party was attacked by
what was estimated to be about 300 Cheyenne warriors. One man was killed
and another severely wounded. One wagon was driven off by the Indians

and then destroyed. Henry and J. A. Fancher were traveling with Joseph, as well as a doctor, Franklin N. Green, who attended to the wounded man.[55]

On June 7, Indians made another attack on the south side of the Arkansas River near the Cimarron Crossing, "and a considerable quantity of stock run off."[56]

June 10: Goose Creek Station was again attacked. This time eight mules were stolen. Robert Boyd, stock tender, was there at the time.

June 11: Indians attacked a forage wagon—not belonging to Wells Fargo—between Castle Rock and Grinnell Springs. The driver was killed as well as a soldier of the 37th Infantry. Lieutenant Joseph C. Coffman also reported another coach attacked at Big Springs, the Indians "killing one soldier, but were driven off after a running fight of four miles." He went on to blame the driver for the soldier's death at Castle Rock, due to the "misrepresentation that I permitted the team to go on with an insufficient guard."[57] When news reached Lieutenant Henry James Nowlan of the 7th Cavalry, stationed with Company F at nearby Monument Station, he took a detail of soldiers to investigate. Nowlan discovered pony tracks of five warriors and followed their trail. Soon he found the forage wagon abandoned in a ravine, the mules gone but surprisingly, the provisions still there, along with the stage driver's rifle and a quantity of ammunition. The scalp of the dead soldier was also lying there. Nowlan had to call off his pursuit due to the poor condition of his horses.[58]

June 12: Indians attacked Cedar Point, Colorado Territory, near present-day Limon. Frank Needham, stock tender, was present when Indians appeared and stole eight horses. Daniel Maloney, a stage driver living at Lake Station eight miles away, also was at Cedar Point when the horses were stolen.

55   Joseph Fancher Indian Depredation Claim #952, Entry 700, Box 9. Record Group 75. The interesting thing about this claim is the fact that it was dismissed as a fraud, on the grounds that the notary who sealed the affidavits in 1870, after which the depredation case lingered without pay until 1890, had no memory of ever signing the affidavit (20 years later), and as a result it was declared invalid. The notary acknowledged the seal with the affidavit was genuine, but because he could not remember the case, and because he felt the signature on the original affidavit was not his own, the case was declared a fraud. And yet, clearly the Fanchers would have had no knowledge of the Wells Fargo telegram verifying that there was an attack and two men killed. It seems perhaps this was a legitimate claim.

56   Major Henry Douglass, 3rd Infantry, "Report from Headquarters Fort Dodge Kansas, June 8, 1867." Record Group 393, Part I, Letters Received, Department of the Missouri, Entry 2593, 1867.

57   Lieutenant J. C. Coffman, "Report Downers Station, June 12, 1867." Record Group 393, Part I, Letters Received, Department of the Missouri, Entry 2593, 1867.

58   Lieutenant Henry J. Nowlan, "Report from Camp of Troop F, Monument KS, June 14, 1867," Record Group 393, Part I, Letters Received, Department of the Missouri, 1867.

June 12: Hugo Springs Stage Station, 25 miles southeast of Cedar Point was also attacked on the same day. Indians charged and stole nine horses and two mules. Napoleon Barker, who later that fall was station keeper at Cheyenne Wells, was at the time the night watchman at Hugo Springs and was present when the Indians made their raid. Daniel Dunsmore, a stage driver living at Downer Station, also was at Hugo Springs when attacked. Phillip Holland lived there and was a stock tender; he was also present. But it wasn't just Wells Fargo property taken in this raid. Anna Holborn, inheriting a freighting business from her husband—who had died the year before—was also at Hugo Springs when this attack was made against the station. She reported that the Indian sortie numbered 45 Cheyenne. She lost 23 mules and five horses from her wagon train.[59] William Kersten was another freighter camping next to Hugo Station. He was freighting from Junction City to Denver and had traveled the Smoky Hill route. He lost four mules.[60]

As this attack was occurring at Hugo Springs, 50 miles further west on the Smoky Hill route to Denver, at Bijou Station, just west of present-day Kiowa, Colorado, 20–25 Indians swooped down of a herd of stock grazing, as a large wagon train comprising 40–45 wagons and 60 men had gone into camp for the evening. Coming from nearby bluffs just before sundown, the Indians yelled, waved their buffalo robes and caused most of the freight stock to stampede. Mary Smith, widowed about three years earlier, with four young daughters and four boys, was with the train. Her destination was Oregon. She lost six mules and a horse. Many of the other wagon owners lost their stock too. A party of men quickly mounted and went in pursuit for about 14 miles, when around sundown they came upon the Indians. A short skirmish followed before darkness ended the fight. Mary's nephew was killed by an arrow wound, a young man named Ben McCulloch. None of the stock was recovered.[61]

June 12: Smoky Hill Stage Station was raided. Sam Connor, stock tender, living that fall at Willow Springs, was present when Indians attacked. The warriors got away with only one horse and one mule. The next day, down on the Santa Fe road a wagon train loaded with supplies en route to Fort Dodge

---

59   Anna Holborn Indian Depredation Claim #333. Record Group 123.
60   William Kersten Indian Depredation Claim #3305. Record Group 123.
61   Mary A. Smith Indian Depredation Claim #8765. Record Group 123.

was attacked by Indians. Two men from Kansas City were in front of the train riding in a buggy when they were shot dead, scalped and mutilated.[62]

That same day, Indian agent Ned Wynkoop reported that Kiowa Indians under the leadership of Satanta, Kicking Bird and Stumbling Bear ran off all the stock from Fort Dodge. Wynkoop wrote to General Hancock that all Indians under his agency were well below the Arkansas River and entirely uninvolved in all the conflicts presently happening.[63] While he may be correct that his Cheyenne, Arapaho and Apache villages remained in their camps south of the Arkansas, he was surely wrong to imply that none of his Indians were engaged in the many raids occurring along the roads to Denver. They were, but they were the ones from Wynkoop's agency who wanted to join other parties in these many raids. Just how many were involved can only be guessed.

Captain William Thompson, Company B, 7th Cavalry, was the officer who lost the horses at Fort Dodge. According to Thompson, the raid by Satanta happened at eight in the morning. Two hundred Indians charged upon a small number of soldiers guarding the horses, within sight of Fort Dodge about a mile off to the east. A total of 71 horses were captured and driven east. Private James Spillman, one of the soldiers guarding the herd, was desperately wounded with three arrows and a pistol shot. He wasn't expected to live. A small number of men from the fort mounted mules and went in pursuit of the fleeing warriors. After about 15 miles, the Indians crossed the river, and escaped to the south. While they were crossing the river the mule-mounted soldiers were able to fire several shots at the raiders, killing one horse and wounding several more, as well as several Indians. Thompson reported that Satanta was wearing the military blouse and officer straps that had been given to him earlier when he had met with Hancock and professed peace.[64]

First Lieutenant Stanley A. Brown, 3rd Infantry, was the officer in pursuit of the stolen horses. Brown:

> I left the post . . . about half an hour after the Indians attacked and run off the cavalry herd. I rode down the river about three miles alone, discovering Indians

62 Captain Edward Byrne, "Report from Camp Grierson and Little Arkansas River, October 27 1867." Record Group 393, Part I, Letters Received, Department of the Missouri, Entry 2593, 1867.

63 E. Wynkoop "Letter to Maj. Gen. W. S. Hancock, Fort Larned, June 13, 1867."

64 Captain Wm. Thompson, "Report from Headquarters, Fort Dodge, June 12, 1867." Record Group 393, Part I, Letters Received, Department of the Missouri, Entry 2593, 1867.

signaling on the opposite bank—exchanged shots with them: the firing brought a few men to me, and in the next mile enough joined me to make my force twelve men, including five citizens. The Indians with the herd kept down the river bottom on the north side. I pushed on as rapidly as possible, a few men joining me on the road. About eighteen miles from the post, I discovered the Indians crossing the river, and came up to the river bank & just as the last had got across: my advance guard reaching the bank in time to cut out six horses and a pony: wounding a few of the Indians, & killing Satanta's (the chief's) horse. The river at this point was swift and deep.... Most of my men were mounted on mules, that would not swim, and I did not deem it practicable to cross in face of such a force.[65]

Major Douglass reported that when Brown hurried off after the fleeing Indians, Captain Thompson put together about 20 infantrymen, driven in wagons, and joined the pursuit, but he soon had to turn back to the fort when he was warned by a messenger that other Indians were approaching the fort from the north. Those reports turned out to be false, but they succeeded in keeping Thompson's small command out of the pursuit that Brown was carrying out. It was soon learned that another herd of stock was under attack to the west of the fort. That herd belonged to the post quartermaster. The soldiers guarding the stock saw the Indians approaching and stampeded the herd in the direction of the fort. None of the government stock was lost, though the stage company and a few civilians lost their stock. Douglass also noted his frustration with a lack of soldiers at the post, due to his having to send so many soldiers out to the various stage stations and to provide support for the arriving and departing stages. Because so few troops were left at the post, there were a minimal number of soldiers who could be assigned to guard the herds. Only a sergeant and four privates were guarding the cavalry horses when they were stolen. Douglass ended his report noting that Private Spillman had died the day after his was severely wounded.[66]

In yet another report, Douglass noted all of his frustrations with trying to secure peace. It is a testament to his inability to be effective in what was expected:

> By the loss of the cavalry herd I am sadly crippled—but one company is hardly sufficient to operate with advantage. The Indians have many war parties out in different

---

65 First Lieutenant Stanley A. Brown, "Report, Fort Dodge Kansas June 13, 1867." Record Group 393, Part I, Letters Received, Department of the Missouri, Entry 2593, 1867.

66 Major Henry Douglass, "Report from Headquarters Fort Dodge Kansas June 14, 1867." Record Group 393, Part I, Letters Received, Department of the Missouri, Entry 2593, 1867.

directions, & while pursuing them in one direction they commit depredations in another. Infantry they will not fight, and easily escape from them—three or at least two companies of cavalry, in fact any number of companies could be used with great advantage in the present state of the country in this vicinity. . . . There is no doubt but that all the Indians in this country are at war with us, their peace promises were only mere pretends to gain time. A little less than three weeks after I gave Satanta the document containing proceedings of the council at Fort Larned, he made an attack on the cavalry herd in person—and I have reason to believe that the Arapahoes are as much engaged as any other band. "Little Raven" may not be favorable to war, but he can't keep his tribe out of it. They are all at war & I do not believe it would be proper to make any distinction. . . . With the Cheyennes and Sioux to the north of us, and the Kiowas and Arapahoes all around us, we have more work in hand than our little garrison can perform—taking into account guards for the lime kiln & stone quarry—escorts to trains to and from those places—escorts to wood trains, escorts to Overland Mail Stage, and escorts to inspectors and paymasters, as they may be called for; we have left barely sufficient for herders and garrison duty.[67]

June 15: Lake Station was again attacked. William M. Keith was the Lake Station stage manager and was present. Two cows were killed by Indians. John Ferris, Chief Division Agent of the Overland Mail Route, owned by United States Express Company, was also present.

June 15: Deering Springs Stage Station, 13 miles west of Cheyenne Wells, was attacked and nine horses and four mules were stolen. James Fahey was a stage driver from Deering Springs and Big Timbers (also called Blue Mound) and was present during the attack. William Saunders, a stock tender, was also present, as was John L. Cisco, Express Messenger.

George Fahrion was also present at Deering Springs during this attack. Coincidentally, he was on his way east from near present-day Kiowa, Colorado, to accept employment with the Quartermaster Department at Fort Wallace, after a verbal invitation from Lieutenant Frederick Beecher. He had loaded his household goods into a wagon and was coming east with his wife, mother-in-law and brother-in-law, James T. Swena. When he got to Deering Springs, a corporal stationed stopped him and said he could not proceed further until there was a sufficient escort to protect him, under the orders of Captain Myles Keogh, commanding Fort Wallace. He and his family had waited for three days when a party of five Indians dashed upon

---

67 Major Henry Douglass, "Report from Headquarters Fort Dodge Kansas June 18, 1867." Record Group 393, Part I, Letters Received, Department of the Missouri, Entry 2593, 1867.

the station. Fahrion was the only person outside; everyone else was inside eating breakfast. Fahrion was shot and severely wounded, and the Indians ran off with his four mules, and 11 horses belonging to the stage company. James Fahey was there and remembered seeing Fahrion leading his mules back to the station when

> I heard several shots, and then stepped out of the barn, I saw Mr. Fahrion coming toward the station and I also saw a number of Indians about 25 or 30 after him shooting at him. He let loose of the mules, and came toward the station as fast as he could. The Indians took the mules . . . . Mr. Fahrion came on to the station, and when he got there I found that he was seriously wounded.[68]

James Swena also recalled what happened:

> They [the stock] were run off in the morning, I saw them run off the mules and horses myself, there were seven Indians that run off the horses, and mules, and a large number of Indians on the hill [a half mile away], at the same time my brother-in-law, Mr. Fahrion was shot and wounded by the Indians, I heard the report of the gun, he was amongst the horses at the time he was shot, and I went to him immediately, and tried to keep the Indians from running off the stock, but they took all the horses but two belonging to the Stage company, and also got the [four] mules belonging to Mr. Fahrion. We remained there at the station—Stage Station—for a day or so, when General Hancock came along with some soldiers, commanded by Captain Keough [sic]. He ordered Mr. Fahrion and myself to come back to Denver, with him, Mr. Fahrion was put in a government wagon, and also the rest of the family, but we were not allowed to bring any goods. He ordered us to leave the goods, except some articles of clothing which we were compelled to have on the road, and the wagon and harness was left there and most all the household goods, in pursuance of this order of General Hancock's.[69]

George Fahrion was unable to return for his wagon for six months. When he sufficiently recovered from his wound and went back to Deering Springs, everything of his was either stolen or destroyed. Fahrion went on to become a judge in Elbert County, and lived in Kiowa. He remained a judge there until 1909.[70]

June 15: Big Timbers (Blue Mound), 22 miles west of Deering Springs was attacked by a band of warriors the same day Deering Springs was attacked.

---

68 George Fahrion Indian Depredation Claim #845. Record Group 123.
69 George Fahrion Indian Depredation Claim #845.
70 Marr, *Douglas County*, 88; Mathews, *Early Days Around the Divide*, 33.

The Indians killed four mules. John L. Cisco, Express Messenger, was present during the attack. James Fahey was driving the coach and reported that the stage was attacked and all four mules were killed. This happened as he was driving between Deering Springs and Big Timbers. The Wells Fargo report of losses did not give the details of what happened. It was a bloody affair. Sergeant Dawson Cain of the 37th Infantry, along with a small detail of soldiers, was escorting a stage coach from Pond Creek to Big Timbers. When the escort and stage coach got within six miles of the station they came under attack by a large body of Indians, at least 200 strong. Cain:

at the first firing we jumped from the coach and commenced firing back; at their first volley they killed a citizen passenger. We fought them to within a mile of the station [Big Timbers] when assistance came to us from the station. I am sorry to report the death of two men of Co. E 3rd Infantry that were escorting the coach and the wounding of one other of the same company. The driver was wounded in the back, one citizen in the shoulder and one in the head. In jumping from the coach the wheel passed over my foot. I had my gun in my hand but in falling I dropped it. On getting up I found my foot badly hurt and my gun some distance from me. The Indians made a rush for me and I ran for the coach & was pulled in. One of the passengers gave me a Spencer carbine which I used during the fight. The escort coach by this time was nearly a mile ahead and we had to fight our way through the Indians until the relief came from the station.

On arriving at the station I found that they had been fighting them all morning. They made an attempt to run off the stock in which they were unsuccessful, the men beating them off and securing the stock. The Indians divided & one party came to attack the coaches and one fought them at the station. . . . The mules in the last coach were all shot and one has died since we arrived.[71]

Lieutenant Joseph Hale wrote from Fort Wallace that when Cain returned to the fort on June 17, the bodies of the soldiers and passenger who had been killed were found on the road, ". . . all had been scalped and so cut up that it was impossible to bring them to this place." General Hancock, with Captain Myles Keogh and an escort of 40 men left the next morning for Denver, well aware of the dangers facing them on their journey.[72]

June 16: Russell Springs was attacked again. This time four horses and

71   Sergeant Dawson Cain, "Report from Big Timbers Station, July [sic] 15, 1867." Record Group 393, Part I, Letters Received, Department of the Missouri, 1867.

72   Lieutenant Joseph Hale, "Report, Headquarters, Fort Wallace, Kas., June 18, 1867." Record Group 393, Part I, Letters Received, Department of the Missouri, 1867.

four mules were stolen. John Collins, stock tender, was there, as was stage driver Richard Wright.

About five miles west of Russell Springs, things turned deadly. Seven wagons were on the Smoky Hill trail when, at around four o'clock in the afternoon, about 200 Cheyenne and a few Sioux attacked the train. In a short fight four of the freighters were killed and three men were taken captive, including J. N. N. Schooler. Schooler was not killed with his friends because some of the Indians recognized him and intervened to keep him alive. Earlier he had lived with Indians for two years, a portion of that time with the Cheyenne. He remained a captive for two weeks and was finally able to escape from their camp on the Republican River, 100 miles away from where he was captured. He lost nine mules, one horse, and two wagons with provisions, a Spencer carbine, two colt pistols and nearly $1,000 in cash.[73]

Also on this day (June 16), several miles to the east on Plum Creek near present-day Holyrood, Kansas, warriors attacked the home of Henry Hegwer, destroying it, as well as his smokehouse and stable, and absconded with seven horses.[74] Coincidentally, nearby at this same moment Lieutenant Thomas Spencer was traveling to Fort Harker to obtain supplies for his command stationed on the Little Arkansas. He was three miles from Plum Creek Ranch—a different ranch than Hegwer's—at about noon when he interrupted an attack upon a wagon train. The freighters were desperately trying to corral their wagons while under attack. The Indians had killed and scalped a man named William Kinney and severely wounded another man, shooting him four times and spearing him with a lance. The two men had been in front of the train and were cut off when the attack began. The Indians had been hiding in a ravine awaiting their opportunity to ambush the freighters. Spencer's timely arrival ended the raid. Fifteen to 20 Indians made the attack, but when Lieutenant Spencer got to the ranch he climbed on top of the building and was able to observe another 40–50 Indians hiding

---

73   J. N. N. Schooler Indian Depredation Claim #?. Record Group 75. Schooler's affidavit was given April 27, 1868, less than a year after the event. The handwritten statement does not indicate what happened to the other two men taken captive, whether they escaped with Schooler or not. This depredation claim does not have a claim number noted on the affidavit, and I failed to note it when I copied it. Because the name does not appear in the index of RG 123, I am assuming I found it in RG 75.

74   Henry Hegwer Indian Depredation Claim #122. Record Group 123. This depredation claim contains no details of the attack.

by a nearby swell.[75] This wasn't the end of the fighting around Plum Creek, however. The next day six settlers raced into Fort Harker and reported a running fight of the day before—June 16—from Plum Creek to nearly Fort Harker. The attack started at dawn and the men fought the Indians for several miles before the attack ended eight miles from the fort. The men thought they wounded at least eight Indians. They lost five horses to the Indians. From the Indians' perspective it was a costly fight.[76]

Also on June 16, down on the Santa Fe road, the wagon train of C. G. Parker was attacked while crossing the river at the Cimarron Crossing. Three men were separated from the train when Indians attacked them. Two were killed, while the third escaped by swimming across the river. Their wagons were plundered and 28 stock driven off. At the same time nearby, about 70 Indians—identified as Kiowa—attacked the stage station at the crossing. They were repulsed by the soldiers stationed there for protection. One soldier was killed by the accidental discharge of his rifle.[77]

William Hartwell, a young man in his early 20s and one of the partners of the stage stop and ranch at Cimarron Crossing, was there that day. He recalled Parker's train was coming from Santa Fe and was attempting to cross the river from the south. Due to high water they made the attempt above the normal crossing. As the wagons were being crossed a herd of mules had been set to grazing on the south side of the river, guarded by four men. The Indians saw their chance and went after the men and mules, as well as the wagons still at the crossing. Hartwell remembered what happened next, observing from the ranch on the north side of the river:

> Puffs of smoke and crack, crack, crack arose from the tall grass in the circle, the red-skins sheering off at each shot, only to rush on again between fires, and yet the men gained their wagons, where one of them fell shot dead. The second one broke for, and gained the waters of the friendly river, while the third, a Frenchman, hurriedly climbed into a wagon loaded with wool and crawled under the sacks. The Indians gathered around, stripped off the cover, ripped open the packs and pulled the unhappy wretch out by the hair of the head.

75   Lieutenant Thomas J. Spencer, "Report from Fort Harker, June 17, 1867." Record Group 393, Part I, Letters Received, Department of the Missouri, 1867. See also Major Meredith H. Kidd, "Report, Headquarters, Fort Larned, Kas., June 22, 1867." Record Group 393, Part I, Letters Received, Department of the Missouri, 1867, Entry 2593.

76   Captain Verling K. Hart, "Report, Headquarters, Fort Harker, June 17, 1867." Record Group 393, Part I, Letters Received, Department of the Missouri, 1867.

77   Major Henry Douglass, "Report from Headquarters Fort Dodge Kansas June 18, 1867."

We could hear his shrieks, *Maria, Dias, mia*—but an Indian is an utter stranger to pity. . . . A pistol shot, and all was over with the unfortunate man. The one that made for the river escaped, and fortunately, for the fourth one, he had crossed and come up to the ranch, just before the attack.

The next day another person arrived at the ranch, and he knew the man killed at the wagon. His name was Curtis Hill, about 22 years old. Mabillion McGee wrote to Hill's father that day and told him of his son's death: "Hill had a good rifle and revolvers. He had nineteen shots and emptied evry one. He was kill rite between the wheels. The rest of the men was in and on the other side of the river. The Indians got every thing he had."[78]

June 17: Stormy Hollow Stage Station, near present-day Hays, Kansas, was attacked and one horse stolen. James M. Carlton, the stock tender, was present.

June 20: Monument Station, 35 miles east of Fort Wallace, was attacked at night. Oliver Perry Wiggins, the station keeper, reported that Indians attacked and stole one horse. Frederick Heigele and John Collins, stock tenders, were also there. Also on this day, Russell Springs was again attacked. Two horses and a mule were stolen. They were grazing too far from the station to be protected by the infantry stationed there and the Indians were easily able to drive them off.[79]

On the same day Monument Station was attacked, another raid was happening on the Santa Fe road in Colorado Territory, east of Fort Lyon. Kiowa and Cheyenne were together in this raid, perhaps as many as 400. A train was traveling from New Mexico to Leavenworth, loaded with sheep wool in several wagons. Eighteen men were with the train. As the men went into their noon camp, they were secluded in a hilly area on the road, with the Arkansas River to the south. Suddenly the men were attacked. Antilaus Trujillo described what happened:

all at once we heard the Indians hallowing . . . the Indians surrounding us and firing shots all around the train. We had our train so fixed that it formed a square like a corral, and we all rushed in there, dodging around the best way we could. The Indians kept firing at us, and we fired a few shots at the Indians, the Indians could not easily hit us in the way we were fixed, and we could not hit the Indians because

78   Louise Barry, "The Ranch at Cimarron Crossing," *The Kansas Historical Quarterly* (Topeka, KS: Kansas State Historical Society, Volume XXXIX, Autumn, 19730, 354–355.

79   Lieutenant Joseph Hale, "Report, Headquarters, Fort Wallace, Ks, June 20, 1867." Record Group 393, Part I, Letters Received, Department of the Missouri, 1867.

we were badly scared and hid. The Indians remained there during all that day. We could not attempt to fight the Indians because there were so many of them, and when night came, sometime between eight and ten o'clock when it was very dark, we made our escape. But while yet inside the enclosure the Indians started the grass on fire all around us, when the fire was close up to the wagons there was only one side for us to escape through the high grass . . . we left and went to Ft. Lyon.[80]

The entire wagon train and wool was burned and destroyed, but apparently all the freighters were able to flee to safety.

June 21: Henshaw Springs was again attacked. Henry Finley, stock tender, was present when Indians attacked about noon and stole nine horses. When news of this came to Fort Wallace more men were added to protect the stages. The next stage leaving Fort Wallace had an escort of 10 infantrymen and six cavalrymen.[81]

Back at Fort Wallace, things turned deadly near the post. About noon, several wagons used to haul stone from the quarry came under attack while still within sight of the post. One wagon was captured and the driver killed. Lieutenant Owen Hale ordered 7th Cavalry Lieutenant James Bell and all available soldiers at the post, which amounted to only 27 men, to charge at the warriors, resulting in a two-hour fight. The Indians tried unsuccessfully to get the soldiers out beyond vision from the fort, where Hale believed they would have been killed to the man. The soldiers fought hard to prevent being turned away from their retreat to the fort. Finally, the Indians withdrew to the east. When it was over two soldiers had been killed, Sergeant William H. Dummell and Private Frederick A. Bacon. Two soldiers were wounded. Sergeant Dummell was able to make a statement before he died. He recognized the leader of the warriors as the person who was given rations nearly a year earlier at Fort Zarah. He also "recognized among the Indians one 'Charlie Bent' who was employed formerly as an Indian scout." The soldiers who had been cutting the stone at the quarry stayed out of the fight, but observed the action from a high bluff, and they reported the Indians at least 1,000 strong. It was believed that as many as 10 Indians were killed in the skirmish.[82]

Seventh Cavalry Captain Albert Barnitz arrived at Fort Wallace with

---

80 Antilaus Trujillo Indian Depredation Claim #6381. Record Group 123.

81 Lieutenant Owen Hale, "Report, Headquarters, Fort Wallace, Ks, June 23, 1867." Record Group 393, Part I, Letters Received, Department of the Missouri, 1867.

82 Lieutenant Owen Hale, "Report, Headquarters, Fort Wallace, Kas., June 22, 1867." Record Group 393, Part I, Letters Received, Department of the Missouri, 1867.

Company G three days after this attack. He wrote to his wife Jennie what he had heard regarding the death of Sergeant Dummell. "He had but 3 soldiers and a citizen with him. The soldiers were all killed [*sic*], and the citizen, being finely mounted, barely escaped." Barnitz went on to state that Dummell probably would not have been killed had he been supported by Company I Sergeant William Hamlin, who with eight soldiers under him had been ordered to charge at the same time but failed to do so.[83] Barnitz would not forget this episode.

June 22: Cedar Point was again attacked. This time eight horses were stolen. At the same time this raid occurred, further east near present-day Russell, Kansas, another attack occurred. At six o'clock in the morning, on June 22, George Hall had nine horses and eight mules stolen. He had earlier contracted with the railroad to build along the line at Fossil Creek and had moved there with six wagons of provisions loaded with enough household goods to furnish a large house. He lost everything. His family of four children, along with his wife, apparently was there at the time of the raid, for among the losses was everything belonging to his family.[84] Also on June 22, John Smith, who the next year lost his father and brother to an Indian raid near Delphos, Kansas, was also working for the railroad. He lost two mules in a morning raid. Smith reported that he "was working for a man [Hall] who had a contract with the K. P. Railroad. I was going after my mules when I saw the Indians so I ran back to the camp and the Indians took the mules from where they were picketed. At this same time a young man was killed and I helped carry him into camp."[85]

83   Robert M. Utley, edited, *Life in Custer's Cavalry: Diaries and Letters of Albert and Jennie Barnitz, 1867–1868* (New Haven and London: Yale University Press, 1977), 63–64.

84   George H. Hall Indian Depredation Claim #7368. Record Group 123. The depredation claim contains no details of the attack, nor is there supporting statements from other witnesses. George Hall died within a month of the June attack, leaving his family destitute.

85   John S. Smith Indian Depredation Claim #10346. Record Group 123. When Smith's brother Alexander was killed in 1868, John Smith later married his widow. See Broome, *Dog Soldier Justice*, 47–49. It is interesting to note that the depredation claim of John S. Smith, the Indian interpreter who was at Sand Creek when his half-breed son Jack was killed in 1864, also filed a claim for this same loss at Fossil Creek. The claim was filed by Mrs. Mary Witherall, the heir to John S. Smith's estate. The claim does not identify her as a remarried widow, though this is likely the case. In this file, Charles Le Fevre testified that he and John S. Smith erected the first building in what became Denver. He also noted that Smith's daughter Armanie died of smallpox in 1868. Son Gilpin Smith died in Oklahoma in 1879. John S. Smith was said to have died at the Cheyenne Agency in 1872. It is a mystery to me how the two John Smiths had the same claim for June 22. It is clear in the first John Smith that he was the one present when the stock was stolen, and it is verified with other witnesses. The Indian interpreter Smith was in all likelihood not there. That the two Smiths are not one and the same person is obvious.

FIGHT NEAR FORT WALLACE, AGAINST
CHEYENNE INDIANS, JUNE 26, 1867.
Seventh Cavalry Sergeant Frederick Wyllyams was killed at this fight. Etching by
Theodore R. Davis, *Harper's Weekly* (August 17, 1867). *Author's collection.*

Thaddeus E. Playter was yet another victim of the raid. He lost four mules, two tents and the provisions that stocked the tents.[86] Thomas Lannon was in the camp when Smith came running in to report the Indians stealing the stock. He lost 10 mules and one horse. Lannon reported that three half-breeds named Bent had earlier come to him to hire out some stock for the railroad work.[87] That was apparently declined and the next thing that happened was the raid at about sunrise. Lannon:

> We had breakfast ready for the men to go to work, and I was in the house, and one of the men ran in and told me the Indians were taking my stock, and I run and took up a carbine, an old Spencer carbine and I ran out; one of my teamsters [Smith] had his hat in his hand and was running in towards the camp and I run toward the Indians and got down on my knees with my carbine, and the old carbine wouldn't

---

86 Thaddeus E. Playter Indian Depredation Claim #550, Entry 700. Record Group 75.

87 Bent reports that the Indians doing these raids were Dog Soldiers. Lannon's memory of the three Bent brothers being present would place them with the Dog Soldiers during these summer raids, contrary to Bent's assertion that at this time he was south of the Arkansas River and avoiding participation in the present conflicts. See Hyde, *Life of George Bent,* 272.

go off for me; I tried three shells on him, but wouldn't one of them go off for me; it was one of those old Spencers; they had no arms on the road at the time.... [The Indians] shot one of my men, one of my teamsters, a little further out, put an arrow blade right through his shoulder and a bullet through his back.[88]

On June 24, a wagon train was attacked down on the Santa Fe road near Plum Buttes. One man was killed.[89] Back on the Smoky Hill trail on the same day, a wood train came under attack near Castle Rock Station. The train was under attack for nearly a mile as it retreated back to the station.[90] At around 11 that night, a band of about 20 Indians tried to stampede the stock at Fort Larned, but were fired on by the guard and fled. The night was too dark to order pursuit.[91]

On June 23, Kiowa Indians attacked a ranch owned by Mr. Vogal, situated along the Arkansas River in Colorado Territory about 12 miles east of Fort Lyon. He lost all of his stock. Nearby at another ranch a worker was killed. Seven Indians were fired on by a couple of soldiers who discovered them lurking among bushes across the river. Soon a search party was organized under the command of Lieutenant Matthew Berry of the 7th Cavalry. After a southern chase of two days the men returned without having overtaken the raiders. Near Pretty Encampment, close to Fort Lyon, warriors were observed on the southern side of the river with the cavalry horses that had earlier been stolen at Fort Dodge.[92]

June 26: Pond Creek Stage Station, two miles west of Fort Wallace, was boldly attacked. James Fahey, driving a stage, was at the station when the attack occurred. Eight horses were stolen. John Collins, stock tender at Cedar Point, was also present as was George Williams, who was living at the time at Cheyenne Wells and driving a stage. H. R. Wyatt, a freighter, was also there, as was Pond Creek butcher R. F. McClure.

This attack at Pond Creek Station quickly brought 50 7th Cavalry troopers under the command of Captain Albert Barnitz. They galloped three miles

88   Thomas Lannon Indian Depredation Claim #2197. Record Group 123.
89   Captain Edward Byrne, "Report, Camp Grierson and Little Arkansas River, October 27, 1867." Record Group 393, Part I, Letters Received, Department of the Missouri, 1867, Entry 2593.
90   Captain Arthur B. Carpenter, "Report, Downers Station, Kansas, June 25, 1867." Record Group 393, Part I, Letters Received, Department of the Missouri, 1867, Entry 2593.
91   Major Meredith H. Kidd, "Report, Headquarters, Fort Larned, Kansas, June 27, 1867." Record Group 393, Part I, Letters Received, Department of the Missouri, 1867, Entry 2593.
92   Captain William H. Penrose, "Report, Headquarters Fort Lyon, C.T., June 29, 1867." Record Group 393, Part I, Letters Received, Department of the Missouri, 1867.

northwest in an attempt to overtake the raiding Indians who were seeking to escape to the north. A sharp gun and saber battle ensued. Soon the Indians were reinforced by another band appearing from the northwest, and for a time the fight was desperate. When the Indians finally withdrew, six soldiers had been killed and another six wounded. In his report of the fight—dated June 28—Captain Barnitz said one of the wounded, Corporal James Ludlow, was hurt so badly he was not expected to recover. He had been shot with a "revenge Arrow" which went completely through his abdomen. But in fact Ludlow did not die, and shortly after he was promoted to sergeant. However, he apparently never fully recovered. In April 1868, he was discharged with a surgeon's certificate of disability. Sergeant Frederick Wyllyams was scalped and mutilated. The other dead included bugler Charles Clarke, Corporal James Douglass, and Privates Frank Reahme, Nathan Trail, and John Welch. Welch's body was never recovered, even though several search efforts were made to find his body. The Indians probably lost a few more in killed and wounded.[93]

In this fight Captain Barnitz personally witnessed the action of Sergeant Hamlin and, remembering his actions five days earlier at the quarry, he ordered him arrested and court-martialed.

His court-martial record provides interesting information about the June 26 fight. His trial—for cowardice—began eight days later, on July 4. Three officers of the 3rd Infantry as well as three officers of the 7th Cavalry presided. Captains Myles Keogh and Albert Barnitz, and Lieutenant James Bell were the 7th Cavalry officers. However, Keogh was excused, as he was accompanying General Hancock on a stage to Denver. Still, the trial proceeded. Hamlin strenuously objected to Barnitz being present, arguing he was prejudiced against him and he would not receive a fair trial. The court ruled the objection "frivolous and unfounded," and Barnitz remained.

Testimony showed that Barnitz had ordered Hamlin to take his platoon and deploy them as skirmishers in support to the left of a platoon of Barnitz's Company G. When Hamlin began to move his men into position the other company was heavily engaged. As Hamlin's men got near the action, instead of deploying for support his troopers began to retreat, leaving the platoon

---

93   Utley, *Life in Custer's Cavalry*, 75–77. Returns From Regular Army Cavalry Regiments 1833–1916, Microfilm Roll 71, Seventh Cavalry, June 1867. Muster Roll, Company G, 7th Cavalry, Record Group 391. Entries for June 1867 through April 1868.

under Barnitz exposed to a flank attack. Hamlin ordered his men to halt, but to no avail. Company G Sergeant William Harris recalled:

> I with eight (8) men went upon the brow of a hill, with some Indians in the bottom beyond us, upon whom I ordered a charge when one of the men said if you are so fast charging look to the rear—I looked to the rear and saw Sergeant Hamlin's party three hundred yards in rear of us. I also saw a party of forty (40) Indians moving between Sergeant Hamlin's party and my own. When Sergeant Hamlin broke, a part retreating still farther to the rear of us, and a part standing firmly in front and rear of us we had a running fight for half a mile.

Company G Private Samuel Martin testified that he heard Hamlin order his men to retreat, "and at the time I heard a man [Captain Barnitz] call him a cowardly son of a bitch, and tell him to go back to the post." Another private from Hamlin's company testified that Hamlin "ordered a retreat and led it himself. I stopped and took two shots, after which he was one hundred yards ahead of me. I saw no more of him till after the halt. He ordered the retreat by saying 'Retreat God damn you. Retreat, there are too many'." The Indians were about 400 yards away when the retreat was ordered.

Yet another private of Company I—Christopher Colgan—recalled that Hamlin advanced ahead of his men and "when they commenced to break, seeing he was outnumbered he got out of the way in a short while. While retreating some of the men were in the front and some in rear of the sergeant. He tried to stop them at first. I was in the rear of him on the retreat."

Hamlin made his own statement about what happened:

> At the alarm of Indians on June 26th at 6 A.M. having got all of my troop some fourteen in number, I was ordered by Lieut. Hale, 3rd U.S. Infantry to report to Captain Barnitz—G Troop, 7th U.S. Cavalry, which I did, and fell on the left of his troop. We started on a gallop and N.W. some three or four miles, until we got in range of the enemy. Then Capt. Barnitz deployed his right as skirmishers, and I the left as skirmishers, we advanced some five hundred yards to the front. The enemy flanked us on the right and left—and then charged for us, which caused the troops to give way in spite of my endeavors to stop them. I kept with them, encouraging them to <u>fire</u> as they retreated, 'till I finally got them to halt some three-quarters of a mile from the start. Then the captain [Barnitz] asked me why I did not stop the men from retreating. I answered it was impossible to do so as the men would not obey my command, then the captain got the troop to dismount (for to fight on foot), they then advanced on the Indians. I was ordered by Captain Barnitz to take charge of the horses, and kept them in the rear. I did so until the Indians retreated to their horses and mounted. I was put under arrest, and ordered to the fort by Captain Barnitz.

Hamlin was found guilty, and ordered "to be dishonorably discharged from the service of the U.S. and to have his head shaved and drummed out of camp." The record was forwarded to headquarters and, on August 10, it was determined the board did not follow procedure in its organization—the record does not say if it was because Keogh's absence was not replaced, or whether there was an impropriety in keeping Barnitz on the board after Hamlin objected—and Hamlin was ordered to be restored to duty. Hamlin apparently had no desire to continue his service in the 7th Cavalry. One day after he was restored to duty, he deserted.[94]

One of the more famous photographs of the entire Indian war era on the Plains was that taken of Sergeant Frederick Wyllyams, one of the dead. Barnitz probably felt Wyllyams might not have died had Hamlin not retreated during the skirmish. In a letter to his wife, Barnitz wrote of Wyllyams: "The Indians had stripped, scalped and horribly mutilated his body. I dare not tell you how fearfully! He had fought bravely, but had incautiously become separated from the command, and was surrounded by overwhelming numbers."[95]

Dr. William A. Bell took the photograph. He was associated with the railroad being built at that time along the Smoky Hill route. He had met Wyllyams only the day before and together they were going to print copies of pictures Bell had recently taken. Little did he know that his next picture would be of the mutilated remains of his new British friend. Bell wrote of Wyllyams:

> A portion of the sergeant's scalp lay near him, but the greater part was gone; through his head a rifle ball had passed, and a blow from the tomahawk had laid his brain open above the left eye; the nose was slit up, and his throat was cut from ear to ear; seven arrows were standing in different parts of his naked body; the breast was laid open, so as to expose the heart; and the arm, that had doubtless done its work against the red-skins, was hacked to the bone; his legs, from the hip to the knee, lay open with horrible gashes, and from the knee to the foot they had cut the flesh with their knives. Thus mutilated, Wyllyams lay beside his mangled horse.[96]

---

94 Court-Martial Cases #00-2525, Record Group 153. Desertion noted in Regimental Returns of the 7th Cavalry.

95 Utley, *Life in Custer's Cavalry*, 72–77. Captain Barnitz., in his report, says the Indians were successful in stealing only two horses and one mule, not the eight horses reported in the Wells Fargo claim.

96 William A. Bell, *New Tracks in North America* (London: Chapman and Hall, 1870), 62–63. Barnitz, in a letter to his wife after the fight, said that Bell made his photograph of Wyllyams after he was brought back to Fort Wallace. Thus it is possible two of the seven arrows fell off of the body as it was carried back to the post, since the photograph shows five arrows and not seven, as Bell reported. See Utley, *Life in Custer's Cavalry*, 74.

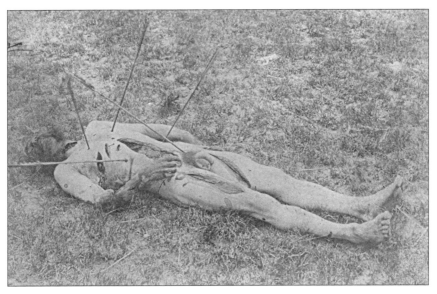

Wyllyams probably had a different, real name. He had enlisted in the 7th Cavalry after coming from England, due to a moral failure. He told others he was a graduate from Eton College, Oxford University, and was from a prominent family in England, and was hiding his true identity by enlisting under an alias. His true identity still eludes discovery. It was believed, at the time of his death, that the specific mutilations done to his body identified which Indians were responsible. Cheyenne "Cut Arms" hacked his arms, the nose mutilation indicated the "Smeller Tribe" of the Arapaho, and the throat slashing marks was the work of Sioux. *Photo courtesy of Dan Larson, Littleton, Colorado.*

Bell said Wyllyams had been educated at Eton College in England, and came from a good family but had a moral indiscretion—"a fatal alliance"—in London, and came to America after being disowned by his relations. Recent research has revealed that Wyllyams had married in Bristol in late 1865, and had a daughter born seven months later, thus indicating the alliance Bell spoke of led to pregnancy and marriage. No evidence could be found confirming the sergeant used his real name in filing his marriage certificate, nor do Eton records bear any person with the name, Wyllyams. Presumably that name was an alias to conceal his true identity when he married Eliza Matilda Turner, a 31-year-old domestic servant from Bristol.

When Wyllyams' daughter was barely five months old, he enlisted in the 7th Cavalry, leaving his wife and child in Newport, South Wales. After he was killed, his widow filed and received a widow's pension, as well as a pension for their daughter, Eliza Louisa. But Mrs. Wyllyams did not learn of her husband's death until six months after he was killed, and by the time her pension was approved their daughter had died from bronchitis, even though her pension continued to include two dollars per month for the deceased daughter. But the tale gets even more bizarre when—two years after Wyllyams' death—his widow gave birth to a second child, a boy, and named him after her deceased husband, and claimed he was the natural father, which was clearly impossible. Bell's account, therefore, that Wyllyams had come from a respectable family in England, might well be the truth, with the addendum that the alias was used to hide his real identity. This secret still eludes resolution to this day.[97]

On the same day Captain Barnitz had his fight near Fort Wallace—June 26—7th Cavalry Company D, under Custer's command—having returned to Kansas after spending some time near Fort McPherson along the Platte River in Nebraska—had a running fight about 30 miles north of Fort Wallace. The company was escorting 12 wagons back to Custer's campsite near present-day Benkelman, Nebraska, after replenishing supplies at Fort Wallace. They had left Fort Wallace on the evening of June 25, and were attacked on the morning of the 26th about 10 miles south of present-day Edson, Kansas. The running fight lasted about three hours. When it was over at

---

97   Wyllyams' interesting story, as well as mystery, has been well told by Peter Russell. See "The Slain Sergeant," *The Crow's Nest: The Journal of the Custer Association of Great Britain*, Spring/Summer 2007, Volume 7, Number 1, 5–12.

least five Indians were killed and many more wounded. George Bent identified the Indians as Dog Soldiers and Pawnee Killer's Sioux. He said no
Indians were killed.[98]

With Custer, there remains controversy to this day with regard to his
motives in sending his wagons 77 miles south to Fort Wallace, when he
had earlier been told that supplies would be available at Fort Sedgwick on
the Platte, roughly the same distance to the north. He had his command
camped near the Republican River, along the three borders of Kansas,
Nebraska and Colorado. Historians chastise Custer for disobeying his
orders to remain on the Denver road, by venturing south down to his June
22 campsite near Benkelman. They further accuse him of then sending
his wagons south to Fort Wallace, because of his hope that his wife Libbie
would be there, awaiting an escort to join Custer on his summer campaign.
One author notes that when Custer sent his wagons south to Wallace he
also sent Major Joel Elliott, a scout and 10 men up to Sedgwick to

> Bring back any orders Sherman may have left for Custer there. Both were bad deci-
> sions, perilous not only to the two groups of soldiers traveling alone through Indian
> territory but to Libbie as well. He was deliberately exposing his men and his wife to
> great danger just so they could be together while he was in the middle of a military
> campaign against Indians. . . . It was reason enough for a career to end in disgrace,
> but for Custer it was only a temporary setback on the road to everlasting glory.[99]

Such judgments could not be further from the truth, and only reflect
shallow research and understanding of the events unfolding in Custer's first

---

98   See Broome, *Custer into the West*, 66–69, for an account of this fight from the military perspective. See
      also Hyde, *Life of George Bent*, 273. Hyde in covering this fight confuses Bent's account, believing Bent
      was talking about Pawnee Killer's raid upon Custer's campsite near Benkelman on June 24. Bent was
      instead talking about the attack upon the wagon party on June 26. Hyde says Custer claimed several
      Indians were killed in this attack. Custer never claimed any Indians were killed in the June 24 attack
      on his campsite, but he did report of Indians being killed in the wagon train fight on June 26, of which
      he was not present.

99   Duane Schultz, *Coming Through Fire: George Armstrong Custer and Chief Black Kettle* (Yardley, PA:
      Westholme Publishing, LLC, 2012), 177. A similar criticism of Custer can be found in Chalfant, *Han-
      cock's War*, 339. Chalfant apparently had this letter Custer entrusted to Elliott but ignored it when
      making the claim that either route—Sedgwick or Wallace—was easily passable with wagons. However,
      to anyone who has ever spent any time in the area between Benkelman and Sedgwick, or Benkelman
      and Wallace, one can easily perceive that Custer's scouts advised him correctly. Yes, one can venture
      to Sedgwick following water routes and avoiding high cut-banks of the Republican River valley, as
      Chalfant claims, but the journey would about double the distance than going straight south to Fort
      Wallace. Chalfant ignores that observation, perhaps to make his interpretation—Custer wanted to
      get his wife Libbie at Fort Wallace—appear sound.

Indian campaign. Custer was south of the Denver road because General William Sherman ordered him down there to find Pawnee Killer, who had earlier told Custer that his camp was near the Republican River. Once down there, Custer sent Major Elliott to Sedgwick to inform Sherman of important information he had since learned. The letter to Sherman that he sent with Elliott has recently surfaced and bears reading in its entirety, as it explains everything regarding Custer's actions:

> Camp of the 7th U.S. Cavalry
> Near the Fork of Republican River
> June 22, 1867

Brev. Major General C. C. Augur
  Commdg Dept of the Platte
    Fort Laramie, D.T.
      General,

In obedience to instructions received from the Lieut. General Commdg Military Division of the Missouri, I have the honor to report the location of my command and the probable time of arrival at Fort Sedgwick. My command arrived at this point today. *Before leaving McPherson I had two interviews with Pawnee Killer, a Sioux Chief, whose band is reported as being on Beaver Creek some forty or fifty miles distant. At these interviews it was agreed that Pawnee Killer and his entire band should remove at once to a point on North bank of Platte, near McPherson, forty days was fixed as the limit within which this move must be made.* I regard this agreement if successfully executed as of no little importance. Pawnee Killer's band being the owners of the lodges burned by General Hancock's command on Pawnee Fork. General Sherman rather mistrusted the sincerity of Pawnee Killer. I do not. *I was directed [by order of Sherman] to send this band in to McPherson under escort, it being supposed I would meet them en route to that post.* They have not had time to move. I am now seventy five miles south east of Sedgwick, the same distance north east from Wallace. I have sent one squadron this evening to Beaver Creek forty five miles distant to bring Pawnee Killer and band to my camp. From Beaver Creek to Wallace it is thirty miles. I send one company of the squadron detached as above to proceed to Wallace from Beaver Creek with twelve wagons to procure supplies, while the other company under Captain West is collecting Pawnee Killer's band. *My supplies can be drawn to this point from Wallace with greater facility than from Sedgwick. The Guides informing me it is almost impossible to conduct a train across the country south of Sedgwick, there being no water for fifty five miles.* If I can get Pawnee Killer's band north of the Platte, there will be only the Cheyennes to deal with South. I am confident from all the information I can gain that the Cheyennes are the authors of the depredations lately committed in the Platte Route. Pawnee Killer represents the Cheyennes as all intending to move south of the Arkansas, but before doing so parties of their young men numbering from five to fifty have been making raids on the Platte Stations. The Cheyenne village is represented as being south west from this point and on a tributary of the South Republican. Guides and Sioux agree in this opinion. *I think I could do much toward breaking up the raids on the Platte Stations if allowed to scout the country in which this village is represented to be.* No trails of Indians have been discovered between McPherson and this point, which is confirmatory of Pawnee Killer's story. General Sherman in the absence of contrary instructions from you directed me to keep on the move by easy marches and in this way make the Indians in this section feel unsafe. Shall I after scouting up North Republican as far as opposite Valley Station turn and hunt the Cheyenne village. I believe I can find Indians. I will have twenty days rations when my train returns, which will be as soon as the officer bearing this can return. I have about three hundred and fifty men all told, quite a number dismounted, and mounted on unserviceable horses. General Sherman promised me some fresh horses from Omaha. I have six companies and ten officers. I wish I could have twenty five or more of your Pawnees, for trailers. In the absence of definite information as to distance from here to Valley Station by proposed route, I cannot tell the exact day upon which I can make Sedgwick. *I would prefer making the strike for the Cheyenne village before going to Sedgwick, unless you otherwise order.* The officer bearing this to Sedgwick, Major Elliott of 7th Cavalry, will occupy two days in reaching that post. I will instruct him to wait instructions from you until the morning of the twenty seventh, then to rejoin me at this point. I will send messengers to Sedgwick from time to time to receive any instructions sent there and will try and reach that post in ten days from time of return of Major Elliott, unless I go on my proposed scout, which would probably delay my arrival at Sedgwick five days more. Please inform me fully of your wishes and whether my proposition merits your approval.

Very Respectfully, &c

G. A. Custer

Brevet Major. Genl. Commdg[100]

While these attacks were being made near Fort Wallace, the same day—June 26—about 50 miles northeast near Grinnell Stage Station, Thomas

---

100 Part 1, Entry 3731, Letters Received, Department of the Platte, Record Group 393, emphasis added. For further details of Custer's summer campaign, see Broome, *Custer into the West*. This important letter—first published in *Custer into the West*—has never been acknowledged by historians covering this history, and renders otiose the criticisms faulting Custer for his decisions and actions while camped on the Republican. It is interesting that William Chalfant, in *Hancock's War*, cites the letter in a footnote, and notes the advice Custer's scouts gave regarding the terrain forcing a trip to Sedgwick much longer than the trip to Wallace, but he ignores everything else in the letter, which clearly explains Custer's strategy, and exonerates him from being an ineffective commander during his summer campaign. Chalfant apparently did not want the reader to form their own opinion from primary source evidence. See Chalfant, *Hancock's War*, 339.

Greasney, the station stock tender, had a frightening experience. He was driving a wagon loaded with provisions, between Castle Rock and Grinnell when Indians charged and captured him. They took all of his goods, burned his wagon and stole his four mules. Surprisingly they did not kill him. It is not entirely clear how Greasney's life was spared. At about this same day a man named McIrwin was driving a stage for the Express Company on the Smoky Hill road when three Indians came out of a ravine and surprised a man riding about 300 yards in front of the stage, killed him and shot his horse. "The Indians with great boldness dismounted and scalped him; having achieved this they rode off at full speed."[101]

Also on June 26, Bunker Hill Stage Station—30 miles east of Fort Hays—was attacked. F. Frazier was driving a stage and was at the station when Indians came. They stole four horses. John W. Howell, the station blacksmith, also was present. The next day, three Cheyenne Indians returned and stole a horse from Julius Kruiger two miles west of Bunker Hill.[102]

Fossil Creek Stage Station, further east of Bunker Hill and near present-day Russell, Kansas, was raided June 26 as well. J. S. Parker, station blacksmith, but living that fall at Pond Creek, was present when the Indians attacked the station. The Indians got away with four horses. Matthew Orr, stock tender at Pond Creek that fall, also was present. Indians had been around Fossil Creek for several days before the Wells Fargo loss.

While the station was attacked, a little further east the Indians made a deadly attack on a crew working for the railroad. Jacob Van Autiuerp, contracted by the Union Pacific to construct three miles of grading, lost eight mules, one horse and two four-horse wagons. One of the drivers was killed when the wagons were captured.[103]

June 27: Chalk Bluffs Station was again raided. Thomas D. Marshall and John Lewis, stock tenders, were present. Sixteen horses were stolen. On this

---

101 Lieutenant Joseph Hale, "Report, Headquarters, Fort Wallace, Kansas, June 30, 1867." Record Group 393, Part I, Letters Received, Department of the Missouri, 1867.

102 Julius Kruiger Indian Depredation Claim #128. Record Group 75.

103 Jacob Van Autiuerp Indian Depredation Claim #3764. Record Group 75. Van Autiuerp said one witness present during the raid was A. L. Runyon who was living in Pueblo, Colorado, at the time the claim was filed in the 1880s. But when Michael Piggott, the government agent assigned to investigate the claim, questioned Runyon, he denied being present and "said he was then in Manhattan [Kansas] a mere boy learning the printer's trade and knows nothing about the losses." This was the father of Alfred Damon Runyon, the famous baseball writer in the early 20th century who helped make baseball the popular American sport of today. Pueblo's Runyon field is named after him. For more on Runyon see http://en.wikipedia.org/wiki/Damon—Runyon#Life—and—work (accessed February 22, 2013).

same day more than 100 miles to the east and about a mile west of Ellsworth, Kansas, Cheyenne Indians made a dawn raid on a herd of stock guarded by some soldiers from Fort Harker. Several horses and mules were lost. Charles Leiber lost eight horses. Two men were killed four miles away.[104]

Andrew Hunter lost four horses and H. F. Hoesman lost six horses. Benjamin Young and John Henry were two privates stationed as guards to protect the stock belonging to the citizens of Ellsworth. They made a report two days later about what happened:

> we were on duty the night of June 26, 1867, guarding the town of Ellsworth from the Indians. We were stationed about ¼ of a mile above the settlement [west]; about an hour before daybreak we saw 4 Indians who had in their possession a lot of horses, mares and colts, perhaps 15 in all. The stock was driven by the Indians and made considerable disturbance. We recognized them as Indians and after calling them to halt, we fired upon them, but our shots failed to take effect, and they crossed the Smoky Hill River.[105]

June 28: John McNeill was driving a stage and was at Downer Station when Indians attacked the station and stole eight horses. On the night of June 29, Cheyenne under the leadership of Sylvester, or Yamatubee, stole nine horses and one mule from J. A. Cary on the Arkansas River near the mouth of the Little Arkansas. Cary was coming from Texas and driving a herd of cattle, which were not stolen. H.U. Donnell spoke with Yamatubee

---

104 Charles Leiber Indian Depredation Claim #553. Record Group 75. The Leiber depredation claim is useful in understanding how the claims were successfully prepared and investigated. First, the claim was taken to Darlington Agency and in tribal council the Cheyenne admitted to the theft. But the claim was thrown out. Leiber did not say how the horses were stolen, whether he was present during the raid "or any facts connected with the theft." Thus it could not be investigated for further proof. Even so, the scant testimony given in regard to the theft (one, apparently a soldier on guard during the theft), only justified the claim that five horses were stolen, not eight. One could only wish such a scrutiny was made on all pioneer reminiscences coming years after the events, or Bent's own story, for that matter. If a similar scrutiny had been placed upon Bent's letters, they probably all would have been thrown out as unsubstantiated. Yet some historians, it seems to me, are very willing to allow Bent's voice as being accurate while at the same time discounting any civilian accounts coming by way of the depredation claim system, on the grounds that they were prejudiced against Indians and greedy to overinflate losses to increase their monetary award. Such thinking is ludicrous. All accounts of these times should be taken as authentic unless there are good reasons to discount them; and the desire for more compensation—true or not—has no bearing on the facts related to the attack, such as time, numbers of Indians and civilians involved, deaths, etc. There are no good reasons to dismiss the accounts found in the depredation claims different than the same reasons to dismiss other accounts, e.g., contradictory testimony from other reliable sources, etc.

105 Andrew Hunter Indian Depredation Claim #552. Entry 700, Record Group 75. When this claim was taken to the Darlington Agency, the Cheyenne Indians denied committing the theft and said it was done by Sioux.

the next day. The Indians had driven the horses 45 miles away when they came upon Donnell near William "Dutch Bill" Griffenstein's Ranch. Donnell saw the stolen stock, which Yamatubee confessed to stealing the night before. Griffenstein's wife was a Cheyenne and one of the warriors with the Indians was her brother.[106]

On July 2, a coach arrived at Fort Wallace, coming from the west. It was the first stage to come through since June 22, 10 days earlier. The sergeant escorting the train reported that when the coach passed the abandoned Goose Creek station about five miles west of Pond Creek Station, Indians were hiding in the vacant buildings and commenced firing on the stage as it drew near. No one on the stage was hit, but two miles further on the coach came upon a hot fight with 40 corralled wagons and the freighters desperately fighting swarming Indians. The coach joined the corral and the soldiers joined the freighter's fight. The fight did not end for another two hours. Two soldiers with the escort were wounded, both in the foot. When the Indians finally withdrew the ox train turned around and went back to Pond Creek with the stage. Sixty freighters armed with both Henry and Spencer carbines were not deemed safe enough to continue the journey west.[107]

On this same night, Lieutenant David Israel Ezekiel of the 38th Infantry had a skirmish with his company at Chalk Bluffs. His soldiers had also skirmished Indians at Monument Station on the night of June 29. He was en route from Fort Hays with 115 infantrymen to relieve a company of 7th Cavalrymen stationed at Monument Station. When he arrived at Monument on July 3, he began erecting a stone fortification with bastions at diagonal corners, to both house his company and provide secure fortifications against Indian attacks.[108]

Back in Colorado Territory and near Julesburg, on July 7, 15 Oglala Lakota raided a group of Union Pacific Railway workers and drove off a large number of mules and horses. Myron Holmes, one of the workers, lost two mules. He reported that the Indians charged from nearby bluffs at about 11 o'clock in the morning, and carried off all of the mules belonging to the large camp of workers. When queried about this raid at Red Cloud Agency, by Indian

---

106 J. A. Cary Indian Depredation Claim #3439. Record Group 75.

107 Lieutenant Joseph Hale, "Report, Headquarters, Fort Wallace, Kas., July 2, 1867." Record Group 393, Part I, Letters Received, Department of the Missouri, 1867.

108 Lieutenant David I. Ezekiel, "Report, Monument Station, July 11, 1867." Record Group 393, Part I, Letters Received, Department of the Missouri, 1867. Entry 2593.

Agent J. J. Saville, Red Dog, Chief of the Oukape band "of Ogallalla Sioux Indians, ... an Indian by the name of 'Bear Shed Off' told him that he led the party who done this, and that after ... he went into the northern country."[109]

July 10: Chalk Bluffs was again attacked. Thomas D. Marshall and John Lewis were again present during the raid. Records do not make clear what was taken or destroyed.

July 11: Back on the Denver road, Beaver Creek Stage Station—near Fort Morgan—was attacked. Twenty-five tons of hay was burned as was the stable. Eight horses were stolen.

July 12: Indians ran off eight horses belonging to Wells Fargo at Downer Station. Captain Arthur Carpenter, 37th Infantry, reported the theft was entirely due to the carelessness of the stock tender at the station, who had been repeatedly warned not to allow the stock to graze unattended. In fact, he left them in a ravine and the Indians were easily able to run them off.[110]

Also on this day, Indians attacked several large wagon trains in the evening near Downer Station. 7th Cavalry Captain Frederick Benteen had been ordered to escort the trains, but when he arrived on the 13th he learned there were actually seven large trains, and he had an insufficient force to provide protection to each one. Instead he escorted only four of the trains, leaving the other wagons at the station. Benteen reported Indians ran off eight horses at the station. One of the trains the warriors attacked had a man severely wounded in the head, breaking his jaw in two places. Benteen reported "he cannot live," and left him at the Station.[111] The man who died was with a government freight train carrying grain from Fort Harker to Fort Wallace. The war party consisted of Cheyenne and Arapaho. Two mules were badly wounded in the skirmish. Ten days later, when the train was returning to Fort Harker, it was again attacked, Indians killing three mules and wounding 30 more.[112]

July 13: Fifty warriors attacked Coon Creek Station 22 miles west of Fort Larned. There were 11 soldiers stationed there for defense and assigned escort duty for the stages. The station had been earlier redesigned with loopholes

109 Myron Holmes Indian Depredation Claim #731. Record Group 75, Entry 700.

110 Captain Carpenter, 37th Infantry, "Report, Downer's Station, Kansas, July 18, 1867." Record Group 393, Part I, Letters Received, Department of the Missouri, 1867. Entry 2593.

111 Captain Frederick Benteen, "Report, Downer's Station, July 14, 1876." Record Group 393, Part I, Letters Received, Department of the Missouri, 1867. Entry 2593.

112 D. W. Powers and Henry Newman Indian Depredation Claim #not given. Record Group 75, entry 700.

for defense—with a small outside opening but large opening inside for the convenient use of rifles when under attack—and thus no soldiers were hurt. The sergeant stationed there reported at least three Indians killed and seven wounded. Immediately after this attack at Coon Creek the same Indians discovered a Mexican freight train approaching and attacked it, stealing 45 of the stock. The next day a wood cutting party of eight soldiers was attacked 15 miles north of Fort Larned. No injuries were reported. On the next day, July 15, the same band of Indians attacked the post at Fort Zarah. The Indians were soon driven off, several of them wounded.[113]

July 14: Chalk Bluffs was again attacked. This time 18 horses were stolen. When the Indians were discovered coming onto the stock, the sergeant stationed there ordered his men out to retrieve the herd. The soldiers went out 500 yards and got around the herd, driving them back to the station. When they returned, two employees of Wells Fargo came out of the barn and in their excitement "commenced firing promiscuously into the herd," which caused them to stampede away from the station and into the hands of the Indians. The warriors had grown in number and the sergeant felt it unwise to attempt to recover them again.[114]

July 17: Stormy Hollow was again attacked. One horse was stolen. On this day, down on the Santa Fe trail a few miles west of Fort Dodge, Indians made raids on two wagon trains and the stage station at Cimarron Crossing. The next day, Major Douglass ordered Sergeant Stanley Brown, 3rd Infantry, to take seven men from Company B, 7th Cavalry, and another 22 men from Company H, 3rd Infantry to relieve the trains that had been attacked. After 15 miles, Brown came upon one of the trains. It had 15 wagons and 20 men as well as another five convalescent soldiers being transported to Fort Union. There he learned of the fight of the day before. One boy with the train was mortally wounded. In addition, a soldier of the 37th Infantry was wounded, but not mortally. One ox was lost. The train belonged to John Blackman. The Indians making the attack were Cheyenne and were led by "Charles Bent," whom some of the men recognized. The fight went from mid-afternoon until dark.

Sergeant Brown remained with the train until the next morning, when he received a report from a scout that Indians had attacked the mail station

---

113   Major H. H. Kidd, "Report, Headquarters, Fort Larned, Kas, July 17, 1867." Record Group 393, Part I, Letters Received, Department of the Missouri, 1867. Entry 2593.
114   Carpenter, "Report, July 18."

at Cimarron Crossing. Leaving some of his men with the Blackman train, Brown took the rest of the soldiers to relieve those persons at the mail station. When he arrived he discovered another train had been attacked across the river opposite the station. It was a large train of 90 wagons and over 130 men. But only about 60 warriors attacked them. Instead of fighting back—the freighters were all well armed—the frightened men hid behind the wagons. Two men were killed and another three wounded. The two men killed were scalped within 200 yards of the wagons. The number of cattle stolen was 530.

Nobody had been injured across the river at the stage station, but nearby, two men working on a hay-cutting crew were killed. Another was injured. Only one of the four men working the hay escaped unharmed. The wagon train belonged to Jose Gutierrez. They were traveling east. Brown left with them 10 soldiers and a sergeant as escort as far at Fort Lyon. He then brought the wounded men back to Fort Douglas. The night before, a citizen accidentally wounded himself, and died on the road before Brown could bring him to the post hospital. His name was Duncan McBlain.[115]

July 20: Smoky Hill Stage Station was raided. Indians took one horse and one mule. Soldiers of the 38th Infantry were stationed at Monument Station, having relieved troopers of the 7th Cavalry a couple weeks earlier. On the same morning, Indians raided Monument and ran off the government stock which was grazing about 75 yards from the station, leaving the soldiers without mounts. The warriors remained in view of the station all day until nightfall, when they withdrew. At nine o'clock the next morning, the Indians hit a freight train camped about a mile from the post and fought with the freighters all day. Later that night, a stage arrived from the east with an armed escort, and the next morning—July 22—with the additional troops a squad of 20 soldiers went to the relief of the train. A howitzer was taken with them, but the ammunition was defective, only one in four shots exploding. One shot went right in among the Indians, estimated to be about 250 in number, but failed to explode. Still, it was thought between 20 and 30 Indians were injured or killed from the earlier skirmishing. The Indians withdrew, taking the government stock stolen two days before as well as a mule stolen from a citizen.[116]

---

115 Reports from Fort Dodge, Sergeant Stanley Brown, July 21, 1867, and Major Henry Douglass, July 23, 1867. Record Group 393, Part I, Letters Received, Department of the Missouri, 1867. Entry 2593.

116 Lieutenant David I. Ezekiel, "Report, Fort Harker, July 26, 1867." Record Group 393, Part I, Letters Received, Department of the Missouri, 1867. Entry 2593.

July 21: Corporal Alfred Braddon of the 38th infantry, along with 10 soldiers, was escorting a wagon train en route to Fort Wallace, when one mile east of Monument Station, the train came under attack by a party of 25 Indians. Another 300 Indians were observed on the bluffs two miles distant. The Indians fired a few shots at the train and the soldiers and teamsters fired a rather large volley in return. The Indians immediately retreated to the bluffs and joined the larger party of Indians. No further attack was made.[117]

While all the raids were occurring mostly on the Smoky Hill and Santa Fe roads, a party of three buffalo hunters left Mitchell County near present-day Glasco, to hunt buffalo in Smith County, just south of present-day Lebanon. On July 23, the three buffalo hunters were attacked by a party of Indians believed to be Cheyenne, but probably a mix of Lakota and Cheyenne. The three men had been successful in their buffalo hunt and the two wagons were filled with buffalo meat, when the warriors surprised them in their camp. John Higgins was not able to escape to Oak Creek but John Owen did. Owen hid while hearing the gunfire and realized the Indians killed his friends, not knowing the third man also had also escaped. He finally made it back to his settlement nearly 50 miles southeast, and reported the attack. With a party of five men he returned to bury his dead friends, but only Higgins was found. The wagons were still there but severely damaged, and the meat putrid, as well as the body of Higgins. The horses were lost. Their neighbor friend was buried and when the men returned home they learned that the third man, Burg, had arrived back while the men were out searching to bury his body.[118]

July 29: Big Creek Station, 50 miles east of Downer Station, was attacked. Indians stole 40 horses and six mules. Stephen L. Clements, a stage driver, was there. He said "every effort was made to defend and recapture said horses and mules, but the Indian force was too powerful to be overcome." David Haley, stock tender, was present as was Benjamin M. Johnson, a trader with a store there. Ben Wilson, a carpenter, also was present.

With all of these attacks upon stages, stage stations, settlers and railroad workers, both the stagecoaches and railroad construction had shut down. General William T. Sherman arrived at Fort Harker in early July to personally appraise the situation. There he learned that only two stages had

117   Illegible signature, Captain, 38th Infantry "Report Headquarters Post, Fort Hays, KS." Record Group 393, Part I, Letters Received, Department of the Missouri, 1867. Entry 2593.

118   John Owen Andrew Hunter Indian Depredation Claim #3657. Entry 700, Record Group 75.

made it to Denver in June and none yet in July. Stages were to run daily. He rather unwisely concluded that it wasn't Indian troubles that shut down railroad construction; instead it was heavy rainfall, and the stages shut down because of "selfishness and cowardice on the part of the stage company officials."[119] Given all of the raids and attacks noted up until this time, it appears Sherman suffered from an inability to let facts interfere with belief.

What is very interesting about the numerous Indian raids and attacks on all of these Wells Fargo stage stations is the fact that so few persons were reported killed. One might ask, did the Indians try to injure the many men present during all these raids? It appears not, especially when viewing the capture of Thomas Greasney near Grinnell Station on June 26. What is to be made of this? The compelling conclusion is similar to what happened in the June raids in Colorado Territory in 1864, which culminated in the killing of Nathan Hungate, his wife and two young daughters. Evidence there pointed to the hypothesis that Hungate shot at least one Indian as the raiders were stealing his stock, and it was that killing that the Indians then avenged with the death of Nathan and his young family. Perhaps the same thing was occurring along the various stage stations in Kansas and Colorado in the spring and summer of 1867. Whites were killed when it was necessary to retaliate for the killing of an Indian; otherwise they were usually left unharmed. Another possible explanation is an Indian culture that placed more praise on stealing or counting coup on an enemy more so than killing him.[120] This issue exacerbated the whole conflict in this five-year Indian war. It grew to the point that if a white person saw an Indian, they shot first and asked questions later. Brigadier General Christopher C. Augur, commanding the Department of the Platte at this time, issued a directive on March 2, 1867 to that effect, stating it "is a well-known rule with Indians that when injured, they retaliate upon the first favorable occasion that offers."[121] Regardless of what the intentions of the Indians were in 1867, continuing violence was inevitable and soon the Indians were taking every opportunity, in their continued raids, to kill the white man. And the white man responded back.

---

119 Marvin H. Garfield, "Defense of the Kansas Frontier 1866–1867," *Kansas Historical Quarterly*, Number 4, August 1932, 334.

120 Dennis Hagen, "Counting Coup: The Nature of Intertribal Warfare on the Great Plains Considered," The Denver Westerners *Roundup*, Vol. LX, NO. 6, November–December, 2004, 11.

121 C. C. Augur, "General Orders No. 14," Headquarters Department of the Platte, Omaha, Nebraska, March 2, 1867. Record Group 393, Part I, Letters Received, Department of the Platte, 1867.

CHAPTER ELEVEN

Waging Actual War

So long as the two distinct races of people, with such diverse interests as subsists between the roving Indians of the plains and our own white settlers, remain together, so long will actual war exist; and if there be an earnest desire on the part of the law-making power of the government to save the weaker party from absolute annihilation, some provisions must be made for separating the conflicting races.

W. T. SHERMAN, LIEUTENANT GENERAL
"REPORT OF THE SECRETARY OF WAR," JULY 1, 1867
SECOND SESSION, FORTIETH CONGRESS

THE WARRIOR ATTACKS AGAINST THE MANY WELLS FARGO stations, as well as the failed military campaigns of Hancock and Custer, inspired the government to seek another treaty with the Cheyenne and Arapaho. On July 20, 1867, Congress approved the effort to establish peace by way of treaty, ". . . to call together the chiefs and head-men of such bands of Indians as were then waging war, for the purpose of ascertaining their reasons for hostility, and . . . to make treaties with them. . . ."[1] The Medicine Lodge Treaty, later in the fall of 1867, was hoped would finally bring peace to the plains of Nebraska, Kansas and Colorado Territory, especially along the roads leading through each state. Like all earlier treaties with the Cheyenne, though, this one failed to bring peace. Peace was only going to come by way of the sword.

But there was still violence on the plains before the treaty negotiations began. The latter part of July was especially violent just above the Kansas border in Nebraska. On July 22, Albert Kalus left his wife and four small

---

1   "Report of the Indian Peace Commissioners," House of Representatives, 40th Congress, 2d Session, Executive Document No. 97 (Washington, DC: Government Printing Office, 1868), 1.

children, and with his hired hand Joseph Pixta took a wagon in search of a homestead for Joseph. Albert's family had a homestead about six miles southwest of present-day Alexandria and four miles east of Hebron, Nebraska. The men were expected back by nightfall but did not return. They were the first victims of Cheyenne war leader Turkey Leg. Turkey Leg was a Northern Cheyenne who often joined forces with Oglala Pawnee Killer. Earlier that summer both Indian leaders met with Custer when Custer was at Fort McPherson, each professing peace. Pawnee Killer then ventured south into Kansas and was involved in the violence along and near the Smoky Hill road, while Turkey Leg apparently stayed nearer the Platte River.[2]

Albert's wife Margaretha feared the worst regarding her husband's fate, when she learned what happened to her brother-in-law, Peter Ulbrich, the next day—his son and daughter were captured. She later recalled what happened at her home, fearing that her husband was never going to return:

> Of course I became then fearful of the safety of my husband and I and my four little children were sitting day in and day out, from week to week, from morning till night and weeping; crying and weeping, when we got the news that the bodies of my husband and Joseph Piexa [sic, Pixta] had been seen by the drivers and passengers of the Overland stage-coaches, frightfully mutilated and buried by the roadside where found by a scouting party of white settlers from Swan Creek, who placed a headboard on the grave and marked it 'Two men killed by Indians'.[3]

Peter Ulbrich's losses were equally severe. Peter's own voice tells what happened:

> About 9 o'clock on the morning of this terrible day a roving band of Cheyenne Sioux, about thirty in number, came galloping down from the direction of Pawnee Ranche on the Fort Kearney road; a squad of them immediately entered my pasture and seized two horses and a mule of mine, grazing therein.
>
> At the same time others in the party jumped over the fence into the field, where my 13 year old daughter Veeney (Veronica) and my 12 year old son Peter were pulling weeds for the hogs in the potato field, pounced upon the terrified children, began whipping them with their rawhides and driving them in the direction of the house, which we had hastily barricaded. Finding the doors and windows barred, the Indians called out the words in plain English: 'Father, father! Come out, we

2   Hyde, *Life of George Bent*, 276.
3   Margaretha Kalus Indian Depredation Claim #4545. Record Group 123.

VERONICA ULBRICH, CAPTURED BY TURKEY LEG'S BAND OF CHEYENNE, JULY 24, 1867, NEAR PRESENT-DAY FAIRBURY, NEBRASKA.
Veronica was in captivity for six weeks before released—with four other captives—in an exchange of "prisoners." Veronica was 13 when captured, and was terribly abused by the Indians. Her 12-year-old brother, Peter, was taken with her, but was shot after the Indians had ridden a short distance from the Ulbrich cabin. His body was recovered after Veronica—Veeney—was released, and took her father to where she remembered Peter was shot. *Courtesy George Ulbrick, Lawrence, Kansas.*

give you papooses.' From upstairs I had observed Indians on every corner of the house with guns at aim; I could see from their countenances and general conduct and appearances that they were bloodthirsty devils and judged that they would massacre all of us, if I opened the door. Having no other means of defense but an old rusty musket, I preferred to await events. My wife implored them: 'Give the papooses free, you got horses and mule, take it, that is enough.'

Waiting and parlaying quite a while the Indians finally went to my stable and compelled my boy in sight of the house to cut up the double harness hanging there, with a sharp knife they handed him; the bridles, lines and other straps were carried off by them.

About ten o'clock A.M. the Indians lifted my son and daughter on the horses stolen from me, riding off with them in a due westerly course. Arrived at the eastern shore of the Little Blue River they shot and killed my boy while riding in their midst; they left him, where we found his body 4 or five months later, at the exact spot which his then liberated sister had pointed out.[4]

Veronica remained a captive for six weeks until rescued in an exchange of captives with Turkey Leg, who had a female and nephew captured in a

4   Peter Ulbrich Indian Depredation Claim #6220. Record Group 123.

fight with soldiers and Pawnee scouts near the Plum Creek Stage Station.[5] Peter Ulbrich recalled his daughter's condition when rescued: "When I recovered her at the farm of Mr. Campbell, south of Grand Island, she was nothing but skin and bones. Campbell's three or four children and my daughter had been surrendered (or exchanged) to the military authorities at North Platte, Nebraska, and forwarded by the Union Pacific Railroad to Grand Island, where Mr. Campbell received them."[6]

The Campbell family had been captured the day after Veronica was taken, nearly 90 miles away near present-day Doniphan, Nebraska. The father, Peter, and his oldest son were six miles away helping a neighbor with harvest. About three o'clock Peter was notified of the raid. He raced home on his horse and on the way discovered the violence at their closest neighbor, where he "found the mother of the family lying dead on the threshold of the door, clasping her infant son in her arms; and nearby a son, fourteen years of age, lay shot through the thigh."[7]

Veronica recalled joining the Campbell clan in captivity: "I first saw the Campbell children, Jessie about twenty years of age, Catherine about 18 years, Daniel and Peter, both small boys about 5 or 6 years old; I think they were twins. Of course I was glad to have white company in my misery. I was afraid I never could get away and had to stay with these brutes and devils all my lifetime." She never forgot the trauma of her ordeal with Turkey Leg:

Although it is a long time ago I remember yet vividly the hot summer day of 1867 when a band of Cheyenne Indians swept down upon our farm, captured me and my brother Peter. They whipped us with their rawhides and we cried bitterly for help. More dead than alive they took us away from home and three miles later they shot my brother off the horse and left him, where I pointed out the location four months later to my father. . . . They compelled me to travel with them, we were traveling from one place to another, some of the band were on the go all the time. I did not get enough to eat, suffered from thirst, had to wash and do other work; sometimes they whipped me, sometimes they wanted or threatened to kill me. Soon one Indian, soon another belonging to the band forcibly violated my body, causing me immense pain and anguish thereby. This was almost a daily and nightly occurrence which would have killed me, if I had not been liberated almost

5   Broome, *Dog Soldier Justice*, 138. See also Michno, *Encyclopedia of Indian Wars*, 208–209.
6   Peter Ulbrich Indian Depredation Claim #6220.
7   John R. Campbell, "An Indian Raid of 1867," *Collections of the Nebraska State Historical Society*, ed. By Albert Watkins, Volume XVII (Lincoln, NE: The Nebraska State Historical Society, 1913), 260.

exhausted. I used to remember the names of some members of the band, especially of some squaws, but I cannot recollect any more at this time.[8]

In the same area where the Ulbrich family was attacked, James Hanna was traveling on the road, following the Little Blue River, returning to his home in Colorado near Fort Collins. He had three young boys and a man helping him herd over 1,300 sheep. About 12 miles after passing Big Sandy Stage Station, the Indians attacked his small wagon party. They fought off the Indians from 11 o'clock until four that afternoon—July 23. The man, Henry Such, was killed. When the Indians finally left, Hanna sent one of the boys back to Big Sandy to report the fight, while he stayed with the other boys and guarded his stock and property. The boy had not returned by the next morning, so he sent off another boy. Still he waited with the third boy and relief did not come, so he finally took off with the other boy, riding horses and leaving his wagon and sheep unattended. After a few miles the Indians saw them and gave chase. He and the boy galloped on their horses for six miles until reaching Big Sandy Station. When he returned to his wagon the next day, no sheep were found, except at least 150 dead ones lying about, filled with arrows. His wagon was burned and all the contents either stolen or destroyed.[9]

Back in Kansas, things got bloody on August 1. James Campbell and George Clinton were contractors with the Union Pacific Railroad, Eastern Division, hired to build and grade the rail line near Hays. Seven men left their camp early that morning to work the grade where present-day Victoria stands. They were careless, leaving their weapons, which had been provided by the government for protection. But because Indians had not been seen for several days, the men were not concerned to carry their rifles with them. It was a deadly mistake. Near Big Creek, about 30 Cheyenne caught their prey unarmed. Six men were killed outright and a seventh, William Gould, was mortally wounded, and soon died in the Fort Hays post hospital. All of the men were scalped. In addition, the Indians stole five mules and five horses, most belonging to the victims. George Clinton was about a mile away with other laborers. The same Indians also attacked his men but they were armed and were able to fight them off, apparently with no losses. The

8   Peter Ulbrich Indian Depredation Claim #6220.
9   James Hanna Indian Depredation Claim #3111. Record Group 123.

six men killed outright were P. S. Ashley, the foreman, from Broadhead, Wisconsin; Thomas Carney, from Iowa; Charles Watson, from Canada; John Hetherington, from Kansas City; Pat Rafferty, also from Kansas City; Hugh McDonough, from Denver. William Gould was from Illinois.[10]

Captain George Armes was at Fort Hays, when at two o'clock he received a report of the killings on Big Creek. At three o'clock he took a company of 38 men—Buffalo soldiers of the 10th Cavalry—and went north towards the Saline while Captain Henry Corbin took another company and followed the Smoky Hill River to the south, where another report said Indians had just attacked Big Springs Station, nine miles distant, and stole 30 stage horses. At Big Springs, two Indians were killed during the theft. One citizen recognized the leader of the Indians as Roman Nose. Henry C. Corbin took a party of soldiers in pursuit of the Indians that attacked Big Creek Station. He soon discovered tracks showing Roman Nose's party going north off the Smoky Hill in the direction Armes had earlier gone, which was the direction the Indians who killed the railroad workers had gone.[11]

Armes went about 18 miles, until darkness came, but did not catch the Indians. He returned to Big Creek, where Campbell and Corbin had their camp, and from there sent a request west to the fort for a howitzer and an additional 30 troopers. His plan was to leave at daybreak and continue pursuit of the Indians. Four hours passed, and the additional command had not yet reported so Armes left at daylight with 34 men, four men having been left behind due to sickness. Cholera was at that time becoming rampant at the forts along the Smoky Hill trail, and no doubt Armes did not want to

---

10   James Campbell & George Clinton Indian Depredation Claim #1128; Elizur Hills Indian Depredation Claim #1101. Record Group 123. Elizur Hills Indian Depredation Claim #5073; Thomas Hetherington Indian Depredation Claim #1128. Record Group 75. Captain Henry C. Corbin, "Report, Headquarters near Fort Hays, Kansas, August 2, 1867." Record Group 393, Part I, Letters Received, Department of the Missouri, 1867. Entry 2593. Lieutenant Sanders was at Big Creek when the attack was made, and in his report he said the attack occurred August 2. Corbin, however, clearly states that the attack at Big Creek happened "About the same time." See Lieutenant Sanders, "Report Big Creek Station, August 3, 1867." Record Group 393, Part I, Letters Received, Department of the Missouri, 1867. Entry 2593. In 1910 D. Goodrich wrote a letter remembering his near death by the Indians that day. He was with a party of eight men coming from Fort Hays to the railroad camp when he and his partners saw the Indians. They were able to hide behind a slight ridge. A civilian employee from the fort passed his group and was caught not far from where the railroad workers had been killed. His body was "scalped, full of arrows & badly mutilated with butcher knives." See D. Goodrich letter, Kansas State Historical Society, Topeka, Kansas.

11   Captain Henry C. Corbin, "Report, Headquarters near Fort Hays, Kansas, August 2, 1867."

risk the sick men spreading that disease. He had ordered the burial of two cholera victims at Fort Hays the day before the warriors made their attacks.[12]

Twenty-five miles later, Armes discovered about 75 Cheyenne on the Saline. But the Indians proved to be too many for the small command. They flanked the soldiers and set the prairie on fire all around them. Armes ordered a withdrawal back to Fort Hays. Three of his men had their horses shot from under them, and Sergeant William Cristy was shot in the head with a bullet and killed.[13] The warriors followed the men for about 15 miles. The engagement was long and hard. Armes estimated the Indians fired 2,000 rounds in the skirmish. The warriors were all well armed, most with repeating Spencers. Armes received a painful bullet wound in his hip, the bullet later extracted by the post surgeon. Two half-breed white men were with the Indians. No doubt one of them was Charles Bent. In his final report Armes wrote: "It is the greatest wonder in the world that my command and myself escaped being massacred, as we had to retreat fifteen miles through a hilly country, full of canyons, rocks and gullies, fighting our way foot by foot, the Indians dodging from one gully and rock to others and firing on us at every chance."[14]

The Indians seemed to like their chances with railroad contractors. They stayed in the vicinity, and on August 5, made a bold raid on the crew working for Shoemaker, Miller and Company, who had a contract for building the

---

12 For a study of the cholera outbreak in Kansas in 1867 see Ramon Powers and Gene Younger, "Cholera on the plains: the epidemic of 1867 in Kansas," *The Kansas Historical Quarterly*, Number 4, Winter, 1971, 351–393.

13 Captain George A. Armes, "Report Fort Hays, Kas. November 23, 1867." Record Group 393, Part I, Letters Received, Department of the Missouri, 1867. Entry 2593.

14 Armes, *Ups and Downs*, 236–239. The depredation claims associated with the men killed at Victoria noted that the Cheyenne denied involvement in this event, and suggested it was done by Sioux. George Bent said the Cheyenne were south of the Arkansas at this time and uninvolved in any raids. He also said it was Sioux causing the disturbances at this time. The likelihood is that Roman Nose, as well as Dog Soldiers under Tall Bull, the majority Cheyenne warriors, both Northern and Southern, were the ones causing the havoc. Pawnee Killer's Oglala were probably there, too. See Hyde, *Life of George Bent*, 278. What is interesting about identifying the Indians involved at Victoria is the depredation claim of Hiram Hall, who lost stock in a raid five miles west of Fort Hays on either August 4 or August 5. Hall's claim was taken to the Cheyenne leaders in 1875, and they admitted the theft. They denied committing the murders on August 1, when the claims associated with that were presented to them in 1889, saying no Cheyenne were in the vicinity in all of July and August. To admit involvement in the one, yet deny involvement in the other, indicates an inconsistency, resolved by concluding the Cheyenne were the perpetrators in both incidents. Clearly, a large number of Southern Cheyenne were involved in the bloody summer of 1867.

rail grade west of Fort Hays.[15] They had subcontracted to Hiram Hall and William H. Crenshaw, and together there were about 25 men working the grade. They were five miles west of the new Fort Hays, where the new town of Hays City was built. Between one and two o'clock in the afternoon, the men went into camp for the noon meal—"dinner" in the 1860s. Twenty-five or 30 horses and mules were tied to picket lines with their harnesses a short distance from camp, after being fed a meal of corn. As the men were relaxing in their camp, they suddenly heard shots from a nearby hill, the most prominent hill at that spot from Fort Hays, near present-day Yocemento. On top of the hill were four or five buffalo soldiers, assigned for protection to the men working the rail line. The Buffalo soldiers had spied about 100 Cheyenne Indians riding fast from the southwest. They fired at the warriors and shouted to the men in camp 300–400 yards to the north, below the hilltop where the soldiers were. The workers' camp was in a prominent bend on the south side of Big Creek. The Buffalo soldiers' warning allowed the railroad workers time to secure their arms. The raiders descended upon the men in the camp from the west, "under full speed yelling and shooting their guns and revolvers—surrounding the camp—in horse shoe shape and stampeded all the stock in camp."

When the Indians charged ". . . the stock became frantic, pulled up or broke their ropes and stampeded out of the openness left in the partly closed circle of yelling Indians and fled over the open plains to the north." The Indians remained firing on the camp for several minutes while a smaller portion of the warriors followed the stock and took charge of them, riding out of sight and thus preventing any of the men from pursuing the panic-driven horses. The workers were grateful for the quick action of the buffalo soldiers, both in warning them and also in using their long range rifles and firing at the Indians. Had the soldiers not done their duty, "most likely every man in the camp would have been murdered—but being warned—they had time to catch up their arms composed of revolvers, Spencer rifles and about twelve improved Springfield rifles furnished . . . by the government for their protection." It was believed one Indian had been killed and perhaps a few more wounded, probably all by the fire of the buffalo soldiers. The Indians took their dead and wounded when they left. One man present

15 It is difficult to establish exactly when this raid occurred. Three depredation claims all give different dates, August 4, August 5, and August 16.

during the raid, Hiram Hall, got a good look at the Indians and described their war paint: "Hardly two Indians look alike—dressed alike—paint their faces—great daubs of paint on them just as though they stuck their hands in a paint pot and put it on their faces. You could see the finger marks. They were bad looking fellows."[16]

On August 6, apparently the same Cheyenne war party made another raid 30 miles further west from Fort Hays, also on railroad workers. Because of an accident to some of the machinery used to grade the road, only a portion of the stock was put to work, and the remaining 32 horses and mules not being used were set out to graze under the supervision of a lone herder. About four o'clock that afternoon the herder drove the stock to a ravine about a mile from the railroad camp, where there was water for the herd to drink. Out of the blue suddenly appeared 16 Indians, who shot at the herder—missing him—and drove off the stock. When the Indians neared the worker's camp, racing the stock away, some of the Cheyenne made an attempt to capture some additional horses that were picketed nearby. However, the men in camp were able to thwart them. Steven Sharp, J. A. Soward, Edwin Dargus and another man pursued the Indians for about 10 miles, but were unable to recapture the stock.[17] With the railroad workers were 10 buffalo soldiers accompanying them for protection. In a report dated August 6, it was noted that the Indians paid dearly for their theft, several of them dying from the fire of the soldiers.[18]

---

16   George Stackhouse and Cyrus Higginbotham Indian Depredation Claim #334. Hiram Hall Indian Depredation Claim # 7638. Record Group 123.

17   Steven Sharp Indian Depredation Claim #1014. Record Group 123. See also Steven Sharp and Thomas Shaw Indian Depredation Claim #4656. Record Group 123. The latter claim said the men lost 26 horses and nine mules. More details emerge in another claim, by Steven Sharp and Thomas Shaw. See claim #1015. When the claim was brought to the Southern Cheyenne in council, the chiefs adamantly denied any Southern Cheyenne involved. Brinton Darlington, their government agent, believed them. This case illustrates, again, the difficulty of identifying what tribes were guilty for the various depredations. If the chiefs were right in their denial—recall the Southern Cheyenne admission to the theft on August 5, five miles west of Fort Hays (311, footnote 14), does put them in the area and makes their involvement in the various raids quite possible—then the likely guilty Indians were those operating either under Roman Nose, or Tall Bull, or other tribal leaders associated with these war leaders. Claim #1015, however, contains testimony from two men present at the Medicine Lodge Treaty, who saw several Southern Cheyenne and Arapaho riding horses and mules with the brand "S and S," which was the brand Sharp and Shaw used on the stock stolen August 6. See the testimony of Joseph Root—secretary of the Commission at Medicine Lodge—and T. F. Moore.

18   Captain Henry Corbin, "Report Headquarters Post New Fort Hayes," August 6, 1867. Record Group 393, Part I, Letters Received, Department of the Missouri, 1867. Entry 2593.

PRESERVED SCALP OF WILLIAM THOMPSON,
RAILROAD LABORER, WHO SURVIVED BEING SCALPED,
PRETENDING TO BE DEAD, AUGUST 6, 1867.
Thompson took his scalp with him to Omaha, where attempts to reattach it failed.
The scalp was later donated to the Omaha Public Library, and still is occasionally
displayed. It was shown for a few weeks in 2013, when this picture was taken. *Photo
courtesy Tedd Remm, Reunion, Colorado.*

Back on the Platte River road in Nebraska, Turkey Leg was still causing
problems. Late in the evening of August 6, his band of Cheyenne made a
deadly sortie near present-day Lexington. His warriors, as well as some
Lakota, probably Oglala under Pawnee Killer—who had recently returned
from raiding in Kansas—had torn up some of the railroad west of Plum
Creek Station near present-day Lexington. They had also cut down the
telegraph wire.[19] Six railroad workers were sent out west from Plum Creek
Station to repair the telegraph wire, not knowing the railroad was also torn
up. They left about nine o'clock that night. After a little more than three
miles they came to a bend in the track. At that point Indians hiding in the

---

19 Henry M. Stanley, *My Early Travels and Adventures in America and Asia*, Volume 1, Second Edition
     (London: Samson Low, Marston and Company, 1895), 161. From evidences in earlier chapters, Spotted
     Tail worked diligently to keep his warriors at peace, whereas Pawnee Killer was known to be an active
     participant warring in 1867.

tall grass jumped out and surprised them. Three workers were quickly killed and another man, William Thompson, was badly wounded. The other two men were able to escape unharmed.[20]

Train Number One was due from the west at Willow Island—present-day Cozad—at 1:50 the next morning, August 7. When it did not arrive, the station operator sent a telegram expressing concern that the train might have derailed. The night was illuminated by a half-moon and the operator could see a large fire to the east.[21] He was right in his fears. William Thompson, still lying wounded on the prairie, could do nothing to warn the approaching train of its awaiting peril. The Indians had pulled the spikes from the wood and bent one of the rails up in the air about a foot or two. That was all that was needed to derail the train.[22] The engineer, Brooks Bowers, and fireman, Gregory Henshaw, were shot and scalped and their bodies later thrown onto the burning train. The Indians had set it afire after plundering the two flat cars and three box cars, loaded with various kinds of freight, including bricks, cloth and whiskey. The cars apparently stayed on the tracks, only the engine derailing.[23] Four other men were at the end of the derailed train and were able to escape and warn a second train which came along not too long after the derailed train had been wrecked. That train reversed its engine and brought the other surviving trainmen back with them to Plum Creek Station.

William Thompson's story is one of the more thrilling tales in the annals of the Plains Indian wars. When daylight came on the morning of August 7, some men took a handcar from Plum Creek and ventured out to the scene of the derailment. As they were sifting through the debris and recovering what little remained of the two burned men whose bodies had been tossed into the fire, ever watchful for Indians, Thompson slowly walked towards them. At first they thought he was an Indian and were about to shoot him when one of the men recognized him as Thompson. His shirt was missing and his skin was covered with dried blood.[24] Henry Stanley first wrote of Thompson's adventure, recording it in Thompson's voice:

20   Telegram from Mr. Snyder to Col. Potter, Fort McPherson, August 7, 1867. Record Group 393, Part I, Telegrams Received, Department of the Missouri, 1867. Entry 3735.

21   http://eclipse.gsfc.nasa.gov/phase/phases1801.html (accessed June 15, 2013).

22   George Bird Grinnell, *The Fighting Cheyennes* (Norman, OK: University of Oklahoma Press, 1956), 267.

23   http://www.usgennet.org/usa/ne/topic/resources/OLLibrary/pionrem/nepr0050.html (accessed July 1, 2013).

24   Ibid.

We [the six men on the handcar] fired two or three shots . . . and then, as the Indians pressed on us, we ran away. An Indian on a pony singled me out, and galloped up to me. After coming to within ten feet of me he fired, the bullet passed through my right arm; but seeing me still run, he rushed up and clubbed me down with his rifle. He then took out his knife, stabbed me in the neck, and making a twirl round his fingers with my hair, he commenced sawing and hacking away at my scalp. Though the pain was awful, and I felt dizzy and sick, I knew enough to keep quiet. After what seemed to be half an hour, he gave the last finishing cut to the scalp on my left temple, and as it still hung a little, he gave it a jerk. I thought then that I could have screamed my life out. I can't describe it to you. It just felt as if the whole head was taken right off. The Indian then mounted and galloped away, but as he went he dropped my scalp within a few feet of me, which I managed to get and hide.[25]

In a later interview Thompson recalled his experience of surviving being scalped, saying two Indians scalped him:

With the deftness of an expert . . . the [first] savage grabbed my scalp lock in one hand, cut around it again and again, until the edges of the skin were loosened. Then he tore it free. The sensation was about the same as if some one had passed a red-hot iron over my head. After the air touched the wound the pain was almost unbearable. I never felt anything that hurt so much. I had to bite my tongue to keep from putting my hand on the wound. I wanted to see how much of the top of my head was left. . . . Just as [I] was prepared to crawl into the grass [I] was roughly seized, a hand clutched [my] hair [what remained] again, and once more [I] felt a knife. [I] felt that another Indian was scalping [me]. After removing a couple inches of scalp the Indian rushed on.[26]

Thompson was brought to Willow Springs, and from there took a train back to Omaha, where he hoped a surgeon could reattach his scalp, which he had carried with him in a bucket of water. The effort failed. He soon moved back to England, but his scalp remained with the surgeon who had tried to reattach it to Thompson's skull. It eventually ended up in the Omaha Public Library where it is still occasionally put on public display, a unique and gruesome relic of the Wild West.

About 100 miles southeast of where Thompson had his hair-raising encounter with Turkey Leg, another band of Cheyenne and Lakota raided back on the Little Blue near the present-day town of Alexandria.

---

25 Stanley, *My Early Travels*, 156. Stanley in all likelihood wrote the first newspaper account of Thompson's scalp experience. See the *St. Louis Democrat*, August 8, 1867.

26 *St. John Daily Sun*, August 4, 1903. New Brunswick, Canada.

These Indians could have been a sortie attached to Turkey Leg, or perhaps Cheyenne Dog Soldiers under other leadership. They attacked the house of Joseph Walker, burned it down, stole a team of horses and killed one of his workers. Walker remembered what happened:

It was a company of Sioux and Cheyennes. There was a gang of them that had been in the habit of making raids through that section of the country stealing horses, cattle and other property, and about two weeks before the raid on me they had stolen two children [Ulbrich] of a neighbor, and killed a number of people in that vicinity. On that day we were expecting them to make another raid on us. I had two hired men working for me at the time, one by the name of Charles Hunt, and Ignatius Tennish. Hunt was in the field with the reaper cutting wheat or oats, and Tennish was looking after the cattle and working in the harvest field. A man by the name of [Edward] Farrell was at my place and it was the day for us to be on the lookout for that gang of Indians. About ten o'clock we went from the house upon a hill west of my house, and when we got there we saw a squad of Indians coming straight toward my place. They were riding ponies and there were from sixteen to twenty of them. Farrell and I were mounted on horses. As soon as we saw the Indians we turned and went back to the house and they followed us. We rode our horses as fast as we could go trying to get away from them. They tried to overtake us, at the same time they were shooting at us as fast as they could fire. Farrell lost his gun in coming down the hill, and I went to the house to get him a shotgun, and while I was at the house Farrell rode down the road toward his home as fast as he could go. When I saw that Farrell had gone, I left the gun and jumped on my horse and started down the road as fast as my horse could run for Big Sandy, a small village on the Big Sandy Creek. When I got about 80 rods from my house I overtook Ed Hawkes and Joe Baker. At that time Mr. Tennish was down by the corn field driving my cattle. The Indians saw him down there and they rode down and surrounded him, shooting him and filling his body full of arrows. After they killed him they scalped him. At that time Mr. Hawkes and Mr. Baker and myself were but a short distance from Mr. Tennish and we saw the Indians kill him but we were unable to give him any assistance. We went down the river to get help and also to warn the settlers living along the Sandy and Blue. In an hour or two we went backward to my place. About a mile and a half east of my place we saw five of the Indians and we pursued them till we lost them in the hills and breaks south of the river. We then went around up west to see if we could find some of the other Indians, but we could not see or get any trace of them. Then we went back to my house and we found that they had taken away and destroyed the property belonging to me. . . . We followed up the Indians and hunted around to see if we could find any of the property which they had taken away. We then went and buried Mr. Tennish.[27]

27 Joseph Walker Indian Depredation Claim #1180. Record Group 123.

After Turkey Leg's deadly attack and derailing of Train Number One, Major Frank North and his Pawnee scouts were ordered to Plum Creek. On August 17, Indians had again cut the telegraph wire west of the station. North ordered Lieutenant Isaac Davis and 20 Pawnee to investigate the matter. When Davis arrived near the site of the train derailment, to his surprise he found Turkey Leg had come back with women and children—more than 150 Indians in all—to recover more plunder from the train debris. Davis quickly sent word back to Plum Creek, asking for reinforcements. Soon Captain James Murie arrived with 30 more Pawnee. The Pawnee had stripped for battle, but kept their blue military tunics on, attached with just the top button. The Cheyenne thought they were facing soldiers and felt they had the advantage, but to their surprise, when the scouts got in range they removed their coats and revealed themselves as the hated enemy of the Cheyenne. A brisk fight ensued and when it was over between 15 and 20 Cheyenne warriors had been killed and a woman, girl and boy captured. The girl soon escaped. The boy was Turkey Leg's nephew, and his capture eventually led to the release of Veronica Ulbrich and the four Campbell children, earlier captured on July 23 and 24, respectively.[28]

Back down in Kansas, a military expedition was sent out of Fort Hays in search of the Cheyenne that had been making the attacks upon the railroad workers. On August 12, Captain George Armes took command of Company F of the 10th Cavalry, as well as two companies of soldiers in the 18th Kansas Cavalry, Company B under Captain Edgar A. Barker, and Company C under Captain George B. Jennings. The total number of men under his command came to 142.[29] The next day he left the post and ventured north to the Solomon River. From there the command moved to a tributary of the North Fork of the Solomon, and up to the headwaters of Beaver Creek, south of present-day Phillipsburg in Phillips County. On August 17, a large Indian trail was discovered near the Saline River. Armes took three soldiers and went back to Fort Hays, 45 miles south. He wanted to resupply before following the trail. At the fort he loaded five wagons—four with forage and one with rations—and with the drivers went back to his command on the

28   Mark Van De Logt, *War Party in Blue Pawnee Scouts in the U. S. Army* (Norman, OK: University of Oklahoma Press, 2012), 95–97.

29   Armes, *Ups and Downs*, 246. Another 22 soldiers came back with Armes when he journeyed to Fort Hays in the middle of the campaign, to get forage and rations, making his total strength before the fighting started at 164.

Saline. He also brought 22 more buffalo soldiers to guard the train. When reunited with his soldiers, he selected 75 men, and on the night of August 19, he began following the Indian trail. He put Lieutenant Price in charge of the wagons and sent the rest of the men, under the command of Captain Jennings, to a prearranged point on the Solomon River, where Armes intended to meet up with them. His intent was to travel at night and hide the command in the day.

At sunrise on August 21, Armes was on the Solomon, when a lone Indian fired on the advance guard. There soon began a general engagement that included heavy fighting with the other parts of his divided command, covering several miles, all in the vicinity of Prairie Dog Creek. The fight lasted throughout the day, finally ceasing at dark. It continued the next day. Armes' portion of the command suffered 11 soldiers wounded, including his first sergeant, a buffalo soldier named Jacob Thornton, shot below the left leg, which disabled him. That night, Armes moved his command about 12 miles and joined forces with Lieutenant Price and the wagon detail, which he learned had been equally engaged in skirmishing throughout the day, as well as Captain Jennings' command. He sent several soldiers to reinforce Price and bring his men, along with the wounded, back to where Armes was entrenched with his men near the Solomon. The next day—August 23—they continued to be under siege. During the day, about 100 warriors approached Armes' command and waved a flag of truce. Armes sent out his guides to hear their proposal but an Indian recognized one of the scouts, called him by name and fired at him. One Indian called out in plain English "Come here, come here, you sons of guns; we don't want to fight the niggers; we want to fight you white sons of guns."[30] When the scouts came back to Armes, they said they recognized Roman Nose and Charles Bent and other prominent warriors. That night the Indians withdrew. On August 24, Armes returned to Fort Hays, arriving back at the post at five o'clock that evening. In his report on August 24, he listed the names of 26 soldiers wounded, two of whom died on the return to Fort Hays. They were buried on the prairie. In an earlier diary entry he said 35 soldiers had been killed or wounded.[31] Another report from Fort Hays, written by Captain Henry Corbin on the evening of August 23, acknowledged having just received

30 Ibid.
31 Ibid., 244.

information from a scout that Captain Armes and the 18th Kansas Cavalry had engaged the enemy. Thirty-two men were wounded and three men were killed and "left in the field." Yet another report said 35 men were wounded and "three killed which were left on the plains." In still another report it was said 11 men were missing from the 18th Cavalry and presumed captured.[32] All thought many more Indians were killed than soldiers wounded.[33] One report said that 40 horses were lost, the Indians numbered about 1,000, and perhaps as many as 150 warriors were killed.[34]

It was probably the fight by Armes, his buffalo soldiers and the 18th Kansas Cavalry, which triggered the efforts to try to bring the Indians in for another treaty. That, as well as Hancock's spring expedition and Custer's summer campaign, was enough to spark the efforts to get the Indians back in council and finally resolve the issues motivating the warriors to stay on the warpath. That was the hope, anyway. The efforts proved once again to be a failure, though the Medicine Lodge Treaty did define the parameters of the reservation boundaries in what was then called Indian Territory, today's Oklahoma panhandle.

The council began in mid-September, but before that happened, there were more raids made by the Cheyenne and Arapaho. Timothy Crook and William McLennan had a government contract to cut and deliver hay to Fort Dodge and Fort Larned. Crook had the Fort Dodge contract. On September 6, two men were cutting hay four or five miles east of Fort Dodge along the Arkansas River. Suddenly two Indians, believed to be Cheyenne, descended upon the two workers. One man was killed, as was his mule. Three mules were driven off with the wagon they were hitched to.[35] When the attack was reported at Fort Dodge, a detachment of soldiers was sent in pursuit, but they were unable to find the Indians.

Major Henry Douglass wrote a report about the incident, revealing more details. There was only one carbine between the two men, and it was loaded with just three cartridges. Because there had not been reports of Indians near

32   Captain George A. Armes, "Report, New Fort Hayes, Kansas August 24, 1867." Record Group 393, Part I, Letters Received, Department of the Missouri, 1867. Entry 2593.

33   Captain Henry Corbin, "Report Headquarters Post New Fort Hays Ks 9 P.M. Aug 23, '67." Record Group 393, Part I, Letters Received, Department of the Missouri, 1867. Entry 2593.

34   Horace S. Moore, "Report Headquarters 18th Kans Cav Ft. Hays 23 Aug 1867." Record Group 393, Part I, Letters Received, Department of the Missouri, 1867. Entry 2593.

35   Timothy D. Crook and William McLennan Indian Depredation Claim #4839. Record Group 123.

the post for some time, the two men got careless and left their other arms and ammunition at their camp. The man killed was unarmed and had tried to flee on one of the mules, was overtaken and killed, "scalped & otherwise horribly mutilated." The man with the carbine was able to escape by running to the river. From a head ornament found near the attack, Major Douglass believed the Indians responsible were Arapaho and not Cheyenne.

On the same day the hay worker was killed, two other men on their way to Fort Larned from Fort Dodge were also attacked by two Arapaho. The distance between the two attacks precludes the same Indians doing both, though they probably resided in the same camp. The men attacked were armed and defended themselves. One Indian was killed and the other Indian had his horse killed, though he escaped. Nearby the two men saw as many as 200 Indians "on the hills adjoining Little Coon Creek." The man who shot the Indian pony was F. F. Jones, an Indian interpreter. Jones reported hearing the language of the Indians trying to attack him and felt they were definitely Arapaho.[36]

Four days after this attack, eight Indians stole about 200 mules belonging to a large Mexican train on the Santa Fe road. The raid happened about 38 miles east of Fort Dodge. Coincidentally, when this happened, 7th Cavalry Sergeant Charles Price had just gone into his noon camp with six other enlisted men, returning to Fort Dodge from Fort Lyon. The Mexican caravan was about 700 yards away, nestled in their camp. Witnessing the raid, Price and his men immediately gave chase. Price was disturbed by the fact that the Mexicans did nothing to try to recover their stock. They still had about 100 mules but not one Mexican mounted a mule to join the chase, though a handful did run in the direction the Indians went. After going about three miles east down the Arkansas, the eight Indians were joined by about 40 others. They then crossed the river to the south. Sergeant Price was able to recover just one mule. In his report of the affair he noted ". . . the running off of the herds of mules is owing entirely to the cowardice and carelessness of the Mexicans. There were two other herds alongside of this one, that did not lose any stock, simply because their mules were hobbled. The wagon master whose stock was run off had hobbles but neglected to use them."[37]

---

36   Major H. Douglass, "Report Headquarters Fort Dodge, Kansas September 7, 1867." Record Group 393, Part I, Letters Received, Department of the Missouri, 1867. Entry 2593.

37   Sergeant Charles Price, "Report Fort Dodge Kansas September 12, 1867." Record Group 393, Part I, Letters Received, Department of the Missouri, 1867. Entry 2593.

Yet another attack was made on September 7, with deadly results. About 50 miles northeast of where Jones was attacked, a larger party of Indians, believed to be Kiowa and Cheyenne, attacked 12 large freight wagons belonging to brothers Franz and Charles Huning. The two men were long-time merchants in Albuquerque—having operated a mercantile business there the prior 14 years—and were on their way back from Junction City, loaded with freight to sell in their store. Eight mules pulled each wagon which was loaded with 5,000 pounds of goods, wares, merchandise and groceries. Included with the 12 freight wagons were two ambulance wagons and a barouche, an open carriage wagon. The barouche was being driven by Frederick William Franke, a young man in his mid-20s. Sitting beside him was his 75-year-old mother, Martha Maria Franke. "Mother Maria" was accompanying the train because Franz Huning was married to her daughter. The mother and her youngest son were coming to Albuquerque to live with her daughter. In addition to the wagons there were several extra mules brought along.

On the afternoon of September 7—about two hours before sunset—the party was suddenly attacked as the caravan approached Plum Butte, a section of the Santa Fe trail about 4 miles west of present-day Chase, or 16 miles straight east of Fort Zarah. About 100 Indians suddenly appeared, screaming and attacking the wagon train. The warriors were all well-armed with revolvers, rifles, lances, and bows and arrows. They were hiding behind a sand hill to the front and left of the approaching train; ". . . the surprise was so complete that almost before they had a chance to grasp their arms the Indians had swept in a furious charge, shooting and yelling behind, through and ahead of the train, throwing everything into confusion. . . ." The raiders knew what they wanted and quickly separated four freight wagons, the two ambulance wagons and the barouche, "turning four entire teams off from the road, and the carriages, by goading the mules with their lances." The freighters driving the wagons fled their stations and found refuge with the rest of the train. The mother and son, however, were unable to escape. They were tortured, killed and mutilated. The wagons were all burned and the goods in each stolen or destroyed. Forty-two mules were also taken. The remaining wagons were quickly driven to Fort Zarah, arriving about two o'clock the next morning. Five soldiers and five of the freighters returned to Plum Butte the next morning, but were unable to retrieve the bodies of

Mother Maria and her son, as there were now over 200 Indians still min-
gling around their captured booty. Several days later a very large wagon
train, well-armed and operated by Charles Parker, came along the trail,
going west to Albuquerque. When they got to Plum Butte, they found the
dead mother and son and brought them into Fort Zarah, where they were
buried in the post cemetery. When the bodies were viewed, it was obvious
that the Indians "burnt and tortured the old lady and the heart of the young
man had been cut out and his body mutilated in a manner not proper to
mention." It was clear to the Huning brothers that the "attack, murder, and
robbery was unprovoked . . . . and a wanton, cruel, and merciless robbery
and murder . . . only justified by those who are paid by the United States to
calumniate and libel peaceful citizens of the United States in order to justify
and excuse the Indians in the perpetuation of such outrages."[38]

It is quite ironic that the Huning brothers had that assessment regarding what happened, for the Indians were in the vicinity precisely to begin
peace negotiations. By September 14, 1,400 Indians had set up their respective camps along Medicine Lodge Creek, about 60 miles southeast of Fort
Larned. Tribes present were the Kiowa, Comanche, Arapaho and Plains
Apache. The only Cheyenne present was Black Kettle's tribe.[39] But there
were still raids to occur before the treaty talks began, which would not happen for another month. One wonders whether the Indians coming for the
council also took time out to commit raids. Certainly the Huning brothers
believed that was the case.

The violence prior to treaty talks continued. D. B. Powers and Henry
Bowman had a contract to deliver corn to Fort Dodge, and while on the
road between Forts Larned and Dodge—on September 8—about 17 miles
southwest of Fort Larned, Cheyenne and Arapaho Indians attacked the mule
train, killing five teamsters and wounding one, and making off with seven
mules and one wagon loaded with 5,800 pounds of corn. The Indians killed
two other mules and wounded three.[40] Meanwhile, north of this incident,
the next day, September 9, three men were delivering three wagon loads of

---

38 Franz and Charles Huning Indian Depredation Claim #1421, 1423. Record Group 123. Indian Agent
    Brinton Darlington took the claim to the Southern Cheyenne, and they admitted the theft and mur-
    ders. Darlington thought this exonerated the Kiowa, but not if the Cheyenne were the Dog Soldiers,
    for many Kiowa were a part of that warrior society.

39 Kraft, *Ned Wynkoop*, 204.

40 D. B. Powers and Henry Bowman Indian Depredation Claim # not noted in file. Record Group 75,
    entry 700.

cut pine to Bunker Hill Stage Station, about 30 miles east of Fort Hays. They had earlier departed from Ellsworth and were within half a mile of Bunker Hill when about 40–50 Cheyenne Dog Soldiers attacked the small party. Each man lost two mules and a wagon. Thomas Cosby had one wagon. He was severely wounded in the attack, but recovered. He was employed by Andrew Dean to deliver the lumber. Julius Craquer—also spelled Kruiger—was hauling his own cut pine. He lost his wagon and the wood, as well as a horse and camp equipage. Hugh Campbell was also hauling his own cut lumber. He too lost his wagon and mules, but also lost 300 rounds of Spencer ammunition worth $21, placing a value to each casing of $.07.[41]

On the same day, at Big Coon Creek near Fort Larned, Captain Nicholas Nolan, 10th Cavalry, reported that 20 Indians attacked the station at four o'clock that afternoon and made off with seven government mules that were being used in escort service from station to station. The soldiers at the station fired at the Indians but could not prevent the theft. One Indian was wounded.[42]

Back on the Smoky Hill trail, Thomas Dixon had a contract to deliver 100 tons of hay for Downer and Monument Station. He lived in Ogden just outside the military reservation of Fort Riley about half-way between Junction City and Manhattan. He employed 20 men from Ogden and brought them down on the Smoky Hill to cut the hay, putting James Wood in charge as foreman. The men had been working for six days and had already gathered more than 60–75 tons of hay, about 15 tons a day. Much of the hay was already stacked at Downer Station. They were cutting the hay about four miles from the station. Captain Martin Mullins had command of a small number of soldiers at Downer. He had assigned three men to protect the hay workers. On September 12, the men were at work in the field when a party of about 30 Indians, believed to be a mix of Kiowa and Cheyenne, suddenly charged the workers. The Indians had been hiding under the cover of some ravines and thus the attack came as a complete surprise. They overpowered the three soldiers, killing them and one of the workers,

41 Andrew Dean Indian Depredation Claim #183; Julius Craquer Indian Depredation Claim #128; Hugh Campbell Indian Depredation Claim #127. Record Group 123.

42 Captain Nicholas Nolan, "Report, Headquarters, Fort Larned, Kansas, September 11, 1867." Record Group 393, Part I, Letters Received, Department of the Missouri, 1867. Box 31.

a Negro. Everybody else safely fled to Downer Station. The Indians took a pair of mules and destroyed a wagon, as well as the hay machinery. The cut hay was burned and destroyed. After the workers made it to Downer they all quit, and as soon as they could, they went back to Ogden. They felt the protection was wholly inadequate and the wages were not worth the risk.[43]

The contracting firm for building the railroad west of Fort Hays, Sharp and Shaw, had another attack on their camp, 30 miles west of the fort. On September 16, two workers took a wagon from camp to a nearby stream so they could fill some barrels with water. They had not gone far before eight Indians suddenly appeared and attacked them. One of the men was killed but the other escaped. The Indians took a mule and horse.[44]

On September 19, a brisk skirmish occurred west of Fort Harker. First Lieutenant Mason Carter was in charge of 33 government wagons which had left Fort Wallace for Fort Harker on September 6. On the way, soldiers were dropped off at Downer Station and Fort Hays. There were also 10 soldiers with the caravan who were still weak and unable to perform duties, recovering from cholera. After leaving Fort Hays, there were only five soldiers left to guard the wagons, two of those men still sick. Thirty-five miles out of Fort Harker, the wagon train was approaching the crossing at Walker's Creek, having just descended from "a very deep ravine, [and] was attacked by a party of Indians estimated at fifty or sixty." Six of the advance wagons were run off by the Indians for three miles. When recovered, they were plundered and everything of value taken, including the mules. Accompanying the attacking Indians were two white men, one of whom ordered Lt. Carter to surrender. Instead, the soldiers fired and one of the white men demanding surrender was shot. The Indians then withdrew. Once order was restored the wagon master got several of the teamsters mounted on mules, and pursuit of the Indians was made. In the chase two more Indians were killed and several wounded. One teamster was killed and three others wounded. The efforts of the wagon master—a man named Robbins—kept everybody from panicking. The six wagons that were earlier spirited away were recovered. The Indians were preparing to burn them when the countercharge of the teamsters caused the warriors to flee.

---

43 Thomas Dixon Indian Depredation Claim #1949 and 2669. Record Group 123.
44 Steven Sharp and Thomas Shaw Indian Depredation Claim #1014, 1015. Record Group 123.

About an hour after the Indians got away, a detachment of Kansas cavalry—commanded by Lieutenant Kane—arrived on the scene and a new pursuit was made to recover the lost stock. After a jaunt of about 20 miles, the hunt was terminated, due to the trail being lost and nightfall arriving. Eighteen mules were captured and four were killed in the initial assault at Walker's Creek.[45]

In early October, before the council talks began for the Medicine Lodge Treaty, 12 Cheyenne warriors made an attack upon a wood cutting detail 12 miles north of Fort Dodge on Little Creek, also called Saw Log Creek. John Coryell had a contract with the government to provide wood to Fort Dodge for fuel. He had 25 men working on the creek, sawing wood and delivering it to Fort Dodge. Each of the men was armed and knew their danger. The foreman, John Felch and a wood hauler, Henry Jones, were killed despite the fact that Felch was armed with two revolvers and a carbine, and Jones had both a revolver and carbine. When they were killed the Cheyenne took their weapons, as well as three horses. The men were just outside of the camp and thus the Indians were able to overtake them. Their bodies were scalped and mutilated. When the murders were reported to the authorities at Fort Dodge, a party of soldiers was sent out and recovered the dead men and brought them back to the post for burial. Apparently these Indians admitted what they had done when they arrived for the talks at Medicine Lodge Creek a few days after the murders.[46]

Just before the council talks began, there was yet another Cheyenne raid. James Smith and Michael Hufurt were hauling freight in two wagons from Ellsworth to Hays City. They were about eight miles east of the site of the old Fort Hays—five miles south of present-day Walker—when they went into their noon camp on October 15. Suddenly 15–20 Dog Soldiers rushed the camp and made off with two horses and two mules, as well as many provisions. The men escaped unhurt.[47]

Three days before the raid against Smith, the peace commissioners arrived at Medicine Lodge Creek. Soon the treaty talks would begin. By the middle of the month there were over 600 whites present and an estimated 5,000 Indians camped nearby. Among the white population were two companies

---

45 First Lieutenant Mason Carter, 5th U.S. Infantry, Regimental Adjutant, "Report Fort Harker, Kansas Sept. 19, 1867." Record Group 393, Part I, Letters Received, Department of the Missouri, 1867. Box 31.

46 John H. Coryell Indian Depredation Claim #3049. Record Group 123.

47 James Smith Indian Depredation Claim #126. Record Group 123.

of the 7th Cavalry, as well as two companies of the 5th Infantry. Major Joel Elliott commanded the 7th Cavalry, as Custer at that time was involved in his personal court-martial at Fort Leavenworth, where he had been found guilty and suspended from the service for a year.[48]

When the council officially began on October 19, only a few Cheyenne were present. The tension mounted, as many feared the Cheyenne would snub the peace talks. There was good reason to think so. Captain James W. Walsh, commander of Fort Arbuckle on the Canadian River in Indian Territory, forwarded a message to military headquarters at Fort Leavenworth, reporting what had been told to him by George Washington, a chief of the Caddocs. Two half-breed Cheyenne—one must think he was referring to Charles and George Bent—had a large amount of money they bragged was recovered from robbing a "fast wagon" [stage coach] and used that to buy some horses that were worth a lot less. They had bragged about being involved with Turkey Leg and the derailment of the train earlier that summer. But more importantly, they said the Cheyenne were not going to the peace council, because of their belief the council was a ruse to "give them cholera or some other disease, and also that they did not want peace." Instead, their chiefs were going to visit with Comanche not at the council, to join the Cheyenne, "to have one big fight with the white people, and let the prairie be all white with Cheyenne bones."[49]

Finally, on October 27, the reluctant Cheyenne came to Medicine Lodge Creek. Discussions with them began in earnest the next day. A concession was made—the Cheyenne could hunt throughout Kansas and up to the Platte River in Nebraska, "provided they remained ten miles from a public road or fort."[50] But when the treaty was ratified by Congress July 25, 1868, and then proclaimed as law August 25, the hunting rights had been changed from permission to hunt up to the Platte River, to instead say that they had "the right to hunt on any lands south of the Arkansas so long as the buffalo may range thereon in such numbers as to justify the chase."[51]

---

48 Kraft, *Ned Wynkoop*, 206–208. For details of Custer's court-martial, see Lawrence Frost, *The Court-Martial of General George Armstrong Custer* (Norman, OK: University of Oklahoma Press, 1967). For events leading up to Custer's court-martial see Broome, *Custer into the West*.

49 Captain James W. Walsh, "Report Headquarters Ft. Arbuckle, C.R. Octo. 4th, 1867." Record Group 393, Part I, Letters Received, Department of the Missouri, 1867.

50 Kraft, *Ned Wynkoop*, 216.

51 Kappler, *Indian Treaties*, 988.

But what exactly did the Cheyenne understand during the council talks? Major Joel Elliott, in his report, did not believe they understood very much. In fact, Elliott did not express any positive thoughts of the peace commission at all, as reflected in a portion of what he wrote in his report:

The first talk was held with the Arapahoes and Cheyennes on the 13th. Nearly all of the Arapahoes were present but very few Cheyennes. The Arapahoes seemed disposed for peace but the Cheyennes were insolent and by their behavior seemed to prefer war. . . . Notwithstanding the Indians did not promise to make peace or even to refrain from hostilities, the commissioners issued large quantities of goods to those present and promised still more if the others would come in. . . .

The time from the 20th to the 27th of the month was consumed in waiting for the Cheyennes to come in. . . . On the 27th the Cheyennes came in; they came up in regular formation of five bands, each about eighty strong, and were armed with guns and pistols as well as bows and arrows. All their movements were directed by signals from a bugle. They presented quite a warlike aspect.

The Cheyennes refused to go to any reservation, did not want goods, and insisted that all the country between the Arkansas and the Platte belonged to them. The only concession they were willing to make was for the railroad to push through this country. The reservation allotted to them . . . they were not even told where it was located, nor indeed that they were to go on any reservation. They are to have the right to hunt between the Arkansas and the Platte and they understand that the country still belongs to them. . . .

The commissioners issued a large number of "Lancaster Rifles" and "Union Arms Company Revolvers" and a large quantity of ammunition to the Indians. The proceedings throughout were conducted in such a manner that anyone unacquainted with the relative strength of the two contracting parties would have imagined the Indians to have been the stronger. . . .

During the entire time of the deliberations a most determined effort was made by a party of the commissioners to induce the Indians to say that the cause of their making war was the burning of their villages last spring, by General Hancock, but unless it was said in private conversations, none of them referred to that event but invariably speak of the war as beginning prior to that affair.

One of the commissioners told the Indians repeatedly that they did right in making war and that he was only sorry that they had not killed more whites. General Augur was the only member of the commission who protested against allowing the Indians to roam between the Arkansas and the Platte and no attention whatever was paid to his remonstrance.[52]

---

52 Major Joel H. Elliott, Report, Camp Det. 7th U.S. Cav. Near Fort Harker Kansas Nov. 5th 1867." Record Group 393, Part I, Letters Received, Department of the Missouri, 1867. Entry 2593.

While Elliott's impressions of the peace efforts indicated failure, an event soon occurred that contributed significantly to establish this fact. Major Meredith H. Kidd wrote a report on November 24, informing authorities of impending trouble. Three days earlier, on November 21, near Fort Zarah, a fight took place between about 30 Cheyenne and a slightly larger number of Kaw warriors. It was first reported that one Kaw was killed and another wounded, but two days later, two of the Cheyenne involved came in to Fort Larned, and said that five Cheyenne were killed and a larger number wounded, many of those severely. Additionally, 12 horses were lost. Kidd went on to say that the Cheyenne "declared their intention to obtain reinforcements and pursue the Kaws."[53] It was this event that put friction on the treaty being successful and ultimately contributed to further bloodshed on the Kansas prairie.

---

53   Major M. H. Kidd, Report, Headquarters Fort Larned, Kansas November 24th, 1867." Record Group 393, Part I, Letters Received, Department of the Missouri, 1867. Entry 2593.

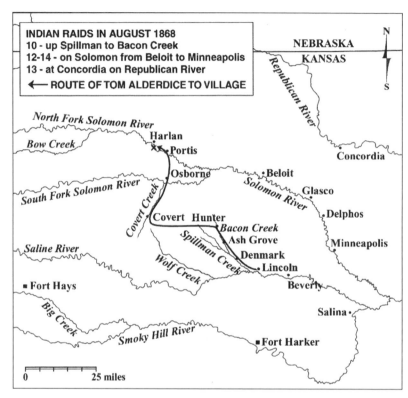

MAP SHOWING AUGUST 1868 RAIDS IN
LINCOLN AND MITCHELL COUNTY, KANSAS; AND
THE ROUTE TOM ALDERDICE TOOK WHEN HE
FOUND TALL BULL'S VILLAGE AFTER THE
SPILLMAN CREEK RAID, MAY 30, 1869.

At about the time Tom found the village, Indians killed Tom's eight-month-old daughter, Alice. Tom later said that Alice was roasted alive. *Courtesy Joan Pennington, Fairfax Station, Virginia.*

CHAPTER TWELVE

Waging Heavy Peace

As long as Indians are allowed to hunt up to our very roads, there will be
constant conflict and consequent murders.

W. T. SHERMAN, LIEUTENANT GENERAL
"REPORT OF THE SECRETARY OF WAR," JULY 1, 1867
SECOND SESSION, FORTIETH CONGRESS

A S IT WAS EACH WINTER, WITH THE EXCEPTION OF 1865,
when the Cheyenne and their allies sought revenge for the atrocities that occurred at Sand Creek the prior November, the winter
of 1867–1868 was relatively free of Indian raids on the roads to Denver. This
is not to say there were not isolated incidents, for there were. O. P. Bicknell was working for Evander Light, who had a contract to provide wood
for the railroad. Light had about 70 men working for him, divided into 10
teams, making both railroad ties and fuel for the locomotives. Bicknell was
working with several men, supervising the wood cutting. Their camp was
about nine miles south of Bunker Hill, Kansas. At about nine o'clock on
the morning of February 20, 1868, as many as 200 Cheyenne charged into
the camp, wounding two men, one of whom later died. The wood chop-
pers lost everything in their camp. Among Bicknell's losses were six oxen
and a wagon, which was burned. Because it was winter, there were several
buffalo robes also lost. Charles Jones lost four mules and a wagon. Two of
three other men also lost their mules and wagons.[1]

---

1   O. P. Bicknell Indian Depredation Claim #3515. Record Group 75. It should be noted here that when
     this claim was investigated by the Department of Interior the agent investigating the claim could not
     find one person who could say anything positive about the character of Bicknell, and thus he could
     not determine whether the claim was authentic or a fraud.

Back in Colorado Territory, on the Denver road in March, the Moore brothers suffered their final raid at Washington Ranch. It was the beginning of a series of raids that once again went along the South Platte trail. A village of about 50 lodges of Sioux and Cheyenne was erected about a half-mile from Washington Ranch, and while camped there on the 20th, the warriors burned the ranch down and destroyed the adobe walls to all the buildings, including the house which had "an adobe wall 252 by 600 feet." Neither Charles nor James was living there at the time. In their absence the property was being managed by someone else. Three days before the burning of the buildings that person had left, in effect abandoning the ranch. Charles described what was destroyed, which ended the history of Washington Ranch:

> They destroyed for us at that time a two-story, shingle roof, adobe walled house worth $3500, all out buildings including the house, and corral [which] were enclosed by an adobe wall 252 by 600 feet. The hay corral was also within the wall, but the Pilgrim house was outside across the road from this enclosure. The Pilgrim house was built of adobe and was 24 by 40 feet and worth $600. There was a frame residence adjoined onto the adobe house inside the corral worth $2100, also an adobe stable 36 feet wide and 250 feet long, with double rows of stalls and an alley between so that you could drive [a wagon] right through those stalls. Those stalls were made out of pine stuff hauled from Denver and the roof was also covered with pine poles and covered with hay like the thatched roof on top of it. The stable and adobe corral together were worth $3000. They burned the frame storage room which was about 12 ft. by 20 feet worth $600. We had 20 cords of wood inside of the enclosure that was worth $20 per cord; we had hauled it 35 miles and some of it 40 miles from Cedar Canyon. They burned, as near as we could estimate, 100 tons of hay which was worth $2500. They destroyed one kitchen stove and two heating stoves worth altogether $75 and household and kitchen furniture worth $200; two mowing machines and hay rakes, $300; seven freight wagons, large wagons worth $100 [each]; six hay racks worth $25 each, and could not have been built for that at that time. On the other side of the river we had a sheep ranch, which they burned, that was worth, with what was left in it, $500.[2]

The railroad had completed track to Cheyenne in late fall, 1867, and once this occurred, there was no longer any sustaining commerce for the Denver road from Julesburg to Denver. By November of that year, freight was

---

2 Charles Moore Indian Depredation Claim #1246. James Moore Indian Depredation Claim #6862 sets the date of the burning of the ranch as March 20. Record Group 123.

shipped via rail to Cheyenne, and from that point freight wagons were used to bring goods into Denver and the surrounding mining communities. Even the stage stations were no longer maintained by Wells Fargo, for mail and passengers used the rail system to Cheyenne.[3] The Denver road was now a thing of the past, and one by one ranch managers left their dwellings. Commerce on the road had disappeared and there was nothing to sustain business. Indians burned other abandoned ranches in the ensuing months, as well as the recently deserted Fort Morgan.

Back in Kansas, raiders struck near present-day Lincoln. On March 30, Frank Schermerhorn had two horses stolen from his ranch. Cheyenne Indians were identified as the perpetrators.[4]

Down on the Santa Fe road, Doctor Lewellen had been operating a trading post on Chisholm Creek near the mouth of the Little Arkansas—near present-day Wichita. Cheyenne Indians made two raids, on April 4 and again on April 6. In the first raid they entered his store—the number of Indians was not given—and robbed Lewellen of much of the provisions he had. Two days later they came back and stole 22 horses and mules. His employee, Phil Block, had lived with the Cheyenne for many years and was fluent in their language, and during the theft of the provisions he pleaded with them not to steal anything, to no avail.[5]

About 50 miles east of where Lewellen suffered his loss by the Cheyenne, Osage Indians committed a murderous raid. Birney Dunn had a ranch in Butler County and had various men working for him, including his brother Samuel T. Dunn. About an hour before sundown on May 17, Samuel and a young man named Anderson were murdered by two Osage Indians. The men were horribly mutilated, including dismembering their heads and fingers. Both men were also scalped. It happened about a half-mile from the ranch home. Soon after the murders, Birney, unaware his brother had just been killed, saw Indians chasing a lot of his horses and two mules. The stock ran past the house and Birney and another man fired at the Osage, who escaped with the two mules. The horses were saved.

---

3   Doris Monahan, *Destination: Denver City*, 242.

4   Frank Shermerhorn Indian Depredation Claim #3491. Record Group 123.

5   Doctor Lewellen Indian Depredation Claim #7331. Record Group 75. George Bent identified Phil Block as one of the men working for the government during the Medicine Lodge treaty. See Hyde, *Life of George Bent*, 201.

The next morning the murders were discovered. Birney Dunn and another man followed the Indian trail for four days, finally arriving in eastern Kansas at the Verdigris River, where the Osage reservation was. Coincidentally, three commissioners were there negotiating a treaty, N. G. Taylor, Thomas Murphy and A. G. Boone. When Dunn brought the charges to the commissioners, the chiefs admitted Osage Indians committed the murders. The two guilty Indians were quickly identified, Wa-Pello and Guernimo, who both belonged to the band of Hard Nose. The two Indians, following the requirements of the treaty, were given up for prosecution. They were taken to Lawrence Kansas, but then released to the sheriff of Butler County, and while being brought back for trial, they escaped.

Back in Ellis County, several young men were living in dug-outs built on Ash Creek, about five miles southeast of Ellsworth, just below Fort Harker. On May 28, Cheyenne Indians raided the dugouts, killing one man and taking the provisions of Matthew McCune, who barely escaped by jumping into Ash Creek, hiding alongside the heavy brush.[6]

As indicated by the attack on McCune, it appeared the Cheyenne were once again ready to commit depredations along the roads and settlements in Kansas. It didn't surprise the settlers, ranch workers or soldiers. To those living and surviving earlier raids, only the naïve would think there was going to be peace following the Medicine Lodge Treaty. But the real beginning of the war wasn't against the whites. The Cheyenne retaliation was in response to the earlier fight between the two tribes near Fort Zarah the prior fall, on November 21. But in the course of this pay back, many white settlers were victimized. Indeed, the Cheyenne acted so brazenly in their assault that the government delayed until late in July in giving them the promised weapons, a perk for signing the Medicine Lodge Treaty.

It is difficult to determine exactly how many Cheyenne were involved in the raid, but when it was over three Cheyenne and one Kaw were wounded.[7] The Cheyenne were led by Tall Bull and Little Robe. The latter had under him 150 warriors. Tall Bull had at least that many and perhaps twice more.[8] The Cheyenne approached the Kaw Agency near Council Grove on June 1.

---

6   Matthew McCune Indian Depredation Claim #621. Record Group 123.

7   Kraft, *Ned Wynkoop*, 233.

8   Reports of A. G. Boone and E. W. Wynkoop, July 20, July 23, 1868. *Annual Report of the Commissioner of Indian Affairs for the Year 1868* (Washington, DC: Government Printing Office, 1868), 66–67.

Settlers in Marion County felt threatened and feared having their property taken or destroyed. Indian agent A. G. Boone and Major Stover started for the Kaw Agency on that day, having received reports of the advancing Cheyenne. They arrived on the morning of June 3, and witnessed the "fight" from the beginning. The Kaws were very excited and ready to defend their agency. As Boone and Stover were talking with the Kaw and assessing the situation, suddenly about 80 Cheyenne, Arapaho and Kiowa charged the Kaw camp, but didn't fire a shot. However, the Kaw did, firing about 20 rounds at the advancing and menacing war party, but the trespassing warriors were too distant to be hit. The Cheyenne then began to form on a nearby hill. Soon a Cheyenne messenger came to Boone, saying they had learned he had come, and requested he visit with them. He and Stover got on horses and rode out to where the Cheyenne were amassed on the hill. The Indians were friendly, and Boone explained he was there to prevent a fight. They expressed a willingness to make peace, but as this conversation was being made, Boone said, ". . . just then the Kaws fired on us and some of the balls passed to Major Stover and myself; some passed over our heads and some fell short; he [Stover] wheeled and went to the Kaws, while the Cheyennes and myself changed position." Soon the firing began on both sides. ". . . they fought as all Indians, by charging, circling, and firing all the while at random; the fight was on open ground, and lasted from three to four hours; we stood over them, seeing it all."[9]

When it was over, the Cheyenne remained in the area for another day or two before returning to their villages near Fort Larned, from where they had come to engage the Kaw. During the time they were near Council Grove, they raided numerous settler homes. James McAlister lived in the area, and when he learned of the hundreds of Cheyenne warriors approaching the settlement, he made a midnight ride on his horse to all the homes near Marion, telling them of the advancing war party. George Morrell lived 11 miles from Marion; he fled to the town for protection. He stayed away for a month, unable to tend to his crops. All the settlers expected the Cheyenne to return in larger numbers.[10] David Lucus also stayed away for a month. Before fleeing he talked to a few Cheyenne, who said they were with Little

9   A. G. Boone Report, June 4, 1868, *Annual Report*, 64–65.
10   George Morrell Indian Depredation Claim #3616. Record Group 75.

Robe. Lucas estimated there were 400 warriors. Each warrior rode one horse and led another. The warriors were spread out for a distance of seven miles. He had been alerted by McAlister at two o'clock in the morning of June 1. At daylight he took his family and some clothing and fled to Marion.[11]

John Nance didn't flee right away, and on the evening of June 1, about 20 Cheyenne came to his house. He fed them, but then they robbed him of a gun and took two of his cows to feed the other Indians. After they left, he took his family and retreated to Marion.[12] Aaron Grigsby was living on Muddy Creek about six miles from Marion. About 30 Indians had stopped at his house at five in the morning, on June 1. They said there were 1,500 warriors coming to fight the Kaws. They came into Aaron's yard and spilled over into his corn field. He had several acres of corn which was about four feet tall. The Indians turned their horses on the corn and vegetables. The entire crop was destroyed. They stayed about two hours, during which time he fed them everything he had to cook. The Indians killed several of his chickens. Before they left they ransacked the house, stealing everything they wanted. Once they departed, he took his wife and children and fled into Marion. When he came back the contents of his house were destroyed or stolen. Dishes were broken and the bedding was torn up. Everything in the house was destroyed. Aaron's young family consisted of five boys, the youngest just seven. They were all frightened by the presence of the Indians.[13]

Homer Winters was also alerted in the early morning hours of June 1 by the warnings of James McAlister. He too took his family to Marion for protection. He lost his crops because, and like the others, he stayed away for a month. All the settlers feared another attack.[14] Robert McAlister—the brother of James—had a similar experience as Williams. He said when everyone got to Marion they were advised to remain there for the next month, until soldiers could come out and provide protection. During that time the refugees built a seven-foot stone wall around the Marion court house for protection.[15]

11   David Lucas Indian Depredation Claim #1169. Record Group 123.

12   John Nance Indian Depredation Claim #178. Record Group 123.

13   Aaron Grigsby Indian Depredation Claim #178. Record Group 75. Also, claim #175. Record Group 123. A report in Grigsby's file (RG 75) by Wynkoop, dated June 12, says "One Kaw, three Cheyenne and a few horses wounded, two Indians houses burned and several others robbed, together with several houses belonging to whites plundered of everything, was about the amount of damage done from the raid."

14   Homer Winters Indian Depredation Claim #3773. Record Group 75. See also claim # 1170. Record Group 123.

15   Robert McAlister Indian Depredation Claim #3639. Record Group 75.

The next day, June 2, Patrick O'Byrne, who lived 12 miles west of Council Grove on Dodd Creek, was visited in the morning by several Cheyenne, who took over his house and stayed there for two days. He didn't go to Marion. Instead he took his family and fled to Cottonwood Falls. When he returned several days later the household contents were pretty much all destroyed.[16]

After the fight with the Kaw on June 3, it appeared the Cheyenne were upset that more retaliation didn't occur in their brief skirmish. They took it out on area settlers. When it was over, Wynkoop wrote a report giving the Cheyenne version of what happened. He noted that when the warriors approached the Kaw agency before the skirmish, they did not disturb the area settlers, though they did take seven cattle and slaughtered them for food, as the area was devoid of any game for the Cheyenne to procure. The settlers all became frightened and fled when they saw the warriors in the neighborhood, but Wynkoop insisted they did not disturb the abandoned homes. Upon leaving after the skirmish, the Cheyenne came across a large cattle drive coming up from Texas. Wynkoop said the man in charge gave the Indians four steers for food. According to Little Robe, that is all that happened in the settlements.[17]

Little Robe was truthful in the first part of his statement, for the most part, but clearly untruthful in his second part. A. G. Boone said the Cheyenne burned two buildings owned by half-breeds, and robbed three other homes.[18] One of those homes burned may have belonged to Louis Pashall. He was married to a Kaw woman and had several small children. The Cheyenne came to his home—two miles from the Kaw agency—at about noon June 3, and burned it to the ground. He lost everything in the house.[19] Moise Bellmard was also married to a Kaw woman named Hattie and had several children. Their home was a half-mile closer to the Kaw Agency than Pashall's home. It too was burned to the ground, and everything inside destroyed.[20] William Crowe lived about three miles from Council Grove. Indians ransacked his home and then burned it to the ground. Everything was lost. Crowe reported that his neighbor, James Omeshe, also had his

---

16   Patrick O'Byrne Indian Depredation Claim #177. Record Group 123.
17   Wynkoop, Report, June 12, 1868. *Annual Report*, 65–66.
18   Boone, Report, June 4, 1868. *Annual Report*, 65.
19   Louis Pashall Indian Depredation Claim #200. Record Group 123.
20   Moise Bellmard Indian Depredation Claim #199. Record Group 123.

house burned to the ground. The two men shared a business together and their buildings adjoined each other.[21] Omeshe said that the burning happened at about five o'clock in the afternoon on June 3. The Cheyenne entered his dwelling and set it on fire, destroying everything inside.[22]

About a half-mile from the Kaw Agency resided William Polk, who lived there with his three sons and daughter. The older son, John, was one of the first to alert the Kaws of the approaching Cheyenne. The Agency was about two miles from Council Grove. John stayed away from his house until after the Cheyenne left and when he went back he found everything in the house was destroyed or stolen. Feather beds and pillows were ripped to shreds, and everything of value in the house that was not stolen was purposely broken and rendered useless.[23] Hubert Pappan lived about a mile from the Kaw Agency. His house was also raided and everything inside destroyed. Elizabeth Pappan was at home, when at noon the Indians entered the house and began their destruction.[24] The same thing happened to the house of William Polk, who was probably the brother of John. Earlier that day, Polk had volunteered, at the request of Major Stover, to travel to Fort Riley to request military support. Later that day, while he was gone, the Indians ransacked his house and took everything of value.[25]

As the war party retreated further from the Kaw Agency, they still continued their raids against settlers. Seven miles from Council Grove, along the Santa Fe road, David Robertson had his home on Elm Creek. During the afternoon of June 3, about 50 Cheyenne entered his home, took what they wanted, which included all the food, cutlery, ammunition, and anything else of value that the warriors desired. Robertson's wife Caroline, and friend Elizabeth Abbington, were in the home when the Cheyenne came in. The Indians destroyed the furniture in the house.[26] Robinson Lockwood also lived on Elm Creek. The Indians kidnapped Caroline and Elizabeth, forcing them to go to the Lockwood dwelling about a mile away. Before they came to the Lockwood home, the Cheyenne entered the home of a neighbor named Sheppard and trashed it. Ellen Lockwood saw the

21   William Crowe Indian Depredation Claim #missing. Entry 700. Record Group 75.
22   James Omeshe Indian Depredation Claim #605, Entry 700. Record Group 75.
23   John Polk Indian Depredation Claim #1212. Record Group 123.
24   Hubert Pappan Indian Depredation Claim #179. Record Group 123.
25   William Polk Indian Depredation Claim #135. Record Group 123.
26   David Robertson Indian Depredation Claim #182. Record Group 123.

Indians enter that home, and fearing for her safety, she fled to Council Grove. When the family later returned, their home was equally trashed and important household goods stolen.[27] Elizabeth lived on Four Mile Creek with her husband, Lafayette Abbington. While she was undergoing her kidnapping ordeal, her husband was outside his house and he saw the Indians enter it, robbing it of everything of value.[28] Also living on Four Mile Creek was Charles Sheppard. Like his neighbors, the contents of his house were stolen, including his carbine and pistol.[29] When Thomas Tedstone saw the Cheyenne approaching his house that same day, he also fled. His home was along the Santa Fe road, on Six Mile Creek. When he returned the next day, as with everyone else, he found the contents of his home either destroyed or stolen.[30]

John Edwards also lived on Six Mile Creek. He lost 15 cattle, all taken for the Cheyenne to eat. The Cheyenne later said Edwards willingly gave the cattle to them, but Edwards said it was under duress. Perhaps compounding the difference of understanding was what the Cheyenne thought about a letter they had, signed by Wynkoop, which they gave to Edwards as they took the cattle. The letter stated that the Cheyenne were there "to protect their borders against the Kaw and Osage."[31] Possibly the Cheyenne felt this permitted them to take provisions. Asbury Dickinson was another neighbor on Six Mile Creek. He lost one heifer and had his household goods stolen and destroyed.[32]

J. H. Costello lived on the Santa Fe road along Lost Springs, in Marion County. He had a ranch serving travelers. When he saw about 30 Indians approaching the store, he, a herder and his store clerk locked up the front of the building and would not let the Indians in. The warriors were insolent and demanded to be let in. They were all armed with rifles, pistols and bows and arrows. They threatened violence if they did not get what they wanted. While this confrontation was going on in front of the store, several warriors went to the rear, where they found a crib of corn, and where the kitchen was separated. They entered the kitchen and took what goods they wanted, took

27   Robinson Lockwood Indian Depredation Claim #201. Record Group 123.
28   Lafayette Abbington Indian Depredation Claim #203. Record Group 123.
29   Charles Sheppard Indian Depredation Claim #205. Record Group 123.
30   Thomas Tedstone Indian Depredation Claim #2753, 202. Record Group 123.
31   John M. Edwards Indian Depredation Claim #2754 and 133. Record Group 123.
32   Ashbusy Dickinson Indian Depredation Claim #204. Record Group 123.

the corn, destroyed the crib and burned the stable and hay that was stacked out back. Costello was able to keep the Indians from forcefully entering the store building. The three men were armed and the Indians apparently did not want to risk death by storming the front of the store.[33]

Twenty-two miles west of Council Grove, Charles Owens lived on the Santa Fe road at Drummond Creek. He fled his house when the Indians came through on their way to the Kaw Agency, and he stayed away until the Indians were gone. When he returned to his ranch on June 4, he found the place ransacked. He was robbed of clothing, bedding and other household goods that belonged to his wife and children. His wife Mary stated everything of value in the house was taken.[34]

With all of this devastation going on in Morris County, and the Cheyenne hanging around for several days, obviously taking whatever they wanted from any home they came across, it was clear something must be done. The insolent Cheyenne needed a response from the government. They could not go unpunished, given all the property damage to so many settlers in Marion County. On June 6, a letter was written, addressed to Governor Samuel Crawford, informing him that at least eight families had been robbed and the Cheyenne were killing all the stock, leaving the poor with nothing. They had even taken "baby close [clothes]." The letter acknowledged no one was killed ". . . but it is bout [sic] as bad to take the last head of stock from a poor man. . . . They [sic] is no use of my trying to tell you of the damage that they have done. . . ." The letter pleaded for protection, saying the residents cannot tend to their crops and are all staying away in Marion.[35]

When word of the extent of depredations against citizens reached the government, Cheyenne agent Wynkoop investigated the matter. In his letter to Thomas Murphy, Superintendent of Indian Affairs, he basically staked his reputation in defending Little Robe's declaration that the Cheyenne did little more than take 11 cows for provisions, and did not molest any settlers. Wynkoop gave his reasons: "I am perfectly confident that Little Robe's statement is perfectly correct, for the reason that with my whole

33   J. H. Costello Indian Depredation Claim #2034. Record Group 123..

34   Charles Owens Indian Depredation Claim #136, 3874. Record Group 123.

35   A. A. Moore, Letter to Governor Crawford, June 3, 1868. Archives Department, 970; 516. Kansas State Historical Society, Topeka, Kansas.

connection with the Indians belonging to my agency there has been no instance in which I have been deceived by them with reference to a matter of that character."[36] Wynkoop was either incredibly naïve or duped. It was all an ugly and untimely prelude to much more deadly deception—deception he would finally admit—that would follow early in August.

Back near Fort Hays, Isaac Losee had a contract to freight for the military, back and forth from the different forts along the Smoky Hill trail, as well as occasional trips to Denver. This time he was taking freight to Denver, and was about 60 miles west of Fort Hays, perhaps a mile east of Kyote railroad station, when he put his freight wagons in camp. It was early June when the attack came; suddenly between 50 and 60 Dog Soldier Indians attacked his camp, ". . . whooping and firing army pistols there at, making such a noise that they frightened the mules and the whole camp." Four men were guarding the mules and fired at the Indians but to no avail. Forty-one mules were lost. The remaining stock was found scattered about on the prairie. The Indians were identified as Cheyenne under a warrior named Powder Face. One herder guard—Hugh Bay—was badly wounded and taken back to Fort Hays, where he eventually recovered.[37]

The immediate result of the Cheyenne raid against the Kaw was an order dated June 25, by N. G. Taylor, the Commissioner of Indian Affairs, to Superintendent Thomas Murphy. He stated that the arms and ammunition, scheduled to be distributed to the Cheyenne, would now not be given. In order to get them, they would first have to prove their peace to the whites, by first abiding by the terms of the Medicine Lodge Treaty. There was no date set for when the arms might be distributed, but clearly, it was going to take time, time for the Cheyenne to show by their behavior that they would keep the peace.[38] General Sheridan wrote to Governor Samuel Crawford on June 16 that he had ordered portions of the cavalry to scout up to Marion Center as well as to the mouth of the Little Arkansas, which would hopefully assure the settlers just affected by the Cheyenne raid in that area that all was well. He then assured the governor that the Cheyenne and Arapaho

36   E. W. Wynkoop Report, June 12, 1868, *Annual Report*, 66.
37   Isaac Losee Indian Depredation Claim #2573. Record Group 123. George Bent says there was a Cheyenne named Powder Face who was a Dog Soldier warrior with Tall Bull and killed at Summit Springs in 1869. Hyde, *Life of George Bent*, 334
38   N. G. Taylor to Thos. Murphy, June 25, 1868, *Annual Report*, 66.

would keep peace, and "do not intend to engage on hostilities. It is small prowling bands that may give us trouble."[39] What soon unfolded was much more than small prowling bands. It would shock Wynkoop and surprise Sheridan. And it led to Black Kettle's death.

The annuities promised to the various tribes of the Medicine Lodge Treaty came to Fort Larned a month later, and Wynkoop reported back regarding how the Cheyenne felt when informed no arms or ammunition were being distributed to them. They refused any of the other goods and said they would wait to receive annuities until they got the arms and ammunition. They were disappointed, but said they would comply with the demand. Still, they felt, first, they were not being treated fairly and that the whites were violating the treaty; and second, they cited several instances where whites had mistreated them and they did not retaliate. Wynkoop ended his report with a plea that the arms be distributed "as soon as possible, and am in hopes daily of receiving an order to that effect."[40]

Commissioner Taylor soon received reports that the Cheyenne were threatening to go to war if they didn't get their arms. Consequently, on July 23, he sent an order to Superintendent Murphy rescinding his earlier order regarding the arms and ammunition, and instead deferred the decision to distribute back to Murphy and Wynkoop, asking them to confer together and decide when the Cheyenne could receive their weapons. On August 1, at Fort Larned, Murphy met with Wynkoop and all the tribes involved with the Medicine Lodge Treaty except the Cheyenne, who were not there. They were expected to report to the fort on August 3, at which time Wynkoop, upon his assurance the Cheyenne would reciprocate peace, would then be permitted to distribute the arms and ammunition to the Cheyenne.[41]

At this point there is an historical controversy that bubbles to the surface. On what day did Wynkoop distribute the weapons and ammunition to the Cheyenne? The Arapahoe were given theirs on August 1, but the Cheyenne could not be given theirs that day because they were not present, and not expected for two more days. That means the earliest Wynkoop could give the weapons out was August 3, and indeed, that is the date some historians

39   Maj. Gen. P. H. Sheridan, to S. G. Crawford, June 16, 1868. Kansas State Historical Society, Archives Department 970.56 513, Topeka, Kansas

40   E. W. Wynkoop to Thos. Murphy, July 20, 1868. *Annual Report*, 66–67.

41   Taylor to Murphy, July 23, Murphy to Taylor, August 1, 1868. *Annual Report*, 67–69.

say the Cheyenne received them.[42] Yet other historians insist the Cheyenne did not receive their arms until August 9, making it impossible for the Cheyenne to have the arms to use in the deadly raid that began 75 miles northwest on August 10.[43] Regardless of where the truth might lie, Indians were splendidly armed since 1864, and there were many other ways in which warriors could procure arms: from traders, both legal and illegal; from raids, in trades with other Indians, and of course, from the government.[44] And it really did not matter when Wynkoop distributed the arms, because David Butterfield, with George Bent as his employee and translator, had illegally armed the Cheyenne in the early spring.[45]

Getting arms from the government bothered nearly all people living on the plains in the 1860s. The letter Captain Barnitz wrote to his wife, when he saw Wynkoop begin to distribute the weapons to his tribes on July 31, 1867, reflected the standard sentiment on the plains at that time: "I believe—maybe they will feel very brave when they get those arms, and will begin to turn their thoughts to war again! Who knows. It is certainly very foolish to fight Indians with one hand, and to make presents, and give them arms with the other!"[46] Captain Myles Keogh wondered the same thing earlier, in an article in the *New York Times*: "He asks why is it that the Interior Department, thorough its agents, should furnish them with the very means of committing massacres, while the War Department is furnishing troops to prevent them. There must be a screw loose somewhere."[47]

Unknown to Barnitz when he sent that letter to his wife, indeed the Cheyenne were turning their thoughts to war again, and it appears they couldn't wait to get started. It began quite suddenly, and violently, on Spillman Creek and the Saline River in Lincoln County, on August 10. It continued further north into Mitchell County for several more days. When it was

42 See Marion H. Garfield, "Defense of the Kansas Frontier 1868–1869," *The Kansas Historical Quarterly*, Number 5, November 1932, 456.

43 Kraft, *Ned Wynkoop*, 238–239.

44 I used the phrase "splendidly armed" to support George A. Forsyth's same phrase in his report of his fight with the Cheyenne at Beecher's Island September 17–25, 1868. See his report, "On Delaware Creek, Republican River September 19, 1868": "They were splendidly armed with Spencer and Henry rifles." Record Group 393, Part I, Letters Received, Department of the Missouri, 1868.

45 David Butterfield Indian Depredation Claim #531. Record Group 75.

46 Utley, *Life in Custer's Cavalry*, 174–175.

47 *New York Times*, January 13, 1867.

over nearly two dozen men and women were killed, one teenager taken captive, as well as two children, who were soon released, and several women were viciously gang raped. Wynkoop wrote in one of his reports, seeking an explanation for why this outbreak occurred, saying that the younger warriors of the Cheyenne were particularly angered at the government for the delay in the distribution of the weapons. And, as Wynkoop reported it, "had I been allowed to issue the arms and ammunition to them at the time promised, they still would have been contented, *from the fact of them having means to procure game*; but the failure of the government to fulfill its promises . . . incensed some of the wilder spirits among them, and, consequently, the outrages committed on the Saline River."[48] Sherman immediately saw the outrages as an act of war. That the chiefs did not restrain their warriors from committing the acts, plus the fact that the tribes did not give up the guilty for punishment, led Sherman to conclude that the Medicine Lodge Treaty "is therefore clearly broken by them. . . ."[49] Superintendent of Indian Affairs Thomas Murphy concurred: "They have violently broken their treaty pledges. . . ."[50]

This was the fulcrum that ultimately led to the winter campaign that resulted in the destruction of Black Kettle's village—and his death, as well as that of his wife—on the Washita River in present-day Oklahoma, on November 27, 1868.

One thing that should be cleared up is the issue of the necessity of the Indians to have arms and ammunition in order to hunt and provide meat for their tribes. People who were living on the plains and who understood Indian culture knew better. One journalist said it this way: ". . . the Indian never kills the buffalo with a gun, but always uses his bow and arrow, saving the gun to go to war with."[51] George Bent explained why Indians never used guns to hunt: "Arrows were *always* used by the hunters, *to avoid quarrels*, for each man had his marks on his arrows and he could tell by the arrows which animals belonged to him. *If guns had been used there would have been constant squabbling*."[52] Clearly, Wynkoop was either naïve or did not fully

---

48   E. W. Wynkoop to Charles E. Mix, October 7, 1868. *Annual Report*, 82, emphasis added.
49   W. T. Sherman, "Headquarters Military Division of the Missouri," September 17, 1868. *Annual Report*, 76.
50   Thomas Murphy to Charles E. Mix, September 19, 1868. *Annual Report*, 76.
51   *Junction City Weekly Union*, November 28, 1868.
52   Hyde, *Life of George Bent*, 199–200, emphasis added.

LON SCHERMERHORN AND FAMILY.

The Schermerhorn ranch was a gathering place for families in Lincoln County during Indian raids, from 1867 to 1869. It was here that General P. H. Sheridan enlisted nearly two dozen civilians to join with Col. George A. Forsyth's company of scouts. Most of the men who enlisted here fought at Beecher's Island, September 17–25, 1868. Mrs. Schermerhorn, as a young teenager, gave birth to her first child while Indians were attacking the ranch in 1868. *Courtesy of Mary Jo (Schermerhorn) Dolinsky, Fort Calhoun, Nebraska.*

understand Indian culture, by believing the Indians needed their arms and ammunition to hunt game. *That was not the case.* The buffalo hunt was one of the more manly things a warrior could do, other than touching an enemy with a coup stick during a battle. The race to get close to a buffalo and bring him down with an arrow showed exceptional courage and masterful horsemanship. All of that was lost when guns were used for hunting. The buffalo hunt was an important part of Indian culture, and extended way beyond simply procuring food. The use of guns took away the evidence Indians had for knowing when an Indian distinguished himself in a hunt. No, the Indians did not need nor want the guns and ammunition for hunting purposes. Wynkoop should have known better. Clearly, Indians would occasionally use a gun to shoot an animal—when convenient, but never during their organized hunts, as Bent makes clear. And the argument the Cheyenne was giving to Wynkoop and others, was that the guns were needed for their organized hunt. It was a deceptive lie.

The August raids on the Saline and Solomon rivers have been detailed in *Dog Soldier Justice: The Ordeal of Susanna Alderdice in the Kansas Indian War,* and does not need to be again described here.[53] However, it would be useful to identify the more horrifying settler accounts, and look at those alongside what Wynkoop reported in his investigation of the matter. It is ironic that Wynkoop penned his letter about the distribution of arms to the Cheyenne on August 10, for it was the very day of the deadly and murderous Cheyenne raid. His next letter on August 19 conceded being deceived: "I am sorry to admit, that the Cheyennes are guilty." He recognized that he would not be able to get the guilty ones turned over to the government for prosecution—a treaty requirement—and he instead devised a plan of letting the Cheyenne who were committed to peace—the majority of the elders—to live next to Fort Larned, where they would be safe and where the government would see that they would not be involved in the ensuing war. This would then allow for the guilty parties to be found and punished.[54] His advice was ignored.

Wynkoop interviewed Little Rock (not Little Robe, who was in the Kaw skirmish) and gave the Cheyenne version of the raid. According to Little Rock, the war party consisted of 10 Sioux [Oglala] lodges—which would mean about 20 warriors—four Arapaho and the rest, about 200 Cheyenne. The Cheyenne represented nearly all of the young warriors in the Southern Cheyenne camps. Little Rock said their intent was to strike the Pawnee in a retaliatory raid for the August 1867, fight they had with the Cheyenne near present-day Lexington, Nebraska, when Turkey Leg was defeated by Major Frank North's Pawnee Scouts. When they got up to the Saline River, the majority of the warriors turned toward the white settlements along the river, only a small party of 20 fighters continuing in the northern path to the Pawnee village. Once on the Saline, White Antelope's brother, Oh-E-Ah-Mohe—White Antelope was the principal chief killed at Sand

53   Broome, *Dog Soldier Justice,* 7–34.
54   E. W. Wynkoop to Thomas Murphy, August 19, 1868. *Annual Report,* 71.

Creek in 1864—and another Cheyenne, Red Nose, went to the first house and captured a woman (Mary Jane Bacon), bringing her to the village. This surprised the rest of the Indians, who then took possession of her and returned her to her house. The two Indians had raped her before bringing her to camp. Wynkoop's report then said after the woman was returned to her house, the Indians left the Saline and went north 30 miles to the Solomon River. When in sight of the settlements, the white men fired on them. Oh-E-Ah-Mohe fired back but missed, and another Indian killed one of the white men. Then a woman was killed. Until that point, most of the warriors admonished those warriors who participated in the raid, "but finding it useless to contend against these outrages being committed without bringing a strife among themselves, they gave way, and all went in together. They then went to another house in the same settlements, and there killed two men and took two little girls prisoners."[55] As when Wynkoop heard about the skirmish with the Kaw, and the ensuing depredations against settlers near Council Grove, he was not told the horrific truth. Indeed, Edmund Guerriere, an interpreter who lived among the Cheyenne for years, was present, and in his sworn affidavit, stated the warriors were composed of Indians from the bands of Little Rock—whom Wynkoop turned to for the Indian version of the deadly raid—Black Kettle, Medicine Arrow and Bull Bear, led by Oh-E-Ah-Mohe and Red Nose.[56]

The events from what the military found, according to General Sherman:

> On the 10th they appeared on the Saline, north of Fort Harker, where the settlers received them kindly; they were given food and coffee, but pretended to be offended because it was in "tin cups," they threw it back in the faces of the women and began at once to break up furniture and set fire to the houses. They seized the women and ravished them, perpetrating atrocities which could only have been the result of premeditated crime. Here they killed two men. Thence they crossed over to the settlements on the Solomon, where they continued to destroy houses and property, to ravish all females, and killed thirteen men. Going on to the Republican, they killed two more men and committed other acts of brutal atrocity.[57]

---

55   E. W. Wynkoop to Thomas Murphy, August 19, 1868. *Annual Report*, 72.

56   Edmund Guerriere, "Headquarters Department of the Missouri, In the Field, Medicine Bluff Creek, February 9, 1869," *Report of the Secretary of War*, 2d Session, 41st Congress, House of Representatives, Ex. Doc.1, Pt. 2 (Washington, DC: Government Printing Office, 1869), 41.

57   Lieutenant General W. T. Sherman, "Report November 1, 1868." *Executive Documents of The House or Representatives, Third Session of the Fortieth Congress 1868–1869* (Washington, DC: Government Printing Office, 1869), 3

General Philip Sheridan added more detail, saying the women were raped from 40 to 50 times, "and, in one instance, the fortieth or fiftieth savage drew his saber and used it on the person of the woman in the same manner."[58]

That person so abused was 22-year-old Mary Jane Bacon, who was living on Bacon Creek—a small creek that flows into Spillman Creek, about 18 miles north of the Saline River—with her husband David and their toddler son. She took the time shortly after her trauma to give a sworn statement to what happened:

> on the 10th day of November, AD 1864 I was married to one David G. Bacon, that in the fall of AD 1865 I removed with my husband to Lecompton, Kansas and that in the spring of AD 1867 I removed with my husband to Spillman Creek Lincoln County in the state of Kansas where my husband provided to erect a house and improve a farm under the homestead act, that the country was sparsely settled and that the nearest neighbor was 1½ mile distant [Simeon Shaw house], that while living there on the 10th day of August AD 1868 the house was visited by three Indians, I being in the house with my infant child [William Edmund, born August 17, 1866], my husband being in the field at work, that the Indians first provided to take the dishes out of the cupboard that I told them, they must not disturb anything, that one of them grabbed for a revolver which was in the cupboard, which I endeavored to get away from him—but failed to do so, I hollered for my husband whereupon one of the Indians got on his pony and rode off towards my husband, while the other two remained at the house, my husband as he afterwards stated to me, heard me holler and started to the house, but met the Indian who pointed the revolver at him and compelled him to run the other way and that my husband did not return to the house at all, that when my husband had been driven away the other Indian returned to the house. While the one Indian was absent, the other two Indians knocked me down senseless — when I came to, one of them was holding me down and the other violating my person, that afterwards the one who had been holding me down violated my person while the other held me, that subsequently the Indian who had been in the field returned and violated my person, and that then they commenced to search the house and carried away and destroyed property for which my husband made out a bill and placed in the hands of General Sheridan and to which reference is hereby made for a part of the claim.
>
> I further state that one of the said Indians was painted red and called himself a Sioux Chief—he was a short heavy set man with a large nose and wore a cross hanging from his neck, the second of said Indians was painted red and had one black stripe running down the face under each eye, and called himself an Arrappahoe

---

58   General Philip H. Sheridan, "Report," *Messages and Documents of the Second Session of the Forty-First Congress, Volume I* (Washington, DC: Government Printing Office, 1869), 48.

[sic], he was a tall man, the third Indian had a black stripe under each eye and a black stripe across his forehead[,] was a tall man and called himself a Cheyenne and I further state, that after said three Indians had abused my person, they took my clothing out in the yard and stomped on them and tore them to pieces together with sheets, bedclothes, household linen, and then carrying away with them what they did not destroy, leaving the house entirely destitute, they then left when I started into the field with my infant to hunt my husband whom I failed to find, that I saw the three Indians going in the direction of my nearest neighbor's house, whereby I was inclined to start with my child to the next nearest neighbors about 2½ miles distant, that on the road there I heard guns firing and soon after saw persons riding fast on horseback and supposed they were white men who had been hunting and had seen Indians and were going home to protect their families—I was in a valley at the time, heard some one hollering on the bluff above me and when I looked up saw they were Indians, that I then started with my child in my arms, to get into the timber. One Indian rode between me and the timber who pointed his revolver at me to stop me and hollered to the rest—Squaw! Squaw! Then 40 or 50 Indians came down and surrounded me, then all the Indians got off of their ponys [sic] when 4 Indians seized me, threw her down and one held each hand and each foot—my child was lying on the ground near me, there a lot of Indians again violated my person a lot of them would violate my person and go off and then another lot would come and do the same thing, I fainted and upon coming to was again violated by still another lot of Indians then I saw a man among the Indians whom from his features I knew to be a white man [probably Edmund Guerrier or George Bent] and implored his protection and asked him what he would think if he had a wife in my place and if he would not take his revolver and guard me, he drew his revolver out of his belt and said "I will"—I at this time was so much exhausted that I immediately fainted again when I came to, he the white man, was gone and when I raised up other Indians, about a dozen came down the hill and treated me as the others had done, that I was then so exhausted that I could not sit up or help myself, that upon being allowed a short time to revive myself, I was put upon a horse and told to go to one of the neighbor's houses, where they intended to camp that night. The horse had been stolen from a Mr. Shaw whose wife and sister-in-law the Indians then had as prisoners—Mr. Shaw was my nearest neighbor to whose house I saw the three Indians going after they left my house. Where Mr. Shaw and family now reside I do not know.

I further state, that with my child in my lap, I rode to a branch of Spillman Creek and made believe, I was hunting a crossing by riding up and down the creek until after dark, that I might thereby deceive the Indians and then turn and go the other way [east] to a settlement 16 miles distant called the Indiana settlement—In the dusk I saw the Indians ride down and cross the creek—as I was in a little bend of the creek, I suppose they did not see me, I then turned my horse and started for the aforesaid settlement. After riding about eleven miles having no saddle or bridle and being unable to guide the horse, I fell from the horse and into the creek [Lost Creek or Beaver Creek] in which there was however but little water, I crawled out upon the bank with my child, where I laid till next morning, when I started to walk towards the settlement and heard someone calling my name [Mart Hendrickson] when I answered and thereupon settlers from Indiana settlement came up to me—I went with them to the settlement where I found my husband. And we afterward took refuge in Fort Harker—I further state that I from said time and up to the present spring [June 7, 1869] I have been sick and entirely unable to work and earn a living and that even now I am not fully restored to my health, which sickness was and is caused by the treatment received from said Indians—that my husband in consequence of the facts stated has grown cold and harsh towards me and has lately entirely left and abandoned me, that I have no means of living and am a charge of at present with two small children upon my father and friends—the Indians I saw after leaving the house were painted differently as were those I saw at the house and called themselves Sioux, Arrappahoes [sic], and Cheyennes, they said they know all the people on the creek and their voices and had been around spying all summer....[59]

Military records noted two citizens were killed along the Saline River, 17 on the Solomon River, and another three killed on the Republican River.[60] It is difficult today to learn the names of all the victims, as frontier newspapers were not yet near the scenes of the Indian raids, but from records in the National Archives, one can put together this much: Other victims of rape included Mrs. Simeon Shaw and her 16-year-old sister, Miss Foster. They were raped repeatedly alongside Mary Jane Bacon for part of their ordeal. Simeon Shaw was gravely wounded by a war-club blow to the head.[61] By August 12, the band of Indians had moved on up to the Solomon River in Mitchell County, just east of present-day Beloit. They remained there for three days and committed numerous atrocities. At one home they killed David Bogardus and his brother-in-law, Braxton Bell, after whipping them and making them run around their cabin. They also raped the wives of both men, Hester Ann Bell/Bogardus and 21-year-old Elizabeth, Braxton's wife. The warriors tried to take Elizabeth captive but "when a short distance from the house, she jumped from the horse and started to run back but was shot

59   David and Mary Jane Bacon Indian Depredation Claim # not given. Entry 210, Box 6 Record Group 75. The file has a statement from Pine Ridge acknowledging that the Sioux involved in the August raids were Oglala, which probably means once again Pawnee Killer's band was present.

60   Eric S. Johnson, compiled by, *No Greater Calling: A Chronological Record of Sacrifice and Heroism During the Western Indian Wars, 1865–1898* (Atglen, PA: Schiffer Military History 2012), 83–84.

61   Simeon Shaw Indian Depredation Claim #6441. Record Group 123.

by an Indian."[62] She lived for two weeks and then died. In the dead arms of her husband Braxton was found his nine-month-old daughter, Ella, still alive but horribly mutilated about the face with a sharp spear.

Inside the ransacked home were two nieces, daughters of Aaron Bell. Those girls, eight-year-old Ester and six-year-old Margaret, were taken prisoner and finally released later when the band returned down to the Saline River, and were spotted and chased by a company of 7th Cavalry troopers that had just arrived from Fort Zarah, commanded by Captain Frederick Benteen. The Indians let the two young captives go because they were hindering their escape from Benteen's trailing troopers. The girls wandered alone and hungry on the prairie for two days before finally being found and rescued. Young Ester later recalled her ordeal:

> David Bogardus was my uncle. I was visiting at his house on the day the Indians came, with my sister. My sister was six years old and I was eight. After they killed my uncle and raided the house, they took me and my little sister and kept us until the next day [August 13] and dropped us on the prairie. We wandered there. We slept out two nights with nothing to eat, until a searching party found us and took us to Fort Harper [Fort Harker] and turned us over to our father. . . . The Indians were Cheyennes and Arapahoes. They took us over on the Saline. There must have been 50 or 60 Indians in the party, some squaws with them. . . . There were no squaws at first with them but we met some others who joined the party among which were some squaws.[63]

While Indians remained in the vicinity until August 14, the band responsible for the murders at the Bogardus/Bell home left the area the next day and went back to the Saline, where Captain Benteen encountered them and effectively drove them away.

On August 13, John Baertoche went on a buffalo hunt in celebration of his son's third birthday. He took with him his neighbor Henry Hewitt and Henry's young son, Major. They only got about a mile or two from their home when the Indians surprised them, killing both men and wounding young Major. The boy ended up back at the Hewitt home, which the Indians

---

62   1924 news clipping, date and paper not given. Mitchell County Historical Society, Beloit, Kansas.

63   Hester Snow Indian Depredation Claim #10350. Record Group 75. Ester said the girls slept in an abandoned dugout the first night, and outside under a big tree the second night. They were found the following afternoon by two settlers who first thought they might be Indians and were about to shoot them "when one of the settlers observed a white rag wrapped around Ester's head." Clipping in Mitchell County Historical Society, Beloit, Kansas.

soon raided, raping Mrs. Hewitt and wounding her with an arrow in her side. She recovered. John Baertoche's family fled their home when they saw Indians approaching it, and lost all contents. John's body was found many days later, all of the flesh eaten by wolves.[64]

The same day Baertoche and Hewitt were killed near present-day Glasco, the Indians moved further east into Cloud County, and near the Republican River just west of present-day Concordia. There they raided the house of Benjamin White and captured his 17-year-old daughter, Sarah. A few miles to the north they caught Sarah's father and killed him. His three sons were able to escape by hiding in the tall grasses of the Republican River.[65]

On August 14, the Indians were still terrorizing the neighborhood. Three Randall brothers lived nearby on the Solomon. Spencer Randall was not present when the raids began. He had earlier taken a wagon into Salina for supplies. When he returned on August 14, the Indians caught him, killed him and plundered the wagon.[66]

That same day, several settlers were in one house for protection. It had been quiet all day so brothers John and Abraham Marshall, both Union veterans of the Civil War, went to investigate the area about a mile from the house. Riding with them was a young boy named Andrew Thompson. When they got to their dugout two Indians ran out and across the prairie. "They chased them but had only one gun. They were led into an ambush and were surrounded by forty or fifty Indians who killed them all before they could get back to their friends. John Marshall, though fatally shot, kept on his horse until he got within site of the camp, when he fell to the ground dead."[67] They lay dead on the prairie, scalped and otherwise mutilated, until a rescue party finally arrived in the neighborhood a couple days later.

Like many other settlers who moved to the new settlements, the Marshall family was an extended one. In addition to the dead brothers, their parents,

---

64 Lena Baertoche Indian Depredation Claim #3530. Nancy Hewitt Indian Depredation Claim #333. Record Group 123.

65 Mrs. E. F. Hollibaugh, *Biographical History of Cloud County* (Logonsport, IN: Wilson, Humphrey & CO, 1903), 49. See also Bazil Saunders Indian Depredation Claim #3698. Record Group 75.

66 Marvin and Lyman Randall Indian Depredation Claim # not given. Record Group 75.

67 *The Beloit Gazette*, August 8, 1928. Mitchell County Historical Society, Beloit, Kansas. In Julia Marshall's depredation claim (#3361 and 6840), she said her sons each had two pistols, which the Indians took. Some might think this was an exaggeration about lost property, but also, it appears quite incomprehensible that the two men would venture out with only one pistol. A wise person would be heavily armed. Julia's assertion is quite believable.

Julia and Abraham, Senior, also claimed a homestead on Asher Creek. Four grown daughters joined the large family, some already married and beginning their own families. They were all victims of the raids, and were huddled together with other settlers in one large house during the raids. Abraham Marshall, Senior, never emotionally recovered from the loss of his sons. He died in 1882, leaving Julia destitute and alone, entirely dependent upon her other grown children for support. She remained justifiably bitter the rest of her life, recalling years later, "my boys fought for to help save our union and had to be slashed up like dogs by the hands of these reptile snakes of the forrist [sic] and it sets pretty hard on me and be sides all the boys I had in the world for my support." She even wrote to President Garfield expressing her bitterness: "They had to be shot down like dogs to rot on the prairie or be devoured by wild wolves. Oh think of it how would u felt if it had bin your children and be sids all the boys I had for my support and scence my husband has died and left me I'm sirley a lone and am old and feable and cant work."[68] Julia outlived her husband by 15 years, but remained a broken and bitter woman, the result of her terrible loss in 1868. Her voice yet speaks of how this raid pained her.

Continuing with their raids, at least 60 warriors rode north, up the Republican River into Republic County about 30 miles and there caught a pioneer unarmed. About a mile southwest of present-day Republic, settlers had built a sort of fortress consisting of eight log cabins providing shelter to more than 20 men, women and children. Gordon Windbigler was one of the men living there. On August 15, he was about three miles north of the settlement with two other men, making hay in the river valley. Only one of the men, Alexander Lewis, was armed with a Spencer. The men were working in the hay field when dozens of warriors charged at them, firing revolvers in an attempt to shoot them down. A pair of horses was hitched to the hay wagon, which left Windbigler to ride the lone horse. The three men fled in the direction of the fortress, the Indians circling the men and trying to cut them off from their intended target. Windbigler was in the lead and would have reached the building, but as he was racing his horse his hat fell to the ground. He pulled up to retrieve it, the wagon passing him as he reached down and snagged his hat. He then ran his horse to the

---

68   Julia Marshall Indian Depredation Claim #3361 and 6840. Record Group 123.

front of the wagon, but by now the Indians realized he was unarmed. He should have stayed with the wagon. The warriors focused their pursuit on him and away from the other two men, where Lewis was firing his Spencer to keep the Indians at bay. As the Indians rushed in on Windbigler, one warrior shot him with a pistol. Windbigler fell from his horse, and then the warriors descended upon him, sticking him with their lances. One thrust hit his jugular, which immediately left him dead where he lay. Lewis ran from the wagon firing at the Indians, driving them away from Windbigler. He could do nothing to bring life back to his friend, but he did save the body from being mutilated.[69]

There was yet another death during this time that warrants mention. The day after Windbigler was killed—August 16—two scouts, both of whom knew and had lived among the Indians, and also had assisted the military as scouts, were sent to Turkey Leg's village to ascertain for the military whether those Indians were again turning hostile. Turkey Leg, after his killing of the railroad workers August 6, 1867, near present-day Lexington, Nebraska, had by August 1868, settled his village back down in Kansas on the Solomon River, not far from Monument Station, about 50 miles northeast of Fort Wallace. Lieutenant Frederick H. Beecher, stationed at Fort Wallace, sent Abner "Sharp" Grover and William Averill "Medicine Bill" Comstock to the village. The men arrived at Fort Hays and stayed two days before journeying northwest to where Turkey Leg was reported to be. They arrived at the village sometime that Sunday and were taken in and treated as friends. That night, however, other Cheyenne came to the village and reported their fight with Captain Benteen on the Saline River, at the end of the deadly Mitchell and Lincoln County raids, which had occurred a few days earlier. One military report indicated Benteen had killed four Indians and wounded two. Once Turkey Leg learned of Benteen's fight, Grover and Comstock were ordered to leave the village. Seven Indians—three of them boys—escorted the two scouts about two miles from the village, when suddenly both men were shot in the back. Comstock was instantly killed, and reports differ about Grover. Some say he pretended to be dead and walked to Monument Station the next day to report the attack. Others say he used Comstock's body as a defense and fired back at the Indians

---

69   I. O. Savage, *A History of Republic County, Kansas* (Beloit, KS: Jones & Chubbic, Art Printers, 1901), 49–51.

until they retreated. In either case, Grover made it back to Fort Wallace and reported what happened. If he had been wounded it must not have been serious, for he recovered within the next month and was able to participate as one of George A. Forsyth's scouts at Beecher's Island. Grover would survive that fight but not for long. He was killed in a brawl at Pond Creek Station just west of Fort Wallace, on January 16, 1869.[70]

The Indian version of the killing of Comstock differs importantly. Dog Soldier leader Bull Bear had personally escorted the men into Turkey Leg's village. When the Indians soon after learned of Benteen's fight on the Saline, Bull Bear again escorted the two men from the village and to safety. It was after that when some other Cheyenne, also returning from their skirmish with Benteen, found the men and fired on them, killing Comstock. In this Indian version, Grover fought off the Indians and eventually made his way to near Monument Station, where he was picked up by a railcar and then brought to Fort Wallace. In this Indian version there was no treachery from any of Turkey Leg's warriors.[71]

Clearly these August attacks on the pioneers were quite terrorizing and violent. Compounding the suffering was the fact that this was at the end of the summer, and when the winter came, so very many settlers were destitute of all means to survive the cold season. Everything they had for sustenance had been destroyed, including clothing, weapons and tools. At least 46 families were the victims of these deadly raids.[72] There was no agency of the government that could provide anything to assist them. The only social program run by the government involved Indians. Given the numerous amount of annuities awarded to the raiding Indians as a part of the Medicine Lodge Treaty, it is easy to understand the bitterness of the settlers against a government that would use large amounts of tax dollars to provide for a people who caused so much devastation and suffering upon the citizens the government was there to protect. And the Indians seemed to know the people would suffer, for when they made their raids they destroyed everything they didn't steal. The coming winter was especially hard on the surviving settlers.

---

70   John S. Gray, "Will Comstock—The Nutty Bumppo of Kansas," (*The Westerners Brand Book*, Volume XVIII, Number 12, February 1962, The Chicago Corral of Westerners, Chicago, IL: 1962), 95–96; Criqui, *Fifty Fearless Men*, 32–40.

71   Hyde, *Life of George Bent*, 309.

72   *Forty-first Congress, 2nd Session, House of Representatives, Mis. Doc.* No. 20, Denver Public Library, 3–7.

As a result of this devastation in Lincoln, Mitchell and Cloud County, Colonel George Forsyth was given permission to organize a company of scouts to locate the marauding Indians. This led to the famous battle of Beecher's Island in northeastern Colorado, south of present-day Wray, on September 17–25. There, 51 men fought a three-day battle and subsequent siege, until rescued nine days later. Five men were killed, including Lieutenant Frederick Beecher, for whom the battle was named.[73]

The Indians, however, were not done with their raiding along the Solomon River, nor did their fight at Beecher's Island slow them down. They returned on October 13, this time concentrating their deadly attacks a few miles further east along the Solomon, near present-day Delphos, in Ottawa County. But it was a different band of raiders, probably not connected directly with the August raids. These raiders were Lakota. In this sortie, another woman was taken captive, 23-year-old Mrs. Anna Morgan, who had been married exactly one month when she was captured. Her husband James was severely wounded. She would soon—a month later—join Sarah White in Sarah's Cheyenne village. She and Sarah would remain together in captivity until rescued by General Custer in the Texas Panhandle in March 1869. In her account of her capture Mrs. Morgan said it was Sioux who captured her and Sioux who eventually traded her to the Cheyenne. She was also the subject of Indian lust throughout her captivity.[74]

The October raids included more settler murders. Near the capture of Mrs. Morgan, the Indians raided the home of Alex Smith. His father, mother and brothers all had joined him in his house because of the earlier raids in August. It was thought the extended family would have more protection together. But three of the brothers joined the militia to protect area residents. When the Sioux attacked the home, the women were able to escape into the nearby woods. The contents of the house were destroyed. But Alexander, Junior, and his father, Alexander, Senior, were together working the fields nearby, and unaware of what was going on at the home. One brother—John—described what he discovered when he came upon the home, after learning the Indians had attacked people in the neighborhood:

---

73 See Broome, *Dog Soldier Justice*, 35–44. For a comprehensive account of the battle presenting both Indian and settler views, see Monnett, *The Battle of Beecher Island*.

74 James Morgan Indian Depredation Claim #3644. Record Group 75. See also Broome, *Dog Soldier Justice*, 52–55.

When I [finally] got down to the home ranch there was no one to be found. It was dark. I found the ranch vacant and no one there and things all mixed up. They had taken the feather beds, cut the ticks and emptied the feathers out, took the flour that was in the house, cut the sacks open and emptied the flour into the dug out. And took the sorgum [*sic*], I think that there was two or three barrels, and emptied them among the flour and feathers and made a general mix up. They took all of the blankets and bed clothing that was around the house.... I called and hunted around the place to see if there was anyone around there. I got no reply from anyone. [The next morning] I hunted around and found father had crawled into an out house that had been built for a chicken coop. He had been shot through the right lung and they had thrust a lance and it had gone through his mouth and come out on the left side of his neck. He gave me to understand that he wanted some water.... After we got him into the house he lived about an hour. It was two days after that before we discovered my brother, Alex, in the river. It seemed he had attempted to cross the river at that place and had failed. He had got his arm hooked around a limb that was sticking out of the water and sand and that was how we came to discover him. We saw his arm over the limb. He had been shot in the small of the back. The bullet did not come through.[75]

In addition to the killing of the two Smith men, the Indians also killed two other people near present-day Glasco. John Andrews was killed and scalped. About 30 minutes before he was killed, seven-year-old Benjamin Misell was with his two older brothers, both children, in their dugout when Indians approached their home. The three boys ran to their neighbor's house. Their father was helping another neighbor with crops and was not present. Little Benjamin could not keep up with his older brothers and the Indians shot him in the back, killing him.[76]

After the killings in October, General Sheridan set forth his winter campaign, knowing the raiding Indians would by then have returned to their individual villages. In the winter, when the Indians stayed in their villages, the military could deliver a blow against the guilty parties. The result was Custer's one victory in fighting Indians. The Battle of the Washita was fought on November 27, 1868.[77]

---

75 Mary E. Smith Indian Depredation Claim #3736. Record Group 75.
76 Thomas Misell Indian Depredation Claim #3629. Record Group 75.
77 For Custer's fight at the Washita see Greene, *Washita*.

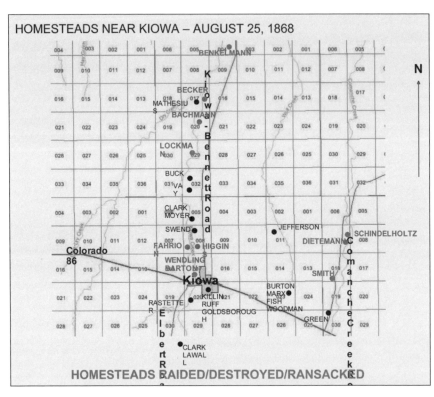

HOMESTEADS NEAR KIOWA – AUGUST 25, 1868

HOMESTEADS RAIDED/DESTROYED/RANSACKED

MAP SHOWING HOMESTEADS RAIDED IN
ELBERT COUNTY, COLORADO, AUGUST 25, 1868.
In these raids, Arapaho Indians killed 31-year-old Henrietta Dietemann
and her five-year-old son, John. *Courtesy Ric Morgan, Elbert, Colorado.*

CHAPTER THIRTEEN

Colorado Indian War

*As to the frontier settlements, I have again and again warned the governors
and the people, that until this Indian matter was finally concluded, these
people should not spread out so much. These isolated farms, with horses
and cattle, are too tempting to hungry and savage bands of Indians.*

W. T. SHERMAN, LIEUTENANT GENERAL
THE CHEYENNE STAR, SEPTEMBER 15, 1868

T HE CHEYENNE OUTBREAK IN KANSAS ON AUGUST 10–14,
1868, while intensely violent in its concentration, was but one
event in an unfolding Plains Indian war along the three roads to
Denver. Military records show the killing of 46 citizens in Colorado and
Kansas after August 14, and before the fight at Beecher's Island on September 17, as well as another 16 dead between Beecher's Island and the battle
on the Washita on November 27.[1] Revenge appears to motivate all of the
violence. And it seemed to always originate in retaliation against other
Indian tribes. Beginning with the Kaw tribe in early June, the Indians who
brought violence on the Saline, Solomon and Republican Rivers were initially going after the Pawnee. In a similar action, violence that spilled over
into Colorado in the last part of August began as a retaliatory raid against
the Utes. These Indians were Cheyenne and Arapaho, numbering about
75. They passed through Colorado City and were sullen in their demeanor,
but showed papers from the recent Medicine Lodge Treaty which said
they were friendly and should not be molested. They indicated that they
were going to fight the Utes. Shortly after that they found their enemy in
South Park, near present-day Hartsell, and killed six warriors, two or three

---

1   Johnson, *No Greater Calling*, 84–99.

women, as well as taking a young Ute boy captive. It was in returning from this violent foray that Colorado citizens suffered.[2] The Pueblo *Colorado Chieftain* later reported that 75–100 Arapaho under Little Chief came into the Fountain Valley and Colorado City. They were all dressed in war paint and were armed with everything from breech loading carbines to revolvers and bows, with 100 arrows to each warrior. Announcing they were going into the mountains to fight the Utes, it was later believed that in fact they went up there to rendezvous with another war party and made their plan to attack the Colorado settlements. Upon arriving back at the end of August, they divided into a war party that raided and killed around Colorado City and Fountain, and another war party that went up Monument Creek and into the Bijou Basin.[3]

Before the trek into Colorado, events unfolded near Fort Larned indicating a continuation of war. On August 1, 20 Kiowa Indians were charged with burning the ranch and toll bridge of Christopher Weidner at Pawnee Fork, four miles east of the fort. This was the popular crossing from north to south at Pawnee Fork on the Santa Fe road. The ranch, with all household contents, was burned, as were all the other outbuildings.[4]

On August 17, Antonio Luna had brought 17 wagons from New Mexico, loaded them with freight at Hays City, and had gone into camp on Big Creek, 12 miles west of Fort Hays. At about eight o'clock that morning, a band of Southern Cheyenne Indians approached the camp from the east. When they got between the herders and the camp they raised their war whoop and scattered about 160 horses and mules. The freighters were able to catch up to the Indians several miles later and recovered about half of the stolen stock, but still lost 96 mules and 10 horses. When this raid was brought to the Cheyenne in council at Darlington Agency, they admitted the theft.[5] Two days later, on August 19, probably the same band of Indians struck in the same area near Pawnee Fork, this time attacking a large freight

---

2   Irving Howbert, *The Indians of the Pikes Peak Region* (New York, NY: The Knickerbocker Press, 1914), 191–194. See also Howbert, *Memories of a Lifetime in the Pike's Peak Region* (New York and London: G. P. Putnum's Son's, 1925), 179–183.

3   *Weekly Colorado Chieftain*, September 11, 1868. Copy in Philip Gomer Indian Depredation Claim #2788. Record Group 123.

4   Charles Weidner Indian Depredation Claim #121. Record Group 123. One statement in the file said the theft occurred on August 28.

5   Antonio Jose Luna Indian Depredation Claim #2163. Record Group 123.

train. They stole 55 mules and a horse belonging to George Maxwell, and seven mules belonging to Martin Baca.[6]

On August 21, yet another band of Cheyenne and Arapaho Indians appeared on the Santé Fe road. Major Douglass—commanding Fort Dodge—was informed that the Indians were going to burn and murder everyone at Cimarron Ranch, located on the Arkansas River 25 miles west of Dodge, as well as anyone else they could find. The ranch was owned by Andrew Anthony since 1867, and served as a stage station, changing horses and serving meals to passengers, as well as a store along the trail for freighters to purchase various items as wagons passed by. One building was the store and dining room, and other buildings included a large stable, a warehouse and a granary to store hay. When Douglass learned of the war party, he sent a messenger to Anthony, warning him to flee for his life. He also called back to the post the small detail of soldiers which had been assigned to the ranch for protection, knowing the Indians were too many for the soldiers to fight if attacked. The messenger sent to warn Anthony—R. M. Wright—left Fort Dodge about sundown, August 19, and Anthony arrived at the post about 10 o'clock the next day. Once he was informed of the danger, he only had time to gather his stock and a few of the more valuable possessions from the ranch. He retreated to the fort. That night his ranch was burned and everything inside the ranch buildings was either taken or destroyed. He also lost over 100 tons of hay, three mowing machines and three wagons, all burned.[7]

Indians next struck on the Smoky Hill road, 12 miles west of Fort Wallace. William H. Bush was in partnership with Seth J. Clark & Company to provide hay for Fort Wallace, at $35 a ton. At nine o'clock in the morning on August 21, the workers were harvesting hay when suddenly a band of Cheyenne warriors attacked them, forcing them to flee. The Indians burned all the hay—as much as 200 tons—and destroyed three haying machines. They also took two mares and seven mules. In the next three weeks the Indians returned and stole two more mares and 11 mules.[8]

Thomas Milhoun had a government contract to deliver beef to Forts Harker, Hays and Wallace. Acquiring 225 cattle at Junction City, he

---

6   George Maxwell Indian Depredation Claim #2105. Record Group 123.

7   Andrew J. Anthony Indian Depredation Claim #1313. Record Group 123.

8   William Bush Indian Depredation Claim #1440. Seth and William Clark Indian Depredation Claim #530 and 4846. Record Group 123. One witness said the attack happened on July 10, but that date does not fit with the other depredations happening in the area that summer.

delivered 75 beeves to Harker, and the same number to Hays. He then proceeded with the remaining 175 to Fort Wallace, eventually arriving at Sheridan, a few miles down the Smoky Hill River, east of Wallace. The day before the attack, two companies of soldiers had been camping about 200 yards away from the cattle camp, but they were ordered back to Fort Wallace. That was probably the break the Indians were looking for. Southern Cheyenne attacked the camp and made off with 100 beef cattle as well as two horses. The attack began about 10 o'clock, on the morning of August 24.[9]

Not too far from where these raids were made near Fort Wallace, James Woodworth—"Muggins" was his nickname—lived his final moments. He was traveling from his ranch at the site of the old Fort Lyon, going from stage station to stage station by night—to avoid being caught alone by Indians—and staying at the stations during the day. He was involved with a railroad contract and was coming to Wallace to pay his workers. He made it as far as Big Timbers Station, which was about a mile into the Kansas border alongside the Smoky Hill River, 16 miles east of Cheyenne Wells Station. Soldiers were stationed there, and on the morning of August 23,

> he and the soldiers were shooting at a mark with revolvers. His oxen [for use in the railroad construction] were out half a mile. After he had fired all the shots out of his revolver he saw a band of [Cheyenne] Indians coming up the valley making for his oxen. He jumped on his mule and started to bring the oxen into the station. After he got away from the station another band of Indians came down the gulch about a quarter of a mile from the station, fell in behind him, pursued him, overtook him and killed him.[10]

He lost his mule, his pistol, saddle, and all the money he was carrying to pay his workers, $2,020, worth more than $34,000 in today's value.[11] Coincidentally, not long after Woodworth left his home at old Fort Lyon, it was burned down by another band of Cheyenne Indians. Woodworth was 35 and had married Eliza Jane, the daughter of James Smith. They had a newborn daughter in 1868. Eliza's father came to visit his daughter in the late afternoon of August 26. He had not been there for more than 30 minutes when one of the Bent boys, probably George, ran his horse up to the ranch and announced that Cheyenne Indians were approaching from Black

---

9   Thomas Milhoun Indian Depredation Claim #589. Record Group 123.
10   James Woodworth Indian Depredation Claim #4761. Record Group 123.
11   http://www.westegg.com/inflation/infl.cgi (accessed May 30, 2013).

Kettle's band and they were going to kill everyone and burn the ranch. Bent had earlier worked with Woodworth and was coming to warn everyone to flee. Smith, his daughter and grandchild and another worker quickly left in a wagon, and fled to the new Fort Lyon about 18 miles distant. After they had ridden about two miles, Smith looked back and could see a large fire where the ranch was. All the buildings were burned down and dozens of hogs were shot with arrows and killed. Everything was lost. It wasn't long after the burning of the ranch that Eliza learned of her husband's death. According to her father, Eliza never recovered from her grief. The baby died shortly after and Eliza went insane and died the next year.[12]

Well into Colorado on the Denver road, near present-day Evans, Indians stole numerous horses from area pioneers. Andrew Getz lived two miles east of the not yet established town. He lost just one horse. He was out working hay near his ranch and was high on a stack when he observed two Indians riding away with his horse from across the South Platte River. He knew it was his horse as he had it picketed near the river and close to where he saw the Indians running a horse. Coming off the stack and going to the river he saw the Indians had five or six horses, one of which was his. Getz said it was the day before when two men were killed by Indians about six miles away.[13] Actually it was three men and they were apparently killed the same day. Mary Bailey lost two horses and another was taken that belonged to her brother-in-law. She lived two miles further east from Getz. At about noon on the same day Getz lost his horse, she saw Indians:

---

12   Woodworth's depredation claim has conflicting dates when everything happened, including his death. The claim was filed years later by Woodworth's father-in-law. Some accounts say Woodworth was killed as early as August 16, and August 22, and 28th. The burning of the ranch is also given varying dates, some accounts saying it was burned two days before Woodworth was killed, and other accounts say two days after. The military records of civilians killed near Big Timbers indicate a single citizen was killed on August 23, between Pond Creek Station (Kansas) and Lake Station (Colorado), and one citizen was killed between Fort Lyon and Fort Sheridan, Kansas on August 27. See Johnson, *No Greater Calling*, 87. Woodworth is likely killed on the earlier date, as the *Rocky Mountain News*, August 26, reports "'Muggins' as he is known and called through all this country" had been killed at Big Timbers." The *Rocky Mountain News*, August 29, 1868, said he was killed on the evening of August 22. Further compounding the matter is that another person, Charles J. Woodworth also filed a claim for compensation. No details are in this depredation claim. It states Woodworth was killed at Big Timbers, on August 22. But Charles says he was the surviving son of James, whom he identified as John, not James Woodworth. See #10741, Record Group 123. It is possible that James had earlier been married and Charles was at the time of Woodworth's death living with his mother—learning later of his father's death—and that his father had remarried Eliza Smith and started a second family. But it's also possible the claim was a fraud. James Smith said Woodworth had a brother in New York by the name of Charles Woodworth.

13   Andrew Getz Indian Depredation Claim #6849. Record Group 123.

come up close to our house and took two of my horses with a lot of others belonging to the neighbors and drove them off south over the bluffs. I lived on the south bank of South Platte River, Mr. [Oscar] Ennes lived about half a mile west of us on the same side of the river. I saw the Indians cross the river, the same river, on the north bank from Mr. Ennes, driving five or six horses; they got some others at Mr. Ennes and came to our place and got about seventeen head of horses there, two of which were mine, one of which was picketed west of the house, and they cut the rope, the other sixteen, one of which belonged to me. The other horses belonged to my brother-in-law, Daniel Bailey, and were grazing near the house at the time they were driven off by the Indians. They went in a southeasterly direction over the hills, my husband and a man by the name of Frank Kees, and another man by the name of Billy, that worked for Mr. Ennes, I don't know what his other name was, and Mr. Oscar and Walter Ennes were present or saw the horses in the possession of the Indians.

Mary was certain the Indians who took the horses were Sioux and Cheyenne because two weeks earlier they had come to Denver to receive annuities, and on their return camped near her ranch "and came here every day to get something to eat for about two weeks."[14]

Bailey's ranch was co-owned by a man named Christopher McLemore. Together they also operated a store for travelers on the road to and from Denver. Four men were at or near the ranch—brothers Sam and Granville Ashcraft, Oscar Ennes and Jim Bailey, Mary's husband. Mary and Jim had married earlier that June. The four men went out to try to recover the horses, and chased the Indians 25 miles but were unable to overtake them. They did, however, during the chase, come upon the bodies of William Brush and two of his herders, who had been killed by the same Indians and their horses stolen too. The Indians—as few as seven—were mostly Cheyenne and belonged to Grayhead's band. A dead Indian was found on an island in the South Platte six days after the raid. Soldiers were thought to have shot him.[15]

Sam Ashcraft remembered that day:

Just after twelve o'clock I was on my ranch on the north side of the river, I took my glasses and went on top of my house and saw five Indians driving a band of horses down to the river from up the road towards Bailey's ranch; two of the Indians got into the river on these horses and came across and got a couple of my horses that were loose, and started back to the other side to where Bailey's horses were; my two horses refused to go into the river and turned around and came back, and the

---

14   Mary Bailey Indian Depredation Claim #6851. Record Group 123.

15   Daniel Bailey and Christopher McLemore Indian Depredation Claim #1258. Record Group 123.

Indians went on across; my brother and I shot at them; we caught these two horses, got on them and went after the Indians; but before we started we went across and got a man with two horses, his name was Ennis; his horses were about the only two horses left on the south side of the river; we then went to Bailey's ranch and got Jim Bailey, and we four followed the Indians, and got in sight of them, but not very close; at Gary's [Gerry's] ranch they recrossed to the north side; Jim Bailey rode one of Ennis' horses, there were no horses left on Bailey's ranch; we found Jim Bailey in the house eating dinner, when we reached there; I do not know how many horses Bailey and McLemore had, fifteen or sixteen, I think; once we were within two hundred yards of these Indians; they were Cheyennes and belonged to Grayhead's band; I heard them talk and they did not talk Sioux; I knew a Cheyenne Indian when I saw him; I could not see exactly how many horses the Indians had with them, they drove away twenty-five or thirty head from the river there. . . . On that same day they killed William Brush and his two herd hands and took his horses on the Gary [Gerry] ranch about twelve miles away; the closest I was to the Indians was down at the ford when they were crossing the river; I saw one dead Indian on an island while they crossed the river to Gary's [Gerry's] ranch; it was five or six days after the raid that I saw this Indian.[16]

While Indians were molesting ranchers along the Denver road, more warriors went to the western edge of the Smoky Hill trail and conducted a series of thefts and murders near present-day Kiowa, Colorado. Like other raids, the warriors—a mixed band of Cheyenne and Arapaho—divided up into smaller parties and covered a wide area. Some raids happened simultaneously with others. The Indians appeared in the vicinity a few days before they began their thefts and murders, which was on August 25. There was a party of at least 100 warriors that camped in the Bijou Basin. They carried papers saying they were friendly and were authorized to hunt.[17] Living in the Basin was Lewis Hayden. His daughter Isabelle was married to a Mr. Holden, and lived about a mile from Hayden's ranch. On August 24, eight Indians came to her house. She had an infant asleep in a crib in her cabin. The Indians showed her papers saying they were friendly. After she fed them they lingered around for awhile and then left. The next day Indians, presumed to be the same ones that were fed the day before, came to her father's ranch and stole eight horses, 50 cattle, and destroyed a wagon and hay making machine.[18]

16   Daniel Bailey and Christopher McLemore Indian Depredation Claim #1258. Record Group 123.

17   Elisha Baldwin Indian Depredation Claim #455. Alfred Butters Indian Depredation Claim #9548. Record Group 123.

18   Lewis Hayden Indian Depredation Claim #6473. Record Group 123.

The warriors apparently came to Bijou Basin from the northwest, for one or two days before they appeared in the Basin they appeared upon Running Creek, which, like Kiowa and Comanche Creek, runs north through present-day Elizabeth, 10 miles west of Kiowa. Four Indians appeared at the ranch of brothers Alfred and Pinckney Butters, asking to be fed. While feeding them other Indians killed two of his cows. Pinckney recalled:

> I gave them something to eat, and at the time these four Indians were in the house getting something to eat, or within an hour of that time, a squad of Indians were on the hill not a quarter of a mile away, I heard them shoot and saw them gather up in a squad at a particular place, and a few days after I found the remains of a young cow killed at that particular place, belonging to me. I found the remains of the other cow about two miles from my house, in Cherry Gulch, having the appearance of having been killed at the same time as the other.

The dead cows had chunks of meat cut out to feed the Indians. About 100 Indians camped below the house that night, moving on to Bijou Basin the next day. On August 25, the Indians returned and stole three horses. Pinckney:

> at noon, I saw my brother's three horses grazing upon that bluff, about a quarter of a mile from the house. Just after dinner, about 1 o'clock, the same day, I noticed a man coming down the creek running his horse as fast as he could, and when he got to my brother's place, this man, on horseback coming with such haste, said to me that the Indians were in the country, and stealing all of the horses in the neighborhood.[19]

South of where the Butters brothers lived, Philip Gomer operated a mill, which was located on Kiowa Creek about a mile south of present-day Elbert. Living next to him was Elisha Baldwin. When the Indians stole the horses from Butters, they also stole five horses belonging to Baldwin.[20] With Baldwin's horses was one owned by John Riley. It was taken with the others.[21] The Indians returned to Gomer's Mill a week later and killed a young boy named Leona Johnson.[22]

Back near present-day Kiowa, the Indians raided the ranch of Henry

---

19   Alfred Butters Indian Depredation Claim #9548.
20   Elisha Baldwin Indian Depredation Claim #455.
21   John Riley Indian Depredation Claim #6712. Record Group 123.
22   September 4, 1868. Coroner's Inquest, Territory of Colorado, County of Arapahoe. Philip Gomer Indian Depredation Claim #2788.

Wendling and shot and killed 10 cattle.[23] Near Wendling's place was a ranch owned by John Benkelman. Benkelman recalled the events:

I resided in Central City, Colo., or a suburb of Central called Bortonburg, Colo. I was engaged in the butchering business at that place and had a ranch, a cattle ranch near Kiowa, Elbert County, Colorado. I had horses and cattle on this ranch in the year 1868. I had a loss by reason of Indian depredations. I lost two head of horses and five head of cattle. I had gone there to Kiowa, to my ranch, after some beef cattle, and the morning of the raid which the Indians made [August 25], I was in the house where my herder lived with some other parties [three men], and it was about the hour of nine o'clock A.M. We were waiting for the men that had gone out to gather up horses which we intended to ride that day. He had been out longer than we expected, so we heard some horses a coming, in the house, and on going out we see that there was a number of Indians driving the horses towards the house. The Indians were coming down the creek with the horses and our men who were bringing in some horses were coming up the creek with some horses; part of the Indians run round shooting at the men who were driving the bunch of horses and got the two bunches of horses together; there was I think two horses lariated close to the house; they cut the lariats with their knives and drove them along too. The man that brought in the horses had his horse saddled; he loaded the double barrel rifle and followed the Indians with two Shepherd dogs; the dogs were well trained, and he succeeded to turn the horses and run them towards the house, but in corralling the horses, the Indians run part of them in another direction; then there was another man that was my herder; he saddled the horse that we had got in the corral, and the two went after the Indians again, but when they got out on the flat between Dry Creek and Kiowa Creek, there were more Indians coming in and they was run into a house on Kiowa where a man by the name of Lockman lived. I was left at the ranch, my ranch, with a young man about 16 years of age. I was trying to guard the horses in the corral. But after the Indian had the men who were after them run into the house of Lockman, they came back to the ranch where I was; there was a high bluff on the side where they were coming to the creek and they had gathered up there for some purpose to consult one another, I suppose, but they divided into two parts, one part went up the creek and the remainder went down the creek and crossed below. I had no arms except some old muskets which had been left there by the freighters. When the party coming down the creek was coming, I drew my old rusty musket on them and they turned, but when I turned around and looking for the other party they had already turned the horses out of the corral, and driving them over the bluffs. By that time I had a horse saddled, and the young fellow who was with me had a horse saddled, I wanted him to go along

---

23   Henry Wendling Indian Depredation Claim #4937. Record Group 123.

with me, but he was scarred so, he wouldn't come with me. He took the horse in the house and stayed there, and I went and hunted up the other parties who were going after the Indians in the first place. Three of my horses were in among the horses which the Indians drove off. One of them I found the next day; the rope was on the horse had got fast when they were driving through the brush, and the horse was still fast when I found him. The five head of cattle I found the next day on my ranch, about five miles below on Kiowa Creek. It looked like the Indians had camped there, where the cattle had been killed. There were some signs where they had shot the cattle with arrows and bullets, and some of those cattle there had been pieces cut out of, probably for meat they used to eat. That is the way the Indians usually did. I found these cattle which were dead, the next day after the horses were taken. I was familiar with the Indian tribes at that time and saw the Indians that took the horses and know the Indians that were in that locality at that time and am satisfied that they were Cheyenne and Arapahoes that committed this depredation.[24]

One of the young men with Benkelman was Thomas Morrison, a Canadian. He had come to America in 1858, when he was 11. His father took a homestead at present-day Morrison, Colorado. The town was named after him. Young Tom was working for Benkelman and living in his house. Before anyone realized Indians were making a raid, they were expecting another herder to bring horses to the house. When horses were heard approaching, Morrison recalled:

I said, "Boys, the horses are coming." Mr. Benkelman ran out the door, and he said, "The Indians." When I got outside there was two Indians going up the creek [south], and they had cut the lariat of one horse and one of the strans [sic] on another one that was picketed there behind the house, and were driving the horses up the creek; and our attention was drawn to Andy Hemey coming down the creek, and the Indians fired at him as he went by; he came down and got his gun and pistol. I took one, and we started up the hill toward the horses, toward the west and south, and I gave back [out] and came back. Andy Hemey went on with the two dogs. I took the horse that was there lariated and tied him inside the corral, and then I heard Andy and the horses and the dogs coming, and we went out and turned the horses in the corral. . . . I saddled up my horse, and Andy Hemey and I went after the five [horses] that the Indians had taken, and we did not get in the corral. We got the five horses away from the Indians and took them to John Lockman's, at the next ranch, and the Indians were so many between Mr. Lockman's and our camp that we couldn't get back to our camp.[25]

---

24   John Benkelman Indian Depredation Claim #4936. Record Group 123.
25   Thomas Morrison Indian Depredation Claim #4865. Record Group 123.

Benkelman makes it clear that both Morrison and Hemey acted courageously:

I think it was about 9 o'clock before we heard some horses coming, and I stepped out of the house, and I see some Indians driving a bunch of horses; at the same time Andy [Hemey] was coming from another direction with another bunch of horses; there was two horses staked close to the house, tied with a rope. I saw two Indians had cut the ropes of the horses, and some of the other Indians run around towards Andy where he had the bunch of horses, and shooting at him, so they got the two bunches of horses together and started over the hill with the horses—over the bluff. Andy went after his gun in the house, and carried a pistol also, and he called the dogs—they were well-trained shepherd dogs—and went after the Indians. By this time the Indians and horses were out of sight over the bluffs, but he overtook them soon after that and the dogs turned the horses toward the ranch. It wasn't but a short time when the horses, dogs, Andy, and all together, came down the hill and the Indians firing at every jump. We got most of the horses in the corral; we were watching for them when they came and headed them off and got them in the corral. The Indians, however, ran some of them by the corral across Dry Creek, and Mr. Morrison and Andy Hemey followed them up to get the horses away from them again, what they had taken along. I stayed at the ranch to guard the horses in the corral. I heard quite a deal of firing and shooting, and I learned thereafter that the Indians run Morrison and Andy Hemey into the ranch of John Lockman, on Kiowa Creek. I think it was about an half an hour when the Indians came back to the ranch; they came upon a high bluff on the east side of Dry Creek, where our house was on the west side of the creek, and it looked to me like they held a council, and thereafter separated, half of them going up the creek and the others going down. I see the ones that went up the creek cross the creek and come down toward me at the house; I had picked up an old gun that had been left at the ranch by some freighters, and when the Indians came up pretty close I drawed the old gun, pointing at them, and they turned run up the creek. By that time I turned and was looking toward the corral, and the other part of the Indians had just turned the horses out of the corral and going over the hill with them, and that was the bunch of horses that the three belonging to Mr. Morrison were with. All this time there was a young fellow of the age of 16 years with me, and while the Indians was off after the small bunch of horses, we saddled a horse each of the ones that were in the corral, and I wanted the young man to go along with me to hunt Mr. Morrison and Andy, but he wouldn't go with me; he took his horse in the house and stayed in the house himself, and I rode over toward Kiowa where I heard the shooting, and there I found my man, Mr. Morrison, which I thought was killed, probably, and Mr. Bachman and Andy Hemey, at Mr. Lockman's ranch. We was holding some consultation as to whether it was best to go after the Indians or not, but we concluded it was best not to go as there was so few of us and so many of them to fight. The same time we looked down Kiowa Creek, and there we see the Indians driving the horses across and going in a northeast direction as fast as they could drive them.[26]

There were three men living in Benkelman's house besides the young herder: Andy Hemey, Tom Morrison and Fred Bachman. But Bachman was not the 16-year-old boy who became frightened, for he was born in 1833, and was thus 35 at the time of the raid. He married the next year and raised a family in the Kiowa area.[27] He lost 11 horses and a bull in the raid.[28] He recalled what happened in the early morning when the Indians appeared:

> I left about that time to go to Kiowa to get the mail, when I got about two miles away from the cabin I saw the Indians on Kiowa Creek and I started to go back to the camp, but the Indians were shooting around and I couldn't get back, then I started for Kiowa again and went to the house of William Buck and stayed there until Andy Hemey and Mr. Morrison came over from our cabin to the Lockman ranch with a bunch of horses. I went out to the [Lockman] corral when Mr. Morrison and Hemey came up and opened the gate for him, and put in the horses; there were five of them and they were my horses. Andy hadn't gotten up to the corral yet; the Indians were shooting and chasing him. I waited at the corral until Andy got up there; a few minutes after that, and while I was still at the Lockman corral, Mr. Benkelman came over the bluff and said he [the Indians] had taken all the horses. About that time I saw the Indians crossing Kiowa Creek with a bunch of horses. They were nearly two miles off and I couldn't distinguish the horses at the time. Then I and Andy Hemey went over to our cabin to see if the Indians had gotten our horses, and they were all gone. Eleven of mine, three of Mr. Morrison's and two of Benkelman's.[29]

At about the same time this raid was happening near the Benkelman ranch, about five miles further east on Comanche Creek, things turned deadly. Apollinaris Dietemann had only lived on Comanche Creek two months, having moved there on June 19. He earlier lived on Plum Creek, just north of present-day Castle Rock, from 1862 to 1868, where he operated a hotel, bought and sold cattle and made and sold butter. He was married to 31-year-old Henrietta and had a young family; John, who was five,

---

26 Thomas Morrison Indian Depredation Claim #4865.

27 http://www.findagrave.com/cgi-bin/fg.cgi?page=gr&GSln=bachmann&GSfn=fred&GSbyrel=all&GSdyrel=all&GSst=7&GScntry=4&GSob=n&GRid=13460918&df=all& (accessed February 22, 2012). My thanks to Mike Day of Wichita, Kansas, for assistance in searching out Bachman's genealogy.

28 Fred Bachman Indian Depredation Claim #4865. Record Group 123.

29 Thomas Morrison Indian Depredation Claim #4865.

and three-year-old Henrietta, "Hattie." Mrs. Dietemann was in her third
trimester with her third pregnancy when her life ended on this day. The
Dietemanns had recently sold their business on Plum Creek and moved
to Comanche Creek where Apollinaris intended to expand his cattle business. He had sold 300 head of cattle when he sold his ranch and hotel in
Castle Rock and brought almost $8,000 to Comanche Creek, intending
to purchase new cattle from Arkansas once the family got settled at their
new home. He was in business with another German/Swiss immigrant,
Anton Schindelholz, who lived on Comanche Creek since 1867. He had
about 1,000 cattle and 75 horses. Anton was engaged to Apollinaris' sister,
Maria, who had just moved from Germany in early May. Two days before,
on August 23, Schindelholz and Dietemann had taken a wagon into Denver
to purchase a marriage license and procure furniture and groceries. As soon
as they were back from Denver, Anton was going to marry Maria, and did
on August 27, despite the family tragedy. They were due back on the day
of the raid. Staying at the ranch while the two men were gone were Maria,
Henrieta Dietemann and her two children, as well as two hired men, Mr.
Lawrence and Benedict Marki.

　　Maria vividly remembered what happened:

> On Tuesday morning about eight o'clock, the 25th of August, 1868, about twenty-
> five or thirty Indians came right near our houses, with a herd of horses that they
> had stole all over the country; and one of the Indians came up to the house and took
> two horses that were picketed in front of the house, one of which was my brother's
> [Apollinaris] and the other A. Schindelholz's, and they took all the horses, about

seven or eight in number, that were grazing near the house; and two mares and a colt, belonging to my brother, were taken at that time. I saw the Indians drive them off. I know that they were Indians, and the people told me that they were Cheyenne and Arapahoe Indians. After they had the horses away we got frightened and thought it wasn't safe there, and my brother's wife wanted to go away to some neighbors, and those neighbors were ten miles away; so we took all the valuables along that we had in the house that we could carry, and my brother's wife and children and the two hired men, Benedict Marki and Mr. Lawrence, and myself, started up the creek to the nearest neighbor, which was about ten miles. It must have been about nine o'clock when we started; as we was about half the way we seen five or six horses grazing in a gulch, and one of the hired men (Lawrence) wanted to go and take one of those horses and ride over to Kiowa to tell the people we were in trouble, but as we neared the horses some Indians came out of a ravine and shot at us, about five or six in number, and they commenced to shoot at us and we commenced to run, and my brother's wife wasn't able to run, and the Indians overtook her and shot her, killed her and scalped her, and the little boy [John] I had hold of with my hand, but he run towards his mother, as he thought he was safer with her, and they took a hold of him and killed him. . . . The balance of us turned our course and went to Middle Kiowa [today's Kiowa Creek]. All of the white people in that neighborhood was together there at Middle Kiowa, as it was safer, and we stayed there until all the trouble was over and we knew that the Indians were gone. I saw them shoot my sister-in-law with a revolver, in the breast, and they shot the boy with arrows, and one of them took a hold of him and twist his neck. This occurred about ten o'clock. After we was at Middle Kiowa about two or three hours my brother came from Denver and A. Schindelholz, also, and about half a dozen of the men went with him to hunt the remains, which they found at the place we left them, and the next day they fetched them in to Denver to be buried.[30]

Benedict Marki added some details, including the claim that the fleeing party went up the creek and not down. Comanche Creek, like Kiowa and Running Creek, flowed north, not south. He and Mr. Lawrence ate with the family but slept outside in a wagon box. Marki:

On the morning of the 25th I went about two miles north of where Dietemann lived after three head of horses belonging to Dietemann. I brought them home and picketed one of them. The Indians were chasing me and [I] did not have time to picket the other two horses. They cut the horse loose that I had picketed and drove the others off. . . . After the horses were taken Mrs. Dietemann, two children, his

30 Apollinaris Dietemann Indian Depredation Claim #4941. Record Group 123. Apollinaris insisted that his wife carried $7500 on her body when she fled the house and that the Indians took the money from her when they killed her.

sister and the hired man and me, walked up the creek about 4 miles when we were attacked by another body of Indians. I was carrying the little girl on my back and Mrs. Dietemann was a little behind. I also had the little boy by the hand. I walked up the hill and looked back and saw the Indians as they grabbed Mrs. Dietemann and shot her in the breast with a pistol. The little boy was with me and ran back [to] his mother and the Indians killed him. We then went [about six miles] to Kiowa where people had gathered and after Mr. Dietemann came we organized a party and went back and found the bodies of Mrs. Dietemann and the boy. Mrs. Dietemann was nearly naked. Her dress was over her face and she was scalped and the little boy had been shot by arrows, lanced and stabbed all over. The bodies were found right close together.[31]

One of the men who went with the search party was John Benkelman. He was also a member of the coroner's inquest, held shortly after Henrietta and her son were brought to Denver the next day. As with the Hungate family in 1864, Henrietta and John were put on public display in Denver: "The remains were taken to an empty house in front of the Tremont House, where for an hour or two people came and viewed them."[32] The *Rocky Mountain News* reported Benkelman's testimony:

so we joined in with two men who were present when the deceased were captured. They guided us to the place where it occurred, and we found the little boy about thirty yards from the place where first captured, dead. After making further search, we found the mother about fifteen yards from where the boy lay. We then sent four men after a wagon, to convey the bodies to Denver, where they now lay. These Indians are supposed to be Arapahoes. The deceased were both about four miles from their home, in company with some others, trying to make their escape to a neighbor's house, but from fatigue from traveling, were a little behind their comrades, when they were cut off by some Indians concealed under a bank. When we found the said bodies, they were horribly mutilated; the mother was shot (by a gun or pistol) in the front of the right shoulder, her face badly bruised as though she had been beaten with a revolver or club, bruises were also found nearly all over her body; she was also scalped. I think she must have been dead about five hours; she had, also, from evident signs, been ravished, which was the conclusion of myself, and those that were with me, signs of great struggle were also visible where she lay.

W. F. McClelland was sworn in as the surgeon for the Coroner's Inquest. He testified that the cause of death of the mother was a gunshot and other violent

---

31   Apollinaris Dietemann Indian Depredation Claim #4941.

32   *Rocky Mountain News*, August 27, 1868. The paper reported many of the comments made on viewing the remains, all calling for immediate action.

bruises. The boy had five arrow shots and many bruises. He concluded: "I give as my opinion professionally that the mother is pregnant about seven months gone."[33] This would explain why Henrietta was walking at a slower pace than her comrades when she was captured and killed. The *Rocky Mountain News,* on August 26, reported that the Indians doing the raids on Kiowa Creek were the same band of Indians that had committed all the murders on the Saline and Solomon River earlier in the month. The Denver *Daily Colorado Tribune* reported, on September 2, that the Indian Bureau in Washington identified the raiders as 250 Cheyenne, Arapaho and Sioux Dog Soldiers.

When it was safe to return to the two houses it was discovered that "all of the household goods were destroyed as well as the clothing. The dresses of the women were torn up and scattered in the yard and the dishes in the house broken, the table and chairs broken to pieces. The only thing that was left of any value at all was a little bedding...."[34] The $8,000 in cash that Apollinaris had from selling his business on Plum Creek was never found, and witnesses said that before fleeing her home Henrietta put the "green-backs" in a money belt, as well as several hundred dollars in gold coin. The money belt was missing as were the gold coins, when Henrietta's body was discovered. If indeed the Indians took this money after killing and raping Henrietta, they absconded with the equivalent of $136,000 in today's value, an incredible amount of money to lose at that time. And indeed, Indians by this time knew the value of money.

Anton Schindelholz added a few more details about what transpired to Mrs. Dietemann and her son on August 25. When he and Apollinaris were returning to their adjacent cabins on Comanche Creek, they met a stage at the Running Creek Stage Station near present-day Bennett. They were told by the stage driver going west that the Indians had made a raid in the Kiowa/Comanche Creek area and on Comanche Creek killed a woman and her boy. Anton and Apollinaris knew that was the wife and son of Apollinaris because that was the only family with children living at that time on Comanche Creek. Their fears were realized when they arrived in Kiowa. When they found the bodies later that day, near sundown, the boy had not been scalped. Schindelholz lost 73 horses and 50–60 head of cattle, noting "I am very positive that I found at least twenty carcasses on the trail

33   *Rocky Mountain News,* August 28, 1868.
34   Apollinaris Dietemann Indian Depredation Claim #4941.

of the Indians where they went, the cattle belonging to me, branded with my brand, branded "T" on the right hip. It was easy to trace the way they started with my stock by their tracks."[35]

Henry Smith was a neighbor of Dietemann and Schindelholz. He had lived on Comanche Creek since 1867, alone, about three miles south of them. He lost two horses, which were herded with the Schindelholz horses. He learned of the raid when the fleeing Dietemann party came by his house about 10 o'clock that morning and told him the Indians were raiding. Mrs. Dietemann was killed not far south of the Smith house. When learning from the Dietemann party that the Indians were north, he walked southwest to Kiowa, not having a horse on his ranch. When he returned to his house the Indians had taken or destroyed everything: "I went back to my place on my ranch that night, and when I got there I found that the Indians had been in the house and destroyed everything there was in it; they took everything that they wanted to carry away, and what they didn't want to carry away they destroyed, and cut to pieces and threw away." When asked what Indians did this Smith answered, rather caustically: "They were Cheyennes and Arapahoes. That was a hard thing to find out; nobody could run and ask them what Indians they were. They were Cheyennes and Arapahoes, that's what all the people said. There were lots of the same kind of Indians all over in the county."[36]

On August 27, Indians, thought to be Northern Cheyenne but possibly Southern Cheyenne who had wandered further north, made a deadly raid just outside the new town of Cheyenne, Wyoming. Benjamin J. Everett was coming from California to Illinois, bringing with him 31 horses and 3 mules, as well as one wagon. He had with him a herder, Edmund M. Pratt, and a cook, Crawford Farwell. They had been in camp—a little more than a mile east of Cheyenne—since the day before. Everett had been to town and purchased some provisions and was told that there had been no Indian trouble since the town had been built. People were freely traveling without molestations from Cheyenne to Denver. About an hour after sunrise on the 27th, as they were about to have breakfast, Pratt was about 80 rods away when Everett walked out to call him to breakfast. When he got within 20 rods of Pratt he saw five Indians on horseback approach his herder. Pratt

35   Anton Schindelholz Indian Depredation Claim #4939. Record Group 123.
36   Henry G. Smith Indian Depredation Claim #6696. Record Group 123.

HENRIETTA AND JOHN DIETEMANN GRAVE MARKER,
MOUNT OLIVET CEMETERY, WHEATRIDGE, COLORADO.
Mrs. Dietemann and her son were killed on Comanche Creek, five miles east
of Kiowa, Colorado, on August 25, 1868. The young mother and boy were fleeing to area settlers, after seeing Indians at their ranch. When Mrs. Dietemann
was attacked and struck down, five-year-old John ran to her side, and was
immediately killed by an Arapaho warrior. Like the Hungate family in 1864,
the mutilated bodies were briefly displayed in Denver before burial. *Courtesy
Tedd Remm, Reunion, Colorado.*

was holding a bridle in his left hand and a mule with a picket rope in his
right hand. The Indians appeared to be conversing with him when Everett
yelled for Pratt to come to breakfast. Suddenly the Indians shot Pratt and
then advanced towards Everett. Everett ran back to his wagon, picked up
two guns—both unloaded—and with his cook fled on foot to Cheyenne.
The Indians left them alone, going back after the stock and then rode off in
the opposite direction. When Everett got to town he went to the livery and
was loaned a horse, which he then rode out to Fort Russell at the other end
of town. There an officer told him he would take a squad of men and pursue
the Indians, but refused to let him go with them. The soldiers disappeared
over the hill and came back after sundown saying they could not catch the
Indians. Everett also heard that the soldiers simply went into camp when
they got out of sight, and came back after dark.

While the soldiers were being summoned, five citizens from Cheyenne took a two-horse wagon out to the camp and found Pratt, still alive. James Abney, the owner of the livery business, used his wagon and got other volunteers to join him. When they got to where the victim was lying on the ground, Abney said Pratt was "on his stomach, so to speak, who had evidently been shot by the Indians. The first thing he asked for was water. Three of the men got out of the wagon and placed him in the wagon. We looked over towards the south, probably, half a mile and saw four to six Indians standing on a knoll. We brought this man here to the hospital." Pratt had been shot twice, had three arrows in his body and had been scalped. They brought him to the hospital of Latham and Corey. Pratt lived a couple hours and then died. The *Cheyenne Ledger* newspaper reported the next day that a memorandum book found on Pratt indicated he served in the Union Army during the Civil War and named 27 engagements he had fought in, noting "Truly this is a sad end for a brave man who had done his country such noble service."[37]

Two days earlier, an unidentified man was killed in Box Elder. His body was brought into Fort Collins the next day. An arrowhead was still in him. The *Rocky Mountain News* reported "No clue to the name of the man could be discovered. Three fingers of his left hand were missing."[38] While this violent encounter was occurring near Cheyenne, Indians were still hanging around Elbert County. Raids were soon again turning deadly, beginning near present-day Colorado Springs, and continuing near present-day Elbert. On August 28, three days after the two murders of the Dietemann family, Indians stole 14 horses and three colts from George Sanborn. Sanborn lived with his family not far from Reed Springs Stage Station, which is about 3 miles northwest of present-day Simla. The family was eating dinner when a neighbor, George Smith, interrupted them and informed them that two Indians had taken Sanborn's horses. Eating with Sanborn was Rollin Sherman. Sherman recalled what transpired next:

> I ran outside and saw the Indians coming by the house with the horses. I got Mr. Smith's horse and Mr. Sanborn got one that was in the barn and we followed the Indians about 5 miles. Mr. Sanborn said that he thought that we had better go back home as the Indians might go to the house and kill his family. When we turned

37   Benjamin Everett Indian Depredation Claim #917, 1291. Record Group 123. Claim # 789, Entry 700, Record Group 75.

38   *Rocky Mountain News*, September 1, 1868.

back the Indians were about a mile and a half or two miles from us. They had driven the horses pretty nearly due south.[39]

Coincidentally, as this same time Oliver P. Wiggins was in the area, and observed through his army field glass the Indians running the horses. He saw two white men come from the next hill, and then they turned back. But Wiggins felt the Indians were Arapaho, as earlier he had spoken with about 50 Arapaho that were camped at the toll road nine miles east of Denver. Those Indians said a portion of their band was hunting out east, right where these raids occurred. Wiggins: "They showed me their passes from the commander of the post at Fort Laramie, and I examined them and found that they were Arapahoes, and there were a few of Standing Elk's Cheyennes with them but the whole was under the command of Roaring Wind, an Arapahoe Chief, ..."[40] Wiggins statement is validated by a report in the *Rocky Mountain News* on August 31: "A good many indications lead to the belief that the Indians numbered about 150, that they were Northern Arapahoes, as they were armed with certificates dated at Laramie."

Recall that in the middle of August, a party of 75–100 Cheyenne and Arapaho ventured through Colorado City on their way to fight the Utes in South Park near present-day Fairplay. When they came through in August they camped on the field of Harlow M. Teachout's neighbor, Eugene Roberts, who in 1869 owned the Elephant Corral in downtown Denver. Roberts lived on Monument Creek near present-day Garden of the Gods in Colorado Springs.[41] When the warriors returned back through Colorado City, more mayhem and murder followed. But before this outbreak of murder and theft, there had been the violence in Elbert County, where Mrs. Dietemann and her son were killed. News of those raids soon got back to Colorado City, and rumors reported that Fleming Neff and his family had been victims and were all killed. Neff lived between Kiowa and Colorado City. The *Pueblo Weekly Chieftain* publicized these rumors, on September 3: "The horrible murder of Mr. Neff, his wife, and seven children, on the Kiowa by Indians, should convince us all that they mean war—bloody, exterminating war."

---

39 George Sanborn Indian Depredation Claim #5749. Record Group 123. The claim was filed many years later and the dates say August 28 as well as August 8. Because of the nearby raids happening on August 25, I place this raid on August 28.

40 George Sanborn Indian Depredation Claim #5749.

41 Harlow M. Teachout Indian Depredation Claim #7726. Record Group 123.

In late August, Eugene Roberts and four other volunteers left the Colorado City area and went 20 miles northeast to the dairy ranch of Neff, only to discover his family was alive and well, and apparently unaware of the murders and raids further east, nor of their demise as reported in the paper. The five men stayed the night at the Neff ranch—no doubt relieved to learn the rumors were just that, rumors—and went back to Colorado City the next day. But they had only gone six miles when they discovered a war party of 65 Indians. Isaac Yoho agreed to go back and warn the Neff family that the Indians were nearby. Neff immediately abandoned his dairy ranch and fled with his family to near Denver, stopping on Dry Creek in Elbert County, where he remained for the next year. In leaving his house he lost his potato garden, and when he returned nearly a year later he discovered his ranch had been burned. Locals who had remained in the neighborhood said the Indians set the ranch on fire.[42]

The raids in late August prompted Colorado Governor Frank Hall to telegraph military authorities begging for assistance: "The Arapahoes are killing settlers, destroying ranches in all directions. For God's sake, give me authority to take soldiers from Fort Reynolds [east of Pueblo]. The people are arming and will not be restrained."[43]

Cheyenne and Arapaho warriors finally came into the outskirts of Colorado City and right into the heart of what would later become downtown Colorado Springs, still unbroken prairie in 1868. Horses were in abundance along the land and the taking of stock was in most cases quite easy. The Indians seemed to tarry in the neighborhood for a couple days. Andrew Jackson Hearst lost 86 horses.[44] On September 1, Indians struck a large herd of horses owned by four Teachout brothers. The herd was kept at Harlow Teachout's ranch on Monument Creek near where the present-day northern boundary is for Colorado Springs. Harlow lost 82 horses and six mules. Allen lost three horses. Edward lost 74 horses, and Henry Teachout lost 155 horses.[45] William Coplen lost four horses that were grazing with

42 Fleming Neff Indian Depredation Claim #6695. Record Group 123.

43 Gregory F. and Susan J. Michno, *Forgotten Fights: Little Known Raids and Skirmishes on the Frontier, 1823 to 1890* (Missoula, MT: Mountain Press Publishing Company, 2008), 268.

44 Andrew Jackson Hurst Indian Depredation Claim #6695. Record Group 123. Hurst filed his claim in 1891 and gave no details. It is possible he is one of the people who exaggerated losses.

45 Harlow M. Teachout Indian Depredation Claim #7726; Edward C. Teachout Indian Depredation Claim #1848; Allen Teachout Indian Depredation Claim #7882; Henry Teachout Indian Depredation Claim #808. Record Group 123.

the Teachout herd. The horses were grazing on Cottonwood Creek near Coplen's ranch when the Indians drove them off.[46]

Allen Teachout recalled the events preceding the loss of his three horses:

> I let my brother take my team [two work horses and a colt] to go down to another brother's [Harlow]. That evening he turned out my team and colt, with a band of horses that were running on the range belonging to my brother, and the next day, the first day of September, the Indians came and drove off the band of horses, and my team and colt were in the band. I was notified immediately and in company with ten or a dozen others, started in pursuit. . . .[47]

Harlow Teachout was there when the horses were taken. About eight o'clock that morning, he and a herder went out to gather the horses, which were scattered. Harlow:

> We rode slowly through them, and when we commenced to drive the herd to the corral, we saw two mounted Indians rushing around the horses, and looking to my right, I saw 15 or 20 Indians in single file riding at full speed to meet the other two Indians I first saw. They were all mounted and well armed. They stampeded the stock and drove them off in an easterly direction. I do not think it was ten minutes from the time I first saw the Indians until they had the stock out of sight. After going a short distance towards the house, I saw my band of 21 head of colts, that were in the habit of running by themselves, and we struck out, and when we got near them two Indians made their appearance coming in full tilt for the colts. I got to the stock first and had them started for the corral, but the Indians commenced shooting at us, and we had to run for the safety of our lives. The Indians then dashed in and captured the colts, the last of my stock except one young colt not able to travel.[48]

After the Indians took the horses, local residents hastily organized a posse to pursue the raiders and recover the stock. The trail was easy to follow since there were about 300 horses leaving tracks. The warriors ventured east and back into Elbert County. Samuel Slane was living along the path the Indians were driving the horses. The Indians had at least 400 horses taken from as many as 25 or 30 different ranchers. Slane—still a teenager—lost 17 horses which were jointly owned by him and his father, Andrew. Neither Slane saw the horses taken but rather heard what happened from their herder, a Ute Indian raised by Mexicans named Antonio Madril. Madril recalled

46 William Coplan Indian Depredation Claim #7536. Record Group 123.
47 Allen Teachout Indian Depredation Claim #7882
48 Harlow M. Teachout Indian Depredation Claim #7726.

he came in that day about noon, cooked his dinner; that his horse that he was riding he had tied two or three hundred yards from the house where there was some grass, while he was cooking his dinner. He . . . heard a noise like a bunch of horses running; he went out to see and he saw a bunch of Indians—Cheyenne and Arapahoes . . . running the loose horses right to where the horse was he had been riding was tied and he said he went back to the house to get his gun and by the time he got out the horse that he had picketed was loose, going with the bunch . . . that he run at them afoot and shot at the Indians; they turned on him and shot at him and run him in the brush.[49]

After the Indians took the Slane horses, they ventured into Bijou Basin, just east of present-day Elbert. The posse organized by the Teachout brothers numbered 18. They camped, on the night of September 1, at a ranch about three miles from a saw mill owned by C. R. Husted. While at the ranch two local men approached them, Job Talbert and Edward Davis. They wanted to join the posse and hoped to be loaned horses and guns at the ranch. They had walked from a nearby mill. However, there weren't any extra horses or guns, so the next morning they walked back to the mill. They never made it back and were killed, scalped and mutilated by the Indians. The posse continued to follow the horse trail and on the way came to a ranch owned by a man named Brackett. The house had been desecrated by the warriors, and after a short search Brackett's mutilated body was found. He too was scalped and his stock driven off with the growing herd. Soon after that the posse joined up with another eight men and continued pursuit. The men stayed another night and found two more mutilated bodies of ranchers, whom they buried. By the next day, the men figured the Indians had made their escape to the eastern plains and came back through Bijou Basin—still 15 miles distant, when they spotted a few Indians on a nearby hill.[50]

It was not long before the men were greatly outnumbered by the Indians. They eyed an isolated ridge that abruptly dropped off on three sides. Quickly the men rode their horses into the ridge and a brisk little skirmish ensued. Several of the horses were wounded. The fight lasted until night came on. Believing they could not withstand a concentrated attack, and thinking that would surely happen in the early morning, it was decided to

---

49 Samuel Slane Indian Depredation Claim #737. Record Group 123.

50 Howbert, *Memories of a Lifetime*, 187–189. Figures were changed to fit the additional information coming from depredation claims. See also David A. Wiser and Gary T. Wright, *Shamrock Ranch* (Boulder, CO: Johnson Books, 2009), 60.

send one of the party back down to Colorado City for help. A man by the name of Wild Bill volunteered. Leaving the party at night, his goal was to secure reinforcements from their neighbors.

The night being "moderately dark," the Indians saw Wild Bill and made an effort to cut him off. However, he was able to escape capture and made it back to Monument Creek, where reinforcements were summoned. The next day they were on their way when the besieged party met them. When morning had come the entrapped pioneers realized the Indians had left.[51] William Buzzard was a Teachout neighbor and recalled the incident:

> a party of men of about twenty . . . followed the Indians on the plains a ways, and was chasing the Indians too close, and the Indians surrounded the party and set up a fight; and the men got a little frightened in the fight, which was about sundown, and a man by the name of Texas Bill broke ranks and came into my house and said they would have to have help that night or else the Indians would kill the whole of them; and we gathered a posse of men to go and relieve the outfit, and we met the party coming home; the Indians had withdrawn, taking the horses with them.[52]

The *Rocky Mountain News* reported the fight occurred about eight miles northeast of Bijou Basin, and involved about 75 Indians. The engagement went from three o'clock until sundown. Eighteen horses were killed or wounded, and two men were wounded.[53] Milton M. DeLano was a partner with Philip Gomer in running a saw mill on Kiowa Creek. He submitted a report on the escape of Wild Bill, which was printed in the *Daily Colorado Tribune* on September 5, and gave some further details of the location and fight. The party of men had traveled to Reed Springs Stage Station, several miles northeast of Bijou Basin. At that point, they turned back southeast towards the Big Sandy, and when about eight to 10 miles from Bijou Basin, they were attacked by the warriors, who succeeded in cutting off escape in any direction. They dismounted and formed a circle inside their horses, and the fight continued until dark. The Indians did not venture into rifle range except occasionally. The men expended most of their ammunition when nightfall came, as their weapons had a longer range than the Indians' rifles. "They selected a daring man called "Wild Bill," put him on their fleetest horse and started him to the Basin for relief. He ran the gauntlet through

51   Howbert, *Memories of a Lifetime*, 190–192.
52   Henry Teachout Indian Depredation Claim #808.
53   *Denver Rocky Mountain News*, September 9, 1868.

the enemy's line, receiving only a slight wound in his foot, and reached the Basin at 8 o'clock."[54]

There has been some confusion with careless historians in thinking that the Wild Bill associated with this Colorado incident was the same James Butler "Wild Bill" Hickok who was killed by an assassin's bullet in Deadwood August 2, 1876. It was first proclaimed by the son of Philip Gomer, a young teenager at the time of this incident in 1868. In 1909, he published his remembrances while living at Gomer's Mill. He identified the Wild Bill as Wild Bill Hickok, and many biographers since then have continued to do so. The noted expert on Wild Bill Hickok—Joe Rosa—has correctly attacked this myth and attributed its beginnings to Alva Gomer.[55]

Before the posse came into the Bijou Basin area in search of the stolen stock, some of the warriors had earlier made a quick raid on Gomer's Mill. There they stole one horse. But that isn't all they did. Two young boys were playing outside the cabin used to house and feed the eight men working the mill. One of the boys was an orphan, the grandson of the cook and housekeeper, Mrs. Louisa A. Johnson. "Three Indians dashed in from the timber near the Mill and seeing two little boys out at play a short distance from the house they shot and killed one of them and then rode rapidly away." Leona Johnson was only six when he was murdered. Little Leona was taken to Denver the next day and buried. On September 4, 30 Indians returned to the mill and stole 27 work mules and five horses.[56]

Once the Indians killed the little Johnson boy, Philip Gomer organized a group of eight men to pursue the fleeing warriors. Late in the day they joined the party of 18 men chasing the Indians who had taken the Teachout herd. They met them in the basin and were a part of the fight when the Texan "Wild" Bill was sent for reinforcements. On September 2, Gomer organized another party of 10 men to join the other 26 men, not knowing they had withdrawn

---

54 Philip Gomer Indian Depredation Claim #2788.

55 The early Colorado newspapers did identify the messenger correctly as Wild Bill, but no paper made the connection that this was the Wild Bill whose fame was growing at that time in Kansas. Indeed, it was a man named Wild Bill, but, as noted in the documents used to tell this story, he was also called Texas Bill. Gomer's account was published in *Trail* I, 1909, and reprinted in the popular 1931 biography by Wilbert E. Eisele, *The Real 'Wild Bill' Hickok* (Denver, CO: William H. Andre, Publisher), 141–149. See especially 145. This myth was continued in the 1959 biography by Richard O'Connor, *Wild Bill Hickok* (New York, NY: Konecky & Konecky, 1959), 118–121. Joe Rosa reported the facts accurately in *Wild Bill Hickok: The Man and the Myth* (Lawrence, KS: University Press of Kansas, 1996), 88.

56 Philip Gomer Indian Depredation Claim #2788.

after the Indians left them on the night of September 1. When this second posse learned the other posse had withdrawn, they continued to pursue the Indians further east. About four miles after leaving Bijou Basin, they found two Indians and gave chase. But, as they were pursuing them, a much larger party of Indians emerged from the heavily wooded pinery and gave chase to the men, forcing them to withdraw. There was a running fight back through the Basin. For five miles the Indians sought to cut off the small party of men but were unsuccessful. Milt Garrison, one of Gomer's men, killed one Indian and severely wounded another. The dead Indian had his revolver pointed at another man when the shot by Garrison saved his partner's life. One man had his mule shot from him, and the Indians had three ponies killed in the fight. The Indians withdrew as the men neared Gomer's Mill.[57]

Marmaduke Green operated a country tavern and dairy 12 miles east of Colorado City. The day after Mrs. Dietemann and her son were murdered, some travelers stopped by to eat at Green's tavern—known as Franceville or Big Springs, but mostly called Jimmy's Camp—and told them they had just come from Bijou Basin. Their destination was the San Juan Valley. They reported the Dietemann murders to Green. Green's family, which included young wife Nancy and a baby, were warned that the Indians were prowling on the warpath. As the men were eating and discussing their danger, Isaac Hutchins—a relative of Marmaduke—came from the west running his wagon as fast as it would go. He came to warn them that the Indians were raiding around Colorado City and they should immediately leave their ranch or risk being killed. The family fled to a fortress in Fountain, 14 miles to the south. When they returned to their tavern/ranch several weeks later, most of their stock was killed and the dwellings plundered. Nancy reported that 13 people had been killed within 35 miles of their ranch.[58]

Naming the dead is difficult, especially since newspapers were not readily available to report the names of victims. But these are the known ones, which fits the numbers that Nancy Green claimed were killed: Mrs. Dietemann and her son, John; Job Talbert and Edward Davis; Mr. Brackett; Charley Everhart; two young sons of Thomas H. Robbins, 11-year-old George and eight-year-old Franklin; Jonathan Lincoln; John Choteau; John Grief (Griff) and Jonathan Tallman; six-year-old Leona Johnson. Talbert,

---

57   *Daily Rocky Mountain News*, September 3, 1868. Philip Gomer Indian Depredation Claim #2788.
58   Nancy J. Green Indian Depredation Claim #4940. Record Group 123.

Davis and Brackett were all victims of the Indians as they fled east with the horses stolen near Colorado City, on September 1. The *Daily Colorado Tribune* on September 5, 1868, reported that three men were killed on the (Big) Sandy on September 2. One man's name was Mr. Moss, the other was John Griff (not Grief), and the third man's name was unknown.[59] This would raise the known dead to 15, only one victim still unnamed.

Little George and Franklin Robbins were killed in the downtown area of present-day Colorado Springs. Charley Everhart was tending cattle his father had grazing on the open prairie. He saw the Indians as they came to him from the north. Howbert noted what followed:

> Everhart had reached a point near what is now the intersection of Platte and Cascade Avenues, when a shot from one of the savages caused him to fall from his pony. One of the Indians then came up, ran a spear through his body and scalped him, taking all the hair from his head except a small fringe around the back part. This tragic occurrence was witnessed from a distance by several persons. An hour later, when the Indians had gone and it was safe to do so, a party went out to where the boy's ghastly, mutilated body lay and brought it in to Colorado City.[60]

After killing Everhart and critically wounding a man named "Judge" Baldwin—a sheep herder—the Indians divided into two parties, one venturing northeast and soon joined by other warriors, and the other venturing south along the Fountain Valley, just east of present-day Interstate 25, in downtown Colorado Springs. The young Robbins brothers were taking care of their father's sheep, not far from where Everhart was killed. The Indians easily caught them. Howbert:

> It was said that one of the boys fell upon his knees to be begging the Indians to spare his life, but the savages never heeded any such appeals. Two Indians reached down from their horses, each grabbing a boy by the hair held him up with one hand, and with a revolver in the other, shot him through the head, and then flung the quivering lifeless body to the ground.[61]

The *Rocky Mountain News*, September 4, said the boys were eight and 10, but that the Indians "did not scalp them. They also killed Charley Everhart

---

59   Philip Gomer Indian Depredation Claim #2788. Howbert says Grief and Talbert were killed on east Bijou Creek, which is about seven miles from the Big Sandy.

60   Howbert, *Memories of a Lifetime*, 195–196. I have discovered in using the many documents from the National Archives, that Howbert's accounts of the Indian raids in both of his books are remarkably accurate.

61   Howbert, *Memories of a Lifetime*, 197–198.

and took his scalp, leaving his skull bare." One young woman remembered vividly what she saw when the dead boys were brought into Colorado City. Hattie L. Hedges Trout came to Colorado City with her family when she was a young girl. They had been in the settlement less than a year when the raids occurred. She never forgot the sight of the boys when their lifeless bodies were brought into Colorado City:

> Those were very exciting days as the Indians were on the war path here. People for miles around came and brought their families for protection from them, and were forted up in the old Anway house which was located at 2618 West Pikes Peak. As I remember it was a log house with a stairway going up on the outside. It still stands but has been remodeled and sided up and painted so no one could recognize it now. We were with others in the fort while my Father and other men stood guard on the hill north of town. We were living here when the three boys were killed by the Indians near where the Antler's hotel now stands. They were herding cattle when they were watched by the Indians from the hills. The oldest of the boys was young Everhart. I believe he was twenty one years old. The Robbins boys were younger. They were brought here and laid out in the old log building which was the first state house. It was located on the north side on Colorado Avenue between 26th and 27th streets. I can just remember of going with my sister to see the bodies as everyone was flocking there so horrified and grieved over it. Oh they were a terrible sight scalped and speared and they had placed their guns to their eyes and blew them out and faces and necks all powder burnt. Even after all these years I dread to recall the awful sight for at that time I hid behind my sister after a horrified glance at them. Oh those were terrible times for everyone so filled with fear and dread.[62]

After the Indians swept through the Colorado Springs area in late August and early September, some of them apparently remained around for a couple weeks at least, taking advantage of opportunities for plunder or murder. Jonathan Lincoln was killed during this time. Somewhere just beyond the El Paso County line and present-day Highway 83, Lincoln and another man were out working a harvest on a ranch on Cherry Creek, when Indians approached the men. The one man fled, but Lincoln "folded his arms and calmly awaited the coming of the savages. Without hesitation they killed him, took his scalp and departed. . . ." At the same time and further north on Cherry Creek the Indians killed Choteau.[63] On September 6, 12 Indians

---

62   http://history.oldcolo.com/index.php?option=com–content&view=article&id=179:reminiscences
     -of-the-early-days-in-colorado-transcribed-edition&catid=61&Itemid=92 (accessed July 11, 2013).
     The cabin where the boys were brought is now a protected historical building in the central park of
     Old Colorado City.
63   Howbert, *Memories of a Lifetime*, 205–206.

were spotted near present-day Franktown. One Indian was reported killed in that area the day before.[64]

During this time, settlers took refuge together in various stone houses. Near present-day Monument, one such house was owned by a man named David McShane. As recalled years later, one of the families staying there was named Trigg. The little boy of Jacob Guire asked to play outside in the yard. Not long after he went out to play, Mrs. Trigg saw an Indian in war paint "dash over a knoll nearby with a tomahawk in his hand. She jumped through the open door, seized the boy and threw him into the kitchen just as the Indians swooped by." The Indian threw his tomahawk at Mrs. Trigg. It missed her but embedded in the door. As quickly as he appeared, he disappeared over the knoll.[65]

Catherine McShane, David's wife, recalled what happened. Ten families were staying at the McShane house after the nearby September 1 raid, when the Teachout brothers had all their horses stolen. The men were all gone in their hunt to recover the stolen stock, including McShane. The families staying together at his house were all women and children. One of the men in the party trying to recover the stolen horses was riding one of McShane's horses. Andrew DeMasters had borrowed the horse to join the pursuit of the Indians. During their engagement near Bijou Basin, the horse was shot and killed. It was during the time that the men were gone, perhaps 10 days after the stock was stolen, when Indians reappeared near Monument and struck at the McShane house. As David recalled,

> We sent all the men we could raise, the country being sparsely settled, to recapture the Teachout herd, and they were surrounded by the Indians and had a skirmish and about 18 of their horses killed and wounded, amongst which two were mine; then the Indians came back and caught the most of us away from home, and took off all of the loose stock in the neighborhood; at that time they took 11 head of horses from my place and my wife stood at the door and kept them off from the house with a gun.

Catherine McShane said that the 10 families staying at her house never left the cabin while the men were chasing the Indians. But some of the Indians had apparently remained behind and returned. She remembered:

> The Indians came to our place between 12 and 1 o'clock in the day, and our children and a lady who was with me were playing outside the home when we saw

---

64   *Daily Rocky Mountain News*, September 9, 1868.

65   Mathews, *Early Days Around the Divide*, 15.

the Indians coming; we got them in the house and put them under the bed to get them out of sight of the Indians, and the lady and I both stood at the door with our guns to protect ourselves and the house, and the Indians went around and took the horses out of the pasture, all except one which was picketed in the field near the house, and one Indian tore the fence down and went and took her and her colt.[66]

The Indians then ventured further north to present-day Castle Rock, and, on September 20, made a raid on settlers living along Plum Creek. Isaac Hopkins lost 10 horses, several hogs and had the contents of his house stolen or destroyed. He was at a neighbor's house a mile away, while his son, Obadiah, was working in the field stacking hay. About three o'clock that afternoon, Obadiah was alerted by another neighbor that Indians had taken the horses. He and another man followed the trail and came to the Indians. They could do nothing to recover the stock. In coming back to the ranch they came upon another small band of Indians. The Hopkins family then left their home and went to another neighbor's cabin. They were staying at Benjamin Quick's place and two days later learned their cabin had been looted and a neighbor's cabin burned. It was then that the hogs were killed. Bedding and household goods were torn apart and scattered about the yard. Hopkins had a library of over 100 books. They were all torn apart and thrown about the yard.[67]

---

66   David McShane Indian Depredation Claim #1452. Record Group 123.
67   Isaac Hopkins Indian Depredation Claim #689. Record Group 123.

CHAPTER FOURTEEN

Fights and More Raids

In all the treaties by the Indian Peace Commission was a clause of doubtful wisdom, viz., leaving the Plains Indians the right to hunt buffalo as long as they lasted, outside of their reservations. Without this condition, it was contended, no peace could be concluded, and though the members varied in opinion, this concession was made by a decided majority and tied on, as long as the Indians maintained peace. But as they have broken the peace, I have ordered the military to renew their efforts to remove to their proper reservations all Indians who have not been drawn into war, and to kill, destroy and capture all who have been concurred in the recent acts of hostilities.

W. T. SHERMAN, LIEUTENANT GENERAL
THE CHEYENNE STAR, SEPTEMBER 15, 1868

WITH THE MURDERS IN COLORADO IN THE LATE SUMMER, 1868, the Indians were basically finished with their raiding in southern Colorado. Unknown to all at the time, however, the warriors had a rendezvous with their allies in the Republican River valley at the Kansas, Nebraska and Colorado state lines. The Battle of Beecher's Island was about to begin.[1] In their venture east, several warriors saw opportunities on the Denver road. The Indians escaping with the Teachout horses made it to the South Platte River. Some of them ventured near Fort Morgan—a now abandoned post—and were looking for victims. They found them on September 3. Twenty-seven-year-old Michael Tamney-—an Irish Immigrant—was with an ambulance wagon, drawn by two mules and riding a horse in the lead. With him was a man named

---

1 See Monnett, *The Battle of Beecher Island.*

Daniel Jones—driving the wagon—and a boy, Will Sinnott. Tamney had loaded goods at Julesburg to sell in Central City, consisting of hundreds of jeans and socks, and dozens of boots, shirts and vests. Instead of following the traditional road on the south side of the Platte, he was driving on the north side. When he got near the junction of Beaver Creek and the South Platte, a party of 40 Arapaho Indians surprised him. He soon reported what happened:

The Indians were mounted on horseback and charged down upon me and party while traveling upon the main highway or wagonroad from Julesburg to Denver about half-past four o'clock [September 3]; the party in attack killed my comrades and captured our wagon, stock and property. . . . I discovered the Indians first in corral when about one-half mile distant, and while engaged in making observations with a field glass, and consulting with my partner or comrade, Daniel Jones, we were charged upon by forty mounted Indians (or more) from the bluffs on the north side of the wagon; the Indians were armed with revolvers and knives; they commenced firing upon me and my comrades when about ten rods distant; immediately after the firing commenced Daniel Jones, who was driving the team at the time, fell from the wagon, and as he fell remarked to me "I am killed, save yourself;" as Daniel Jones fell, I could plainly see the bullet wounds made by two balls from the revolvers in the left breast of Daniel Jones; the boy whose Christian name was William was, at the time the firing commenced, sitting upon one of the boxes of goods in the wagon, but I did not see him killed. Immediately after Jones fell wounded, I turned my horse eastward and endeavored to make my escape, closely followed by seven of the Indians who were firing upon me rapidly, one ball passing through the "cape" of my saddle and two struck the rear of the saddle; I was pursued for about two and one-half miles when my horse plunged into a slough immediately in my front, burying my horse all except his head and throwing me forward in the same slough; while lying in the mud where I first fell there were not less than twenty-five shots fired at me by the Indians; when I had wiped the mud sufficiently from my eyes I saw four Indians out of the seven draw their knives and begin to search in a northerly direction for a place to cross to where I lay and the remaining three start in a southerly direction for the same purpose; upon this I drew my boots (filled with mud) from my feet and started on the run bareheaded and barefoot for the Platte River, in plain sight of the Indians all the time until I reached the bank of the river when I jumped down about nine feet into the main channel of the Platte River; changing my mind in regard to concealing myself upon or under the bank of the river, I waded about six rods through about five feet of water to two small islands separated by a narrow ditch of water; I crawled up the ditch about three rods and concealed myself among the willows and grass leaving as little trail behind me as possible; I had scarcely concealed myself when the seven Indians crossed the river on their horses and came upon the island where I lay, searching the island over thoroughly and during the search came so near me several times that I could have touched them, but having searched until after the sun had set and finding nothing they left. I lay in this position from about five o'clock on Thursday afternoon until dark the next Friday, not daring to crawl for water during that time; I traveled eastward on Friday night for about ten miles when I saw what I supposed the be the fires of four Indians lodges, then I lay on an island in the Platte River from that time until Saturday night, when I resumed my travels and by running almost all the way for about fifty miles I came opposite another island in the Platte River to which I waded, as upon the night previous, and lay for about two hours, when becoming desperate I determined to travel during the day (Sunday); I traveled until about three o'clock that afternoon, when I heard a shot and thinking they were Indians I concealed myself in a bunch of sunflowers on the road and began picking the mud from the tubes of my revolver preparing to defend myself; while so engaged I heard another shot and within about one hour and a quarter I saw two soldiers coming west with their rifles on their shoulders, which eventually proved to be members of the 18th U. S. Infantry; I arose and spoke to them and as I spoke fell to the ground exhausted; I was picked up by the soldiers and carried to the wagon which was about two miles in the rear, coming west, and put in the wagon which turned and traveled about sixteen miles when they reached Fort Sedgwick; the sergeant of the provost guard took me to headquarters and from there I was taken to the hospital where I remained from the 6th day of September, 1868, until the 25th day of September, 1868, when I left Fort Sedgwick and came to Cheyenne by way of the Union Pacific Railroad on a purse raised for me among the soldiers and citizens of Fort Sedgwick.[2]

There are a few things confusing about the story. In addition to his statement above, he said the raid happened near the old Lillian Springs stage station, but that station was 30 miles east of Beaver Creek. His story is confirmed by other witnesses, which makes it credible, and pinpoints the raid as happening near the old Lillian Springs Stage Station, near present-day Proctor. Cecil Deane was a U.S. Deputy Surveyor in 1868. That summer he had been working with a crew of three men from the Lodge Pole stage station down to the South Platte, and from there to Denver. He said he came upon the damaged wagon and the two dead freighters on September 4, in Township 7 N. Range 53 East. But this would place the event near present-day Atwood, 18 miles west of Lillian Springs. Tamney's long statement

2   Michael Tamney Indian Depredation Claim #1726. Record Group 123.

was made within a month of the raid. Having survived his ordeal, one can understand his inability to be precise in stating where it happened. But Deane's survey description contradicts his other statement, of finding the bodies and damaged ambulance near where the Crook railroad station was, which is just east of the old Lillian Springs Stage Station. The likely place of the event, then, is just north of Lillian Springs, below and just east of Proctor. Deane described what he found:

> On the forenoon of September 4, 1868, while in Tp. 7 N. Range 53 East, I came to an abandoned ambulance and saw the bodies of a man and boy who had apparently been killed but a few hours. Several dozen parts of pairs of new boots, having the top or leg cut off at the instep were scattered around the ambulance, also a number of cardboard and wooden boxes, ordinarily used to contain underwear, boots and heavy clothing were observed at same place. A large quantity of buttons, used on ordinary clothing, were observed scattered on the ground. Leatherwork of ambulance was cut and destroyed. . . . The body of the man found dead had been scalped [in a statement several months earlier Deane said "the body of the man found dead had been scalped, his privates had been cut off and partially forced into his mouth."]. The body of the boy had not been mutilated except by two bullets, shot through his body, which caused his death. . . . About a month subsequent . . . while making further government surveys in this locality, . . . I caused the body of the boy to be buried, and also the remaining bones of the body of the man, as his body had been eaten by wolves.

In a later statement survivor Tamney added a few other details:

> we were attacked by a large band of Indians, Arapahoes and Sioux; about eighty of these Indians attacked us, drove me away on my horse, run me into Pawnee Creek, where my horse mired; they shot me through the left leg; I escaped from them and concealed myself, after swimming about one and one-half miles, on a small island in the South Platte River, where I lay for forty-eight hours. . . . About four weeks afterwards I met Mr. C. A. Deane in Denver, who informed me he had found the bodies of the man and boy, the ambulance and the remains of the venture at a point opposite Lillian Springs; through his assistance I afterwards regained the ambulance.

Deane clearly shows the murders happened near Lillian Springs. Late in the day of September 3, just after the man and boy had been killed, and the Indians had left, Deane and two other men came from the north down to the South Platte River,

> on the north side nearly opposite old Lillian Springs stage station, on the old Overland Stage Mail Route, now near Crook Station, on the Julesburg Division of the

Union Pacific Railway: it was night when I reached the river, and the next morning I observed an ambulance standing beside the road near where I camped; upon reaching it, I first observed the mutilated bodies of a white man and boy, both dead, lying by the side of the ambulance, the boy shot through the body and head, and the man shot twice through the breast; I also saw several Indian arrows, part on the ground and part sticking in the woodwork of the ambulance. . . . The man and the boy had evidently been killed but a few hours at the time I first saw them, judging from my experience as a soldier in the inspection of gunshot wounds. . . .

Deane's story was also reported in *The Colorado Transcript* (Golden City) on September 16, quoting from an earlier statement in the *Tribune* on September 10:

He reports on Friday last (September 4) forty miles east of Fort Morgan [which would put the incident between Atwood and Sterling], he discovered a government ambulance, and near it the bodies of a man and boy, dead, but not scalped, although otherwise most horribly mutilated. They appeared to have been dead only one day. Their pockets were turned inside out, and the only thing found about them was a letter in the Welsh language. . . . Mr. Dean's party consisted of only three persons, therefore it was not considered sage to tarry and fully investigate the affair. They saw no Indians but did see numerous signs.[3]

Deane's earlier statement that he returned a month later and buried the bodies is corroborated in a letter written to General George Ruggles by Colonel Henry Carrington, commanding the post at Fort Sedgwick. On October 2, four weeks after the murders, Carrington acknowledged the bodies were still unburied next to the abandoned wagon, but said they were 90 miles distant—"nearly opposite the mouth of Beaver Creek"—and he didn't feel at liberty to send the necessary detail of men without prior approval from higher authorities. Carrington concluded, "Possibly the trip might have advantages as it will directly strike the north and south trail; but the value of the property is so small that I prefer not to deplete the post of troops and teams. . . ."[4] Carrington did not seem concerned that American citizens were rotting on the prairie without burial, the remains subject to the hunger of wolves and other animals. Instead, it appears the value of the plundered property to his thinking did not justify sending the troops. He

---

3   Marc H. Abrams, *Newspaper Chronicle of the Indians Wars, Volume 2, 1867–1868* (Brooklyn, NY: Abrams Publications, 2010), 312.

4   Col. Henry Carrington, "Letter, Fort Sedgwick Col. Ter. Oct. 2, 1868." Record Group 393, Part I, Department of the Platte, Letters Received, Box 6, 1868.

might have felt different had the young boy been his son. But he also showed the confusion of exactly where the incident occurred, quite probably due to Tamney's explanation of where the incident happened—he was recovering at the post hospital and no doubt Carrington talked with him personally. It is clear, from Deane's later testimony, that the attack was not a 90-mile journey from Sedgwick to the bodies. It was about half that distance.

Carrington's letter suggests something else about the South Platte road to Denver in 1868. The railroad was advancing on the north side of the river. In 1867, it was at Julesburg, and by November 13, of that year, the track was laid to Cheyenne, a distance of about 125 miles.[5] The railroad was built on the north side of the river. It would make sense that in 1868 there were two roads, the old road on the south side, but now a more conveniently traveled road on the north side, following the railroad. Indeed, by 1868, the south side of the trail—the original Denver road—was mostly abandoned. There would still be traffic to and from Denver, but not enough to maintain businesses, and the ranches that had been engaged in the commerce of freighters and settlers were gradually abandoned, one by one. Many of the buildings burned in the summer of 1867 were not rebuilt, as they had been when they were burned by the Indians in 1865. Indeed, Wells Fargo stopped running the stage to Denver in late November—instead moving it to run from Cheyenne to Denver—further hindering commerce along the old South Platte road.[6] Supplies were more readily available on the north side of the river because of the new towns built in conjunction with the railroad. Freight going to Denver was now conveniently brought by rail to Cheyenne, and from there freighted by wagon to Denver, eliminating about a month's travel by wagon over the old Platte River route from Julesburg to Denver. Passengers could take a more comfortable ride on rail to Cheyenne and then from there take a stage to Denver. The same was true with the contract Wells Fargo had with the U.S. mail. This change in late 1867 explains why Tamney was traveling on the north side of the road when his one-wagon train was attacked.

A newspaper at the time reported that another survey party had seen a large Indian trail near Fort Morgan numbering in the hundreds, and maybe

---

5   E. O. Davis, *The First Five Years of the Railroad Era in Colorado* (no city listed, but Denver, CO: Sage Books, Inc., 1948), 13.

6   Doris Monahan, *Julesburg and Fort Sedgwick Wicked City—Scandalous Fort* (Sterling, CO: published by Doris Monahan, 2009), 177. Monahan, *Destination: Denver City*, 242.

as many as 1,500, which consisted "principally of Arapahoes with their families." It was believed the party included the same Indians that had just finished their deadly raids around Colorado City and Kiowa.[7] And indeed, it wasn't just Tamney's two friends who had been killed during this time, for Deane saw other atrocities too—awful ones. His narrative continued:

> the next night, on passing old Fort Morgan, about sixty miles from the ambulance, I observed the burning of the abandoned government buildings by the Indians, whom I could see by the light of the flames, and I could also see that they were burning a man, evidently a white man whom they had captured, and I heard his screams while he was so burning; about eight o'clock the following morning, near the mouth of Crow Creek I found where several stacks of hay and grain had been burned, and two cabins, which had also been burned, were still smoking at that time; I also observed at the same place a large number of cattle, some of which had been killed and the others hamstrung, the latter still alive but worthless; when I reached the mouth of Crow Creek I found the bodies of three men festered and putrefying near a herder's cabin.[8]

Fort Morgan had been closed in May 1868, the government foreseeing the end of freight lines through the old Denver road. But this decision was perhaps one season premature, for it left people in that area quite vulnerable to the violent attacks occurring later that summer. Who these additional unfortunate victims were that Deane observed will probably never be known. Similar to what happened with the forts built on the Bozeman trail two years earlier, once abandoned by the military; the Indians burned them at their first opportunity. Unfortunately a white man was brought to death by the torture of fire when the buildings at Fort Morgan were burned.[9]

While Indians were roaming along the old Denver road, other Indians were looking for victims along the other trails in Kansas, Nebraska and Colorado. They caught some careless soldiers between Forts Larned and Dodge, and one man was awarded a Medal of Honor for joining the fracas. Leander Herron was a corporal in Company A, 3rd Infantry, and was

---

7   Abrams, *Newspaper Chronicle*, 312.
8   Michael Tamney Indian Depredation Claim #1726.
9   Don English, in *The Early History of Fort Morgan, Colorado* (Fort Morgan, CO: The Fort Morgan Heritage Foundation, 1975), 14, said the buildings and moveable material was sold at public auction and that the locals living in the area used what remained. Given the credible testimony of Deane this is clearly false. In the summer of 1868, the road that Fort Morgan had earlier protected was no longer safe once the post was ordered closed, and there were no local ranchers living in the area. It was still desolate and dangerous, even more so with the closing of the fort.

stationed at Fort Larned. During this time, voluntary couriers would run military reports between the two forts, always traveling at night to avoid detection. Herron had volunteered to bring the mail and dispatches from Fort Larned to Dodge, a distance of a little more than 50 miles. On his night trip to Dodge, he came upon a mule-team heading north, bringing wood to a post on Little Coon Creek between the two forts. On the creek was a small sod post, at which a sergeant and 10 men were stationed. But there was no wood nearby, and the men relied upon a supply of wood delivered periodically to the little post. Herron spoke to the four men bringing the wood and advised them—for their own safety—to remain at the post until there was a larger train coming from the east to attach with before riding back to Dodge. He then went on to deliver the mail at Fort Dodge.

The next night—September 2—Herron was ordered back to Larned with important dispatches from Dodge. He was given a man to accompany him, Patrick "Paddy" Boyle of the 7th Cavalry. The two men had ridden for about 12 miles in the dark—near present-day Bellefont and Spearville—when they heard firing in the distance.[10] They rode to the sound of the fight. As they got closer, they saw it was a wagon under attack. The citation for Herron's medal simply said that while "detailed as mail courier from the fort, voluntarily went to the assistance of a party of four enlisted men, who were attacked by about 50 Indians at some distance from the fort and remained with them until the party was relieved."[11] Herron recalled what happened next: "We got ready and rode straight for the wagon train. If the Indians saw us they took us for members of their own party." To Herron's surprise the wagon was the wood-wagon he had passed the night before. The soldiers did not heed his advice to stay at Coon Creek.

Herron:

> The Indians followed close on our trail and five minutes after we reached the wagon we were fighting to repulse a desperate charge they made upon us. But we repulsed it all right. Six men with guns can do heavy execution when they know their scalps and lives depend upon their aim.

10   Johnson, *No Greater Calling*, 88–89.

11   Vance Hartke, Chairman, *Medal of Honor Recipients 1963–1973* 93d Congress 1st Session, Committee Print No. 15 (Washington, DC: U. S. Government Printing Office, 1973), 296. The book says citation unknown when given, but the following link notes that he received the award 50 years later on the Eddie Rickenbacker radio show. http://www.milettavistawinery.com/?page—id=265 (accessed July 10, 2013).

CORPORAL LEANDER HERRON,
COMPANY A, 3RD INFANTRY.
Herron was awarded a Medal of Honor for his
action on September 2, 1868, while carrying
dispatches between Forts Larned and Dodge.
Courtesy Jacquie Herron Kilgren, great-
granddaughter of Corporal Herron, Spokane,
Washington.

After this I looked over the ground and found a mighty poor place to defend a wagon. We talked the matter over and it was determined that Paddy Boyle should attempt to get away and ride to the fort [Dodge] for assistance. Shaking hands all around, Paddy sneaked away on his horse and a few minutes later we heard a bunch of shots and yells. Then things quieted down again and we knew Paddy had been killed.

Our wagon team [mules] had been killed and up to that time the men had fought from behind the wagon. But we knew, with daylight, that the Indians would begin circling around us and would certainly get us. So I scouted around a little and close by found a deep buffalo wallow. We five men managed to push the wagon until it stood right over the deep wallow. We got into this and found our position very much improved.

But our ammunition was getting low. Since Paddy had been killed we knew there was mighty little chance that we would ever escape. So we agreed to fight until each man had just one bullet left. That last bullet was for the men themselves. We were not going to be tortured. We would kill ourselves with our last shot.

The Indians charged us repeatedly, uttering the most blood-curdling yells. Most of the time they would be on the side of their horses, but once in a while we would send a bullet all the way through the pony and get the man on the other side. Several times their charges brought them within a few feet of our wagon, but the boys were calm and with deadly aim managed to drive them back.

At this time we were getting in mighty bad shape. Goodman, one of the men, had been wounded seven times by arrows and bullets [Corporal James Goodwin, Co. B, 7th Cavalry, gunshot wound, shoulder]. O'Donald had been struck in the head by a tomshawk [*sic*] during a hand-to-hand fight [John O'Donnell, Co. A, 3rd

Infantry, gunshot wounds, thigh, neck and face]. Nolan was wounded with both bullet and arrow [Charles Faxton, gunshot wounds, arms, buttocks]; Hartman, the fourth soldier, was wounded but not seriously. I was unwounded. I would load my Remington revolver and hand it to Nolan, who was obliged to fire with his left hand, his right arm having been shattered by a bullet. It was only by the most desperate exertions that any of us escaped death during the many charges the Indians made upon us, only for the fact that the Indians stopped to carry off their dead prevented them from killing us during any of their charges.

Finally we were reduced to twelve rounds of ammunition each, and that's how I won my congressional medal. The Indians were preparing for another charge, and we knew this would be the last. We reminded each other to save the last shot for ourselves, and then we got ready to meet the rush.

But the rush did not come.

From what we could see, the Indians had divided themselves into two parties, and were coming from two directions at us. We prepared to divide our forces, to face both charges. But only one division charged. Before we could fire at it we heard a call in English:

"Don't fire."

We thought it a ruse to get close to us, as many of the Dog Soldiers could speak good English. But suddenly a man threw his carbine in the air. Then we recognized him and shouted.

It was Paddy Boyle. He had gotten through after all. And he got to the fort all right too.

The Indians broke and fled. The white soldiers rode up to us. Every last man was dressed in white.

"What kind of uniforms do you call this?" I asked Paddy.

"Well, the boys were asleep when I reached the post," he answered, "and they didn't take time to dress. They ain't got on anything but their underclothes."

Which was a fact. The men didn't wait to dress.[12]

Seventh Cavalryman, Private Winfield Scott Harvey, was at Dodge— arriving on September 3—and kept a diary, an unusual activity for enlisted men. He wrote about this incident in his entry for September 5. The Indians no doubt had been alerted to the rushing cavalrymen and left the fight just before they arrived:

---

12   Leander Herron typed manuscript, Kansas State Historical Society, Topeka, Kansas. In my years of research I learned early to make individual notations of every document I copied. However, in the beginning of this journey, I sometimes forgot to do this. This manuscript is one of those. The markings, writing his name on the top of the document, follow what is found with the various individual archive materials at the KSHS, and I am assuming this is where that document is housed. If not there, perhaps the Nebraska State Historical Society, in Lincoln, Nebraska. The New York Times, January 26, 1919, contains a similar account, and notes that the relief came at dawn.

There was a wagon attacked at Little Coon Creek last night at about eleven o'clock. Three soldiers belonging to the 3rd Infantry were wounded, and the mail coming at the same time is all that saved them from being killed, as one of the men with them gave the alarm at the post and Company B, 7th U. S. Cavalry, stationed at this post, went out to bring them in, but saw no Indians. They had fled and disappeared.[13]

The timing of the rescue of the 7th Cavalry, minus uniforms, apparently was never a feature in any Hollywood westerns. But it was not the only time the cavalry arrived in the nick of time, and that was a story-line in early western movies.[14]

On September 7—on the Smoky Hill trail—a few miles east of Fort Wallace Indians made an attack upon 20-year-old Archibald Gardner, who was driving a wagon loaded with hay near Sheridan. He was killed and scalped and two horses hitched to the wagon stolen. His family had emigrated from Scotland five years earlier and his father had taken a job with the railroad and was sent out to Sheridan in 1867. By 1869 his mother was a poor widow.[15]

The Indians, Dog Soldiers, remained in the area. An unnamed man was killed at Sheridan on September 8. West of Fort Dodge 26 miles, on the Cimarron crossing, warriors killed 17 citizens. The next day six more were killed at Sheridan.[16] On September 10, Indians at Sheridan stole two horses belonging to Marshall Riley.[17] Two days later, they caught another hay wagon going to the hay camp operated by Tim McCarty, about three miles from Sheridan. Edward Carson was driving a wagon owned by Jordan Scott. Carson was overcome and killed. He was speared and scalped and his revolver and two horses were stolen.[18]

After these deaths near Sheridan were reported to the commander at Fort Wallace, Colonel George A. Forsyth and his 50 scouts—recently arrived at the post from Fort Hays—were sent on the trail. The Indians had ventured north after committing murders and theft at Sheridan. As the party followed

13   Shirk, George H., "Campaigning with Sheridan: A Farrier's Diary," *Chronicles of Oklahoma*, Volume 27, 1959, 73.

14   See Gregory F. and Susan J. Michno, *Circle the Wagons! Attacks on Wagon Trains and Hollywood Films* (Jefferson, NC, and London: McFarland & Company, Inc., Publishers, 2009). The authors show how Hollywood created stories that followed real-life cavalry rescues. See, e.g., the Fisk train 1864, 104; the Cooke (Custer) train 1867, 127; the Lyman train 1874, 136; the Sawyers train 1865, 150.

15   Jeanette Day Indian Depredation Claim #1097. Record Group 123.

16   Johnson, *No Greater Calling*, 89–90.

17   Marshall Riley Indian Depredation Claim #3680. Record Group 75.

18   Jordan Scott Indian Depredation Claim #3734. Record Group 75.

the trail the tracks grew bigger and bigger, so big, in fact, some of the men with Forsyth felt it was suicidal to continue with such a small party. The Indians were reuniting with the other bands that had raided into Colorado, Nebraska and Wyoming. The result was the Battle at Beecher's Island, which began September 17, and continued for three days. The column was not relieved until September 25. Six men died, including Lieutenant Frederick Beecher, a nephew of famed abolitionist, Reverend Henry Ward Beecher. Eighteen men were wounded.[19]

Meanwhile, down on the Santa Fe road near Fort Lyon, Cheyenne and Arapaho Indians were again making deadly raids. At seven o'clock on the morning of September 8, about 50 Indians killed dozens of sheep belonging to Robert Lambert and Frank Smith, who had a ranch on the Purgatory River. It was Election Day in that area and a man was working as a clerk for the election. He was out riding his mule and when the Indians saw him they surrounded him, killed him and took his mule. The unfortunate murder victim was Tom Kinsie (or Kinsey). Silas Wright remembered: "Tom Kinsie was passed our house as we were sitting down to breakfast and wanted me to go to the election. I told him I would overtake him before he got there. We started down and I tried to overtake Kinsie, but unsuccessfully. While we were unhobbling our horses the Indians killed Kinsie."[20]

At the same time this was happening, about four miles away at a ranch run by Charles Boggs, his brother Thomas and Leftrick Allen, Indians ran off 32 mules and six horses. Seven oxen were killed. The herd was about a half-mile from the ranch tended by two herders—Kinsey and Hart— whom the Indians killed. It is unclear if the Kinsey killed was a brother of Thomas Kinsey. The election was supposed to be held at the Bogg's Ranch (Boggsville). A third herder—William Allen—was able to escape back to the ranch. The military at Fort Lyon, just four miles away, were notified and immediately sent out a company of 40 7th Cavalrymen under command of Lieutenant Henry Abell, and Captain William Penrose, 3rd Infantry. The Indians were caught after several miles and in a fight four warriors were killed, including one known as One-Eyes Cheyenne. Two cavalrymen were

19   Michno, *Encyclopedia of Indian Wars*, 223–224. Monnett, *Battle of Beecher Island;* Bob Snelson, *The Solomon Avengers: The Battle of Beecher Island September 17–25, 1868* (self-published, 2006); Criqui, *Fifty Fearless Men.*

20   Robert Lambert Indian Depredation Claim #7336. Record Group 123.

killed, Company L privates Phillip Sheridan and Henry Rickie. The pursuit ended at darkness. The stock was not recovered.[21]

The *Rocky Mountain News,* on September 17, gave details of this fight. The company of cavalrymen and infantry left the post within 15 minutes of the report of the raid and soon saw 15 Indians running the stolen stock in their front. They chased them for as many as 20 miles, greatly exhausting both the Indian ponies and the larger cavalry mounts. Penrose ordered Abell to advance with his best horses, and with 10 men he took off after the Indians. The chase lasted about two miles when the troopers caught up to the band. Abell and five troopers separated from the rest and as they got closer to the Indians, four of them turned back and charged the pursuing soldiers. Penrose saw the skirmish unfold and ordered more men in a flank movement on the four Indians and got them surrounded. "The four Indians fought with desperation, but were soon all killed. The fight lasted but a few minutes. The Indians killed two of the cavalry, and wounded one slightly." As this fight was unfolding, the remaining raiding warriors switched from their tired ponies to the stronger and fresher stock they had just stolen and in this way eluded capture.

On September 12, John Banning lost 28 mules and 20 horses near the Wyoming border. He was working for the railroad helping to build the spur line connecting Cheyenne to Denver. About 10 miles south of Cheyenne, in what he said was a place known as the "natural corral," nine Indians, believed to be Cheyenne, suddenly appeared in the early morning, chased the herder back to the camp where the men were living as they worked the railroad, and ran off the stock. Banning and six other men pursued the Indians for as many as 40 miles but could not catch them.[22]

Back on the Denver road, two men—Fletcher and Thomas—had a beef contract with Fort Sedgwick, and employed three men to care for a large cattle herd near the post. On September 20, the cattle were about three quarters of a mile from their ranch—located near Fort Sedgwick—when the men went to breakfast. After eating his meal, one man went out to check on the herd and noticed 46 cattle were missing. The herders looked around

---

21   Charles A. Boggs and Leftwick Allen Indian Depredation Claim #928. Record Group 123. Johnson, *No Greater Calling*, 90.

22   John A. Banning Allen Indian Depredation Claim #2655. Record Group 123. See also statement in Charles A. Boggs and Leftwick Allen Indian Depredation Claim #928.

for almost two hours before finding a trail nearly five miles away. The cattle had been run into a sand creek, the ground being very hard which left a very faint trail. The men followed it another three miles when the ground became soft, and then they could plainly see the trail and what was happening. There were about 20 different pony tracks mixed among the cattle, but their feet had been muffled. Soon the herders came upon a feather lying in the trail "notched and painted in Indian style." Another mile further the men discovered a muffle that had fallen from one of the legs of an Indian pony. After another four miles, four Indians appeared just over a bluff a half-mile in the distance. The warriors saw the three men as the cattlemen saw them. There were only two revolvers among the three men, and, as the Indians began to ride towards them the three men withdrew. The Indians followed them five miles until darkness came. When the men came back to the fort, they reported the theft to Col. Henry Carrington, who ordered a column of 35–40 infantry soldiers, drawn in wagons, to pursue the warriors the next day. About 25 miles were traversed and the trail became difficult to follow; the officer leading the detail decided to turn north to the Platte rather than continue to follow the disappearing trail south in the direction of the Republican River. Two of the herders continued south and in about four miles, the trail again became readily visible. But when they got back to the command they could not convince the officer in charge to return to the trail they had verified going south, allowing the Indians to escape.[23]

By the time October rolled around, Indians had made several raids on and near the roads to Denver. In late September, warriors raided settlers living along Sharp's Creek, a small stream that flows into the Smoky Hill River southeast of present-day Marquette, in McPherson County, Kansas. One settler was killed, and the wife of Warren Bassett was stripped of her clothes and raped. She was later found alive and naked in the woods along with her week-old baby. Mrs. Bassett claimed the Indians who raped her numbered about 40.[24] Several horses were stolen from various settlers.

23 Fletcher and Thomas Indian Depredation Claim #3487. Record Group 75.
24 Henry Weber Indian Depredation Claim #3790. Record Group 75. Johnson, *No Greater Calling*, 94. See also Warren Bassett Indian Depredation Claim #3393. Record Group 123. Bassett had two claims, another one for 1870. He identified Osage Indians as the tribe involved in both incidents; however, the investigation in the Henry claim indicated it was Cheyenne and possibly Kiowa Indians involved in the 1868 incident. Further investigation in the Bassett claim indicated the 1868 incident was not committed by Osage Indians but rather Kiowa.

Eleven more citizens were killed near the trails to Denver in Kansas and Colorado, from October 1 to the 12th.[25]

On October 1, northwest of Fort Collins, Elias Whitcomb lost seven horses on Box Elder Creek. Cheyenne were identified as the culprits, but this far north, they were probably Northern Cheyenne who had ventured down from Wyoming.[26] On October 9, just south of the Smoky Hill River near Ellsworth, Cheyenne Indians targeted horses owned by two men named George Sanderson and James White, stealing seven.[27] The two men also declared a loss of 60 horses earlier in September, but a government investigation into those losses revealed both men were connected with an elaborate plan of horse stealing, especially government horses from nearby Fort Harker, using their livery as a means to cover it up. Indeed, violence seemed to follow them throughout their time in Ellsworth. Sanderson especially had a violent temperament and a compulsive love of gambling. Indian Agent Michael Piggott, in investigating the claim, said both men "were a hard lot of citizens, enjoying the general reputation of 'horse thieves,' ready to shoot and kill each other as well as those who interfered with their business. J. R. White, one of the claimants, was killed by one of his own men in a quarrel about stolen horses. C. B. Whitney, also one of their men, was killed, besides a number seriously wounded."[28] The dead Whitney was one of the veterans of Beecher's Island, and when killed, was serving as sheriff of Ellsworth County.[29]

This does not mean, however, that Indians were not raiding in the area at this time. Indeed, Cheyenne Indians came upon a dugout five miles southeast of Ellsworth about mid-October and caught a roommate of Matthew McCune outside the dugout. He was killed and scalped and left next to the creek. Two or three other men were able to escape. The Indians destroyed the contents of the dugout and made off with a team of horses belonging to McCune.[30] It was also during this time that two herders were caught by the Cheyenne, the same distance south from Fort Harker, stripped and

25   Johnson, *No Greater Calling*, 95–96.
26   Elias Whitcomb Indian Depredation Claim #719. Record Group 123.
27   Sanderson and White Indian Depredation Claim #1011. Record Group 123.
28   Sanderson and White Indian Depredation Claim #1010. Record Group 123. This depredation claim is an excellent example of how government investigation of the claims were able to flesh out frauds.
29   Jim Gray, *Desperate Seed: Ellsworth, Kansas on the Violent Frontier* (Printed in USA: Kansas Cowboy Publications, 2009), 37.
30   Matthew McCune Indian Depredation Claim #3641. Record Group 75. See Gray, *Desperate Seed*, 21. The undated story there may well connect to McCune's story.

tied to the ground. Fires were built around their staked bodies, and the men were slowly burned to death. Townspeople in Ellsworth could hear their cries late into the night. The next morning "the blackened and half-burned bodies were found still fastened to the ground, not only scalped, but horribly mutilated."[31]

Two incidents happened, one in Kansas and one in Colorado, which resulted in well-known captivity stories of the time. They occurred five days apart, on October 9 and October 13. On the 9th, Richard Blinn was returning to Kansas with his young wife, 19-year-old Clara and their two-year-old toddler son, Willie. They were in a train consisting of eight wagons and had left from Fort Lyon earlier, following the Arkansas River east. When they had traveled between 45 and 50 miles, near the border between Colorado and Kansas, a war party of anywhere from 75 to 200 Cheyenne warriors caught the small train just as it was departing from the noon meal. Unfortunately, Clara was in the lead wagon, containing the family's entire possessions. Little Willie Blinn was with her, asleep in the wagon. The Indians fired on the men in the other wagons and were thus able to overtake Clara and drive her wagon east away from the others. Richard—Dick—and his brother Hubble chased the wagon for about 300 yards, trying to shoot one of the oxen driving the wagon—hoping that would halt it—but failed to do so. The besieged men could only watch as Clara and Willie were taken captive and the wagon, beyond rifle fire, was pillaged and burned.[32] The same day, closer to Fort Lyon, Chaney Owen was attacked on the Santa Fe road. He lost 98 cattle, two mules, four freight wagons and all the contents, which contained provisions and clothing.[33]

---

31 Roenigk, *Pioneer History of Kansas*, 362. Roenigk claims it was the memory of this and similar events in Ellis County that led citizens to chase Pawnee scouts who stopped in Ellsworth after the Washita, on their way home to their reservation in Nebraska. They were chased from town and as many as six of the friendly scouts were killed. Roenigk's account is verified in a report from Fort Harker dated March 16, 1869. See Captain Edward Leib, "Letter, Headquarters, Fort Harker, Kansas, March 16, 1869." Record Group 393, Letters Received, Department of the Missouri, part 1, Entry 2601, 1869. Both Roenigk and Leib condemn the action. This event often gets confused with yet another killing of Pawnee Indians in Lincoln County, which happened in late January. See Broome, *Dog Soldier Justice*, xvii–xix. See also Van De Logt, *War Party in Blue*, 111–112. See also Johnson, *No Greater Calling*, 105.

32 Richard Blinn Indian Depredation Claim #1564. Record Group 123. See also Judith P. Justus, "The Saga of Clara Blinn at the Battle of the Washita," *Research Review the Journal of the Little Big Horn Associates*, Vol. 14, No. 1, Winter, 2000, 11–20; and Broome, *Dog Soldier Justice*, 62–65.

33 Chaney Owen Indian Depredation Claim #3314. Record Group 123.

The other white captive was taken along the Solomon River in Ottawa County, Kansas, near present-day Delphos. James Morgan was helping a neighbor in his field when he left his newly married wife, 23-year-old Anna, at their home. Not long after James left, his horse ran back to their cabin. Unknown to Anna, James had been seriously wounded, shot in the thigh by a band of Lakota Indians who had come into the Solomon Valley from the north. Anna mounted the horse and was riding to where her husband was working when she came upon the warriors that had shot James. She was captured and a month later traded to the Cheyenne, shortly before General G. A. Custer attacked Black Kettle's village on the Washita River on November 27.[34]

Unknown to Custer at the time he captured Black Kettle's lodges, Clara and Willie were killed in one of the adjoining villages during the battle. Their frozen bodies were found two weeks later, a few miles from where Custer attacked Black Kettle's camp. Custer's casualties were two officers and 20 enlisted men killed, as well as several wounded. Indian casualties, according to Custer's report, included 103 warriors killed, and 53 women and children taken captive. Custer soon revised his report up to 140 warriors killed. Some historians question that amount and lower it to a significantly smaller number, anywhere from 29 killed, down to 12 warriors and about that same number of women and children.[35]

Custer's fight at the Washita had among the Indian casualties Black Kettle and his wife, Medicine Woman. Both had survived the attack on Sand Creek two days shy of exactly four years earlier, but they were not fortunate in Custer's fight. As Bent recalled, during the fight Black Kettle "mounted a horse and helped his wife up behind him and started to cross the Washita River, but both the chief and his wife fell at the river bank riddled with bullets; the horse was also killed at the same time."[36] With the death of Black Kettle, the Southern Cheyenne lost their great peace chief, the one Cheyenne who appeared repeatedly trying to secure peace between the

---

34 James Morgan Indian Depredation Claim #3644. Record Group 75. Broome, *Dog Soldier Justice*, 52–55.

35 Greene, *Washita*, 136–137; Richard G. Hardorff, *Washita Memories: Eyewitness Views of Custer's Attack on Black Kettle's Village* (Norman, OK: University of Oklahoma Press, 2006), 397–403. Bent said the losses were 11 warriors, 12 women and six children killed at the Washita. Two Arapaho were killed in the fight that killed Major Elliott and his party. Hyde, *Life of George Bent*, 320, 322.

36 Hyde, *Life of George Bent*, 316–317.

Southern Cheyenne and the military. Throughout the years his efforts were unsuccessful. It's probably ironic that the war party trail Custer followed into the Washita led the cavalry right into Black Kettle's village. Guilty or not, Black Kettle was unable throughout the Cheyenne war to control the younger Cheyenne.

With Black Kettle's death, opinions varied regarding the role he played during these tumultuous times. Superintendent Thomas Murphy called him "one of the best and truest friends the whites have ever had among the Indians of the plains."[37] General Sheridan called him a "nominal chief—a worn out and worthless old cipher."[38] To freighters who knew him and who survived attacks by raiding Indians, the feeling was that Black Kettle acted as a spy for the militant warriors. Freighter Samuel Monk recalled that Black Kettle's village

> had the reputation of being the headquarters for the depredating Indians who were making these raids on the emigrants and freighters, while they professed to be friendly. I have seen Black Kettle in here pretending to be friendly . . . they made signs of friendliness while here, but the best authorities—those who knew them best—state they were the headquarters between the whites and Indians; they came in to learn our position and what we were doing, and those people who were raiding the trains came into their camp and got information.[39]

After the Washita fight, Custer was not finished with his winter campaign. There were Cheyenne tribes that escaped, and they still held captive Sarah White, captured in the August raids near the Republican River, and Mrs. Anna Morgan, captured two months later. He finally found the village, actually two, on March 15, 1869. One contained about 200 lodges, the other about 60 lodges, several miles further away along the Sweetwater River in the Texas Panhandle. The Dog Soldier Indians were in the villages. Through negotiation, Custer was able to free the two women, both pregnant by their captors, and avoided a fight.[40]

---

37 Greene, *Washita*, p. 166.

38 General P. H. Sheridan, "Report to General W. T. Sherman, November 1, 1869." Report of the Secretary of War, Forty-First Congress, 2d Session, Volume 1, Executive Document, Pt 2 (Washington, DC: Government Printing Office, 1869), 46.

39 Sallena Grant Indian Depredation Claim #9942. Record Group 123.

40 Broome, *Dog Soldier Justice*, 66–71. If Sarah was pregnant, she probably lost the baby before birth. She did not raise a half-breed child, nor do descendants today have any knowledge that she was pregnant when rescued. Email correspondence from Tracy White, June 6, 2013.

Both Custer and Sheridan thought the fight at the Washita, as well as the negotiations Custer brought to the Sweetwater—where the Indians agreed to go to their reservation—were the end of the Cheyenne war. Custer ended his long report on his late winter expedition with this concluding sentence: "This I consider as the termination of the Indian war."[41] He was mistaken. Tall Bull, Whistler and their band of Dog Soldiers instead sought to go north into the Powder River country and there associate with their northern allies, especially the Oglala Sioux Pawnee Killer. They escaped from Custer on the Sweetwater. The result was yet another deadly raid into north-central Kansas. Thirteen more settlers would be killed in Lincoln County, and two more women taken captive. Many other victims would enter the eternal prairie-sleep, before and after the murderous raid along Spillman Creek and the Saline River, the same area the Dog Soldiers wrought such violence in early August 1868. It would take yet another military expedition—this time the 5th Cavalry under Brevet Major General Eugene A. Carr—to finally bring the war to an end in Kansas, Nebraska and Colorado, though war would continue down in Texas through 1875. That war would claim another family in a deadly Indian raid near the Smoky Hill trail on September 11, 1874. The German family consisted of husband John, wife Lydia, and their seven children, son Stephen, and daughters Rebecca Jane, Catherine, Sophia, Joanna, Julie and Addie. When attacked several miles east of Fort Wallace along the Smoky Hill River, all were killed except 17-year-old Catherine, 12-year-old Sophia, seven-year-old Julia and five-year-old Addie. The young girls remained in captivity for weeks and were eventually released separately as pairs, as part of the Red River War.[42]

Before the rescue of Mrs. Morgan and Sarah White, while Custer's regiment was recuperating from the fight on the Washita, Indians came down from Red Cloud Agency near present-day Crawford, Nebraska, and took a lot of stock belonging to Jim Moore and Elias Whitcomb. Jim had been in partnership with his brother Charles on the Denver road running Washington Ranch, a few miles east of present-day Sterling. Charles recalled,

---

41   Maj. Gen. G. A. Custer, "Report to Major General P. H. Sheridan, March 21, 1869." Record Group 393, Part I, Entry 2601, Department of the Missouri, Letters Received, 1869.

42   See Arlene Feldman Jauken, *The Moccasin Speaks: Living as Captives of the Dog Soldier Warriors Red River War 1874–1875* (Lincoln, NE: Dageforde Publishing, Inc., 1998). For Indian captivities, see Michno, *A Fate Worse Than Death,* 158–164.

"upon account of the railroad destroying our ranch business [1867]" the brothers decided to divide their stock, which included horses, mules, cattle and sheep. Working for a time at Julesburg, until all their cattle and sheep had been butchered and sold, Jim then took the remaining stock and moved to Cheyenne—giving his brother Charles in March 1867, a promissory note for $10,000—and then opened a livery business with a partner named H. H. Hook in August, calling it Hook and Moore, Livery. Jim entrusted Hook to run the business, as he had successfully ran a similar business near Fort Kearny, Nebraska. Jim Moore then went back home to Ohio to visit family and friends and get married. When he returned, he discovered that Hook had taken the profits and squandered the money on his own personal debts. As a result he bought Hook out in the middle of July 1868. He then ran the livery under the name James A. Moore, Livery, until Indians took his considerable number of horses and mules, quartered on a stock ranch northwest of present-day Laporte, Colorado, where he had them cared for. Moore lost a total of 96 horses and mules, his entire stock necessary to run his livery business in Cheyenne. The loss closed his business.

The theft occurred December 25. Eleven Lakota—Oglala—under an Indian named Swift Bird—silently mingled among the herd, concealing themselves from the herders, until the stock was taken from their corrals and put to pasture. Suddenly seven of the Indians stampeded the herd and drove them all away, except for one mare. They went in an easterly direction and soon came upon the ranch of Elias Whitcomb, and from his ranch stole an additional 19 horses. From there the Indians went down to the South Platte River below the mouth of the Cache La Poudre and at Elbridge Gerry's ranch stole additional stock from him. Together Moore and Whitcomb went to Fort Russell, and reported the theft to Major James Van Voast. Van Voast then ordered two officers and 152 men in pursuit. Joining them were an additional 19 citizens—including Whitcomb and Moore. They found the trail going south from Gerry's ranch, and pursued the party all the way to the Republican River east of present-day Wray and near the Colorado-Kansas border. At that point an Indian village was discovered, but the officers thought it prudent not to attack the large camp and the soldiers returned to Fort Russell empty-handed.[43]

---

43   James Moore Indian Depredation Claim #6862. Record Group 75; Elias Whitcomb Indian Depredation Claim #720. Record Group 123.

Jim Moore's short life had interesting events. In addition to surviving the serious neck wound in a skirmish with raiding Indians at his ranch on the Denver road in 1865, he was earlier one of the famed riders with the short-lived Pony Express. While riding for them in 1860, he set a record for perhaps the longest and quickest ride of a Pony Express rider. His route went from Midway Station—about half way from Fort Kearny to Fort McPherson—east to Julesburg Station. It was 140 miles one way, and Moore would make the trip once a week, changing horses at each station, located from 10 to 14 miles apart. Riders were preferred smaller in size and weight, but Moore stood six feet and weighed 160 pounds. For his feat, the company gave him a gold watch.[44] Frank Root recorded the events that put Moore in one of the greatest exploits of the Pony Express:

> Moore made a remarkable ride on the 8th day of June, 1860, when the pony line had been in operation little more than two months. He was at Midway Station—the half-way point between the Missouri River and Denver—when a rider bearing a highly important government dispatch for the Pacific coast arrived. Without losing a minute, Jim mounted his pony and was off for old Julesburg, in the northeast part of Colorado, 140 miles distant. He made his ride as quickly as possible, fleet animals being placed at his disposal at intervals along the route. Reaching Julesburg, he met the east-bound rider with another important Government dispatch from the Pacific, destined for the national capital.
>
> Unfortunately, as it happened, the rider who should have been the bearer of this dispatch east had been killed the day before. With less than ten minute's rest, and without even stopping to eat, Moore jumped into the saddle, and, in a twinkling, was raising a terrible dust down the Platte toward Midway. He made the round trip of 280 miles in fourteen hours, forty-six minutes, an average of over eighteen miles an hour.[45]

After the loss of his livery business in Cheyenne, Moore moved to Sidney, where his brother Charles had moved after closing Washington Ranch in late 1867. Both brothers owned separate stores for general merchandise, as well as a bar and billiard room. The businesses were three blocks apart in downtown Sidney. Jim Moore apparently continued to keep some stock down at Washington Ranch, though the ranch no longer served travelers on the Denver road, the road no longer being operational. Charles had his own

---

44   William Lightfoot Visscher, *A Thrilling and Truthful History of The Pony Express or Blazing the Westward Way* (Chicago, IL: The Charles T. Powner Co., 1946), 39.

45   Root and Connelley, *Overland Stage*, 128.

stock ranch on Rush Creek, northwest of Sidney. On September 22, 1873, Jim was working a haying operation outside of Sidney when he fell from a high-baled hay wagon. The load of hay fell on top of him; ". . . breaking his spinal column and producing absolute and complete paralysis of all of that portion of his body below the injured part. . . ."[46] The *Cheyenne Daily Leader* on September 24 reported that Moore was injured "while riding on top of a large load of baled hay; the load upset upon him, injuring his spine, and giving him serious internal injuries. The surgeon of the post at Sidney despairs of his recovery. Dr. Corey went down yesterday to attend him." The *Laramie Daily Sentinel* reported the accident, saying Moore's back was broken and his breast-bone crushed. "The doctor thinks the chances of the recovery of Mr. Moore are quite hopeless."[47] Jim was only 33 when he died three months later.[48] He had married Mary C. Bean November 16, 1867, when he had gone to Ohio and left Hook in charge of the livery. Together they had three children, Blanche (1869), Granville (1872), and James Alexander. Little James was born just five days after his father was mortally injured. Moore had a ranch called the JM Ranch north of Fort Laramie. The Wyoming town of Jay Em was named after him. After Moore's death, Mary remarried Renslaer S. Van Tassell in 1880.[49] She only lived three more years, dying December 3, 1883.[50] Jim's brother Charles, however, ultimately prospered in Sidney, raising his own family there—several descendants still living there—and died at the age of 82, on October 15, 1915. An historic building still survives in Sidney with the name Moore on the front.[51]

---

46   James Moore Indian Depredation Claim #6862.

47   *Laramie Daily Sentinel*, September 26, 1873.

48   Obituary, *Cheyenne Daily Leader*, December 16, 1873.

49   After Jim Moore's death, Charles Moore sued his widow for payment of the $10,000 promissory note. She finally settled for half the amount, and probably incurred lasting animosity between the surviving families. See James Moore Indian Depredation Claim #6862.

50   Obituary, *Cheyenne Daily Leader*, December 11, 1883.

51   See the Charles A. Moore history, written by his great-grand-daughter, Glenna Belle Moore Niebaum, *History of Cheyenne County Nebraska 1986* (Curtis Media Corporation, 1987), 790–792.

CHAPTER FIFTEEN

Tall Bull's Revenge

All Indians are lawfully under the control of the Interior Department, by and through civilian agents; but that department is extremely jealous of any interference by the military, so that our officers and soldiers have no right to anticipate Indian hostilities, but can only act against Indians after the commission of hostile acts.

W. T. SHERMAN, LIEUTENANT GENERAL
THE CHEYENNE STAR, SEPTEMBER 15, 1868

GEORGE A. CUSTER'S NOVEMBER 27, 1868, FIGHT ON THE Washita resulted in five months of no raids along the three roads to Denver. That would change in May 1869. It began with two fights with Brevet Major General Eugene A. Carr and seven companies of the 5th Cavalry. Carr was moving his command from Fort Lyon, Colorado Territory, north through Kansas and into Nebraska, where he had been ordered to report to Fort McPherson. Carr's command was one of the military units engaged in the 1868–1869 winter campaign, when Custer had his fight on the Washita and Black Kettle was killed. Carr's command had spent the winter down in New Mexico and had returned to Fort Lyon on the Santa Fe road when he was ordered to Fort McPherson on the Platte River road. Tall Bull and his Dog Men had escaped from Custer on the Sweetwater in

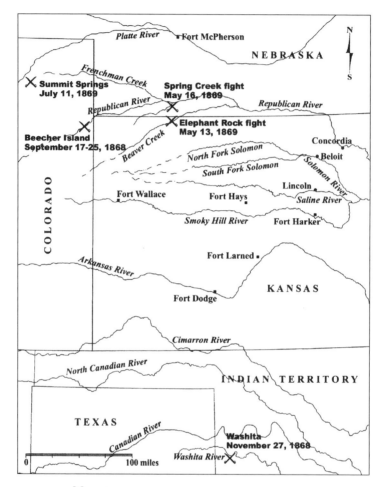

MAP SHOWING MILITARY ENGAGEMENTS
WITH THE CHEYENNE, 1868–1869.
Courtesy Joan Pennington, Fairfax Station, Virginia.

March. He was moving his village north to the Powder River country when Carr's 5th Cavalry fortuitously crossed paths with Tall Bull's warriors in northwest Kansas near present-day Traer, at a place known as Elephant Rock. A sharp fight ensued, on May 13, and when it was finished at least 25 warriors were dead, as well as four soldiers. Twenty-five lodges were captured and burned. Three days later, May 16, yet another fight happened, just inside the Nebraska border on Spring Creek, about midway between present-day Oxford and Atlanta. In this fight it was unknown how many Indians were killed, but about two dozen were known wounded. Carr's men did not sustain any deaths, but three enlisted men were wounded. Both fights involved as many as 200 warriors.[1]

After this second fight, Carr's command arrived at Fort McPherson. Tall Bull returned south near present-day Portis, Kansas, and from there organized a series of deadly retaliatory raids against innocent Kansas settlers. It was the Indian way: avenge death by striking back at the tribe who killed them. The tribe this time was whites. It would mark the beginning of the end of the Tall Bull's Dog Soldier society. The first raids began on May 23, against a newly arrived group of Swedish immigrants on White Rock Creek in Jewell County, just west of present-day Lovewell. In late spring, a large colony of 100 Swedish immigrants joined into a company called Excelsior Colony, under the leadership of Lewis A. Walker, from Long Island. The area along White Rock Creek had earlier been selected for establishing adjoining homesteads, and from Chicago via Long Island, the immigrants arrived in Kansas. Typical of the colonists was the family of Gustavus Norlin. He left his large family—13 children—at Junction City and only brought his three oldest boys to White Rock Creek. The plan was to build a cabin and then retrieve the rest of his family out to their new homestead. The Norlins had only been on White Rock Creek for two weeks when the Indians made their deadly visit.

A day or two before—probably May 20—warriors had killed four men in a buffalo hunting party of seven, not far north from White Rock Creek, on the Republican River. On that day, three men came down from their hunting camp into White Rock City, and said the Indians had just attacked

1   Broome, *Dog Soldier Justice*, 72–75.

them on the Republican River and killed four of the party.[2] Several men in the settlement—about 20—upon learning of the hunters' deaths, went out to bury the bodies. It was while these men were gone on this burial detail that the Dog Soldiers came into the new settlement. The dead hunters the burial party went to bury were just inside the Kansas border with Nebraska, about 10 miles north in the northeast corner of Jewell County.

Peter Tanner and Charles Hogan had built a cabin on one side of a small creek spilling into White Rock, and about 100 yards apart from a cabin on the other side of the creek, built by brothers Paul and Martin Dahl. Inside the Tanner and Hogan house were two sons of Gustavus Norlin. With them was another young man named Bergland. The oldest son, Ernest, was with his father and the burial party and missed the raid. Fourteen-year-old Charles Norlin saw the Indians as they rode into the newly formed settlement from the northwest. They were about a mile away and he mistook them for soldiers and went out to greet them. It was a Sunday. The Indians, from 60 to 100, were riding in military fashion and carried their spears and carbines straight up, resting the bottom of the carbine on the horse. They were all dressed in blue overcoats, which initially misled Charles in what he was seeing. It was his first sight of an Indian, and he was not prepared for what would happen. Half of them, upon seeing him, turned their horses toward him. As he was approaching the Indians, he was near the Dahl brother's house when he heard two shots coming from inside the home. He then discovered the men on horseback were Indians and not soldiers. At first he was paralyzed with fear and could not move. But the Indians chasing him got distracted when they heard the shots from inside the Dahl house. They momentarily turned away from Charles and rode toward the house, probably thinking the Indians that had entered there might have encountered resistance. That delay allowed Charles the short time necessary to regain his wits. He immediately ran back to the Tanner and Hogan house and the three young boys—Bergland was 18 and brother Christopher was 16—fled in the opposite direction, where they fortuitously found a fallen log near the creek. A hole was left where the tree had fallen, and it was just enough room for the three boys to hide inside. They remained there a day,

2   Winsor and Scarbrough, *History of Jewell County*, 12.

not daring to move, before the burial detail returned from the Republican River and found them.[3]

The Indians were ready to inflict violence upon entering the Dahl cabin. Brothers Martin and Paul had earlier gone out on a long walk and missed the raid. Their 16-year-old nephew, Thomas Voarness, stayed at the house and was preparing supper when the Indians came upon him. The two shots Charles heard were from the Indians shooting young Voarness. Charles Norlin later recalled that Voarness was found "in a hole that was made by taking sods for the roof of the building; [he] was still living and covered with feathers. He had been shot in the head and had an arrow in his bowels. He was only able to say 'Squaw' when found, and was taken to White Rock, where he died."[4]

The Dahl brothers remembered the incident differently. Upon returning home from their walk they first came to the Tanner/Hogan cabin and saw it pillaged and household contents destroyed and spread outside the house. They then became concerned for their place, according to Martin,

> and hurried over to their house where they found their nephew lying by the fire-place shot through the body. He lived 10 or 12 hours and told them a short time after they left and while he was cooking dinner, he heard a noise at the door and when he looked the door was filled with Indians. He reached for his carbine but before he could get it the Indians shot him through the body and he fell. They payed [paid] no more attention to him but went about the house and broke open trunks and ransacked everything as they had done at Hogan's. What the Indians could not take away they destroyed.[5]

The Dahl brothers used a door from their cabin and put the mortally wounded Voarness on it "and took our wounded nephew to White Rock City, which was about seven miles. We carried him on a stretcher, to that place, and we thought we might find a doctor there, but there was none

---

3   Gustavas Norlin Indian Depredation Claim #8908 and Peter Tanner Indian Depredation Claim #9807. Record Group 123. Ernest Norlin exaggerated the distance to where the buffalo hunters had been killed, saying it was 40 miles north, which was way beyond the Republican River.

4   Peter Tanner Indian Depredation Claim #9807.

5   Charles Hogan Indian Depredation Claim #3119. Record Group 123. See also Martin Dahl Indian Depredation Claim #no number in file. Entry 700, Box 9. Record Group 75. Dahl says one of the dead buffalo hunters was a man named Thomas Warney or Warner and that he was from the White Rock Creek settlement and had been killed on May 21. See also Paul O. Dahl Indian Depredation Claim #3466. Record Group 75.

there and the boy died that night, and we buried him the next day at that place, White Rock City."[6]

Paul Dahl remembered:

> It was this way. It was on a Sunday morning [May 23] and my brother and I had gone down White Rock Creek for a walk to put in the time, and when we left that morning there was no disturbance on or near Hogan's place. Hogan with a number of settlers all around there had gone away to bury some men who had been killed by the Indians some two or three days before this [May 20–21], and was not at home. We of course knew where they had gone at the time, and we were away from the place about three, maybe four hours. We had done some work on our clothes that morning before we had gone on that trip, and we came back by way of Mr. Hogan's place, and we saw things all scattered around the place, groceries and provisions all mixed and on the ground all spoiled; furniture all broken and cut up with hatchets, bedding all torn to pieces and his trunks had been broken open and everything that was left was in such a torn and bad condition that it was impossible to make any use of what was left. This could only have been but a short time after the Indians had been there. We then hurried to our place, where we left our nephew Thomas Voarness, to get dinner for us, and after seeing what had taken place at Hogan's house we hurried to [our] own place and there we found our house raided and everything taken or destroyed, and our nephew shot through the body. We had nothing to fall back on as the Indians had taken or destroyed everything we had in the house as well as shot our nephew. We only had our shirts and overalls on. The rest of our clothing was taken or destroyed, as well as at Hogan's, and I know that everyone in our neighborhood lost everything they had, and I know that there was not a horse left in the neighborhood, only those that was ridden to that funeral, of those men who had been killed by the Indians. This nephew of ours told us that he heard a noise at the door of our house and turned to see who it was, and there he saw the Indians, and when he tried to get his gun they shot him right through the body and left him where he fell, and did not bother him after he fell. As soon as we could we fixed something to carry him on, and we carried him to White Rock City, where we thought we might be able to get a doctor, but there was none there, and our nephew died that night from the shot in the body, where he was shot by the Indians. He told us as soon as we got to the house that day he told us what happened and who it was who done it.[7]

The men who had gone up to Nebraska to bury the dead buffalo hunters returned back to White Rock City later that night. Richard Stanfield recalled coming back to the raided settlements:

6   Charles Hogan Indian Depredation Claim #3119.

7   Charles Hogan Indian Depredation Claim #3119.

We had gone up above Hogan's place on the creek, to bury four men who had been killed by the Indians a few days before. There were about twenty of us, as we got nearly all the men on the creek to go up for protection; we had buried those men who had been killed and was returning to our homes, and on our way back, we could see that the Indians had raided all along the creek, at different places taking what they wanted to carry and destroying what they did not take. Clothing, furniture, groceries and provisions were scattered all along and broken up. At night about dark we came to the place called White Rock City and there we saw the Dahl brothers, with their nephew, a boy that had been shot by the Indians that day. He was dead when we got to the place. The Dahl brothers had improvised a stretcher out of one of the doors, and had carried the body from where he had been shot to the place where we saw them, and that was several miles. . . .[8]

The Norlin family after the raid decided it was unsafe to continue to live along White Rock Creek and instead, after the deadly raids, settled further east along the Republican River in what became Concordia. Two years later, another son was born into the large family.[9] George Norlin grew up to be an attorney, like his elder brother. He eventually became the long-termed and endeared president of the University of Colorado at Boulder, after serving as a Greek language and literature professor.[10] Today's prestigious Norlin Library is named in his honor. There well might not have been a "Norlin" Library had his father chosen to remain at White Rock Creek instead of volunteering to assist with his eldest son in the burial party of the dead buffalo hunters.

The Dog Soldiers remained in the area and eventually moved further east, but while they were doing this, another group of Indians made a raid 150 miles southeast, near Fort Wallace. One might think it must have been a different band of Indians but in fact it wasn't, for stock stolen near Sheridan, Kansas, were recovered at the fight at Summit Springs six weeks later, showing that the Indians associated with Tall Bull had divided into several smaller parties and covered a large area in their raids. When found at Summit Springs there were about 200 warriors, and about that same number had

---

8   Charles Hogan Indian Depredation Claim #3119.

9   U. S. Census: 1880—Sibley, Cloud, Kansas, Page 16, Sup Dist., 3, Enum Dist., 36; Indexed as George Norline, line 40. See also: https://secure.ancestry.com/register/guestregistration.aspx?rtype=1&f name=&lname=&dbid=6742&kurl=http%3a%2f%2fsearch.ancestry.com%2fcgi-bin%2fsse.dll%3fdb %3d1880usfedcen%26h%3d48960441%26indiv%3dtry%26o-vc%3dRecord%3aOtherRecord%26tid% 3d24057605%26tpid%3d12964882144%26rhSource%3d1876%26nreg%3d1 (accessed March 23, 2013).

10   http://en.wikipedia.org/wiki/George–Norlin (accessed June 15, 2013). During my graduate studies at the University of Colorado, I spent many hours in Norlin Library, seeing Norlin's inscription every time I entered. My interest in the Indian wars began just as I was ending my graduate studies in philosophy.

left the Summit Springs village shortly before Tall Bull was caught there.[11] Thus the Indians connected with all the raids in Kansas during this time numbered as many as 400.

William Moore, Adolph Vorenberg and Bradford Daily, together, had a large freighting firm delivering freight to Fort Union. They had come from the New Mexico fort to Sheridan, Kansas, to load their empty wagons with freight to take back to Fort Union. Sheridan at the time was an important terminus for the railroad and freighters going south and west from there would get their freight at Sheridan. The men had filled at least 10 wagons with goods when the Indians successfully ran off their stock. About 15 warriors at the noon hour, on May 26, charged the herd, which was grazing about one mile from Sheridan. They made off with 232 mules and a few horses. Sixty-seven of those mules were recovered at Summit Springs and eventually returned to the freighters.[12] This helps to explain why Carr, in following Tall Bull's trail in June, found many mule shoes at each Indian camp the command came upon in the trek ending at Summit Springs.[13]

Two days later—May 28—Indians again struck near White Rock Creek, this time back on the Republican River about 10 miles north of present-day Scandia, and a few miles northwest of White Rock City. It was another buffalo hunting party that was victimized. A group of men, along with a couple sons, decided to leave their homes near Waterville and come west to hunt buffalo. The men brought two wagons, one for provisions and one for what they harvested from their buffalo hunt. The hunters consisted of 42-year-old Rueben Winkleplect and his son Alonzo and nephew Edward Winkleplect, fellow Civil War veteran Philip Burke—Burke and Winkleplect served together in the same regiment in the Union Army for three years and then homesteaded near Waterville after the war—a man named Mr. Cole and his son, and John McChesney. They left Waterville on May 10, and ended up a successful hunt on the Republican River north of Scandia, called Scandinavis in 1869. In addition to a wagon load of buffalo meat, Mr. Cole had captured a buffalo calf which he was taking back to Waterville to raise.

---

11   Broome, *Dog Soldier Justice*, 172.
12   Adolph Vorenberg Indian Depredation Claim #584–585, William Moore Indian Depredation Claim #1474, Bradford Daily Indian Depredation Claim #585. Record Group 123.
13   Broome, *Dog Soldier Justice*, 155.

They were in camp—their last night before returning home—near the mouth of White Rock Creek and the Republican when about dark they found signs of Indians. They quickly put out their fire, went to bed without eating and early the next morning—May 28—they began to move their camp. They got to near the Republican when they were attacked. The Indians numbered from 75 to 100. The buffalo hunters—all but two of them sitting in the wagons—whipped the horses and made a mad dash to the river. Everyone jumped off of the wagons and into the Republican River, swimming for dear life for the other side. None survived making it across. The Indians caught them and killed them all. Because McChesney could not swim, when he got to the edge of the river he hid in the tall grass. The Dog Soldiers, in their haste to catch the fleeing hunters, failed to see one did not jump into the river, and that was how he survived. McChesney felt if the party could have made it to the tall willows on the other side of the Republican they might have saved themselves. He remained hidden while the Indians killed the rest of the party. He did not move the rest of the day. The next day, he walked down to Scandia and reported the fight. Another burial party was sent out and buried the six dead men and boys. The dead hunters were all stripped of their clothing and one man was scalped. Winkleplect "made a hard fight. He was a big strong man and he was shot with arrows and gunshot wounds and was badly mutilated." One of the arrows was so deeply imbedded in him that McChesney had to put his feet on the body to pull the arrow out. His gun was still there but had been destroyed by the warriors.[14]

S. Rowland was in Scandia when McChesney came to town. The burial party waited two days before venturing out to bury the dead, fearing Indians might still be hiding in the area awaiting opportunity for further attacks. They had probably learned from the earlier effort to bury dead hunters when the Indians raided the settlement while the men were away. It was better to wait a couple days, to make sure the Indians were not waiting for the men to leave so they could more easily molest the settlers remaining behind. The warriors had been making attacks in the vicinity for a week. Rowland was part of the burial detail, as he was with the earlier one that buried the four men killed not far from where this party was caught:

---

14   Maria Winkleplect Indian Depredation Claim #10100. Philip Burke Indian Depredation Claim #10553. John McChesney Indian Depredation Claim #9260. Record Group 123.

Sunday morning [May 30] we got a team and wagon and four or five men and went from Scandinavis to a man by the name of Fisher's [place] on White Rock Creek. At Mr. Fisher's we got his two boys and a man that we called Buckskin and went to hunt for the bodies. When we reached the Republican River we ran across two wagons loaded with buffalo meat. The party then divided, some going up the river, I with McChesney, and four or five others crossing the river and coming across the bodies on the other side of the river. The bodies were all stripped of their clothing and one man was scalped, the scalp lying by his side. Mr. McChesney pointed out to me Mr. Burke, Mr. Winkleplect and the others whose names I have forgotten. One of the men had two arrows fast in his back. After looking at the bodies we buried them there. The wagons were left just as they were unhitched from, seemed to be, and the harness were all cut to pieces about a foot in length. There was a gun lying by the side of one of the wagons which was broken up and the barrel was bent at about right angles. A frying pan was all we could see of the camp outfit.[15]

Rowland went on to say that the Sunday following, June 6, two Indians "rode up within 20 rods of the hotel at Scandinavis and killed a boy who was herding some horses there and drove away the horses that he was herding, and drove them down along the Republican River." That boy was a teenager named Malcolm Granstadt. Two of the horses belonged to a Union veteran who had homesteaded in the area in 1868, Robert Watson.[16] Watson himself was nearly killed as he was plowing in his field. The Indians cut him off from retreating to his house. Just as things appeared hopeless, a widow named Mrs. Frazier, who was living in a nearby cabin, ran out with a loaded shotgun and fired at the Indians, driving them back and giving Watson enough time to escape.[17] Grandstadt and another boy were taking care of five horses. There had been a sentry on the high hill in Scandia, but he had left his post, which allowed two Indians to ride down a ravine east of town unseen, until just about upon their prey. One of the boys saw the Indians coming and fled into a building, but Malcolm was clubbed with a pistol, which knocked him down. As he was lying on the ground, one of the Indians shot and killed him and took the horses.[18]

Richard Stanfield recalled what happened to him after leaving the home on White Rock Creek where Thomas Voarness had died on the night of May 23:

---

15   Maria Winkleplect Indian Depredation Claim #10100.

16   Robert Watson Indian Depredation Claim #3787. Record Group 75.

17   Winsor and Scarbrough, *History of Jewell County*, 14.

18   Savage, *A History of Republic County, Kansas*, 55.

Young teenager Malcolm Granstadt was killed by Dog Soldiers as he was protecting horses in the newly established village of Scandinavis, nestled along the Republican River. *Painting by James Davis Nelson, Jewell, Kansas. Courtesy Duane Gile, Scandia, Kansas.*

I went on to my own claim, and it was only a day or two after this [May 28] that the Indians, coming from the direction of [Charles] Hogan's place, attacked my claim. There with me at this time Clark TenIck [Tanick], . . . O. C. Davis, . . . and W. [William] P. Phillips, ... When we saw the Indians coming we were all together on my place. We made for my cabin and I drove my team of horses into the cabin and saved them. Davis had a team of mules lariated out near the cabin. The Indians got those mules and drove them away. . . . The Indians attacked us early in the afternoon, firing on us and as we were all well armed we made a spirited reply and they, seeing we were prepared for them, after keeping up the fight for about 5 hours, until about dark when they left us. . . . [where the buffalo hunters were killed] was only a short distance from where we had the fight with them [and] we heard the shooting, and knew it was some fighting from the way the firing was; but we were not close enough to see or help them. A couple of days after the fight at our place we waited until we thought everything was quiet and then we went to Scandia, Kansas. It was centrally located and was the largest place around here at the time, and when we got there we heard of those six hunters being killed. There was seven of them in the party, but one of them got away from the Indians, and got to Scandia, and reported the killings by the Indians of his partners, and I went with the party to assist in the burying of those six men who had been killed at that time. . . .[19]

Another member of the Excelsior Colony was Ernest Ackerly. He had just arrived with his wife at White Rock Creek when the raids began. Married just three months earlier in Brooklyn, he and his new wife had come out west to begin their life together. Once they learned of the raids, Ackerly hired brothers Frank and William Frazier to haul their wagon—loaded with all of the family possessions—18 miles back east to where present-day Belleville is. Another single man, Walter Jackson, decided to leave with Ackerly. The party was attacked about half-way to their destination. Everything was lost. This included such things as clothing, dresses, linen, bonnets, shoes, cooking utensils, culinary ware, bedding, books, family bible, tools, provisions, all loaded in the wagon and all either stolen or destroyed. It was an entire household of goods. They were lucky to escape with their lives. Ackerly:

In April, 1869, I joined the Excelsior Colony of which Lewis A. Walker of Long Island was president; for the purpose of going to Kansas to settle permanently at a place called White Rock in Jewell County where the colony's lands had been selected. In May 1869 I went to Kansas with my wife. We carried with us such household goods, clothing and property as I owned, including many articles, which had been given as wedding presents at the time of our marriage. At Washington, Kansas, I employed one Lyal Pasco to guide us to the settlement of the Excelsior Colony and to haul our goods there in his wagon. We reached the camp of the colony on May 23, 1869. On the second day thereafter, reports reached us that the Indians had killed several white settlers, and were committing depredations a few miles to the west of our camp. Not deeming it safe to remain there longer, I employed one William Frazier and his brother Frank to take us and our goods back to their house some eighteen miles east of our camp. My wife and I left the camp on May 28, 1869, with William and Frank Frazier, accompanied by one Walter Jackson who was also a member of the Excelsior Colony. When about eight miles from the camp we were attacked by a body of Indians numbering about eighty as nearly as we could judge. William Frazier and his brother unhitched their horses from the wagon and rode back to the camp to notify the colony of its peril. My wife, Jackson and myself had to take to the woods and conceal ourselves for eight hours under the brush to save our lives. The Indians surrounded the wagon in which were my goods and stole and destroyed everything therein. We could hear them as they opened boxes and shouted, but were powerless to prevent their depredations. We

19   Charles Hogan Indian Depredation Claim #3119. Oren Davis Indian Depredation Claim #2712. Record Group 123.

remained hid in the timber until after dark when we left and worked our way east along a creek to Frazier's house. While on our way we passed the dead body of a white man who had been recently killed by the Indians. It was between two and four o'clock on the morning of May 29 that we reached the Frazier's. Here we met Mr. Walker, the President of the Colony, who had with him a number of white men who had volunteered to go with him to the relief of the Colony. One of the men was Mr. C. M. Murdoch, a public officer, I think a deputy sheriff of Washington County, Kansas. We also met at Frazier's an old hunter and guide named William Harrington [Buckskin]. He had lived among the Sioux Indians for about eight years and could speak their language. He told us that he had been attacked by the Indians the day before but had succeeded in escaping from them. That while they had him 'corralled' in the timber he had talked with these Indians and knew that they were Sioux. They told him they would kill every white man they could catch. My wife and I remained at Frazier's a few days while Mr. Walker, Murdoch and the relief party went on to the camp of the Colony. While we were at Frazier's, a white man I think from Chicago, came there from further west [John McChesney]. He was one of a party of seven who had been hunting buffaloes at the Big Bend of the Republican River. The Indians had surprised and attacked them and had killed six of the party. The survivor [McChesney] had, with great difficulty succeeded in escaping from them, and getting to Frazier's place. On June 1st, 1869, Mr. Walker with the relief party, and all the remaining members of the Colony, reached Frazier's with such of the goods and effects of the Colonists as they had been able to haul away in wagons. They reported that they had passed Frazier's wagon, in which my goods had been hauled, about four miles above the 'Rice Place' and that all of the contents of the wagons, except what the Indians had carried off, were lying around torn up and destroyed. On June 2, 1869, we left Frazier's place with many of the other Colonists and went back with them to Washington, Kansas. One of my books, an old family Bible containing the record of the Ackerly family, was alone worth to me several hundred dollars. For its loss, no money allowance could compensate.[20]

The Indian raid destroyed all the dreams and hopes of the colony. William Frazier confirmed Ackerly's memory. As he recalled, they were on the road hauling the family goods for Ackerly and Jackson. The wagon had become stuck in John's Creek. The Frazier brothers had taken their boots off and were working to free the wagon when the Indians struck. The two brothers quickly removed the horses from the wagon, mounted them and fled

20 Ernest Ackerly Indian Depredation Claim #809. Record Group 75. Winsor and Scarbrough claim Buckskin's encounter with the Dog Soldiers consisted of his hiding unseen in White Rock Creek all night, nearly causing him to freeze to death, and that he was later teased about hiding in the water so long. See *History of Jewell County*, 14.

east, leaving Ackerly, his wife and Jackson to seek shelter in the tall grasses surrounding the creek. The Indians chased the brothers for about three miles, which probably saved Ackerly and his wife, until finally the brothers abandoned their tiring horses and made for the creek, hiding among the thick growth. The Indians captured the horses.[21]

William W. Newlon was not a part of the Swedish colony, but he shared an interesting tale that happened in the same area where the two parties of buffalo hunters had been killed. He had taken a claim near Hogan's place, having been over the area the summer before, in 1868. Newlon's story is grammatically corrected to make for easier reading, as it was dictated to type when made. To read the whole account gives a voice to a long lost pioneer:

> In May 1869, about the middle of the month, my brother Joseph Newlon (now dead), John McFarlane, and Joseph Myers, . . . and myself started from our homes to go on a buffalo hunt in Western Kansas. On the second night out, one of Myers' horses got away and the next morning Myers got on his other horse, and started on the back trail after the lost horse, and he followed it back to his home. We had a wagon and two yoke of cattle to it, Myers had his team of horses and a wagon, we waited at the place we had camped until about nine o'clock, then we wrote a note, and pinned it on Myers' wagon telling him when he got back to follow our trail, and placing some provisions in his wagon. My brother, McFarlane and myself with the other wagon and oxen started on West. We camped on the Republican River, and continued up the Valley of the Republican River, until about four o'clock that same afternoon when I saw an object moving ahead of us crossing the valley about two miles distant. I had a field glass with me and I got them and looked at the object that was moving and made out an Indian pony with an Indian lying flat on its back. I had not long to look when it disappeared over the ridge out of sight.
>
> I told my brother and McFarlane what I had seen, but we continued on up the valley, and when we reached the point where this pony had disappeared over the Ridge I got off the wagon and crawled up to the place where I had seen the pony and looked over the Ridge and when I looked over the other side I saw on the flat over the Ridge a large band of Indians mounted. I counted seventy of them and there were probably more than that. On our way up the valley we had noticed ahead of us a grove of timber and we had made up our minds to make for the mote of timber as we thought that there would be a spring of water in that mote. I noticed that those mounted Indians were also headed for that timber so as to intercept us before we would reach the timber. They from their actions had thought that we were headed for that grove to camp for the night before we saw those Indians. There was a creek

---

21   William Frazier Indian Depredation Claim #3485. Record Group 75.

on the other side of this ridge, and the Indians were going to follow this creek and keep out of sight. As soon as I saw the Indians I signaled my brother and McFarlane to stop and come up to where I was. This they did and when they reached me I told them what I had seen and gave the glasses to McFarlane, who was an old trapper and hunter on the Frontier. As soon as he looked he said it was a big band of Indians, as he said it is certainly Indians. In the meantime I had been looking around for the best place to make a stand if we had to fight and made the discovery that about two hundred yards from where we were back from this place was a large blow out or hole in the ground large enough to put our entire outfit into and have them out of sight. McFarlane said "What shall we do?" I said it is no use trying to get away with our oxen as we cannot, as the Indians are all on horseback and would overtake us in a short time, so we had best prepare for a fight. "You two go and put the wagon and oxen in the blow out, unhitch the oxen and fasten them on the hind wheels, a yoke on each hind wheel. Fasten them by the heads with chains." This they did and in the meantime I was watching the Indians, or watching for them as they were out of sight in this creek hollow, and I expected them to appear at any time. After my brother and McFarlane had got the wagon and oxen in the hole and the oxen fastened they came back to where I was. The Indians had not yet appeared. I told them to wait and watch and I went to the wagon and got our guns and revolvers and the ammunition all in shape to be gotten readily. We had three rifles and three revolvers, each having a rifle and revolver. After making everything ready for a fight I went back up to where the boys were; in a few moments the Indians appeared in the valley and charged on this grove of timber and surrounded it on all sides. It was apparent from their actions that they expected us to be there, as they had given us time to get there. They approached the grove very cautiously, until they made the discovery that we were not there. Then they made another charge down to a bend in the river, where there was quite a bunch of timber, and from their actions they must have thought that we had gotten into that timber. They scouted around through this timber cautiously and as soon as they made the discovery that we were not there they went to the first grove of timber that they had charged, and there they gathered together as if they were having a pow-wow or council. And it was while they were together there that I counted them or seventy five of them, and I think that there was some that I did not count; after holding this pow-wow they headed straight for the place where this Indian had crossed the ridge. After seeing them well on their way I went to the place where we had our outfit and got our guns all ready for the fight that we expected; in less than five minutes they rode up on the ridge where I had been lying, and stopped and looked all around and soon discovered the position that we were in. They then backed down from the ridge and surrounded the place where we were.

We supposed they did not like the place we were in and thought it was too dangerous for them to charge. We could hear the stamping of the horses and the noise they made and we knew we were surrounded it seemed as if they intended to starve us out, or get us in some other way than by charging on our position; that is the way it appeared to us in that hole.

We three talked the matter over and concluded that we could not get our outfit away with us, and that without it we might be able to give the Indians the slip during the night, so about nine o'clock we crawled up from the hole and followed a little depression in the ground that ran toward the valley. We saw their pickets on duty as we passed them on the right of where we passed about thirty paces, another on our left about the same distance. We saw them clearly outlined against the sky as we were lower than they. We were very careful until we passed their lines, it being very dark that night. We struck on down the valley as fast as we could travel, travelling all that night. About eight or nine o'clock in the morning we came to a place where there was six men working. They had located claims and were working on them and had just got one log house built in which all of them it seemed lived while they were on work on the claims. To them we gave the alarm; they had three horses there, I got one, McFarlane got one and two of the men who was there got on one, and . . . went to Lake Sibley, to give the alarm, and to get assistance. As the captain of a militia company lived there and the guns were kept there, I went to Salt Creek our home (on foot) to give the alarm and the other men whose names I do not remember went to White Rock settlement and other settlements for help and to alarm the settlements, and we were to get all the help we could and to return to this place as a rendezvous. My brother Joe remained at this place waiting our return.

The next day we all reached this place where we were to meet and we had quite a bunch of mounted men then from the different places. After getting together we started for the place where we had left our outfit; when we got there the Indians were gone but their fires were still burning, and we found our outfit just as we had left it. It seemed to us that the Indians had seen us coming and had got out of sight of us. After leaving our oxen drink and feed awhile we took the back track, got back to the place where those six men were located and had built the log house, and there we separated and all went to our several homes. About two hours after we had left that place the Indians rode up and acted as if they would attack this log house; it seems as if they had followed us right up. It seems there was a few shots fired at this place, but the Indians saw it was too strong a place and too many men there so they went away, towards some other settlement.[22]

Newlon learned later that Hogan's place had been destroyed at about the same time as his encounter with Indians. The two sites were about 20 miles apart. He was also correct that the Indians had targeted another settlement. That raid—May 30 on Spillman Creek—would be their deadliest and most

22   Charles Hogan Indian Depredation Claim #3119. See also Broome, *Dog Soldier Justice*, 79–80. Winsor and Scarbrough, *History of Jewell County*, 14–15, seem to confuse this story and place Lovewell as the man who saw the Indians peering over a hill and charging three Swedes. Newlon's account must be taken as authentic.

violent thrust in 1869. And it would prompt the demise of Tall Bull's Dog Soldier band six weeks later at Summit Springs.

Before the warriors' coup de grace on Spillman Creek they would carry out two more opportunistic attacks south and west of White Rock Creek. The first happened near Fossil Creek Station, near present-day Russell, Kansas; on the same day McChesney's buffalo hunting partners were killed on the Republican River—May 28—another band of Tall Bull's warriors caught a party of laborers working the Kansas Pacific Railway, a mile and three-fourths west of Fossil Creek Station. Among the men was a teenager named Adolph Roenigk, who had come to Kansas in 1867, and in 1868, was living and working at Fossil Creek. About a week earlier the men heard reports that Indians were again on the prowl in north-central Kansas. The seven workers had taken a handcar on the tracks to work the rails. Roenigk, George Seely and Charles Sylvester[23] brought their seven-shot Spencer carbines, as did an unidentified man who unfortunately left his ammunition in the bunkhouse. Three other men—George Taylor, Alexander McKeefer and John Lynch—were unarmed. Not far east of where the men were working was a fork of a deep ravine capable of hiding Indians, making their work area vulnerable to a surprise attack. A deeper ravine was to the west. As was often the case when confronting potential danger, some of the men scoffed at caution, when one of the workers thought he saw an Indian in the distance. Roenigk thought it wise to get his Spencer from the handcar parked nearby, but as he walked to retrieve it he was teased for his fears. He left his Spencer on the handcar where the other carbines were, and returned to where the men were working.

The men continued to work and soon forgot their earlier scare. An hour later the warriors came out from hiding and one of the men yelled "Yes, there are Indians." Roenigk remembered what happened next:

> After that first shout of alarm, I saw Indians mounted on ponies, coming out of the ravine west of us yelling like demons. One can imagine I did not wait for the last Indian to emerge from the ravine but ran for my gun, seized my cartridge bag and slung the strap over my shoulder the way I carried it. I grabbed a handful of cartridges, loading in such haste that I got in one cartridge too many and was

---

23   For further information on Charles Sylvester—quite likely the same person—see the account of the 14-year-old Sylvester's escape from seven years of Indian captivity in the late fall, 1865, in Colorado Territory, at Mound Station, on the Denver road. See Chapter Eight, 201, note 72. If the two Sylvesters are the same person, then Charles Sylvester in 1869 was 18 years old, and, after recovering, lived at North Platte, Nebraska. Roenigk was also a teenager when wounded in this same incident. The uniqueness of the name suggests it is the same person.

unable to close the magazine. To correct this mistake consumed several precious moments. By this time the savages were almost upon us. They were firing rapidly and the bullets made the dust fly on every side. I heard one of the men call out "Come on," and looking up, saw the others were on the car and already thirty yards away. I had barely enough time to reach the car or be left, but I ran the gauntlet of the Indians' shots and got on the car.

The Indians seemed to be more excited than we were, for of all the miserable marksmanship I ever saw in my life this was the worst. Many shots were fired at us and we had gotten nearly half a mile before any one was struck.

Our main effort was to get the car under good headway and if we had succeeded the Indians could have done us little or no injury. We had gone but a short distance when Indians came out of the branch ravine in front of us, and the next minute we were surrounded. They were firing into us from all sides and we had to take our guns, which slackened the speed of the car. Our assailants were in danger of shooting each other, so they opened in front and allowed us to pass, keeping up the fire from both sides and behind. I thought it impossible to reach the station amidst the flying bullets. A culvert was ahead of us and I called to the boys, "Let's get in the culvert." Someone said "No," and on we went. It was impossible to get the car under headway as the Indians, seeing we were about to escape, pressed momentarily closer, and we were obliged to take up our guns in defense.

As we raised our guns to our shoulders the Indians would glide to the other side of their ponies, but we continued to fire as best our position would allow. About half way to the station Alexander McKeefer and John Lynch were killed and fell from the car. Both fell within a distance of two hundred yards. Each time a man fell a crowd of Indians sprung from their ponies and gathered around the victim. The last one when struck exclaimed, "Oh, God." I turned to look at him and saw he was shot and while I turned back to face the Indians, he tumbled from the car. Again the Indians gathered around the fallen man, and I fired a shot into their midst, with what effect I do not know. When the savages had emptied their guns we received a shower of arrows, most of which went wild. George Seely was struck in the thigh by one but he jerked it out the next moment. I saw the boys bleeding, but so far I had not received a scratch, but just as the last three shots rang out I felt a sting in my breast, spurts of blood came from my mouth and nose, and I felt that my time to live was short. We were now within half a mile of the station and the Indians turned and left us. When near the station we met John Cook coming toward us carrying his rifle.

We all retired to the large dugout and prepared for an attack. The ammunition was placed on a table in the center of the room where it would be handy and thus we waited the return of the foe. During the time I examined my wound and found it to be a bullet hole in the center of my breast. Some one had spread blankets on the floor and on these I laid down and said my prayers—I was raised a Lutheran.

George Seely, Charlie Sylvester and George Taylor were also wounded and lay down on the floor, subject to call should the Indians attack the dugout. The man who was not wounded and John Cook kept watch. Indians hovered about the station all the afternoon.[24]

Roenigk learned that night the bullet that hit him passed through his body, which gave him hope that he might live. He had been shot through both lungs but eventually recovered. The two men who fell from the rail car "were stripped of clothing and horribly mutilated, having been scalped, stuck full of arrows and rings of telegraph wire pierced through the calves of their legs and other parts of their bodies."[25] When word of the raid reached Fort Hays, a company of troopers in Custer's 7th Cavalry was ordered to Asher Creek in Mitchell County, near where the deadly raids in August 1868, had occurred. It was thought the Indians might return for another raid on the settlements there. The troopers arrived on the Saline River near present-day Lincoln on the evening of May 30, just in time to hear firing signaling the conclusion of an afternoon of mayhem and murder along the Saline.[26]

A day after the violent attack on the railroad workers—May 29—warriors caught a group of four buffalo hunters on a tributary of the south fork of the Solomon River north of Fossil Creek in Osborne County, near present-day Covert, Kansas. The men had left Lincoln County near present-day Beverly two weeks earlier, just at the time General Carr was having his two fights with Tall Bull near Elephant Rock and Spring Creek. Napoleon "Dick" Alley, Henry Trask, William Earle and Solomon Humbarger had taken two wagons to carry their supplies as well as the many buffalo skins, tallow, tongues and meat they anticipated gathering. They had a successful and uneventful hunt; in five days they killed at least 80 buffalo.

Hunting buffalo with a rifle was truly an art. The experienced buffalo hunter, as was Humbarger, knew this. He had hunted buffalo for 10 years. If you shot a buffalo in the heart, it would kill him, but not before the beast bawled, kicked and ran a short distance. The commotion usually caused

24 Roenigk, *Pioneer History*, 172–174. Text corrected from misspellings in original account.

25 Roenigk, *Pioneer History*, 176. Roenigk lived a long life. He eventually settled in Lincoln, Kansas and became known as an excellent saddle maker. When he died he was buried where his parents were in Morganville, Kansas, about 60 miles northeast of Lincoln. The Kyne Museum in Lincoln has a display of two of Roenigk's saddles. I had admired them for many years when one day I looked at who donated them. To my surprise, they were donated by the father of my good school friend, when a cadet at St. John's Military School in Salina in 1971. Unfortunately the family was deceased by the time I discovered this and I was unable to ask about the saddles. No one in the museum knew anything regarding the generous donation.

26 *The Davenport Daily Gazette*, June 1, 1869.

the herd to stampede. So, shooting a buffalo in the heart meant one would probably only get one buffalo each time a herd was found grazing. But if the buffalo was shot in the lungs, the animal would not stampede; rather, it would cough, the blood dripping from its nostrils. Smelling blood, other calves would approach the distressed buffalo, often pawing the earth and bellowing, not understanding what was happening to the wounded one. If the hunter was against the wind, the buffalo's great sense of smell would not detect the hunter, and the hunter could get off several more fatal lung shots into the curious herd before the uninjured buffalo would finally understand something was amiss, and run.[27]

This was what these successful buffalo hunters had done on their hunt. As they were just finishing up preparing everything for their journey home, the Indians came upon them. Trask and Humbarger had done the hunting, while Earle and Alley prepared the carcasses for what would be harvested and brought back to their settlements. It was raining and the men were in no hurry to return home in the rain. They were relaxing in their camp about noon when the Indians attacked them. Humbarger shot and killed one Indian, and then was severely wounded in the thigh with an arrow. The other men escaped injury. They were able to get into the thick timber of the nearby creek, and the Indians were unwilling to venture forth.

Humbarger had been resting under one of the wagons when the Indians attacked, and upon being aroused, he quickly grabbed his rifle in one of the wagons—in his haste he grabbed the wrong rifle—a single shot Sharps—and then joined the other two men in the creek timber. Alley had taken a walk away from camp when the Indians made their charge and was unaware of what had happened.

Humbarger leveled the Sharps carbine at an Indian,

a sub-chief, who, with his bow and arrow was close upon the heels of the fleeing men. This savage, in his frenzied pursuit of scalps, caught sight of Humbarger with his upraised rifle, and knowing the sights were trained in his direction, began dodging back and forth as he ran in order to present a more difficult mark. "But I caught him," Humbarger said. With unerring aim he pulled the trigger at the right instant. The large bullet passed through the redskin's body, struck a sapling beyond, from which it glanced with a whistling sound through the air. The savage fell back mortally wounded.[28]

27 *Beverly Tribune*, May 26, 1926.
28 Roenigk, *Pioneer History*, 224.

After he shot the Indian, Humbarger tried to run further into the creek timber and while running got hit with an arrow in his thigh. The men were in a predicament, for their ammunition was in the wagons, and the wagons were between the Indians and where the men took their shelter. Earle had his Spencer but was too terrified to fire. It was left to Trask and Alley, who had rejoined his partners after escaping from the Indians who had tried to trap him away from the creek, to make a dash for the wagons to retrieve Alley's rifle and the ammunition. They succeeded without being hit.

Napoleon Alley's escapade during this time was remarkable. He had been attacked before the Indians charged the camp where his three friends were. He had earlier decided to take a walk up the creek. When he had ventured outside the timber a short distance he heard, first, an owl hoot and then a wolf bark. Both calls did not sound right, giving him caution, but he didn't want to return to the camp to report his concerns, thinking the other men would tease him for being scared. He thus continued to venture up a hill when he heard and then saw the Indians come charging at him:

> They came out of the woods on their ponies in a semi-circle between him and the camp. The only direction he could go was straight ahead up the hill. So Alley started with the Indians yelling behind him. . . . His only hope was to get into the timber again. The creek made a bend so that by running over the hill and down the other side he could reach the creek again if he could keep ahead of the Indians. To his surprise they didn't seem to try very hard to catch him. So he reached the top of the hill, ran down the other side and reached the creek bank. Then he understood why the Indians had let him get away so easily.
>
> The Indians possessed a sort of grim humor and they were playing with him somewhat as a cat plays with a mouse. They had spread out behind him so as to force him to the creek bank at a point where the bank was a rocky bluff, too steep to climb down and so high that to leap off seemed certain death. Here they came yelling like fiends. Dick looked back at the Indians and down at the creek below. Capture by the Indians meant certain death, and to jump seemed to mean the same thing. But death on the rocks in the creek bed was preferable to torture by the Indians. So he picked out the place where the water looked deepest and leaped for it.
>
> Fortune favored him. He landed in a hole in the creek where a freshet had washed in some mud, and it was deep enough to break his fall . . . it seemed to him he would never stop going down. He landed on his feet, and sunk in the mud to his knees before his feet hit the hard bottom. Then his back gave way and he went on down till his hands were down in the mud, and when they reached the bottom his elbows gave way and he went on down in the mud before he stopped. He got his face out of the mud so he could breathe and lay there getting his breath back.

The Indians gathered on the bank above him but didn't shoot, evidently thinking he was killed. When he had got his breath back so that he felt able to make another effort, he worked his arms loose from the mud so that he could raise up. The timber came down to the bank of the creek on the other side, and if he could get into the timber he stood some chance of escape; but he knew that as soon as the Indians saw him move they would begin to shoot at him. Finally he concluded to make the effort. So he raised up and threw himself over on the other bank and tried to get his legs out of the mud. The Indians began to yell and shoot at him, and arrows struck all around him, but as they were shooting almost straight down most of them passed over him. . . . It seemed to him that he would never get his legs out of the mud, but finally got them loose and scrambled up the bank and out into the timber. The Indians sat on their horses for a while upon the top of the bluff watching for a chance to shoot at him, but he got into the thick timber where they couldn't see him. Finally they turned and started off down the creek toward the camp.[29]

Alley heard the firing on his comrades and did not know if they were dead or alive, as shortly after all the commotion he heard, it got silent. He waited some time before venturing back to camp, staying concealed in the creek bed. There he discovered the men were still alive, though Humbarger was wounded. But the men lost everything they had in the wagons. After dark they walked the creek beds—mostly dry with pockets of water—a journey of two days to get home, but they could only go about 15 miles before Humbarger's arrow wound made it so that he was no longer able to walk. Alley—Humbarger later married Alley's sister—then stayed with Humbarger while Trask and Earle continued east until they reached Spillman Creek in the northwest section of Lincoln County, when they discovered the Indians had just raided there.[30] Indeed, the Dog Soldiers had attacked the settlement along the Saline River and Spillman Creek the day after their encounter, on Sunday, May 30.

---

29 *Beverly Tribune,* June 17, 1926, and June 24, 1926.

30 William Earle Indian Depredation Claim #840; Napoleon Alley Indian Depredation Claim #8179. Record Group 123. Adolph Roenigk letter, October 24, 1906, Archives, Kansas State Historical Society. See also http://www.kansasmemory.org/item/219590/page/8. Roenigk says in *Pioneer History of Kansas* that the men were attacked June 2, but the depredation claims make it clear they were attacked on May 29 and before the Indians made their deadly raid on Spillman Creek. Roenigk has an interesting account of the attack. See *Pioneer History,* 221–227. See also *Beverly Tribune,* June 24, 1926.

CHAPTER SIXTEEN

Bury My Heart
at Spillman Creek

If God Himself placed these markings upon the soul . . .
Why then would a gentle Spirit be so hard to control . . .
Please then let me try to explain, even then knowing,
That to enlighten can be a very dangerous game
An unbroken horse can be gentle
But it does not then follow that he will be soft, docile, or tame
For a tamed expression is devoid of all energy
And is ill-calculated to inspire the mind
With any feelings whatsoever, of any kind
For to be noble of character is to witness bravely
And to know this: along with our forefathers
Who might be inclined to agree
That there is a price to be paid; my friends
If we're to be, gentlemen and free.

POETRY BY STANLEY (SKIPPER) WINDER
GREAT-GREAT-GRANDSON OF SUSANNA ALDERDICE
AND GREAT-GRANDSON OF WILLIS DAILY

SUNDAY, MAY 30, 1869, WAS A WARM, BEAUTIFUL KANSAS spring day. It was also the first day America was nationally celebrating what is today called Memorial Day. Recognized and popular the year before, 1869 was the first year "Decoration Day" was observed across the nation.[1] Memorial Day recognizes those American soldiers whose lives were sacrificed in the preservation of freedom. Before this day was over,

---

1   http://en.wikipedia.org/wiki/Memorial–Day#Early–history (accessed March 23, 2013).

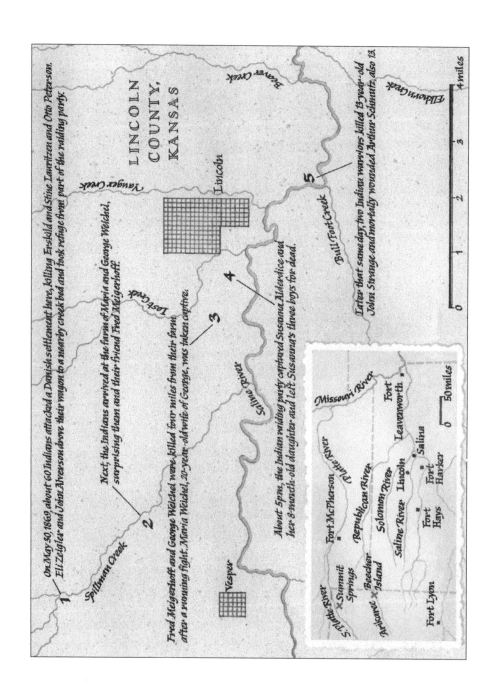

LINCOLN COUNTY, KANSAS

On May 30, 1869 about 60 Indians attacked a Danish settlement here, killing Erskild and Stine Lauritzen and Otto Petterson. Eli Zeigler and John Alverson drove their wagon to a nearby creek bed and took refuge from part of the raiding party.

1

Spillman Creek

2

Next, the Indians arrived at the farm of Maria and George Weichel, surprising them and their friend Fred Meigerhoff.

Lost Creek

3

Fred Meigerhoff and George Weichel were killed four miles from their farm after a running fight. Maria Weichel, 20-year-old wife of George, was taken captive.

Vesper

4

Saline River

About 5 p.m., the Indian raiding party captured Susanna Alderdice and her 8-month-old daughter and left Susanna's three boys for dead.

Yauger Creek

Lincoln

5

Bull Foot Creek

Later that same day, two Indian warriors killed 13-year-old John Strange and mortally wounded Arthur Schmutz, also 13.

Beaver Creek

Elkhorn Creek

0   1   2   3   4 miles

Missouri River

Fort McPherson

S. Platte River
×Summit Springs

Platte River

Republican River

Beecher
×Island

Arikaree

Solomon River

Fort
Leavenworth

Saline River   Lincoln
Fort Hays   ●Salina

Fort Harker

Fort Lyon

0   50 miles

434

the first Americans to enter perpetually into this national recognition were not soldiers but rather Kansas citizens, victims of the Cheyenne war. Nine men, women and children poured their blood out as the price of the prairie. No one would pay a higher toll than did a young pioneer mother, Susanna Alderdice, just 24 years of age. Two of her four children died on this day, a third joining her two brothers three days later. The young mother would enter the eternal sleep of her children in the unknown, six weeks later, at her failed rescue at Summit Springs, bringing the final number of dead Americans in this tragic rampage to 11. One lone child of Susanna's young family would spill as much blood on the prairie as did his siblings, but the uncaring ground would spare demanding his heartbeat.

Learning the correct names of all the victims is not easy because many years later different names and spellings were given.[2] A memorial to the dead was erected in Lincoln, Kansas, in 1910. The names on the pioneer monument were given as E. Lauritzen [sic], Stine Lauritzen [sic], O. Petersen [sic], F. Meigherhoff [sic], G. Weichell, F. Alderdice, J. Daily, J. H. Strange, and A. Schmutz.

The raid began in mid-afternoon at about three o'clock. Eli Zigler, Susanna's 19-year-old brother and John Alverson, Susanna's brother-in-law, had lunch—"dinner"—with Susanna and her children on the Saline River, about a mile and a half west of present-day Lincoln, late in the morning. Susanna's husband, Tom Alderdice, as well as other men in the settlement, were away filing land claims and procuring provisions. They would return the next day, only then learning what happened the day before. Eli and John had finished their visit and had left Susanna, and were driving a wagon

---

2   See Adolph Roenigk Letter, January 24, 1908. Archives, Kansas State Historical Society, Topeka, Kansas. See also http://www.kansasmemory.org/item/219590/page/14 (accessed July 1, 2013).

SPILLMAN CREEK RAID, MAY 30, 1869.
(*opposite*) Map details Tall Bull's Dog Soldier raid into Lincoln County. Nine settlers were killed that day. Maria Weichell was taken captive, as was Susanna Alderdice and her eight-month-old daughter, Alice. Alice was brutally murdered in Tall Bull's village three days later. Susanna was killed at her rescue at Summit Springs, July 11, 1869. Maria Weichell was gravely wounded at her rescue, but recovered. She later married John Mantz, and lived near San Francisco. She died in 1890, at the age of 45. *Courtesy Joan Pennington, Fairfax Station, Virginia.*

Tom Alderdice, Susanna Zigler Daily's second husband.
They married in 1866, at Salina, Kansas. Susanna was a young widow with two boys. Together she and Tom had a boy, Frank (1867), and daughter, Alice (1868). Both young children were killed during Susanna's ordeal, which began May 30, 1869, near Lincoln, Kansas. Tom learned of Susanna's death 11 days after she was buried on the battlefield, where her attempted rescue failed, when she was killed by Tall Bull. The military at the time called the fight at Summit Springs "Susanna Springs," in honor of Susanna. *Author's collection.*

loaded with supplies northwest. Their destination was the juncture of Bacon and Spillman Creek, where they intended to take over a staked homestead that had been abandoned as a result of the deadly Cheyenne raid in August 1868. As they were driving along the high ground, just north of present-day Denmark, they could see a cabin on the south side of Spillman Creek, about a half-mile to their south. The newly-built cabin housed several members of Swedish, Danish and German families. Looking to the north of the cabin, Eli and John saw what appeared to be about 60 soldiers approaching from the west. The cavalrymen were riding four abreast and wearing blue tunics. It seemed the "soldiers" spotted the two men in the wagon at about the same time. John was arguing with Eli, saying the men were Indians and not soldiers, when all doubts were erased. About 15 warriors turned toward the cabin, the rest charging at Alverson and Zigler. Eli was driving the wagon. Realizing his danger, Eli quickly turned the wagon about-face and drove his team of horses as fast as the wagon could go to Lost Creek, which they had crossed earlier. Eli:

> When we got to the creek the Indians were close behind us. I looked across the
> creek and thought there was a little bank on the other side that would protect us

MARY ZIGLER ALVERSON. Susanna Alderdice's closest sister in age, Mary married John Alverson, who narrowly escaped death at the beginning of the Spillman Creek raid May 30, 1869, when Susanna was captured and her children killed. There is no known picture of Susanna, but this picture of her sister gives a glimpse of how Susanna might have looked in 1869. *Author's collection, courtesy Gary Bathurst, Spokane, Washington.*

some. So I drove across, but John misunderstood me and jumped out into the creek and I drove up the bank. John ran along under the bank on the side I was on; the Indians were coming across the creek within a few yards of us, shooting and yelling. John was calling for me to get out of the wagon, when I got to that little bank, I stopped the horses, seeing nothing more could be done to save the team and that we must defend ourselves, I dropped the lines, grabbed my gun and jumped out on the off side of the wagon. Reaching in the box for my cartridges, I could only get the box, about 20 rounds. While I was getting the cartridges the Indians were close all around. One of them rode up and picked up the lines just as I had laid them down and he held the horses. I thought sure I'll put a hole through you, but before I could get my gun around he jumped off his pony down beside the wagon, and still held the horses. The Indians were shooting all this time. John was calling for me to get under the bank. Just then another Indian darted up right close to the wagon and I thought I would get him, but before I could cover him with my gun he jumped his pony on the opposite side of the wagon, so I could not get him.

John was still begging me to jump over the bank and I had about made up my mind to. As I stepped out from the wagon I looked toward the rear and behind the wagon and saw three Indians standing about four rods away, having me covered with their guns. I had no time for a shot, so made a spring for the creek bank; my foot slipped and I fell just as they fired. I think they over shot me. I also think that the slip is what saved me. I kept going on my hands and feet over the bank. As they were pouring their shots right at us at short range we saw a log lying up the bank a little below us, we ran to that, thinking that would protect us on the side.[3]

The Indians were unwilling to risk their lives shooting at armed men protected in a deep creek bank, forcing the Dog Men to be exposed in order to aim at their target. They left the men alone and contented themselves with taking the horses, pillaging the contents of the wagon and then destroying it. The Dog Soldiers then sought other victims. The two lucky men, however, were unwilling to climb out on the prairie and expose themselves. Instead, they slowly made their way back to the settlements, walking in Spillman Creek until they found a narrow place with steep banks. There they hid until dark, and then cautiously made their way inside the creek bed for about six miles, until coming to the Saline River. From there they went east to Elkhorn Creek, and then south another four miles to Lon Schermerhorn's ranch. That ranch was the preferred place for settlers to gather for protection during Indian raids. Zigler and Alverson were covered with mud and their clothes were in shreds by the time they ended their journey to safety.[4] Once there, the men would learn the tragic fate of Susanna and her children.

The warriors ignoring joining their comrades in chasing the Alverson wagon hit pay dirt, making their target the lone cabin on Spillman Creek. The home was built on Danish native Askel Martin Lauretson's land claim. In this small cabin lived six families, totaling 11 adults and five children. Laurence Christensen was there and recalled, less than two months later, what happened:

> I have taken the oath of allegiance to and applied to become a citizen of the United States. I have resided in the United States about two years. In March of this year, myself, John Peter Christiansen, Askel Martin Lauretson and Otto Peterson, made a settlement on the public lands of the United States, on Spillman Creek, a tributary of the Saline River, in Township 20, Range West, and in April, we were joined by Fritz Myhoff and Weitzel Weitzel; Mr. and Mrs. Weichell and Lauretson, myself & brother had wives [Stine, Maria and Nicoline] and Lauretson a son about twelve years old, named Marcus Lauretson. I had one child [Mary] and my brother three children [Christian, Helena and Hans] the whole of us comprising six families, occupied one house but each was engaged in improving separate tracts of the

---

3   Bernhardt, *Indian Raids*, 36–37. Washington Smith, *Saline Valley Register*, July 5, 1876. See also http:// skyways.lib.ks.us/genweb/lincoln/stories36.htm (accessed February 22, 2012).

4   John Alverson Indian Depredation Claim #8206, Record Group 123. *Saline Valley Register*, July 5, 1876.

public land, with a view to making separate homesteads.[5] The house occupied [by] us was built on Lauretson's land over 24 feet square, with a lean-to or shed used as a kitchen. . . .

On Sunday the 30th day of May last our place was attacked by Cheyenne Indians. The attack was made in the afternoon of the day. At the time our party was disposed of about as follows: Weichell and his wife [Maria], Lauretson and his wife [Stine], and [Otto] Peterson and [Fritz/Fred] Myhoff, had started up the creek, to look at their respective claims. Myself and brother with our wives, my own child, the three children of my brother and Lauretson's boy were in the house. Weichell and Myhoff had guns with them. The first notice we had of the attack was the firing of the Indians upon Lauretson and his wife, who was only about 30 rods [495 feet] from the house. The Indians were concealed in the timber. Lauretson and his wife were both killed. On hearing the firing, myself and my brother opened the door with a view of going to their aid, but on our doing so the Indians fired at us, their balls passing close by the door. We then went back into the house, and making holes through the walls of the house, we fired several times at such of them as came within our range. I do not know that any of the Indians were hurt. There were about sixteen of them engaged in the attack upon the house. They approached the house and got upon the top of it and into the shed, in which latter they destroyed our cooking stove, cooking utensils and dishes. They made several attempts to fire the house, but the roof was of earth and the logs green, and we continued to fire upon them, they were not able to burn the buildings. Their attack on the house continued from three o'clock till just before dark, when they drew off, soon after which we left the house and succeeded in reaching the settlement on the Saline, on the road we were fired on by the Indians, but there was no harm done. The next day a party of the settlers went out and found and buried Lauretson and his wife, Weichell, Myhoff & Peterson. Mrs. Weichell was not found, and the opinion was that she was carried off a prisoner by the Indians. During their attack the Indians broke up and destroyed the cooking stove, the dishes and other household kitchen implements in the shed, and also 1 hoe; they also carried off three axes & a chest of tools, consisting of planes, files, braces, bits, chisels, hatchets Etc. The stove cost $30 in Chicago and was worth where destroyed $45; the dishes and the household implements were worth $25; the axes were worth $2.25 each; the hoe was worth $1.25; the chest of tools was worth at least $25. They also carried off two feather pillows worth $2.50 each.

A few days before the attack we had made a purse to buy a team with, to which I had contributed one hundred and fifty dollars, my brother, J. P. Christiansen had contributed one hundred and fifty dollars, and A. M. Lauretson, one hundred and fifty dollars and Otto Peterson was to, but had not yet, contributed a like sum. All

---

5   Broome, *Dog Soldier Justice*, 93.

the money paid was in the possession of, and on the person of A. M. Lauretson, when he was killed, and the whole of it was stolen by the Indians. It was in United States currency and amounted in the aggregate to the sum of four hundred and fifty dollars.[6]

Lauretson and his wife "were mutilated in a fiendish manner, too horrible to describe on paper."[7] Peterson was found on the opposite side of Spillman Creek—south—than the Lauretsons.[8] George Weichell, his 23-year-old wife Maria—who was three months pregnant with her first and only child—and Fritz Myhoff/Fred Meigerhoff had earlier taken a stroll along Spillman Creek to enjoy the Sunday afternoon.[9] The Indians—about a dozen—caught them out on the prairie and unable to retreat back to the cabin. But both men were armed and fought off the warriors. Had Maria not been with them, perhaps the Dog Men would have considered a fight a poor risk, but a potential female captive was enough to make that risk worth taking. It's not known if either man wounded or killed any Indians, but they were able to go south almost five miles before running out of ammunition, approximately a mile north of the Saline River and a mile and a half west of Lincoln. Once the men used up their ammunition, the Indians were able to come in for the kill. The time now was early evening, probably five o'clock. The warriors mutilated the men, and cut off the finger of George, taking his wedding ring.[10] The killings happened about a mile northwest of where another party of Indians at about that time descended upon Mrs. Alderdice and her children.[11]

---

6   Laurence Christensen Indian Depredation Claim, Settled Indian Account #1325, Record Group 217. The first-hand document in this claim was written two months after the raid by the Christensen brothers, who knew the victims. They were careful in spelling out the names of the other adults living in the cabin. I take these spellings as definitive in learning the accurate names of the victims of the Spillman Creek raid.

7   Roenigk Letter, January 24, 1908.

8   Bernhardt, *Indian Raids*, 28, 40. Bernhardt believed Peterson was found on the north side of Spillman Creek, while Eli Zigler believed the body was found on the south side of the creek. All state he was not found at the time the other victims were found, which lends credence to Zigler's claim.

9   In *Dog Soldier Justice* I incorrectly spelled the Weichell name as Weichel. The Christensen depredation file—which I did not have when I wrote *Dog Soldier Justice*—as well as the pioneer monument, gives credence to the correct spelling as Weichell. But more definitively is the 1880 census which shows the name of the unborn baby Maria was carrying when she was captured, Minnie Grace Weichell. See http://search.ancestry.com/iexec?htx=View&r=an&dbid=6742&iid=4239985-00140&fn=Mary&ln=Mantz&st=r&ssrc=&pid=20511061 (accessed February 22, 2011).

10   Broome, *Dog Soldier Justice*, 95.

11   *Saline Valley Register*, July 5, 1876. Bernhardt claimed the two events happened within a quarter-mile of each other. Bernhardt, *Indian Raids*, 30.

THE CAPTURE OF 23-YEAR-OLD MARIA WEICHELL, MAY 30, 1869.
When Maria was captured her husband George was killed, along with family friend
Fritz Myhoff/Fred Meigerhoff. She was rescued at Summit Springs six weeks later.
She was three months pregnant when captured. Painting by James Davis Nelson,
Jewell, Kansas. *Courtesy Jeanette Lyon, Tucson, Arizona.*

With Maria as an unfortunate captive, that band of Indians rode west until they felt safe from anyone finding them. Then they took Maria and "laid her on the ground and with four holding her arms and legs they all ravished her. She was then gone about three months in pregnancy."[12] Her inhumane treatment would continue for six more weeks.

As these warriors were chasing and capturing Maria, another sortie of six Dog Soldiers come up the Saline River looking for plunder west of Lincoln. They well might have been with the party that earlier attacked Eli Zigler and John Alverson. If so, then the warriors, after attacking the two men, continued south on Lost Creek until reaching the Saline where they divided, half going west and half going east. Both parties would succeed in their murderous intent.

There were several homes near each other, just south and west of where Maria was captured. Indians first entered the home of Tim and Bridget Kine on the Saline River. Further west of the Kine house was the home of Michael Haley, and west of that was the home of Nicholas Whalen.[13] Between those two homes was the home of Thomas Alderdice and his wife Susanna. A day or two before the raid, Alderdice, Kine and four other men had left the settlements to file land claims in Junction City and then, on the return home, they purchased supplies in Salina, 35 miles east.[14] Kine's wife Bridget, along with their two-month-old daughter, Katherine,[15] Susanna and her four children had agreed to stay in the Haley home, along with Nicholas Whalen and Thomas Noon and his wife. Haley had taken his wife and three young daughters south to Fort Harker, as news of the Indians raiding along

---

12 Eugene A. Carr, Letter to William F. Cody, July 2, 1906, Box 3, E. A. Carr Papers, U.S. Army Military History Institute, Carlisle Barracks, PA.

13 Nicholas Whalen says in the Timothy Kine depredation claim that at the time of the raid, he was living with Michael Haley. Haley and Whalen were cousins, so it is possible that Whalen in 1869 had not yet built his house, and if so, then reference in 1869 to the Haley house and the Whalen house are one and the same. If this is the case, then there were three houses near each other on the Saline. See Indian Depredation Claim #7455, Record Group 123.

14 The earlier pioneer reminiscences as well as Timothy Kine's Indian Depredation claim indicate the men had gone to Junction City to file a land claim. If this was true then they would have left earlier and could have come back through Salina for supplies.

15 Timothy Kine states in his depredation claim that his daughter was two months old at the time of the raid. He also signs his name Kine, and not Kyne, though there is another signature of a witness spelled Pat Kyne, as witness for Bridget's testimony, as she could not spell, and her statement is marked with an "X," with Pat Kyne as witness. The claim was dated 1874. It is possible Kine at the time of the raid had changed his spelling from Kyne to Kine. The historical museum in Lincoln has the last home that Kine built, and it is called the Kyne home. See Indian Depredation Claim #7455.

WILLIS DAILY, AT TIME OF MARRIAGE,
MARCH 25, 1886.
Willis was the only child of Susanna Alderdice
to survive the May 30, 1869 raid in Lincoln
County, Kansas. Willis was tortured and
abused, before five arrows were shot into his
back. He was four and a half years old when
gravely wounded. Other accounts indicate
he was also shot twice and speared in the left
hand. In the 1960s, one of his children wrote
that one could clearly see the five scars from
the arrow wounds when Willis worked his
farm shirtless, in Blue Rapids, Kansas. Willis
died of cancer June 16, 1920, at the age of 55.
Author's collection.

White Rock Creek had filtered into the settlements, and Haley feared for
his young family's safety. With everybody staying together in one house,
including Whalen and Noon there to protect the young mothers from an
Indian attack if one came, it was felt safe to leave the women on the Saline,
while their husbands were away filing land claims and getting supplies.

Susanna's life had already included hardship. Only 24 years old, she had
married James Alfred Daily in the fall of 1860, when she was just 15 years old
and he was 20. July 1, 1863, her son John was born near Salina. He was not yet
six years old on May 30. On October 5, 1864, a second son was born, Willis.
But James was not present for the birth of Willis, for he was at that moment
in the middle of a 100-day enlistment with the 17th Kansas Infantry. He
had responded to a call for volunteers to protect the Kansas border from
the threat of a Confederate invasion during the Civil War. His enlistment
was due to expire in November, but James came down with typhoid fever
and died at Fort Leavenworth November 25, leaving Susanna a teenaged
widow. She moved into the home of her parents, Michael and Mary Zigler,
who were living at the time near the Solomon River just north of Salina.
At about this time, Tom Alderdice took the Oath of Allegiance at Rock
Island, Illinois, where he had been a Confederate prisoner of war after his
capture at the battle of Chickamauga the year before, and joined the 2nd

U. S. Volunteer Infantry. His regiment was sent to Kansas, and soon Tom met Susanna while stationed near Salina. They wed June 28, 1866, and a year later had a son, Frank, and in 1868 a daughter, Alice. Now in late May, Susanna was about five months pregnant with her fifth child.[16]

Bridget Kine recalled the terrifying moment when she saw the Indians. She had heard a noise and looked east from the Haley yard to where her cabin was, and there she saw warriors taking her husband's mare and colt from the front of the yard. In that moment of fright, she was paralyzed with fear and unable to react. But Tom Noon, his wife and Nicholas Whalen had no such paralysis. They had horses picketed nearby, and promptly jumped on them and rode off to the west, forgetting their earlier promise to protect the young mothers and children. A handful of Indians chased them but soon returned, unable to catch them. Susanna and Bridget were suddenly alone with their children. Bridget recovered her senses, and with her daughter in her arms, ran south to the Saline River. The distance must have been several hundred feet; in her scamper she could hear the Indians on horseback gallop in pursuit. Susanna followed her, but with her pregnancy and four children, she realized she was not going to be able to get away. One account said Susanna pleaded with Bridget to help her. Bridget replied back that she could do nothing but save herself. Another account said Bridget was carrying one of Susanna's children—probably Frank, as John and Willis were capable of running alongside their terrified mother—and seeing she could not make the river with him holding her hand, Bridget laid the child down in the tall blue stem and told him to lie still, and then ran down the bank and into the river.

Bridget was up to her waist in the water, holding little Katherine above the water level. To her fortune, there had been a large cottonwood tree that had earlier toppled into the water. It left a deep-hanging bank, which barely hid her from approaching eyes. Little Katherine remained awake and did not make a sound. Had she cried, Bridget later reported, she was prepared to use her apron and suffocate the newborn, to keep her silent. A later report

---

16 James A. Daily Military Service Record and Pension File. Record Group 94. Broome, *Dog Soldier Justice*, 1–4. In *Dog Soldier Justice* I misrepresented Susanna's age as being five years older, which was a mistake. After *Dog Soldier Justice* was published I heard from descendants of Susanna's older sister, Sophia Zigler Norton, who died in 1905. They had each U.S. Census following the Zigler family, which clearly showed Susanna was born in 1845, and not 1840, as I first thought.

said Bridget could hear an Indian speaking in plain English, telling his comrades that one woman made it to the river. As Bridget hid, she could see the moccasins of some of the Dog Men as they sought to find her.[17]

The Indians knew they couldn't linger long, for armed settlers could emerge at any moment. Still, there was enough time for them to "torture and abuse" Susanna's three boys before killing them. The little children were stripped of their clothing, and when found the next day had numerous arrow and gunshot wounds in their back.[18] The Indians then tied Susanna to a horse, and allowed her to hold eight-month-old Alice between her arms. At least she had her daughter with her—something to give her hope alongside her anguish—though she had to endure the rest of her short life with the awful images of watching her young boys tortured and murdered.

In this mass of murder emerged an incredible story of survival, unknown to Susanna. The day after the raid, when soldiers and settlers were retracing the murderous path of the Dog Soldiers, lying unconscious next to his two dead brothers, with multiple wounds—all in the back—four-year-old Willis Daily was found still breathing. He had five arrow wounds, and other accounts indicated additional gunshot wounds as well as a spear wound in his left hand. He was taken to the home of one of the settlers, but no one was able to locate a doctor willing to treat him—it was still quite dangerous to venture about—and there, the unfortunate child agonized in pain for two days with an arrow imbedded in him so deep no one could pull it out. Finally, one of the settlers held Willis down while another used a bullet mold as pliers, and yanked the arrow from his back. A young boy in the house at the time later recalled what happened. Little Willis

> begged so hard to have it taken out that a man by the name of Phil Lantz said that if someone would hold him down, he could pull it out and a man by the name of Washington Smith said he would hold him. Lantz pulled the arrow out with a pair of bullet molds of my father's and as luck would have it, the spike came out but no one thought he would live....[19]

Willis surprised everyone and recovered. He was raised to adulthood by Susanna's parents, Michael and Mary Zigler. In 1886, he married Mary

---

17   Broome, *Dog Soldier Justice*, 98.
18   Broome, *Dog Soldier Justice*, 96–99.
19   Hendrickson, "Memories," *The Lincoln-Sentinel Republican*, February 8, 1934.

Twibell and soon moved to Blue Rapids, Kansas, where he raised his three children to adulthood. He died in his home from the ravages of cancer on June 16, 1920, at the age of 55.[20]

While Susanna was experiencing her terrible ordeal, the other Dog Soldiers who ventured east along the Saline found their prey, in a field just south of present-day Lincoln, near where other settlers had built their homes. Two boys, 13-year-old Arthur Schmutz and 13- or 14-year-old John "Harrison" Strange were digging for turnips on a hill. When the boys spotted two Indians approaching them, they began to run back to a home but the older Indian called out that he was a good Pawnee, intending to assure the boys they wouldn't be harmed. They stopped running and the older Indian passed them on his horse, taking time to lean over and touch each boy on the shoulder with his spear, thus counting coup, an Indian custom bestowing honor to a warrior who touches an enemy. The experienced warrior then went after some unharnessed horses nearby. The younger Indian—not much older than the two boys—approached them, and raised himself up on his horse, ready to swing a big pine club at Strange. Schmutz reported, "Young Strange saw the blow coming, and with the words 'Oh, Lord!' half expressed, he fell and died almost immediately, his skull having been broken in near the crown. The club broke and was left lying on the ground nearby." At that, Schmutz tried to run while the young warrior shot arrow after arrow at him, apparently hitting him several times. As he ran, he pulled the arrows out, but one metal point remained lodged deep in his side. The Indian would have caught up to him except that two of Strange's younger brothers looked from their cabin and saw the young warrior assaulting the two defenseless boys. They ran outside, firing a shotgun at the Indian, who then galloped off. Schmutz was taken down to Fort Harker, and there lingered in the post hospital for 10 weeks before he died.[21]

Coincidentally, Company G of the 7th Cavalry, under the command of Lieutenant Edward Law, had just arrived on the south side of the Saline River a bit further east of where the Strange boy was killed, near the mouth of Bullfoot Creek and the Saline. As the soldiers were preparing for camp, they heard the firing of the shotgun by the two younger Strange boys, but

---

20   Broome, *Dog Soldier Justice*, 187–195. That arrow was kept as a souvenir and eventually donated to the Lincoln County Historical Society, and is on display in the town museum in Lincoln.

21   Broome, *Dog Soldier Justice*, 100–102. *Saline Valley Register,* July 5, 1876.

took it to be firing from settlers hunting. Very soon, however, pioneers fled across the river and reported the raid. Law earlier had orders to go 30 miles north to Asher Creek after the Fossil Creek raid, and he had arrived in the Saline valley just as the Spillman Creek raid was ending. With some of his troopers and a few settlers, they started out west, pursuing one party of raiders, the ones that had Susanna. They saw them, but were unable to overtake them before darkness ended the chase.[22]

The next morning, Tom Alderdice and the other men in his party were returning home, and when a few miles east he heard a report that his family had been killed. He and Kine then galloped their wagons to the Shermerhorn ranch, where they got further details. Bridget was there and reunited with her husband. Her trauma affected her for the rest of her life, eventually leading to two hospitalizations in the Kansas Insane Asylum in Topeka.[23]

In an interview late in life, Tom Alderdice discussed what happened when he returned to his homestead. The young family had just moved to their land claim on the Saline, and had not had time to erect a house. His young family was living in a double tent, southeast of where Whalen finally built his cabin. Tom's memory of that sad moment never waned:

> I kept on west on the south side of the river until I got opposite to my home and then forded the river. I went up to the bank and looked to where the tent was when I left and I saw that it was down. I walked north to the tent. I had a garden south of the tent and when I got to the garden I found that the flour that I had left in the house was sown and scattered over the garden. I then saw John Daily lying on the prairie near the tent. He was lying on his back and he was dead. He had seven arrows in his body. A little north of where John Daily was lying I found Frank Alderdice, my oldest child, about two years old, with six arrows in him. He was lying on his back. ... I placed the children side by side and covered them and the next morning went back and was preparing to make a coffin for them. Mike Haley came over to where I was and said "It's hard Tom for a man to be making a box for his own children." He helped me to make the coffin.[24]

22 Broome, *Dog Soldier Justice*, 104–106.

23 "Report of Commission and Judgment in the Probate Court of Lincoln County, Kansas," February 23, 1906, 104. A. Artman, Probate Judge. Copy in the personal papers of Craig Walker, Lincoln, Kansas.

24 *Lincoln Republican*, January 25, 1923. Coincidentally, Mike Haley was the great-grandfather of my history teacher, when I went to St. John's Military School, in Salina. I did not learn this until Virgil "Lefty" Loy had retired, but, hearing that I was giving a talk at St. John's about the Indian raids in Lincoln County, he came to hear me. Lefty grew up hearing family stories of Susanna and the 1869 Indian raid. He went to school in Beverly, and as a young boy, he was enthralled with listening to the stories of J. J. Peate, the Indian fighter who ended up with the arrow pulled from the back of Willis Daily.

Tom went on to say that the arrow that went into Willis—the one that was so difficult to remove—"was below the breast bone and went straight through the body." Tom prepared his children for burial, and then did something only a desperate husband and father could imagine doing: he struck out on his own after the Indians, hoping to find their trail and follow it to their village. He knew a bit about tracking. Indians did not ride horses with horse shoes. They generally spread out when traveling across the prairie, so the tall buffalo grasses would not imprint their tracks. But so too, Indians seldom wandered on the open prairie when out on the warpath. Instead, they would follow single file inside the deep creek and river beds, only occasionally rising on the prairie to cross open ground, until they could enter another creek. In this way Tall Bull's Dog Soldiers went back to their main village. And Tom found it. And when he got there, nearly 100 miles to the northwest, he observed warriors coming and going from the village. They were obviously still seeking plunder and murder.

As suspected, the Indians did raid on the Solomon between present-day Beloit and Concordia. On June 2, they cornered a young 12-year-old boy, Ezra Adkins, near where Sarah White had been captured in 1868. They shot him in the head. Reverend Nels Nelson, a neighbor, witnessed the murder and told the Adkins family. Together about dark, Nels and Ezra's father went out to retrieve the body. The boy's dog led them to little Ezra:

> The scene was a ghastly one, with the brains oozing from the gunshot wound that had been inflicted about seven hours earlier. The grief of the family was terrible to behold and a scene never to be forgotten by the little group of settlers gathered there, where a few hours before the family had rejoiced in dreams of a future happy home.[25]

---

25 Hollibaugh, *Biographical History of Cloud County*, 54. After *Dog Soldier Justice* was published, I received a call from the son of Alan LeMay, who wrote the novel, *The Searchers*, which in 1956 became the screenplay for what many people think was John Wayne's greatest movie, of the same title. He told me he always believed his father's story, while set in Texas, actually reflected events in Kansas. His family had followed Nels Nelson from Sweden, and settled in Republic County. When he read about Nels Nelson in my book, he called me to tell me I had found the verifying link to convince him *The Searchers* was really about Kansas Indian raids and not Texas, as the movie depicted. Alan LeMay grew up as a little boy listening to his grandmother tell him thrilling stories of Indian raids in Kansas when she was a child. The father of one family in the movie is named Nels. Alan's son has since published a biography of his famous father. See Dan LeMay, *Alan LeMay: A Biography of the Author of* The Searchers (Jefferson, NC: McFarland & Company, Inc., Publishers, 2012). Coincidentally, shortly after LeMay published his book about his father, Glenn Frankel published *The Searchers: The Making of an American Legend* (New York/London/New Delhi/Sydney: Bloomsbury USA, 2013). Frankel argues LeMay's novel was all about Cynthia Ann Parker, the Texas captive who was re-captured years after her captivity, but remained defiantly Indian throughout her remaining life.

Once Tom located the village, he then traveled east all the way to Fort Leavenworth, and there reported to General John Schofield what he had discovered. He wrote what he had observed:

> I started in pursuit on the 1st of June, traveled from Saline River three miles east of Spillman Creek, north by west striking the north branch of Salt Creek. Distance 12 miles. Traveled west by north up north branch of Salt Creek, striking Spillman Creek about ½ mile above main fork. Distance 9 miles. Traveled up west fork of Spillman to head of creek traveling west by north, crossed to Wolf Creek striking east fork; went up east fork about 4 miles, crossed to west fork. Found trail. Followed trail to creek, name unknown. Traveled north to Solomon up north fork of Solomon. Saw Indians (3 in number) hunting, still further up creek Indians. I supposed a large camp above, secreted myself in ravine to watch movements. Could see nothing but Indians going out and returning to creek. Returned back to settlement for help.[26]

The village was in the Solomon Valley between the present-day towns of Harlan and Portis. At the same time Tom gave this report to Schofield, he also provided details regarding Susanna:

> Description of Mrs. Susan Alderdice, captured by Indians on Saline River, Lincoln County, Kans, May 30th, 1869.
> Height: Medium
> Complexion: Light
> Hair: Light Brown
> Age: Twenty Two years
> Eyes: Blue[27]

Unknown to Tom, about the time he found the village, the Indians had tired of little Alice's incessant crying and killed her. She was killed three days after her capture. Tom said he "learned that my child had been roasted alive before the death of my wife."[28] Other accounts said she was dismembered and thrown into a creek, or she was strangled and hung in a tree.[29]

---

26 Alderdice, Tom, "Letter dated June 21, 1869," Part 1, E2601, Department of Missouri, Letters Received, 1869, Record Group 393.

27 Alderdice, "Letter." When Tom arrived at Fort Leavenworth, he got there at the end of the day, June 19, and was not permitted to see Schofield until the next day. General George Custer was visiting in the city with his wife, and together they met with Tom. The meeting was widely published in newspapers, and in her last book, *Following the Guidon*, Libbie Custer wrote about meeting with Tom. This is all covered in *Dog Soldier Justice*, 119–122. The other thing interesting to note is that Tom named Susanna, "Susan," which indicates this was her preferred name. Census records also verify this. He apparently was wrong in giving her age, as census records consistently indicate she was born in 1845, making her in all likelihood still 24 when captured.

28 *Lincoln Republican*, January 25, 1923.

29 Broome, *Dog Soldier Justice*, 124–125.

Regardless of the manner of little Alice's death, Susanna's terrible ordeal took from her hands her last child. She would never know Willis had survived. General E. A. Carr later said Tom found the remains of his baby daughter in the Indian village.[30] If that is true, then Tom went back to the village after reporting its location to General Schofield at Fort Leavenworth.

While Tom was finding the village and reporting it to the military, the decision had earlier been made to send Brevet Major General Eugene A. Carr and several companies of the 5th Cavalry out of Fort McPherson near present-day Maxwell, Nebraska, down into north-central Kansas, to try and locate the raiding Indians. On June 9, he left the fort with eight companies. Three additional companies of Pawnee Scouts joined the expedition, under the command of Major Frank North. One company of the 5th Cavalry was soon returned to McPherson and given duty guarding the Platte River in Nebraska, leaving Carr with a total of 10 companies, comprising just less than 500 men. After Tom Alderdice informed General Schofield where the Indian village was, that information, along with his description of Susanna, was telegraphed to Fort McPherson and then couriered to Carr in the field.[31] The soldiers now knew they were on a rescue mission to find the two women captives taken in the Spillman Creek raid.

When Carr went south from Fort McPherson, he almost immediately came into contact with the Dog Soldiers. As Tall Bull's village was moving away from their camp where Tom Alderdice found them, warriors were still jaunting off into small groups, looking for opportunities to murder and plunder. It was these small bands of warriors that permitted Carr to stay on track of the Dog Soldier village. Once he found their trail, he had four fights with the Indians, the last one when he found and destroyed their entire village at Summit Springs, on July 11.[32]

Tall Bull might well have escaped north into the Powder River country, had 50 of his warriors not misinterpreted Carr's intentions, believing wrongly the soldiers had withdrawn from their pursuit. Earlier, three

---

30 Carr, E. A., "Letter to Bill Cody, July 2, 1906, New York City," Box 3, E. A. Carr Papers, U.S. Army Military History Institute, Carlisle Barracks, PA. See also Carr, "Reminiscences of Indian Wars," Box 3, Indian Wars 1868–1892. Eugene A. Carr Papers, United States Army Military History Institute, Carlisle Barracks, PA, 25.

31 Broome, *Dog Soldier Justice*, 154.

32 Eugene A. Carr, "Letter to Washington Smith, February 24, 1887." Washington Smith Indian Depredation Claim #3951, Record Group 75.

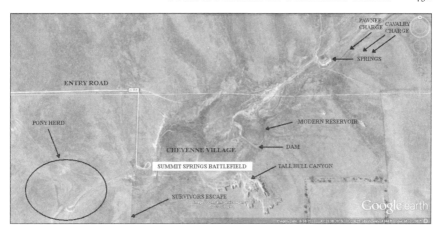

SUMMIT SPRINGS, JULY 11, 1869.
The fight at Summit Springs effectively ended raids committed by Tall Bull's band
of Dog Men. Tall Bull and as many as 75 other warriors were killed at Summit
Springs, near present-day Sterling, Colorado. *Map courtesy Chuck Jones, Aurora,*
Colorado.

companies of Carr's command had a skirmish with the Dog Soldiers on
July 5. Earlier—July 2—Carr's men had camped on the South Fork of
the Republican River about a mile southwest of present-day Benkelman,
Nebraska. The next day Carr went west, on the north side of the Republican
15 miles, and went into camp just west of present-day Haigler, Nebraska.
Scouting parties, especially the Pawnee contingent, were sent out to search
for any trails the Indians might have left. Carr was getting closer to his prey,
and the Dog Soldiers knew it. For that matter, Carr knew that warrior spies
were tracking his movements as well. He was able to average about 30 miles
a day, while the village, slowed by the enormous meat, plunder and camp
equipage, was able to travel half the distance Carr did. The longer Carr's
troopers were in the field, the closer they were getting to Tall Bull's village.[33]

Carr's scouting parties returned, and the Pawnee reported finding the
Indian camp, abandoned about 36 hours earlier. Examination revealed the
village contained between 160 and 200 tepees. That would have included
more than 400 warriors. The next day—July 4—Carr sent Companies A, E,
and M, under the command of Brevet Major William Bedford Royall, along

---

33   Carr, "Reminiscences of Indian Wars."

with one company of Pawnee, to track the village trail west. While Royall went off on his expedition, Carr took the rest of the command and went south on the Arikaree Fork of the Republican, finally going into camp near where the September 17–25, 1868, Beecher's Island battle had been fought. Coincidentally, Forsyth's small command of Kansas scouts who fought in that famous battle included Susanna's brother Eli—the youngest scout at 18—and Tom Alderdice, Susanna's husband. It was while Tom was away fighting for his life at Beecher's Island that Susanna gave birth to Alice, who was now dead, murdered by her captors a month earlier.

On July 5, Royall sent a courier to Carr and reported he had passed several abandoned Indian camps. After that courier had been sent to Carr, Royall's command came upon a war party of about a dozen Indians returning to their village. They were carrying with them a wounded, young warrior. The Cheyenne were about 30 miles north of the Republican, a few miles southwest of present-day Holyoke, Colorado. A sharp fight ensued. The Pawnee with Royall killed three warriors, including the injured boy, and wounded at least three others. The surviving Dog Soldiers escaped north. George Bent later identified the wounded Cheyenne warrior, killed by the Pawnee, as Howling Magpie. He had been shot through both thighs in an earlier skirmish with Carr's troopers. His cousins, Shave Head and Little Man, were with the party, bringing the wounded Howling Magpie back to the village when they were all killed.[34] Meanwhile, once Carr learned that Royall was on the Indian trail, he left his Arikaree camp on July 6, and brought his command northeast 20 miles, camping a few miles east of present-day Haigler, Nebraska. The next day, Royall joined Carr in camp, having exhausted his rations. On July 8, Carr moved his command east and away from the Dog Soldiers, finally going into camp near their earlier July 4 campsite, just west of Benkelman. This campsite was a mile east of their July 4 camp.

It was this move which fooled Tall Bull. A party of about 50 Dog Soldiers followed Royall back to Carr's camp, and continued following Carr's command as they ventured east 15 miles, to the forks of the Republican. In the early evening, some impatient and incautious warriors trailing Carr's movements made a rush on the cavalry camp, their intent probably to capture some horses. The warriors were repulsed. When they returned to Tall Bull's village, they reported that Carr had turned east, which led Tall Bull

---

34 Hyde, *Life of George Bent*, 330–331.

to wrongly believe Carr had withdrawn from the field. Why else would the command go east, when they knew the Dog Soldiers were traveling west?

One Pawnee distinguished himself in the skirmish on July 8, and later that summer was awarded the Medal of Honor, a very rare feat for an Indian scout. Pawnee Sergeant Co-rux-te-chod-ish (Mad Bear) ran out of the camp and boldly charged the Dog Soldiers when they made their assault, but in the din of the fight and the dusk of the evening, Mad Bear was accidentally shot in the back by one of Carr's troopers. He was gravely wounded and spent the rest of the campaign in an ambulance wagon, missing the important fight at Summit Springs three days later. His boldness to fight the Dog Soldiers impressed General Carr, and he made his recommendation for the Medal of Honor. Unfortunately, Luther North's reminiscences, written years later, declared that Carr's recommendation for the medal was really meant for Traveling Bear, who had fought bravely at Summit Springs. However, the papers for the Medal of Honor, housed in the National Archives, as well as Carr's reminiscences and military reports, clearly indicate the medal was for Mad Bear's heroic action on July 8. Carr also cited Mad Bear for killing two of the Dog Men caught by Royall's command on July 4. Historians have repeatedly cited Luther's false account, and wrongly named the Medal's actual recipient.[35]

Another heroic action occurred earlier in the day, on July 8, and also resulted in a Medal of Honor. The soldier's story, both before and after receiving the Medal of Honor, is so interesting it bears briefly telling here. After Royall returned to Carr's camp near present-day Haigler, he reported that he had abandoned an exhausted cavalry horse of Company M. Corporal John Kile volunteered to take two men, and retrieve the horse several miles northeast from the camp. Meanwhile, Carr moved his command east towards present-day Benkelman. After the horse was found—probably a few miles northwest of present-day Parks, Nebraska—the three soldiers were returning to Carr's eastern camp, when a band of Dog Soldiers discovered them. Thinking they could easily overcome three cavalrymen, the adrenaline-filled warriors charged at the soldiers. The citation written for the award was short on detail: "This soldier (Kyle [Kile]) and two others were attacked by eight Indians, but beat them off and badly wounded two of them."[36]

---

35 Broome, *Dog Soldier Justice*, 157–158.
36 Anonymous, *The Medal of Honor of The United States Army* (Washington, DC: Government Printing Office, 1948), 211.

George Price, who in 1869 was a 1st Lt. with Carr's command, later wrote of Kile's heroic fight: ". . . on the afternoon of the 8th Corporal Kyle [Kile] and three men of Company M had a brilliant affair on Dog Creek, where, although surrounded by thirteen Sioux warriors, they succeeded in killing three and compelling the others to retreat north of the Republican River, when they leisurely retired and rejoined the command twelve miles below."[37]

Lieutenant William Volkmar's journal, written on July 8, gave more details, but misspelling Kile's last name as Kyle:

> In the morning a small detachment of "M" Troop, 5th Cavalry, under Corporal Kyle [Kile], was sent from Black Tail Deer Creek, over to Rock Creek to recover, if possible, an exhausted horse, abandoned there by the troop in returning with Col. Royall; Whilst engaged at this, they were attacked by a much superior force of Indians, of whom they killed and wounded three and made their escape.[38]

Carr, in his report written July 20, also mentioned Kile's fight:

> During the day [July 8] three men of Company "M" who were several miles in the rear of the column bringing in a given-out horse, were attacked by eight Indians. They got near a large rock for a breastwork on one side, and killed the horse as a defence on the other, and beat off the Indians, wounding two badly.
>
>   Corporal John Kyle [Kile], Company M 5th Cavalry was in charge of the party; he showed especial bravery on this, as he had done on previous occasions.[39]

Kile's heroic action, as it was soon reported to Carr—who noted in his report that Kile had acted bravely earlier—included the desperate fight Company M had at Spring Creek, on May 16. And of course, there was still the fight to be had at Summit Springs three days later, where Kile again demonstrated "especial bravery."

Enlistment records show that John Kile first enlisted as a teenager in the 5th Cavalry on December 9, 1865. On November 20, 1866, he deserted.

---

37 George F. Price, *Across the Continent With the Fifth Cavalry* (New York, NY: Antiquarian Press LTD, 1959. Originally published in 1883), 136. If Price was accurate in his location, then the fight happened near the Republican River between Haigler and Parks, Nebraska.

38 Record Group 393, Part 1, Department of the Platte. Letters Received, 1869, Box 12. Volkmar is officially the first officer to misspell Kile's name as Kyle. Not being in his company, when he heard of Kile's heroic exploits he wrote his last name as he thought it was spelled, Kyle. Carr, nearly two weeks later, when he wrote his report, and probably having Volkmar's Itinerary report in front of him, repeated the misspelling, as did Price when he wrote his account about a dozen years later. All of the Medal of Honor books continue misspelling Kile's actual name.

39 Record Group 393, Part 1, Entry 3731, Department of the Platte, Letters Received, 1869.

Three days later, on November 23, he re-enlisted under the alias John Kelley into the 7th Cavalry. On June 20, 1867, he deserted from the 7th Cavalry, while Custer was camped near Fort McPherson and in the midst of his first independent Indian campaign.[40] On July 24, he re-enlisted as John Kile into the 37th Infantry, hoping to avoid detection from his earlier desertions from the cavalry. On May 1, 1868, he was court-martialed in New Mexico and given a dishonorable discharge, as well as a three-year prison sentence. In a drunken escapade on Christmas Day, 1867, he had broken into the sutler's store at a new post—Fort Lowell—his company was helping to construct. After being sentenced, he was never escorted to prison, escaping before he could be delivered to Jefferson City, Missouri. He then turned himself in—in Tennessee—on August 19, 1868, to face a court-martial for his 5th Cavalry desertion of 1866. That episode, as with all the others, involved incidents with alcohol. He was sentenced to 12 months of hard labor, but had four months taken off for voluntarily surrendering himself, and, upon conclusion of that sentence in May 1869, he was promoted to corporal and received the Medal of Honor in late August, for his heroic action on July 8. On May 17, 1870, he finished his 5th Cavalry enlistment as a first sergeant, a soldier described as having good character. On June 1, he re-enlisted—using the misspelled name cited in his recommendation for the Medal of Honor, as John Kyle—into the 1st Infantry in Buffalo, New York. He deserted the next day, and then re-enlisted one last time, back in the 7th Cavalry, on June 9—as John Kile—reporting for duty at Fort Hays, on June 26. He was immediately recognized as the 1867 deserter John Kelley, but upon showing his Medal of Honor papers to General Custer, as well as his record serving in the 5th Cavalry, and discharge papers showing his rank as a first sergeant, Custer absolved him from any charges from his earlier desertion.[41] Things appeared to look good for Kile. But that changed shortly when, on July 17, he went into Hays City to celebrate, got drunk, and was mortally wounded in a wild brawl with Wild Bill Hickok. He died the next morning in the post hospital.[42]

---

40 See Broome, *Custer into the West*, 50–57.

41 Sandy Barnard, edited, *Ten Years With Custer: A 7th Cavalryman's Memoirs* (Terre Haute, IN: AST Press, 2001), 121–122.

42 For further details of his interesting story see Jeff Broome, "Wild Bill Hickok's 1870 Hays City Brawl With Custer's Troopers," *Journal Wild West History Association*, Volume IV, Number 6, December 2011, 19–32; "An Accident in History: The Incredible Story of the Soldier Killed by Wild Bill Hickok in the Hays City Brawl," *The Journal of America's Military Past*, Volume XXXVII, Winter (*continued*)

Once Kile returned back to Carr's camp on July 8—and Mad Bear had his heroic action later that day—Carr continued his pursuit of Tall Bull, following Royall's route northwest, back into Colorado Territory. On July 9, Carr marched his men 32 miles northwest, leaving the Republican River and traveling through several difficult sand hills before camping. Lieutenant Volkmar reported in his itinerary journal that the hot winds rendered the day's march "very trying. Large quantities of slaughtered buffalo were found during the day. *And the Indian trail became very heavy.*"[43] The Dog Soldiers, thinking Carr had retreated, had become careless. Worse still, they did not assign any warriors to scout and verify that the cavalry had indeed withdrawn from pursuit. Captain Luther North later explained Tall Bull's behavior. When an Indian "knows that an enemy is after him it is impossible to take him unawares but let him think himself safe and he is the most careless being on earth...."[44] One more day's march, and the soldiers would be within striking distance of Tall Bull's village.

On July 10, Carr's command marched northwest 32 miles, and camped on a fork of Frenchman Creek, probably about five miles south and halfway between present-day Holyoke and Haxtun, Colorado. The stage was now set for Carr's attack on Tall Bull's hidden village at Summit Springs, 36 miles distant. At 5:30 on the morning of July 11, Carr's command proceeded northwest, following the clearly defined and very fresh Indian trail. Soon the command reached a high ridge, from where the South Platte could be observed to the north. It also exposed the soldiers for a considerable distance to any observant Indian eyes. Because of that, the men dismounted and hurried their horses over the ridge as quickly as possible, and reformed the command in steep ravines, where the Indian trail was faint, as they had been able to spread out for a considerable distance in the ravines. The

---

2012, Whole Number 18, 28–44; "The Soldier Who Almost Killed Wild Bill Hickok: John Kyle, John Kelley or John Kile?," The Denver Westerners *Roundup*, March—April 2012, Vol. LXVIII, no. 2, 3–30; "Wild Bill Hickok's Hays City Brawl With Soldiers of Custer's 7th Cavalry," *The Brand Book of the English Westerners' Society*, Volume 45, No. 1, Winter 2011, 2–32; "Tom Custer & Hickok's 1870 Brawl with Company M, Seventh Cavalry," *Research Review The Journal of the Little Big Horn Associates*, Vol. 26, 2012 Annual, 2–12; "Wild Bill's Brawl With Two of Custer's Troopers," *Wild West*, December, 2012, 50–57. The article in *Journal Wild West History Association* won the 2012 Wild West History Association Six-Shooter Award for "Best Article on Wild West History."

43 Lieutenant William J. Volkmar, "Journal Entry for July 9," emphasis added. "Journal of the March of the Republican River Expedition," Department of the Platte, Letters Received, 1869, Record Group 393.

44 Donald F. Danker, ed., *Man of the Plains: Recollections of Luther North, 1856–1882* (Lincoln, NE: University of Nebraska Press, 1961), 302.

soldiers were now basically paralleling westward with the Platte, several miles south of present-day Crook, Proctor and Iliff. The Pawnee reported that when they were on the ridge they could see what was believed to be a large herd of horses, signaling to Carr that the village was nearby. In addition, a very heavy Indian trail was discovered going southwest. That trail would take Carr and his men right into Summit Springs.[45]

When this heavy trail was found going opposite where the Pawnee reported seeing a large number of horses, Carr divided his command, sending half with Royall to follow the Pawnee lead, while Carr took one company of Pawnee and the rest of the soldiers—Buffalo Bill Cody included—and followed the heavy trail southwest. When the command marched from their camp early that morning, they left a company of soldiers to guard the wagon train, while it slowly followed the command in pursuit of the Cheyenne village. It wasn't long before the Pawnee with Carr said the village would be found following Carr's route. With that, Carr ordered his command to gallop, which they did until about 1:30, at which time Royall's command rejoined Carr. Royall's "horses" turned out to be bushes near the Platte. Within 10 minutes after Royall reconnected with Carr, the village location was now confirmed. Because the ground was very hilly, Carr was able to get within three miles northeast of the village without being discovered.

Carr divided the command into four columns, and the men prepared for battle. The columns moved a mile closer and arranged themselves behind "the crest of a hill." An additional column of soldiers was held in reserve. Volkmar wrote in his journal what transpired at 1:50:

> All being ready the trumpets rang out the "charge" and with hurrahs the columns and reserve dashed over the hill, down the slope towards the village, the columns forming lines as they ran. The surprise was complete—the Indians having made a desperate attempt to run off their stock, offering the most resistance on the left, but half the reserve being thrown in there, the fight was quickly over and ended with a running pursuit of six or eight miles when it had to be abandoned on account of the exhausted condition of the horses.[46]

---

45 Volkmar, "Journal Entry for July 11."

46 Volkmar, "Journal Entry for July 11." When reading Lt. Volkmar's journal, it is clear that Carr used Volkmar's itinerary to reconstruct his report on the fight, distances marched, etc. However, Carr made a mistake and said the charge was made from the northwest, when in fact it is clear from the lieutenant's journal that the cavalry never ventured north and west of the village. They charged from the northeast, as Volkmar accurately reported.

When the charge was sounded to attack, there was a very strong breeze which, fortunate for the cavalry and unfortunate for Tall Bull's warriors, was blowing from the south, thus carrying the sounds of the charge away from the village, allowing the surprise to be even more complete.[47] Luther North later told the story of a young warrior, probably about 15 years old, who had been herding the village's giant horse herd to the south of their camp. As the cavalry raced two miles into the village, the young warrior was able to see them from where he was overseeing the pony herd. There wasn't time for him to run into the village to sound the warning, but he might get the attention of the villagers if he ran the herd into their camp. The race to the village was on between the young Indian boy and the cavalry. He did not win the race, and died in his effort. North later observed, "No braver man ever lived than that fifteen year old boy."[48]

The cavalry was lucky, in more ways than one, in making their attack at Summit Springs. The day before they found the village—according to the later reminiscences of Bent—nearly half of Tall Bull's warriors—the Lakota contingent—had forded the South Platte River to the north. That reduced the tepees remaining down to 84. From the earlier estimates in examining abandoned village sites, this would confirm what the Pawnee had estimated the size of the village to be. This also meant Carr's command included roughly the same number of soldiers as were warriors left in Tall Bull's reduced village. At the time of the Summit Springs fight, the warriors who had left Summit Springs were many miles away, having safely escaped from Carr. George Bent claimed that the warriors knew the cavalry was trailing them. Tall Bull wanted to wait another day before crossing the river, recently swollen due to rains. It was a fatal mistake, and according to the Indian view, the Cheyenne blamed Tall Bull for their defeat.[49]

When the cavalry attacked the village, most of the warriors as well as the women and children were able to escape to the southeast. There were as many as 500 Indians in the village, and anywhere from 52 to 76 were reported killed. But a band of warriors remained at the southeast end of the village, where there were deep ravines, and there they made a stand, though a few sought to hide. In a few short minutes they were all dead,

---

47 *New York Times*, July 26, 1869.
48 Danker, *Man of the Plains*, 115.
49 Hyde, *Life of George Bent*, 331–332.

including Tall Bull. Luther North later stated his brother Frank had killed Tall Bull with a shot to the head, as the warrior carefully stuck his head up at the top of one of the ravines. But this account contradicts all other accounts of Tall Bull's death, including the Cheyenne. The likely killer of Tall Bull was a young sergeant, "Dannie" McGrath. Buffalo Bill Cody and Lieutenant George Mason are also possible candidates, as well as an unidentified Pawnee.[50]

It was in front of the ravines where the most serious fighting took place. Bent told the story of one warrior killed there, connecting his death to a custom involving bravery with Dog Soldiers in combat:

> A young Dog Soldier, named Wolf with Plenty of Hair, was very brave and staked himself out with a dog rope at [the] head of the ravine. It was the custom for the Dog Soldier wearing a dog rope to pin himself down in running fights or when a party was taken by surprise as in this case. The fighting was so hot around the ravine that no one had time to pull the picket pin for Wolf with Plenty of Hair, and after the fight was over he was found where he had staked himself out.[51]

The Indians fleeing the village were chased for several miles by many troopers and Pawnee. Indeed, only one cavalry horse was killed in the fight, apparently McGrath's horse. But 11 horses were ridden to death chasing the fleeing Indians. It was a grueling march to arrive at Summit Springs; and the horses were ridden hard for two miles in charging the village. The village was the end of a fast march of more than 35 miles from the morning camp. The horses were simply unable to maintain pursuit of the fleeing Indians and were ridden to death, which explains why so many Indians were able to escape.[52] Still, according to the Indian view of the fight, it was the Pawnee during this chase that succeeded in killing many of the Cheyenne, most of them women and children. In fact, Cheyenne oral history indicates the Pawnee did most of the killing at Summit Springs.[53]

Where in the unsuspecting village were the two women captives that had been captured near Spillman Creek back in May? One can only imagine Susanna Alderdice's and Maria Weichell's fright and hope, when the first shots of the fight signaled an attack. All knew Indians kill their captives

50 Broome, *Dog Soldier Justice*, 167–172.
51 Hyde, *Life of George Bent*, 334.
52 Broome, *Dog Soldier Justice*, 166.
53 Hyde, *Life of George Bent*, 333–334.

rather than let them be rescued. And, sadly, that is what happened to Susanna, now about seven months into her final pregnancy. Luther North said he found Susanna near the stream—White Butte Creek—flowing from the springs. He reported she had been killed by a tomahawk.[54] Carr said that Susanna "was shot over the eye and had her skull broken in.... She was of middle age and looked badly, and evidently had been hardly [*sic*, badly] used and treated as a slave."[55] Sun Dance Woman, one of Tall Bull's wives who was captured at Summit Springs, later admitted it was Tall Bull who killed Susanna, but not with a tomahawk. Rather he brained her with his rifle, used as a club. She said she "knew that Susanna was dead or would die, from the sound of the rifle blow when it hit her head. It cracked like a split from a ripe pumpkin."[56]

Susanna had apparently made it outside Tall Bull's Tepee when the vengeful warrior killed her. Maria Weichell, on the other hand, was found inside the chief's tepee, gravely wounded by a pistol shot to her back, as she too tried to flee at the start of the battle. In a 1917 interview, Luther North claimed:

> When we charged into the village, Cushing [North's brother-in-law and one of the officers commanding a Pawnee Company] stopped in a teepee to get a drink of water out of a keg and the wounded white woman ran up and grabbed hold of him almost frightening him to death. She afterwards said Tall Bull in person had shot her.[57]

North's memoirs added additional details. Captain Sylvanus E. Cushing had taken a drink of water from the keg and then handed it over to his cousin, Frank North:

> About this time a woman came crawling out of the lodge, and running to Capt. Cushing fell on her knees and threw her hands about his legs. We now saw she was a white woman. She was bleeding from a bullet wound through her breast. She was a Swede [German] and could not talk English, and had been taken prisoner several months before [six weeks to the day], when this band of Cheyennes had raided a Swedish settlement in Kansas. Tall Bull had taken her for his wife,

---

54 Danker, *Man of the Plains*, 115–116.
55 Carr, "Reminiscences of Indian Wars," 25.
56 C. Jefferson Cox, "Summit Springs," *Denver Westerners Roundup*, Vol. 26, #3, March 1970, 21.
57 Bruce Liddic and Paul Harbaugh, ed., *Camp on Custer: Transcribing the Custer Myth* (Spokane, WA: The Arthur H. Clark Company, 1995), 174.

and when we charged his camp he tried to kill her, but only made a flesh wound through her breast.[58]

General Carr later wrote that Maria was shot "with a pistol bullet in the back—it broke a rib, but passed around and lodged under the left breast, and was removed by my surgeon."[59] Louis Tesson, the surgeon accompanying Carr's expedition, had an Army tent set up on the battlefield, and removed the bullet from Maria's back. Maria was carried in an ambulance wagon back to Fort Sedgwick, where she remained in the post hospital until August 4.[60]

Seven years after Maria was rescued at Summit Springs, the first report was published suggesting what became of her. Washington Smith was living near the Saline River in Lincoln County when the May 30 raid happened. He said in a local paper: "She afterwards came into the settlements. The soldier who first reached her in the rescue was one whose time had about expired, and Mrs. Weichell afterwards became his wife."[61] General Carr corresponded with Smith, and from him he learned the story; and from there historians have referred to Carr's claim that Maria Weichell later married a hospital steward at Fort Sedgwick.

There are two things important in Smith's claim. First, Maria had returned to the settlements after her rescue and before 1876, and she had come accompanied by her new husband, from whom Smith learned her story. Maria had come back because she wanted to retrieve her property that was in the Lauretson home, when she was captured on Spillman Creek. Indeed, she did recover much of her possessions, including several dresses that had been taken from the Lauretson home after it was abandoned following the May 30 raid. The *Kansas Daily Commonwealth* reported on June 20, 1869, that Maria's goods "have since been stolen by some devils with no less moral principal than the savages themselves." George Green, one of the Beecher's Island survivors, later said that he had taken possession of two boxes of goods belonging to Maria and "returned and delivered them to her." Green had traced the missing property to two men, one named Johnson, who refused to give them up. He had to get an arrest warrant in

---

58   Danker, *Man of the Plains*, 115–116.

59   Carr, "Letter to Washington Smith," Washington Smith Indian Depredation claim #3951. Record Group 75.

60   "Letter to Clarence Reckmeyer from the Adjutant General's Office, August 2, 1929," Manuscript Collection #504, Box 1, Folder 1929. Kansas State Historical Society, Topeka, Kansas.

61   *Saline Valley Register*, July 4, 1876.

MARIA WEICHELL'S RESCUE AT SUMMIT SPRINGS.
Captain Luther North, commanding a company of Pawnee at the
battle, wrote that Maria, once she realized the military was in the
village, clung to the leg of the officer who entered the tepee where
she had been shot in the back, by Tall Bull. Tall Bull was shortly after
killed in the ravines, just southeast of the village. Painting by James
Davis Nelson, Jewell, Kansas. *Courtesy Jeanette Lyon, great-great-
granddaughter of Maria Weichell, Tucson, Arizona.*

order to recover them. The thieves said they were saving the goods until they could be returned to their rightful owners. With the law behind him, Green recovered the property and returned it to Maria.[62]

Both Green and Smith acknowledged Maria had returned to Lincoln County to retrieve her possessions. And, according to Smith, she was married. Indeed, she had married a man named John Mantz, but records have not yet been found to verify that he was in the military. The 5th Cavalry muster rolls for 1869 do not have him listed as a soldier. It is possible he had enlisted under an alias, or he was a teamster with Carr in 1869, but apparently he was not an enlisted man in the 5th Cavalry, using the name Mantz. By 1880, Maria was living near San Francisco, and in 1890, she was dead, having died at the age of 45 on September 20. Her obituary in the September 23, *San Francisco Morning Call,* said she was a native of Bavaria and that she was "45 years, two months and 2 days" when she died. This would place her birth on July 18, 1845. Maria was one week short of her 24th birthday when rescued at Summit Springs. Her only child, Minnie Grace Weichell, was born in Omaha on December 18, 1869, confirming Carr's earlier report that Maria was already pregnant when captured.[63]

When the battle at Summit Springs ended and the soldiers and Pawnee returned to the village after chasing the fleeing Indians, ominous clouds formed over the eastern Colorado skies. Soon—four o'clock according to Lieutenant Volkmar's itinerary journal—a violent thunderstorm erupted across the plains. Wind, lightning and large hail burst forth from the clouds and pelted the ground. The hail was so big and dangerous the soldiers had to run for shelter inside the captured tepees. Lightning struck a horse, while a cavalryman was still mounted on the mare. The horse was killed, but the soldier was only dazed. In fact, there was only one soldier injury in the entire events of the day, and his wound was nothing more than a slight cut on his ear, from a glancing arrow that missed its intended target. Clearly, in all of the Plains Indian wars, of which Summit Springs was a part, there was no fight in which the margin of victory and the drama of defeat were greater for the U.S. military. It was a remarkable fight with a resounding consequence in ending civilian violence to this part of the western plains.

---

62   Lena Baertsche Indian Depredation Claim #3530, Record Group 123. See also Broome, *Dog Soldier Justice*, 279.

63   Broome, *Dog Soldier Justice*, XVI–XVII.

And yet, Summit Springs—called by the officers at the time Susanna Springs—is today mostly unknown to students of the Indian wars. It does not deserve the neglect modern history has given it. It effectively ended the Cheyenne war.

After the storm moved off to the east, the soldiers settled down for their evening meal. At dusk, one cavalryman noticed some kind of movement on the top of the bluffs where Tall Bull and most of the warriors had been killed earlier in the day. The moving object was small and at first thought to be a coyote, but soon it was recognized to be a three- or four-year-old Indian child. Somehow the little boy had been able to hide and survive the carnage in the ravines. Had a Pawnee seen him during the fight, he would have been killed. Now, cold and hungry, the little boy sought sanctuary back in the captured village. He was placed among the 17 other female and child Indian captives.[64] By nine o'clock that night the supply and ambulance wagons arrived at the battlefield, having taken that long to get to Summit Springs from the morning camp on Frenchman Creek. It was nearly a 36-mile drive.

Carr had ordered a board of officers to take inventory of the captured village. The findings were enormous:

>56 rifles
>22 revolvers
>40 sets bows and arrows
>20 tomahawks
>47 axes
>150 knives
>50 pounds powder
>20 pounds bullets
>14 bullet moulds
>8 bars lead
>25 boxes percussion caps
>17 sabres
>17 war shields
>9 lances
>13 war bonnets
>690 buffalo robes
>552 panniers [baskets carried on horses]
>152 moccasins
>319 raw hides

---

64   Roenigk, *Pioneer History*, 275–276. Broome, *Dog Soldier Justice*, 168.

PORTRAIT OF MARIA WEICHELL.
After her rescue, Maria had one daughter,
Minnie Grace Weichell, born December 18,
1869. By 1880 she was married to John Mantz
and living in San Francisco, California.
She died September 20, 1890. *Courtesy
Jeanette Lyon, Tucson, Arizona.*

361 saddles
31 mess pans
52 water kegs
67 brass & iron camp kettles
200 raw hide lariats
16 bottles strychnine
84 lodges, complete
125 travois
9,300 pounds meat, dried
160 tin cups
180 tin plates
200 dressing knives
8 shovels
75 lodge skins (new)
40 saddle bags
75 bridles
28 woman dresses
50 hammers
9 coats
100 pounds tobacco
200 coffee pots (tin)
1,500 dollars (in gold & national bank notes)
horses & mules killed 25

MINNIE GRACE WEICHELL,
MARIA'S ONLY CHILD.
She survived in her mother's wound during
Maria's captivity ordeal. After Maria died
in 1890, her daughter—married to Ben
Wurthmann—contacted the government
in 1904, asking for a copy of an interview
Maria gave to military authorities, when
she was in the hospital in Omaha, giving
birth to Minnie Grace. It is not known if
the report was given to Minnie Grace. It has
not been found in the National Archives.
Mrs. Wurthmann died in 1945, almost 100
years to the day when her mother was born.
Courtesy Jeanette Lyon, Tucson, Arizona.

The board continued with this report:

Besides the above mentioned articles the Board is of the opinion that there was at
least ten (10) tons of various Indian property, such as clothing, flour, coffee, corn
meal, saddle equipments, fancy articles, etc., destroyed by the command before
leaving the camp, by burning [July 12].

There was also found in the different lodges, articles which had undoubtedly
been stolen from white settlements: albums, containing photographs, daguerreo-
types, watches, clocks, crockery ware, silver forks and spoons etc.

In making examination preparatory to burning the camp, quite a number of
white scalps were found attached to wearing apparel, lances and children's toys,
some of which appeared to be very fresh.[65]

This wasn't all that was found. Hundreds of horses and mules were also
captured. There was the additional gruesome discovery of a necklace made
from human fingers. Recall that George Weichell had his finger cut off and
his wedding ring taken, when Maria was captured. That ring was found, as
well as a sizable amount of money, and given to Maria.[66] Meanwhile, Louis
Tesson erected his hospital tent on the battlefield, and after treating Maria,

65   Royall, Major W. B., "Camp, Republican River Expedition, July 11, 1869," Part 1, E3731, Department
      of the Platte, Letters Received, 1869, Record Group 393.
66   Broome, *Dog Soldier Justice*, 181–182.

he then prepared Susanna's body for burial. She was buried in a deep grave on the cold prairie the next morning, at eight o'clock. Louis Tesson read an Episcopal prayer for the dead, while the soldiers gathered around in solemn silence. One man remembered the funeral: ". . . the cavalry sounded the funeral dirge, and as the soft, mournful notes died away many a cheek was wet that had long been stranger to tears." A headboard was placed at the grave, "with an inscription stating that we knew of her."[67]

There was one more duty to be performed before the command could march back east. The village had to be destroyed. This was an enormous village, with its large contents abandoned when the Indians fled under attack. Carr was able to load six of his wagons with captured plunder, most of which was personal property belonging to victims of the Dog Soldier raids into Kansas, Colorado and Nebraska. Everything else was burned. What was set afire was so large it was necessary that 160 individual fires were built, to ensure destruction of everything abandoned in the village. In addition to all the goods and plunder, there were several Indian dogs lingering about the now destroyed village. As Carr later recalled, when the command marched away from Summit Springs and back to the old wagon road on the South Platte River, dozens of dogs "gathered on a hill and set up a Wagnerian accompaniment in a gamut of discontent howls. . . ."[68]

That "Wagnerian accompaniment in a gamut of discontent[ed] howls" was more than a lament to the destruction of the Indian village. It was also a symbolic representation of the demise of the Cheyenne Dog Soldier society, a final cry officially marking the end of the annual deadly Indian raids across Kansas, Nebraska and Colorado Territory that began in 1864, and finally ended at Summit Springs in 1869. Peter John Powell, the Cheyenne apologist who felt the violent murders Tall Bull's warriors committed in

---

67   Cyrus Townsend Brady, *Indian Fights and Fighters* (New York, NY: McClure, Phillips & CO., 1904),178; General Eugene A. Carr, "Republican River Expedition, Letter to General G. D. Ruggles, July 20,1869," Department of the Plate, Letters Received, Part 1, Entry 3731, Record Group 393; Volkmar, "Journal Entry for July 12"; Hercules Price, "Letter to Ferdinand Erhardt, December 6, 1907, January 19, 1908, August 10, 1910." Price Letters, Kansas State Historical Society, Topeka, KS. In 2012, History Colorado, formerly the Colorado Historical Society, awarded a grant to Arapahoe Community College in Littleton, to use modern technology, including ground penetrating radar, to try and locate Susanna's unmarked grave at the Summit Springs battlefield. Doug Scott is the archaeologist working with the college in this archaeological project. If found she will be exhumed and returned to Lincoln County, Kansas, where she will be buried next to the grave of her one son—Willis Daily—who survived the family massacre and lived until 1920.

68   Carr, "Reminiscences," 29.

Kansas were excusable retribution for what the U.S. Military had earlier done to the Cheyenne, acknowledged that with "that defeat, the power of the Dog Men all but disappeared, blown away like wind blows the buffalo grass."[69] Truer words could not be spoken.

Carr's march from Summit Springs back east to Fort Sedgwick, on the now abandoned wagon road on the south side of the Platte River, was no doubt a silent march of 61 miles, marked everywhere with the silent memories of those who endured—so many of whom died—the five-year Cheyenne war on the roads to Denver.

---

69   Powell, *People of the Sacred Mountain*, 735.

APPENDIX

Locating Stage Stations on the Denver Road

THE STUDY OF HISTORY HAS MANY ASPECTS THAT DRAW various people into its snare. For many, that draw includes spending much time traversing the actual grounds where history was made. The focus of this book covers hundreds of miles inside three states, making it nearly impossible to intimately explore the entire region in which this five-year Indian war occurred. One is left, then, to focus on where numerous people would congregate during their journey into the west. Those places include the old forts, many of which are preserved or restored as national historic sites. Of course, many other sites have not been preserved, and are now under cultivation with minimal local acknowledgment of the great historic significance associated with that site. Forts Zarah, Sedgwick, Wallace, Reynolds, and others have been swept away by the progress of civilization. A few have memories preserved in local historical societies near where the forts once stood. Fort Wallace is probably the best example of a local community working hard to preserve its history. Cities have buried other fort locations such as Fort Harker, where the city of Kanopolis now stands, with a building or two from the old fort still standing. Forts Laramie and Larned are two outstanding national historic sites, with Fort Larned the best preserved of all original forts in the region this book covers. These are wonderful places to visit, and being on site stirs a deep curiosity of what it must have been like to have been there when the site was active.

While the settlers, freighters and passengers on the stage lines would frequent these bastions of protection, it was the old stage stops themselves that everyone encountered in their journey west. And it was the stage stops that disappeared from the collective memory once they closed and the people who experienced them aged and died. For one studying this history today, most of these sites have been lost and one is left with only wonderment with where they actually stood. Efforts were made early in the 20th century to mark several of these sites along the Santa Fe trail, the Smoky Hill trail, and even the Pony Express.[1] Unfortunately no such effort has been made to locate sites along the South Platte trail, with one exception. Glenn Scott made a series of trail maps more than twenty years ago, using modern USGS maps, and on these he superimposed old survey field notes when the land was eventually surveyed and opened for homesteading.[2]

Scott's short narrative accompanying his historical trail map of northeastern Colorado concluded with this charge: "Perhaps this historic trail map will encourage historians to use metal detectors or some other means to accurately locate the poorly placed stations and ranches and to report these. . . ."[3] It was this charge that inspired me to seek out the private land owners of the old stage stops between Julesburg and Denver, in an effort to verify some of the long lost sites. One of these sites I was particularly interested in was Riverside Station, so important to my earlier study of Custer's first Indian campaign in 1867 which culminated in *Custer into the West*. It was at Riverside Station that Custer experienced the largest number of men to desert while directly serving under his command.[4] In 2004, I met with Russ and Bob Talbot, owners of the historic land I was interested in exploring. They graciously allowed me to metal detect their untouched cattle land, where both Riverside Station and the Custer campsite were located, the

---

1   Two books helpful in locating sites on the Smoky Hill trail are Margaret Long, *The Smoky Hill Trail* (Denver, CO: The W. H. Kistler Stationary Company, 1941), and Wayne C. Lee and Howard C. Raynesford, *Trails of the Smoky Hill* (Caldwell, ID: The Caxton Printers, Ltd, 1980). For the Santa Fe trail, see Marc Simmons & Hal Jackson, *Following the Santa Fe Trail*, Third Edition/Revised and Expanded (Santa Fe, NM: Ancient City Press, 2001), and William E. Hill, *The Santa Fe Trail Yesterday and Today* (Caldwell, ID: The Caxton Printers, Ltd., 1992). For the Pony Express, see Joe Bensen, *The Traveler's Guide to the Pony Express Trail* (Helena, MT: Falcon Press Publishing, 1995), and William E. Hill, *The Pony Express Trail Yesterday and Today* (Caldwell, ID: The Caxton Press, 2010). For sites related to Custer, see Jeff Barnes, *The Great Plains Guide to Custer* (Mechanicsburg, PA: Stackpole Books, 2012). The book on sites relating to Indian encounters covering the events in this book has not been written, though there are two related books: John D. McDermott, *A Guide to the Indian Wars of the West* (Lincoln and London: University of Nebraska Press, 1998), and Paul L. Hedren, *Traveler's Guide to the Great Sioux War* (Helena, MT: Montana Historical Society press, 1996).

2   Glenn R. Scott, *Historic Trail Maps of Eastern Colorado and Northeastern New Mexico* (Boxed Set: U.S. Department of the Interior, U. S. Geological Survey, limited to 500 copies, 2004).

3   Scott, "Historic Trail Maps of the Sterling 1 × 2 Quadrangle, Northeastern Colorado, 2."

4   Broome, *Custer into the West*, 71–77.

place when 34 men of the 7th Cavalry deserted on the nights of July 5–6, 1867. The two sites were one mile apart.

Glenn Scott's historic trail map put me in the general vicinity of Riverside Station, and, using that as a guide, the stage stop was promptly located, where, using a metal detector, the numerous relics were awaiting discovery. Having located the station, it was relatively easy to find Custer's campsite, due to the itinerary journal kept by Custer's engineer officer, Lieutenant Henry Jackson. He wrote in his journal, on July 5, that the men camped "1 mile west of Riverside Station and 45 miles west of Fort Sedgwick." Even better, his drawn map showing the camp indicated the men camped on a hill.[5] To no surprise, the Talbot land indeed had a sand hill one mile west of where we had located the station. The moment I used my detector on the hill, I immediately uncovered an Army eagle button from a soldier's uniform. Shortly after that initial find, I personally collected 92 Army eagle buttons and over 70 unfired Spencer cartridges, as well as an officer's broken presentation cavalry spur, pieces of a broken Spencer carbine, and a Company M, Kepi brass pin. Friends collected nearly as many military accoutrements as I did.

Both of these sites on the Talbot land were located, and today plans are underway with the Overland Trail Museum in Sterling, to erect a marker alongside the county road where one can see the campsite from which Custer's men deserted, just south of Iliff. To be able to stand on those sites and visualize in my mind the daily comings and goings of the Concord stages, the Indian raids on the station and the nearly countless passing of freighters in their journey to and from Denver—daily in the summer and frequent in the winter—fueled my desire to write *Cheyenne War*. Finding the numerous artifacts from these times kept my mental energies flowing to complete this task.

While Riverside Station was an important stop on the Denver road, especially with its connection with Custer—he learned here that Lieutenant Kidder had missed connecting with his command, when Custer left Kansas and ventured into Colorado—it was the other, more obscure stations and ranches I was equally interested in locating. Glenn Scott's map indicated likely sites where many of these stations once stood. In 2000, I met Nell Brown Probst, author of *Forgotten People: A History of the South Platte Trail*

---

5   Broome, *Custer into the West*, 107, 132.

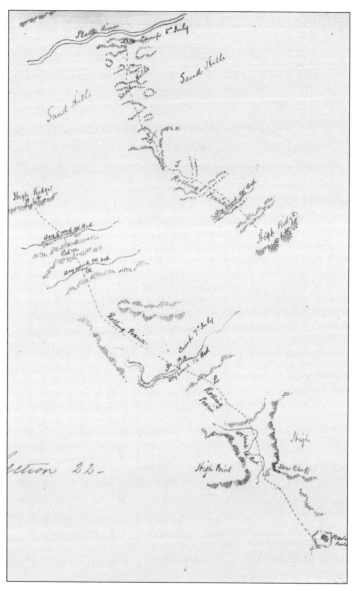

LIEUTENANT HENRY JACKSON'S MAP OF
CUSTER'S CAMP ON JULY 4–5, 1867,
ONE MILE WEST OF RIVERSIDE STATION.
Thirty-four troopers deserted from this campsite, the largest contingent of soldiers to desert while serving with Custer. *Courtesy National Archives Building, Washington, DC.*

and told her of my interest in locating some of the stage stops identified in Scott's maps. She directed me to a local rancher, who she knew shared a love of this history, William Condon. Bill at one time owned the land, which is presently under the auspices of the Division of Wildlife, covering an area on the south side of the Platte River, from several miles east of Crook, and all the way west to Proctor. Bill had managed the land since 1944. By the time I met Bill, he owned the land that the Denver road ran, from Crook west nearly to Proctor. Before he sold the land which became the DOW in the 1980s, he first erected monuments denoting Spring Hill Station and Lillian Springs. The evidences of each site were still liberally sprinkled on the ground, when Bill came onto the land in 1944. Those monuments today are on DOW land.

As a private landowner, Bill could not have a bigger interest in the history of his land. When I met him in 2000, he already knew about the two lost stage stops on his land, Riverside Ranche and Mound Station. He had Scott's maps and from Scott's work had a general idea where they might have been, but that only meant that one was within about a mile of where a station had once operated. Bill was very interested in allowing me to use a metal detector to hopefully find these sites. If the sites could be located, Bill was interested in erecting additional monuments identifying the stations. I could not begin to count or estimate the many times I spent entire days scouring the area with my metal detector, hoping to find the stations. With several friends assisting me with their metal detectors, we finally found Riverside Ranche, but Mound Station remained elusive, until a few trips with friends from the Eureka Treasure Hunters Club brought success. The Eureka Club has a long history of locating artifacts associated with historic sites. Several members make up what they call their HART team, which stands for Historic Artifact Recovery Team. It was with members of HART accompanying me on Bill's land that we had our "eureka" moment and finally located Mound Station.

In 2009, Bill, working with the Crook Historical Society, finally succeeded in erecting beautiful stone monuments depicting the location of Riverside Ranche and Mound Station. The full history of the two sites remains somewhat elusive. In what year did they begin operations? That's unclear. They are not identified as being burned in the 1865 attacks on Julesburg and the area ranches and stage stops. Lillian Springs, as well as

VIEW OF RIVERSIDE STATION.

Riverside Station was an important telegraph link on the Denver road. It was subject to several Indian raids from 1865 to 1867. Custer camped there July 4–5, 1867, with about 350 troopers of the 7th Cavalry. The land is owned by Mildred, Russ and Bob Talbot, Iliff, Colorado. *Author's collection.*

MILITARY ARTIFACTS RECOVERED AT RIVERSIDE STATION,
JUST BELOW PRESENT-DAY ILIFF, COLORADO,
10 MILES EAST OF STERLING.

(*opposite*) It was at Riverside Station that Lt. Col. Custer learned that Lt. Lyman Kidder had failed to meet up with Custer's command. In back-tracking from Riverside, Custer on July 12, 1867, discovered the remains of Kidder and his men, a few miles north of present-day Goodland, Kansas. *Author's collection.*

Spring Hill were burned in 1865. Spring Hill was rebuilt and again burned when the road was abandoned in late 1867. Lillian Springs was probably not rebuilt, for there are no records of its existence after its burning in 1865. It is likely, then, that both Mound Station and Riverside Ranche were erected and operating following the 1865 attacks, and they probably remained on location until the railroad made its way to Cheyenne, and the stage route changed, running from Cheyenne to Denver. When that occurred, there was no longer any need for the stations to exist, because freighters could

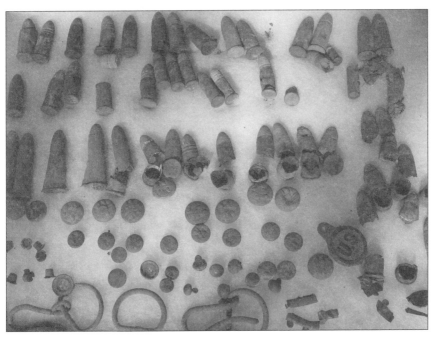

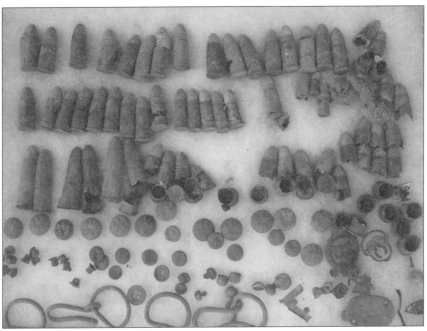

MOUND STATION ARTIFACTS.
These military artifacts were recovered at Mound Station, 25 miles east of Sterling, Colorado, on the Condon Ranch. Mound Station was one of the stage stops on the Denver road, and was subject to Indian attacks from 1865 to 1867.

load freight brought by rail to Cheyenne, for a much shorter trip down to Denver.

But in the summer of 1867, both sites were still operating, and the threat of Indian raids was very real. On August 1, 1867, Brevet Brigadier General Joseph Haydn Potter, commanding Fort Sedgwick, ordered one corporal and four privates to serve at Mound Station for protection against Indian raids. An equal number of soldiers were put out at several of the stations between Fort Sedgwick and Fort Morgan.[6] But by 1868, the stations were no longer operating, and reports indicate the abandoned stations were burned by late summer. Buildings at both sites were probably sod, and it

6   Bvt. Brig. Genl. J. H. Potter, "Report Headquarters, Fort Sedgwick, C.T. August 4, 1867," Record Group 393, Part I, Letters Received, Department of the Platte, Entry 3731, 1867.

MOUND STATION MEMORIAL MARKER,
CONDON RANCH, CROOK, COLORADO.
Jeff Broome and Bill Condon at dedication ceremony, 2008. Marker erected by the
Crook Historical Society, after the station was recently discovered by the author.
Mound Station was where 14-year-old Charles Sylvester appeared in November
1865, after escaping from a seven-year ordeal of Indian captivity (see Chapter 8).
Author's collection.

was not long before the structures melted back into the prairie. There, their
location remained lost, until now. If only long lost memories could once
more speak. . . .[7]

In an Appendix to *Dog Soldier Justice* I wrote about the possibility of
locating Susanna Alderdice's unmarked grave at Summit Springs. I gathered
all the primary source evidence available to show that she was buried in a
deep grave on a small hill in the middle of the Cheyenne village. Wrapped
in lodge skins and a buffalo robe, there was a strong probability that her
remains, if found, might be well preserved. There was also oral history,
passed down by the family who owns Summit Springs, now cared for by
Gary Ramey and his sister, Kathy, and brother-in-law, Gene Miller. In 1963,
Bill Ramey, now deceased, contracted with a local man—Bill Lively—to

7   Several artifacts from Riverside Station, Wisconsin Ranch, Mound Station, as well as Riverside Ranche,
     have been donated to the Overland Trail Museum in Sterling, and are on display for visitors to see.

MILITARY ARTIFACTS RECOVERED AT RIVERSIDE RANCHE.
Riverside Ranche—not to be confused with Riverside Station—was situated
on the Denver Road, 27 miles east of Sterling, Colorado, on the Condon Ranch.
Author's collection.

dig the land at Summit Springs and build a small reservoir. After Mr. Ramey finished his project he informed Bill that in the process of cutting the land with heavy equipment to form the reservoir, he had come across a body wrapped in a buffalo robe. When he discovered the remains, he thought they belonged to an Indian, reburied them and worked around it. He wasn't going to say where it was because he didn't want anyone later digging it up.

Mr. Lively did not know the history of the battle, and in fact, no one at that time was aware from the military reports, surfacing in some publications in later years, that Susanna had been buried in a buffalo robe. The likelihood that Bill Lively's account involved Susanna's body is high. Bill Lively's character was that of a man who would not place human remains under the soon to be filled reservoir, so there is a strong likelihood that

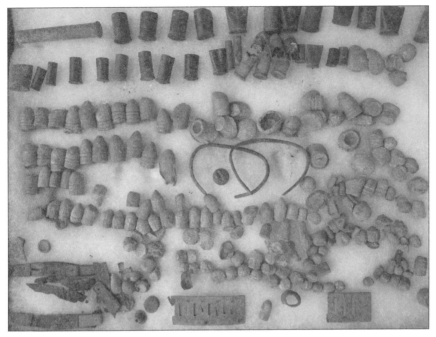

ARTIFACTS RECOVERED FROM WISCONSIN RANCH,
A FEW MILES WEST OF STERLING, COLORADO.
Wisconsin Ranch was attacked by Indians in January 1865, as well as later times.
Author's collection.

Susanna is today buried somewhere near the reservoir. In 2012 Arapahoe
Community College entered into a grant agreement with History Colorado
to use professional archaeological techniques, including ground penetrating radar as well as magnetic and resistivity geophysical surveys to try and
locate Susanna's long lost grave. In the spring of 2012, ground penetrating radar collected data and further field work, under the direction of Dr.
Douglas Scott, did not yield results. However, as is often the case with
archaeological field work, collecting, processing and testing information
is slow and tedious.

It is still the hope that this grant will yield the location of Susanna's body.
Descendants of Susanna desire to have her remains reposed at Spillman
Cemetery in Lincoln County, Kansas, to rest alongside the grave of her

MEMORIAL MARKER AT SUMMIT SPRINGS, HONORING SUSANNA ALDERDICE. The monument was unveiled on the anniversary of the Summit Springs fight, July 11, 2004. Susanna lies in an unmarked grave near the man-made reservoir at Summit Springs. Six direct descendants of Susanna attended the dedication. *Author's collection.*

WILLIS DAILY WITH HIS WIFE, MARY TWIBELL DAILY,
AND THEIR THREE CHILDREN.
From left to right: Rhoda Ann ("Anna") Daily Waters, James Alfred Daily (the same name as Willis's father, who died of typhoid fever during the Civil War, just weeks after Willis was born, in 1864), Elsie Daily Horton. Picture circa 1910. *Author's collection.*

only surviving child, who was critically wounded at her abduction in 1869. Perhaps it is fitting to quote here, the inscription on the outside of the National Archives and Record Administration building in Washington, DC: "What is Past is Prologue."

Bibliography

If a source was used in Cheyenne War, *it is noted here in bold.*

ARTICLES

Barry, Louise, "The Ranch at Walnut Creek Crossing," *The Kansas Historical Quarterly*, Volume XXXVII, Summer, 1971, Number 2, 121–147.

Bradley, Evelyn, "The Story of a Colorado Pioneer," (*The Colorado Magazine*, Vol. 2, No. 1, January 1925), 50–55.

Broome, Jeff, "On Locating the Kidder Massacre site of 1867," The Denver Westerners *Roundup*, July—August, 2000, 3–18.

———, "Libbie Custer's Encounter With Tom Alderdice . . . The Rest of the Story," *Custer and His Times, Book 5*, ed., John P. Hart (La Grange Park, IL: Little Big Horn Associates, Inc., 2002), 63–93.

———, **"Custer, Kidder and Tragedy at Beaver Creek," *Wild West*, June, 2002, 30–37.**

———, "Death at Summit Springs: Susanna Alderdice and the Cheyennes," (*Wild West*, October, 2003), 38–45.

———, "Indian Depredation Claims: One of the Many Roads to the Little Big Horn," *The Brian Pohanka 20th Annual Symposium Custer Battlefield Historical & Museum Assn., Inc. Held at Hardin, Montana on June 23, 2006*, (Hardin, MT: Custer Battlefield Historical & Museum, Inc., 2006) 73–90.

———, "Custer's Summer Indian Campaign of 1867: New Information on the U.S. Seventh Cavalry Desertions at Riverside Station," *Research Review: The Journal of the Little Big Horn Associates*, Vol. 20, No. 2, Summer, 2006, 17–30.

———, "Custer's First Fight with Plains Indians," (*Wild West*, June, 2007), 28–35.

———, "Custer's Summer Indian Campaign of 1867: New Information on Custer's First Skirmish with Hostile Indians," *Custer and His Times, Book 5*, ed., John P. Hart, (Little Big Horn Association, Inc., forthcoming, 2008).

———, "The Soldier Who Almost Killed Wild Bill Hickok: John Kyle, John Kelley, or John Kile?," The Denver Westerners *Roundup*, March–April 2012.

———, "Custer's Summer Indian Campaign of 1867," The Denver Westerners *Roundup*, July–August 2008.

————, "Wild Bill Hickok's Hays City Brawl with Soldiers of Custer's 7th Cavalry," *The Brand Book*, The English Westerners' Society, London, Volume 45, No. 1, Winter 2011.

"Wild Bill Hickok's Hays City Brawl with Custer's Troops," *Journal Wild West History Association*, Volume IV, Number 6, December 2011.

————, "An Accident in History: The Incredible Story of the Soldier Killed by Wild Bill Hickok in the Hays City Brawl," *The Journal of America's Military Past*, Volume XXXVII, Whole Number 18, No. 1, Winter 2012.

————, "Wild Bill's Brawl with Two of Custer's Troopers," (*Wild West*, December, 2012), 50–57.

————, "Tom Custer & Hickok's 1870 Brawl with Company M, Seventh Cavalry," *Research Review: The Journal of the Little Big Horn Associates*, Vol. 26, 2012 Annual, 2–12.

Carey, Raymond G., "Another View of the Sand Creek Affair," *Denver Westerners Roundup*, Vol. XVI, #2, February 1960.

Case, Frank, "Experiences on the Platte River Route in the Sixties," (*The Colorado Magazine*, Volume V, No. 4, August 1928), 146–151.

——————, "The Pawnee Scouts *and the* North Brothers," (*The Trail Guide of the Kansas City Westerners*, Vol. XI, Number 1, March 1966), 1–13.

Coad, Mark M., "Indian Fighting in 1864," (*Nebraska History*, Vol. VI, No. 4, October–December 1923), 102–108.

Cox, C. Jefferson, "Summit Springs," *Denver Westerners Roundup*, Vol. 26, #3, March 1970.

Davis, Theodore R., "A Stage Ride to Colorado," (*Harper's New Monthly Magazine*, Vol. 35, No. 206, July 1867), 137–150.

————, "A Summer on the Plains," (*Harper's New Monthly Magazine*, Vol. 36, No. 213, February 1868), 292–307.

Dixon, David, "Edmund Guerrier: A Scout With Custer," (*Research Review*, Vol. XIV, No 12, December 1980), 3–8.

————, "A Scout With Custer: Edmund Guerrier on the Hancock Expedition of 1867," (*Kansas History*, Vol. 4, No. 3, Autumn, 1981), 155–165.

Faller, Lincoln B., "Making Medicine Against 'White Man's Side of Story': George Bent's Letters to George Hyde," (*American Indian Quarterly*, Vol. 24, No. 1, Winter, 2000), 64–90.

Farley, Alan W., "An Indian Captivity and Its Legal Aftermath," (*Kansas Historical Quarterly*, Vol. XXI, No. 3, Winter, 1954), 247–256.

Garfield, Marvin H., "The Military Post as a Factor in the Frontier Defense of Kansas, 1865–1869," (*Kansas Historical Quarterly*, Vol. I, No. 1, November 1931), 50–62.

————, "Defense of the Kansas Frontier, 1864–1865," (*Kansas Historical Quarterly*, Vol. I, No. 2, February 1932), 140–152.

———, "Defense of the Kansas Frontier, 1866–1867," (*Kansas Historical Quarterly*, Vol. I, No. 4, August 1932), 326–344.

———, "Defense of the Kansas Frontier, 1868–1869," (*Kansas Historical Quarterly*, Vol. I, No. 5, November 1932), 451–473.

Gray, John S., "Will Comstock—The Nutty Bumppo of Kansas," (*The Westerners Brand Book*, Volume XVIII, February 1962, Number 12, The Chicago Corral of Westerners, Chicago, IL: 1962).

Grimes, Richard S., "The Ascent of the Cheyenne Dog Soldiers, 1838-1869" (*Journal of the Indian Wars*, Vol. 1, No. 4, 2000), 51–69.

Hall, J. N., "Colorado's Indian Troubles as I View Them," (*The Colorado Magazine*, Vol. XV, Number 4, July 1938), 121–129.

Hagen, Dennis, "Counting Coup: The Nature of Intertribal Warfare on the Great Plains Considered," The Denver Westerners *Roundup*, Vol. LX, No. 6, November–December, 2004.

Harris, T. Keith, "Charles Autobee," *Denver Westerners Roundup*, Vol. XIII, #4, April 1957.

Hodder, Mrs. Halie Riley, "Crossing the Plains in War Times," (*The Colorado Magazine*, Vol. X, Number 4, July 1933), 131–136.

Justus, Judith P., "The Saga of Clara Blinn at the Battle of the Washita," *Research Review the Journal of the Little Big Horn Associates*, Vol. 14, No. 1, Winter, 2000, 11–20.

Lambert, Julia S., "Plain Tales of the Plains," (*The Trail*, Vol. VIII, No 12, May 1916), 5–13.

Malin, James C., "Dust Storms, Part Two, 1861–1880," (*The Kansas Historical Quarterly*, Vol. XIV, No. 3, August 1946), 265–296.

Mathews, Carl, "Pioneering on the Divide," *Denver Westerners Roundup*, Vol. XII, #2, February 1957.

McDermott, John D., "No More Snowstorms, Tears of Dying," (*Wild West*, February 2006), 24–29.

Michno, Gregory F., "The Perils of Plum Creek," (*Wild West*, April, 2001), 32–38; 76–77.

Millbrook, Minnie Dubbs, "The West Breaks in General Custer," (*Kansas Historical Quarterly*, Vol. XXXVI, No. 2, Summer, 1970), 113–148.

———, "Custer's First Scout in the West," (*The Kansas Historical Quarterly*, Vol. XXXIX, No. 1, Spring, 1973), 75–95.

Monnett, John, "Reimagining Transitional Kansas Landscapes: Environment and Violence," (*Kansas History: A Journal of the Central Plains*, Volume 34, Number 4, Winter 2011–2012), 259–279.

Montgomery, Mrs. Frank C., "Fort Wallace and its Relation to the Frontier," (*Collections of the Kansas State Historical Society 1926–1928*, Vol. XVII, 1928), 189–282.

Mumey, Nolie, "John Milton Chivington The Misunderstood Man," *Denver Westerners Roundup*, Vol. XII, #11, November 1956.

Pattison, John J., "With the U S Army Along the Oregon Trail, 1863–66," (*Nebraska History*, Vol. 15, 1934), 78–93.

Powers Ramon, and Younger, Gene, "Cholera on the plains: the epidemic of 1867 in Kansas," *The Kansas Historical Quarterly*, Number 4, Winter, 1971, 351–393.

Root, George A., and Russell K. Hickman, "Pike's Peak Express Companies: Part II—Solomon and Republican Route—Concluded," *Kansas Historical Quarterly*, Volume XIII, Number 4, November 1944, 221.

—— **"Part III—The Platte Route," *Kansas Historical Quarterly*, Volume XIII, Number 87, November 1945, 485.**

Russell, Peter, "The Slain Sergeant," (*The Crow's Nest: The Journal of the Custer Association of Great Britain*, Spring/Summer 2007, Volume 7, Number 1), 5–12.

Shirk, George H., "Campaigning with Sheridan: A Farrier's Diary," (*Chronicles of Oklahoma*), Volume 27, 1959, 68–105.

Skogen, Larry C., "The Bittersweet reality of Indian Depredation cases," *Prologue, the Journal of the National Archives*, Vol. 24 (Fall 1992), 290–296.

Thomas, Gary M., "The Custer Scout of April 1867," (Kansas City, KS: Westport Printing, 1987), 1–36.

Trenholm, Virginia Cole, "Amanda Mary and the Dog Soldiers," (*Annals of Wyoming*, Volume 46, Spring, 1974, Number 1), 5–46.

Verney, Edmund Hope, "An Overland Journey From San Francisco to New York, by way of the Salt Lake City," *Royal Good Works and Sunday Magazine*, Vol. 7, June 1, 1866), 378–393.

Watson, Elmo Scott, "John W. Powell's Colorado Expedition of 1867," (*The Colorado Magazine*, Vol. XXVII, No. 4, October 1950), 302–311.

White, Lonnie, "The Hancock and Custer Expeditions of 1867," (*Journal of the West*, Vol. 5, No. 3, July 1966), 355–378.

Whiteley, Lee, "Running Creek: Elbert County's Stream of History," *Denver Westerners Roundup*, Vol. LI, #3, May/June 1995.

BOOKS

Abrams, Marc H., Compiled and Edited, *Newspaper Chronicle of the Indian Wars, Volumes, 1, 2, 3* (Brooklyn, NY: Abrams Publications, 2010).

Afton, Jean, David Fridtjof Halaas, and Andrew E. Masich, *Cheyenne Dog Soldiers: A Ledgerbook History of Coups and Combat* (Niwot and Denver, CO: Colorado Historical Society and the University Press of Colorado, 1997).

Anonymous, *The Medal of Honor of The United States Army* (Washington, DC: Government Printing Office, 1948).

Appleby, Susan Consola, *Fading Past: The Story of Douglas County, Colorado* (Palmer Lake, CO: Filter Press, LLC, 2001).

Armes, Col. George A., *Ups and Downs of an Army Officer* (Washington, DC: self-published, 1900).

Ayers, Nathaniel M., *Building A New Empire* (New York, NY: Broadway Publishing Co., 1910).

Barnard, Sandy, *Ten Years With Custer: A 7th Cavalryman's Memoirs* (Terre Haute, IN: AST Press, 2001).

Barnes, Jeff, *The Great Plains Guide to Custer: 85 Forts, Fights & Other Sites* (Mechanicsburg, PA: Stackpole Books, 2012).

Barr, Elizabeth N., *Souvenir History of Kansas* (self-published, 1908).

Barton, Bea W., *The Mormon Battalion Mississippi Saints and Pioneers Douglas County, Colorado: Honorable Remembrance to the Latest Generation* (Aardvark Global Publishing, 2008).

Becher, Ronald, *Massacre Along the Medicine Road: A Social History of the Indian War of 1864 in Nebraska Territory* (Caldwell, ID: Caxton Press, 1999).

Bell, William A., *New Tracks in North America* (Albuquerque, NM: Horn and Wallace, Publishers, 1965).

Bensen, Joe, *The Traveler's Guide to the Pony Express Trail* (Helena, MT: Falcon Press Publishing, 1995).

Bernhardt, Christian, *Indian Raids in Lincoln County, Kansas, 1864 and 1869* (Lincoln, KS: The Lincoln Sentinel Print, 1910).

Berthrong, Donald J., *The Southern Cheyennes* (Norman, OK: University of Oklahoma Press, 1963).

Bisel, Debra Goodrich and Martin, Michelle, *Kansas Forts and Bases Sentinels on the Prairie* (Charleston and London: The History Press, 2013).

Brady, Cyrus Townsend, *Indian Fights and Fighters: The Soldier and the Sioux* (New York, NY: McClure, Phillips & Co., 1904).

Broome, Jeff, *Dog Soldier Justice: The Ordeal of Susanna Alderdice in the Kansas Indian War* (Lincoln and London: University of Nebraska Press, 2009). First published in 2003, Lincoln, KS: Lincoln County Historical Society.

———, *Custer into the West, With the Journal and Maps of Lieutenant Henry Jackson,* (El Segundo, CA: Upton and Sons, Publishers, 2009).

Brotemarkle, Diane, Hawkbells and Horseshoes on the Platte Colorado's Elbridge Gerry (Platteville, CO: Platteville Historical Society, 2011).

Burkey, Blaine, *Custer, Come at Once!* (Hays, KS: Society of the Friends of Historic Fort Hays, 2nd ed., 1991).

Brown, Dee, *Bury My Heart At Wounded Knee: An Indian History of the American West* (New York, NY: Bantam Books, Inc., 1971).

Carlson, Paul H., *The Plains Indians* (College Station, TX: Texas A&M University Press, 1998).

Carroll, John, edited, *The Benteen-Goldin Letters on Custer and His Last Battle* (New York, NY: Liveright, 1974)

———, with an introduction, **The Sand Creek Massacre: A Documentary History** (New York, NY: Sol Lewis, 1973).

Chalfant, William Y., *Hancock's War: Conflict on the Southern Plains* (Norman, OK: The Arthur H. Clark Company, 2010).

Chronological List of Actions, Etc., With Indians From January 15, 1837 to January, 1891, Introduction by Floyd, Dale E. (No town listed, Old Army Press, 1979).

Clark, C. M., M.D., *A Trip to Pike's Peak and Notes by the Way, etc.* (Chicago, IL: S. P. Round's Steam Book and Job Printing House, 1861. Reprinted The Talisman Press, 1958).

Coel, Margaret, *Chief Left Hand Southern Arapahoe* (Norman, OK: University of Oklahoma Press, 1981).

Coffin, Morris H., *The Battle of Sand Creek* (Waco, TX: W.M. Morrison, Publisher, 1965).

Conklin, E. B., *A Brief History of Logan County, Colorado, With Reminiscences by Pioneers* (Denver, CO: Welch-Haffner Printing Co., 1928).

Corbett, Christopher, *Orphans Preferred The Twisted Truth and Lasting Legend of the Pony Express* (New York, NY: Broadway Books, 2003).

Cozzens, Peter, edited, *Eyewitnesses to the Indian Wars, 1865–1890* (Mechanicsburg, PA: Stackpole Books, 2003).

Crawford, Samuel J., *Kansas in the Sixties* (Chicago: A. C. McClurg & Co., 1911).

Criqui, Orvel A., *Fifty Fearless Men* (Marceline, MO: Walsworth Publishing Company, 1993).

Custer, Elizabeth B., *Boots and Saddles, or Life in Dakota with General Custer* (New York, NY: Harper and Brothers, 1885).

———, *Tenting on the Plains, or General Custer in Kansas and Texas* (New York, NY: Charles L. Webster & Company, 1887).

———, *Following the Guidon* (New York, NY: Harper & Brothers, 1890).

Custer, Gen. G. A., *My Life on the Plains, or, Personal Experiences With Indians* (New York, NY: Sheldon & Co., 1874).

Czaplewski, Russ: *Captive of the Cheyenne: The Story of Nancy Jane Morton and the Plum Creek Massacre* (Kearney, NE: The Dawson County Historical Society, 1993).

Danker, Donald F., ed., *Man of the Plains: Recollections of Luther North, 1856–1882* (Lincoln, NE: University of Nebraska Press, 1961).

Davis, E. O., *The First Five Years of the Railroad Era in Colorado* (no city listed, but Denver, CO: Sage Books, Inc., 1948).

Dawson, Charles, *Pioneer Tales of the Oregon Trail and of Jefferson County* (Topeka, KS: Crane and Company, 1912).

Di Certo, Joseph J., *The Saga of the Pony Express* (Missoula, MT: Mountain Press Publishing Company, 2002).

Dodge, Col. Richard Irving, *Our Wild Indians: Thirty-three Years' Personal Experience Among the Red Men of the Great West* (New York, NY: Archer House, Inc., 1959. Originally published in 1890).

————, *The Plains of the Great West and Their Inhabitants* (New York, NY: Archer House, Inc., 1959. Originally published in 1877).

Downey, Fairfax, *Indian Fighting Army* (Fort Collins, CO: Old Army Press, 1971).

Dudley, First Lieutenant Edgar S., compiled by, *Roster of Nebraska Volunteers From 1861–1869* (Hastings, NE: Wigton & Evans, State Printers, 1888).

Eisele, Wilbert E., *The Real 'Wild Bill' Hickok* (Denver, CO: William H. Andre, Publisher).

Ellenbecker, John G., *Tragedy at the Little Blue: The Oak Grove Massacre and the Captivity of Lucinda Eubank and Laura Roper* (Kearney, NE: Prairie Lark Publications, 1993. Revised Second Edition).

Ellis, Richard N., *General Pope and U.S. Indian Policy* (Albuquerque, NM: University of New Mexico Press, 1970).

Englert, Lorene and Kenneth, *Oliver Perry Wiggins Fantastic, Bombastic Frontiersman* (Palmer Lake, CO: Filter Press, 1968).

English, Don, *The Early History of Fort Morgan, Colorado* (Fort Morgan, CO: The Fort Morgan Heritage Foundation, 1975).

Fischer, David Hackett, *Historians' Fallacies: Toward a Logic of Historical Thought* (New York, Evanston, and London: Harper & Row, Publishers, 1970).

Forsyth, George A., *Thrilling Days of Army Life* (New York and London: Harper & Brothers, 1900).

————, *The Story of the Soldier* (New York, NY: D. Appleton and Company, 1900).

Frost, Lawrence A., *The Court-Martial of General George Armstrong Custer* (Norman, OK: University of Oklahoma Press, 1967).

————, *General Custer's Libbie* (Seattle, WA: Superior Publishing Company, 1976).

Fry, James B., *Army Sacrifices; or, Briefs From Original Pigeon-Holes* (New York, NY: D. Van Nostrand, Publisher, 1879).

Goodrich, Thomas, *Scalp Dance: Indian Warfare On The High Plains 1865–1879* (Mechanicsburg, PA: Stackpole Books, 1997).

Gray, Jim, *Desperate Seed: Ellsworth, Kansas on the Violent Frontier* (Printed in USA: Kansas Cowboy Publications, 2009).

Greene, Jerome A., *Washita: The U.S. Army and the Southern Cheyennes, 1867–1869* (Norman, OK: University of Oklahoma Press, 2004).

———— and Douglas D. Scott, *Finding Sand Creek: History, Archeology, and the 1864 Massacre Site* (Norman, OK: University of Oklahoma Press, 2004).

Grinnell, George Bird, *The Story of the Indian* (New York, NY: D. Appleton and Company, 1896).

———, *Two Great Scouts and Their Pawnee Battalion: The Experiences of Frank J. North and Luther H. North*, forward by King, James T. (Lincoln, NE: University of Nebraska Press, 1973. Originally published in 1928).

———, *The Fighting Cheyennes* (Williamstown, MA: Corner House Publishers, 1956. Originally published in 1915).

Halaas, David & Masich, Andrew, *Halfbreed: The Remarkable Story of George Bent Caught Between the Worlds of the Indian and the White Man* (New York, NY: Da Capo Press, 2004).

Hardorff, Richard G., *Washita Memories: Eyewitness Views of Custer's Attack on Black Kettle's Village* (Norman, OK: University of Oklahoma Press, 2006).

Hartke, Vance, Chairman, *Medal of Honor Recipients 1963–1973 93d Congress 1st Session, Committee Print No. 15* (Washington, DC: U. S. Government Printing Office, 1973).

Hatch, Thom, *Black Kettle: The Cheyenne Chief Who Sought Peace but Found War* (Hoboken, NJ: John Wiley & Sons, Inc., 2004).

Heitman, Francis B., *Historical Register and Dictionary of the United States Army, Vol. 1* (Washington, DC: Government Printing Office, 1903. Reprinted Urbana, IL: University of Illinois Press, 1965).

Hick, John, *Between Faith and Doubt: Dialogues on Faith and Reason* (New York, NY: Palgrave Macmillan, 2010).

Hill, William E., *The Santa Fe Trail Yesterday and Today* (Caldwell, ID: The Caxton Printers, Ltd., 1992).

———, *The Pony Express Trail Yesterday and Today* (Caldwell, ID: The Caxton Press, Ltd., 2010).

Hoebel, E. Adamson, *The Cheyennes: Indians of the Great Plains* (New York, NY: Holt, Rinehart and Winston, 1960).

Hollibaugh, Mrs. E. F., *Biographical History of Cloud County* (Logonsport, IN: Wilson, Humphrey & CO, 1903).

Holmes, Louis A., *Fort McPherson, Nebraska, Fort Cottonwood, N.T.: Guardian of the Tracks and Trails* (Lincoln, NE: Johnson Publishing Co., 1963).

Howbert, Irving, *The Indians of the Pikes Peak Region* (New York, NY: The Knickerbocker Press, 1914).

———, *Memories of a Lifetime in the Pike's Peak Region* (New York and London: G. P. Putnum's Son's, 1925).

Hungate, Carroll P., *The Hungate Family*, five volumes (Kansas City, MO: Universal Publications, 1974–1976).

Hutton, Paul Andrew, *Phil Sheridan and His Army* (Lincoln and London: University of Nebraska Press, 1985).

Hyde, George E., *Spotted Tail's Folk: A History of the Brule Sioux* (Norman, OK: University of Oklahoma Press, 1961).

———, *Life of George Bent Written From His Letters* (Norman, OK: University of Oklahoma Press, 1968).

James, William, *The Will to Believe and Other Essays in Popular Philosophy* (New York, NY: Dover Publications, Inc., 1956. Originally published in 1897).

Jauken, Arlene Feldman, *The Moccasin Speaks: Living as Captives of the Dog Soldier Warriors Red River War 1874–1875* (Lincoln, NE: Dageforde Publishing, Inc., 1998).

Johnson, Eric S., Compiled, *No Greater Calling: A Chronological Record of Sacrifice and Heroism During the Western Indians Wars, 1865–1898* (Atglen, PA: Schiffer Military History, 2012).

Jones, Douglas C., *The Treaty of Medicine Lodge* (Norman, OK: University of Oklahoma Press, 1966).

Jones, Robert Huhn, *Guarding the Overland Trails: The Eleventh Ohio Cavalry in the Civil War* (Spokane, WA: The Arthur H. Clark Company, 2005).

Kappler, Charles J., compiled and edited, *Indian Treaties 1778–1883* (Mattituck, NY: Amereon House, 1972).

Keenan, Jerry, *Encyclopedia of American Indian Wars 1492–1890* (Santa Barbara, Denver and Oxford: ABC-CLIO, Inc., 1997).

———, *The Wagon Box Fight: An Episode of Red Cloud's War* (Conshohocken, PA: Savas Publishing Company, 2000).

Kelly, Fanny, *Narrative of My Captivity Among the Sioux Indians*, edited by Clark and Mary Lee Spence (Chicago, IL: R. R. Donnelley & Sons Company), 1990.

Kelman, Ari, *A Misplaced Massacre: Struggling Over the Memory of Sand Creek* (Cambridge, MA: Harvard University Press, 2013).

Kerner, Gaiselle, compiled by, *Preliminary Inventory of the Records of the United States Court of Claims (Record Group 123)*, (Washington, DC: The National Archives, 1953).

Klokner, James B., *The Officer Corps of Custer's Seventh Cavalry 1866–1876* (Atglen, PA: Schiffer Military History, 2007).

Knight, Oliver, *Following the Indian Wars: The Story of the Newspaper Correspondents Among the Indian Campaigners* (Norman, OK: University of Oklahoma Press, 1960).

Kraft, Louis, *Ned Wynkoop and the Lonely Road from Sand Creek* (Norman, OK: University of Oklahoma Press, 2011).

Larimer, Mrs. Sarah L., *The Capture and Escape; or, Life Among the Sioux* (Philadelphia, PA: Claxton, Remsen & Haffelfinger, 1870).

Lawrence, Deborah and Jon, *Violent Encounters: Interviews on Western Massacres* (Norman, OK: University of Oklahoma Press, 2011).

Lee, Wayne C. and Raynesford, Howard C., *Trails of the Smoky Hill: From Coronado to the Cow Towns* (Caldwell, ID: The Caxton Printers, Ltd., 1980).

LeMay, Dan, *Alan LeMay: A Biography of the Author of The Searchers* (Jefferson, NC: McFarland & Company, Inc., Publishers, 2012).

Liddic, Bruce, and Harbaugh, Paul, ed., *Camp on Custer: Transcribing the Custer Myth*, ed., (Spokane, WA: The Arthur H. Clark Company, 1995).

Llewellyn, Karl N. and Hoebel, E. Adamson, *The Cheyenne Way: Conflict and Case Law in Primitive Jurisprudence* (Norman, OK: University of Oklahoma Press, 1941).

Long, Margaret, *The Smoky Hill Trail* (Denver, CO: The W. H. Kistler Stationary Company, 1941).

Mails, Thomas E., *Dog Soldiers, Bear Men and Buffalo Women: A Study of the Societies and Cults of the Plains Indians* (Englewood Cliffs, NJ: Prentice-Hall, Inc., 1973).

Marr, Josephine Lowell, *Douglas County: A Historical Journey* (Gunnison, CO: B & B Printers, 1983).

Mathews, Carl F., *Early Days Around the Divide* (St. Louis, MO: Sign Book CO., 1969).

Mattes, Merrill J., *The Great Platte River Road* (Lincoln, NE: Nebraska State Historical Society, 1969).

———, *Platte River Road Narratives* (Urbana and Chicago, IL: University of Illinois Press, 1988).

McChristian, Douglas C., *Fort Laramie: Military Bastion of the High Plains* (Norman, OK: The Arthur H. Clark Company, 2008).

McDermott, John D., *Forlorn Hope: The Battle of White Bird Canyon and the Beginning of the Nez Perce War* (Boise: Idaho State Historical Society, 1978).

———, *Frontier Crossroads: The History of Fort Caspar and the Upper Platte Crossing* (Casper, WY: City of Casper, 1997).

———, *Circle of Fire: The Indian War of 1865* (Mechanicsburg, PA: Stackpole Books, 2003).

———, *Red Cloud's War: The Bozeman Trail 1866–1868* (Norman, OK: The Arthur H. Clark Company, 2010).

McGinnis, Anthony, *Counting Coup and Cutting Horses: Intertribal Warfare on the Northern Plains 1738–1889* (Evergreen, CO: Cordillera Press, Inc., 1990).

McReynolds, Robert, *Thirty Years on the Frontier* (Colorado Springs, CO: El Paso Publishing Co., 1906).

Mead, James R., *Hunting and Trading on The Great Plains 1859–1875*, edited by Schuyler Jones (Norman, OK: Oklahoma University Press, 1986).

Meline, James F., *Two Thousand Miles on Horseback. Santa Fe and Back. A Summer Tour Through Kansas, Nebraska, Colorado, and New Mexico, in the Year 1866* (New York, NY: Hurd and Houghton, 1867).

Michno, Gregory F., *Encyclopedia of Indian Wars: Western Battles and Skirmishes, 1850–1890* (Missoula, MT: Mountain Press Publishing Company, 2003).

———, *Forgotten Fights: Little-Known Raids and Skirmishes on the Frontier, 1823–1890* (Missoula, MT: Mountain Press Publishing Company, 2008).

———, *Battle at Sand Creek: The Military Perspective* (El Segundo, CA: Upton and Sons, Publishers, 2004).

————, *Dakota Dawn: The Decisive First Week of the Sioux Uprising, August 17–24, 1862* (New York and California: Savas Beatie, 2011).

———— and Susan Michno, *A Fate Worse Than Death: Indian Captivities in the West, 1830–1885* (Caldwell, ID: Caxton Press, 2007).

———— and Susan Michno, *Circle the Wagons! Attacks of Wagon Trains in History and Hollywood Films* (Jefferson, NC, and London: McFarland & Company, Inc., Publishers, 2009).

Monahan, Doris, *Destination: Denver City the South Platte Trail* (Athens: Swallow Press/Ohio University Press, 1985).

————, *Julesburg and Fort Sedgwick Wicked City—Scandalous Fort* (Sterling, CO: Published by the author, 2009).

Monnett, John H., *The Battle of Beecher Island and the Indian War of 1867–1869* (Niwot: University Press of Colorado, 1992).

————, *Where a Hundred Soldiers Were Killed: The Struggle for the Powder River Country and the Making of the Fetterman Myth* (Albuquerque, NM: University of New Mexico Press, 2008).

Moore, John H. *The Cheyenne Nation: A Social and Demographic History* (Lincoln and London: University of Nebraska Press, 1987).

Morris, Maurice O'Connor, *Rambles in the Rocky Mountains: With a Visit to the Gold Fields of Colorado* (London, Smith, Elder and Co., 1864).

Niebaum, Glenna Belle Moore, *History of Cheyenne County Nebraska 1986* (Curtis Media Corporation, 1987), 790–792.

Norton, David Fate and Popkin, Richard H., edited, *David Hume: Philosophical Historian* (New York, NY: The Bobbs-Merrill Company, Inc., 1965).

Nye, Wilbur Sturtevant, *Plains Indian Raiders* (Norman, OK: University of Oklahoma Press, 1968).

Oliva, Leo E., *Soldiers on the Santa Fe Trail* (Norman, OK: University of Oklahoma Press, 1967).

————, *Fort Wallace, Sentinel on the Smoky Hill Trail* (Topeka, KS: Kansas State Historical Society, 1998).

Pohanka, Brian C., edited, *A Summer on the Plains with Custer's 7th Cavalry: The 1870 Diary of Annie Gibson Roberts* (Fredericksburg, VA: Schroeder Publications, 2004).

Poole, Captain D. C., *Among the Sioux of Dakota* (New York, NY: D. Van Nostrand, Pub. 1881).

Portrait and Biographical Record of the State of Colorado (Chicago: Chapman Publishing Company, 1899).

Potter, James E., *Standing Firmly by the Flag: Nebraska Territory and the Civil War* (Lincoln & London: University of Nebraska Press, 2012).

Powell, Father Peter John, *People of the Sacred Mountain: A History of the Northern Cheyenne Chiefs and Warrior Societies 1830–1879 With an Epilogue 1969–1974* (San Francisco: Harper and Row, Publishers, 1981).

————, *Sweet Medicine: The Continuing Role of the Sacred Arrows, The Sun Dance, and the Sacred Buffalo Hat in Northern Cheyenne History* (Norman, OK: University of Oklahoma Press, 1969).

Price, George F., *Across the Continent With the Fifth Cavalry* (New York, NY: Antiquarian Press LTD, 1959. Originally published in 1883).

Probst, Nell Brown, *Forgotten People: A History of the South Platte Trail* (Boulder, CO: Pruett Publishing Co., 1979).

Rath, Ida Ellen, The Rath Trail (Wichita, KS: McCormick-Armstrong CO, Inc., 1961).

Record of Engagements With Hostile Indians Within The Military Division of the Missouri From 1868 To 1882, Lieutenant-General P. H. Sheridan, Commanding (Washington: Government Printing Office, 1882; reprinted Fort Collins, CO: Old Army Press, 1972).

Ricker, Eli S., *Voices of the American West, Volume 1: The Indian Interviews* (Lincoln, NE: University of Nebraska Press, 2005).

————, *Voices of the American West, Volume 2: The Settler and Soldier Interviews* (Lincoln, NE: University of Nebraska Press, 2005).

Reilly, Hugh J. *Bound to Have Blood: Frontier Newspapers and the Plains Indian Wars* (Lincoln and London: University of Nebraska Press, 2010).

Rickey, Donald, Jr., *Forty Miles a Day on Beans and Hay: The Enlisted Soldier Fighting in the Indian Wars* (Norman, OK: University of Oklahoma Press, 1963).

Rister, Carl Coke, *Border Captives: The Traffic in Prisoners by Southern Plains Indians, 1835–1875* (Norman, OK: University of Oklahoma Press, 1940).

————, *Border Command: General Phil Sheridan in the West* (Norman, OK: University of Oklahoma Press, 1944).

Roberts, Gary Leland, *Sand Creek: Tragedy and Symbol* (Ann Arbor, MI: UMI Dissertation Services, 1984).

Roenigk, Adolph, *Pioneer History of Kansas* (Self-published, 1933).

Root, Frank A., and William E. Connelley, *The Overland Stage to California* (Topeka, KS: Self-published, 1901).

Rosa, Joe, *They Called Him Wild Bill: The Life and Adventures of James Butler Hickok* (Norman, OK: University of Oklahoma Press, 1964).

————, **Wild Bill Hickok: The Man and the Myth (Lawrence, KS: University Press of Kansas, 1996).**

Russell, Don, *The Lives and Legends of Buffalo Bill* (Norman, OK: University of Oklahoma Press, 1960).

Savage, I. O., *A History of Republic County, Kansas* (Beloit, KS: Jones & Chubbic, Art Printers, 1901).

Schultz, Duane, *Coming Through Fire: George Armstrong Custer and Chief Black Kettle* (Yardley, PA: Westholme Publishing, LLC, 2012).

Scott, Glenn R., *Historic Trail Maps of Eastern Colorado and Northwestern New Mexico* (Denver, CO: U.S. Department of the Interior, U.S. Geological Survey, 2004).

Shaw, Luella, *True History of Some of the Pioneers of Colorado* (Denver, CO: Press of Carson-Harper Co., 1909).

Sheridan, P. H., *Personal Memoirs of P. H. Sheridan, Volume II* (New York, NY: Charles L. Webster & Company, 1888).

Simmons, Marc & Jackson Hal, *Following the Santa Fe Trail*, Third Edition/Revised and Expanded (Santa Fe, NM: Ancient City Press, 2001).

Skogen, Larry, *Indian Depredation Claims, 1796–1920* (Norman and London: University of Oklahoma Press, 1996).

Smith, Shannon D., *Give Me Eighty Men: Women and the Myth of the Fetterman Fight* (Lincoln and London: University of Nebraska Press, 2008).

Snelson, Bob, *Solomon Avengers: The Battle of Beecher Island September 17–25, 1868* (self-published, 2006).

Spring, Agnes Wright, *Caspar Collins: The Life and Exploits of an Indian Fighter of the Sixties* (New York, NY: Columbia University Press, 1927).

Springer, Charles H., *Soldiering in Sioux Country: 1865*, edited by Benjamin Franklin Cooling III (San Diego, CA: Frontier Heritage press, 1971).

Spurr, Dick & Wendy, *Historic Forts of Colorado* (Grand Junction, CO: Centennial Publications, 1994).

Stafford, Mrs. Mallie, *The March of Empire Through Three Decades* (San Francisco: Geo. Spaulding & Co., 1884).

Stanley, Henry M., *My Early Travels and Adventures in North America, Vol. 1* (London, England: Sampson Low, Marston and Company, 1895).

Tate, Michael L., *The Frontier Army in the Settlement of the West* (Norman, OK: University of Oklahoma Press, 1999).

———, *Indians and Emigrants: Encounters on the Overland Trail* (Norman, OK: University of Oklahoma Press, 2006).

Tebbel, John, and Jennison, Keith, *The American Indian Wars* (New York, NY: Bonanza Books, 1959).

Thrapp, Dan L., *Encyclopedia of Frontier Biography, in Three Volumes* (Glendale, CA: The Arthur A. Clark Company, 1988).

Unrau, William E., edited, *Tending the Talking Wire: A Buck Soldier's View of Indian Country 1863–1866* (Salt Lake City: University of Utah Press, 1979).

———, *Indians, Alcohol, and the Roads to Taos and Santa Fe* (Lawrence, KS: University Press of Kansas, 2013.

Utley, Robert M., *Frontiersmen in Blue: The United States Army and the Indian, 1848–1865* (New York, NY: The Macmillan Company, 1967).

————, *Frontier Regulars: The United States Army and the Indian, 1866–1891* (New York and London: Macmillan Publishing Co., Inc. and Collier Macmillan Publishers, 1973).

————, **edited,** *Life in Custer's Cavalry: Diaries and Letters of Albert and Jennie Barnitz, 1867–1868* **(New Haven and London: Yale University Press, 1977).**

————, *The Indian Frontier of the American West 1846–1890* (Albuquerque, NM: University of New Mexico Press, 1984).

Van De Logt, Mark, *War Party in Blue: Pawnee Scouts in the U.S. Army* **(Norman, OK: University of Oklahoma Press, 2010).**

Vaughn, J. W., *The Battle of Platte Bridge* **(Norman, OK: University of Oklahoma Press, 1963).**

Vestal, Stanley, *Warpath and Council Fire: The Plains Indians' Struggle for Survival in War and Diplomacy 1851–1891* (New York, NY: Random House, 1948).

Visscher, William Lightfoot, *A Thrilling and Truthful History of The Pony Express or Blazing the Westward Way* **(Chicago, IL: The Charles T. Powner Co., 1946).**

Wagner, David E., *Powder River Odyssey: Nelson Cole's Western Campaign of 1865* (Norman, OK: The Arthur H. Clark Company, 2009).

————, *Patrick Connor's War: The 1865 Powder River Indian Expedition* **(Norman, OK: The Arthur H. Clark Company, 2010).**

Ware, Eugene F., *The Indian War of 1864* **(Topeka, KS: Crane & Company, 1911). Reprinted in 1960 (New York, NY: St. Martin's Press).**

The War of the Rebellion: A compilation of the Official Records of the Union and Confederate Armies, **70 Volumes (Washington, DC: Government Printing Office, 1896).**

Wellman, Paul I., *Death on Horseback: Seventy Years of War for the American West* (Philadelphia & New York: J. B. Lippincott Co., 1947).

West, Elliot, *The Contested Plains: Indians, Goldseekers, and the Rush to Colorado* (Lawrence, KS: University Press of Kansas, 1998).

Williams, Dallas, *Fort Sedgwick Colorado Territory: Hell Hole on the Platte* **(Julesburg, CO: Fort Sedgwick Historical Society, 1996).**

————, **ed.,** *Fort Sedgwick Colorado Territory: Hell Hole on the Platte* **(Julesburg, CO: Fort Sedgwick Historical Society, 1996).**

Williams, Scott C., compiled, *Colorado History Through the News (a Context of the Times.) The Indian Wars of 1864 Through the Sand Creek Massacre* **(Aurora, CO: Pick of Ware Publishing, 1997).**

Wilson, D. Ray, *Fort Kearny on the Platte* (Dundee, IL: Crossroads Communications, 1980).

Winsor, M., and Scarbrough, James, *History of Jewell County, Kansas, with a full account of its early Settlements and the Indian Atrocities Committed Within its Borders* **(Jewell City, KS, 1878).**

Winks, Robin W., Editor, *The Historian as Detective: Essays on Evidence* (New York, NY: Harper & Row, Publishers, 1968).

Wiser, David A., and Wright, Gary T., *Shamrock Ranch* (Boulder, CO: Johnson Books, 2009).

Wynkoop, Edward W., *The Tall Chief: The Unfinished Autobiography of Edward W. Wynkoop, 1856–1866*, ed., Gerboth, Christopher B., (Denver, CO: The Colorado Historical Society, Monograph 9, 1993).

Young, Charles E., *Dangers of the Trail in 1865: A Narrative of Actual Events* (Geneva, NY: Press of W. F. Humphrey, 1912).

Young, Frank C., *Across the Plains in '65* (Denver, CO: privately printed, 1905).

RESEARCH INSTITUTIONS, MUSEUMS, AND LIBRARIES

Buffalo Bill Museum and Grave, Golden, Colorado

Colorado Springs Pioneer Museum, Colorado Springs, Colorado

Colorado State Historical Society, Denver, Colorado

Crook Historical Museum, Crook, Colorado

Denver Public Library, Western History Department, Denver, Colorado

Ellis County Historical Society, Hays, Kansas

Fort Hays State Historic Site, Hays, Kansas

Fort Hays State University, Special Collections Archives, Hays, Kansas

Fort Sedgwick Historical Society, Julesburg, Colorado

Friends of Historic Fort Logan, Englewood, Colorado

Hays Public Library, Hays, Kansas

Kansas State Historical Society, Topeka, Kansas

Lincoln County Historical Society, Lincoln, Kansas

Logan County Historical Society, Sterling, Colorado

McCracken Research Library, Buffalo Bill Historical Center, Cody, Wyoming

Nebraska State Historical Society, Lincoln, Nebraska

Overland Trails Museum, Sterling, Colorado

Salina Public Library, Kansas Room, Salina, Kansas

United States Army Military History Institute, Carlisle Barracks, Pennsylvania

White Swan Research Library, Little Bighorn Battlefield National Monument, Crow Agency, Montana

Yale Collection of Western Americana, Beinecke Rare Book and Manuscript Library, New Haven, Connecticut

NATIONAL ARCHIVES AND RECORDS ADMINISTRATION

Record Group 75, Indian Depredations Claims.

Record Group 94, 7th U. S. Cavalry, Muster Rolls, 1867.

Record Group 75 and 123, Indian Depredations Claims.

Record Group 393, Department of the Missouri, Letters Received, 1867–69.

Record Group 393, Department of the Missouri, Letters Sent, 1867–69.

Record Group 393, Department of the Platte, Letters Received, 1867–69.

U.S. GOVERNMENT DOCUMENTS

Atkins, J. D. C., Commissioner, "Letter from the Secretary of the Interior," *49th Congress, 1st Session, House of Representatives, Ex. Doc. No. 125* (Washington, DC: Government Printing Office, 1886).

———, "Letter from the Acting Secretary of the Interior," *49th Congress, 2nd Session, House of Representatives, Ex. Doc. No. 77* (Washington, DC: Government Printing Office, 1887).

General Philip H. Sheridan, "Report," *Messages and Documents of the Second Session of the Forty-First Congress, Volume I* (Washington, DC: Government Printing Office, 1869).

General U. S. Grant's report to the President of the United States, "Difficulties With Indian Tribes," (Washington: Government Printing Office, 1870), House of Representatives, 41st Congress, Executive Document #240.

House Executive Documents, **41st Congress, 2nd Session, 1869–1870.**

House of Representatives, 40th Congress, Third Session, Executive Document #1.

Lieutenant General W. T. Sherman, "Report November 1, 1868." *Executive Documents of The House or Representatives, Third Session of the Fortieth Congress 1868–1869* (Washington, DC: Government Printing Office, 1869).

"Protection Across the Continent," Letter from the Secretary of War, House of Representatives, 39th Congress, Second Session, Executive Document #23.

"Report from Fort McPherson, August 21," and "Fort Sedgwick August 24, 1866," Lieutenant General Sherman, 39th Congress, 2d Session, House of Representatives, Ex. Doc No. 23 (Washington, DC: Government Printing Office, 1867).

"Report of General C. C. Augur," 40th Congress, Second Session, Executive Document #1.

"Report of J. M. Schofield, Secretary of War." (Washington, DC: Government Printing Office, 1868).

Report of Mr. Doolittle, *Condition of the Indian Tribes: Report of the Joint Special Committee* (Washington, DC: Government Printing Office, 1867).

Report of the Commissioner of Indian Affairs for the Year 1864 (Washington, DC: Government Printing Office, 1865).

Report of the Commissioner of Indian Affairs for the Year 1866 (Washington, DC: Government Printing Office, 1866).

Report of the Commissioner of Indian Affairs for the Year 1868 (Washington, DC: Government Printing Office, 1868).

"Report of the Secretary of War: Report of Lieutenant General Sherman, St. Louis, MO., October 1, 1867." Second Session of the Fortieth Congress (Washington, DC: Government Printing Office, 1867).

Report on Indian Affairs, by the Acting Commissioner, for the Year 1867 (Washington, DC: Government Printing Office, 1868).

"Report of the Indian Peace Commissioners," House of Representatives, 40th Congress, 2d Session, Executive Document No. 97 (Washington, DC: Government Printing Office, 1868).

Report of the Joint Committee on The Conduct of the War (Washington, DC: Government Printing Office, 1865).

Second Lieutenant Henry Jackson, *Itinerary of the March of the Seventh United States Cavalry*, Record Group 393, Part 1, Entry 2593, Department of the Missouri, Letters received, 1867, National Archives Building, Washington, DC.

Senate Executive Documents, 40th Congress, 2nd Session, 1867–1868.

Senate Executive Documents, 40th Congress, 3rd Session, 1869.

Sheridan's report to General Sherman, Forty-First Congress, 2d Session, Volume I, Executive Document, Pt. 2 (Washington, DC: Government Printing Office, 1869).

"Testimony as to the Claim of Ben Holladay," 46th Congress, 2d Session, Mis. Doc. No. 19 (Washington, DC: Government Printing Office, 1880).

U.S. Secretary of War, *Annual Reports*, 1867–1870.

Index

Page locators in italics indicate illustrations.

Abbington, Elizabeth, 338, 339
Abbington, Lafayette, 339
Abell, Henry Harrison, 236–38, 238n46, 239, 400, 401
Abney, James, 377
Ackerly, Ernest, 422–24
Ackley, George B., 156
Ackley Ranch. *See* Gillette's Ranche
Adams, Harriet. *See* Eubanks, Hattie
Adkins, Ezra, 448
Adkins, John, 245
Adle, John, 204, 205
adobe buildings, 34, 65, 140, 169, 213, 215, 332
African Americans: buffalo soldiers, 241n53, 257, 310, 312, 313, 319, 320; soldiers, treatment in raids, 61, 324; traders and freighters, 213, 324
alcohol: drunkenness, Indians, 95, 96, 152, 162, 227, 228, 271; drunkenness, military, 60, 111, 455; trade, 60, 79n29, 139; traps, 142n28, 149
Alderdice, Alice, 330, 435, 444, 445, 449, 452
Alderdice, Frank, 435, 436, 444, 447
Alderdice, Susanna, *434*, 435–36, 437, 440, 442–45, 447, 449–50, 449n27, 459–60; books about, 14, 346, 477; burial and grave, 467, 467n67, 477–80, *480*; family, 433, 435, *437, 443*, 443–46, 444n, 445, 447–50, 449n27, 479–80, *480*
Alderdice, Thomas, 330, 435, 436, 442, 443–44, 447–50, 452
aliases, 291, 292, 454–55, 463
Alkali Station, 125, 163, 164, 201–202, 204–205; attacks and battles around, 206, 207–209,

210, 214–15, 261, 267; employees, 206, 211, 215n100, 267
Allen, Leftrick, 400
Allen, William, 400
Alley, Napoleon, 429, 430, 431–32, 432n30
Alverson, John, 434, 435–38, 442
Alverson, Mary Zigler, 437
ambulance wagons, 389–90, 392–93, 464
American Ranche, 33, 65, *134*, 141; abandoned site, 178; Indian raids, 52–53, 56, 139, 140–41, 140n23, 141n25, 147n37, 155, 159, 269; mail station, 31, 32
American westward expansion. *See* westward expansion
Anderson (victim), 333
Andrews, John, 357
Andrews, John (and family), 108, 109
Angell, Herman, 108
animal thefts. *See under* horses; livestock
annuities to Indians: power/leverage, 16, 16n9, 17, 265; settlers' opinions, 355; weapons, treaty-related, 328, 341, 342–43, 344
Antelope Station, 33, *135*; mail station, 32; raid/burning, 139, 168, 169
Anthony, Andrew, 361
Anthony, Scott, 196, 196n61
Apache tribes: camps, 186; clashes/raids, 1864, 37; depredation claim records, 50; peace councils, 323; territory, 188
Appleby, Susan Consola, 122n19
Arapaho tribes: captives, 114–16, 189; Cheyenne relations, 189–90; clashes/raids, 1864, 37, 54, 56, 67, 113–16, 128–29;

Arapaho tribes (*continued*): clashes/raids, 1865, 133, 155, 161, 182–83, 191, 202; clashes/raids, 1867, 230, 265, 271–72, 278, 299, 305, 320–21, 323; clashes/raids, 1868, 342–43, 346, *358*, 359, 361, 365, 368, 370–81, 390–92, 395, 400; depredation claim futility, 50; depredation claim records, 15; friendly tribes, 179–80; Hungate family attack (1864), 54; Kaw battles, 335; peace councils, 222, 323, 328; "Smeller" tribe, 291; territory, 188; treaties history, 219–20, 305, 328, 342; villages/ lodges, 115, 129, 133, 186, 189–90. *See also* Little Raven (chief)

archaeological study and excavations: Alderdice grave, 467n67, 477–79; Hungate homestead, 55; stations and ranches, 470–71, *473, 475, 476*

Armes, George A., 230n29, 232, 233–34, 235, 240–41, 241n53, 310–11; cavalry forays, 318–20; works, 241n53, 311n14, 318n29

Armijo, Peodoro, 195

arms. *See* weapons and ammunition

arrows: human attacks, 290, 290n96, *291*, 428, 429, *443*, 445, 446, 447–48; hunting, 344–46; poison, 193

arson/burning: bodies, 87, 88, 150, 153, 178, 206, 208, 253, 259, 330, 395, 403–404; family homes, 54–55, 55n54, 72, 75, 76, 80, 118, 122, 142, 144, 332, 337–38, 347, 360, 362–63; of Indian villages by military, 253, 294, 328, 413, 466, 467; posts, ranches, and stations, 50, 70, 76, 78, 79n29, 83–84, 85, 87, 90, 118, 127, 135, 139, 140n23, 141n25, 142, 143, 148, 149, 150, 156, 161, 163–64, 165, 168, 170, 206, 212, 214, 215–17, 253, 254, 260, 266–68, 269n48, 299, 325, 332, 333, 360, 361, 363, 395, 474, 476; prairie, 51, 122, 125–26, 126n34, 311; prevention, due to materials, 140; railroad trains, 315; used as self-defense, 37, 46; wagons, 77, 80, 101n22, 107, 183, 192, 193, 194, 205, 207, 209, 267, 284, 296, 309, 322, 331, 361, 404; wood, 230, 243–44, 243n56

Asbury, Henry, 41n9, 219, 244–45, 245n60

Ashcraft, Grant, 123–24

Ashcraft, Sam and Granville, 364–65

Ashcraft, Samuel, 225

Asher, Ambrose, 69, 72, 73–74, 91, 93n9, 94

Asher Creek attacks, 353, 429, 447

Ashley, P. S., 310

Atchison, Kansas, 32, 33, 67

Atkinson, Alfred M., 59

Augur, C. C., 268n45, 294–95, 303, 328

Autobees, Charles, 113–14

Baca, Jose, 195

Baca, Martin, 361

Baca, Monico, 195

Baca y Ortiz, Ramone, 195

Baca y Ortiz, Servando, 195

Bachman, Fred, 370

Bacon, David, 348, 350

Bacon, Frederick A., 284

Bacon, Mary Jane, 347, 348–50

Bad Face Oglala Sioux, 222

Bad Wound, 161

Baertoche, John, 351, 352

Bagwell, Anderson, 229

Bailey, Daniel, 364

Bailey, Jim, 364, 365

Bailey, Mary, 363–64

Bainter, James, 78, 79–80

Baird, A. J., 42

Baker, Joe, 317

Baker, Lewis, 118, 197, 198, 198n66

Baldwin, Elisha, 366

Baldwin, "Judge," 385

Bancroft, Samuel, 134, 156

Banning, John, 401

Barker, Edgar A., 318

Barker, Napoleon, 275

Barnard, Edwin, 214

Barnes, Jeff, 470n1

Barnett, George, 138

Barnitz, Albert, 284–85, 287–90, 290n96, 343

Barret, Richard, 61

Barron, J. W., 266

Barton, Bea W., 122n19

Barton, David H., 101

Barton, G. C., 105

Bassett, Warren, and wife, 402, 402n24

Bates, Lt., 189

Battey, Stephen, 64

Battle at Sand Creek: The Military Perspective (Michno), 105n24, 130n46

The Battle of Platte Bridge (Vaughn), 24n26

Battle of the Washita (November 27, 1868), 344, 357, 405–406, 405n35, 407, 411, 412

Baxter, Lenox, 51

Bay, Hugh, 341
Bean, Mary C., 410
Bear Shed Off, 299
Beauvais, Gemenien, 137n12–138n12, 162
Beauvais Ranch, 162, 174
Beauvais Station, 162, 227
Beaver Creek Station, 33, *134*, 299; mail station, 31, 32, 52; personal travel accounts, 43, 44, 171n45, 294; raids, 65, 139; rescues, 143
Becher, Ronald, 67n2, 70n5, 78n23, 79n29, 81n31, 90n5, 100, 101n22, 109n32
Beck, St. Ledger, 139n18, 155–56
Beecher, Frederick, 235n40, 278, 354, 356, 400
Beecher, Henry Ward, 400
Beecher's Island Battle (September 1868), 356, 359, 389, 400, *412*; casualties, 199n69; fighters, 57, *345*, 355, 400, 403, 452, 461; relief, 230n28; site, 25, 452
Bell, Aaron, 351
Bell, Braxton and Elizabeth, 350–51
Bell, Ester, 351
Bell, Hester Ann, 350
Bell, James, 284, 288, 292
Bell, William A., 290, 290n96
Bellmard, Moise, 337
Benkelman, John, 367–70, 373
Bensen, Joe, 470n1
Bent, Charles, 38, 105, 107, 119, 120, 121, 205, 212, 284, 300, 311, 319
Bent, George: battle and raid accounts, 24n25, 73, 109n33, 110–11, 164–65, 167, 190, 197–98, 198n66, 213, 229, 248, 286n87, 293, 297n104, 311n14, 458; biography, 37–38; on Black Kettle, 161; Butterfield employ, 247–48, 343; on "friendly tribes" and treaties, 179–80, 188, 189, 220, 220n5, 246–47; on hunting, 345, 346; on Indian losses, 155n, 176, 176n3, 189n41, 293, 405n35, 452; interpretations, 164n25; Southern Cheyenne group, 211; warnings to travelers, 362–63
Bent, William, 37, 38, 187
Benteen, Frederick, 299, 351, 354, 355
Bent's Fort, 29, 38
Bergland (settler), 414
Bernhardt, C., 440n8, 440n11
Bernhardt, M., 262–63
Berry, Matthew, 287
Berthong, Donald, 147, 147n37
Beson (guard), 121, 122

Bickford, Harvey, 63
Bicknell, O. P., 331
Bicktold, John, 78
Big Belly's Ranch, 45
Big Coon Creek, 324
Big Creek Station, 302, 310
Big Crow (chief), 98–99, 109–10, 109n33
Big Head, 188
Big Hoo, 240
Big Sandy, 113, 129, *250*
Big Sandy Stage Station, 71, 309
Big Springs Station, 163, 258, 310
Big Thunder, 80–81
Big Timbers, 262, 278, 279–80, 362, 363n12
Big Turkey Creek, 63
Big Wolf (chief), 101, 124
Bijou Creek Ranch, 42, 53, 64, 267, 275, 385n59
Bisel, Debra Goodrich, 212n95
Bishop's Ranch, 235, 270
Bissonette, Joseph, Jr., 95
Bissonette, Joseph, Sr., 93, 95
Black Bear, 189–90
Black Foot (chief), 73, 110
Black Hawk, 201
Black Kettle (chief): 1864 movements, forces, and attacks, 48, 49, 99n16, 106n, 113–14, 115, 129, 130–31; 1865 movements, forces, and attacks, 161; 1868 movements, forces, and attacks, 347, 362–63; 1867 movements and forces, 244, 247, 248; children in captivity, 72, 91, 94; conferences, 115, 323; death, 342, 344, 405–406; reputation/war vs. peace, 106n, 131, 161, 184, 229n22, 241n53, 405–406; Sand Creek massacre (1864), 38, 113, 129, 130–31, 130n46; treaties, 187
Blackman, John, 300–301
Blakely, William, 78n23
Blinn, Clara, 404, 405
Blinn, Richard, 404
Blinn, Willie, 404, 405
Block, Phil, 333, 333n5
Blondeau, Bernard, 89–90
Blue Mound Station, 262, 278, 279–80
Blue Nose, 161
Blufton Station, 212
Blunt, James G., 122–23
Bogardus, David, 350, 351
Bogart, James and David, 157
Boggs, Charles, 400

Bone Scraper Society (Cheyenne warrior society), 38

Boone, A. G., 334, 335, 337

Boughton, Edson, 224–25

Boughton, M. V., 224–25

Bowers, Brooks, 315

Bowman, Henry, 323

Bowstring Men (Cheyenne warrior society), 38

Box Elder Creek massacre (1864). *See* Hungate family attack (June 11, 1864)

Boyd, Robert, 266, 274

Boyle, John, 198

Boyle, Patrick, 396, 397, 398

Boyle, Thomas, 51

Bozeman Trail: fort abandonment and burning, 395; official road, and construction, 222; source of 1866–1867 conflict, 229, 244

Brackett, Mr., 381, 384–85

Braddon, Alfred, 302

Bradley, Henry, 47–48

branding, 45, 120, 121, 313n17, 375

Brandly, J. G., 42

Bremer, F. J., 125

Bretney, Lt., 181

Brewer, John S., 163, 164

Brine, Peter, 158

Brings Water, 221–22, 222n8

Broken Horn, 185

Broome, Jeff, 239n, 249n, 258n21, 293n98, 295n, 346, 406n40, 440n9, 448n, 455n42, 469–80, 477

Brown, Albert L., 51

Brown, John, 53

Brown, Joseph, 266

Brown, Junius, 53

Brown, Mahlon H., 163

Brown, Melvin, 76–77

Brown, Stanley A., 276–77, 300–301

Brown's Ranch, 235

Brugh, Andrew, 214

Brugh, Spangler, 214

Brule Sioux, 26; clashes/raids, 67, 91n6, 155, 161, 191; friendly tribes, 179–80; treaties history, 221, 222, 223

Brundage, Hiram, 138

Brush, William, 364

Buck, William, 370

buffalo: food for captives, 99; food for travelers, 195; hunting methods, 344–46, 429–30;

resource tensions and war, 41–42, 222, 244; treaty hunting rules, 263–64, 327, 331, 344–46, 365, 389; whites' hunting, 302, 418–19, 427, 429

"Buffalo John." *See* Hiteman, John H.

buffalo soldiers, 241n53, 257, 310, 312, 313, 319, 320

Buffalo Springs Ranch, 68, 85, 87, 139, 159, 168, 169

Bulen, E. D., 138, 138n15, 159, 170

Bulen Ranch. *See* Connally and Bulen Ranch

Bull Bear (chief), 40, 91, 99, 99n16, 105, 235, 246, 347, 355

Bull Soldiers (Cheyenne warrior society), 38

Bullock, Captain, 114

Bunker Hill Stage Station, 296, 324

Bureau of Indian Affairs: compensation rules, 248; reports, 93n10

burial parties, 74–75, 253, 302, 326, 393–94, 413–15, 416–17, 419–20, 422, 466–67

Burke, John, 88

Burke, Patrick, 79, 79n28, 82, 83, 86

Burke, Philip, 418–19, 420

burning. *See* arson/burning

Bursell, L. C., 267

Bush, William H., 361

Butler, B. W., 164n25

Butterfield, David, 246–48, 343

Butters, Alfred and Pinckney, 366

Buzzard, William, 382

Cady, William J., 156

Cain, Dawson, 280

Cain, Riley, 198

California Ranch, 122

Camp Cottonwood. *See* Fort McPherson

Camp Douglas, 183

Camp Fletcher, 212, 212n95

Camp Osborn, 126

Camp Rankin: change to Fort Sedgwick, 218; defenses, 138, 158n, 160, 162–64, 166, 167, 171; history, 133–37, 134n. *See also* Fort Sedgwick

Camp Sandborn, 42, 52

Camp Wardwell. *See* Fort Morgan

Campbell, Hugh, 324

Campbell, James, 309, 310n10

Campbell, Peter, 308

captives: children, 57, 58–59, 69, 69n3, 70, 71, 72, 74, 91, 92–93, 93n9, 94, 96, 98, 99n16, 116, 142, 144, 146, 183–85, 188, 189, 195, 196,

199–201, 272, 306–309, 344, 347, 351, 351n63, 407, 435; exchanges, 307–308, 318; films about, 448n; informers, 53; interviews, 95–96; intra-tribe, 39, 359–60; memoirs and memories, 57n60, 58–59n62, 59n64, 96–98, 99n16, 109n32, 111, 115, 144–46, 146n36, 184–85, 187, 196, 200–201, 201–202n72, 308–309, 351; Mexican, 116, 195, 196; photographs, 93, 93n9, *94*, *465*; rescue attempts, 93, 95, 404, 435, 436, 450; rescues, 144, 145, 188, 189, 308, 351, 351n63, 356, 406, *441*, 460–63, *462*, 477; taken by U.S. military, 190, 307–308, 318, 405, 464; women, 52n43, 57–58, 57–58n60, 69, 69n3, 70, 71–72, 74, 87, 91, 93, *94*, 95–99, 99n16, 109–10, 114–16, 116, 142, 144–46, 200, 200n, 254, 255, 256–57, 338–39, 347, 352, 356, 404–405, 406, *434*, 435–36, 440, *441*, 442–45, 447, 449–50, 459–61, *462*, 465, 466–67

The Capture and Escape; or, Life Among the Sioux (Larimer), 59n64, 96, 109n32–n33, 201–202n72

Carlton, James M., 283

Carney, Thomas, 310

Carpenter, Arthur, 299

Carpenter, Col., 230n28

Carr, Eugene A., 407, 411, 413, 418, 429, 442n12, 450–54, 450n30, 456–58, 457n46, 460, 461, 463, 467, 468

Carrington, Henry, 222, 258, 393–94, 402

Carroll, John M., 130n46

Carson, Edward, 399

Carson, Kit, 215n100

Carter, Mason, 325

Cary, J. A., 297

Case, William and Charles, 51

cash, 186–88, 281, 327, 362, 372n, 374, 439–40, 466

Cassil, Lewis, 223–24, 224n14

Castle Rock Station, 274, 287, 296

cattle. *See* livestock

Cedar Point, 274–75, 285, 287

Central Overland California and Pike's Peak Express Company, 31, 32

Chalfant, William Y., 220n5, 251n2, 293n99, 295n

Chalk Bluffs Station, 214, 234–35, 266, 296–97, 298, 299, 300

"Charley." *See* Bent, Charles

Charr's Creek Ranch, 63

Chase, Dewitt, 204

Cherry Creek, 29, 133, 144, 155

Cheyenne tribes: clashes/raids, 1864, 48, 52, 54, 56–57, 69, 84–88, 89–111, 113–15, 124–25, 128–29; clashes/raids, 1865, 24, 133, 155, 161–74, 175, 177, 181–83, 191, 195–96, 197–98, 202, 205, 210–11, 214–15; clashes/raids, 1866, 223–25, 224n14, 226; clashes/raids, 1867, 234–35, 244–45, 254, 255, 255–61, 264–65, 273–75, 278, 281, 283–84, 284–87, *286*, 290–93, *291*, 294–97, 299, 300, 302, 305–309, 311n14, 312–30; clashes/raids, 1868, 331, 333–57, 359–88, 399–400, 402–405, *412*; clashes/raids, 1869, 411, *412*, 413–32, 433–68; depredation claim records, 15, 50, 311n14, 313n17; Kaw battles, 329, 335, 336, 337, 341, 347, 359; overall war involvement, 37, 39, 40, 48, 49, 67, 124, 406; Pawnee battles, 189, 318, 359, 459, 464; personalities, 244; territory, camps, and villages, 186, 188, 189, 252, 332; treaties history, 219–21, 305, 327–28, 342–43; warrior societies, 38–39. *See also* Northern Cheyenne tribes; Southern Cheyenne tribes

Cheyenne War: 1864, 38, 39–66, 67–88, 89–111, 113–31; 1865, 133–53, 155–74, 175–218; 1866, 190, 219; 1867, 242–48, 250, 251, 253–54, 257–58, 263–303; 1868, 331, 333–58, 359–88, 411, *412*; 1869, 411, *412*, 413–32, 433–68; battles geography, 24–25, 31–32, *412*; battles timeline, 24–25, 32, 34, 37, 42, 220–21, 331; end, assumptions, 407; end, reality, 463–64

Chicago Ranche, *134*, 198–99, 199n68, 201n, 223, 254

Chief Left Hand Southern Arapaho (Coel), 93n9

Chivington, John M., 46, 47, 52, 129–30, 181, 193

cholera, 310–11, 311n12, 325, 327

Choteau, John, 384, 386

Christensen, Laurence, 438–39, 440n6

Christiansen, John Peter, 438, 439

Christie, Augustus, 211

Christy, Charles, 230, 230n28

Cimarron Crossing, 274, 282, 300–301, 399

Circle of Fire: The Indian War of 1865 (McDermott), 24n26, 109n32, 110n34, 147n37

Cisco, John L., 268, 278, 280

citizen affidavits. *See* Indian Depredation Claims

Civil War (1861–1865): art, 212; casualties, 133–34; Cheyenne fighters, 51, 175, 191; Confederate prisoners, workers, 206, 443–44; Confederate soldiers, 38, 40–41; Union veterans, 352–53, 377, 418, 420, 443

civilian offensives, 190–91, 345
"civilian perspective" and focus, 13–14, 20–21, 25
Civilization and Education Acts (1796), 16
claims, depredations. *See* Indian Depredation Claims
Clark, Benjamin H., 230, 230n28, 243
Clark, C. M., 34
Clark, Victor, 267
Clarke, Charles, 288
Clarke, Milton, 128
Cleave, Richard, 163, 163n22, 166n30
Cleaves Ranche, 236
Clements, Stephen L., 302
Clinton, George, 309, 310n10
Cloud, W. F., 224n14
Co-rux-te-chod-ish, 453
coaches: operation and travel, 33–34. *See also* stage service
Coad, John F., 123, 140n23, 147–50, 170n39, 215–16, 230–32, 233–34, 234n36
Coad, Mark M., 123, 133, 140n23, 147–50, 152–53, 172, 215–16, 230–32, 234n36
Coburn, Watson, 140n23, 198, 199, 199n68, 199n69, 201n, 223, 242, 254
Cody, William F., 442n12, 450n30, 457, 459
Coel, Margaret, 93n9
Coffey, Capt., 206
Coffey, Jules, 95
Coffin, Morse, 124
Coffman, Joseph C., 274
cold. *See* weather, and effects
Cole, F., 50
Cole, Mr., 418–19
Cole, Nelson, 189, 190, 190n45
Colgan, Christopher, 289
Colley, Samuel G., 47
Collins, Caspar, 176n2, 181–82, 182n19, 191
Collins, John, 267, 281, 283, 287
Collins, William O., 110, 175, 176, 182n19, 223–24, 224n14
Colorado: geographic history, 29, 219–20; maps, 134–35, 358, 412, 470, 472; political history, 29, 39; raids and attacks, 13, 358, 359–88, 389, 404. *See also* Denver City; Denver Road
Colorado City, 378–79, 386, 395
Colorado Springs, 379, 385, 386
Colorado Territory, 29, 192. *See also* Denver road; Smoky Hill trail

Colorado Voluntary Cavalry, 92, 105n24, 113, 123, 172
Colorado Volunteer Artillery, 46
Comanche tribes: clashes/raids, 1864, 37, 63; peace councils, 323
Coming Through Fire: George Armstrong Custer and Chief Black Kettle (Schultz), 293n99
compensation for depredations: amounts, 17, 19–20, 23, 104, 105, 248; claim processing, 16–19, 19n16, 21–23, 74n10, 90n5, 230n28, 243n56, 265, 274n55, 296n103, 297n104; rules and laws, 16, 18, 248. *See also* Indian Depredation Claims
Comstock, Erastus, 78
Comstock, George, 78
Comstock, William Averill, 354–55, 355n70
Comstock Ranch, 88
Condon, William, 473, 477
Conklin, Emma Burke, 35
Connally, Guilford D., 138, 138n15, 159, 170
Connally and Bulen Ranch, 135–36, 135n3, 136, 137, 138, 138n15, 139, 159, 168, 170–71
Connor, Patrick, 110n34, 189–90
Connor, Sam, 275
Connor Fight (1865), 24
Constable, George, 76
Cook, John, 429
Cook, William E., 186n31
Coon Creek Station, 299–300, 396–97
Coplen, William, 379–80
Corbin, Henry, 310, 310n10, 313n17, 319–20, 320n
coroners' reports, 373–74
corpses: animal involvement, 214, 253, 352, 392, 393; discovery and identification, 259, 306, 307, 393; Indian remains, 178; military remains, 259, 290, 291; public displays, 373, 385–86
Coryell, John, 326
Cosby, Thomas, 324
Cosbyn, John H. "Jack," 64
Costello, J. H., 339–40
Cottonwood Springs. *See* Fort McPherson
Cottrill, W. H., 265, 266
counting coup, 150, 303, 446
court-martials, 288–90, 327, 454–55
Court of Claims, 17–18
Courts, Caspar, 122n19
Cow Creek, 56–57

Cow Creek Station, 63, 177–78
Crane, Jesse, 47, 49n28, 60
Craquer, Julius, 324
Crawford, Samuel, 224n14, 255, 340, 341
Crazy Dogs (Cheyenne warrior society), 38
Crenshaw, William H., 312
Cristy, William, 311
"critical trust" principle, 20
Crocker, W. D., 47
Crook, Timothy, 320
Crooked Lance Society (Cheyenne warrior society), 38
crop failures, 51
Crow, Jerome, 61
Crowe, William, 337–38
Curtis, Dick, 273
Curtis, F. R., 48
Curtis, Samuel R., 60, 64
Curtis, T. R., 50, 50n33
Curtis, Winty, 50, 50n33
Cushing, Sylvanus E., 460
Custard, Amos, 181–82
Custer, George A., 184–85, 230, 252; accounts, 230n28, 407; Tom Alderdice meeting, 449n27; Battle of the Washita (November 27, 1868), 230n28, 344, 357, 405–406, 407, 411, 412; campsites, 1867, 134, 250, 293n98, 470–71, 472, 474; captive rescues, 356, 406; Cheyenne war leadership, 249, 249n, 250, 252–53, 258, 259, 268, 292–95, 305; court-martial, 327; Lyman Kidder communications, 258, 259, 471, 474; peace parleys, 306; travel debate and controversy, 250, 293–95, 293n99, 295n, 471, 472
Custer, Libbie, 293, 293n99, 449n27
Custer into the West with the Journal and Maps of Lieutenant Henry Jackson (Broome), 239n, 249n, 258n21, 293n98, 295n, 470
Cut Arms, 291
Cut Nose, 184, 185
Cutler, M. B., 107, 208
Czaplewski, Russ, 69n3, 93n10, 110n34

Dahl, Martin, 414, 415–16, 415n5, 417
Dahl, Paul, 414, 415–16, 417
Daily, Bradford, 418
Daily, James Alfred, 443, 444n
Daily, James Alfred (Jr.), 480
Daily, John, 435, 443, 447

Daily, Mary Twibell, 480
Daily, Willis, 433, 443, 445–46, 447n24, 448, 450, 467n67, 479–80, 480
Daily Colorado Tribune, 374, 382, 385
Dangerous Duty: A History of Frontier Forts in Fremont County, Wyoming (McDermott), 24n26
Danielson, Benjamin, 133, 147, 149–51, 153, 215–17
Dargus, Edwin, 313
Darlington, Brinton, 313n17, 323n38
Darrah, Thomas, 54
Darrow, George, 272
Davis, Daniel, 254
Davis, Edward, 381, 384–85
Davis, Evan, 191, 210, 210n90
Davis, Hiram, 159–60, 169
Davis, Isaac, 318
Davis, O. C., 421
Davis, Theodore, 212, 213–14, 259, 273, 286
Dean, Andrew, 324
Deane, Cecil, 391–93, 394, 395, 395n9
death, feigning, 120–21, 269–70, 314, 354
death customs, 110, 222, 447, 467
"Decoration Day," 433
Deer Creek Station, 58, 59, 93, 109
Deering Springs, 266, 278–80
defenses, against Indians: added fortifications, 298, 299–300, 336; feigning death, 120–21, 269–70, 314, 354; fire, 37, 46; firepower, 70, 76, 78, 86, 117, 119, 128, 129, 140, 142–43, 148–49, 150, 152–53, 162, 164, 165–66, 178, 211, 213, 224, 225, 241, 261, 286–87, 301, 311, 312, 313, 326, 352n67, 353, 420, 421, 425, 427–28, 430–31, 437–38, 440, 446–47; hiding, 90, 100, 195, 213, 227n20, 284, 301, 302, 310n10, 334, 352, 390–91, 419, 422–23, 423n, 425–26, 444–45; hopelessness without, 97; safety in numbers, 82–83, 84–87, 96–97, 122, 127, 149, 178, 182, 183, 190, 191, 225, 353, 356, 387–88, 438–39, 443; sticks, 67, 86; superstition and fears, 203; topography, 79–80, 397; volunteer cavalries, 123; wagon formations, 117, 148, 152–53, 158n, 160–61, 283, 397, 425
DeLano, Milton M., 382
DeMasters, Andrew, 387
Dennison Station, 33, 66, 134, 139n18; abandonment, 155–56; mail station, 32
Denver City, 29; culture, 101–104;

Denver City *(continued)*: gold rush travel, 30; mail, freight, and stage service, 31–33, 43, 64, 80; political center and isolation, 41, 113, 151. *See also* Denver road

Denver City Trail. *See* Denver road

Denver Road, *134–35*; alternative roads, 192, 211; battles, overviews, 13, 24–25, 37, 123–24, 135; buildings and development, 31, 32, 33, 41, 176, 178, 190, 394, 473; Custer routes, *250*, 253, 293–95, 295n; forts and stage stations, *68*, 75–76, *134–35*, 139–41, 162, 394, 469–80; gold rush travel, 30; mail travel, 31–32, 333; personal travel accounts, 34–35, 43–46, 390–93; raids and attacks, 37, 54, 56, 65, 67, 69, 75, 76, 135–44, 192–94, 197–99, 209–11, 214–17, 224–25, 230–34, 239–43, 249, 254–55, 257–62, 268–72, 332, 363–65, 389–93, 401–402; railroad effects, 258, 332–33, 394; ranch/station abandonment, 135, 167–68, 169, 298, 332, 394; stage service, 31–32, 33–34, 65, 68, *134–35*, 169, 268–69, 332–33, 469–80; telegraph lines, 65, 66, 143, 164, 164n24, 192

Department of the Interior: authority and range, 251, 411; depredation claims processing, 16–19, 248; Indian arming, 343

Department of the Missouri, 249, 294

depredations: burning bodies, 87, 88, 150, 153, 178, 206, 208, 253, 259, 330, 395, 403–404; corpse mutilation, and witnesses, 55, 56, 71, 74–75, 86–87, 115, 116n8, 213, 253, 259, 280, 290–92, *291*, 322–23, 326, 333, 352, 373, 385–86, 393, 403–404, 429, 440; corpses, discovery and identification, 259, 306, 307, 393; government investigations, 106n; nature of war, 249, 265, 277–78; photographs, 290, *291*; punishment policy and authority, 251; source material and claim files, 13, 15–26; souvenirs, 124, 144, *314*, 316, 466; tribe-specific mutilations, 291. *See also* horses; Indian Depredation Claims; livestock; scalping; sexual abuse and rape; torture

derailed trains, 315, 318, 327

desertion, military, 237–39, 239n, 253, 290, 454–55, 471, 472

Destination: Denver City The South Platte Trail (Monahan), 139n18, 141n25, 151n43, 269n48

Diamond Springs Station, 227, 228

Dickinson, Asbury, 339

Dicus, Samuel, 266

Dietemann, Apollinaris, 370–73, *371*, 372n, 374

Dietemann, Henrietta, 358, 370–74, *376*, 384

Dietemann, John, 358, 370–71, 372, 373, 374, *376*, 384

Dietemann, Maria, 371–72

Dietemann family attack (August 25, 1868), *358*, 370–74, *371*, *376*

Dillon, William, 171

Dimick, Frank, 151–52

Dimon, Charles Augustus, 145–46

diseases, spread: cholera, 310–11, 311n12, 325, 327; to Indians, from whites, 41, 327; scurvy, 263; typhoid fever, 92, 94

Dixon, David, 14

Dixon, Thomas, 324

Dock Billy, 80–81

doctors: attacks on, and supplies, 136, 333; military surgeons, 461, 466–67; needs for, 274, 416, 445; treating captives, 92

Dodd, John, 49–50

Dodge, Richard I., 235, 235n42, 236, 257–58

Dog Soldier Justice: The Ordeal of Susanna Alderdice in the Kansas Indian War (Broome), 14, 17n13, 146n36, 285n85, 346, 406n40, 440n9, 448n, 477

Dog Soldiers/Dog Men (Cheyenne warrior society), 38–39; captives, 91, 99, 186, 435–36, 437, 438, 440–46, 459–61, 462, 463; English, 398, 445; fighting customs, 459; gathering forces, 133, 246, 407, 411, 413, 450; Kiowas, 323n38; military ruses, 452–53, 456; raids and attacks, 69, 79, 91, 106n, 103–31, 205, 223, 255, 293, 311n14, 324, 326, 341, 374, 399, 407, 413–22, *421*, 433, 434, 435–53, 467–68; scapegoating, 130–31, 286n87; treaty attempts, 188–89

dogs, 367, 368, 369, 467

Dolan, Peter, 101, 107, 124

Donnell, H. U., 297–98

Donohue, Thomas, 225

Douglas, W.A., 63

Douglas Ranch, 76–77, 143

Douglass, Henry, 41n10, 245–46, 268n46, 272, 277–78, 300, 320–21, 361

Douglass, James, 76, 78

Douglass, Cpl. James, 288

Downer Station, 211, 212, 214, 253, 266, 275, 297, 299, 324–25

Downing, Jacob, 42n13, 52–53

drunkenness, 60, 95, 96, 111
Dudley, Edgar S., 204n76
Dummell, William H., 284, 285
Dunlap, B. H., 128
Dunlop, Captain, 62
Dunn, Birney, 333, 334
Dunn, Clark, 42
Dunn, Samuel T., 333
Dunn's fight (April 12, 1864), 42, 45
Dunsmore, Daniel, 275
Dupries, Mr. and Mrs., 90
Dyche, Calvin, 230, 230n28, 243n56

Eagle Head, 184
Eagle's Nest Stage Station, 126
Earle, William, 429, 430, 431, 432
Eaton Station, 263
Eayre, George S., 46–49, 52
Edwards, John, 339
Elephant Rock fight (May 13, 1869), 412, 413, 429
11th Ohio Cavalry, 175
Elk Creek, 118
Ellenbecker, John, 69n3
Elliott, Joel, 293, 293n99, 294, 295, 327, 328–29, 405n35
Ellsworth, William, 175
Elm Creek Ranch, 68, 80
Emery, Bob, 77
Emery, Charles, 75n11, 77, 78n23, 79n28, 82, 83–84
Encyclopedia of Indian Wars: Western Battles and Skirmishes 1850–1890 (Michno), 135n3, 139n18, 175, 400n19
Engel, George, 122
Englert, Lorene and Kenneth, 215n100
English, Don, 395n9
English language, use by Indians, 125, 180, 200, 201, 270, 306–307, 319, 398, 445
Ennes, Oscar and Walter, 364, 365
Ennis, William, 50, 50n35
Eubanks, Hattie, 69, 70, 70n5, 71, 79n29
Eubanks, Isabella, 72, 91, 91n7, 94
Eubanks, Joseph, 69–70, 69n3, 70n5, 71, 72, 73–74
Eubanks, Joseph, Jr., 69, 70, 70n5, 71, 74
Eubanks, Lucinda, 69, 70, 70n5, 71, 72–73, 72n7, 74, 87, 91n7, 99n16, 109, 110–11, 179
Eubanks, William, 69, 70, 71, 179

Eubanks family attack (August 1864), 69–75, 70n5, 86, 88
Eubanks Ranch, 68
evacuation, settlers, 335–36
Evans, John: concerns and conferences, 39, 40, 41, 47, 67, 75, 115; war proclamation, 113; White Antelope's confession, 89, 91n6, 94
Everett, Benjamin J., 375, 376
Everhart, Charley, 384, 385–86
Excelsior Colony, 413–24
Ezekiel, David Israel, 298

facts, nature of, 13–14, 20–21, 23–24, 73, 297n104
Fahey, James, 278, 279, 280, 287
Fahrion, George, 278–79
Fairview Ranch. *See* American Ranche
Faller, Lincoln, 164n25
family attacks, 355; Alderdice family (Spillman Creek Raid, May 30, 1869), 434, 435–45, 443, 447–50; Andrews family/Gilman Ranch (August 8, 1864), 108; Baker family (August 18, 1864), 118; Blinn family (October 9, 1868), 404; Bogardus/Bell family (August 1868), 350–51; Campbell family (July 25, 1867), 308; Dietemann family (August 25, 1868), 358, 370–74, 371, 376; Eubanks family (August 1864), 69–75, 70n5, 86, 88; Fletcher family (July 31, 1865), 182–86, 188; German family (September 11, 1874), 407; Gillett family/Gilman Ranch (August 8, 1864), 108–109; Hanna family (July 23, 1867), 309; Hungate family (June 11, 1864), 54–56, 75, 303, 373; Kalus/Ulbrich family (July 22, 1867), 305–306, 317; Kelley family (July 12, 1864), 57–58; Kine family (May 1869), 442; Larimer family (July 1864), 58–59; Marshall family (August 1868), 352–53; Martin family (August 19, 1864), 119–21; Morris family (January 15, 1865), 52n43, 141–42, 141n26, 144, 152; Penny family (November 1, 1865), 126–27, 209–10; Swedish immigrants (May 1869), 413–23
Fancher, Henry, 274
Fancher, J. A., 274
Fancher, Joseph, 273, 274n55
Farley, Alan W., 58n62, 201n
farms, arson, 51
Farrell, Edward, 317

Farwell, Crawford, 375

Fast Bear (chief), 213

A Fate Worse Than Death: Indian Captivities in the West (Michno and Michno), 69n3, 70n5, 72n7, 91n7, 146n36, 186n31

Faxton, Charles, 398

Felch, John, 326

Ferguson's Ranch, 270, 271

Ferris, John, 266, 267, 278

Fetterman, William J., 229–30

Fetterman Fight (December 21, 1866), 24, 229–30; books about, 230n26; spoils, 234, 245

5th Cavalry Regiment (United States): 1868 campaigns, 407; 1869 campaigns, 411, 413, 418, 429, 450–68

Finding Sand Creek: History, Archeology, and the 1864 Massacre Site (Greene and Scott), 131n49

Finley, Henry, 272, 284

firearms. *See* weapons and ammunition

fires. *See* arson/burning

firewood and lumber, 230, 243–44, 243n56, 245, 323–24, 326, 331, 396

1st Colorado Cavalry, 42, 46, 52

1st Nebraska Cavalry, 105, 125, 163, 208

Fisher, Samuel, 254, 255

Fleming, Rufus, 208

Fletcher, Amanda, 183–84, 185–86, 186n31, 187, 188, 189

Fletcher, Jasper, 182–83, 184, 185, 186–87, 186n31, 186n32, 188

Fletcher, John, 93, 95, 107

Fletcher, Lizzie, 183, 184–85, 188

Fletcher, William, 93, 100, 107

Fletcher family attack (July 31, 1865), 182–86, 188

food: bargaining power, 63, 95, 123, 125–26, 191; captives', 73, 99, 257, 308; grocery freight and transportation, 86, 87, 157, 159, 193, 194, 195, 196, 202, 204, 205, 209, 211, 247, 274, 322, 323; personal travel accounts, 44; ruses, raids, 60, 116, 254–55, 256, 365–66; sharing meals, 194; waste, theft, and abuse, 88, 121, 208, 336, 337, 338, 339–40, 347, 357, 367, 368, 466

Foolish Dogs (Cheyenne warrior society), 38

Forgotten People: A History of the South Platte Trail (Probst), 139n18, 471, 473

Forsyth, George A.: 1868 offensives, 356, 399–400; Beecher's Island fight (1868), 57, 230n28, 343n44, 345, 355, 400, 452

Fort Arbuckle, 327

Fort Aubrey, 268

Fort Cass (trading fort), 30

Fort Dodge, 412; attacks at, 276–77; attacks near, 122, 195–96, 230, 300, 321, 326, 361, 399; captives, 186; communications delivery, 396–99; defenses, 195–96, 276, 277, 361; employees and supplies, 243, 243n56, 272, 320, 323, 326; Satanta at, 245–46, 276

Fort Harker, 250, 255, 281, 282, 302, 412, 469; attacks near, 347–51; as destination/place of safety, 442–43; horse theft, 403; supplies, 361–62

Fort Hays, 250, 252, 253, 268, 298, 310, 312, 319, 330, 412; defenses, 429; supplies, 361–62

Fort Kearny, 68; attacks, 229, 260; as destination/place of safety, 67, 85, 86, 90, 90n5, 179, 180, 201, 204, 238; detachments, 106; horses, 121; Indians' views, 180; mail routes, 31, 81

Fort Laramie: communications, 181, 294–95; hangings, chiefs, 109–11, 109n33, 110n34; historic site, 469; military offenses, 175, 178–79; nearby Sioux raids, 59, 64; peace council, 1866, 221, 222–23, 227; stage route, 64, 183; treaty, 1851, 219, 223

Fort Laramie: Military Bastion of the High Plains (McChristian), 24n25, 109n33, 221n7

Fort Larned, 47, 48, 49, 60, 62, 250, 412; annuities, 342; captives rescued, 189; defenses, 244, 287, 395–96; historic site, 469; negotiations, 1867, 219, 251–52; trade route, 127

Fort Leavenworth: mail route, 30; military HQ, 327, 449, 449n27; trade route, 61, 62, 122, 127, 225

Fort LeDuc (trading fort), 30

Fort Lupton (trading fort), 30

Fort Lyon, 38, 47, 56, 92; as destination/place of safety, 114, 301, 363; Fort Wise history, 220; military maneuvers, 129, 400–401, 411; site, 362

Fort McPherson, 90n5, 101n22, 107–108, 109, 127, 191, 237, 412; military travel, 235, 294, 411, 413, 450; peace parleys, 306

Fort Morgan, 134, 171n45; attacks near, 299, 389, 393, 395; burning and abandonment, 135, 333, 389, 395, 395n9; defenses, 192, 238, 239, 395, 476; employees, 224–25; mail station/area, 31, 32, 52; records, 225, 225n16

Fort Phil Kearny. *See* Fort Kearny

Fort Reynolds, 379, 469

Fort Rice, 144, 145

Fort Riley, 49, 237, 249

Fort Russell, 408

Fort Sedgwick, 134n, *135, 218, 250,* 469; arrests, 236; defenses, 192, 231–32, 233–34, 235, 240, 257–58, 260, 270, 294, 391, 476; mail station/area, 31, 32; name history, 133–34; supplies, 231, 293, 294, 295, 401; thefts, 257–58

Fort St. Vrain (trading fort), 29

Fort Sully, 57

Fort Uncompahgre (trading fort), 30

Fort Union: military travel, 300; trade route, 61, 62, 116, 122, 128, 418

Fort Wallace, *250, 412,* 469; attacks on, 284, *286;* defenses, 192, 284–85, 294; employees, 278; reports from, and attacks near, 258, 262, 264, 292–93, 295, 354–55, 361–62, 399, 417–18; supplies, 293, 294, 361–62

Fort Wicked. *See* Godfrey's Ranche

Fort Wise Treaty (1861), 40, 220

Fort Zarah, 469; burials, 322–23; communications, 230; defenses, 351; location, 50, 61; raids, 63, 128, 229, 300, 322, 323, 329, 334, 351; rations, 284; Satanta at, 63, 244

forts, maps, *68, 134–35, 412,* 469, 471, 473

Fosdick, H. M., 114

Fossil Creek, 257, 296, 429, 447

Fossil Creek Stage Station, 201n, 285n85, 296, 427

Foster, Horatio M., 157–58, 157n4, 160

Fott, John, 224n14

Fouts, William D., 179, 180–81

Fox Tail, 229

Franke, Frederick William, 322–23

Franke, Martha Maria, 322–23

Frankel, Glenn, 448n

Frazier, F., 296

Frazier, Frank, 422–24

Frazier, Mrs., 420

Frazier, Robert W., 134n

Frazier, William, 422–24

Freas, Lorenzo M., 83n35, 157n4, 157n5

Freeman, Daniel, 74–75, 87–88

freeways, *134–35*

Fremont Station, 225

Fremont's Orchard(s), 42, 45

Fremont's Springs, 270

Frenchman's Creek, 43, 207, 209

Friday (chief), 161

friendly fire, 453

"friendly" tribes: Pawnee, 125, 318, 453; Pawnee impersonations, 446; peace attempts, 184; relocation attempts, 178–80; scouts, 189, 206, 257–58, 318, 346, 404n31, 450, 451, 457

Frontier Crossroads: The History of Fort Caspar and the Upper Platte Crossing (McDermott), 24n26, 182n19

frostbite, 176, 208, 234, 238, 240

fur trade routes, 29–30

Galbreth, Mr., 261

Gallagher, Benjamin, 90n5

Gardner, Archibald, 399

Gardner, Benjamin, 51

Garfield, James, 353

Garfield, Marvin H., 303n119

Garrison, Milt, 384

Garton, Elijah, 205–206

Garton, Ellis, 205, 206

Garton, Hamilton B., 204, 205–206

Gaskell, Albert, 205

Gentry, Albert, 62

German family attack (September 11, 1874), 407

Gerry, Eldridge, 39n4, 40, 408

Getz, Andrew, 363

Giersch, Peter, 51

Gillett, Chauncey, 108, 109

Gillett family attack (August 8, 1864), 108–109

Gillette, Lewis B., 156, 157n4, 158n, 168

Gillette's Ranche: description and raids, 156–59, 156n3, 160, 161n11, 168, 169; location, *135;* mail station, 32

Gilman, Jeremiah, 107–109

Gilman, John, 107–109

Gilman Ranch, 101n22, 107–108

Gilpin, William, 39

Gleason, Timothy, 267

Goddard, Jay, 165n27

Godfrey, Holan, 52n43, 139, 140, 140n22, 140n23, 142, 143, 269

Godfrey's Ranche, 52n43, 134; attacks, 139, 140, 140n22, 140n23, 143, 159, 269, 270; mail station, 31, 32

gold rush: land demands and treaties, 219; routes and travel, 29, 30

Gomer, Alva, 383, 383n55
Gomer, Philip, 54, 56, 157, 157n4, 157n5, 168, 360n3, 366, 382, 383–84
Gonzales y Baca, Miguel, 195
Goodrich, D., 310n10
Goodwin, James, 397
Goose Creek Station, 264, 266, 267, 274, 298
Gordon, G. A., 186n32, 187–88, 188–89
Gould, William, 309, 310
governors: Colorado, 39, 40, 41, 47, 67, 75, 113, 379; Kansas, 224n14, 255, 340, 341; military warnings to, 359
Graham, Jesse, 127
Granstadt, Malcolm, 420, 421.
Grant, Sallenna, 130n46, 194
Grant, Ulysses S., 251
Graves, E.S., 83
Gray, William, 138
Graybeard (chief), 161
Greasney, Thomas, 295–96, 303
Green, Franklin N., 274
Green, George, 56–57, 461, 463
Green, Marmaduke, 384
Green, Nancy, 384
Green, P.H., 63
Greene, Jerome A., 131n49, 220n3, 405n35
Greyhead, 364, 365
Griff, John, 384, 385
Griffenstein, William, 298
Grigsby, Aaron, 336, 336n13
Grinnell, George Bird, 167, 189n41
Grinnell Stage Station, 295–96, 303
Grover, Abner "Sharp," 354–55
Grummond, Lt., 229
Gruwell, James, 204
Guernimo, 334
Guerriere, Edmund, 347, 349
Guire, Jacob, 387
guns. See weapons and ammunition
Guthrey, Patrick, 192, 192n52
Gutierrez, Jose, 301

Hackney Ranch, 68, 78, 78n23
Hagen, Dennis, 303n120
Hain, William, 258–60
Hale, Owen, 185, 229n24, 280, 284, 289
Haley, David, 302
Haley, Michael, 442–43, 442n13, 447, 447n24
Hall, Frank, 379

Hall, George, 285, 285n84
Hall, Gus, 142–43
Hall, Henry, 138
Hall, Hiram, 311n14, 312–13
Halladay, Albert, 78, 78n23, 79n28
Halleck, H. W., 64
Hamilton, Alexander, 136
Hamlin, William, 285, 288–90
Hammond, Andrew, 80
Hampton, John W., 190n45
Hanchett, Alanson, 138
Hancock, W.S.: attack investigations, 279; correspondence, 224n14, 239, 249, 251, 253, 255, 276; Indian relations, 246; interpreters, 273; military/Indian councils, 251–52, 268, 276; war culpability/role, 248, 249, 251, 251n2, 252, 253–54, 273, 294, 305, 328
Hancock's War (Chalfant), 220n5, 251n2, 293n99, 295n
Hanger, Charles, 186, 186n31, 187, 188
hangings: chiefs, 109–11, 109n33, 110n34; fraudulent businessmen, 79n29; women, 115–16
Hanna, James, 309
Hard Nose, 334
Hardy, Cpt., 47
Harlow, William H., 158–60, 159n7, 161n11, 169
Harlow's Ranche, 134, 158–60; described, 169; mail station, 32; raid/burning, 139, 168
Harmon, Patrick, 100, 100n22–101n22
Harmon, Thomas, 75n12, 107
Harper's Weekly (periodical), 212, 273, 286
Harrington, William, 423, 423n
Harris, John H., 126
Harris, William, 289
Hart (herder), 400
Hartman (soldier), 398
Hartwell, William, 282
Harvey, Winfield Scott, 398–99
Hatch, Thom, 220n5
Hawkes, Ed, 317
Hayden, Lewis, 365
Haynes, John, 224, 224n13, 224n14
Haynes, Walter, 223–24, 224n14
Hays, Laurence, 100
Hays, Truman B., 43–46
Hearst, Andrew Jackson, 379
Heath, Herman H., 204–205, 207–209, 209n87
Hedren, Paul L., 470n1

Hegwer, Henry, 281
Heigele, Frederick, 266, 267, 283
Hemey, Andy, 368–69, 370
Hendrickson, Mart, 350
Henning, Conrad, 127
Henry, John, 297
Henshaw, Gregory, 315
Henshaw Springs Station, 272, 284
Herd, John, 127
Herron, Leander, 395–98, 397, 398n
Hetherington, John, 310
Hewitt, Henry, 351
Hickok, James Butler "Wild Bill," 383, 383n55, 455, 455n42–456n42
Higgins, John, 302
Hiles, John, 61
Hill, Curtis, 283
Hill, Louis M., 79–80, 79n29
Hill, William E., 470n1
Hills, Elizur, 310n10
Hinds, James, 147, 152
historic preservation, 469–70, 473
historical fact. See facts, nature of
Hiteman, John H., 159, 159n7, 160, 169
Hockaday, John, 30
Hodder, Halie Riley, 173–74, 174n49, 178
Hoel, Aaron, 37, 42–46
Hoesman, H. F., 297
Hogan, Charles, 414, 415, 415n5, 416, 417, 421, 426
Hogbin, Aquila, 271
Holaday's Ranch, 237
Holborn, Anna, 275
Holden, Isabelle, 365
holidays, 433, 435
Holladay, Ben, 31, 32, 33, 65, 79n29, 136n6, 166n31, 167, 169–70, 170n39
Holland, Phillip, 275
Hollibaugh, E. F., 448n
Holmes, Myron, 298
Hook, H. H., 408
Hopkins, Isaac, 388
Hopkins, Obadiah, 388
Horse in the Road, 240
horses: deserters, 237, 238; killings, 119, 121, 267, 311, 459, 463, 466; payment of Indians' ponies, 228; Pony Express, 409; race horses, 225; recovery attempts, 276–77, 300, 302, 364–65, 367–68, 369, 380–84, 387, 408;

taking of Indians' ponies, 53; thefts, 49–50, 52–53, 54, 60, 62, 63, 64, 72, 75, 78, 80, 98, 108–109, 113–14, 119, 121, 126, 175, 176, 177, 180, 183, 191, 192, 198, 210, 225, 226, 229, 231, 239, 257–58, 260, 266, 267, 269, 272, 274–75, 276, 278, 279, 280–81, 283, 284, 285, 296–98, 297n104, 300, 301, 302, 307, 310, 313, 317, 333, 360–61, 361, 362, 363–65, 366, 367–70, 371–72, 375, 377–78, 379–83, 387–88, 389, 399, 400, 401, 402, 403, 408, 418, 424, 438, 444; travel challenges, 44, 179, 207, 252–53, 262, 274, 277, 282, 401, 453, 459. See also livestock
Horton, Elise Daily, 480
hotels, 65, 82, 370
Houston, John, 51–52
Howbert, Irving, 385
Howell, John W., 296
Howling Magpie, 452
Hufurt, Michael, 326
Hughes, Andrew, 166–67
Hugo Springs Stage Station, 275
Humbarger, Solomon, 429, 430–31, 432
Hume, David, 13
Hungate, Nathan Ward, 54–55, 55n54, 55n55, 303
Hungate family attack (June 11, 1864), 54–56, 75, 303, 373
Huning, Franz and Charles, 322–23
Hunt, Charles, 317
Hunt, George, 78, 88
Hunter, Andrew, 297, 297n105
hunting: areas, 41; treaty rules and complications, 263–64, 327, 331, 344–46, 365, 389; by whites, 52, 84, 302, 418–19, 427, 429–30. See also buffalo
Husted, C. R., 381
Hutchins, Isaac, 384
Hyde, George, 38, 49n28, 109n33, 135n3, 164n25, 176n3, 189n41, 220n5, 221n7, 222n8, 293n98, 311n14

Iams, Sarah J., 141
Iliff, W. Charles, 91, 100, 107
Indian agents: councils, 194–95, 251–52; investigations, 21–22, 74n10, 105, 161, 186, 243n56, 296n103, 340–41; power and authority, 16–17, 251. See also Wynkoop, Edward "Ned"

Indians and Immigrants: Encounters on the Overland Trails (Tate), 14–15
Indian attacks, accounts. *See under* personal memory accounts; revenge attacks
Indian culture, 110, 303, 344–46, 446
Indian Depredation Claims: amounts paid, 17, 18, 19–20, 23, 265; captives and families, 93n9, 99, 99n16; cash, 186; examples, 37, 50, 56–58, 58n62, 67, 74n10, 75n12, 81n31, 83n35, 99, 101–105, 137, 168, 169–70, 247, 332; filing and investigation processes, 16–19, 19n16, 21–23, 74n10, 90n5, 230n28, 243n56, 265, 274n55, 296n103, 297n104; fraud, 17, 21–22, 23, 23n23, 74n10, 79n29, 81n31, 90n5, 137n9, 168, 170n39, 203n73, 247–48, 274n55, 331n, 363n12, 403; futility of filing, 50; historical worth and usefulness, 13, 15–16, 20–26, 100, 100n22–101n22, 101, 140n23; legislation, 16, 18; organization and extent, 15n8, 17–18, 17n12, 19–20; re-filing, 18–19; Sand Creek–related, 130n46, 285n85; victims lists, 70n5, 75n11, 139n18. *See also* Court of Claims
Indian Depredation Claims, 1796–1920 (Skogen), 17–18
Indian depredations. *See* depredations
Indian Peace Commission, 305, 389
informed consent, 220
Ingham, Frederick, 211
Ingham, S. A., 211
insurance claims and fraud, 17, 20, 23
interpreters. *See* translators
Interstate 76 (I-76), 134–35
Iowa Cavalry, 56, 95, 118, 137, 163, 175, 177, 197, 199, 207, 208
Irwin, Jackman and Company (government contractors), 46, 47
Ishman, David, 138
Ivory, William W., 198

Jackson, Hal, 470n1
Jackson, Henry, 471, 472
Jackson, Walter, 422–23
Jacques, Francis "Frank," 147, 148, 150–51, 152, 153
James, William, 96
Jenness, John C., 232–33
Jennings, D. D., 228
Jennings, George B., 318, 319
Johnson, Benjamin M., 302

Johnson, Charles T., 138
Johnson, Hervey, 110
Johnson, Leona, 366, 383, 384
Johnson, Louisa A., 383
Jones, Charles, 331
Jones, Daniel, 389–90
Jones, F. F., 321
Jones, Henry, 326
Jones, John S., 30, 31
Jones, Mr. (interpreter), 246
Jones, Robert, 176n2
Jones, William, 209, 210
Jordan, James, 138
Joy, Margaret, 100, 101n22
Julesburg Stage station, 33, 136, 136n6, 139, 167; attacks (winter, 1865), 24n25, 159, 160–61, 163–67, 168, 206, 473; journeys, 159–60, 162, 166
Junction Ranch, *68*, 224–25

Kalus, Albert, 305–306
Kalus, Margaretha, 306
Kalus/Ulbrich family attack (July 1867), 305–309, *307*, 317
Kane, Lt., 326
Kansas: Civil War, 51; Denver road travel route, 32–33, 41, *68*; maps, *412*; raids and attacks, 13, 39, 47, 48, 51–52, 60–64, 67, 116, 122, 128–29, 220, 309–10, 330, 333–34, 347–57, 359, 404, 413–32, 433–38, *434*, 467–68; statehood, 29; treaties history, and lands, 219–20, 327
Kansas Cavalry, 62, 207, 318, 320, 326
Kansas Pacific Railway, 427
Kansas Stage Company, 50
Kansas Territory, 29
Kappler, Charles J., 220n3
Kasson, John A., 199–200
Kaw tribes: fights, 329, 334–35, 336, 337, 341, 347, 359; intermarriage, 337–38; misidentification, 51
Keenan, Jerry, 189n40
Keith, William M., 278
Kelley, Capt., 210
Kelley, John, 454–55
Kelley, Michael, 52–53, 56, 65, 87, 88, 140, 141, 141n25
Kelley's Station. *See* American Ranche
Kelly, Fanny, 57–58, 57–58n60, 58–59n62, 200n, 201n

Kelly, Josiah, 57
Kelly, Mary, 57
Kelly, Melan C., 78, 87
Kelly, William, 100
Kelman, Ari, 131n49
Kelso, Ed, 158
Kennedy, Judson, 140n23, 147n37, 148, 149, 150, 152, 171n44, 172
Kennedy, William, 86–87, 88
Keogh, Myles, 234, 234n39, 235, 235n41, 262, 263–64, 278, 279, 280, 288, 343
Kersten, William, 127, 275
Kicking Bird (chief), 62, 63, 64, 247–48, 276
Kidd, Meredith H., 329
Kidder, Lyman S., 258, 259, 471, 474
Kidder massacre site, 250, 258, 259
kidnapping. See captives
Kilburn, E. B., 269n48, 270
Kile, John, 453–56, 454n38
Kine, Bridget, 442, 442n15, 444–45
Kine, Timothy, 442, 442n13–n15, 447
Kinna, John, 81n31
Kinney, William, 281
Kinsie (Kinsey), Tom, 400
Kiowa Station, 68, 70, 76, 107
Kiowa tribes: boasts, 64; clashes/raids, 1864, 37, 47, 60–64, 128–29; clashes/raids, 1865, 178; clashes/raids, 1867, 244, 247, 272, 276, 278, 282, 283–84, 287, 322–23; clashes/raids, 1868, 360, 402n24; depredation claim records, 15, 50, 323n38; Kaw battles, 335; peace councils, 323. See also Satanta (chief)
Kit-fox Men (Cheyenne warrior society), 38
Knox, George, 21–22
Koons, Anthony, 138
Kraft, Louis, 220n3
Kruiger, Julius, 296
Krumme, Henry, 207, 208–209
Kyne, Pat, 442n15
Kyne Museum (Lincoln, Nebraska), 429n25

Lake Station, 267, 268, 274–75, 278
Lakota tribes. See Sioux tribes
Lambert, Julia S., 115, 115n5
Lambert, Robert, 400
lands, Indian: resource tensions and war, 41–42, 41n9; treaties history, 219–20, 320; treaty reductions and effects, 40, 220
lands, white settlements: Indian designs,

early reports, 39, 42, 47; lawfulness and protection, 251
Lane, J. G., 199n68, 204, 205, 206n79
Lang, George, 257
Lannon, Thomas, 286–87, 286n87
Lantz, Phil, 445
Lapier, H., 254–55
Larimer, Sarah, 58–59, 58–59n62, 59n64, 95–96, 109n32, 179, 180–81, 200, 201–202n72
Larimer, William J., 58, 58n62
Larimer family attack, 58–59, 58–59n62, 59n64
Laurance, Coleman, 126
Lauretson, Askel Martin and Stine, 434, 435, 438–40
Lauritzen, Erskild and Stine. See Lauretson, Askel Martin and Stine
Law, Edward, 446–47
Lawrence, Mr., 371, 372–73
Le Fevre, Charles, 285n85
Lean Bear (chief), 48, 49, 49n28
Leavenworth and Pike's Peak Express Company, 30
Lee, Billy, 241
Lee, Wayne C., 212n94, 470n1
Left Hand (chief), 129
legislation, 16, 18
Leib, Edward, 404n31
Leiber, Charles, 297n104
LeMay, Alan, 448n
LeMay, Dan, 448n
Lentz, Henry F., 198–99, 205–206
Leonard, P. L., 266
letters. See under military reports; personal memory accounts
Lewellen, Dr., 333
Lewis, Alexander, 353, 354
Lewis, John, 296–97, 299
Lewis Ranch, 234
Lewis's Canyon, 172
Liberty Ranch ("Liberty Farm"), 77, 82, 83–84, 85
Life of George Bent (Hyde), 38, 49n28, 109n33, 135n3, 176n3, 189n41, 220n5, 293n98, 311n14
Light, Evander, 331
Lillian Springs Ranch, 134; mail station, 31, 32; modern monuments and study, 473–74; personal accounts, 34, 199n68, 391–93; raids/burning, 139, 167–68, 391–93
Lincoln, Abraham, 39

Lincoln, Jonathan, 384, 386

Lippincott, Davis, 138

Litchfield, Abram T., 166n30, 167

Little Arkansas Treaty (October 1865), 187, 188, 197, 212, 220–21, 220n5, 249, 263–64

Little Bighorn battle (1876), 230

Little Blue River, 68, 77

Little Blue River attacks (August 1864), 67, 69–88, 74n10, 80, 89, 94, 105–107, 131, 161

Little Blue Station, 68, 75, 76–77, 78, 237

Little Cheyenne Creek, 224

Little Chief, 360

Little Coon Creek, 321, 396, 399

Little Heart (chief), 62, 63

Little Horse, 240, 240n50, 242

Little Man, 452

Little Raven (chief), 41n10, 113, 114, 189, 230, 243, 245, 278

Little Robe, 334, 335–36, 337, 340–41

Little Rock, 346

Little Thunder (chief), 106, 161

Lively, Bill, 477–79

livestock: freighter losses, 157–58; killings, 61, 63, 70–71, 72, 80, 83–84, 88, 119, 128, 140, 165, 171, 195, 205, 206, 208, 278, 309, 326, 337, 363, 366, 367, 368, 374–75, 388, 395, 400; ranch-to-ranch sales, 66; recovery attempts, 46–48, 54, 63, 64, 106, 171–72, 171n45, 193, 198, 203–204, 210, 240–41, 242–43, 258–59, 260–62, 321, 400–402, 408; replacements, 62; thefts, 42, 46–48, 49–51, 53–54, 60, 61, 62, 63, 64, 66, 70–71, 77, 78, 108–109, 125, 127, 129, 161, 162, 163, 167, 171–72, 173, 177, 192, 193, 194, 195, 197, 198, 203, 208, 210, 214, 223, 225, 226, 229, 231, 239–40, 242–43, 246, 253, 258, 260, 264, 267, 268, 271–72, 273, 274, 275, 278, 279, 281, 283, 286, 287, 296, 297, 298, 300, 301, 317, 321, 326, 336, 339, 340, 341, 360–61, 361, 362, 365, 383, 400, 401–402, 404, 408, 418; transportation, 43, 44–45; valuing, in claims, 90n5. See also horses

Living Springs Ranch, 156–57

Livingston, Robert R., 125–26, 136n7, 139, 140n23, 163–65, 164n25, 167–68, 171n44

Lockman, John, 367, 368, 369, 370

Lockwood, Ellen, 338–39

Lockwood, Robinson, 338

Lodgepole Creek Station, 175, 196, 198, 214, 233, 262, 391

Logston, Fleming, 192, 192n51

Lone Tree Station, 68

Long, Margaret, 470n1

Long Chin, 39n4

Looking Glass Creek, 56

Lookout Station, 253, 266

Losee, Isaac, 341

Lottinville, Savoie, 109n33

Louisa Springs, 212

Lovewell, Thomas, 255–56

Loy, Virgil "Lefty," 447n24

Lucus, David, 335–36

Ludlow, James, 288

Ludwickson, John, 209n87

Luna, Antonio, 360

Luna, Don Jesus, 272

Lynch, John, 427, 428

Mad Bear, 453, 456

Madril, Antonio, 380–81

Mahohivas (Cheyenne warrior society), 38

mail delivery, 30–31, 33; attacks and plunder, 75, 136, 137, 396; defenses, 195, 215; railroad, 333, 394; volunteers, 396–99. See also Pony Express

Maloney, Daniel, 268, 274–75

Maloney, James K., 225

Maloney, Lent, 266

Man Afraid of His Horse, 161

Man-shot-by-a-bee, 39n4

Mantz, John, 435, 463, 465

Marble, Ann, 89, 91, 92–93, 93n9, 94

Marble, Daniel, 69n3, 72, 89, 91, 92–93, 93n9, 94, 98

Marble, Joel, 91

Marble, William, 91–92, 97, 100, 107

Markham, Joseph, 85

Marki, Benedict, 371, 372–73

marksmanship, 428

Marling, Elizabeth, 226–27, 227n20, 254

Marling, John, 226–27, 227n20

Marr, Josephine Lowell, 122n19

Marshal, George, 91

Marshall, Abraham, Jr., 352

Marshall, Abraham, Sr., 353

Marshall, John, 352, 352n67

Marshall, Julia, 352–53, 352n67

Marshall, Thomas D., 266, 296–97, 299

Martin, George, 113, 119, 120

Martin, Henry and Robert, 119–21

Martin, Michelle, 212n95
Martin, Samuel, 63, 289
Martin, William, 119–20
Martin family attack (August 19, 1864), 119–21
Martinez, Daloreo, 195, 196
Mason, George, 459
Mason, Joseph, 177
Massacre along the Medicine Road (Becher), 67n2, 70n5, 78n23, 79n29, 81n31, 90n5, 100, 109n32
Maxwell, George, 361
Maxwell, John, 171
Maynadier, Henry, 221, 222
McAlister, James, 335, 336
McAlister, Robert, 336
McArthur, Amos, 138
McBlain, Duncan, 301
McCarty, Tim, 399
McChesney, John, 418–19, 420, 423, 427
McChristian, Douglas C., 24n25, 109n33, 221n7, 222n8
McClelland, W. F., 92
McClure, R. F., 287
McCulloch, Ben, 275
McCune, Matthew, 334, 403
McDermott, John D., 17n13, 24n26, 109n32, 110n34, 147n37, 182n19, 221n7, 470n1
McDonough, Hugh, 310
McDowell, James L., 128, 129
McFarlane, John, 424–26
McGarret (teamster), 106
McGee, Mabillion, 283
McGee, Thomas, 201, 203n73
McGillycuddy, Valentine T., 105; interviews, 21–22; raids statements, 74n10, 161
McGrath, Dannie, 459
McIrwin, Mr., 296
McKan, Hugh, 156n3, 157–58, 157n5, 158n, 161n11
McKeefer, Alexander, 427, 428
McKenny, Thomas I., 49, 60
McLelland, W. F., 373–74
McLemore, Christopher, 364, 365
McLennan, William, 127, 320
McNeill, John, 297
McShane, Catherine, 387–88
McShane, David, 387
Medal of Honor recipients, 395, 397, 453, 454n38, 455
Medicine Arrow (chief), 93, 347

Medicine Lodge Creek, 323, 326–27
Medicine Lodge Treaty (1867), 248, 305, 313n17, 320, 326–27; attacks following, 333–41, 343–44, 359–60; attacks prior, 323, 326; gifts and annuities, 328, 334, 341, 342–43, 344, 355; papers and proofs, 359, 365
Medicine Woman, 405
Meigerhoff, Fred, *434, 435, 438, 439, 440, 441*
Melrose, Hugh, 105n24, *129*
Melrose, Melvin, 105n24
Memorial Day, 433, 435
memory accounts. *See* personal memory accounts
Merwin, Fred, 212–13
metals, trade, 81, 100
Metcalf, Newton/Merritt, 79n29
Mexican Army, 238
Mexican freighters, 116, 117, 195–96, 321
Michno, Gregory and Susan, 69n3, 70n5, 72n7, 91n7, 105n24, 130n46, 135n3, 146n36, 186n31, 399n14
Midway Station, 409
Miles, John D., 247
Milhoun, Thomas, 361–62
military artifacts, 473, 474, *475, 476, 478, 479*
military court-martials, 288–90, 327, 454–55
military escorts: civilian offenses, 190–91; mail, 195, 215, 278; railroad workers, 312, 313; relocating tribes, 178–79; resources needed, 278, 299; wagon trains, 151, 156–58, 160, 182–83, 212, 280, 284, 301, 302, 324, 325
military offensives: Alkali Station area, 1865, 202–205, 207–209; attack investigations, 130–31, 197; Bozeman Trail, 1865–1866, 229–30; Camp Rankin/Julesburg, 1865, 134–38, 164, 165–67; campaigns, 1865, 178–79; campaigns, 1867, 249, 250, 251–54, 255, 260, 261–64, 284–85, 287–303, 305, 310, 318, 471; campaigns, 1868, 341–42, 356, 357, 407, *412*; campaigns, 1869, 411, *412,* 413–32, 446–47, 450–61; Colorado, Volunteer Cavalry Regiment, October 1864, 123–24; livestock and horse recovery, 171–73, 171n45, 180, 210, 232, 240–41, 242–43, 260, 261–62, 276–77, 300, 321, 326, 400–402, 408; Mud Springs, 1865, 24n26, 175–76; Nebraska Territory, August 1864, 118; Powder River campaign (July 1865), 24n26, 189–90; prairie burning, 125–26; Sand Creek, 24–25, 38, 113, 129–30

military reports: area attacks, 100n22–101n22, 105–107, 163, 164–65, 167–68, 232, 234, 257–58, 263–64, 319–20, 347–48, 404n31, 449; award-related, 453–54; Battle of Pointed Rock (1865), 207–208; Chalk Bluff, 235; chases and horses, 179, 240–41, 276–77; chiefs, 41n9, 241n53, 244; delivery, 395–96; diaries, 199, 199n68, 398–99, 454, 456, 457, 457n46, 463, 471; errors, 24n25; fort reports, 227n21, 238n46, 239n, 320–21, 395–96; vs. Indian reports, 48–49; inventories, 464–66; letters, 224n14, 234, 244, 290, 290n96, 294–95, 393–94; as limited resource, 24; parleys, 191; prairie burning, 125–26; resource woes, 277, 278; Sand Creek investigation, 130–31; on treaties, 188–89, 191, 328–29; war forecasts/plans, 244–45, 249, 251, 277–78
military uniforms, 191, 398, 399, 414, 436, 471. *See also* war dress
Mill, John Stuart, 25
Miller, Gene, 477
Milligan, Joseph, 85, 86, 87
Minimic, 184, 185–87
Minnecongues, 144–45, 146
Misell, Benjamin, 357
A Misplaced Massacre: Struggling Over the Memory of Sand Creek (Kelman), 131n49
Missouri Cavalry, 199, 215–16
Mitchell, Robert B., 99n16, 126n34
Mix, John, 240, 241, 242, 257, 260–62
Mobley (ranch owner), 236
Moffat, David, 101–104
Moffitt, John and Thomas, 51
Monahan, Doris, 139n18, 140n23, 141n25, 151n43, 269n48
Monk, Samuel, 130n46, 406
Monnett, John H., 24n26, 57n59, 146n36, 230n26, 356n73
Montana. *See* Bozeman Trail
Monument Station, 235, 267, 268, 274, 283, 298, 301, 324
monuments, 473, 477, *480*
Moonlight, Thomas, 180
Moore, Charles A., 31, 140–41, 239–40, 332, 409–10, 410n49; first-hand accounts, 172–73, 242, 407–408; losses/Indian depredation claims, 34–35, 53, 65–66, 75, 141n25–26, 155, 171, 171n44, 172, 173, 332, 408
Moore, Edson, 138

Moore, James A., 31, 35, 52–53, 53, 65, 75, 140–41, 141n25–26, 240n50, 332, 409–10, 410n49; first-hand accounts, 242; injuries, 173–74, 174n49, 239–40, 409, 410; losses, 171, 332, 407–408; raids, 172–73
Moore, William, 418
Moore Ranch. *See* Washington Ranche
Moran, Daniel, 247
Morgan, Anna, 356, 405, 406
Morgan, James, 356, 405
Mormons, 123
Morrell, George, 335
Morris, Maurice, 34
Morris, Sarah, 140n23, 141–42, 141n26, 144–46, 146n36, 152, 153, 178
Morris, William, 140, 141–42, 141n25, 178
Morris family attack (January 15, 1865), 52n43, 141–42, 141n26, 144, 152
Morris Ranch. *See* American Ranche
Morrison, Sarah, 52n43, 141n26
Morrison, Thomas, 368–70
Morrison, William, 52n43
Morrison, W. W., 51
Morrison Ranch. *See* American Ranche
Morrow, Jack, 118, 235
Morton, Nancy, 69n3, 72, 91, 93, 95, 96–99, 99n16–17, 109–10, 115–16
Morton, Thomas, 93, 95, 97, 99, 100, 107
Moschel, Conrad, 122, 122n19
Moss, Mr., 385
Mound Station, 134; captives at, 199–200, 199n70–200n70, 201n, 427n, 477; defenses, 476; mail station, 32; modern study, 473–74, 476
Mud Springs Station, 24n26, 175–76, 198
Mudge, Elizabeth, 88
Mudge, William, 67, 79n29, 85, 87
mules. *See* livestock
Mullahla's Station, 125
Mullins, Martin, 324
Murdoch, C.M., 423
Murie, James, 318
Murphy, Edward B., 137
Murphy, John, 83n35, 107
Murphy, Thomas, 334, 340, 341, 342, 344, 406
Murphy's Ranche, 236
Murray, Bridgette, 56
Murray, Michael, 143
Murray, Patrick, 56, 56n57

Murray Ranch. *See* Douglas Ranch
Myers, Joseph, 424–26
Myhoff, Fritz, *434,* 435, 438, 439, 440, *441*

Nance, John, 336
Narrative of My Captivity Among the Sioux Indians (Kelly), 57n60, 201n
National Archives and Record Administration building (Washington, DC), 480
National Archives material. *See* Indian Depredation Claims; primary and secondary source documents
natural resources: tensions, and war, 41, 41n9, 219, 222, 243–44; water, 41n9, 244; wood, 41, 243–44, 245
Nebraska, *412*
Nebraska Territory, 29; Denver road travel route, 43, *68;* military attacks on Indians, 118; raids and attacks, 13, 39, 67, 69–88, 94, 105–107, 113, 119–22, 124–25, 127. *See also* Denver road
Nebraska Volunteer Cavalry, 107, 198, 204, 207, 208
Needham, Frank, 274
Neff, Fleming, 378
Nelson, James Davis, *441, 462*
Nelson, Nels, 448, 448n
Nesbitt, Joseph H., 65–66, 141, 141n25, 171
New Fort Hays, 312
Newlon, William W., 424–27, 426n
newspaper accounts: battles, 378, 382, 401, 461; captives, 461; depredations, 15, 95, 100, 101n22, 116n8, 141n25, 196, 196n61, 198–99, 224n14, 256, 257, 261, 269, 360, 363n12, 373, 373n32, 374, 377, 385–86, 393, 449n27; depredations claims filing information, 18–19, 19n16; military and government structures, 411; railroads and effects, 41–42; trade trends, 40
Nichols, David H., 123, 124
Nichols, H., 266
Nolan, Nicholas, 324
Nolan (soldier), 398
Noon, Thomas, 442–43, 444
Norlin, Charles, 414, 415
Norlin, Ernest, 414, 415n3
Norlin, George, 411, 417, 417n9, 417n10
Norlin, Gustavus, 413, 414, 415n3
Norris, George, 208
North, Frank, 189, 318, 346, 450, 459, 460

North, Luther, 453, 456, 458, 459, 460, 462
North, Robert, 39–40, 39n4, 42
Northern Cheyenne tribes: clashes/raids, 1864, 37, 67, 73; clashes/raids, 1865, 161, 205, 211; clashes/raids, 1867, 239–41, 305–306, 311n14; clashes/raids, 1868, 375, 378, 403; overall involvement, 37; peace talks, 222
notaries, 274n55
Nowlan, Henry James, 274
Nye, John A., 80, 81n31, 105, 105n24–106n24, 107

Oak Grove Ranch, *68,* 78, 87
O'Brien, Nicholas J., 134–35, 136–37, 137n9, 161, 163, 165, 166–67, 166n30
O'Byrne, Patrick, 337
O'Donnell, John, 397–98
O'Fallon's Bluffs, 118, 193, 197, 207
Official Records of the War of the Rebellion, 99n16, 140n23, 147n37
Oglala Sioux, 26; chiefs, 73, 110, 222–23; clashes/raids, 1864, 57, 67, 98, 133; clashes/raids, 1865, 191, 196–97, 205, 211, 214–15, 222; clashes/raids, 1867, 231–32, 298–99, 311n14, 314; clashes/raids, 1868, 408; friendly tribes, 179–80; locations, 407; peace talks, 222–23; reputation, 98
Oh-E-Ah-Mohe, 346–47
Ohio Cavalry, 175
Oklahoma, treaties and lands, 220, 320
Old Fort Lyon, 362
Old Torchee (chief), 116
Old Wolf, 123
Omaha Public Library, *314, 316*
Omeshe, James, 337–38
One Eye, 184
One-Eyes Cheyenne, 400
Oregon Trail, 181
Orr, Matthew, 296
Osage Indians, 333, 334, 339, 402n24
Ostrander, Nelson, 78, 88
Otero, Vicente, 62–63
Overland Stage Company, 81, 126; attacks, *221,* 254; employees, 163n22, 167, 206, 235; home station, 139
Overland Stage route, 84–85, 87, *134–35,* 267
Overland Trail, *134–35,* 181
Overland Trail Museum, 471, 477n
Owen, Chaney, 404

Owen, John, 302
Owens, Charles, 340
Owl Woman, 38

Pacific Ranche, 236
Page, John H., 245
Palmer, John, 69, 70, 71
Palomas Springs, 62, 63
Pappan, Hubert and Elizabeth, 338
Parker, C. G., 282
Parker, Charles, 323
Parker, Cynthia Ann, 448n
Parker, Daingerfield, 255, 255n14
Parker, J. S., 296
Parmetar, J. W., 48, 50n30, 60
Pasco, Lyal, 422–23
Pashall, Louis, 337
Pattison, John J., 199, 199n68, 199n70–200n70,
    204n75, 208n84, 208n85
Pawnee Indians: alliances, 125, 318, 453;
    Cheyenne battles, 189, 318, 359, 459, 464; Dog
    Soldier impersonations, 446; livestock theft/
    property crime, 226, 226n17; scouts, 189, 318,
    346, 404n31, 450, 451, 457; settler attacks, 255;
    as victims, 404n31
Pawnee Killer, 133, 244, 252, 293, 293n98,
    294–95, 306, 314, 314n19, 407
Pawnee Ranch, 67, 68, 79–80, 79n29, 82–83,
    84–87
Pawnee Rock, 129
"peace chiefs," 48, 99n16, 106n, 184, 189, 194–95,
    228, 228n22–229n22, 241, 241n53, 405–406
peace councils, 221, 222–23, 306, 323, 326–27
peace treaties: creation and inclusion, 220,
    222–23, 328; failures, 219, 220, 227, 229–48,
    278, 305, 320, 329, 334, 344, 389; history, 40,
    219–20, 249, 326–27; Indians' breaks, 196,
    197–98, 212–13, 227, 343–44, 346, 389; Indians'
    desires and conditions, 175, 184, 188–89, 191,
    194–95, 220, 246; whites' breaks, 219–20, 342.
    See also Fort Laramie; Little Arkansas Treaty;
    peace treaty–engaged Indians
peace treaty–engaged Indians: effects, 1866,
    223, 226, 227–28; first-hand accounts, 196,
    197–98; geographic loopholes, 272; hunting,
    263–64, 327, 331, 344–46, 365, 389; penalties
    for depredations, 16, 17, 228, 241, 265, 334,
    341; pre-treaty depredations, 323, 326. See
    also Spotted Tail (chief)
Peate, J. J., 447n24

Pennock, Frank, 157, 157n4
Penny, Jacob, 209–10, 260–61
Penny family attack (November 1, 1865),
    209–10
Penrose, William, 400, 401
pensions, 292
Perkins, Eli and Margaret, 140, 172
Perrin, Lewis, 211–12, 213–14
personal memory accounts: beginning of
    war, 43–46, 48–50, 49n28; captives, 57n60,
    58–59n62, 59n64, 95–96, 96–99, 109n32–33,
    111, 115, 144–46, 146n36, 184, 187, 196,
    199–201, 201–202n72, 308–309, 351, 460–61;
    complementary source, 21, 23–24; diaries,
    199, 199n68, 208n84, 208n85, 230n28; family
    losses, 353, 447–48, 449; Indian accounts of
    war, 37–38, 48, 73, 164–65, 176; Indian attacks,
    46, 58–59, 67, 69, 69n4, 71, 74–88, 96–99, 108,
    117, 119–21, 128–29, 133, 140, 140n23, 141–42,
    142n27, 144, 147–53, 172–73, 198–99, 202–203,
    204, 205–206, 210, 212–13, 213–14, 215–17, 224,
    225, 231–32, 254–56, 262–63, 269–70, 271–72,
    279, 280, 282–84, 286, 297, 306–307, 310n10,
    315–16, 317, 348–50, 356–57, 362, 363–65,
    366, 367–70, 371–73, 380–81, 385, 387–88,
    390–93, 395, 396–99, 415–17, 419–22, 422–23,
    424–26, 427–29, 430, 431–32, 436–38, 438–40,
    440n6, 444, 447, 448; injuries treated, 445;
    interviews, 95–96, 316; letters, 38, 93n9,
    109n33, 141n26, 150–51, 164n25, 200n, 224,
    244, 290, 290n96, 294–95, 310n10, 343, 449,
    449n27; limitations and flaws, 24n25, 76n15,
    140, 140n23, 151n45, 152, 158n, 166–67, 224n14;
    military accounts of war, 124, 165–66,
    207–208, 289, 396–99, 400, 453–54, 457, 458,
    459, 460–61; peace struggles, 241–42; Sand
    Creek massacre, 130n46; scalping, 315–16;
    time and, 21, 25–26; travel, 34, 43–46, 173–74,
    178, 179, 409; trustworthiness of information,
    21, 23–24, 73, 76n15, 215n100, 453; wagon
    formations, 117, 397. See also "civilian
    perspective" and focus; military reports
Peterson, Otto, 434, 435, 438, 439, 440, 440n8
Phillips, William P., 421
Phipps, William, 194
photographs: captives, 93, 93n9, 94, 465;
    civilians, 345, 371, 436, 437, 443; soldiers,
    dead, 290, 290n96, 291; soldiers, heroes, 397
Pierce, John, 138
Piggott, Michael, 243n56, 296n103, 403

Pike's Peak Express and Stage Company, 32, 65

Pine Ridge Station, 177

Pioneer History of Kansas (Roenigk), 201n, 223–24, 224n14, 404n31, 429n25, 432n30

Pixta, Joseph, 306

Plains Indians: fur trade, 29; war encouragement and causes, 40, 389. *See also* Apache tribes; Arapaho tribes; Cheyenne tribes; Comanche tribes; Kaw tribes; Kiowa tribes; Sioux tribes

Platte Bridge Station and fight (1865), 24, 177, 181–82

Platte River/Platte River road: mail delivery routes, 30–31; major travel route, 31, 43; personal travel accounts, 44, 106; raids, 52, 118, 124, 125, 127, 133, 175, 314, 389–94

"playing dead," 120–21, 269–70, *314*, 354

Playter, Thaddeus E., 286

Plum Butte, 322–23

Plum Creek attacks (August 8, 1864), 69, 69n3, 72, 73, 74n10, 89–101, 130–31; documentation, 100n22–101n22, 105–107; responsible parties, 89, 94, 105, 109n33, 161; victims, 107, 124

Plum Creek Station, 89, 90, 96, 100, 100n22, 107, 272–73, 281–82, 315, 318

Plumb, Preston B., 177

poetry, 433

Pointed Rock, Battle of (1865), 207–208

poisoned arrows, 193

Pole Creek Station, 175, 196, 198, 214, 233, 262, 391

Polk, John, 338

Polk, William, 338

Pond Creek Station, 234, 264, 280, 287–88, 296, 298, 355, 363n12

Pony Express, 31, 163n22, 409, 470, 470n1

Poole, L.H., 22

population depletion, 41

Porter, Charles F., 100, 105–107

Potter, Carroll H., 227, 228, 228n22–229n22

Potter, James E, 197n64, 209n87

Potter, J. H., 261, 262, 268n45

Potter, Joseph Haydn, 476

Powder Face, 341, 341n37

Powder River campaign (July 1865), 24n26, 189–91

Powder River country, Indian populations, 182, 190–91, 197, 222, 407, 413, 450. *See also* Bozeman Trail

Powder River Odyssey: Nelson Cole's Western campaign of 1865 The Journals of Lyman G. Bennett and Other Eyewitness Accounts (Wagner), 24n26, 189n40

powder wagons, 37, 46

Powell, James, 233

Powell, Peter John, 91n6, 467–68

Powers, D. B., 323

Powers, John, 47

Poysell (interpreter), 186

Prairie Dog Creek, 319

Pratt, Edmund M., 375–77

Pratt, Matthew, 99, 99n17

Prentice, L. J., 267

Pretty Encampment, 268, 287

Price, Charles, 319, 321

Price, George, 454, 454n37

Price, Sterling, 51, 175, 191

primary and secondary source documents: depredations compensation claims, 19, 20–22, 23–24; passage of time, 25–26; ranches and stations, 34–35; used in book's creation, 13, 15, 15n8, 17n12, 20, 23–24, 25–26. *See also* military reports; newspaper accounts; personal memory accounts

principle of critical trust, 20

prisoners. *See* captives

Probst, Nell Brown, 139n18, 140n23, 471, 473

protections, against Indians. *See* defenses, against Indians

pseudonyms, 291, 292

public viewings, mutilations, *314*, 316, 373, 385, 386

publishing lawsuits, 58–59n62

punishment policy and authority, depredations: economic, 265; government bodies, authority, 251, 341, 344, 411; treaties, 334, 341

Quick, Benjamin, 388

Quinn, Michael, 231

Rafferty, Pat, 310

railroads: attacks, 262, 298–99, 302, 309–10, 311–15, *314*, 318, 325, 354, 427, 429; Cheyenne line, 135, 394, 401, 474, 476; derailing, 315, 318, 327; effects on Indians, and Indians' responses, 41–42, 41n9, 244, 245; effects on ranches, 258, 333, 394, 407–408, 474, 476; mail delivery, 333, 394; newspaper accounts, 41–42; stage replacement, 258, 332–33, 394, 474, 476; Union Pacific, 120, 134–35, 201, 260, 296, 298, 309–10;

railroads (*continued*): workers, 285, 296, 298, 309, 310, 311–13, *314*, 314–15, 325, 331, 354, 362, 427, 429
Rainey, Austin, 90
Ramey, Bill, 477–78
Ramey, Gary and Kathy, 477, 478
ranches: attacks, 75–76, 78–79, 106–107, 367; railroad effects, 258, 333, 394, 407–408, 474, 476; routes and locations, 31–32, *68*, 469–80. *See also* Denver Road; specific ranches
Randall brothers, 352
ransom goods, 95
Rath, Charles, 50
Raynesford, Howard C., 212n94, 470n1
re-enlisting, 455
re-filing of claims, legislation, 18
Reahme, Frank, 288
Red Bead, 257–58, 259
Red Cloud (chief), 50n33; family, 50; peace talks, 222–23; tribes and territory, 179–80, 229
Red Cloud's War: The Bozeman Trail 1866–1868 (McDermott), 24n26
Red Dog, 299
Red Nose, 347
Red River War, 407
Red Shields (Cheyenne warrior society), 38
redheads, 203
Rees, John, 226n17
reservations: creation, 220, 320, 328; Indians moved, 389, 407
retreats: described, 311; incorrect orders, 285, 288–89
revenge attacks: Hungate family, 54–56, 303; Indian motivation/plans, 133–35, 303, 337, 359, 411, 413–32; inter-tribe, 346, 359, 413; "Jack," among Arapaho, 56n57; military campaigns and acts, 251, 253–54; railroad worker attack retaliation, 318–19; Sand Creek massacre, 130, 331; stopped, by chiefs, 228; weaponry, 288
Reynolds, Ezekiel, 53
Reynolds, John, 151, 151n45
Rice, Bartlett, 255, 256
Richards, William, 271
Richmond, John, 93, 93n10
Rickey, Don, 239n
Rickford, Harvey, 50
Rickie, Henry, 401
Riggs, James, 61
Riley, John, 366

Riley, Marshall, 399
Ripley, W. D., 42
Rising Sun Ranch, 210
Riverside Ranche, *478*; mail station, 32; study, 470–71, 473–74, *475*, 478
Riverside Station, *134*, *250*, *474*; attacks near, 192, 268, 269; Custer campaigns, 253, 470–71, 472, 474
roads. *See* Denver Road; Platte River/Platte River road; Santa Fe trail; Smoky Hill trail
Roaring Wind, 80–81, 378
Robbins, Franklin, 384, 385–86
Robbins, George, 384, 385–86
Robbins, Thomas H., 384
Roberts, C. R., 63
Roberts, Eugene, 378, 379
Roberts, Nathan, 267–68
Robertson, Caroline, 338
Robertson, David, 338
Rock Creek Station, 182, 183, 237
Rock Forehead, 188
Rocky Mountain News, 55n53, 115, 116n8, 141n25, 198–99, 240, 363n12, 373, 373n32, 374, 377, 378, 382, 385–86, 401
Roenigk, Adolph, 201n, 223–24, 224n14, 404n31, 427–28, 427n, 429n25, 432n30
Roman Nose (warrior), 38, 199, 199n69, 310, 311n14, 313n17, 319
Romine, James G., 170–71
Root, Frank A., 81–82, 174, 409
Root, Joseph, 313n17
Roper, Fred, 78n23
Roper, Laura, 69n4, 72, 87, 91, 93, 93n9, 94, 115
Rosa, Joe, 383
Roswel, Nahum C., 157
Routh (guide), 46
Rowland, S., 419–20
Roworth, William, 157
Royall, William Bedford, 451–52, 453, 454, 456, 457
Ruggles, George, 393
Running Creek Stage Station, 374
Runyon, A. L., 296n103
Runyon, Alfred Damon, 296n103
Rush Creek, 24n26, 176, 410
Russell, Peter, 292n
Russell, William H., 30, 31
Russell Springs, 263, 267, 280–81, 283
Ruthden Station, 212, 214

Sa-tan-ke (chief). *See* Satanta (chief)

Sage Creek Station, 177

Sallee, Lt., 199

Salt Lake City: freight routes, 121, 123, 193; mail routes, 30–31; stage routes, 192

Sanborn, George, 377

Sand Creek massacre (November 29, 1864), 24–25, 75, 89, 113, 129–30, 229n22; casualties, 89, 105n, 161, 184, 346–47; investigation, 106n, 130–31; site, *250*; study and legacy, 130–31, 130n46, 131n49; survivors, 38, 133, 184, 223, 252, 285n85, 405; war effects, 75, 131

The Sand Creek Massacre: A Documentary History (Carroll), 130n46

Sand Hill, 182, 188, 210n90

Sand Hill Station, 198, 204, 210

Sandborn, George L., 42

Sanders, Lt., 310n10

Sanders, William, 266

Sanderson, George, 403

Santa Fe trail, 13; defenses, 129–30; freight travel, 62; gold rush travel, 30; raids and attacks, 56–57, 62, 63–64, 114, 122, 128, 195–96, 243, 268, 272, 275–76, 282, 283, 287, 300, 302, 321–23, 333, 338–40, 360–61, 400, 404–405; utility and history, 29, 244, 470, 470n1

Saracino, Jesus, 264

Sargeant, Nelson, 137

Satanta (chief), 60, 63, 116; attacks, 1867, 276–77, 278; on causes of conflict, 41n9, 219, 244; movement and war preparation, 1867, 245–46

Saunders, William, 278

Saville, J.J., 298–99

Saw Log Creek, 326

Sawyers, James, 190–91

scalping: family raids, 55, 71, 74–75, 76, 98–99, 108, 142, 146, 372, 373; process, 181, 316; soldiers, 274, 288, 290, *291*; souvenirs, 124, 144, *314*, 316, 466; trade route and ranch raids, 61, 64, 73, 79, 83, 98–99, 115, 116n8, 117, 167, 253, 266, 274, 276, 280, 281, 296, 301, 309, *314*, 315–16, 317, 321, 326, 333, 352, 357, 372, 381, 385–86, 399, 403–404, 419, 420, 429; warnings, 196–97

Scandinavian immigrants, 413–23, *434*, 436, 438–39

Scarbrough, James, 224n14, 256n16

Schermerhorn, Frank, 333

Schermerhorn, Lon, *345*, 447

Schindelholz, Anton, 371, 372, 374

Schmutz, Arthur, *434*, *435*, 446

Schofield, John, 449, 449n27, 450

Schooler, J. N. N., 281, 281n73

Schuler, Jacob S., 59

Schultz, Duane, 293n99

Scott, Douglas D., 131n49, 467n67, 479

Scott, Glenn R., 30n, 470, 471, 473

Scott, Jordan, 399

Scott, Thomas, 138

scurvy, 263

The Searchers (LeMay), 448n

2nd Colorado Cavalry, 63, 178

secondary source documents. *See* primary and secondary source documents

Sedgwick, John, 133–34

Seely, George, 427, 428

Selby, George, 205

self-fulfilling prophecies, 96

self-injury, 282, 301

Sergent, Thomas, 167

Seth J. Clark & Company, 361

7th Cavalry Regiment (United States): organization, 249; peace summits, 327; spring 1869 campaigns, 429, 446–47; summer 1867 campaigns, 268, 276, 284–85, 287–95, 298, 299–300, 318–19, 321, 470–71, 474; summer 1868 campaigns, 351, 396–402; travel woes and desertion, 237–39, 239n, 455, 472

7th Iowa Cavalry, 56, 95, 118, 137, 163, 175, 177, 197, 199, 207, 208

sexual abuse and rape: captives, 72–73, 75, 110, 146, 146n36, 308, 356, 442; Indian attacks, 55, 226, 344, 347, 348–50, 352, 402; port-mortem abuse, 115, 116n8; soldiers' abuses of Indians, 180

Sharp, James, 51

Sharp, Steven, 313, 313n17

Sharp and Shaw, 313n17, 325

Shave Head, 452

Shaw, Luella, 140n23, 142n28

Shaw, Mrs. Simeon, 349, 350

Shaw, Simeon, 348, 349, 350

Shaw, Thomas, 313n17

Sheppard, Charles, 339

Sheridan, Kansas, 418

Sheridan, Michael, 238–39, 239n, 242–43

Sheridan, Philip, 238, 241n53, *345*, 348, 357, 406, 407

Sheridan, Phillip, 401

Sherman, Rollin, 377–78

Sherman, William T.: appraisal of attacks, 302–303, 344, 347; on causes of conflict, 305, 331; Interior Department and Indians, 411; orders, 251, 293, 294, 295; peace attempts, 341–42, 389; tours and surveys, 227, 227n21, 248; warnings to settlers, 359

Shoemaker, Miller and Company, 311–12

Shrouf, George, 42n13, 127

Shull, Alfred, 226n17

Siegenfuhr, August, 127

Simmons, Marc, 470n1

Simonton, T. H., 80, 81, 81n31

Sinnott, Will, 390, 392–93

Sioux tribes: clashes/raids, 1864, 37, 47, 57, 58–59, 67, 84–88, 98; clashes/raids, 1865, 133, 155, 161, 176–77, 191, 193, 196–97, 198–99, 202, 205, 222; clashes/raids, 1867, 231–32, 255, 261, 271–72, 278, 281, 292–93, 293, 294–95, 298–99, 302, 314, 316–17; clashes/raids, 1868, 356, 364, 408; depredation claim records, 15, 57–58n60; Dog Soldiers mixing, 38; false Sioux, and depredations committed, 56; Minnesota uprising, 1862, 40; peace talks, 222–23; treaties history, 221; villages, 332. See also Spotted Tail (chief)

Sitting Bear (chief). See Satanta (chief)

Skogen, Larry, 17–18, 20–21, 23

Slane, Andrew, 380

Slane, Samuel, 380, 381

Slusher, William, 121

smallpox, 81–82

"Smeller" Arapaho tribe, 291

Smith, Adam, 56

Smith, Alexander, 285n85, 356, 357

Smith, Andrew W., 226

Smith, D. Tom, 81n31

Smith, Dan, 176

Smith, Frank, 400

Smith, Frederick, 90, 90n5

Smith, George, 271, 377

Smith, Henry, 375

Smith, Horace G., 80, 81, 81n31

Smith, James, 362, 363n12

Smith, James (freighter raided October 1867), 326

Smith, James (Marble family group member), 91, 100, 101n22, 107

Smith, John, 356–57

Smith, John S., 188, 223, 224n14, 285, 285n85, 286

Smith, Mary, 275

Smith, Robert, 226

Smith, Thomas R., 77n20

Smith, Washington, 445, 461, 463

Smith, W.F., 89, 92

Smith, William, 114, 116n8

Smoky Hill River, 25, 47, 133, 250, 297, 310, 330, 362, 402

Smoky Hill Stage Station, 275–76, 301

Smoky Hill trail, 13; attacks, 192, 211–14, 217, 221, 234–35, 260, 262–63, 275, 281, 296, 301–302, 306, 324, 361, 365, 399, 407; Custer travel, 250, 253; defenses, 192; gold rush/mail travel, 30; livestock travel and theft, 46, 47, 272; site preservation, 470; treaty condition, 188

The Smoky Hill Trail (Long), 470n1

snow, 43, 44, 204, 209, 231, 232, 235, 236, 237, 238, 240, 252. See also weather, and effects

Snow, Hester, 351n63

Snyder, Anna, 114–16, 116n8

Snyder, John, 114, 115, 116n8

Snyder, N. D., 116n8

South Platte road. See Denver road

Southern Cheyenne tribes: clashes/raids, 1864, 37, 61, 73, 89, 94, 180; clashes/raids, 1865, 197–98, 211; clashes/raids, 1867, 311n14, 323n38; clashes/raids, 1868, 346, 360, 362; depredation claim records, 15, 313n17; overall involvement, 37. See also Black Kettle (chief)

Soward, J. A., 313

Spanish language, 116

Spencer, Chester, 193

Spencer, Thomas, 281, 282n75

spies, 406, 451

Spillman, James, 276, 277

Spillman Creek, 434, 436–38, 440

Spillman Creek Raid (May 30, 1869), 407, 426–27, 432, 432n30, 433–68, 461; personal accounts, 436–38, 438–40; routes taken, 330; stages and areas, 434

Spotted Tail (chief), 105, 107; family, 221–22, 222n8; forces, 133, 179–80, 227–28, 241, 242, 244, 258; as peace leader, 221, 222, 223, 227–28, 227n22–228n22, 240, 241, 241n53, 242, 314n; raids, identification, 211

Spotted Tail's Folks (Hyde), 221n7, 222n8

Spring, Agnes Wright, 176n2

Spring Creek fight (May 16, 1869), 412, 413, 429

Spring Hill Station, 33, *134*, 169, 170n39; mail station, 31, 32; monuments, 473; personal accounts, 34, 169–70, 170n39; raid/burning, 139, 168, 169–70, 474

Spring Ranch, *68*, 78–80

Springer, Charles H., 190n45

"Squaw men," 22

St. Clair, Mr., 91, 100, 107

Stafford, Mallie, 178

stage service: attacks and accounts, 81–85, 87, 107, 212–13, 269–71, 280, 296, 297, 298, 302–303, 361; Denver road, 31–32, 33–34, 65, *68*, *134–35*, 169, 268–69, 332–33, 469–80; railroad replacement, 258, 332–33, 394, 474, 476; schedules, 303; stations maps, *68*, *134–35*, *470*, *471*, *473*

Stage Station, 45

Standing Elk, 205; forces, 228, 378; raids, identification, 211

Stanfield, Richard, 416–17, 420–21

Stanley, Francis M., 204

Stanley, Henry M., 314n, 315–16

Stanley, Orsen, 63

Stapleton, James, 201, 203, 203n73

Stapleton, Michael, 203n73

stationers, 101–104

Stebbins, Joel, 138

Stevenson, Thomas, 79n29

stock. *See* livestock

Stormy Hollow Stage Station, 283, 300

storytelling. *See* personal memory accounts

Stover, Maj., 335, 338

Strange, John, *434*, 435, 446–47

Street, David, 269, 270–71, 272

Strew, Moses, 260

Stultzman, Jacob, 266

Stumbling Bear, 276

Such, Henry, 309

suicide, 115–16, 397

Summers, S. W., 107

Summit Springs: captives at, 435, *441*, 459–61, *462*, 463, 464, 467, 477–80, *480*; fight (July 11, 1869), 25, 131, 341n37, *412*, 427, 450, *451*, 453, 458–67; location, and Indian base, 123, 124, 417–18, 450–53, *451*, 456–58

Summit Station, *68*

Sun Dance Woman, 460

superstitions, 203

surprise attacks: Indians, 60, 74, 76, 116, 118, 135, 139, 181–82, 191–92, 193, 194, 196, 197, 229–30, 296, 314–15, 322; military, 123–24, 129–30, 165–66, 207–208, 457–58

Sutherland, James, 157–58, 157n4, 157n5, 161n11

Sutzer, Mrs., 254, 255, 256

Sweetwater meeting and escape, 406, 407, 411, 413

Sweetwater Station, 181, 182

Swena, James T., 278, 279

Swift Bird, 408

swimming skills, 179, 270, 419

Sylvester, 297–98

Sylvester, Charles, 199–201, 200n, 201–202n72, 427, 427n, 429–30, 477

Talbert, Job, 381, 384–85

Talbot, Russ and Bob, 470, 471, 474

Talbott, Walter, 138

Tall Bull, 79, 133, 201n, 311n14, 313n17; death, 458–59, 462; 1869 forces, movements, and revenge, 411, 413–32, *434*, 452–53, 456, 467–68; forces, 334, 341n37, 458–59; Indian population shifts, 407, 411, 413, 450; village and Summit Springs fight, *330*, 417–18, 448, 450–53, 456–67. *See also* Dog Soldiers/Dog Men (Cheyenne warrior society); Spillman Creek Raid (May 30, 1869); Summit Springs

Tallman, Jonathan, 384

Tamblyn, William, 212

Tamney, Michael, 389–94

Tanick, Clark, 421

Tanner, Peter, 414, 415

Tappan, John, 243n56

Tate, Michael, 14–15

Taylor, E. B., 265

Taylor, George, 427, 429–30

Taylor, James, 51–52

Taylor, N. G., 334, 341, 342

Teachout, Allen, 379, 380, 387, 389

Teachout, Harlow M., 378, 379, 380, 387, 389

Teaskey, A. D., 229

Tedstone, Thomas, 339

telegraph lines: Denver Road, 192, 268, 269, 272–73, 474; Overland/Oregon trails, 181–82; peaceful times, 227; Platte River Road, 314, 318; repair and maintenance, 269

Temple, James H., 197, 198

Templeton, Andrew, 105n24

Tennish, Ignatius, 317

Tesson, Louis, 461, 466–67
Texas: maps, *412*; tribe moves, 244, 356, 406; war timeline, 407
theft, animals. *See under* horses; livestock
3rd Colorado Cavalry, 75, 129
13th Missouri Cavalry, 199, 215–16
Thirty-Two Mile Station, *68*, 78, 107, 238
Thompson, Andrew, 352
Thompson, Frank, 158
Thompson, James, 225
Thompson, William, 276, 277, *314*, 315–16
Thompson Ranch, *68*
Thorne, Albert, 169, 170n39
Thornton, Jacob, 319
Thrapp, Dan L., 212n96, 215n100
Thurmond, W. E., 247–48
timber resources, 41, 41n9, 41n10, 243–44, 245
Time, Kellsto. *See* Fletcher, Lizzie
timeline and studies or war, 14–15, 24–25, 37, 49n28, 220–21, 331
To Strike, 242
Todd, G. D., 171
Torrez, Juan, 195
Torrez, Tino, 195–96
torture: accounts, 99, 146, 206, 213, 322, 323; burning, 206, 259, 395, 403–404; children, 206, 322–23, *443*, 445, 449
trade goods: alcohol, 65, 79n29; cash, use, 187–88; clothing, 390; merchandise examples, and losses, 63–64, 101–104, 123, 137, 137n9, 157, 194, 209, 247, 265, 390; weapons stockpiling (Indians), 39–40, 246, 247–48; wood, 230–31, 323–24. *See also* wagon trains
trading, captives, 72–73, 91, 93, 99n16, 110, 185–86, 187, 188, 356, 405
trading posts and forts, 29–30; inclement weather, 43, 44; personal accounts, travel, 34, 43–46, 48; thefts and raids, 47–48, 50, 65, 333
Trail, Nathan, 288
trail-making: cattle, 402; Indians, 197, 207, 255, 264, 274, 448, 456–57; military forces, 452–53, 456
trail mapmaking, 470, 471, 473
trains. *See* railroads; wagon trains
Tramp, David, 247
translators: Indian/English, 186, 201, 223, 228, 245, 246, 248, 273, 343; Spanish, 116
Thrapp, Dan L., 158n
Trask, Henry, 429, 430, 431, 432
Traveling Bear, 453

treaties. *See* peace treaties
Trees, L. M., 157
trials, Indian chiefs, 110
Trigg family, 387
Triggs, Jeremiah H., 72, 95, 109, 115
Tritch, George, 19n16, *80*, 81–82
Trout, Hattie L. Hedges, 386
True History of Some of the Pioneers of Colorado (Shaw), 140n23, 142n28
Trujillo, Antilaus, 283–84
truth, interpretation, 13–14, 20, 21, 23–24, 73, 297n104
Tulley, Elizabeth, 105
Tulley, Michael, 100, 101, 105, 107
Turkey Leg, 306, 307–309, 314, 318, 327, 346, 354, 355
Turner, Eliza Matilda, 292
Twenty-Five Mile Point Ranch, 90
Two-Face (chief), 67, 72–73, 74n10, 80–81, 105, 110
typhoid fever, 92, 94

Uhlig, Edmund, 76n15
Uhlig, Johanna, 76, 76n15
Uhlig, Theodore, 76, 88
Ulbrich, Peter (Jr.), 306, 307, 308
Ulbrich, Peter (Sr.), 306–307, 308
Ulbrich, Veronica, 306–309, *307*, 318
Ulbrich/Kalus family attack (July 1867), 305–309, *307*, 317
Union Pacific Railroad, 120, 134–35, 201, 260, 296, 298, 309–10
Union Vedette (newspaper), 95
University of Colorado at Boulder, 411, 417, 417n10
University of Oklahoma Press, 93n9
Unrau, William E., 110n34, 229n22
Upper Arkansas Agency, 114
Ups and Downs of an Army Officer (Armes), 241n53, 311n14, 318n29
Ute tribes, 115n5, 196, 359–60, 378

Valley Station, 33, *134*; defenses, 123, 149, 153, 155–56, 167, 171n45; mail station, 31, 32; raids, 139, 143, 148–51, 192; site state, 35, 240; telegraph station, 65, 66, 143. *See also* Washington Ranche
Van Autiuerp, Jacob, 296, 296n103
Van Tassell, Renslaer S., 410
Van Toast, James, 408

Varney, Isaac, 76
Vaughn, J. W., 24n26, 182n19
Verney, Edward, 192–93, 192n53
Voarness, Thomas, 415–16, 417, 420–21
Vogal, Mr., 287
Volkmar, William, 454, 454n38, 456, 457n46, 463
Vollintine, T. W., 258, 260
Vorenberg, Adolph, 418

Wa-Pello, 334
Wadsworth, James, 235
Wagner, David E., 24n26, 189n40, 189n41
Wagon Box Fight (August 2, 1867), 233
wagon trains: banding and defenses, 84–86, 96–97, 151, 156–58, 160–61, 178, 182–83, 190, 191, 225, 299, 302, 324, 325; casualty totals, 101n22; formations, 100, 116–17, 158n; Indian raids, 61–62, 63, 69, 70–71, 75, 76–77, 79–81, 80, 89–92, 99, 100, 101n22, 106–107, 116–18, 122, 123, 124–28, 139, 158n, 192–94, 195–97, 197–98, 201–202, 204–206, 209–11, 214–15, 271–74, 275, 280–81, 282–84, 285, 287, 299, 300–302, 321–23, 325, 341, 360–61, 389–93, 394, 396, 404, 418–19, 422–23, 434; Mormons, 123; railroad replacement, 258, 332–33, 394; regulations, 178, 182, 183, 190, 191, 225
Walker, Alexander, 202–203, 203n73, 204
Walker, Craig, 447n23
Walker, James, 201
Walker, Joseph, 317
Walker, Lewis A., 413, 422–23
Walker, Samuel, 189, 190, 207
Walker's Creek attack (September 19, 1867), 325–26
Walker's Creek Stage Station, 266, 267
Wall, Jas K., 106
Walnut Creek station, raids, 49–50, 64
Walsh, James W., 327
Walter, Albert, 151, 151n45, 156–58, 156n3, 157n5, 160, 172
Wanless, John, 151
war dress, 86, 97, 123, 313, 318, 348–49, 360, 414, 436. See also military uniforms
Ward, Mrs., 254–57
Ward, Nicholas, 254–56
Ward, Richard, 255
Ware, Eugene, 126n34, 134n, 138, 163, 165–67
warrior societies, 38

Washington, George (chief), 327
Washington Ranche, 134; building information, 35, 65, 141, 141n25, 240, 332, 407–408, 409–10; horses, 53; mail station, 31, 32; raids, 65, 139, 171, 172–73, 239–40, 268, 269, 332; travelers, 173–74
Washita fight. See Battle of the Washita (November 27, 1868)
water resources, 41n9, 244
Waters, Rhoda Ann Daily, 480
Watson, Charles, 310
Watson, Robert, 420
Watson, Sarah, 131
Watson, William, 121
Watson, William A., 105n24, 115n5
Waugh, James, 204
Wayne, John, 448n
weapons and ammunition: arson losses, 267; Indians' gifts (treaties), 328, 334, 341, 342–43, 344; Indians' rights to, 179, 342; Indians' stockpiling, 39–40, 246, 247–248; Indians' variety, 42, 76, 246, 322, 328, 343, 343n44, 344, 360, 428, 464; military, 137, 164, 165–66, 191, 198, 208, 236, 237, 240, 241, 311, 396–98; poisoned arrows, 193; self-injury, 282, 301; settlers', traders', and workers' defenses, 70, 76, 78, 86, 117, 119, 128, 129, 140, 142–43, 148–49, 150, 152–53, 162, 164, 165–66, 178, 211, 213, 224, 225, 241, 261, 286–87, 301, 311, 312, 313, 326, 352n67, 353, 420, 421, 425, 427–28, 430–31, 437–38, 440, 446–47; thefts, 236, 281, 324, 336, 339; trades, and Indian arming, 236, 237, 247–48, 343; unarmed settlers, traders, and workers, 261, 272, 309, 320–21, 353–54, 427
weather, and effects: all 1867, 219, 231, 234, 235–36, 237, 238, 240, 251–52; fall 1865, 208, 209; freight and trade travel, 43, 44; rainfall, and assumptions, 303; rainfall, and field conditions, 263, 264; summer 1866, 219; winter 1868, 355; winter 1865–1866, 190, 219
Weichell, George, 434, 435, 438, 439, 440, 440n9, 466
Weichell, Maria, 434, 435, 438, 439, 440–42, 440n9, 441, 459–61, 462, 465, 466, 466–67
Weichell, Minnie Grace, 440n9, 463, 465, 466
Weidner, Christopher, 360
Welch, John, 288
Wells Fargo and Company: attacks against, 249, 265–70, 274n55, 275, 299, 300, 303, 305; claims, 265, 280; service stoppage, 394;

Wells Fargo and Company (continued): stage
stations, 333
Welte, Lorenz, 122, 122n19
Wendling, Henry, 366–67
Wentworth, H. H., 64
westward expansion: Indian responses and
policies, 245; tracing places, 469–70, 471;
treaties history and changes, 219–20
Whalen, Mike, 201
Whalen, Nicholas, 442–43, 442n13, 444
Where a Hundred Soldiers Were Killed: The
Struggle for the Powder River Country and the
Making of the Fetterman Myth (Monnett),
24n26
Whistler, 407
Whitcomb, Elias W., 196–97, 403, 407–408
White, A.G., 86
White, Benjamin, 352
White, James, 403
White, J. R., 403
White, Sarah, 352, 356, 406, 406n40
White Antelope (chief): attacks and fights, 61,
91n6, 94, 105, 106n, 107, 109n33, 124–25, 131;
forces, 129; Sand Creek massacre (1864), 89,
105n, 130n46, 131, 161, 346–47
White Horse, 79
White Man's Fork (creek), 43, 207, 209
White Rock Creek area raids: 1866, 226; 1867,
254–55; 1869, 413, 415n5, 416, 417, 418, 419–21,
422, 423n20, 427, 442–43
White White (chief), 144–45, 146
Whiten, James, 83, 83n35
Whitney, C. B., 403
Wiechselbaum, Theodore, 230, 230n28, 243n56
Wiggins, Martha, 267
Wiggins, Oliver Perry, 158n, 206–207, 208n85,
211, 214–15, 215n100, 267, 283, 378
Wilcox, John, 179, 197, 197n64, 199–200, 200n
Wild, William, 23n23
"Wild Bill," 382–83, 383n55
Wiley, Charles, 116–18
Williams, George, 287
Williams, Robert, 21–22
Williford, George W., 175, 190–91
Willow Creek Stage Station, 266, 267, 275
Wilson, Ben, 302
Wilson, Robert P., 157, 157n4
Windbigler, Gordon, 353–54
Winder, Stanley, 433
Winkleplect, Alonzo, 418–19, 420

Winkleplect, Edward, 418–19, 420
Winkleplect, Rueben, 418–19, 420
Winsor, M., 224n14, 227n20, 256n16
Winters, Homer, 336
Wisconsin Ranche, 134, 140n23; artifacts,
479; Indian threats, 123; mail station, 31, 32;
military base, 123; personal travel accounts,
43, 44–45; raids/burning, 139, 143, 147–53,
159, 215–17, 269n48, 479; rebuilding, 215
Wisely, Joel, 136, 137n9
Witherall, Mary, 285n85
Wolf Warriors (Cheyenne warrior society), 38
Wolf with Plenty of Hair, 459
wolves: and corpses, 214, 253, 352, 392, 393;
whites' killing, 42
Wood, James, 324
Woods, John, 93
Woodworth, Charles J., 363n12
Woodworth, Eliza Jane, 362–63, 363n12
Woodworth, James, 362, 363, 363n12
Woolworth, Calvin C., 101
Wright, Richard, 267, 281
Wright, R. M., 361
Wright, Silas, 400
Wurthmann, Ben, 466
Wyatt, H. R., 234, 234n39, 287
Wyllyams, Frederick, 286, 288, 290–92, 290n96,
291, 292n
Wynkoop, Edward "Ned," 273; attack
investigations, 49, 272, 340, 346–47;
captives releases, 72, 73, 94, 99n16, 184, 186,
187, 188–89; defenses of Cheyenne, 337,
339, 340–41, 342, 344–46; depredations
accounts, 224n14, 243n56, 276, 336n13, 347;
treaties, 187, 188–89; weapons distribution,
342–43, 344–46
Wyoming: battles, 24; pre-state territory, 13;
raids history, 13, 176–77. See also Bozeman
Trail

Yamatubee, 297–98
Yellow Woman, 38
Yoho, Isaac, 379
Young, Benjamin, 297
Young, Brigham, 123
Young, Frank C., 142n27

Zigler, Eli, 434, 435–38, 440n8, 442, 452
Zigler, Mary, 443, 445
Zigler, Michael, 443, 445

Dedication

THIS BOOK IS DEDICATED TO BILL CONDON, LANDOWNER of a portion of the Denver trail, and steward of its history. I first met Bill in 2000 as I began my research on the rich history of eastern Colorado. I had come to learn that most of the stage stops and pilgrim ranches along the Denver trail had been lost to history, with an historical hint hidden in survey records housed in the Bureau of Land management office in Lakewood, Colorado. A few years earlier Glenn Scott R. Scott had published a series of historic trail maps, superimposing over modern maps approximate locations of the long lost ranches and stage stops.

Four of these stops were on land that had been owned or still presently owned by Bill. Indeed, more than a dozen years before I met Bill he had remembered from back in the 1940s where the location of two important stops were on his land, viz., Spring Hill and Lillian Springs. He had been responsible for erecting historic markers identifying both sites, those markers presently on land managed by the Division of Wildlife. But the other two sites, one a ranche—Riverside Ranche—and the other a stage stop—Mound Station—had been lost. It was my hope that I could possibly find those historic sites that led me to my first meeting with Bill Condon. That was more than a dozen years ago, and as a result my life has been richly rewarded with the warm friendship that has grown between Bill and myself. Indeed, in some ways, Bill has been to me a surrogate father, my own father dying when I was a teenager.

But more importantly, Bill for me has served as an inspiration of the American Spirit—which same spirit so many of our long forgotten pioneers embraced as they pursued the American dream along the Denver trail. People like Charles Moore, co-owner of Washington Ranch, the Coad brothers, owners of Wisconsin Ranch, Holan Godfrey of "Fort Wicked," Watson Coburn, owner of Chicago Ranche, William Morrison, killed at

American Ranch in 1865, and many more embodied this spirit. These men are important members of America's First generation, a designation I give to those people—women too—who were the first generation of Colorado pioneers following the discovery of gold near Denver, which includes my own great-great grandfather, William A. Watson. Those who lived a long life all succeeded very well and are an inspiration to us all of what is instilled in the American spirit. Hard work, honestly, rock solid character, steward of talent and a deep love of hard work as the path to success. Bill embodies all of these character traits, and more. And it is to him this book is dedicated. Without his encouragement and support over many long years, this book would have never been born.

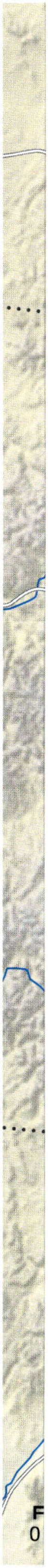
F
0